ISSUES IN NEWS AND REPORTING

Sara Miller McCune founded SAGE Publishing in 1965 to support the dissemination of usable knowledge and educate a global community. SAGE publishes more than 1000 journals and over 800 new books each year, spanning a wide range of subject areas. Our growing selection of library products includes archives, data, case studies and video. SAGE remains majority owned by our founder and after her lifetime will become owned by a charitable trust that secures the company's continued independence.

Los Angeles | London | New Delhi | Singapore | Washington DC | Melbourne

ISSUES IN NEWS AND REPORTING

SELECTIONS FROM *CQ RESEARCHER*

FOR INFORMATION:

CQ Press

An Imprint of SAGE Publications, Inc.

2455 Teller Road

Thousand Oaks, California 91320

E-mail: order@sagepub.com

SAGE Publications Ltd.

1 Oliver's Yard

55 City Road

London EC1Y 1SP

United Kingdom

SAGE Publications India Pvt. Ltd.

B 1/I 1 Mohan Cooperative Industrial Area

Mathura Road, New Delhi 110 044

India

SAGE Publications Asia-Pacific Pte. Ltd.

3 Church Street

#10-04 Samsung Hub

Singapore 049483

Printed in the United States of America

ISBN (pbk): 978-1-5443-2225-4

Library of Congress Control Number: 2017964358

This book is printed on acid-free paper.

Acquisitions Editor: Terri Accomazzo

Production Editor: Kimaya Khashnobish

Typesetter: C&M Digitals (P) Ltd.

Proofreader: Sarah J. Duffy

Cover Designer: Candice Harman

Marketing Manager: Allison Henry

Certified Sourcing
www.sfiprogram.org
SFI-00453

18 19 20 21 10 9 8 7 6 5 4 3 2 1

Contents

Annotated Contents

TRUST IN MEDIA

Journalism is facing a credibility crisis. Declining faith in government and other institutions and a decades-long assault by conservatives have hurt mainstream news outlets. And President Trump has called journalists "the enemy of the American people." Recent incidents involving public figures, including a Montana congressional candidate's alleged assault on a reporter, have underscored the hostility that journalists face. Some traditional media also have suffered from self-inflicted wounds by blurring the lines between news and commentary and ignoring the interests of rural readers to focus on well-off urbanites. Ad revenue and subscriptions at newspapers have plummeted, in part due to the rise of the Internet and changing consumer habits. Meanwhile, social media have fostered "echo chambers" in which people seek out news that affirms their beliefs. Journalists and those studying the news business say mainstream outlets must be more transparent about how they do their jobs and more skillful at explaining events to survive.

MEDIA BIAS

An unprecedented number of Americans view the news media as biased and untrustworthy, with both conservatives and liberals complaining that coverage of political races and important public policy issues is often skewed. Polls show that 80 percent of Americans believe news stories are often influenced by the powerful, and nearly as many say the media tend to favor one side of issues over another. The proliferation of commentary by partisan cable broadcasters, talk-radio hosts and bloggers has blurred the lines between news and opinion in many people's minds, fueling concern that slanted reporting is replacing media objectivity. At the same time, newspapers and broadcasters — and even some partisan groups — have launched aggressive fact-checking efforts aimed at verifying statements by newsmakers and exposing exaggerations or outright lies. Experts question the future of U.S. democracy if American voters cannot agree on what constitutes truth.

FREE SPEECH AT RISK

Governments around the globe have been weakening free-speech protections because of concerns about security or offending religious believers. After a phone-hacking scandal erupted in the British press and Muslims worldwide violently protested images in the Western media of the Prophet Muhammad, European nations enacted new restrictions on hate speech, and Britain is considering limiting press freedom. Autocratic regimes increasingly are jailing journalists and political dissidents or simply buying media companies to use them for propaganda and to negate criticism. Muslim countries are adopting and rigidly enforcing blasphemy laws, some of which carry the death penalty. Meanwhile, some governments are blocking or monitoring social media and cybertraffic, increasing the risk of arrest for those who freely express their thoughts online and dashing hopes that new technologies would allow unlimited distribution of information and opinion.

PRESS FREEDOM

Press freedom around the globe declined for the eighth year in a row in 2009, with more than three quarters of the world's population now living in countries without a free press. It was once thought that new technologies — such as cell phones and the Internet — would help to open up repressive societies. But as fast as reporters in those countries adopt technologies that enable them to connect to the outside world, authoritarian governments like China, Iran and Russia devise sophisticated new tools to control the flow of online information. Meanwhile, dictatorial regimes continue to use heavy-handed, old-school methods to control the world's

media, including intimidation and violence. Fifty-two journalists were murdered in 2009, most of them while investigating corruption or politics. Another 136 journalists were jailed — the highest number since 2003 and a 68-percent increase over 2000. Such trends alarm media experts, who say press freedom is a prerequisite for economic development and a harbinger for the future direction of political and social freedoms.

JOURNALISM STANDARDS IN THE INTERNET AGE

Press critic A.J. Liebling of *The New Yorker* wrote in 1960 that "freedom of the press is guaranteed only to those who own one." A half-century later, everyone with an Internet connection owns a virtual press. And many of them scorn the journalism standards that have guided America's mainstream media since before Liebling penned his famous aphorism. Among those standards: accuracy above all else, plus fairness, balance, thoroughness, independence, civility, decency, compassion and responsibility — along with a clear separation of news from opinion. Now, operators of some news-like websites unabashedly repeat rumors and throw accuracy to the wind. Vile, anonymous reader comments on mainstream media websites mock civility. Add the pressures of Internet speed and shrinking news staffs, and serious journalists wonder what kind of standards — if any — will prevail during the next 50 years.

PRESS FREEDOM

Wrenching changes in the news business are starting to alter the legal landscape for journalists. The federal Freedom of Information Act and "shield" laws in many states give reporters access to official documents and offer some protections against prosecutors who demand to know their confidential sources or information that reporters have gathered. But amid catastrophic revenue declines, media companies struggling to stay afloat have less money to throw into court fights to enforce their journalistic rights. And the increasing numbers of online bloggers — including those who call themselves independent journalists — have even fewer resources. Moreover, politicians have been arguing over which kinds of bloggers — if any — should be defined as journalists entitled to free-press protections. The debate on that issue has stalled progress on a proposed federal shield law in the Senate, though backers were hopeful of reaching a compromise.

POLARIZATION IN AMERICA

Americans have become familiar with the kind of high-decibel, no-compromise political warfare between Republican and Democratic officeholders that led to a government shutdown last fall and threatened default on the national debt. While bitter partisanship is nothing new in American history, some social scientists fear the current wave is dangerously undermining national unity and the country's democratic traditions. Even the two main political parties are embroiled in infighting, with Republicans increasingly engaged in conflicts between traditional conservatives and those further to the right, and some liberal Democrats trying to push their party further to the left. Polarization in America is not limited to politics, either. People are moving into neighborhoods populated by others with like-minded views. And market researchers, pollsters and political scientists are discovering left/right preferences about what to drink, where to shop, how to be entertained and whom to marry.

PRIVACY AND THE INTERNET

In decisions with far-reaching implications on both sides of the Atlantic, European courts and regulators have ruled that Google and other search engines must delete links to Europeans' unwanted personal information from the Web, reinforcing a "right to be forgotten" that has a long legal tradition on the continent. A French regulator's order applying that doctrine to the Google .com search page used by Americans is widely seen as conflicting with the U.S. Constitution's guarantee of free expression. Even so, some privacy advocates say Americans should have a right to erase some information from the Web, such as embarrassing photos or postings that could damage their reputation or prevent them from getting a job. So far, federal and state laws allow only certain kinds of data, such as bankruptcy records, to be expunged online after a certain period of time. But

polls suggest Americans want more control over other kinds of personal information online.

DIGITAL JOURNALISM

More and more people in the United States and around the world are getting their news online instead of in print or via radio or television — the so-called legacy media. Digital news sites allow news to be continually updated, with few if any of the space or other constraints that apply to print publications or radio and television newscasts. With lower upfront costs, journalism entrepreneurs can start businesses more readily than in the past. Witness the new digital-only news sites just started by high-profile journalists who left prestigious traditional newspaper companies. Yet some observers complain about the increased partisanship seen in digital publications and the increased risk of error with less careful editing than in traditional news media. And the business plans for the new digital sites are works in progress, with uncertain long-term prospects. Meanwhile, traditional news organizations are reinventing themselves to remain relevant and profitable in the digital age.

CONSPIRACY THEORIES

President Barack Obama is a foreign-born radical plotting to establish a dictatorship. His predecessor, George W. Bush, allowed the Sept. 11 attacks to occur in order to justify sending U.S. troops to Iraq. The federal government has plans to imprison political dissenters in detention camps in the United States. Welcome to the world of conspiracy theories. Since colonial times, conspiracies both farfetched and plausible have been used to explain trends and events ranging from slavery to why U.S. forces were surprised at Pearl Harbor. In today's world, the communications revolution allows conspiracy theories to be spread more widely and quickly than ever before. But facts that undermine conspiracy theories move less rapidly through the Web, some experts worry. As a result, there may be growing acceptance of the notion that hidden forces control events, leading to eroding confidence in democracy, with repercussions that could lead Americans to large-scale withdrawal from civic life, or even to violence.

INTERNET ACCURACY

The Internet has been a huge boon for information seekers. In addition to sites maintained by newspapers and other traditional news sources, there are untraditional sources ranging from videos, personal Web pages and blogs to postings by interest groups of all kinds — from government agencies to hate groups. But experts caution that determining the credibility of online data can be tricky, and that critical-reading skills are not being taught in most schools. In the new online age, readers no longer have the luxury of depending on a reference librarian's expertise in finding reliable sources. Anyone can post an article, book or opinion online with no second pair of eyes checking it for accuracy, as in traditional publishing and journalism. Now many readers are turning to user-created sources like Wikipedia, or powerful search engines like Google, which tally how many people previously have accessed online documents and sources — a process that is open to manipulation.

Preface

Can news outlets regain the public's confidence? Can governments control the press in the internet Age? Should Americans have a right "to be forgotten"? We feel that students need objective, yet provocative examinations of these issues to understand how they affect citizens today and will for years to come. This annual collection aims to promote in-depth discussion, facilitate further research and help readers formulate their own positions on crucial issues. Get your students talking both inside and outside the classroom about *Issues in News and Reporting*.

This first edition includes sixteen up-to-date reports by *CQ Researcher*, an award-winning weekly policy brief that brings complicated issues down to earth. Each report chronicles and analyzes executive, legislative and judicial activities at all levels of government. This collection is divided into six diverse policy areas: environment; business and economy; rights and liberties; social policy; health; and national security—to cover a range of issues found in most American government and public policy courses.

CQ RESEARCHER

CQ Researcher was founded in 1923 as *Editorial Research Reports* and was sold primarily to newspapers as a research tool. The magazine was renamed and redesigned in 1991 as *CQ Researcher*. Today, students are its primary audience. While still used by hundreds of journalists and newspapers, many of which reprint portions of the reports, the *Researcher's* main subscribers are now high school, college and public libraries. In 2002, *Researcher* won the American Bar

Association's coveted Silver Gavel award for magazine excellence for a series of nine reports on civil liberties and other legal issues.

Researcher writers—all highly experienced journalists—sometimes compare the experience of writing a *Researcher* report to drafting a college term paper. Indeed, there are many similarities. Each report is as long as many term papers—about 11,000 words—and is written by one person without any significant outside help. One of the key differences is that writers interview leading experts, scholars and government officials for each issue.

Like students, writers begin the creative process by choosing a topic. Working with the *Researcher's* editors, the writer identifies a controversial subject that has important public policy implications. After a topic is selected, the writer embarks on one to two weeks of intense research. Newspaper and magazine articles are clipped or downloaded, books are ordered and information is gathered from a wide variety of sources, including interest groups, universities and the government. Once the writers are well informed, they develop a detailed outline and begin the interview process. Each report requires a minimum of ten to fifteen interviews with academics, officials, lobbyists and people working in the field. Only after all interviews are completed does the writing begin.

CHAPTER FORMAT

Each issue of *CQ Researcher*, and therefore each selection in this book, is structured in the same way. Each begins with an overview, which briefly summarizes the areas that will be explored in greater detail in the rest of the chapter. The next section chronicles important and current debates on the topic under discussion and is structured around a number of key questions, such as "Is the U.S. power grid vulnerable to major attack?" and "Do high development costs justify soaring drug prices?" These questions are usually the subject of much debate among practitioners and scholars in the field. Hence, the answers presented are never conclusive but detail the range of opinion on the topic.

Next, the "Background" section provides a history of the issue being examined. This retrospective covers important legislative measures, executive actions and court decisions that illustrate how current policy has evolved. Then the "Current Situation" section examines contemporary policy issues, legislation under consideration and legal action being taken. Each selection concludes with an "Outlook" section, which addresses possible regulation, court rulings and initiatives from Capitol Hill and the White House over the next five to ten years.

Each report contains features that augment the main text: two to three sidebars that examine issues related to the topic at hand, a pro versus con debate between two experts, a chronology of key dates and events and an annotated bibliography detailing major sources used by the writer.

ACKNOWLEDGMENTS

We wish to thank many people for helping to make this collection a reality. Thomas J. Billitteri, managing editor of *CQ Researcher*, gave us his enthusiastic support and cooperation as we developed this eighteenth edition. He and his talented editors and writers have amassed a first-class library of *Researcher* reports, and we are fortunate to have access to that rich cache. We also thankfully acknowledge the advice and feedback from current readers and are gratified by their satisfaction with the book.

Some readers may be learning about *CQ Researcher* for the first time. We expect that many readers will want regular access to this excellent weekly research tool. For subscription information or a no-obligation free trial of *Researcher*, please contact CQ Press at www.cqpress.com or toll-free at 1-866-4CQ-PRESS (1-866-427-7737).

We hope that you will be pleased by the seventeenth edition of *Issues for Debate in American Public Policy*. We welcome your feedback and suggestions for future editions. Please direct comments to Monica Eckman, Executive Publisher for CQ Press, an imprint of SAGE, 2600 Virginia Avenue, NW, Suite 600, Washington, DC 20037; or send e-mail to *Carrie .Brandon@sagepub.com*.

—The Editors of CQ Press

Contributors

Alan Greenblatt covers foreign affairs for National Public Radio. He was previously a staff writer at *Governing* magazine and *CQ Weekly*, where he won the National Press Club's Sandy Hume Award for political journalism. He graduated from San Francisco State University in 1986 and received a master's degree in English literature from the University of Virginia in 1988. For *CQ Researcher*, he wrote "Confronting Warming," "Future of the GOP" and "Immigration Debate." His most recent *CQ Global Researcher* reports were "Rewriting History" and "International Adoption."

Chuck McCutcheon is a former assistant managing editor of *CQ Researcher*. He has been a reporter and editor for *Congressional Quarterly* and Newhouse News Service and is co-author of the 2012 and 2014 editions of *The Almanac of American Politics* and *Dog Whistles, Walk-Backs and Washington Handshakes: Decoding the Jargon, Slang and Bluster of American Political Speech*. He also has written books on climate change and nuclear waste.

Jennifer Koons teaches journalism at Northwestern University's satellite campus in Doha, Qatar. Previously, she was a Washington, D.C.-based journalist writing about national politics and legal issues, including cases before the U.S. Supreme Court, the 2008 and 2004 presidential campaigns and congressional action on Capitol Hill. Her work has appeared in *The New York Times, The Washington Post, San Diego Union Tribune* and *Inside Mexico*, among other publications. She earned a master's degree in journalism from

Northwestern's Medill School of Journalism and a master's degree in law from Northwestern's School of Law. She was the McCormick Journalism Fellow at the Reporters Committee for Freedom of the Press in Rosslyn, Va.

Kenneth Jost has written more than 160 reports for *CQ Researcher* since 1991 on topics ranging from legal affairs and social policy to national security and international relations. He is the author of *The Supreme Court Yearbook* and *Supreme Court From A to Z* (both CQ Press). He is an honors graduate of Harvard College and Georgetown Law School, where he teaches media law as an adjunct professor. He also writes the blog Jost on Justice (http://jostonjustice.blogspot.com). His previous reports include "Blog Explosion" and "Future of Newspapers" (both 2006).

Peter Katel is a *CQ Researcher* staff writer who previously reported on Haiti and Latin America for *Time* and *Newsweek* and covered the Southwest for newspapers in New Mexico. He has received several journalism awards, including the Bartolomé Mitre Award for coverage of drug trafficking, from the Inter-American Press Association. He holds an A.B. in university studies from the University of New Mexico. His recent reports include "Mexico's Drug War," "Hate Groups" and "Vanishing Jobs."

Robert Kiener is an award-winning writer based in Vermont whose work has appeared in *The London Sunday Times, The Christian Science Monitor, The Washington Post, Reader's Digest,* Time Life Books and other publications. For more than two decades he worked as an editor and correspondent in Guam, Hong Kong, Canada and England. He holds an M.A. in Asian studies from Hong Kong University and an M.Phil. in international relations from Cambridge University.

Sarah Glazer is a London-based freelancer who contributes regularly to *CQ Researcher*. Her articles on health, education and social-policy issues also have appeared in *The New York Times* and *The Washington Post*. Her recent *CQ Researcher* reports include "European Migration Crisis" and "Free Speech on Campus." She graduated from the University of Chicago with a B.A. in American history.

Staff writer **Marcia Clemmitt** is a veteran social-policy reporter who previously served as editor in chief of *Medicine & Health* and staff writer for *The Scientist*. She has also been a high-school math and physics teacher. She holds a liberal arts and sciences degree from St. John's College, Annapolis, and a master's degree in English from Georgetown University. Her recent reports include "Climate Change," "Health Care Costs," "Cyber Socializing" and "Student Aid."

Tom Price, a contributing writer for *CQ Researcher*, wrote "The Future of Journalism" for the March 27, 2009, edition. Currently a Washington-based freelance journalist, he previously was a correspondent in the Cox Newspapers Washington Bureau and chief politics writer for the *Dayton Daily News* and *The Journal Herald* in Dayton. He is author or coauthor of five books, including *Changing The Face of Hunger* and, most recently, *Washington, DC, Free & Dirt Cheap* with his wife Susan Crites Price. His work has appeared in *The New York Times, Time, Rolling Stone* and other periodicals. He earned a bachelor of science in journalism at Ohio University.

1

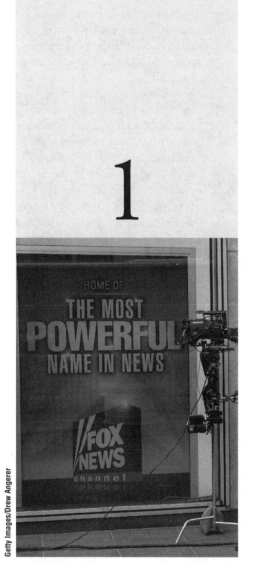

Fox News proclaims its clout at its New York studios. Attitudes about media outlets, particularly Fox and *The New York Times,* reflect partisan views. According to a recent poll, 73 percent of Republicans found Fox credible – compared to 45 percent of Democrats. *The Times* drew a 76 percent credibility rating from Democrats versus 52 percent from Republicans.

From *CQ Researcher,*
June 9, 2017

Trust in Media

*Can news outlets regain
the public's confidence?*

Chuck McCutcheon

The annual White House Correspondents' Dinner is known for its movie stars and not-so-gentle ribbing of the president. But this year's event was different. For the first time in 36 years, the president didn't attend. And one of journalism's legendary figures offset the glamour and jokes with a sober assertion countering criticism of the mainstream media as biased.

"Journalists should not have a dog in the political fight except to find that best obtainable version of the truth," *Washington Post* reporter Bob Woodward, whose work uncovering the Watergate scandal in the 1970s helped spur President Richard M. Nixon's resignation, said in a speech at the April gala.[1]

That same night, 95 miles away, at a rally in Harrisburg, Pa., to mark his 100th day in office, President Trump delivered a different message about journalists. "Their priorities are not my priorities, and not your priorities," Trump told a cheering, partisan crowd. "If the media's job is to be honest and tell the truth, the media deserves a very, very big fat failing grade."[2]

Woodward's and Trump's remarks illustrate the conflicting views that confront traditional news outlets as they try to rebuild public trust in the media that polls show has hit bottom. Those outlets — newspapers, magazines, websites and broadcast networks with professional, nonpartisan staffs — are victims of an overall decline of faith in government and nongovernmental institutions, as well as constant assaults from politicians that have put them in the crosshairs of today's polarized political climate. Trump is the latest leader of the assaults, labeling journalists "the enemy

Views of Media's Performance Show Partisan Divide

Democrats are more likely than Republicans to say the national news media do a very good job of keeping people informed. The percentage of Republicans with that view dropped 6 points over the last year, while the percentage of Democrats who feel that way increased by 5 points.

Percentages of U.S. adults who say national news media do "very well" or "fairly well" at keeping them informed:

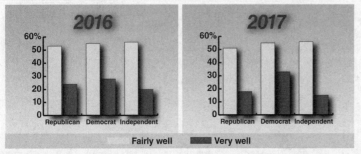

Source: Surveys conducted March 13-27, 2017, and Jan. 12-Feb. 8, 2016, "Americans' Attitudes About the News Media Deeply Divided Along Partisan Lines," Pew Research Center, May 10, 2017, https://tinyurl.com/lwvktsu

of the American people" and dismissing unfavorable coverage of him as "fake news."*[3]

The media also have deeply fragmented as the internet has given rise to a cacophony of voices casting doubt on traditional-media staples — notably the use of anonymous sources and the concepts of neutrality and dispassionate reporting. Facebook and other social media have fostered that cacophony by creating "echo chambers" that affirm people's beliefs and enable them to spread information — accurate and inaccurate — faster than ever.

But trust in the media also has been hurt by self-inflicted wounds, including blurred lines between news and commentary; fabricated stories written by rogue reporters; a focus on well-off urbanites while giving less attention to rural Americans; and the post-9/11 failure to

---

* While Trump defines unfavorable coverage as "fake news," the accepted definition is fabricated stories, posted on obscure websites, intended to disparage politicians and generate ad revenue through clicks after readers share them.

aggressively challenge the unfounded claim that Iraq had weapons of mass destruction. In addition, competition for readers has led some outlets to focus on "clickbait" — frivolous and incendiary stories, some untrue — at the expense of substantive topics.

Journalists and those studying the news business say mainstream media outlets must rise to the challenge by performing skillfully in the face of greater outside pressure and shrinking resources. They also must devote more energy to educating readers, listeners and viewers about how they operate.

"Journalism has a trust problem. . . . There's a growing rift between news organizations and the consumers they exist to serve," said Benjamin Mullin, managing editor of Poynter.org, the website for the Poynter Institute, a journalism-training center in St. Petersburg, Fla.[4]

Recent Gallup polls suggest the rift is wide:

- Just 32 percent of Americans trust the media, the lowest level recorded since Gallup began asking the question in 1972.[5]
- Forty-one percent of the respondents to another survey asking about the honesty and ethical standards of 22 professions ranked journalists "low" or "very low." Only members of Congress and car salespeople scored lower.[6]
- Sixty-two percent of Americans said the media favor one political party over the other, compared with 50 percent in past years.[7]

News organizations' failure to engender trust could cause society to splinter even further, warns Tom Rosenstiel, executive director of the American Press Institute and a senior fellow at the Brookings Institution, a centrist Washington, D.C., think tank.

"The press needs to rebuild its trust with the public," Rosenstiel says. "We've got to create [news stories] in such a way that people will say, 'I don't like the tone of that, but yeah, I'll accept it, because it's probably true.'"

The two biggest reasons people do not trust news are that they consider it one-sided or inaccurate, according to a 2016 poll by the Press Institute — a nonpartisan media-research organization in Arlington, Va.[8]

Yet the entire notion of "wrong" has become politicized. Trump made so many assertions judged false that the Oxford Dictionaries named "post-truth" its 2016 word of the year.[9] One of his advisers, Kellyanne Conway, caused an uproar in January when she described a questionable assertion about the size of Trump's inauguration crowd as an "alternative fact."[10] Another aide defended giving Trump a false magazine cover warning of a forthcoming ice age instead of global warming at a briefing by contending the information it contained was "fake but accurate."[11]

But more than most issues, Gallup and other polls show, media mistrust reflects the country's entrenched political divide.

A Pew Research Center poll in May found a 47 percentage-point gap between Democrats and Republicans over whether criticism from the media helps keep politicians honest — the largest gap since Pew began asking the question in 1985.[12] And according to a Morning Consult poll in December, 73 percent of Republicans found GOP-leaning Fox News credible — compared to 45 percent of Democrats. *The New York Times* drew a credibility rating of 76 percent from Democrats versus 52 percent from Republicans.[13]

Mistrust of the media is not a strictly partisan issue. African-Americans have accused the media of failing to recognize the Black Lives Matter movement as well as the importance of events fueling its rise.

Media scholars say some outlets have fueled the divide by coarsening discourse and lambasting news organizations whose politics differ from theirs. They also say the growth of watchdog groups, such as Media Matters and the Media Research Center, has added to

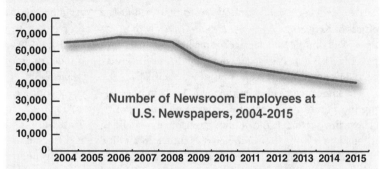

Newspapers Slashing Editorial Staffs

Newspapers in the United States cut more than 24,000 newsroom jobs — a decline of 37 percent — between 2004 and 2015, the most recent year data were available. Layoffs and buyouts among reporters and editors are expected to continue as newspapers struggle with falling circulation and ad revenue.

Number of Newsroom Employees at U.S. Newspapers, 2004-2015

Source: "Newspapers Fact Sheet," Pew Research Center, June 1, 2017, p. 8, https://tinyurl.com/yb8g77ht

the divide. Wealthy partisans finance many of those groups, which track inaccurate reporting, media bias and political gaffes.

Journalists of late have had to endure additional abuse. Four incidents occurred in May:

- A Federal Communications Commission (FCC) guard allegedly pinned a reporter for *CQ Roll Call* against a wall as he sought to ask commissioners a question at FCC headquarters in Washington, then forced him to leave a public meeting. An FCC commissioner apologized for the incident.

- In Montana, Republican congressional candidate Greg Gianforte was charged with misdemeanor assault after he allegedly threw a reporter to the ground who asked him a question. After winning the special election for the state's at-large House seat, Gianforte apologized for his conduct.

- Dan Heyman, a Public News Service reporter in West Virginia, was arrested after trying to question Health and Human Services Secretary Tom Price in a state Capitol hallway. Heyman said he was holding his phone toward Price to record him; police said he was trying to bypass Price's security detail.

- Reporter Nathanial Herz of the *Alaska Dispatch News* said state Sen. David Wilson (R-Wasilla) slapped him across the face after he asked the senator a question. Herz filed a police report, and the case has been turned over to the state's Office of Special Prosecution.[14]

Also in May, several windows were shattered at the offices of Kentucky's *Lexington Herald-Leader,* with investigators attributing the damage to small-caliber bullets, or possibly a BB gun. Newspaper publisher Rufus M. Friday cited a rise in hostile rhetoric toward journalists.[15]

For some media veterans, the media's role in uncovering inaccurate statements by Trump and other politicians while serving as the public's government watchdog is the biggest barometer of the media's future credibility.

"If the media for whatever reason fails to meet this challenge, then democracy as we have known it will slowly die," longtime television network correspondent Marvin Kalb, a professor emeritus at Harvard University's Kennedy School of Government and founding director of its Shorenstein Center on the Press, Politics and Public Policy, said in March.[16]

Those on the political right, however, see the mainstream media — or what they call the "legacy media" — as facing an insurmountable obstacle to rebuilding public trust. Above all, perhaps, they consider the media guilty of hypocrisy for its perceived bias against Republicans while insisting it favors neither party.

"The biggest challenge facing journalists today is a self-inflicted problem: too many activists with bylines posing as neutral observers, and they've been found out," says John Bicknell, executive editor of Watchdog.org, a network of websites covering local and state government funded by the Franklin Center for Government & Public Integrity, a news organization based in Alexandria, Va., with a free-market, limited-government perspective. "Once you've destroyed your own credibility, it's very difficult to get it back — and we see that in many, if not most, legacy newsrooms."[17]

Both conservative and liberal journalism observers say generalizing about "the media" is difficult, in large part because it encompasses an ever-growing array of news and information sources, each with its own mission and leanings.

"Lumping these disparate entities under the same single, bland label is like describing the denizens of the ocean as 'the fish,'" wrote *Washington Post* media reporter Paul Farhi.[18]

Despite such media diversity, the public tends to focus on national — not local — outlets when expressing mistrust. Joy Mayer, a consulting fellow at the University of Missouri's Donald W. Reynolds Journalism Institute, says she noticed this when speaking with readers and viewers around the country for a project she leads on media trust-building.

"I couldn't believe how quickly, in most people's minds, 'the media' jumps to national political coverage," Mayer says. "I tell them, 'The media are people who cover your local school board and high school sports.'"

The notion of "journalist" also is being expanded with the phenomenon of cellphone video capturing news incidents and social media's ability to give members of the general public the power to give direct on-the-scene reports while sharing information among friends.

Social media have created what Rosenstiel calls the "atomization of the news," in which people place more trust in who shared information with them than in the quality of news brands. That phenomenon, he says, helped fuel the "fake news" phenomenon.

As journalists, academics and others debate trust in the news media, here are some of the questions being raised:

Are traditional standards of objective journalism outdated?

One of the bedrock principles of traditional journalism is objectivity, generally defined as not playing favorites despite one's personal views. But the notion of objectivity has come under attack from critics of President Trump, who say his unfitness for the presidency demands the media take up an advocacy role to portray the truth more directly and accurately.

Many veteran journalists say objectivity is essential to developing trust. Media outlets, they say, have an obligation never to identify with any side in a conflict or other issue.

"Journalists in this tradition [of objectivity] have plenty of opinions, but by setting them aside to follow the facts — as a judge in court is supposed to set aside prejudices to follow the law and the evidence — they can often produce results that are more substantial and more credible," former *Times* executive editor Bill Keller said.[19]

In January, Lewis Wallace was fired from his job as a reporter for the syndicated business radio show "Marketplace" after publishing an article on the website *Medium*.[20] Journalists, Wallace wrote, "need to become more shameless, more raw, more honest with ourselves and our audiences" instead of simply reacting passively to what he predicted would be arrests and other attempts to curtail media freedom of speech under Trump.[21]

Among the most vocal critics of objectivity is American journalist Glenn Greenwald, whose articles in London's *Guardian* contained classified information on U.S. government surveillance in 2013 released by former national-security contractor Edward Snowden. "This voice that people at NPR and PBS and CNN are required to assume, where they're supposed to display this kind of non-human neutrality about the world in which they're reporting, is a deceitful, artificial one," said Greenwald, editor of the national-security website *The Intercept*.[22]

Kerry Lauerman, executive editor of the liberal-leaning news and commentary website *Mic*, which targets Millennials, encourages reporters not to hide their views. "We're stronger by having people with different points of view approach things with those points of view," Lauerman said. "It probably does further erode the sort of old-fashioned notion of objectivity. But I think that's better for journalism, too."[23]

Some critics of traditional media point to earlier eras to argue that mainstream journalism never has been truly objective — and should stop pretending it is.

Objectivity "has seldom existed in American history, and has especially been scarce since the 1960s, when activist journalism came out of the closet with its ideological coverage of Vietnam and then Watergate, all perfumed with the spurious claim to journalistic integrity and public service," said Bruce Thornton, a fellow at Stanford University's Hoover Institution.[24]

Other critics fault the language of objectivity. *National Review* columnist Jonah Goldberg pointed to The Associated Press stylebook's barring the use of "illegal immigrants," though "illegal immigration" is still permitted. Instead, The AP and other outlets have recommended terms such as "unauthorized" and "undocumented" for immigrants.

That usage, Goldberg said, is part of left-wing pro-immigration activists' agenda "to blur the distinctions between legal and illegal immigration. . . . As a matter of

fact and logic, the difference between an 'unauthorized immigrant' and an 'illegal immigrant' is nonexistent."[25]

Many journalists say absolute objectivity is impossible, given the inherent subjective nature of choosing one fact over another in telling a story.

But they say that something close to it can be achieved by doing rigorous reporting offering deep insights. That includes weeding out extremist voices and specious claims in favor of provable facts.

"Objectivity is all about doing your job well as a journalist," says Ken Paulson, a former editor of *USA Today* who is president of the First Amendment Center, which studies free-expression issues. He also is dean of Middle Tennessee State University's College of Media and Entertainment. "The question is, can you get up every morning and write what you find out — accurately write about what you've discovered?"

Paulson and many journalists say objectivity is rooted in fairness — conveying the arguments of all sides of an issue. But, they add, fairness does not mean "he said, she said" reporting — the oft-criticized practice of unquestioningly giving both sides equal weight.

"Good journalism doesn't require perfect balance," said Michael Kinsley, founding editor of *Slate* magazine. "In fact, perfect balance may be a distortion of reality. But journalism gains credibility when it gives all sides their due."[26]

The American Press Institute's Rosenstiel says one means of bolstering media trust — greater transparency — is enhancing objectivity by borrowing the methods of science and demonstrating to readers and viewers how news outlets arrive at their conclusions.

The Post, in publishing an e-book biography of Trump last year, put online an archive of most of its research materials, including thousands of pages of interview transcripts, court filings, financial reports, immigration records and other material.[27]

"There's this discipline of verifying — making sure you have enough sources and describing as much as [you] can about your sources, like showing your math in a school assignment that proves to the teacher that you did the work yourself," Rosenstiel says. "That's what the idea of an objective method of journalism is about."

Are the national news media out of touch with ordinary Americans?

Critics of mainstream journalism question whether staffers at national outlets are disconnected from people in

AP Photo/Sathi Soma

Edgar Maddison Welch surrenders to police in Washington, D.C., on Dec. 4, 2016. Armed with an assault rifle, the Salisbury, N.C., man drove to Washington to try to stop what online conspiracy theories falsely said was a child sex ring being run by Democratic presidential candidate Hillary Clinton out of a local pizza restaurant. Media experts and scholars say many voters were swayed during the presidential campaign by the proliferation of so-called fake news spread by alternative news websites and social media.

blue-collar jobs who often live outside of the metropolises of the East or West coasts. But journalists at those outlets dispute the charge.

The debate is an old one. In a 1996 article, "Why Americans Hate the Media," *Atlantic* national correspondent James Fallows said national political journalists fixate on tactical matters at the expense of issues that the public cares about more deeply.

"When ordinary citizens have a chance to pose questions to political leaders, they rarely ask about the game of politics," Fallows wrote. "They want to know how the reality of politics will affect them — through taxes, programs, scholarship funds, wars."[28]

Those tendencies have only worsened over the last two decades with the explosion of the internet and interest in polls and celebrity at the expense of more time-consuming, deeply reported pieces, media observers say. As the news business has shrunk, it has concentrated in New York, Washington and California.

The result, those observers say, helps explain the traditional media's failure to anticipate the outcome of 2016's election, in which Trump defied almost all polls and pundits to win the Electoral College despite losing the popular vote.

"Much of the East Coast-based media establishment is arguably out of touch with the largely rural population that voted for Trump," said Mathew Ingram, a *Fortune* senior writer covering the media.[29]

Dean Baquet, the *Times'* executive editor, said he is proud of his paper's campaign coverage. But he said after the election: "The New York-based and Washington-based media powerhouses . . . don't get the role of religion in people's lives."[30]

Veteran reporter and author David Cay Johnston, former board president of the group Investigative Reporters and Editors, said today's journalists no longer closely share their audience's concerns.

"There's been a tendency in the news to focus very much on, 'What's going on with the internet? What's going on with these exciting new gizmos?' As opposed to, 'What's happening to people who work in factories in Iowa and Michigan and their concerns?" Johnston said.

Johnston attributed the shift to changing demographics. In 1960, nearly one-third of reporters and editors had never attended a single year of college; in 2015, that figure was down to 8 percent — 38 percentage points below the number of adults 25 and older nationwide.[31]

College-educated journalists "began making newspapers move up the income ladder and the wealth ladder in terms of readership and lost sight of this mass audience they used to have," he said. "And a result, the coverage and what newspapers defined as important tended to be the concerns of the upper-middle class."[32]

Too many of the journalists are liberal, putting them further out of touch, says Watchdog.org's Bicknell. "If mainstream news organizations want to regain credibility with the public, they should begin by hiring young conservative journalists," he says.

The White House Correspondents' Dinner, which has evolved from an intimate gathering in 1921 into a televised gala of hundreds of journalists and politicians — and the celebrities they invite — often is cited as symbolizing the gulf between the national media and public. *The Times* stopped attending the dinner in 2008, saying it sent a misleading signal that the paper was too chummy with politicians.[33]

Criticism of the national media's aloofness from America extends beyond economic class and politics into race.

African-American talk show host Tavis Smiley cited the Trayvon Martin case as evidence that newsrooms have "the same unconscious bias that exists in police departments" because they lack staffers who understand black America. Martin, an unarmed 17-year-old African-American, was shot and killed in 2012 by neighborhood-watch volunteer George Zimmerman in a gated Florida community. Zimmerman, who is white, pleaded self-defense and was acquitted of second-degree murder.[34]

"The reality is that that story would never have made it to the front pages were it not for black media," Smiley said. "Oftentimes the mainstream media — particularly where people of color are concerned — is on the late freight."[35]

However, a number of academics and journalists say major news outlets are responding to such criticisms.

"That is something that needs a correction, and the correction has begun," former *Post* executive editor Leonard Downie, now a professor of journalism at Arizona State University, says of the accusation of being out of touch.

Downie and other media observers cite *The Times'* and other newspapers' detailed stories explaining the impacts of Trump's policies. That includes the White House's proposed budget, which calls for slashing or eliminating federal programs important to small communities and rural areas that backed Trump.

They also note that while the number of minorities at media outlets is still too low, it is on the rise. An American Society of News Editors survey found the minority workforce rose 5.6 percent from 2015 to 2016 among the 433 news organizations that took part in both years' surveys. Overall, minorities made up 17 percent of workers at daily print newspapers and 23 percent of employees at digital-only publications.[36]

Media observers are encouraged by journalists' willingness to "crowd-source" reporting — asking the public directly for help, expanding their networks and building credibility. *Post* reporter David Fahrenthold won a Pulitzer Prize in April for his work investigating Trump's charitable contributions, in part by soliciting information

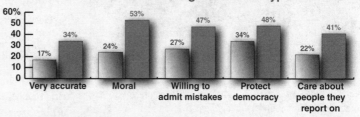

Most People Trust Media They Use

Americans tend to trust the news sources they rely on but distrust "the news media" as an abstract concept. For example, just over half of those surveyed viewed the news sources they consult as moral, but only 24 percent said that about the media in general.

Percent who said the following about each type of media:

Source: "'My' media versus 'the' media: Trust in news depends on which news media you mean," American Press Institute, May 24, 2017, p. 2, https://tinyurl.com/ya32z2za

from readers about whether they belonged to organizations that had been promised or received contributions.

When looking into whether Trump used $10,000 of charitable money to buy a portrait of himself, Fahrenthold recalled, "I asked my readers and Twitter followers for help, and they amazed me with their ingenuity. They found things that I never would have thought to find on my own."[37]

Times domestic-affairs correspondent Sheryl Gay Stolberg also cites "Anxious in America," a 2016 series to which she contributed, as another example of reporting about everyday Americans. It explored economic and social concerns in rural Appalachia, among African-Americans at a Philadelphia food pantry and evangelical Christians in small-town Iowa as well as other places.[38]

While acknowledging that the national media focuses too much on polls and "horse-race" journalism, Stolberg says of her paper, "I disagree that we don't reflect America."

Does the use of anonymous sources erode trust in journalism?

Critics of the use of anonymous sources call it a significant contributor to the erosion of trust in the media, while the practice's defenders say that — when done

Comedian Melissa McCarthy parodies White House press secretary Sean Spicer on "Saturday Night Live" on May 13, 2017. In recent weeks, assistant press secretary Sarah Huckabee Sanders has been giving press briefings instead of Spicer, who has had a rocky relationship with the press. Spicer faced withering criticism after President Trump pulled out of the Paris climate accord, telling reporters he did not know whether Trump accepted climate change science.

judiciously — it gets closer to the truth than quoting people only by name.

The use of such sources requires the public to place considerable faith in journalists, said Mary Louise Kelly, who covers intelligence agencies for NPR. "If I am using an anonymous source, I have given my word that I will not reveal their identity," Kelly said. "But I am asking you, the listener, to trust me that I have done everything in my power to make sure this person is who they say they are, that they have access to the information and also to weigh what's their motive."[39]

A Morning Consult/*Politico* poll in March found that 44 percent of those surveyed said it is likely reporters make up unnamed sources. As with other polls involving media trust, the poll showed a deep partisan split: 65 percent of Republicans said journalists made up sources, while just 24 percent of Democrats agreed.

The poll also showed that half of those surveyed didn't consider it appropriate for the media to use anonymous sources when reporting on government business. That issue also broke along partisan lines: 66 percent of Republicans considered it inappropriate compared to only 36 percent of Democrats.[40]

Trump has fed public mistrust about the practice. Reporters "have no sources; they just make them up when there are none," he said in February.[41]

The Times tightened its requirements for the use of unnamed sources in 2016 in response to two erroneous articles. One was based on unnamed officials who said inspectors general asked the Justice Department to open a criminal investigation into whether Hillary Clinton had mishandled sensitive information on a private email account she used as secretary of State. *The Times* later clarified that the referral was not criminal and did not name Clinton as a focus.[42]

Nevertheless, when *The Times* this year published a string of exclusive stories about Trump, the paper drew a warning from Liz Spayd, the paper's public editor.* She noted the articles relied heavily — some entirely — on unnamed sources. "The descriptions [of sources' identities] generally tilt far more toward protecting the sources than giving readers confidence in what they said," Spayd wrote.[43]

Conservative political commentator Mollie Hemingway, a senior editor at the *Federalist* magazine, responded to a slew of critical articles about Trump in May with a sarcastic tweet: "I didn't go to journalism school, but should our media really privilege unaccountable, anonymous sources to on-the-record accountable ones?"[44]

However, many in the news business say mainstream media outlets do a largely successful job in drawing a distinction between unnamed sources with a partisan ax to grind and those wanting to provide helpful information without risking their jobs.

Of those in the latter camp, "These are not people who pull us aside because they want to screw Donald Trump," *The Times*' Baquet said. "These are people who are worried about the direction of government."[45]

Reporters who make the most frequent use of anonymous sources have accumulated considerable trust with those sources, which should persuade the public to have confidence in those reporters, said Dana Priest, a Pulitzer Prize-winning national security reporter at *The Post*.

---

* *The Times* announced on May 31 that it was eliminating the public editor position, and Spayd resigned. The paper has recently created the Reader Center, which it described as a way to "build even stronger bonds with our readers."

Those reporters "are pretty good at judging the character of somebody that they actually quote without their name," Priest said. "And that's how we do that business. It would not happen without it, because they're really not supposed to be talking to us."[46]

The use of anonymous sources declined in the half-century between 1958 and 2008, reaching its peak in the 1970s, according to a 2011 study.

The study found journalists increasingly described the backgrounds of anonymous sources in some way rather than simply identifying them as "reliable sources." In 1958, 34 percent of stories with unnamed sources used that type of vague language, but that figure fell below 3 percent in 2008. It also found reporters more frequently explained the reasons why they grant anonymity.[47]

Paulson of the First Amendment Center says procedures to discourage reliance on anonymous sources — including having reporters share the names of sources with senior editors — led to a 70-percent reduction in their usage during his stint as *USA Today's* editor from 2004 to 2009.

Relying on unnamed sources while sustaining trust is "a balancing act," he says. "It has to be offset by the importance of the story. We were not going to use anonymous sources to find out the name of the new Taylor Swift album — only to reveal important information about national security."

BACKGROUND

Early Press Coverage

The First Amendment's guarantee of press freedom makes the news media "the only business in America specifically protected by the Constitution," as President John F. Kennedy once observed.[48] Nonetheless, journalists seldom have been held in high public regard.

Thomas Jefferson famously championed free expression: "Were it left to me to decide whether we should have a government without newspapers or newspapers without a government, I should not hesitate a moment to prefer the latter," the author of the Declaration of Independence and the nation's third president once said. Yet he griped about how those papers covered him.

"Nothing can now be believed which is seen in a newspaper," Jefferson wrote in 1787. "Truth itself

CBS News anchor Walter Cronkite, considered the country's most trusted figure during his long tenure, helped change public perception of the Vietnam War when he declared in a 1968 commentary that it was destined "to end in a stalemate."

becomes suspicious by being put into that polluted vehicle."[49]

For much of the 19th century, journalists stressed sensationalism over accuracy, with papers serving as mouthpieces for political parties. "He lies like a newspaper" became a common criticism.[50]

"Editors ran their own candidates — in fact they ran for office themselves, and often continued in their post at the paper while holding office," historian Garry Wills wrote. "Politicians, knowing this, cultivated their own party's papers, both the owners and the editors, shared staff with them, released news to them early or exclusively to keep them loyal, rewarded them with state or federal appointments when they won."[51]

Ulysses S. Grant, the commanding Union general during the Civil War, later served two scandal-filled presidential terms. During his second inaugural address in 1873, Grant railed against reporters, saying he had been "the subject of abuse and slander scarcely ever equaled in political history."[52]

The New York Press in 1897 coined the term "yellow journalism" to describe the fiercely competitive and sensationalistic New York newspapers owned by titans Joseph Pulitzer and William Randolph Hearst. The term came from the comic strip "The Yellow Kid," about a mischievous boy in a yellow nightshirt.[53]

The splashy reporting of Hearst's and Pulitzer's papers was offset by *The New York Times.* Tennessee publisher

Adolph S. Ochs acquired the paper in 1896 and vowed "to give the news impartially, without fear or favor, regardless of party, sect or interests involved."[54]

The emergence of investigative journalists — muckrakers — in the early 20th century helped boost trust. The best known was Upton Sinclair, whose 1906 novel *The Jungle* exposed labor and sanitary abuses in the meatpacking industry. Thirteen years later, Sinclair's *The Brass Check,* a work of nonfiction, compared the brass token used by patrons of prostitutes to wealthy newspaper owners' buying off journalists' credibility.[55] It sold more than 150,000 copies.[56]

Legendary journalist Walter Lippmann helped found *The New Republic* magazine in 1914 and became one of the world's most widely respected columnists.[57] Lippmann warned in a 1920 book that without a "steady supply of trustworthy and relevant news," then "all that the sharpest critics of democracy have alleged is true."[58]

During the 1920s, radio became common in American households. In 1934, President Franklin D. Roosevelt signed a bill into law stipulating that stations could lose their licenses if their broadcasts were considered too controversial. It required stations to offer equal time for political candidates.[59]

With the advent of television after World War II, the federal government again became involved in regulating journalistic content. Lawmakers became concerned that the three TV networks of the era — NBC, ABC and CBS — could misuse their broadcast licenses to advance a biased agenda. The Federal Communications Commission issued the Fairness Doctrine in 1949 requiring radio and TV stations to devote some of their programming to controversial issues and allow the airing of opposing views.[60]

During the 1930s and '40s, polls showed "at best only modest levels of trust in the news media," according to Georgetown University public policy professor Jonathan M. Ladd.[61]

But around midcentury, competition from television led newspapers to expand coverage and offer more deeply sourced and interpretive reporting. Papers also developed, along with magazines, a commercial model that led many of them to be hugely profitable through classified and display advertising.

It was during this period that a few newspapers, including the *Milwaukee Journal* and *Washington Post,*

questioned accusations by Wisconsin GOP Sen. Joseph McCarthy, who led the "Red Scare" investigations of alleged communists in the United States during the 1950s. CBS News reporter Edward R. Murrow, in a 1954 special report, said of the senator: "He didn't create this situation of fear — he merely exploited it, and rather successfully."[62]

By 1956, two-thirds of Americans said in polls that newspapers were fair. Of those charging unfairness, most thought they were too favorable toward President Dwight D. Eisenhower (1953-61) and other Republicans.[63]

Vietnam and Watergate

The Vietnam War hardened partisan attitudes toward the media. Reporters found struggles on the battlefront at odds with the upbeat assessments of military leaders, while TV news broadcast vivid combat images directly into American homes. CBS News anchor Walter Cronkite, considered the country's most trusted figure, changed the public perception of the war when he declared in a 1968 commentary that the war was destined "to end in a stalemate."[64]

Republican Nixon (1969-74) and his first vice president, Spiro T. Agnew, often accused reporters of untrustworthiness. On Vietnam, Nixon said "our worst enemy seems to be the press," while Agnew blasted "the tiny, enclosed fraternity of privileged men elected by no one."[65]

Reed Irvine, a Republican journalist and press critic, in 1969 founded the conservative watchdog group Accuracy in Media to provide what he saw as a check against the media's liberal excesses. It grew within two decades into a 30,000-member organization with a $1.5 million annual budget, drawing praise from GOP lawmakers for its work exposing alleged biases, errors and distortion.[66]

Journalists played the central role in the era's other most significant controversy—the 1972 break-in at Democratic National Committee headquarters in Washington's Watergate office building and subsequent events that culminated in Nixon's resignation in 1974.

Relying on anonymous sources, *Post* reporters Woodward and Carl Bernstein uncovered many of the developments tying Nixon and top aides to the break-in, a cover-up and other misdeeds. A 1976 movie portrayed

C H R O N O L O G Y

1900s-1950s *Newspapers draw competition from radio, television.*

1919 Celebrated muckraker Upton Sinclair, known for attacking his era's social and economic institutions, publishes *The Brass Check,* a nonfiction book equating the brass tokens that brothel patrons used to buy prostitutes' services with the money that newspaper owners paid journalists to influence their reporting.

1949 Federal Communications Commission (FCC) issues "Fairness Doctrine" requiring radio and TV stations to devote some programming to controversial issues and the airing of opposing views.

1954 CBS News correspondent Edward R. Murrow wins praise for commentary highly critical of Wisconsin Sen. Joseph McCarthy's "Red Scare" investigation of suspected communists in the United States.

1956 Two-thirds of Americans say in polls that newspapers are fair, more than twice the percentage as those who consider them unfair.

1960s-1980s *Partisan attitudes harden toward media.*

1968 CBS News anchor Walter Cronkite helps turn public opinion against the Vietnam War by predicting it will end in a stalemate. . . . Republican Richard M. Nixon is elected president and attacks the media's credibility.

1969 Conservative media critic Reed Irvine starts Accuracy in Media to provide what he calls a check against liberal media excesses.

1972 After a break-in at Democratic National Committee offices at Washington's Watergate complex, *Washington Post* reporters Bob Woodward and Carl Bernstein write numerous articles tying Nixon and his aides to the break-in, a subsequent cover-up and other misdeeds, all leading to Nixon's resignation.

1976 Gallup Poll shows public confidence in the media at an all-time peak of 72 percent.

1980 Republican Ronald Reagan is elected president, serving two terms during which his aides sought to aggressively shape media coverage through staged events and other means. . . . Business tycoon Ted Turner launches CNN, the first TV channel providing 24-hour news coverage.

1981 *Washington Post* reporter Janet Cooke wins Pulitzer Prize for "Jimmy's World," an article about an 8-year-old heroin addict that is later exposed as a fabrication.

1987 FCC abolishes "Fairness Doctrine," paving the way for talk radio to become a platform for conservatives and others to regularly attack perceived media bias.

1990s-Present *Internet reshapes public's perception of the media.*

1994 Matt Drudge, an unknown political commentator, starts the news-aggregation website *Drudge Report,* among the first of a number of conservative-leaning media outlets.

1996 Fox News launched; within six years it is the most-watched cable network.

2003 Critics of the Iraq War bash news outlets, saying they didn't aggressively challenge President George W. Bush's assertions that Iraq possessed weapons of mass destruction.

2004 Facebook social network launched; it quickly becomes a massively popular alternative to news outlets by taking their content and tailoring it to users' preferences.

2008 Alaska Gov. Sarah Palin, the GOP vice presidential nominee, lambastes what she calls "the lamestream media."

2016 During the presidential campaign, conservatives accuse mainstream media of under-covering Hillary Clinton's perceived misdeeds and Democrats accuse them of overcovering Donald Trump's rallies in order to boost ratings and online traffic. Some Democrats also accuse Fox News of pro-Trump bias.

2017 President Trump calls the media "the enemy of the American people" amid constant clashes with reporters.

Catching Politicians
With Their "Pants on Fire"

Fact-checking sites perform "very important journalism."

In the media-trust debate, two phrases have become part of the lexicon: "Pants on Fire" and "Pinocchios." The colorful expressions are used, respectively, on the fact-checking websites PolitiFact and Fact Checker, which evaluate the truth of government officials' statements. The sites' popularity has both irked their targets and raised questions about how the administrators of the sites choose which statements to parse.

The two sites are far from alone. U.S. news outlets had 52 separate fact-checking operations in 2016, up by 15 from 2015.[1] The biggest is PolitiFact (www.politifact.com), launched by the *Tampa Bay Times* in 2007, which won a Pulitzer Prize two years later and now has affiliations with news outlets in 18 states, public radio and the Scripps chain of television stations.*[2]

The Washington Post also started its fact-checking site, Fact Checker (https://www.washingtonpost.com/news/fact-checker/), in 2007. Another well-known site, FactCheck.org, was launched in 2003 by the University of Pennsylvania's Annenberg Public Policy Center.[3] On the political right, the website Conservapedia (www.conservapedia.com) — a conservative version of the online dictionary Wikipedia — aims to debunk what it considers overly liberal claims.[4]

At PolitiFact, claims are rated — as shown on an accompanying "Truth-O-Meter" — on a scale from "True" to "Pants on Fire," while Fact Checker assesses the degree of truth of a statement on a scale of zero to four "Pinocchios."

A Fact Checker column on May 18 assigned three Pinocchios to the assertion by House Minority Leader Nancy Pelosi, D-Calif., that 7 million veterans would definitely lose tax credits under the House Republicans' bill to repeal former President Obama's health-care overhaul, the Affordable Care Act. "In reality, it's not so certain," Fact Checker said.[5]

On May 12 PolitiFact gave a "Pants on Fire" rating to President Trump's assertion that allegations that his campaign may have colluded with Russia was a "made-up story" that Democrats used as an excuse for his victory. "Democrats did not create the story, nor do they control the agenda of the House and Senate committees, which are conducting their own investigations," the column declared.[6]

Fact-checking has evolved beyond its origins in the 1990s, when news outlets occasionally assessed claims in campaign advertisements, journalism scholars say. Today, TV networks such as CNN also do on-screen fact-checking during debates.

"It is very important journalism, and it's here to stay," says former *Post* executive editor Leonard Downie, now a professor of journalism at Arizona State University. (As a young deputy metropolitan editor of *The Post*, Downie supervised much of the paper's Watergate coverage by Bob Woodward and Carl Bernstein.)

A Pew Research Center survey last fall found 83 percent of voters consider it the media's responsibility to check the statements of candidates and campaigns. And 77 percent of those who said they planned to vote for Trump saw it as either a major or minor responsibility, compared with 89 percent of Hillary Clinton's supporters.[7]

Politicians have noticed. In a 2015 interview, then-Gov. Rick Perry, R-Texas, — now U.S. Energy secretary — said his state had reduced nitrogen-oxide emissions levels by 63.5 percent. Then he added, "Say 63 percent — that way, we won't get PolitiFacted." (The actual figure was 62.5 percent, the site noted.)[8]

But conservatives have criticized such sites because, they say, no public mechanism exists to show which assertions are fact-checked and which aren't, opening the selection process to bias. "When you're only advocating a political agenda, like PolitiFact, I understand, guys, where you're coming from," Fox News commentator Sean Hannity said in 2015 while disputing a "Pants on Fire" rating for an earlier assertion about Syrian refugees.[9]

In a 2016 study, political scientists Stephen Farnsworth of the University of Mary Washington and Robert Lichter of George Mason University examined hundreds of PolitiFact and Fact Checker evaluations and found that PolitiFact's selections were more critical of Republicans than Democrats "to a statistically significant degree." Fact Checker also was more critical of GOP politicians, they found, but not to as significant a degree.

---

* PolitiFact won the Pulitzer Prize for National Reporting for its coverage of the 2008 election, including its use of "probing reporters and the power of the World Wide Web to examine more than 750 political claims, separating rhetoric from truth to enlighten voters."

Farnsworth and Lichter said the sites should better explain how they choose claims to evaluate. "The lack of transparency from the organizations regarding their selection procedures, and the practical difficulties of content analyzing every controversial statement by every lawmaker, make it difficult to untangle the central question of whether partisan differences in fact-checking reflect the values of the fact-checkers or the behavior of their targets," they said.[10]

PolitiFact creator Bill Adair, now a journalism professor at Duke University who remains a contributing editor at the site, says PolitiFact vigorously tries to avoid bias by examining the most significant or newsworthy statements, regardless of political affiliation.

The Fact Checker's Glenn Kessler responded to complaints about Trump getting more fact-checks in 2016 than Clinton by saying the GOP nominee talked more. "We would have liked to publish a lot more fact-checks of Hillary than we did, but she didn't give many interviews, her speeches were rigidly vetted and didn't vary that much," Kessler said. "Meanwhile, Trump would call in to four to five TV shows and go off the script in rallies."[11]

Tom Rosenstiel, executive director of the American Press Institute, a nonpartisan media-research organization, encourages fact-checking that goes beyond cataloguing assertions. "We've heard fact-checking is more effective if it's viewed as 'Help me understand this issue' rather than just right and wrong," Rosenstiel says. "The idea we have is, let's fact-check a broader issue rather than a specific claim. You would pick issues based on how important they are. Like transportation — what are the key facts? Or water — how clean is the water?"

Several efforts are underway to incorporate new technologies into fact-checking and to present the results in various formats. Studies show that charts and other graphical information can make information stick better in readers' minds, Adair says.

"We need to develop different ways of presenting accurate information," he says.

— *Chuck McCutcheon*

The online fact-checking site PolitiFact has made "Pants on Fire" part of the media-trust lexicon. Fact Checker, with its "Pinocchio" rating, is another popular site that evaluates the truth of government officials' statements.

Screenshot/CQ Researcher Staff

[1] Bill Adair, "Keep on Fact-Checking!" *The New York Times,* Nov. 8, 2016, http://tinyurl.com/l9kwxqj.

[2] Mark Stencel, "The facts about fact-checking across America," ReportersLab.org, Aug. 3, 2016, http://tinyurl.com/ya6fqb4n.

[3] Brooks Jackson, "Is This a Great Job or What?" FactCheck.org, Dec. 5, 2003, http://tinyurl.com/ya4w9btx; Glenn Kessler, "About the Fact Checker," *The Washington Post,* Sept. 11, 2013, http://tinyurl.com/ybsf4v9t; The PolitiFact Staff, PolitiFact.com, http://tinyurl.com/yck9q3pw.

[4] "Conservapedia.com," undated, http://tinyurl.com/2ppol7.

[5] Michele Ye Hee Lee, "Nancy Pelosi's claim that 'seven million veterans will lose their tax credit' under the GOP health bill," *The Washington Post* Fact Checker, May 18, 2017, http://tinyurl.com/ybqrlm2z.

[6] Jon Greenberg, "Donald Trump's Pants on Fire claim Russia story 'made-up' by Democrats," PolitiFact.com, May 12, 2017, http://tinyurl.com/yaktmejd.

[7] Michael Barthel, Jeffrey Gottfried and Kristine Lu, "Trump, Clinton Supporters Differ on How Media Should Cover Controversial Statements," Pew Research Center, Oct. 17, 2016, http://tinyurl.com/ybhyyf3f.

[8] W. Gardner Selby, "Rick Perry gets a laugh out of Texas Truth-O-Meter," PolitiFact Texas, Jan. 15, 2015, http://tinyurl.com/y7stbhgj.

[9] Alex Griswold, "Hannity Blasts 'Left-Wing Website' Politifact For Giving Him 'Pants on Fire' Rating,' " *Mediaite,* Oct. 28, 2015, http://tinyurl.com/oncqu6g.

[10] Stephen J. Farnsworth and S. Robert Lichter, "A Comparative Analysis of the Partisan Targets of Media Fact-checking: Examining President Obama and the 113th Congress," paper presented at the American Political Science Association convention, September 2016, http://tinyurl.com/yabwrdx2.

[11] Alexios Mantzarlis, "Fact-checking under President Trump," Poynter.org, Nov. 10, 2016, http://tinyurl.com/jmbg4sn.

the pair as dogged investigators, and a Gallup poll that year showed public confidence in the media at an all-time peak of 72 percent.[67]

But Republican Ronald Reagan's presidency (1981-89) ushered in greater public skepticism. Some Democrats accused reporters of being reluctant to criticize him out of fear of being cut off from the flow of White House information. They also said reporters were too willing to take part in stage-managed events crafted by Reagan aides with an eye toward enhancing the president's popularity.[68]

In 1987, during Reagan's second term, the FCC abolished the Fairness Doctrine, paving the way for talk radio.[69] Rush Limbaugh, a conservative political commentator and host of a talk show in Sacramento, Calif., made perceived liberal bias one of his signature issues and saw his program become nationally syndicated in 1988 and the nation's most popular radio show.[70]

The Reagan era also saw competitive constraints and government regulation of cable channels relaxed by the Cable Communications Policy Act of 1984. The industry boomed, as all-news "24/7" cable channels such as CNN changed the face of television journalism by reaching a wide audience and offering coverage for longer periods than the TV networks.[71]

Media Scandals

Cable increased pressure on print media, which in the post-Watergate era had boosted in-depth reporting. *The Post's* Janet Cooke won a Pulitzer Prize in 1981 for "Jimmy's World," a lengthy article about an 8-year-old heroin addict that the paper retracted when she admitted the boy was fictitious.[72]

The Cooke controversy was followed by scandals involving other journalists found to have fabricated or embellished their work:

- *The New Republic's* Stephen Glass, who wrote articles in the 1990s about young conservatives, Wall Street traders and Silicon Valley technology entrepreneurs that were found to be entirely or partially false.[73]
- *USA Today's* Jack Kelley, who wrote dispatches from Serbia and other war-torn countries in the 1990s and early 2000s that the newspaper found were substantially inaccurate. Editor Karen

Jurgensen resigned in 2004 over her failure to detect the fabrications.[74]

- *The Times'* Jayson Blair, who was found in 2003 to have copied material from other publications as well as devising fake quotations, then lying about it. The paper's two top editors subsequently stepped down.[75]
- NBC News anchor Brian Williams, who was suspended without pay for six months in 2015 — and eventually lost his anchor post — following a segment in which he exaggerated details of his travels in a military helicopter during the Iraq War. The story opened a controversy involving other instances in which Williams exaggerated or invented dangers he faced.[76]
- Sabrina Rubin Erdely, a journalist for *Rolling Stone*, the magazine and its parent company were found guilty of defamation of a former University of Virginia administrator in a 2014 magazine article about sexual assault on campus that included a debunked account of a fraternity gang rape.[77]

Media trust levels, as measured by Gallup, fell to just over 50 percent of Americans polled through the late 1990s and into the early 2000s. Media credibility has consistently been below 50 percent since 2007.[78]

Democratic President Bill Clinton was a polarizing figure, especially after his sexual relationship with White House intern Monica Lewinsky led to his impeachment and subsequent acquittal. "The Drudge Report," a conservative news-aggregation website launched in 1994, led the charge against Clinton and other Democrats.

Other right-wing outlets that followed in its wake, such as Breitbart News, were aggressively skeptical of President Barack Obama. The outlets gave voice to the "alt-right," a loose coalition of white nationalists, white supremacists, anti-Semites and others seeking to preserve what they consider traditional Western civilization.[79]

Such outlets "were preaching this is the only place you can get news — this is the only place you can trust," said Ted Newton, president of a Washington political communications firm and an adviser to Republican Mitt Romney's 2012 presidential campaign. "All other media outlets are lying to you [they said], so you need to come to us. And so in an attempt to capture an audience, they almost made them slaves to those news outlets."[80]

Cable news discovered that many viewers were hungry for partisanship. Fox News launched in 1996 with a motto to be "fair and balanced," combining straight news reporting with pro-Republican commentary.

Though critics labeled Fox a GOP soapbox for bigotry and propaganda, it struck a chord with viewers who believed the rest of media displayed an overly liberal tilt to become the most-watched cable channel in 2002.[81] Rival cable channel MSNBC, created in 1996 as a partnership between NBC and Microsoft, sought starting in 2007 to become Fox's liberal counterweight.[82]

Critics of the Iraq War blasted Fox and the rest of the media for not more aggressively investigating GOP President George W. Bush's justification of the 2003 invasion — that Iraq possessed nuclear, chemical or other so-called weapons of mass destruction. One *Times* reporter, Judith Miller, came under criticism for writing articles giving credence to Iraqi and U.S. officials who made that claim.[83]

Some journalists said deep public support for Bush after the Sept. 11, 2001, terrorist attacks influenced how aggressively they challenged his claims.

In the run-up to the war, "There wasn't any reporting in the rest of the press corps, there was stenography," recalled John Walcott, Washington bureau chief for McClatchy Newspapers, which published some of the most skeptical coverage about the decision to invade. "The administration would make an assertion, people would make an assertion, people would write it down as if it were true, and put it in the newspaper or on television."[84]

Social Media

Facebook, Twitter and other social-media sites further lessened the need for Americans to rely on newspapers, TV or other news outlets. Facebook's algorithms assessed what people clicked on and then fed them similar content, a development that many experts say further lessened trust in mainstream outlets.

Politicians began recognizing the power of social media in appealing directly to a mass audience. Alaska Gov. Sarah Palin, the 2008 GOP vice presidential nominee, inveighed against "the lamestream media."[85]

At the same time, media watchdog groups formed across the ideological spectrum. On the political right, hedge fund executive Robert Mercer and his daughter

Craigslist founder Craig Newmark, whose website has attracted millions of dollars' worth of ads away from local newspaper classified advertising, has joined several private and nonprofit groups and media organizations in supporting projects aimed at developing faith in the media. "As a news consumer, like most folks, I want news we can trust," Newmark said. "That means standing up for trustworthy news media and learning how to spot clickbait and deceptive news."

Getty Images/Justin Sullivan

Rebecca gave $13.5 million between 2008 and 2014 to the Media Research Center, whose projects include a website (CNSNews.com) that publishes stories it says the mainstream media overlooks.[86] On the left, liberal business magnate George Soros gave at least $1 million to Media Matters for America, which also has obtained funding from or formed partnerships with several groups that Soros funds or has funded.[87]

In the 2016 presidential race, traditional media came under attack from all sides. Hillary Clinton's campaign castigated journalists for lavishing too much uncritical attention on Trump, whose colorful candidacy drew far more coverage than any of his Republican primary rivals.[88] Supporters of Vermont Sen. Bernie Sanders, Clinton's main primary opponent, accused the media of not taking him seriously and undermining his campaign.[89]

Neither Clinton nor Sanders, however, made media criticism as central to their races as Trump. Three months before the election, Trump named Steve Bannon, a founding member of the board of Breitbart, as head of his campaign. He later tapped the controversial Bannon as his chief strategist in the White House.

Trump made, and continues to make, near-daily use of Twitter as a weapon to bypass and attack traditional

Falling Newsroom Employment Erodes Trust

Reporters are "stretched thinner. That hurts trust."

Journalists are having a tough time building trust, in part because there are fewer of them and those who remain are stretched thin.

Declining circulation and falling advertising revenue have led to dramatic downsizing at print, broadcast and digital outfits. Newspapers, for instance, shed more than 24,000 reporting and editing jobs — a 37 percent drop — between 2004 and 2015, the latest year for which figures exist.[1] And the remaining reporters must not only gather the news and write stories but also shoot videos and constantly update their stories in real time using Twitter, Facebook and other social media.

"As newsrooms shrink, there's less time to do stories and they're doing shorter, more incomplete stories," says Tom Rosenstiel, executive director of the American Press Institute, a nonpartisan media research group in Arlington, Va. "As a consumer, you say, 'This paper is thinner,' " he says, while journalists are having to "write a tweet and do a video [so] they're stretched thinner. That hurts trust. You don't have as much time to do everything."

Facing plummeting ad income, Gannett Co., the country's largest newspaper chain and owner of *USA Today* and more than 100 other dailies, reduced its workforce about 2 percent last October.[2] The company also cut staff at its Tennessee and New Jersey papers this year, but has refused to publicize recent cuts, according to the *Columbia Journalism Review.*[3] BH Media Group, a subsidiary of Berkshire Hathaway, the conglomerate headed by Nebraska investor Warren Buffett, announced in April it was cutting 289 jobs at its 31 dailies and nearly 50 weeklies.[4]

And the future economic climate for newspapers could get even worse, said Nicco Mele, former *Los Angeles Times* senior vice president. "If the next three years look like the last three years," he predicted in 2016, "somewhere between a third to a half" of the 50 largest metropolitan papers in the country could go out of business. Mele is now director of the Shorenstein Center on Media, Politics and Public Policy at Harvard University.[5]

Staff cuts have decimated coverage of state legislative news. Between 2005 and 2014, investigative and in-depth reporting on state government declined 30 percent at six major papers, according to a 2016 study by a George Washington University graduate student.[6]

Downsizing local and state government coverage means greater secrecy — and potentially increased corruption — because fewer media outlets are holding state and local institutions accountable, several watchdog groups have warned. "The traditional media, particularly newspapers, have always led the open-government charges if the school board is closing a meeting illegally or the city is denying records or a judge is kicking a reporter out," said Jeffrey Hunt, a media lawyer in Salt Lake City. He sees the media "leaving the field in terms of fighting these battles."[7]

Not all of the economic news is bad — especially for the big media outlets such as *The New York Times*, *The Washington Post* and cable network MSNBC that have devoted substantial resources to the unfolding controversy over Russia's alleged involvement in the U.S. presidential election and ties to President Trump's administration.

In January *The Post* generated more new subscriptions than in any other month, beating what had been a record-setting November.[8] The paper has hired hundreds of reporters and editors since Amazon's Jeff Bezos bought the paper a few years ago, and Jed Hartman, chief revenue officer, predicted that 2017 would be its third year of double-digit revenue growth.[9] And during the first three months of this year *The Times* added 308,000 net digital-only news subscriptions — more than in any quarter in its history.[10] First-quarter revenues increased 5.1 percent over the first quarter of 2016, and circulation revenues jumped 11.2 percent.[11]

Stephen Farnsworth, a professor of political science and international affairs at the University of Mary Washington in Fredericksburg, Va., said the two papers are benefiting from a jump in the number of serious news consumers because of Trump. Those people "are appreciating the media more than they did last year at this time," says Fransworth, who directs Mary Washington's Center for Leadership and Media Studies.[12]

Despite those numbers, *The Times* in late May announced a round of newsroom buyouts aimed primarily at editors. The paper also announced it was abolishing the "public editor," or ombudsman, position held by Liz Spayd. Publisher Arthur Sulzberger said the paper would create a "Reader Center" to interact with the public.[13]

Meanwhile, the left-leaning MSNBC was the second-most-watched cable network during prime time during the week of May 15 — behind TNT, which carried several NBA playoff games. MSNBC's weekday prime-time shows averaged 2.44 million, eclipsing Fox News' 2.40 million for the first time ever.[14] Fox has devoted less coverage to the Russia controversy, and its commentary has been solidly pro-Trump. Some industry analysts wonder if its approach will hurt both its credibility and financial situation.[15]

Numerous advertisers backed away from Fox after commentator Bill O'Reilly was forced out in April amid allegations of sexual harassment and popular Fox commentator Sean Hannity had to apologize for advancing a discredited rumor that a murdered Democratic National Committee staffer was targeted for death by Hillary Clinton and liberal philanthropist George Soros.[16]

No one in the industry, however, has an easy solution for how news organizations can boost revenues while maintaining trust. Some foundations are financing investigative reporting, and some wealthy donors are providing millions of dollars to fight fake news and support in-depth reporting.

Another experiment is emulating the Netherlands' *De Correspondent (The Correspondent),* which recently announced a U.S. prototype. The online news site is funded by 56,000 members, who each pay about $63 a year for work done by its 21 full-time staff and 75 freelancers. The site aims to do in-depth, unique articles without competing against other media for breaking news, said Jay Rosen, a New York University professor of journalism who is helping with the U.S. version's launch.[17]

At journalism conferences, Rosen wrote, he has heard "a very good question: What if news organizations optimized every part of the operation for trust? Not for speed, traffic, profits, headlines or prizes . . . but for trust. What would that even look like? My answer: It would look a lot like *De Correspondent*."[18]

— *Chuck McCutcheon*

[1] "Newspapers Fact Sheet," Pew Research Center, p. 8, June 1, 2017, https://tiny url.com/yb8g77ht.

[2] Philana A. Patterson, "Gannett to reduce workforce by about 2% to help manage costs," *USA Today,* Oct. 24, 2016, http://tinyurl.com/yaknjj3y.

[3] Steve Cavendish, "Gannett Slashes Staffs at Tennessee Papers," *Nashville Scene,* March 28, 2017, http://tinyurl.com/ydff4nfa; Benjamin Mullin, "Layoffs hit North Jersey Media Group, again," Poynter.org, http://tinyurl.com/h8erxqr. Also see David Uberti, "Gannett newspapers are hiding an important local story," *Columbia Journalism Review,* May 5, 2017, http://tinyurl.com/y97jnu7w.

[4] Paul Fletcher, "Berkshire Hathaway's Media Group Cuts 289 Newspaper Jobs Nationwide," *Forbes,* April 4, 2017, http://tinyurl.com/ybwl52l3.

[5] "Nicco Mele — In Search of a Business Model: The Future of Journalism in an Age of Social Media and Dramatic Declines in Print Revenue," Shorenstein Center on Media, Politics and Policy, Harvard University, Feb. 18, 2016, http://tinyurl.com/ya3qes95.

[6] Lauren A. Dickinson, "The Strength of State Government Reporting: How In-Depth News and Investigative Coverage by Six U.S. Newspapers Fared from 2005 Through 2014," master of arts thesis, George Washington University, May 15, 2016, http://tinyurl.com/yb6ajwsl.

[7] Miranda S. Spivack, "Public contracts shrouded in secrecy," "Reveal" (Center for Investigative Reporting), Nov. 16, 2016, http://tinyurl.com/y9jvtrue.

[8] Ken Doctor, "Trump Bump Grows Into Subscription Surge — and Not Just for the New York Times," *TheStreet.com,* March 3, 2017, http://tinyurl.com/y7hu29ff.

[9] James B. Stewart, "Washington Post, Breaking News, Is Also Breaking New Ground," *The New York Times,* May 19, 2017, http://tinyurl.com/y8cs94x2.

[10] Sydney Ember, "New York Times Co. Reports Rising Digital Profit as Print Advertising Falls," *The New York Times,* May 3, 2017, http://tinyurl.com/m72ezr5.

[11] "The New York Times Company Reports 2017 First-Quarter Results," *Business Wire,* May 3, 2017, http://tinyurl.com/y8mr6d8b.

[12] Natalia Wojcik, "Trump has been 'rocket fuel' for NYT digital subscriptions, CEO says," CNBC.com, May 3, 2017, http://tinyurl.com/kyp6y46.

[13] Tali Arbel, "Among the job cuts at The New York Times, the public editor," *Boston.com* (The Associated Press), May 31, 2017, http://tinyurl.com/y88zmdz8.

[14] James Hibberd, "MSNBC weekly ratings beat Fox News, CNN for first time ever," *Entertainment Weekly.com,* May 22, 2017, http://tinyurl.com/m2sntup.

[15] Stephen Battaglio, "Trump-Russia story is a threat to Fox News' ratings dominance," *Los Angeles Times,* May 23, 2017, http://tinyurl.com/y9l5msgq.

[16] Simon Dumenco, "Is the Sean Hannity Advertiser Revolt Bill O'Reilly All Over Again?" *Advertising* Age, May 25, 2017, http://tinyurl.com/ybpayo4k.

[17] Jay Rosen, "Jay Rosen: This is what a news organization built on reader trust looks like," NiemanLab, March 28, 2017, http://tinyurl.com/ktkmpgb.

[18] *Ibid.*

Getty Images/MSNBC/NBCU/Heidi Gutman

Rachel Maddow, host of the "Rachel Maddow Show" on MSNBC, is celebrated by liberals – and reviled by conservatives – for her partisan commentary. In today's highly polarized political and media climate, 62 percent of Americans say the media favor one political party over the other, compared with 50 percent in past years.

media.[90] House Majority Leader Kevin McCarthy, R-Calif., a Trump supporter, said the president's deployment of Twitter is "like owning newspapers."[91]

Facebook came under heavy criticism during the campaign for tailoring stories in users' online feeds to what those users had previously read. That included a substantial amount of fake news, which made the network "a sewer of misinformation," according to Joshua Benton, director of Harvard's Nieman Journalism Lab.[92]

As polls showed trust in the media plummeting, news organizations and outside groups ramped up efforts to rebuild it.

One effort was the Reynolds Institute's Trusting News project, launched in January 2016 to look at how news outlets could rebuild trust through social media. The project found successful social-media posts shared several traits: They were about familiar topics that people were inclined to interact with; they gave people something specific to react to; and they used informal language to be relatable.[93]

A participant, the *Standard-Examiner* in Ogden, Utah, developed a video for Facebook and its website in which local African-Americans and law enforcement officials met to discuss Black Lives Matter.[94] The project

"was a new way for us to see the importance of having a conversation with the readers and being transparent," says Ann Elise Taylor, the paper's news editor.

The Coloradoan newspaper in Fort Collins, Colo., used a hit-and-run bicycle accident as a way to explain how — contrary to some readers' beliefs — journalists regret having to cover bad news. The Facebook post generated more than 3,500 link clicks — far more than expected.[95]

The Cincinnati television station WCPO-TV also took part, using Facebook to explain its commitment to covering child poverty while acknowledging the challenges in exploring the topic because it cannot show children's faces or use their voices on camera.[96]

"With the state of media and the way people think about media, it's crazy not to get involved with a project like this to win their trust," says Mike Canan, WCPO.com's editor.

CURRENT SITUATION
Trump and the Media

The early months of Trump's presidency have been marked by aggressive news coverage — led by *The Times* and *Post* — about whether Russia's government worked behind the scenes to help his campaign and influence his new administration.

A Quinnipiac University poll in early May indicates the media covering Trump may have gained some ground in winning the public's confidence. But it also showed skepticism of journalists remains entrenched.

When asked whom people trusted more to tell the truth about important issues, 31 percent picked Trump and 57 percent cited the media, a rise of 5 percentage points from mid-February, when the president denounced the media as "the enemy of the American people" in a tweet.[97]

However, the poll also showed that voters disapproved, 58 percent to 37 percent, of the way the media cover the president.[98]

Such a split in attitudes reflects the harm inflicted from Trump's attacks, says Bill Adair, a former *Tampa Bay Times* reporter and founder of the fact-checking site PolitiFact who is now a professor of journalism at Duke University.

"Clearly there's been a hunger for accurate, objective news lately — that's been encouraging," Adair says. "But

Should journalists try to be objective?

YES THOMAS KENT
President and CEO, Radio Free Europe/Radio Liberty; Former Standards *Editor, The Associated Press*

Written for *CQ Researcher*, June 2017

Not every journalist needs to be objective. But if sources of objective journalism disappear, society will suffer a tragic loss.

Some claim it's impossible for journalists to be objective; no one, they say, can report the news without a shade of personal opinion.

This might be true if a journalist's job were simply to provide one version of reality. That would open the way for journalists to impose their views on others. But the real goal of objectivity isn't so much about controlling the information available as about making sure readers get all the facts and interpretations they need to make up their own minds.

Smart journalists draw these facts and interpretations not only from their own investigations but also from reporting and reasonable opinions on social networks — making a well-done objective news story deeply democratic, reflecting input from many places. Objectivity demands only that journalists keep their personal views out of their stories. Personal opinions should be saved for opinion columns, where people expect writers to advocate for their points of view.

Critics sometimes claim objective journalism is a robotic, mindless craft of simply writing down what everyone says. It is nothing of the sort. So-called fake news and fantasy narratives have no place in an objective news article. Some things happened; others didn't. A newsmaker spoke in one context; to put his or her words in another is a lie. Journalists remain responsible for the truth of what they publish.

Some critics also accuse objective journalists of scrubbing humanity and emotion out of stories in a bid to avoid any opinion. But objectivity doesn't mean rejection of human feeling. The slaying of children by a gunman at a school can be fairly referred to as horrific; there is no need for a paragraph saying "on the other hand." A photographer covering a war or disaster can put aside his camera when he has a chance to save a life.

The world will be far poorer if journalism is allowed to become nothing but a stream of opinion pieces, which by their nature shortchange some points of view in order to advance the author's argument.

Society must have a place where thoughtful readers without the time to do extensive personal research can find fair, accurate accounts of events as well as a variety of responsible opinion to put them into context. Objective journalism fills this need.

NO BRUCE THORNTON
Research Fellow, Hoover Institution; Professor of Classics and Humanities, Fresno State University

Written for *CQ Researcher*, June 2017

So-called objective journalism is another progressive idea based on scientism, the notion that human behavior and action can be as predictable and reliable as science. In earlier times, media reported obvious facts, but the political interpretation of those facts reflected what James Madison called the "passions and interests" of the competing political factions in a diverse country. The numerous newspapers across the country reflected this diversity, which is why they often had the word "Democrat" or "Republican" in their titles.

After World War II, journalism was professionalized and training happened in "J schools" at liberal universities, which biased much reporting toward liberal and urban sensibilities. The advent of television reduced the number of newspapers that once provided diversity, allowing the liberal interpretation to dominate far beyond the media centers in New York, Washington, Chicago and Los Angeles.

In the 1960s journalism became an activist and advocacy business. Coverage of the Vietnam War and the Watergate scandal interpreted events from a partisan and left-wing perspective that saw U.S. intervention as neocolonial adventurism and President Richard Nixon as a budding tyrant out to destroy the Constitution. As a consequence, South Vietnam was abandoned to the communist North, and Nixon was forced to resign, paving the way for Jimmy Carter's disastrous foreign policy of retreat and appeasement.

The repeal of the Federal Communications Commission's Fairness Doctrine in 1987 was followed by the advent of talk radio, which began to erode the monopoly of the big-three television networks and dominant newspapers like *The New York Times* and *The Washington Post*. Then came cable news with shows like Fox News, and the internet. Now thousands of outlets reflect the diversity of opinion that the First Amendment was written to protect. Where once maybe 50 opinion makers dominated political discourse, now there are hundreds of thousands. Their impact became clear when in 2004 CBS icon Dan Rather was brought down by internet sleuths for reporting "fake news" about George W. Bush's National Guard service.

Today we've returned to a true "marketplace of ideas" in which diverse political perspectives can compete, and ideological biases pretending to be "objective" can be exposed within hours. Once more it is up to the citizens to be informed and use their critical judgment rather than taking on faith the reporting of a handful of media outlets. If they misuse that freedom, that's the price always to be paid when people are free.

Pierre Omidyar, founder of eBay, launched a $100 million global project in April aimed at restoring trust in the media and other institutions. The focus will be on strengthening independent media and investigative journalism, confronting misinformation and hate speech and enabling citizens to better engage with government.

Trump has said some incredibly damaging things about the media."

Both *The New York Times* and *Post* have seen financial gains that media analysts say reflect increased trust.[99]

Barton Swaim, a conservative *Post* columnist, said he expected the mainstream media to aggressively cover Trump's presidency after being demonized during the election. "Even so, the sheer visceral animosity from the media, together with the aggressively insurgent opposition by [Democratic] holdovers from within the government, has shocked me as much as the election itself," Swaim said.[100]

Media scholars and journalists say Trump tacitly understands traditional media's importance. They note that when the initial attempt to overturn Obama's Affordable Care Act could not win enough GOP supporters to be brought up for a House vote in March, the first reporters Trump notified were not from a conservative outlet, but *The Times* and *Post*.[101]

Commentators at Fox News, like other GOP-leaning outlets, have remained supportive of Trump, devoting less airtime to the ongoing investigation's into the Trump campaign's possible collusion with Russia than other outlets. Fox's opinion-givers and other conservatives have echoed the president in arguing that the leaking of classified information to the media is far more serious than speculation of any administration wrongdoing.[102]

William Kristol, a conservative pundit and former Fox commentator, criticized the conservative media, particularly Fox News, for "rationalizing everything" Trump does.[103]

The nonprofit investigative website *ProPublica,* founded in 2008, recently has expanded on its collaborations with other outlets, pairing with *The Times* and The Associated Press in March to rapidly collect White House staffers' financial-disclosure forms.[104] *ProPublica* opened a bureau in Chicago this spring, its first outside Washington and New York.[105]

In the Midwest, Cleveland's *Plain Dealer* and *Cleveland.com* launched the reporting collaboration "Ohio Matters," which has sent reporters to six rural, suburban and urban parts of the crucial swing state to hear concerns. Trump carried Ohio by 8 percentage points in 2016, far above most polls' earlier projections.[106]

To try to show its commitment to watchdog journalism, *The Post* in February put the motto "Democracy Dies in Darkness" below its front-page nameplate. The move led the conservative *Washington Times* to launch its own slogan — "Real News for Real Americans."[107]

Trust-Related Projects

Several private and nonprofit groups have joined media organizations on projects aimed at developing trust.

A global coalition of technology leaders, academic institutions and others announced a $14 million undertaking in April, The News Integrity Initiative, to combat declining trust in media and advance news literacy. Supporters include Craig Newmark, founder of the online classified-ad site Craigslist, which, ironically, has severely crippled newspapers' classified revenues.

"As a news consumer, like most folks, I want news we can trust," Newmark said. "That means standing up for trustworthy news media and learning how to spot clickbait and deceptive news."[108]

The program will be administered by the CUNY Graduate School of Journalism. It will focus in part on helping readers better spot fake news and frivolous "click-bait" disguised as news articles.[109]

The philanthropic investment firm Omidyar Network, the brainchild of eBay founder Pierre Omidyar, in April launched a $100 million project over the next three years aimed at restoring trust in the media and other institutions globally. The funding will focus on strengthening independent media and investigative journalism, tackling misinformation and hate speech, and enabling citizens to better engage with government.[110]

The Reynolds Institute recently wrapped up the second phase of its "Trusting News" project with 30 media outlets around the country. That phase — which will conclude with a report this fall — invited local readers and viewers to describe how news outlets can win their confidence, Mayer says.

In Cincinnati, WCPO.com's invitation for readers to take part drew 463 responses in less than a day — a sign Canan says people care about the issue.

"One of the biggest takeaways is, there's a lot of guilt by association," he says. "As I delved into conversations with people, they said, 'I don't trust the media,' but it was really, 'I don't when [it] comes to politics.' Or they don't trust the national media."

Canan says he has started collaborating with the *Cincinnati Enquirer,* a journalistic competitor, on ways to build trust. Peter Bhatia, the newspaper's editor and vice president for audience development, said he and other editors have been trying to "demystify our process" by explaining how the newsroom operates in talks to tea party as well as progressive groups and when publishing investigative projects or deeply reported work.

Transparency "becomes more of an imperative as we work hard to restore trust lost in the last election cycle, regardless of how fair the charges against us may be," Bhatia said.[111]

The *Standard-Examiner's* Taylor, who also took part in the Reynolds Institute project, agrees on the need for increased transparency. She says a surprising number of readers do not make the distinction between news and commentary, with separate staffs handling each as at most outlets.

"That's knowledge a lot of journalists take for granted," she says. "One thing I'd like to address in being more transparent is explain what is an editorial, what is an opinion piece, how do they differ from a news story and how are all these things connected? That would be a valuable tool people could use as they consume news for the rest of their lives."

Facebook and Google

The twin colossi of the information world are trying to bolster confidence in the media in the face of criticism that they have enabled the spread of fake news and profited from sharing journalism content without paying its producers for it.

Facebook has put out new tools to stem the spread of fake news. If users click on a news story, they now have the option of reporting it as being false. If enough users flag such stories, Facebook will send the article to a factchecking organization such as Snopes. com or PolitiFact — and if those outlets agree, the article will appear on Facebook with a red banner that says "Disputed by third-party fact checkers" and include a link to the explanation.

In addition, Facebook has promised to employ software to help identify fake news stories and has its engineers working on finding websites that impersonate actual news sites.[112]

Founder Mark Zuckerberg published a manifesto in February outlining how the social-media giant can contribute to restoring trust in news and information. One of his aims is to encourage the growth of local news and improve the range of business models on which news organizations rely.[113]

Google's News Lab, launched in 2015, seeks to connect journalists with programs, data and other resources to use in their reporting. It started the First Draft coalition to create standards and best practices for verifying eyewitness media content and combating fake news. The coalition expanded last year to include 80 partners, including Facebook and Twitter, and is working with universities and other organizations around the world.[114]

Critics of Google's and Facebook's efforts, however, say their continued dependence on incorporating news articles in their content compels them to do far more to help the media regain trust.

Steven Waldman, founder of Life-Posts.com, where people share personal stories online, said Facebook and Google should devote 1 percent of their profits for five years to create a $4.4 billion permanent endowment to transform local journalism.

"These companies are among the biggest beneficiaries of the digital disruption that has, among other things, caused the crisis in American journalism," Waldman said. "It's time for the disrupters to solve the problems."[115]

OUTLOOK
Unpleasant Truths

With political polarization deeply rooted in society, journalism scholars and those in the news media predict mistrust of journalists will continue — the question is to what degree.

"The media will never be all that popular; it's in the business of telling unpleasant truths," says Stephen Farnsworth, a professor of political science and international affairs at the University of Mary Washington in Fredericksburg, Va., who directs its Center for Leadership and Media Studies.

The American Press Institute's Rosenstiel says trust levels "are going to continue to slip, because we're in a more polarized world, and I don't see a solution to that on the horizon." Part of the problem, he adds, is the inability of the Democratic and Republican parties to produce leaders who are considered trustworthy to a broad bipartisan audience.

"It's ironic that when he left office, Barack Obama had much higher approval ratings than Trump or any politician has now," he says. "I think there's a sort of nostalgia — we can, in retrospect, appreciate people, but when we're on the field of battle, we retreat to our team."

More conservatives need to have their voices heard in traditional media, said former Wisconsin right-wing talk-radio host Charlie Sykes. If that does not happen, he said, those conservatives will continue putting their faith in outlets that mirror their preconceived views.

"You can do the best reporting in the world, but unless you can find a way to restore that credibility . . . it won't even register," said Sykes, now a contributing *New York Times* columnist.[116]

Benton, of Harvard's Nieman Lab, is particularly interested in seeing whether online outlets such as BuzzFeed and Mic that have marketed themselves to younger, urban readers will start courting conservative readers.

"Do they double down on identity-driven stories embracing the values of diversity and multiculturalism?" he asked. "Or — at a time when many are under their own revenue strains . . . do any of them see a market opportunity in the Trump voter?"[117]

Finding ways to finance quality journalism at larger-scale mainstream outlets will be critical, says Arizona State's Downie, the former *Post* editor.

"I'm pleased to see that audiences are beginning to find ways to pay more for digital subscriptions to the *Times*, support events produced by other news organizations and increase membership in public radio," he says. "Foundations are stepping up and philanthropists are stepping up. But whether that's sufficient five or 10 years from now, I can't say."

The Reynolds Institute's Mayer, who leads the Trusting News project, predicts a split between news organizations catering to polarization and those willing to earn more trust. Of the latter group, she expects an increased effort to listen more closely to readers.

"There's no room in journalism anymore for people who don't see customer service and understanding the audience as part of the job," she says. "People in journalism have to have an entrepreneurial mindset and a customer-service mindset with a focus on, 'Here's what we do.'"

Duke University's Adair, the PolitiFact creator, estimates that if trust levels do pick up, it will take 10 or 15 years. The media "will do better at labeling types of articles and being more transparent," he says. "There's likely to be a renewed effort to invest in news literacy so that people, particularly young people, have a better understanding of the news ecosystem."

Until then, said *Post* media columnist Margaret Sullivan, a former *Times* public editor, young people going into journalism must accept being mistrusted.

"You have to understand there's a mission attached to our job and that we need to do it well," Sullivan told a student audience at the University of Wisconsin-Madison, "and put on our big-boy and big-girl pants and not worry that we're under attack — because it's going to continue."[118]

NOTES

1. Jennifer Calfas, "Read the Advice Bob Woodward and Carl Bernstein Gave at the White House Correspondents' Dinner," *Time,* April 30, 2017, http://tinyurl.com/n7qvosk.

2. Mark Landler, "Trump Savages News Media at Rally to Mark His 100th Day," *The New York Times,* April 29, 2016, https://tinyurl.com/ycvcq7u9.

3. See Chuck McCutcheon, "Populism and Political Parties," *CQ Researcher,* Sept. 9, 2016, pp. 721-744.

4. Benjamin Mullin, " 'I want to see us take journalism to people where they are': A Q-&-A with Jeff Jarvis about restoring trust in journalism," Poynter.org, April 3, 2017, https://tinyurl.com/y6uugszv.

5. Art Swift, "Americans' Trust in Mass Media Sinks to New Low," Gallup, Sept. 14, 2016, https://tinyurl.com/hda5s4u.

6. "Honesty/ethics in professions," Gallup, Dec. 7-11, 2016, https://tinyurl.com/lcer8a.

7. Art Swift, "Six in 10 in US See Partisan Bias in News Media," Gallup, April 5, 2017, https://tinyurl.com/metlvk6.

8. "How trust can be broken, and the decline of confidence in the press," American Press Institute, April 17, 2016, https://tinyurl.com/yadwe7or.

9. "Oxford Dictionaries Word of the Year 2016 is . . . Post-Truth," Oxford Dictionaries.com, Dec. 12, 2016, https://tinyurl.com/kdgknmd.

10. "Meet The Press 01/22/17," NBC News, Jan. 22, 2017, https://tinyurl.com/y7fuxnjy.

11. Shane Goldmacher, "How Trump gets his fake news," *Politico,* May 15, 2017, https://tinyurl.com/kwlt3yl.

12. Michael Barthel and Amy Mitchell, "Americans' Attitudes About the News Media Deeply Divided Along Partisan Lines," Pew Research Center, May 10, 2017, https://tinyurl.com/ydgdyxx.

13. Laura Nichols, "Poll: Majority Find Major Media Outlets Credible," Morning Consult, Dec. 7, 2016, https://tinyurl.com/ya59mcra.

14. Paul Farhi, "Reporters say they are being roughed up. Observers point to Trump," *The Washington Post,* May 26, 2017, https://tinyurl.com/ycfzvlbj.

15. "Windows shattered at Herald-Leader building; suspected bullet damage found," *Lexington Herald-Leader* (Ky.), May 29, 2017, https://tinyurl.com/ycp3c2ds.

16. "Marvin Kalb on Current Challenges to the Freedom of the Press," National Press Club Journalism Institute speech, YouTube.com, posted April 1, 2017, http://tinyurl.com/ycxubgdd.

17. Andrew Collins, "Meet Watchdog editor John Bicknell: journalist, author, history buff," Franklin Center for Government & Public Integrity, Nov. 3, 2015, https://tinyurl.com/y9pwrkyd.

18. Paul Farhi, "Dear readers: Please stop calling us 'the media.' There is no such thing," *The Washington Post,* Sept. 23, 2016, https://tinyurl.com/y9v84hfb.

19. Mathew Ingram, "Glenn Greenwald vs. the NYT's Bill Keller on objectivity and the future of journalism," *Gigaom,* Oct. 28, 2013, https://tinyurl.com/yd76vw7v,

20. Margaret Sullivan, "How one reporter's rejection of objectivity got him fired," *The Washington Post,* Feb. 1, 2017, https://tinyurl.com/y7e98afx.

21. Lewis Wallace, "Objectivity is dead, and I'm okay with it," Medium.com, Jan. 27, 2017, https://tinyurl.com/y8k56rtw.

22. Adam Ragusea, "Glenn Greenwald on the 'adversarial force' of a free press," *Current,* March 29, 2016, http://tinyurl.com/y8zokx8h.

23. "Objectivity: What Is It Good For?" WNYC-FM's "On the Media" transcript, Feb. 3, 2017, https://tinyurl.com/ybg5hlbe.

24. Bruce Thornton, "We Citizens Have to Guard the Media 'Guardians,' " *FrontPageMag,* Sept. 2, 2016, https://tinyurl.com/ya368tpe.

25. Jonah Goldberg, "The Press Is Not the Enemy," *National Review,* Feb. 24, 2017, https://tinyurl.com/yaox2yj7.

26. Michael Kinsley, "Is It Possible There Is Nothing Nice to Say?" *The New York Times,* May 13, 2017, https://tinyurl.com/ybrufzqw.

27. "'Trump Revealed': The reporting archive," *The Washington Post,* Aug. 30, 2016, https://tinyurl.com/h9g6rgg.

28. James Fallows, "Why Americans Hate the Media," *The Atlantic,* February 1996, https://tinyurl.com/y8y9h3st.

29. Mathew Ingram, "Here's Why the Media Failed to Predict a Donald Trump Victory," *Fortune,* Nov. 9, 2016, https://tinyurl.com/z8db88p.

30. " 'New York Times' Executive Editor On The New Terrain Of Covering Trump," "Fresh Air," NPR, Dec. 8, 2016, https://tinyurl.com/jdo6pxg.

31. Andrew McGill, "U.S. Media's Real Elitism Problem," *The Atlantic,* Nov. 19, 2016, https://tinyurl.com/y9jd3fu6.

32. Carrie Sheffield, "WATCH: Journalism used to fight for the working man, now it's a bastion of 'trust fund kids,'" *Salon.com,* March 19, 2017, https://tinyurl.com/yd8esfe3.

33. "History of the WHCA," White House Correspondents' Association, https://tinyurl.com/csdr45h; Jim Romenesko, "Why NYT doesn't attend White House Correspondents' Association Dinner," Poynter.org, May 4, 2011, https://tinyurl.com/yawpvrp9.

34. See Peter Katel, "Racial Conflict," *CQ Researcher,* Jan. 8, 2016, pp. 25-48.

35. Nick Tabor, "PBS?'s Tavis Smiley on What's Wrong (and Right) With the Media," *New York*, July 24, 2016, https://tinyurl.com/yabdclp3.

36. Shan Wang, "U.S. newsrooms seem to be getting a little more diverse. But minority journalists are still, well, a minority," NiemanLab.org, Sept. 9, 2016, https://tinyurl.com/zqkx9zg.

37. "The President and the Press: The First Amendment in the First 100 Days," Newseum.org event transcript, April 12, 2017, https://tinyurl.com/y8yn3o4w.

38. "Anxious in America," *The New York Times,* 2016, https://tinyurl.com/y8dx7ucp.

39. "Why The Media Use Anonymous Sources," "Morning Edition," NPR, Dec. 16, 2016, https://tinyurl.com/hs9a4v4.

40. Eli Yokley, "Voters Skeptical of Anonymous Sourcing, but Still Trust Political Reporting," *Morning Consult,* March 8, 2017, https://tinyurl.com/y7m6dryj; "Morning Consult National Tracking Poll #170301," *Morning Consult,* March 2-6, 2017, p. 265, https://tinyurl.com/ycvdgy5h.

41. Tara Golshan, "Full transcript: President Trump's CPAC speech," *Vox.com,* Feb. 24, 2017, https://tinyurl.com/ybescrr8.

42. "Following Multiple Debacles, NY Times Is 'Cracking Down On The Use Of Anonymous Sources,'" Media Matters for America, March 15, 2016, https://tinyurl.com/yamapyfc.

43. Liz Spayd, "The Risk of Unnamed Sources? Unconvinced Readers," *The New York Times,* Feb. 18, 2017, https://tinyurl.com/yb2wmu3r.

44. Mollie Hemingway, tweet, May 15, 2017, https://tinyurl.com/y9z4rmgv/

45. Jill Disis, "New York Times editor: Why journalists need to use anonymous sources," CNN.com, Feb. 26, 2017, https://tinyurl.com/ycuvz6hd.

46. "Why The Media Use Anonymous Sources," *op. cit.*

47. Steve Myers, "Study: Use of anonymous sources peaked in 1970s, dropped by 2008," Poynter.org, Aug. 9, 2011, https://tinyurl.com/y98utmk9. The study was by Matt J. Duffy, a professor of international media law at Zayed University in Abu Dhabi, and Ann E. Williams, a professor of communication at Georgia State University.

48. "John F. Kennedy Speeches/The President and the Press: Address before the American Newspaper Publishers Association, April 27, 1961," John F. Kennedy Presidential Library and Museum, https://tinyurl.com/zuxwmen.

49. Lindsey Bever, "Memo to Donald Trump: Thomas Jefferson invented hating the media," *The Washington Post,* Feb. 18, 2017, https://tinyurl.com/ybh5hqro; Daniel Lattier, "Thomas Jefferson Had Some Issues With Newspapers," *Intellectual Takeout,* Aug. 28, 2015, https://tinyurl.com/y76v92bt.

50. Ryan Holiday, "Abraham Lincoln as Media Manipulator-in-Chief: The 150 Year History of Corrupt Press," *The Observer*, Nov. 5, 2014, https://tinyurl.com/ycq45rf6.

51. Garry Wills, "How Lincoln Played the Press," *New York Review of Books*, Nov. 6, 2014, https://tinyurl.com/yaoc27mz.

52. "Second Inaugural Address of Ulysses S. Grant," Yale University Law School, Lillian Goldman Law Library, https://tinyurl.com/yb9okf5b.

53. "Yellow journalism," *New World Encyclopedia,* https://tinyurl.com/yagthwpu.

54. "Our History," New York Times Company, https://tinyurl.com/y7hxev7j; "Without Fear or Favor," *The New York Times,* Aug. 19, 1996, https://tinyurl.com/ybtored9.

55. Upton Sinclair, *The Brass Check: A Study of American Journalism* (1919), https://tinyurl.com/y7zsf7um.

56. "Upton Sinclair," https://tinyurl.com/yc2574cl.

57. "Walter Lippmann," *Encyclopaedia Brittanica,* https://tinyurl.com/y93ffgw5.

58. Walter Lippmann, *Liberty and the News* (1920), p. 11.

59. Stuart N. Brotman, "Revisiting the broadcast public interest standard in communications law and regulation," Brookings Institution, March 23, 2017, https://tinyurl.com/kpugnbz.

60. Dan Fletcher, "A Brief History of the Fairness Doctrine," *Time,* Feb. 20, 2009, https://tinyurl.com/yawejko8.

61. Jonathan M. Ladd, *Why Americans Hate the Media and How It Matters* (2013), p. 62, http://tinyurl.com/mljy8vp.

62. "Joseph R. McCarthy," History.com, https://tinyurl.com/o724hco; David Mindich, "For journalists covering Trump, a Murrow moment," *Columbia Journalism Review,* July 15, 2016, http://tinyurl.com/ybhfryk4.

63. Ladd, *op. cit.*

64. "Final Words: Cronkite's Vietnam Commentary," NPR, July 18, 2009, https://tinyurl.com/3wncqv3.

65. Chester Pach, "Public Learned Less After Media Was Blamed for Failure in Vietnam," *The New York Times,* April 29, 2015, https://tinyurl.com/ycult2yx; Christopher Cimaglio, " 'A Tiny and Closed Fraternity of Privileged Men': The Nixon-Agnew Antimedia Campaign and the Liberal Roots of the U.S. Conservative 'Liberal Media' Critique," *International Journal of Communication 10* (2016), https://tinyurl.com/y86wosuv.

66. "The Retromingent Vigilantes Revel," Accuracy in Media Report, October 1989, https://tinyurl.com/y8h26snb.

67. Swift, "Americans' Trust in Mass Media Sinks to New Low," *op. cit.*

68. Mark Hertsgaard, *On Bended Knee: The Press and the Reagan Presidency* (1988).

69. Fletcher, *op. cit.*

70. "Rush Limbaugh," Biography.com, https://tinyurl.com/ce2e5qh.

71. Michael I. Meyerson, "The Cable Communications Policy Act of 1984: A Balancing Act on the Coaxial Wires," *Georgia Law Review 19,* Spring 1985, https://tinyurl.com/y8kfytwm.

72. Mike Sager, "The fabulist who changed journalism," *Columbia Journalism Review,* Spring 2016, https://tinyurl.com/y7rmfgnh.

73. Michael Hiltzik, "Stephen Glass is still retracting his fabricated stories — 18 years later," *Los Angeles Times,* Dec. 15, 2015, https://tinyurl.com/yb3ryk6r.

74. Jacques Steinberg, "Editor of USA Today Resigns; Cites Failure Over Fabrications," *The New York Times,* April 21, 2004, https://tinyurl.com/y8gdzx53.

75. Isabella Kwai, "Why he did it: Jayson Blair opens up about his plagiarism and fabrication at the New York Times," ReportersLab.org, April 12, 2016, https://tinyurl.com/y8msdlel.

76. Paul Farhi, "At long last, Brian Williams is back — humbled and demoted to MSNBC," *The Washington Post,* Sept. 21, 2015, http://tinyurl.com/y7gnkb6c.

77. T. Rees Shapiro, "Jury finds reporter, Rolling Stone responsible for defaming U-Va. dean with gang rape story," *The Washington Post,* Nov. 4, 2016, http://tinyurl.com/ybhzols8.

78. Swift, *op. cit.*

79. See Marcia Clemmitt, "'Alt-Right' Movement," *CQ Researcher,* March 17, 2017, pp. 241-264.

80. Oliver Darcy, "Donald Trump broke the conservative media," *Business Insider,* Aug. 26, 2016, https://tinyurl.com/j8qprjf.

81. "Roger Ailes Looks Back on 15 Years of Fox News," The Associated Press, Fox News.com, Oct. 5, 2011, https://tinyurl.com/y9anos9o.

82. Alex Weprin, "A Brief History Of MSNBC.com And NBCNews.com," *AdWeek,* July 16, 2012, https://tinyurl.com/ydz8jpqz.

83. Erik Wemple, "Judith Miller tries, and ultimately fails, to defend her flawed Iraq reporting," *The Washington Post,* April 9, 2015, https://tinyurl.com/y8occ74s.

84. Max Follmer, "The Reporting Team That Got Iraq Right," *The Huffington Post,* May 25, 2011, https://tinyurl.com/yo99zz.

85. Andy Barr, "Palin trashes 'lamestream media,'" *Politico,* Nov. 18, 2009, https://tinyurl.com/yc9g7ok7.

86. Matea Gold, "The Mercers and Stephen Bannon: How a populist power base was funded and built," *The Washington Post,* March 17, 2017, https://tinyurl.com/m8gctl3.

87. Keach Hagey, "Soros gives $1 million to Media Matters," *Politico,* Oct. 20, 2010, https://tinyurl.com/29da5l3.

88. Nicholas Confessore and Karen Yourish, "$2 Billion Worth of Free Media for Donald Trump," *The New York Times,* March 15, 2016, https://tinyurl.com/z9jkzcn.

89. Nicole Fisher, "Sanders' Supporters: Why Some Won't Back Clinton," *Forbes,* Aug. 17, 2016, https://tinyurl.com/y7kt698g.

90. Robert Draper, "Trump vs. Congress: Now What?" *The New York Times Magazine,* March 26, 2017, https://tinyurl.com/mxl7vvv.

91. *Ibid.*

92. Joshua Benton, "The forces that drove this election's media failure are likely to get worse," NiemanLab, Nov. 9, 2017, https://tinyurl.com/nrccvms.

93. "Trusting News," Donald W, Reynolds Journalism Institute, February 2017, https://tinyurl.com/kbsgehl.

94. "VIDEO: Discussing race and policing in Northern Utah," *Standard-Examiner* (Ogden, Utah), July 27, 2016, https://tinyurl.com/ybp dzlqd.

95. "Newsrooms Partners: The Coloradoan," Trusting News website, undated, http://tinyurl.com/ycyyjwxu/.

96. "WCPO — 9 On Your Side," Facebook post, Sept. 23, 2016, https://tinyurl.com/yb926w5u.

97. Michael M. Grynbaum, "Trump Calls the News Media the 'Enemy of the American People,' " *The New York Times,* Feb. 17, 2017, https://tinyurl.com/js4uyw5.

98. "May 10, 2017 — U.S. Voters Send Trump Approval To Near Record Low; Quinnipiac University National Poll Finds; No Winner In Media War, But Voters Trust Media More," Quinnipiac University, May 10, 2017, https://tinyurl.com/kebfbpv.

99. Sydney Ember, "New York Times Co. Reports Rising Digital Profit as Print Advertising Falls," *The New York Times,* May 3, 2017, https://tinyurl.com/m72ezr5.

100. Barton Swaim, We're not learning from the Trump story — because we've peeked at the last page," *The Washington Post,* May 18, 2017, https://tinyurl.com/y9pj3tbv.

101. Jackie Strause, "After 'Fake News' Claims, Trump's First Calls After Health-Care Defeat Were to N.Y. Times, Washington Post," *Hollywood Reporter,* March 24, 2017, http://tinyurl.com/kxenhcp.

102. Maxwell Tani, "Here's how Fox News responded to reports Trump leaked classified information to Russian officials," *Business Insider,* May 16, 2017, https://tinyurl.com/ycbbmkor.

103. Aidan McLaughlin, "Bill Kristol: Most of Fox News Has Become 'Ridiculous,' "*Mediaite,* May 15, 2017, https://tinyurl.com/mb87gr4.

104. Eric Umansky, "How We're Learning To Do Journalism Differently in the Age of Trump," *ProPublica,* May 8, 2017, https://tinyurl.com/mk2lvhe.

105. Jackie Spinner, "Q&A: Louise Kiernan says ProPublica Illinois will 'find areas where we can have impact,'" *Columbia Journalism Review,* March 6, 2017, https://tinyurl.com/ybj3zgbh.

106. "Ohio Matters: Redesigning Political Coverage in Ohio," *Cleveland.com,* http://tinyurl.com/mvecskx; "Ohio: Trump vs. Clinton," *Real ClearPolitics.com,* http://tinyurl.com/y923vh3u

107. Rachel Stoltzfoos, "The Washington Times Adopts A New Slogan For Trump Era," *The Daily Caller,* March 13, 2017, https://tinyurl.com/y8etm5nq.

108. Benjamin Mullin, "Can trust in the news be repaired? Facebook, Craig Newmark, Mozilla and others are spending $14 million to try," Poynter.org, April 3, 2017, http://tinyurl.com/nyfkvh4.

109. *Ibid.*

110. Margaret Sullivan, "Omidyar network gives $100 million to boost journalism and fight hate speech," *The Washington Post,* April 4, 2017, https://tinyurl.com/y9a84mes.

111. Peter Bhatia, "To Restore Trust, Enhance Transparency," *Nieman Reports,* Feb. 15, 2017, https://tinyurl.com/yb8jh224.

112. David Pogue, "What Facebook Is Doing to Combat Fake News," *Scientific American*, Feb. 1, 2017, https://tinyurl.com/h26du9a.

113. Mark Zuckerberg, "Building Global Community," Facebook, Feb. 16, 2017, https://tinyurl.com/myq4nkf.

114. Steve Grove, "The Google News Lab in 2016, and where we're headed," *Medium.com*, Dec. 6, 2016, https://tinyurl.com/y747x5bt.

115. Steven Waldman, "What Facebook Owes to Journalism," *The New York Times*, Feb. 21, 2017, https://tinyurl.com/y9kjtyf2.

116. Cadence Bambenek, "Recap: Trust, Truth and the Future of Journalism," Center for Journalism Ethics, University of Wisconsin-Madison, April 13, 2017, https://tinyurl.com/ycdxnwxf.

117. Benton, *op. cit.*

118. "Truth, Trust & the Future of Journalism: Keynote Conversation with Margaret Sullivan," Center for Journalism Ethics, University of Wisconsin-Madison, YouTube video, posted April 5, 2017, https://tinyurl.com/y8dpw97y.

BIBLIOGRAPHY

Selected Sources

Books

Anderson, C.W., Leonard Downie and Michael Schudson, *The News Media: What Everyone Needs to Know*, Oxford University Press, 2016.
A media culture professor at the College of Staten Island (Anderson), a former *Washington Post* executive editor (Downie) and a Columbia University journalism professor (Schudson) explain the economic, technological and societal forces that have helped erode trust in journalism.

Carlson, Matt, *Journalistic Authority: Legitimating News in the Digital Era*, Columbia University Press, 2017.
A St. Louis University communications professor examines the cultural, structural and technological factors that prompt readers to accept or reject a journalist's version of events.

Graves, Lucas, *Deciding What's True: The Rise of Political Fact-Checking in American Journalism*, Columbia University Press, 2016.
A University of Wisconsin professor of journalism and mass communication chronicles the evolution of fact-checking websites and their importance in assessing assertions by government officials.

Stone, Roger, *The Making of the President 2016: How Donald Trump Orchestrated a Revolution*, Skyhorse Publishing, 2017.
A political adviser and friend of Donald Trump details how Trump's strategy of castigating mainstream news outlets helped him win the presidency.

Articles

"The Case Against the Media. By the Media," New York, July 25, 2016, https://tinyurl.com/zm2sn6g.
The weekly magazine interviews dozens of print, broadcast and online journalists about what they see as their profession's biggest flaws.

Benton, Joshua, "The forces that drove this election's media failure are likely to get worse," NiemanLab, Nov. 9, 2017, https://tinyurl.com/nrccvms.
The director of Harvard University's media-research center says the problems that led the media to be blindsided by Trump's victory must be corrected.

Rosenstiel, Tom, "What the post-Trump debate over journalism gets wrong," Brookings Institution, Dec. 20, 2016, https://tinyurl.com/h6pgke5.
A senior fellow at the centrist think tank and executive director of the American Press Institute says journalists must embrace new methods to earn trust, such as making documents and other reporting research available for readers to see firsthand.

Shafer, Jack, "How Trump Took Over the Media By Fighting It," Politico Magazine, Nov. 5, 2016, https://tinyurl.com/jqnhfwn.
The political website's media writer says Donald Trump went far beyond any other presidential candidate in condemning reporters.

Thornton, Bruce, "We Citizens Have to Guard the Media 'Guardians,'" *Frontpage Mag*, Sept. 2, 2016, https://tinyurl.com/n86nge5.
A fellow at Stanford University's Hoover Institution says negative coverage of Trump's presidential campaign reflects the mainstream media's longtime bias against Republicans.

Toffel, Richard J., "The Country Doesn't Trust Us — But They Do Believe Us," NiemanLab, Dec. 12, 2016, https://tinyurl.com/n2vjyzy.
The president of the investigative website ProPublica highlights the importance of trust in an essay accompanying interviews with several dozen journalists, academics and others predicting future media trends.

Umansky, Eric, "How We're Learning To Do Journalism Differently in the Age of Trump," ProPublica, May 8, 2017, https://tinyurl.com/mk2lvhe.
ProPublica, a nonprofit online news organization, says it will cover the Trump administration by digging deeper, collaborating, being transparent and being comfortable with uncertainty.

Reports and Studies

"State of the News Media 2016," Pew Research Center, June 15, 2016, https://tinyurl.com/zh7vqdj.
The nonprofit research group says the economic pressures facing the news media intensified in 2015, with average weekday newspaper circulation seeing its biggest drop since 2010.

"Trusting News," Donald W. Reynolds Journalism Institute, February 2017, https://tinyurl.com/kbsgehl.
A research project of the University of Missouri's journalism think tank says news outlets can employ Facebook and other social media to effectively build trust with audiences.

" 'Who Shared It?': How Americans decide what news to trust on social media," American Press Institute, March 20, 2017, https://tinyurl.com/leh49n7.
A collaboration between the American Press Institute and The Associated Press-NORC Center for Public Affairs Research finds that when Americans read news on social media, how much they trust the content is determined less by who creates the news than by who shares it.

Swift, Art, "Americans' Trust in Mass Media Sinks to New Low," Gallup, Sept. 14, 2016, https://tinyurl.com/hda5s4u.
The polling company finds trust in the media at its lowest level since Gallup began asking the question in 1972.

For More Information

Accuracy in Media, 4350 East West Highway, Suite 555, Bethesda, MD 20814; 202-364-4401; www.aim.org. Conservative media watchdog organization that searches for potential liberal bias in news reporting.

American Press Institute, 401 N. Fairfax Drive, Suite 300, Arlington, VA 22203; 571-366-1200; www.americanpressinstitute.org. A nonprofit group that researches journalism trends.

American Society of News Editors, 209 Reynolds Journalism Institute, Missouri School of Journalism, University of Missouri, Columbia, MO 65211; 573-884-2430; www.asne.org. Promotes ethical journalism, supports First Amendment rights and defends freedom of information and open government.

Fairness & Accuracy in Reporting, 124 W. 30th St., Suite 201, New York, NY 10001; 212-633-6700; www.fair.org. Liberal media watchdog organization that monitors bias and censorship in news reporting.

Media Matters for America, P.O. Box 52155, Washington, DC 20091; 202-756-4100; www.mediamatters.org. Liberal media watchdog group that looks for potential conservative bias in news reporting.

Media Research Center, 325 S. Patrick St., Alexandria, VA 22314; 703-683-9733; www.mrc.org. Conservative media watchdog group that searches for potential liberal bias in news reporting.

Nieman Journalism Lab, Harvard University, 1 Francis Ave., Cambridge, MA 02138; 617-495-2237; www.niemanlab.org. Analyzes the news media's future in the internet age.

Pew Research Center for the People & the Press, 1615 L St., N.W., Suite 700, Washington, DC 20036; 202-419-4300; www.people-press.org. Nonpartisan media research organization funded by the Pew Charitable Trusts.

Poynter Institute for Media Studies, 801 Third St. South, St. Petersburg, FL 33701; 727-821-9494; www.poynter.org. Journalism education and research organization and owner of the *Tampa Bay Times;* ethics section of its website includes articles, discussions, tips and case studies.

2

Media Bias

Is slanted reporting replacing objectivity?

Robert Kiener

Getty Images/Chris McKay

Conservative talk show hosts such as Sean Hannity have found huge audiences — mainly among Republicans — at Fox News. Some media critics trace the rise of partisan programming to the government's 1987 decision to abandon the Fairness Doctrine, which required broadcasters to devote airtime to policy debates and offer contrasting views on those issues. The government said the rapid growth of cable outlets made the rule unnecessary.

From *CQ Researcher,*
May 3, 2013

"A total embarrassment." "A fawning interview." "A targeted barrage of softballs."

A wide variety of journalists and media critics used those disparaging terms to attack CBS reporter Steve Kroft's Jan. 27 "60 Minutes" interview with President Obama and outgoing Secretary of State Hillary Rodham Clinton.[1]

The Atlantic compared it to Scott Pelley's earlier, much tougher "60 Minutes" interview with President George W. Bush and proclaimed "a glaring double standard" favoring Democrats.[2] *The Washington Post* called Kroft's sit-down with Obama and Clinton a "soft-as-premium-tissue" interview.[3] Fox News claimed the interview "totally epitomizes liberal media bias in the modern era."[4] *The Wall Street Journal's* editorial page dubbed it "embarrassing" evidence of "the mainstream media fawn-a-thon toward the current president."[5]

The complaints are only the latest in a rising chorus of charges that the nation's mainstream media — major newspapers, newsweeklies and broadcasters — lean either to the left or to the right. And polls show that the perception of media bias is growing, and that it comes from both sides of the political spectrum.

For example, some mainstream media outlets were accused of slanting their coverage of the Senate's recent refusal to mandate background checks on gun purchases. "Television hosts, editorial boards and even some reporters have aggressively criticized and shamed the 46 Senators who opposed the plan, while some have even taken to actively soliciting the public to contact [the senators] directly" to express their displeasure, reporter Dylan Byers

Coverage of Democrats Was More Negative

Republican-oriented sources accounted for about 60 percent of the partisan quotes during three months of media coverage of the 2012 presidential campaign, according to the 4thEstate Project, which conducts statistical analysis of the media. It also found that media coverage of health care, the economy and social issues was more negative for President Obama than for GOP challenger Mitt Romney. Thirty-seven percent of total election coverage during the period was negative for Obama, compared to 29 percent for Romney.

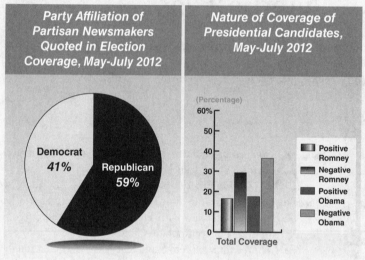

Party Affiliation of Partisan Newsmakers Quoted in Election Coverage, May-July 2012

Democrat 41%
Republican 59%

Nature of Coverage of Presidential Candidates, May-July 2012

(Percentage)

Positive Romney
Negative Romney
Positive Obama
Negative Obama

Total Coverage

Source: "Liberal Media Bias: Fact or Fiction," 4thEstate Project, July 2012, specialreports.4thestate.net/liberal-media-bias-fact-or-fiction/

wrote in *Politico.* "The decision by some members of the media to come down so firmly on one side of a policy debate has only served to reinforce conservatives' long-standing suspicions that the mainstream media has a deep-seated liberal bias."[6]

The Sunday talk shows also are criticized for hosting Republican and conservative guests more often than Democrats or liberals. Of 400 guests hosted by the major Sunday morning talk shows on ABC, CBS, NBC and Fox during the first three months of 2013, 40 percent were either Republicans or conservatives, and only 29 percent were Democrats or liberals, complained the left-leaning media watchdog group Media Matters. Centrist, nonpartisan and ideologically neutral guests made up 31 percent.[7]

The claim that the mainstream media — or as former vice presidential candidate and Alaska governor Sarah

Palin calls them, the "lamestream" media — lean to the left has been a favorite theme of the Republican Party for years. "As a conservative I've long believed that there is an inherent media bias, and I think that anyone with objectivity would believe that that's the case," vice presidential candidate Rep. Paul Ryan, R-Wis., said last September. "I think most people in the mainstream media are left of center."[8]

The media are "out of control with a deliberate and unmistakable leftist agenda," the Media Research Center, a conservative media watchdog group in Alexandria, Va., charged in an August 2012 "open letter" to the "biased" news media during last year's presidential race. "To put it bluntly: you are rigging this election and taking sides in order to pre-determine the outcome."

During the 2012 presidential election, however, Democrats received more negative coverage than Republicans, according to the 4thEstate Project, which examined three months' worth of 2012 election coverage. It found that 37 percent of Obama's coverage was negative, compared to 29 percent of Romney's. About 60 percent of the partisan quotes came from GOP-oriented sources.[9]

Others see a conservative, pro-GOP slant at some popular media outlets. Fox News is "vital" to the conservative movement, said Republican Jim Gilmore, former governor of Virginia.[10] And a 2009 Pew Research poll found that Fox News is considered the most ideological channel in America, with 47 percent of respondents saying Fox is "mostly conservative."[11]

Measuring media bias is an inexact science, and researchers who try to quantify it have found mixed results, with some studies showing a left-leaning bias and some a rightward tilt.

A Media Matters survey found that about 60 percent of the nation's newspapers publish more conservative syndicated columnists than liberal ones every week, and among the country's top 10 columnists (as ranked by the number of papers that carry them), five are conservative, two centrist and three liberal.[12]

A classic study by the media watchdog group Fairness & Accuracy in Reporting (FAIR) found in 1998 that most journalists were relatively liberal on social policies but significantly more conservative than the general public on economic, labor, health care and foreign policy issues. Journalists "nearly always" turn to government officials and business representatives — rather than labor representatives or consumer advocates — when covering economic policy, a practice that critics say led to the nation's business reporters being blindsided by the 2007-09 recession.[13]

Tim Groseclose, a political science professor at the University of California, Los Angeles (UCLA), has developed a statistical model for measuring the "slant quotient" of news stories. In his 2012 book *Left Turn: How Liberal Bias Distorts the American Mind,* he concludes that "every mainstream national news outlet in the United States has a liberal bias." Of the 20 news sources he studied, 18 were left of center, he said.[14]

But David D'Alessio, an assistant professor of communications sciences at the University of Connecticut, Stamford, says his research shows that "while some individuals may produce biased reporting, over time both sides tend to balance one another. There is no clear bias for one side or the other."

Many observers agree that distrust of the media often depends on one's political leanings. "Democrats trust everything except Fox, and Republicans don't trust anything other than Fox," said a Public Policy Polling press release announcing its latest survey of media credibility.[15] "If Fox tilts right, that doesn't bother conservatives; they don't necessarily see it as bias," said Bernard Goldberg, a Fox contributor and author of *Bias* and other books on media partiality. "And when MSNBC goes left, liberals . . . see it as 'truth.'"[16]

"Fox is perfectly entitled to be a conservative news organization" said former *New York Times* executive editor Bill Keller. "I will always defend their right to be that. My criticism of Fox is that a lot of the time they pretend that they're not. And I think that just tends to contribute to cynicism about the media. All news organizations, including the ones that try very hard to play fair and to

be even-handed in their reporting and writing, get tarred by the Fox brush."[17]

Despite the inconclusiveness of the studies, skepticism about media credibility is growing. For instance:

- A 2013 Public Policy Polling survey of news media trustworthiness found that Fox's credibility had dropped significantly: 46 percent of those surveyed said they do not trust the network — up 9 points since 2010.[18]
- A 2011 Pew Research Center poll found that 77 percent of respondents believed news organizations "tend to favor one side" — up from 53 percent in 1985.[19]
- A September 2012 Gallup survey found that 60 percent of respondents said they had "not very much" or no trust or confidence that the mass media report the news fully, accurately and fairly — up from 46 percent in 1998.[20]

"These are big increases, says Mark Jurkowitz, a former *Boston Globe* journalist and media reporter and now the associate director of the Pew Research Project for Excellence in Journalism. "For the last three decades there has been a seriously embedded, growing thought among the public that the media, especially the liberal media, are biased."

Larry Light, editor-in-chief of the financial website AdviceIQ.com, contended that public antipathy toward the news media is the result of what he called the right-wing's ongoing "war against journalists," which he maintained has stepped up its tempo recently. The perception of bias "has nothing to do with people's individual observations" but everything to do with "a juggernaut of conservative, anti-media propaganda that has grown more and more powerful," he wrote. "The propagandists repeat the phrase 'biased liberal media' a zillion-fold everywhere. That it is a crock of baloney is beside the point."[21]

Some observers blame the changing perceptions on the rise of cable television, radio talk shows and Internet sites and blogs, which have enabled thousands of new players to spread their often partisan messages. Commentators such as conservatives Sean Hannity of Fox News and radio personality Rush Limbaugh, and liberals such as Rachel Maddow of MSNBC, along with

Most Americans See Media as Politically Biased

More than three-fourths of Republicans consider the media politically biased, a perception shared by 54 percent of Democrats and 63 percent of Independents. Sixty percent of Americans say they have little or no confidence in the media to report news fully, accurately and fairly.

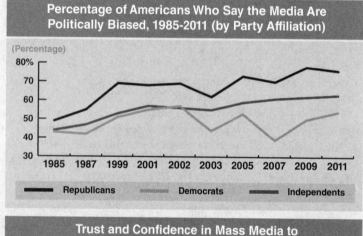

Percentage of Americans Who Say the Media Are Politically Biased, 1985-2011 (by Party Affiliation)

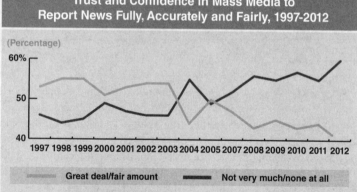

Trust and Confidence in Mass Media to Report News Fully, Accurately and Fairly, 1997-2012

Sources: Lymari Morales, "U.S. Distrust in Media Hits New High," Gallup, September 2012, www.gallup.com/poll/157589/distrust-media-hits-new-high.aspx; "Views of the News Media: 1985-2011," Pew Research Center, September 2011, p. 11, www.people-press.org/files/legacy-pdf/9-22-2011%20Media%20Attitudes%20Release.pdf

Robert Lichter, director of the Center for Media and Public Affairs at George Mason University in Annandale, Va., and co-author of the 1986 book *The Media Elite.*

Indeed, 63 percent of respondents cited cable news — particularly CNN and Fox — when asked what comes to mind when they hear the term "news organizations," according to Pew.[22] Pew also found that opinion and commentary, as opposed to news reporting, fill 85 percent of MSNBC's airtime, 55 percent of Fox's and 46 percent of CNN's.[23]

Some say the public's perceptions about media bias may also have been influenced by the growth of media watchdog groups, such as Media Matters and the Media Research Center, which track inaccurate reporting, media bias and political gaffes. Often financed by wealthy partisans, the groups comb the media searching for examples of perceived right- or left-wing bias.

"Part of their message is, 'The other guy is lying to you,'" says Jurkowitz. That helps to convince the public that "the media are biased," he says.

Others say fact-checking groups such as PolitiFact and FactCheck.org may also have increased the perception that the media are biased.

Surveys repeatedly have shown that most mainstream journalists in New York City and Washington, D.C., have liberal leanings, but most reporters say they separate their personal views from their reporting.[24] "An opinion is not a bias," said Michael Kinsley, former editor of the online publication *Slate.*[25] Longtime *Washington Post* political reporter David Broder once famously declared that "the charge of ideological bias in the newsroom [is] laughable. There

news sites such as the right-leaning Drudge Report and left-leaning *Huffington Post,* have helped blur the line between straight news and opinion. "The public does not always differentiate between these partisan outlets and the more objective mainstream media," says S.

just isn't enough ideology in the average reporter to fill a thimble."[26]

As scholars, journalists and news consumers explore bias in the quickly changing media world, here are some questions they are asking:

Should journalists try to be objective?

As the media landscape grows more varied — with cable broadcasters, bloggers, Twitterers and others adding their often-partisan views to those of the established media — many media analysts are asking if journalistic objectivity is becoming passé.

But for many mainstream media organizations, objectivity is a core part of their brand and very much worth preserving. "Objectivity is like virtue; it's . . . the thing that you always strive toward" in search of the truth, said *New York Times* conservative columnist David Brooks.[27]

He and other journalists say being objective means not playing favorites, regardless of one's personal views. "It means doing stories that will make your friends mad when appropriate and not doing stories that are actually hit jobs or propaganda masquerading as journalism," said Alex S. Jones, director of Harvard University's Joan Shorenstein Center on the Press, Politics and Public Policy and a Pulitzer Prize-winning journalist. "It is essential that genuine objectivity should remain the American journalistic standard."[28]

In its *Handbook of Journalism*, the Reuters news service warns journalists: "As Reuters journalists, we never identify with any side in an issue, a conflict or a dispute."[29]

But many media specialists today question whether journalists can ever be truly objective or neutral. "No journalist is completely objective," says Pew's Jurkowitz. "There are subjective judgments made in every story: what quote a reporter uses in his lead, the prominence he gives to certain facts, who gets one or two quotes, the language used, etc."

"Objectivity is in the eye of the beholder," says Barrie Dunsmore, a former ABC News foreign correspondent. "It's not just reporting both sides, which often aren't equivalent in terms of moral, legal or sociological balance. It has to be coupled with knowledge of a subject. It's easy to be objective if you don't know anything."

"The big problem with objectivity is that it has no bias toward truth," says Eric Alterman, a journalism history professor at the City University of New York (CUNY) Graduate School of Journalism and a liberal journalist. "You can quote both sides of an issue, and they can both be false. This doesn't bring readers any closer to the truth."

"Good journalism, like good science, starts out with a hunch, not with an observation, and then builds its case from there" says Reuters media critic Jack Shafer. "It's the method the journalist uses to arrive at his conclusion that has to be objective."

Some journalists have held that being objective means producing "balanced" stories — stories that give various sides of an issue. But many now see that approach as misleading and often producing weak reporting.

"There is no such thing as objectivity, and the truth . . . seldom nestles neatly halfway between any two opposing points of view," the late Texas columnist Molly Ivins declared. "The smug complacency of much of the press . . . stems from the curious notion that if you get a quote from both sides . . . you've done the job. In the first place, most stories aren't two-sided, they're 17-sided at least. In the second place, it's of no help to either the readers or the truth to quote one side saying, 'cat,' and the other side saying 'dog,' while the truth is there's an elephant crashing around out there in the bushes."[30]

After seeing his reporting reduced to a formulaic, he-said-she-said news story, former *Los Angeles Times* reporter Ken Silverstein complained to his editors that "balanced" reporting can be "totally misleading and leads to utterly spineless reporting." In the end, he continued, "It's just an easy way of avoiding real reporting and shirking our responsibility to inform readers."[31]

Constantly demanding balance can lead to a false equivalence, critics argue. "Al Gore says about 97 percent of climate scientists agree that global warming is real and manmade, but only about 50 percent of news reporting will say that, because they . . . want to give equal weight to both sides," says Alterman.

"The term 'balance' implies equal time, and that's not sufficient for accurate and fair reporting," says Dunsmore. "It is more important to be accurate and fair than merely showing both sides of an issue in order to be balanced."

Longtime Washington observers Norman Ornstein, a resident scholar at the conservative American Enterprise Institute, and Thomas Mann, a senior fellow at the centrist Brookings Institution, recently excoriated the mainstream press for insisting on writing balanced news stories that gave equal weight to often-outlandish political views, such as the comment by former Rep. Allen West, R-Fla., that "78 to 81" members of Congress are communists.

"Our advice to the press: Don't seek professional safety through the evenhanded, unfiltered presentation of opposing views," they said. Instead, reporters should ask: "Which politician is telling the truth? Who is taking hostages, at what risks and to what ends?"[32] Choosing balance over common sense does the public a disservice, they said. Taking a "balanced treatment of an unbalanced phenomenon distorts reality."[33]

Others, such as George Mason's Lichter, differentiate between objectivity and balance. Objectivity is "such a valuable gift from America to the world of journalism that I'd hate to lose it," he says. "We owe a debt of gratitude to the wire services and papers such as *The New York Times* for making objectivity their goal."

But some journalists today argue that reporters should not be afraid to declare their biases. With many new-media platforms producing journalism that is increasingly laced with opinion, it's more important than ever to know a reporter's agenda, says Jurkowitz. "Organizations have to be clear about their motives and agendas. Transparency is the new objectivity," he says.

Has the proliferation of media watchdog groups fostered perceptions of media bias?

Much of the criticism of the "biased right-wing press" and the "lamestream media" has originated with self-styled media watchdog groups that exist mainly to monitor the media in hopes of discovering bias, inaccuracies or inconsistencies. Often funded by politically inspired financial backers such as conservative billionaire brothers Charles and David Koch or liberal financier George Soros, these groups comb the media searching for examples of bias.

"An entire cottage industry exists to highlight the media's alleged failings," wrote Paul Farhi, a reporter at *The Washington Post*.[34]

By publicizing failings, groups such as the Media Research Center (MRC), Media Matters for America, Fairness & Accuracy in Reporting and others also have ratcheted up the volume in the national conversation about media bias. "Their message that the media are biased has certainly seeped into the public consciousness," says Pew's Jurkowitz.

For example:

- L. Brent Bozell, founder and president of the conservative MRC, said the mainstream media are "the 'shock troops' of the Obama administration because they are the ones doing all the dirty work for him so that he doesn't have to do it."[35]
- Left-leaning Media Matters said Fox News often uses "offensive words" to refer to undocumented immigrants. The group claimed that between Nov. 7, 2012, and Feb. 15, 2013, Fox's primetime hosts and their guests used what Media Matters called anti-immigrant language — such as "illegals," "illegal aliens" and "anchor babies" — 99 times."[36] (Recently The Associated Press dropped the term "illegal immigrant" from its *AP Stylebook*.)[37]
- Fairness & Accuracy in Reporting complained that the mainstream media "failed" to properly question the Bush administration's justification for the Iraq War by neglecting to sufficiently question the existence of weapons of mass destruction and other assertions.[38]

These groups have "created the perception that the media is more biased than it really is," says Si Sheppard, an assistant professor of political science at Long Island University and author of *The Partisan Press: A History of Media Bias in the United States.* "That's their objective. They like to say that the media play favorites, but studies have shown that there has not been consistent favoritism in reporting over the last few decades."

Others say that because these groups are open about their own biases, their findings do not unfairly taint the press. "Everyone has to parse everyone's arguments for themselves," says Reuters media critic Shafer. "I find these groups valuable."

But others say the groups have crossed the line from unbiased critics to political partisans. "When watchdog groups push their political agenda to the detriment of facts, they are becoming biased political operators," says Andrew R. Cline, associate professor of journalism at Missouri State University, in Springfield. "They stop doing a good service."

"Media criticism has become political criticism by another name," says George Mason's Lichter.

But the MRC's Bozell disagrees. "Data is data, numbers are numbers. While our interpretation of those facts may be subjective, we aren't forcing the public to see bias everywhere. We are showing them what different news organizations are reporting and the way they are reporting and let them decide."

"By awakening the public to bias, these watchdogs are doing a favor," says UCLA's Groseclose. "They are moving people's perceptions closer to the truth that the media is biased."

However, some media observers say the groups make the media look more biased than they really are. "These groups' criticisms are certainly reinforcing that opinion," says Lichter. "Instead of just beating up the other side, there is more beating up on the media for being biased."

This is more than politically oriented criticism. "The new part of some of these groups' message is, 'the media are lying to you,'" says Jurkowitz. "That has become a significant element of the message that goes out on both sides of the spectrum."

Lichter and others blame the public's declining trust in media in part on the watchdog groups' repeated allegations of bias.

Media Matters executive vicepresident Bradley Beychok disagrees. "The fact that public trust in the media continues to fall says more about the media than it does about media watchdogs. The media landscape is expanding beyond television and newspapers. As it does, there is more of a need to combat misinformation from new sources."

Are the media biased in favor of President Obama?

During the Sept. 16, 2012, presidential debate, Republican candidate Mitt Romney implied that Obama's personal funds likely included investments in China, a charge that had been leveled at Romney.

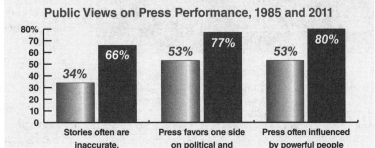

Negative Views of Press Growing

The public's assessment of the press has become increasingly negative since the mid-1980s. Two-thirds of Americans say reports often are inaccurate, compared to about one-third in 1985. Seventy-seven percent say the press shows bias on political and social issues, while 80 percent say the media often are influenced by powerful people and organizations. Experts say the rise of cable television and the Internet has led more media outlets to engage in partisanship, with less regard for accuracy.

Public Views on Press Performance, 1985 and 2011

Stories often are inaccurate: 34% (1985), 66% (2011)
Press favors one side on political and social issues: 53% (1985), 77% (2011)
Press often influenced by powerful people and organizations: 53% (1985), 80% (2011)

Source: "Views of the News Media: 1985-2011," Pew Research Center, September 2011, p. 1, www.people-press.org/files/legacy-pdf/9-22-2011%20Media%20Attitudes%20Release.pdf

1985
2011

"Mr. President, have you looked at your pension?" asked Romney.

Obama shot back, "You know, I don't look at my pension. It's not as big as yours, so it, it doesn't take as long."

In a nearby room where reporters were watching the debate, a round of applause broke out.[39]

While conservative commentators used this outburst as proof of their oft-repeated claim that much of the media favored Obama, others said all it showed was that reporters, like anyone else, enjoy a good debate comeback.

Many conservatives, such as the Media Research Center's Bozell, say the media are pro-Obama and his administration. "Saying the media aren't Obama-biased is like saying ducks don't waddle," says Bozell.

David Freddoso, editorial page editor of the conservative *Washington Examiner* and author of *Spin Masters: How the Media Ignored the Real News and Helped Reelect Barack Obama,* echoes the bias claims but believes that much of it is unintentional. "A lot of the mainstream media's pro-Obama bias is a product of the 'liberal bubble world' most journalists live in," he says. "When you

Conservatives claimed moderator Candy Crowley (center) of CNN favored President Obama when she intervened on his behalf during the Oct. 16, 2012, presidential debate. GOP candidate Mitt Romney repeatedly asserted that Obama took "days" to call the Sept. 11, 2012, attack on the Benghazi consulate in Libya an "act of terror," while Obama insisted he did so the day after the incident. When Romney refused to accept Obama's answer, Crowley said the president "did in fact" call the incident an act of terror on Sept. 12. Crowley later said she was only trying to move the debate along to other topics.

and most of your colleagues are liberal, that can easily skew your perceptions."

Freddoso believes the mainstream media have "misrepresented Obama's so-called economic recovery" in Obama's favor and "emphasized Romney's gaffes during the campaign instead of attacking Obama's handling of the Benghazi attack," in which the American diplomatic mission in Benghazi, Libya, was attacked by insurgents in September, 2012.

Some conservative journalists claim there has been a double standard in coverage of the Obama and George W. Bush administrations. "There was no fear of affronting Bush," said Fred Barnes, executive editor of the conservative *Weekly Standard.* "He faced relentless scrutiny. . . . The media raised questions about his motives, the constitutionality of his policies, his brainpower. . . . Obama's adoption of these same policies has drawn minimal attention."[40]

Lichter disagrees. "While Obama did get extremely positive coverage during his extended honeymoon period in 2009, the press since then has been fairly balanced in its coverage of him and his administration."

Other media critics claim journalists are so swayed by Obama's personal story that it is hard to "resist" him. "He is liberal, Ivy League and a person of color. That is simply too powerful a combination for the media to resist," wrote Peter Wehner, a senior fellow at the conservative Ethics and Public Policy Center. "One gets [the] sense that journalists not only like Mr. Obama; they are in awe of him."[41]

But NBC chief White House correspondent Chuck Todd called such charges "mythology." He said conservatives increasingly believe, without cause, that the "big, bad non-conservative media is out to get conservatives."

However, Light, the editor of AdviceIQ.com, wrote, "anti-media critiques are often absurdly one-sided. Their anti-media world is one where you whine about perceived slights to your side and conveniently ignore bad press that Democrats get. Anything that doesn't embrace the right-wing line is, by definition, biased."[42]

Likewise, Romney strategist Stuart Stevens said after Romney's loss in the election that the media were not "in the tank" for Obama nor were they too sympathetic to him.[43]

The public as a whole believes the press was fair in its coverage of the candidates. During the 2012 election, 46 percent of those polled by Pew said the coverage of Obama was fair, and an equal percentage said Romney's coverage was fair. However, when only Republicans were polled, 60 percent said the press coverage of Obama was "too easy," compared to just 4 percent of Democrats.[44]

While critics point to negative coverage of Romney as an example of media bias, others say it reflected the nature of political reporting: Journalists tend to cover politics as a horse race, and gaffes make for entertaining copy. A lot of Romney's negative coverage, they say, was due to his numerous gaffes, such as his critical comments about how London was handling security for the Olympics or his blaming Palestine's lack of economic success on cultural differences with Israel.

The 4thEstate study found no pro-Obama bias during the election period it examined. From May 1 to July 15, 2012, Republicans were quoted in news reports 44 percent more often than Democrats, and negative coverage of Obama was 17 percent higher than such coverage of Romney, the group said. "Our data does not support the thesis of a liberal media bias as it relates to Election 2012 coverage," 4thEstate said.

"If anything, our analysis suggests a media bias towards both Mr. Romney and Republicans."[45] The organization also found that the media discussed Romney more than Obama: 41.8 percent of the time versus 36.8 percent.[46]

However, a Pew Research poll found that Obama enjoyed a surge in positive coverage during the last week of the campaign.[47]

"But on the whole, both candidates got equally negative coverage," says George Mason's Lichter.

BACKGROUND

Journalism's 'Dark Ages'

Historians are quick to point out that the roots of American journalism were deeply embedded in partisan soil. Bias was the norm during journalism's formative years in this country. Indeed, the very idea of an unbiased press was anathema to the nation's early citizens.

Newspapers reflected the opinions of their owners and publishers. "For most of American history . . . there was only opinion, and highly partisan opinion at that," said Sheppard of Long Island University.[48] In *The Partisan Press*, Sheppard cites several early newspaper owners and publishers who attacked the ideas of balance and objectivity:

- On Sept. 4, 1798, the *Newark Gazette* described giving equal time to both sides of the political divide a "'folly that should not be tolerated.'"[49]
- On July 17, 1799, *The Washington Mirror* said treating parties equally was impossible, and that "printers who 'pretended' neutrality succeeded only in willfully misleading the people."[50]
- On March 10, 1800, the *New York American Citizen* called impartiality "'injurious to the best interests of mankind.'"[51]

Newspapers and their political pamphlet cousins were "mouthpieces" for the political parties of the era.[52]

Many newspapers were even supported directly by politicians. For example, Thomas Jefferson helped pay for the startup and running of the *National Gazette*, and Alexander Hamilton supported the *Gazette of the United States*.

Getty Images/Mario Tama

Antiwar demonstrators protest the mainstream media's Iraq War coverage outside NBC headquarters in New York City on March 15, 2006. Critics said the press was too willing to accept the Bush administration's assertions that Iraq had weapons of mass destruction before the U.S.-led invasion of the country in 2003 No such weapons were ever found.

"This gave an acrimonious tone to public discourse, since newspapers had no incentive to temper the language they used to criticize opponents," wrote George Mason University's Lichter.[53] In addition, newspapers often had lucrative government printing contracts, which also promoted biased reporting.

To temper the political bias of the press, the government — led by President John Adams' Federalist Party — passed the Sedition Act of 1798, which made it a crime to publish "false, scandalous and malicious writing" about the president or Congress. It enabled the government to close down many opposition Republican newspapers but caused such a voter backlash that Adams was not reelected. The act expired in 1801.[54]

The partisan press also placed party above accuracy. Some editors and reporters even worked part-time for politicians.[55] Others were key party leaders.[56] Some have called the first quarter of the 19th century the "Dark Ages of American journalism."[57]

"Even Jefferson, who famously preferred newspapers without government to government without newspapers, later complained that newspapers made their readers less well informed because 'he who knows nothing is nearer to truth than he whose mind is filled with falsehood and errors,'" wrote Lichter.[58]

'Penny Papers'

The rise of the "penny papers" in the 1830s transformed journalism's partisan character. Edited for the middle and working classes rather than for the elites, cheap, tabloid-style papers such as the *New York* Sun were able to prosper by offering an entertaining, informative product less dependent on partisan politics — for a penny apiece.

This was largely an economic decision. A partisan approach would inevitably alienate a large sector of a paper's potential readership, while a less political approach was more inclusive and could, in turn, attract more advertising. By mid-19th century the penny press' less partisan approach dominated journalism.

"Henceforth the reader would typically be viewed as a consumer rather than a partisan, and the nostrums of private enterprise would replace those of political ideology in paying the bills," wrote Lichter.[59]

But the penny papers were not apolitical. They often endorsed candidates, sometimes from more than one party. With "a business model incorporating the independence of action afforded by financial self-reliance, the critical first steps towards objectivity had been established," explained Sheppard.[60]

Toward the end of the 19th century, rapid industrialization and urban growth increased the audience for newspapers. Entrepreneurial publishers such as Joseph Pulitzer and William Randolph Hearst helped develop a profitable formula that relied heavily on a sensationalist mix of sex, crime and gossip that came to be known as "yellow journalism."

A combination of factors soon pushed newspapers to become less sensational. Their increased reliance on advertising made them reluctant to offend readers and led papers to improve their product and expand circulation. The expansion of the railroad and telegraph created new demand for instantaneous news from isolated communities where political sentiments might differ from the paper's hometown. Wire services, such as The Associated Press, formed in 1846, prospered by supplying subscribing newspapers with concise, accurate and objective copy.

When Adolph Ochs purchased *The New York Times* in 1896, he announced his intention, "to give the news impartially, without fear or favor, regardless of any party, sect, or interest involved."[61] As journalism history professor Alterman says, "We can date the beginning of serious,

objective reporting in America with Ochs' purchase of *The New York Times.*"

In part because of Ochs' paper, objectivity began to play a more important role in journalism. Journalism schools proliferated after the turn of the 20th century and taught the importance of objectivity along with accuracy and ethical reporting. According to a study cited by Lichter, the proportion of objective stories in newspapers and on wire services doubled from 1897 to 1914. "Having previously served the common good by standing aside from the world of politics, the press would now do so by standing above it," noted Lichter.[62]

Electronic Media

Radio, which burst onto the scene in the 1920s, soon transformed the media landscape. Between 1927 and 1934 the number of homes with radios jumped from 25 percent to 65 percent. Politicians, some angered by what they perceived as a biased press, saw radio as a medium to get their unfiltered message directly to the public. President Franklin D. Roosevelt famously used his iconic "fireside chats" to circumvent what he considered to be a hostile Republican press and speak directly to the people.

Because the airwaves were considered a public resource, radio was regulated. Under the Communications Act of 1934, created by the Federal Communications Commission (FCC), stations could lose their licenses if their broadcasts were considered too controversial, and stations had to offer equal time for political candidates.

By the 1940s radio was the main source of political information for 52 percent of the public, compared to 38 percent who relied on newspapers, according to a 1940 American Institute of Public Opinion poll.[63]

Meanwhile newspapers continued to become more objective. As publishers realized readers were attracted by objective, authoritative reporting, a church-state-style wall separated the advertising and news sides of the business. Robert McCormick, publisher of the *Chicago Tribune,* took this separation so seriously that he had two sets of elevators installed in his headquarters building in the early 20th century; one was for reporters and editors, the other for the business side.[64]

After World War II, television emerged as the dominant news medium. Nearly half the nation's households had a television as early as 1953, and by 1963 television was America's leading source of daily news.[65]

CHRONOLOGY

1690-1798 *Newspapers move from partisan approach to more independence.*

1690 *Publick Occurrences* becomes first newspaper published in America.

1702 *Daily Courant* becomes first English-language daily newspaper.

1791 First Amendment is added to U.S. Constitution, guaranteeing the right to publish news, information and opinions without government interference.

1798 The Alien and Sedition Acts prohibit publishing anything "false, scandalous and malicious" about the president or Congress. More than 20 editors are arrested; some are imprisoned. The laws later expired or were repealed.

1800s-1900 *Newspapers flourish as the "penny press" gains in popularity; journalism becomes a profession.*

1830 United States has 715 newspapers.

1833 *New York Sun* is launched, marking beginning of "penny press."

1846 Newspapers with varied political views create the nonpartisan Associated Press wire service.

1850 Only 5 percent of U.S. newspapers are "neutral and independent."

1851 Believing that a free, independent press is important to an educated populace, the Post Office offers a cheap mailing rate for newspapers.

1870 Nearly 5,100 newspapers are published in the United States.

1878 University of Missouri begins offering nation's first journalism courses.

1896 Adolph Ochs buys *The New York Times* "to give the news impartially, without fear or favor, regardless of any party, sect or interest."

1900-2000 *Government regulates, then deregulates, the broadcast media. Radio, television and then the Internet change the face of media.*

1934 Communications Act creates Federal Communications Commission (FCC) to regulate radio.

1940 American Institute of Public Opinion says 52 percent of Americans rely on radio for political information; 38 percent rely on newspapers.

1949 FCC's "Fairness Doctrine" requires broadcasters to devote airtime to controversial issues and to offer contrasting views.

1963 TV surpasses newspapers as the leading source of daily news.

1981 Survey by George Mason University journalism professor S. Robert Lichter shows that 81 percent of mainstream journalists voted for Democrats for president between 1964 and 1976.

1985-1986 Non-journalistic corporations buy all three major television networks, sparking cost cutting and staff reductions in the news departments.

1987 FCC drops Fairness Doctrine, saying the growth of cable and broadcast outlets make it unnecessary.

2000-2013 *Newspaper circulation drops; many papers cease publication. Cable broadcasting surges; social media play an increasing role in opinion journalism.*

2001 Fox becomes most-watched cable-news network.

2007 Nearly 1,500 newspapers sell 55 million copies daily.

2012 Gallup survey finds 60 percent of Americans have no or not very much trust that the mass media report the news accurately and fairly, up from 46 percent in 1998. Pew Research Center finds that 36 percent of Twitter users follow the news, compared with 19 percent of social media users.

2013 Pew Research Center finds that opinion and commentary fill 85 percent of MSNBC's airtime, 55 percent of Fox's and 46 percent of CNN's.

Media Bias Seen as Threat to Democracy

"I don't know if democracy can survive without an actively free press."

How important is a free and vibrant press to a healthy democracy? The nation's founders, even though they were not always pleased with the partisan newspapers that proliferated at the time, thought it was vital.

"No government ought to be without censors, and where the press is free, no one ever will," Thomas Jefferson told George Washington in 1792.[1] The First Amendment to the Constitution offered special protection to the press by barring Congress from abridging its freedom.

Throughout American history, the press has been viewed as such an important source of checks and balances on the government that it became known as the "Fourth Estate" — as important to democracy as the legislative, executive and judicial branches of government. However, while the founders stressed the need for a free press, they never claimed, for example, that the press should be nonpartisan.

As Americans increasingly complain that the media are becoming more biased, some media critics are asking if such a trend is healthy for democracy.

"We designed a constitutional system with many checks and balances," said Democratic pollster Patrick Caddell. "The one that had no checks and balances was the press, and that was done under an implicit understanding that, somehow, the press would protect the people from the government and the power by telling — somehow allowing — people to have the truth. That is being abrogated as we speak, and has been for some time."[2]

Caddell and others argue that an increasingly partisan press not only is slanting the news but choosing not to cover news that could cast an ideology or party in a bad light. Such bias by omission, said Caddell, has led the media to make "themselves a fundamental threat to the democracy, and, in my opinion, made themselves the enemy of the American people."[3]

At the 2013 Conservative Political Action Conference (CPAC), an annual political conference attended by conservative activists and elected officials, Rep. Lamar Smith, R-Texas, said, "When the media don't report the facts, Americans can't make good decisions. And if Americans can't make good decisions, our democracy is at risk. So media bias, to me, is a major threat to our democracy."[4] "If society doesn't have knowledge of the workings of government, how can it pass judgment on government?" asks L. Brent Bozell, president of the Media Research Center, a conservative media watchdog group "I don't know if democracy can survive without an actively free press."

Not everyone agrees that today's media threaten democracy. "When anyone tells me that the media is so biased that democracy is at risk, I remind them that even at the beginnings of our democracy the media was much, much more partisan," says S. Robert Lichter, director of the Center for Media and Public Affairs at George Mason University and

To guarantee that the public airwaves exposed audiences to a variety of viewpoints, the FCC's 1949 Fairness Doctrine required broadcasters to devote airtime to controversial matters of public interest and to offer contrasting views on those issues. The act also forbade stations from censoring campaign or political ads. Another FCC rule, calling for "equal time" for political candidates, did not apply to newscasts, documentaries, entertainment programs or political advertising.

Television's popularity was a factor in the closure of the nation's afternoon newspapers, which could not compete with the immediacy of the evening news broadcasts. However, many papers responded to the new journalistic competitor by "expanding their interpretative coverage and news analyses, where print held a competitive advantage," wrote Lichter. "Mainstream journalism began to take on a sharper point of view, often including opinion and advocacy in its reporting. . . . For the next decade, reporters were thrown onto the front lines of political battlegrounds that ranged from the civil rights movement to campus protests, the Vietnam War and the Watergate scandal."[66]

co-author of *The Media Elite.* "There were no boundaries then, and people were accused of all sorts of heinous, outlandish things. We survived then, and we will now."

A continuing decline in the number of journalists and the closure of print and broadcast outlets in recent years could be more of a threat to democracy than partisan media, say other observers. "There is no end in sight to job losses in journalism," says Eric Alterman, a journalism history professor at CUNY Graduate School of Journalism. "Losing journalists means people will be far less informed as citizens, and that's bad for democracy. Also, the bad guys will be able to get away with a lot more because there won't be as many people watching them."

Others are concerned about the growing concentration of media ownership, which could result in corporate influence on what is covered and how it is covered. Six corporations (Disney, News Corp, Viacom, Time-Warner, Comcast and CBS) control 90 percent of the nation's news and entertainment media, up from 50 percent in 1983.[5] "Rupert Murdoch owns *The Wall Street Journal* and *The New York Post,* and he and the Koch brothers are reportedly trying to buy the *Los Angeles Times,*" says Alterman, referring to wealthy, conservative billionaire brothers who have donated millions of dollars to libertarian, free-market advocacy groups and conservative politicians. "That would result in much less of a national conversation."

Former "CBS Evening News" anchor Dan Rather, who recently described a free and independent press as "the red, beating heart of democracy and freedom," warned of the dangers of such concentrated ownership.

"These big corporations, for whom news is only a small part of their business — they manufacture defense products and weapons, they run theme parks, they have all kinds of interests — this makes them dependent in large measure on whoever is in power in Washington," said Rather, who now anchors the news on the cable channel AXS TV. "I think we can all agree that we don't want to have a few very large corporations, working in concert with a powerful political apparatus in Washington, deciding what we see, read and hear — and they do, to a very large degree."[6]

— Robert Kiener

[1] *The Jeffersonian Cyclopedia* (1900), p. 130, http://books.google.com/ books?id= ZTIoAAAAYAAJ&pg=PA130&lpg=PA130&dq=%E2%80 %9CNo+government+ought +to+be+without+censors,+and+where+the +press+is+free,+no+one+ever+will,% E2%80%9D+Thomas+Jefferson+ told&source=bl&ots=vamgnUacT4&sig=gHinV3 U0Chb16W3EjRdu jaEhRo4&hl=en&sa=X&ei=X7x2UZu6lcXy0QGL9oD4Ag&ved =0CEMQ6AEwAzgK#v=onepage&q=%E2%80%9CNo%20 government%20ought %20to%20be%20without%20censors%2C%20 and%20where%20the%20press%20 is%20free%2C%20no%20 one%20ever%20will%2C%E2%80%9D%20Thomas%20 Jefferson%20told&f=false.

[2] Patrick Caddell, "Mainstream media is threatening our country's future," Fox News, Sept. 29, 2012, www.foxnews.com/opinion/2012/09/29/ mainstream-media-threatening-our-country-future/.

[3] *Ibid.*

[4] "Congressman Smith speaks at CPAC 2013 Re: media bias," press release, March 14, 2013, http://lamarsmith.house.gov/news/ documentsingle.aspVDocumentID=324058.

[5] Ashley Lutz, "These 6 companies control 90% of the media in America," *Business Insider,* June 14, 2012, www.businessinsider.com/ these-6-corporations-control-90-of-the-media-in-america-2012-6.

[6] Brad Martin, "Dan Rather warns of media control," *American Libraries,* June 24, 2012, http://americanlibrariesmagazine.org/annual-conference/ dan-rather-warns-media-control.

New Media

The 1980s were marked by major changes in American media. In 1985 and '86, non-journalistic corporations bought all three major television networks, leading to sweeping cost-cutting and staff reductions in the news departments.

Meanwhile, public perceptions that the media were fair were plummeting. By 1984, 38 percent of those surveyed said newspapers were "usually fair," down from two-thirds who felt the press was "fair" in 1937.

The FCC dropped the Fairness Doctrine in 1987, arguing that the growth of cable and broadcast outlets made it unnecessary. The decision, favored by Republicans, is seen as one of the main causes of the rise of conservative talk radio in the 1980s and '90s.[67] Legislation that liberalized media-ownership restrictions, such as the 1996 Telecommunications Act, led to widespread broadcast media consolidation via mergers and buyouts.

Meanwhile, competitive constraints and government regulation of cable channels were relaxed by the Cable

Fact Checkers Proliferate — and So Do Their Critics

Media services expose deception, but partisans often ignore them.

"Here's the truth the president won't tell you," said Rep. Michele Bachmann, R-Minn., at this year's Conservative Political Action Conference (CPAC), an annual political conference attended by conservative activists and elected officials. "Of every dollar that you hold in your hands, 70 cents of that dollar that's supposed to go to the poor doesn't. It actually goes to benefit the bureaucrats in Washington, D.C. — 70 cents on the dollar."[1]

True? Not exactly.

The Washington Post's "Fact Checker" column found that Bachmann was off by at least a factor of 10 — or even a factor of 200 — depending on what was included in her figures. It awarded her four "Pinocchios" — its worst rating — "for such misleading use of statistics in a major speech."[2]

Written by veteran reporter Glenn Kessler, "Fact Checker" is just one of many fact-checking operations that have sprung up over the last decade or so — including those at CNN, The Associated Press, Fox and ABC — to examine the accuracy of statements made by politicians and public officials. Such operations also fact-check major speeches, most notably after presidential debates, major addresses such as the State of the Union and claims made in campaign ads.

Groups such as PolitiFact, the Pulitzer Prize-winning site started in 2007 and a project of the *Tampa Bay Times* (formerly *St. Petersburg Times)*, and FactCheck.org, a project of the Annenberg Public Policy Center of the University of Pennsylvania, describe themselves as nonpartisan.

FactCheck.org, for example, says it is a "nonpartisan, non-profit 'consumer advocate' for voters that aims to reduce the level of deception and confusion in U.S. politics."[3]

But as fact-checking programs have proliferated, so have their critics. Not surprisingly, many of these criticisms fall along ideological lines. On its conservative-leaning editorial page, *The Wall Street Journal* argued that fact checking is "overwhelmingly biased toward the left," while liberals, such as City University of New York journalism professor Eric Alterman, often claim there is a growing conservative bias among the fact checkers.[4]

Likewise, candidates have been accusing the fact checkers of bias. During the 2012 presidential election, fact checkers labeled as deceptive a Mitt Romney campaign advertisement depicting President Obama as saying, "If we keep talking about the economy we're going to lose." Although the fact checkers explained that Obama was merely quoting Republican Sen. John McCain, Romney's strategists quickly went on the offensive. "We're not going to let our campaign be dictated by fact-checkers," said Romney campaign pollster Neil Newhouse.[5] After Romney lost the election, Media Research Center's research director, Rich Noyes, said his defeat was due partly to opponents "pounding Romney with partisan fact checking."[6]

In fact, both parties often attacked or simply ignored fact checkers' claims of inaccuracy or deceit. "Both candidates' campaigns laid out a number of whoppers, got clobbered for doing so, and then kept right on saying them," said *New York Times* media critic David Carr.[7]

Communications Policy Act of 1984. The industry boomed, with hundreds of stations reaching households across the country. Soon, thanks to advances in cable and satellite technology, all-news "24/7" cable channels such as CNN and later Fox News and MSNBC would change the face of television journalism. Outspoken conservative hosts such as Sean Hannity and Bill O'Reilly would find a lucrative audience, mainly among Republicans, on Fox News. And equally sharp-tongued hosts on talk

radio, no longer hampered by the need to present both sides of an issue, filled the airwaves and prospered.

Many journalists were shocked "that they were widely perceived as just another cog in a distant establishment, an elite group of wealthy and influential snobs who had forgotten their roots," said Lichter.[68] Surveys repeatedly confirmed that the mainstream media were generally to the left of the American public on such hot-button issues as gun control and abortion.[69]

Bill Adair, the departing editor of PolitiFact, agrees. "I think there has always been a calculation by political campaigns to forge ahead with a falsehood if they think it will score the points they want to score."[8]

A recent rise in partisan fact-checking organizations, such as Conservative Fact Check and the Media Matters-sponsored Political Correction, has led to even more charges of bias.

"The term 'fact check' can easily be devalued, as people throw it onto any sort of an opinion that they have," said Brendan Nyhan, an assistant professor of government at Dartmouth College. "The partisans who pay attention to politics are being conditioned to disregard the fact checkers when their own side gets criticized."[9]

Fact checking has proved to be a valuable resource, but media experts warn that it is no substitute for sampling a diverse range of news and views. As Northeastern University journalism professor Dan Kennedy noted, "Perhaps the biggest lie of all is that fact-checking can act as some sort of short-cut to the truth. For news consumers, there's really no getting around the time-intensive work of paying attention to multiple sources of information and making their own judgments."[10]

— *Robert Kiener*

The online fact-checking organization PolitiFact — a Pulitzer Prize-winning site started in 2007 by the St. Petersburg Times (now the Tampa Bay Times) — uses a "pants on fire truth-o-meter" to show when a politician is not telling the truth.

[1] Glenn Kessler, "Bachmann's claim that 70 percent of food stamps go to 'bureaucrats,'" *The Washington Post*, March 19, 2013, www .washingtonpost.com/blogs/fact-checker/post/bachmanns-claim-that-70-percent-of-food-stamps-go-to-bureaucrats/2013/03/18/3f85d04 2-8ff5-11e2-bdea-e32ad90da239_blog.html.

[2] *Ibid.*

[3] "About Us," Factcheck.org, www.fact check.org/about.

[4] James Taranto, "The Pinocchio press," *The Wall Street Journal*, Sept. 4, 2012, http://online.wsj.com/article/SB1000087239639044430170457 7631470493495792.html.

[5] As *The New York Times* pointed out," The truncated clip came from a speech Mr. Obama gave in 2008 talking about his opponent, Senator John McCain of Arizona." The full Obama quote was: "Senator McCain's campaign actually said, and I quote, 'If we keep talking about the economy, we're going to lose.'" See Michael Cooper, "Campaigns play loose with truth in a fact-check age," *The New York Times*, Sept. 1, 2012, www.nytimes.com/2012/09/01/us/politics/ fact-checkers-howl-but-both-sides-cling-to-false-ads.html.

[6] Mike Burns, "Fox blames Romney loss on the 'biased' fact-checkers," Media Matters, Nov. 7, 2012.

[7] David Carr, "A last fact check: It didn't work," *The New York Times*, Nov. 6, 2012, http://mediadecoder.blogs.nytimes.com/2012/11/06/ a-last-fact-check-it-didnt-work.

[8] Cooper, *op. cit.*

[9] *Ibid.*

[10] Dan Kennedy, "PolitiFact and the limits of fact checking," *The Huffington Post*, Dec. 13, 2011, www.huffingtonpost.com/dan-kennedy/ politifact-and-the-limits_b_1144876.html.

Many GOP politicians agreed with the perception that the media were left-leaning and fanned the flames. For example, during the 1996 presidential election, Republican candidate Bob Dole exhorted, "We've got to stop the liberal bias in this country. . . . Don't read that stuff! Don't watch television! Don't let them make up your mind for you!"[70]

Also in 1996, Fox News was launched by Australian-born news magnate Rupert Murdoch, who appointed former GOP media consultant Roger Ailes as CEO.

Says Lichter, "The idea that journalists were presenting news from their own point of view was growing among the public."

Blurring the Lines

The growing belief that the media were biased, coupled with liberalizing legislative changes and technological developments, opened a new chapter in the history of the American media. Television and radio airwaves were soon populated with a growing band of commentators and pundits who helped blur the line between journalism and opinion for many media consumers.

The media landscape changed dramatically. Talk radio, cable news networks, Internet-based websites and blogs fragmented the media but also have made them more populist. The new partisan media, much like their historic predecessors, the *National Gazette* and other 18th century publications, have offered a wide variety of ideological slants on the news.

As former University of Wisconsin-Madison journalism school director James Baughman wrote, "In contrast to the fractious newspaper culture of the mid-19th century, today's media culture is in fact divided between the new partisan media of the radio, Internet and cable, and those news outlets that still endeavor to report the news seriously. Serious news services won't, for example, provide platforms for those who insist the president was born in Kenya, or that the Bush administration was behind the destruction of the World Trade Center."[71]

While new media outlets sometimes offer biased slants on the news, the mainstream — or what some term the "elite" — media that still strive to be nonpartisan attract the larger audiences.

But, some media experts say, as the media landscape becomes more partisan, that grip may become more and more tenuous.

CURRENT SITUATION

Agenda-Driven News

Each day in more than 20 states across the country, some 35 reporters are investigating topics such as government waste, corruption and fraud. But they are not employed by traditional newspapers or television stations.

Rather, they are part of a nonprofit media program that has quietly been hiring and training reporters in state capitals. The Franklin Center for Government and Public Integrity is an investigative nonprofit based in Alexandria, Va., that is funded by the State Policy Network — a group of conservative think tanks — and other conservative organizations such as the Richmond, Va.-based Sam Adams Alliance and by the Koch brothers.

The center, which the *Columbia Journalism Review (CJR)* called "the most ambitious conservative news organization you've never heard of," hires journalists to report on government waste and public unions, usually from a pro-free-market, anti-labor viewpoint. Its news stories are published on its website, Watchdog.org, and elsewhere.[72] Often, the stories are picked up by blogs and by often-understaffed regional newspapers, but only some of the papers tell readers the stories originated with the center.

Although the center describes itself as nonpartisan, the liberal *Washington Monthly* called it "more like a political attack machine than a traditional news machine."[73] A Pew Research study of Franklin Center-sponsored stories found that 41 percent were proconservative versus 11 percent that favored the left.[74]

Some media observers also accuse the center of not being transparent. *CJR* said "a reader of one of the local and regional newspapers that run Franklin Center statehouse reporting might not even be aware of the Franklin Center and its agenda or 'point of view.'"[75]

Says Steven Greenhut, Franklin's vice president of journalism, "I reject the description of us as partisan. We have a free-market philosophy and have done plenty of stories that have offended both conservatives and liberals, Republicans and Democrats."

This sort of nonprofit, sometimes agenda-driven, news organization is a relatively new phenomenon. Since 2000, cash-strapped newspapers have lost 30 percent of their news personnel, according to Pew, and few can afford the personnel for complex or investigative stories. Nonprofit organizations have moved in to fill some of that void.

Think tanks and partisan organizations, such as the conservative Heritage Foundation, also have begun hiring "news reporters" to help spread their messages to a wider audience. "This is the wave of the future," says George Mason's Lichter. "Heritage Foundation and others have realized they don't need to depend on a few gatekeepers at major media outlets to run their material. They merely have to put it on the Web themselves."

Nonprofit organizations such as ProPublica produce nonpartisan, nonideological investigative journalism, often in partnership with other major media outlets. The Kaiser Health Foundation produces objective health-related news stories under the brand *Kaiser Health News*. The stories are regularly published by newspapers such as *The Washington Post,* but the stories are clearly identified as coming from those sources.

Do mainstream outlets have a political bias?

YES

TIM GRAHAM
Director of Media Analysis,
Media Research Center,
Alexandria, Va.

Written for *CQ Researcher*, May 2013

One can tell the tilt of the "mainstream" media merely by listening to conservatives and liberals complain about the tone of the news. Conservatives demand that the media cover both sides of public policies and controversies. Liberals such as President Obama lament that the media too often present a "false balance" — that conservatives get any air time to be blatantly incorrect. This suggests the media's default is to favor liberal views and downplay or ignore conservative ones.

In 2011, former *New York Times* executive editor Bill Keller wrote, "If the 2012 election were held in the newsrooms of America and pitted Sarah Palin against Barack Obama, I doubt Palin would get 10 percent of the vote. However tempting the newsworthy havoc of a Palin presidency, I'm pretty sure most journalists would recoil in horror from the idea."

In 2008, the Pew Research Center surveyed 222 journalists and news executives at national outlets. Only 6 percent said they considered themselves conservatives, compared to 36 percent of the overall population that describes itself as conservative. Most journalists — 53 percent — claimed they are moderate; 24 percent said they were liberal and 8 percent very liberal.

Only 19 percent of the public consider themselves liberal. And it's not much of a leap to presume many of the 53 percent who describe themselves as "moderate" are really quite liberal, since Keller thinks most are horrified by a President Palin.

Our studies of TV news repeatedly show a liberal tilt. Media Research Center news analysts reviewed all 216 gun-policy stories on the morning and evening shows of ABC, CBS and NBC in the month after the Newtown, Conn., school shooting. The results showed staggering imbalance: Stories advocating more gun control outnumbered stories opposing gun control by 99 to 12, or a ratio of 8 to 1. Anti-gun sound bites were aired almost twice as frequently as pro-gun ones (228 to 134). Gun-control advocates appeared as guests on 26 occasions, compared to seven for gun-rights advocates.

But the most insidious bias is what the national media choose *not* to cover. For example, in 2012 there was only one network mention (on ABC) that Obama promised to cut the deficit "by half by the end of my first term in office."

Inconvenient clips of tape go missing, while network anchors can find the time to ask the president about Dr. Seuss books and which superhero's power he would like to possess.

NO

S. ROBERT LICHTER
Director, Center for Media and Public Affairs,
George Mason University; Co-Author,
The Media Elite

Written for *CQ Researcher*, May 2013

Liberal media bias is an article of faith to conservatives, who see the news as a reflection of journalists' well-documented liberal perspectives and Democratic voting preferences. However, the truth is more complicated.

First, the media aren't the closed shop they used to be. The Internet hosts a thriving competition between left-wing and right-wing websites and blogs, and any reasonable definition of the "mainstream media" would have to include Fox News and conservative-dominated talk radio.

Second, both conservative and liberal media watchdog groups have long lists of complaints about biased stories. What's missing is evidence of a broad pattern of coverage that consistently favors one side. For example, a meta-analysis of every scholarly study of election news found no systematic bias in the amounts of good and bad press given to Republican and Democratic presidential candidates. Another study compared news coverage of measurable conditions, such as unemployment and murder rates, under Democratic and Republican administrations at every level of government. It too found no consistent evidence of partisan favoritism.

Journalists do suffer bouts of "irrational exuberance," when they wear their feelings on their sleeves. Yet, even Barack Obama's well-documented media honeymoon in 2008 and 2009 soon gave way to the highly critical coverage that every recent president has suffered. By 2012 Obama's campaign coverage was as negative as Mitt Romney's.

So why do conservatives see liberal bias at every turn? One answer is what's called the "hostile media effect." Partisans treat criticisms of their own side as bias, while assuming criticisms of the other side are well-founded.

But some aspects of political journalism don't affect both sides equally. In their role as a watchdog over the rich and powerful, journalists see the world in terms of competing economic and political interests, with the media standing above the battle and serving the public interest. They are sympathetic toward those who define themselves the same way, such as "public interest" groups or social movements demanding equality for excluded groups.

Thus, what conservatives see as liberal bias is often the byproduct of a professional norm that runs parallel to liberal values. And journalists can filter their personal political views out of their stories more easily than their professional identities. So the problem for conservatives is not *just* that journalists are liberals, it's that they're journalists.

Getty Images/Bill Pugliano

Former Republican vice presidential candidate and Alaska governor Sarah Palin has been highly critical of the nation's major newspapers and other mainstream media, calling them the "lamestream media" and alleging they are biased against conservatives. Studies on media bias have produced mixed results.

For-profit ideologically driven journalistic operations also are proliferating. In 2010 the conservative online news site *Daily Caller* was launched with 21 reporters and editors. Other sites such as Breitbart.com report news with a conservative agenda. Liberal, for-profit news sites include *The Huffington Post* and the *Talking Points Memo* political blog.

"Efforts by political and corporate entities to get their messages into news coverage are nothing new," according to Pew. "What is different now . . . is that news organizations are less equipped to question what is coming to them or to uncover the stories themselves, and interest groups are better equipped and have more technological tools than ever."[76]

More is not necessarily better. "I have warned conservatives to be careful what they wish for," explains the Media Research Center's Bozell. "With the old media, at least there were rules, such as the two-source rule. In the new media there's the no-source rule. Stories can be written by innuendo. The public is finding it harder to differentiate between news and conjecture."

Tweeting and More

About 35 percent of Americans turn to online sources for news, and as more and more do so, journalists have responded by using blogs, social media sites like Facebook and, more recently, Twitter to reach their audience.

"Tweet your beat" is a common refrain among online journalists. According to recent surveys, only 3 to 4 percent of the public gets its news either regularly or sometimes via Twitter, but that number is reportedly growing.[77] Twitter's immediate and direct (and usually unedited) nature creates a more intimate relationship between journalist and reader than existed in the past. As a Pew Research Center report noted, "Twitter users appear to be more closely connected to professional journalists and news organizations than their social-networking counterparts when it comes to relying on them for online news."[78]

"Twitter is a venue for news but also opinion," says Pew's Jurkowitz. "It's tempting to say something memorable and pithy in 140 characters or less." As some journalist have found, however, tweeting and blogging opinion can prove disastrous:

- CNN's senior editor for Middle Eastern Affairs, Octavia Nasr, was fired after posting this comment on Twitter: "Sad to hear of the passing of Sayyed Mohammad Hussein Fadallah. One of Hezbollah's giants I respect a lot." CNN called her tweet "an error of judgment," and said, "It did not meet CNN's editorial standards."[79]
- *The Washington Post* rebuked managing editor Raju Narisetti for tweeting, "Sen. Byrd (91) in hospital after he falls from 'standing up too quickly.' How about term limits. Or retirement age. Or common sense to prevail."[80]

Narisetti — who has since moved to Rupert Murdoch's News Corp. as a senior vice president and deputy head of strategy — subsequently closed his Twitter feed. *The Post* promptly drew up new guidelines, saying its journalists "must refrain from writing, tweeting or posting anything — including photographs or video — that could be perceived as reflecting political, racial, sexist, religious or other bias or favoritism that could be used to tarnish our journalistic credibility."[81]

Other papers have drawn up similar conduct codes. "I think that the same guidelines for reporters would hold true in social networking or any other ways they conduct themselves in their life outside of work," said Martin Kaiser, editor of the *Milwaukee Journal Sentinel*. "It's the same way [that] we don't want reporters putting bumper stickers on their cars for candidates."[82]

Those who get their news from social networks prefer unbiased reports, according to a recent Pew poll. More than half of the respondents preferred nonpartisan news: 52 percent of those who get their news on Twitter and 56 percent of those who get news on social networks prefer news sources without a particular point of view.[83] Not all journalists agree that opinion should be banned from reporters' social media outlets. "It's time to get rid of the hoax that all reporters are objective," says journalism professor Alterman. "I am all for journalists exposing their personal biases on Twitter, their blogs or wherever."

Reuters takes a more balanced approach in its social media policy. Acknowledging that posting on Twitter and blogging can be like "flying without a net," it reminds its reporters that "social networks encourage fast, constant, brief communications; journalism calls for communication preceded by fact-finding and thoughtful consideration. Journalism has many 'unsend' buttons, including editors. Social networks have none."[84]

Whatever side a journalist takes on the social media debate, there's no denying the power of the new technology. This February, moments after NBC's Todd claimed that charges of a liberal media bias were "a mythology," his Twitter feed and others were filled with tweets, pro and con. After watching the messages pour in, he tweeted, "when you want to spark a conversation on Twitter, simply talk about media bias."[85]

OUTLOOK

Dizzying Changes

The numbers are grim. Nearly every week brings news of another newspaper or magazine cutting staff, shrinking the publication, reducing frequency or even closing. Television stations, especially local operations, are trimming staff, and national networks are downsizing and closing bureaus.

The Internet has essentially "blown up" the old media world and transformed the way news is delivered and consumed. Given the dizzying changes in the media world and the speed with which they have altered the

landscape, many experts say it's impossible to know the future of bias.

"Remember, it wasn't until the 1990s that we even had Web browsers," says George Mason University's Lichter. "Since then, YouTube, Twitter and Facebook have completely changed the way people interact with media. One thing is sure: We will see a lot more innovations that change the way people think about the media and its biases. It is difficult to see what's ahead, but if current trends continue it looks like the media will be becoming increasingly partisan."

Some even see an end of traditional "hard news" coverage. Bozell believes "journalism is losing its seriousness. The line between news and infotainment is being blurred." Others worry that as newspapers continue cutting back and producing less hard and investigative news, readers will continue to desert them, as the Pew surveys and others suggest.

"Infotainment is luring more and more people away from solid journalism, so I think the news will be playing a lesser role in people's lives than it does today," says Sheppard, the Long Island University journalism professor. "Kim Kardashian has over 17 million Twitter followers, and many of those people are probably following her instead of reading the news. There's a worry for the future of the republic!"

Many media experts claim the media will grow increasingly partisan, resembling the early days of journalism. "I see the wheel turning, not full circle, but toward more partisan narrow-casting," says Sheppard. "We will see the media creating more partisan information, which will then be seized upon by ideological audiences."

According to Sheppard and others, the financial success of Fox News and talk radio will likely spawn even more imitators, each hoping to serve a niche, partisan market. However, if the ideological middle disappears in the media, some worry that new media will merely be "preaching to the choir."

A more fragmented media will offer more choice but would also further change the public's perceptions of the press. "The decay of the traditional agenda-setting function of the press will continue, and with it the idea of 'the public' as a large, interconnected mass of news-consuming citizens," said a recent Columbia School of Journalism study. "Choice in available media outlets will continue to expand, leading not so much to echo chambers as to a world of many overlapping publics of varying sizes."

"Seen in this light, the long-term collapse of trust in the press is less a function of changing attitudes toward mainstream media outlets than a side effect of the continuing fragmentation of the American media landscape."[86]

Will there be an increase in transparency? "The media will be more open about their views because they realize people want a point of view in their news," says CUNY journalism professor Alterman. "There will always be an audience for trustworthy news organizations such as *The New York Times,* but media with strong points of view will increase. Fewer people will complain about media bias."

As long-established and valued newspapers face closure or purchase by partisan owners, many journalists believe the nation will be worse off. Many question how democracy can continue to function if voters become so inundated by "advocacy journalism" that they give up trying to even make an objective, informed decision or simply disengage from the democratic process altogether.

"The world will not be a better place when these fact-based news organizations die," said former *New York Times* correspondent Chris Hedges. "We will be propelled into a culture where facts and opinions will be interchangeable, where lies will become true and where fantasy will be peddled as news. I will lament the loss of traditional news. It will unmoor us from reality."[87]

NOTES

1. "Obama and Clinton: The 60 Minutes interview," "60 Minutes," CBS News, Jan. 27, 2013, www.cbsnews.com/8301-18560_l62-57565734/obama-and-clinton-the-60-minutes-interview/.

2. Conor Friedersdorf, "Steve Kroft's Softball Obama Interviews Diminish '60 minutes,'" *The Atlantic,* Jan. 29, 2013, www.theatlantic.com/politics/archive/2013/01/steve-krofts-soft ball-obama-interviews-diminish-60-minutes/272611/.

3. Erik Wemple, "Kroft on Obama-Clinton interview: 30 minutes not enough!" *The Washington Post,* Jan. 28, 2013, www.washingtonpost.com/blogs/erik-wemple/wp/2013/01/28/ kroft-on-obama-clinton-interview-30-minutes-not-enough/.

4. Noel Sheppard, "The transformation of '60 Minutes' — now the place for swooning, softball interviews," Fox News, Jan. 30, 2013, www.foxnews.com/opinion/2013/01/30/transformation-60-minutes-now-place-for-swooning-softball-interviews/.

5. Peggy Noonan, "So God Made a Fawner," *The Wall Street Journal,* Feb. 7, 2013, http://online.wsj.com/article/SB10001424127887323452204578290363744516632.html.

6. Dylan Byers, "Gun vote triggers media outcry," *Politico,* April 18, 2013, www.politico.com/story/2013/04/gun-debate-triggered-media-bias-90306.html#ixzz2Rsfg1FgP.

7. "REPORT: Partisanship And Diversity On The Sunday Shows In 9 Charts," Media Matters, April 5, 2013, http://mediamatters.org/research/2013/04/05/report-partisanship-and-diversity-on-the-sunday/193482.

8. "Ryan: As a Conservative I've long believed there's inherent media bias," *Real Clear Politics,* Sept. 30, 2012, www.realclearpolitics.com/video/2012/09/30/ryan_as_a_conservative_ive_long_believed_theres_inherent_media_bias.html.

9. "Liberal Media Bias: Fact or Fiction," 4thEstate Project, July 2012, specialreports.4thestate.net/liberal-media-bias-fact-or-fiction/.

10. Quoted in Reed Richardson, "GOP-Fox Circus Act," *The Nation,* April 29, 2013, pp. 11-15.

11. "Fox News Viewed as Most Ideological Network," Pew Research Center for People & the Press, Oct. 29, 2009, www.people-press.org/2009/10/29/fox-news-viewed-as-most-ideological-network/.

12. "Black and White and Re(a)d All Over: the Conservative Advantage in Syndicated OpEd Columns," Media Matters, 2007, http://mediamatters.org/research/oped/.

13. "Examining the 'Liberal Media' Claim," Fairness & Accuracy in Reporting, June 1, 1998, http://fair.org/press-release/examining-the-quotliberal-mediaquot-claim/.

14. David Freddoso, "Press pass: In a new book a journalist explains how the media tilts the scales for Obama," *New York Post,* Jan. 7, 2013, www.nypost.com/p/news/opinion/books/press_pass_CAbPXffNvA4ntrqbMNIkOI.

15. "4th Annual TV News Trust Poll," Public Policy Polling, Feb. 6, 2013, www.publicpolicypolling.com/main/2013/02/4th-annual-tv-news-trust-poll.html.

16. Joseph Cotto, "Bernie Goldberg on media bias in the 'Unites States of Entertainment,'" *The Washington Times,* Oct. 25, 2012, http://mobile.washingtontimes.com/neighborhood/conscience-realist/2012/oct/25/bernie-goldberg-media-bias-united-states-entertain/.

17. Joe Strupp, "Bill Keller Speaks Out On Judy Miller, Iraq War Coverage, And Fox News," Media Matters, June 3, 2011, http://mediamatters.org/blog/2011/06/03/bill-keller-speaks-out-on-judy-miller-iraq-war/180289.

18. "4th Annual TV News Trust Poll," *op. cit.*

19. "Pluralities Say Press is Fair to Romney, Obama," Pew Research Center for the People & The Press, Sept. 22, 1012, www.people-press.org/files/legacy-pdf/9-22-2011%20Media%20Attitudes%20Release.pdf.

20. Lymari Morales, "U.S. distrust in media hits new high," Gallup Politics, Sept. 21, 2012, www.gallup.com/polJ/157589/distrust-media-hits-new-high.aspx.

21. Larry Light, "The right's propaganda victory over the 'liberal' media," *The Huffington Post,* Dec. 11, 2012, www.huffingtonpost.com/larry-light/the-rights-propaganda-vic_b_2279625.html.

22. "The State of the News Media 2013," The Pew Research Center's Project for Excellence in Journalism, 2013, Key Findings, http://stateofthemedia.org/2013/overview-5/key-findings/.

23. *Ibid.*

24. Tim Groseclose, *Left Turn* (2011), pp. 99–110.

25. Michael Kinsley, "Gore Carries Slate," Nov. 7, 2000, *Slate,* www.slate.com/articles/news_and_politics/readme/2000/11/gore_carries_slate.html.

26. David Broder, *Behind the Front Page* (2000), p. 332.

27. David Brooks, "Objectivity in Journalism," Catholic Education Resource Center, www.catholiceducation.org/articles/media/me0054.html.

28. Alex S. Jones, "An Argument Why Journalists Should Not Abandon Objectivity," Nieman Reports, Fall 2009, www.nieman.harvard.edu/reports/article/101911/An-Argument-Why-Journalists-Should-Not-Abandon-Objectivity.aspx.

29. "Freedom from Bias, Reuters Handbook of Journalism," Reuters, http://handbook.reuters.com/index.php?title=Freedom_from_bias.

30. Chris Hedges, "The Creed of Objectivity Killed the News," TruthDig, Feb. 1, 2010, www.truthdig.com/report/item/the_creed_of_objectivity_killed_the_news_business_20100131.

31. Ken Silverstein, "The Question of Balance: Revisiting the Missouri Election Scandal of 2004," *Harpers,* May 8, 2007, http://harpers.org/blog/2007/05/the-question-of-balance-revisiting-the-missouri-election-scandal-of-2004/.

32. Thomas E. Mann and Norman J. Ornstein, "Let's just say it: The Republicans are the problem," *The Washington Post,* April 27, 2012, http://articles.washingtonpost.com/2012-04-27/opinions/35453898_1_republican-party-party-moves-democratic-party/3.

33. *Ibid.*

34. Paul Farhi, "How biased are the media, really?" *The Washington Post,* April 27, 2012, http://articles.washingtonpost.com/2012-04-27/lifestyle/35451368_1_media-bias-bias-studies-media-organizations.

35. "MRC launches $2.1 million campaign demanding liberal media 'tell the truth!'" News-busters, Oct. 5, 2010, http://newsbusters.org/blogs/nb-staff/2010/10/05/new-2-1-million-campaign-demands-liberal-media-tell-truth.

36. Salvatore Colleluori, "Roger Ailes' Latino outreach at odds with Fox News' anti-immigrant rhetoric," Media Matters, Feb. 19, 2013, http://mediamatters.org/research/2013/02/19/roger-ailes-latino-outreach-at-odds-with-fox-ne/192714.

37. Paul Colford, "'Illegal immigrant' no more," *The Definitive Source,* April 2, 2013, http://blog.ap.org/2013/04/02/illegal-immigrant-no-more/.

38. Jim Naureckas, "The media didn't fail on Iraq; Iraq just showed we have a failed media," Fairness & Accuracy in Reporting, March 25, 2013, www.fair.org/blog/2013/03/25/the-media-didnt-fail-on-iraq-iraq-just-showed-we-have-a-failed-media/.

39. Stephen Dinan, "Reporters applaud Obama's slam on Romney's wealth," *The Washington Times,* Oct. 17, 2012, www.washingtontimes.com/blog/inside-politics/2012/oct/17/reporters-applaud-obamas-slam-romneys-wealth/.

40. Fred Barnes, "The four-year honeymoon," *The Weekly Standard,* Jan. 14, 2013, www.weeklystandard.com/articles/four-year-honey moon_693769.html.

41. Peter Wehner, "Media bias in the age of Obama," *Commentary,* Jan. 30, 2013, www.commentarymagazine.com/2013/01/30/media-bias-in-the-age-of-obama/.

42. Light, *op. cit.*

43. Jon Nicosia, "Top Romney strategist Stuart Stevens says media not 'in the tank' for President Obama," Mediate, Feb. 24, 2012, www.mediaite.com/tv/top-romney-strategist-stuart-stevens-says-media-not-in-the-tank-for-presi dent-obama/.

44. "Pluralities say press is fair to Romney, Obama," Pew Research Center for the People & the Press, Sept. 25, 2012, www.people-press.org/2012/09/25/pluralities-say-press-is-fair-to-romney-obama/.

45. "Liberal media bias: fact or fiction?" *op. cit.*

46. "Romney discussed more than Obama in election coverage," 4thEstate, Aug. 1, 2012, http://election2012.4thestate.net/romney-discussed-more-than-obama-in-election-coverage/.

47. "Low marks for the 2012 election," Pew Research Center for the People & the Press, Nov. 15, 2012, www.people-press.org/2012/11/15/section-4-news-sources-election-night-and-views-of-press-coverage/press.

48. Si Sheppard, *The Partisan Press* (2008), p. 19.

49. *Ibid.* pp. 18-19.

50. *Ibid.*

51. *Ibid.*

52. Quoted in *ibid.* pp. 22-23.

53. S. Robert Lichter, "The Media," in Peter H. Schuck, *Understanding America: The Anatomy of an Exceptional Nation* (2009), p. 187.

54. Geoffrey R. Stone, *Perilous Times* (2004), p. 73.

55. James L. Baughman, "The Fall and Rise of Partisan Journalism," Center for Journalism Ethics, University of Wisconsin-Madison, April 20, 2011.

56. Paul Starr, "Governing in the age of Fox News," *The Atlantic,* Jan. 1, 2010, www.theatlantic.com/magazine/archive/2010/01/governing-in-the-age-of-fox-news/307845/.

57. Sheppard, *op. cit.* p. 22.

58. Lichter, p. 187.

59. *Ibid.*, p. 188.

60. Sheppard, *op. cit.* p. 76.

61. William Safire, "On language; default, Dear Brutus," *The New York Times,* Dec. 10, 1995, www.nytimes.com/1995/12/10/magazine/on-language-default-dear-brutus.html.

62. Lichter, *op. cit.* p. 190.

63. *Ibid.* p. 32.

64. Bill Kovach and Tom Rosenstiel, *The Elements of Journalism* (2001), p. 62.

65. Alan Greenblatt, "Media Bias," *CQ Researcher*, Oct. 15, 2004, p. 866.

66. Lichter, *op. cit.* p. 194.

67. Peter J. Boyer, "Under Fowler, FCC treated TV as commerce," *The New York Times*, Jan. 19, 1987, www.nytimes.com/1987/01/19/arts/under-fowler-fcc-treated-tv-as-commerce.html.

68. Lichter, *op. cit.* p. 205.

69. For survey results, see Sheppard, *op. cit.* p. 284.

70. Quoted in *ibid.* p. 280.

71. Baughman, *op. cit.*

72. Justin Peters, "Serious, point of view journalism?" *Columbia Journalism Review*, Sept. 13, 2012, www.cjr.org/united_states_project/serious_point-of-view_journalism.php?page=all.

73. Laura McGann, "Partisan Hacks," *The Washington Monthly,* May/June 2012, www.washington-monthly.com/features/2010/1005.mcgann.html.

74. "Non-profit News: Assessing a New Landscape in Journalism," Pew Research Center, July 18, 2011, p. 11, www.journalism.org/sites/journalism.org/files/Non-profit%20news%20study%20FINAL.pdf.

75. Peters, *op. cit.*

76. "The State of the News Media 2013," *op. cit.*

77. "In Changing News Landscape, Even Television Is Vulnerable," Pew Research Center for the People & The Press, Sept, 27, 2012, www.people-press.org/2012/09/27/section-2-online-and-digital-news-2/.

78. *Ibid.*

79. James Poniewozik, "CNN, Twitter and Why Hiding Journalists' Opinions Is (Still) a Bad Idea," *Time,* July 8, 2010, http://entertainment.time.com/2010/07/08/cnn-twitter-and-why-hiding-journalists-opinions-is-still-a-bad-idea/.

80. John Morton, "Staying Neutral," *American Journalism Review,* Dec./Jan. 2010, www.ajr.org/article.asp?id=4837.

81. Stephanie Gleason, "Going Public," *American Journalism Review*, December/January 2010, www.ajr,org/article.asp?id=4846.

82. *Ibid.*

83. "In Changing News Landscape, Even Television is Vulnerable," *op. cit.*

84. *Handbook of Journalism,* Reuters, http://handbook.reuters.com/index.php?title=Reporting_From_the_Internet_And_Using_Social_Media.

85. "Chuck Todd discusses the 'mythology' of media bias against conservatives," *Twitchy*, Feb. 19, 2013, http://twitchy.com/2013/02/19/chuck-todd-discusses-the-mythology-of-media-bias-against-conservatives/.

86. C. W. Anderson, Emily Bell and Clay Shirky, "Post-Industrial Journalism," Columbia Journalism School, 2013, p. 108, http://journalistsresource.org/wp-content/uploads/2013/01/TOWCenter-Post_Industrial_Journalism.pdf.

87. Hedges, *op. cit.*

BIBLIOGRAPHY
Selected Sources
Books

Alterman, Eric, *What Liberal Media? The Truth About Bias and the News,* Basic Books, 2004.
A City University of New York journalism professor and liberal journalist says the news media are far more slanted toward conservative than liberal thought, contrary to the claims of many conservative media critics.

Freddoso, David, *Spin Masters: How the Media Ignored the Real News and Helped Reelect Barack Obama,* Regnery Publishing, 2013.
The editorial page editor of the conservative *Washington Examiner* contends the mainstream media manipulated coverage of the 2012 presidential candidates, were obsessed with Mitt Romney's gaffes and refused to cover stories that could have portrayed President Obama in a negative light.

Groseclose, Tim, *Left Turn: How Liberal Media Bias Distorts the American Mind*, St. Martin's Press, 2011.
A UCLA political science and economics professor concludes that nearly all mainstream media have a liberal bias, based on a formula he uses to analyze political content in news stories.

Hunnicut, Susan (ed.), *At Issue: Media Bias,* Greenhaven Press, 2011.
Media experts explore the history of bias, the meaning of objectivity, whether the mainstream media are biased toward Democrats or Republicans, whether bias in financial reporting contributed to the nation's financial crisis and more.

Sheppard, Si, *The Partisan Press: A History of Media Bias in the United States,* McFarland & Co., 2008.
An assistant political science professor at Long Island University places the debate about media bias in historical context. He tracks media bias from the early days of the nation's partisan press to the rise of objectivity in the 20th century to today's technology-driven media alternatives.

Stroud, Natalie Jomini, *Niche News: The Politics of New Choice,* Oxford University Press, 2011.

A journalism professor at the University of Texas-Austin explores how consumers navigate the increasingly crowded and diverse new-media market and investigates the political implications of those choices.

Articles

Alterman, Eric, "Think Again: Why Didn't the Iraq War Kill the 'Liberal Media'?" American Progress, April 4, 2013, www.americanprogress.org/issues/media/news/2013/04/ 04/59288/why-didnt-the-iraq-war-kill-the-liberal-media.

In reporting on the Iraq War, reporters ignored traditional journalistic practices in order to dismiss counter-evidence provided by numerous experts, says the author. Because of these lapses, the author claims, the bulk of the mainstream media and much of the blogosphere showed bias in favor of the war.

Carr, David, "Tired Cries of Bias Don't Help Romney," *The New York Times*, Sept. 30, 2012, www .nytimes.com/ 2012/10/01/business/media/challenging-the-claims-of-media-bias-the-media-equation .html?_r=0.

Although the press is frequently accused of exhibiting a liberal bias when conservative candidates drop in the polls, the media increasingly are made up of right-leaning outlets, says the *Times* media critic.

Chozik, Amy, "Conservative Koch brothers turning focus to newspapers," *The New York Times*, April 21, 2013, www.nytimes.com/2013/04/21/business/media/koch-brothers-making-play-for-tribunes-newspapers.html?page-wanted=all.

Charles and David Koch, the billionaire supporters of libertarian causes, reportedly are considering trying to buy the Tribune Co.'s eight regional newspapers, including the *Los Angeles Times* and *Chicago Tribune*. Some in the media industry are asking whether they would use the papers to further a conservative agenda.

Friedersdorf, Conor, "Steve Kroft's Softball Obama Interviews Diminish '60 Minutes,'" *The Atlantic,* Jan. 29, 2013, www.theatlantic.com/politics/archive/2013/01/steve-krofts-soffball-obama-interviews-diminish-60-minutes/272611.

An Atlantic staff writer argues that "60 Minutes," which prides itself on tough investigations and probing interviews, limited its interview with President Obama and Secretary of State Hillary Rodham Clinton to "softball" questions.

Stray, Jonathan, "How do you tell when the news is biased? It depends on how you see yourself," Nieman Journalism Lab, June 27, 2012, www.niemanlab .org/2012/06/ how-do-you-tell-when-the-news-is-biased.

Recent research shows that people detect and judge bias in news reporting based on such factors as how they see themselves, not on what journalists write.

Reports and Studies

"The State of the News Media 2013: An Annual Report on American Journalism," The Pew Research Center's Project for Excellence in Journalism, March 18, 2013, http://stateofthemedia.org.

The nonpartisan research group's annual study includes reports on how news consumers view the media's financial struggles, how the news landscape has changed in recent years, an analysis of the main media sectors and an essay on digital journalism.

For More Information

Accuracy in Media, 4350 East West Highway, Suite 555, Bethesda, MD 20814; 202-364-4401; www.aim.org. Conservative media watchdog organization that searches for potential liberal bias.

American Society of News Editors, 209 Reynolds Journalism Institute, Missouri School of Journalism, Columbia, MO 65211; 573-884-2405; www.asne.org. Promotes ethical journalism, supports First Amendment rights, defends freedom of information and open government.

Center for Media and Public Affairs, 933 N. Kenmore St., Suite 405, Arlington, VA 22201; 571-319-0029; www.cmpa.com. Nonpartisan research and educational organization that studies the news and entertainment media.

Fairness & Accuracy in Reporting, 104 W. 27th St., Suite 10B, New York, NY 10001; 212-633-6700; www.fair.org. Liberal media watchdog organization that monitors bias and censorship.

Media Matters, P.O. Box 52155, Washington, DC 20091; 202-756-4100; www.mediamatters.org. Liberal media watchdog group that looks for potential conservative bias.

Media Research Center, 325 S. Patrick St., Alexandria, VA 22314; 703-683-9733; www.mrc.org. Conservative media watchdog group that searches for potential liberal bias.

Pew Research Center for the People & the Press, 1615 L St., N.W., Suite 700, Washington, DC 20036; 202-419-4300; www.people-press.org. Nonpartisan media research organization funded by the Pew Charitable Trusts.

Poynter Institute for Media Studies, 801 Third St. South, St. Petersburg, FL 33701; 727-821-9494; www.poynter.org. Journalism education and research organization; ethics section of its website (www.poynter.org) includes articles, discussions, tips and case studies.

Society of Professional Journalists Ethics Committee, 3909 N. Meridian St., Indianapolis, IN 46208; 317-927-8000; www.spj.org/ethics.asp. Advises journalists on ethical matters; website contains ethics resources and a blog.

3

AFP/Getty Images/Khaled Desouki

Egyptian political satirist Bassem Youssef arrives at the public prosecutor's office in Cairo on March 31. Police questioned Youssef for allegedly insulting President Mohammed Morsi and Islam. The government filed charges against hundreds of Egyptian journalists but dropped them earlier this month. Free-speech advocates worry that journalists, bloggers and democracy supporters worldwide are being intimidated into silence.

From *CQ Researcher,*
April 26, 2013

Free Speech at Risk

Will it survive government repression?

Alan Greenblatt

I t wasn't an April Fool's joke. On April 1, "Daily Show" host Jon Stewart defended Egyptian political satirist Bassem Youssef, who had undergone police questioning for allegedly insulting President Mohammed Morsi and Islam.

"That's illegal? Seriously? That's illegal in Egypt?" Stewart said on his Comedy Central show. "Because if insulting the president and Islam were a jailable offense here, Fox News go bye-bye."

Stewart was kidding, but Youssef's case has drawn attention from free-speech advocates who worry Egypt's nascent democracy is according no more respect toward freedom of expression than the regime it replaced.

The U.S. Embassy in Cairo, which had linked to Stewart's broadcast on its Twitter feed, temporarily shut down the feed after Egyptian authorities objected to it. Egypt's nascent government also has filed charges against hundreds of journalists, although Morsi asked that they all be dropped earlier this month.

Concerns are widespread that commentators, journalists, bloggers — and, yes, even comedians — are being intimidated into silence. And not just in Egypt.

Free speech, once seen as close to an absolute right in some countries, is beginning to conflict with other values, such as security, the protection of children and the desire not to offend religious sensibilities, not just in the Middle East but in much of the world, including Western Europe.

In many cases, freedom of speech is losing. "Free speech is dying in the Western world," asserts Jonathan Turley, a George Washington University law professor. "The decline of free speech

Democracies Enjoy the Most Press Freedom

Democracies such as Finland, Norway and the Netherlands have the most press freedom, while authoritarian regimes such as Turkmenistan, North Korea and Eritrea have the least, according to Reporters Without Borders' 2012 index of global press freedom. European and Islamic governments have enacted or considered new press restrictions after a recent phone-hacking scandal in Britain and Western media outlets' irreverent images of the Prophet Muhammad triggered deadly protests by Muslims. Myanmar (formerly Burma), which recently enacted democratic reforms, has reached its greatest level of press freedom ever, the report said.

Press Freedom Worldwide, 2013

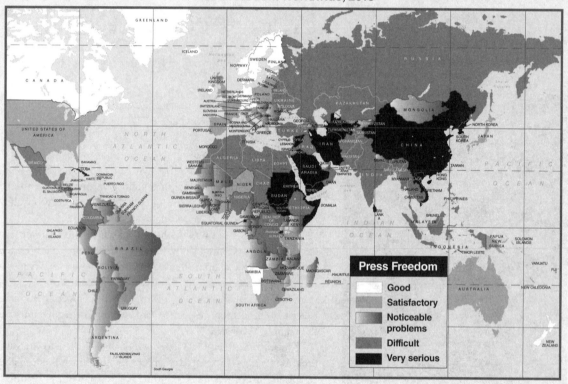

Source: "Freedom of the Press Worldwide in 2013," Reporters Without Borders, http://fr.rsf.org/IMG/jpg/2013-carte-liberte -presse_1900.jpg

has come not from any single blow but rather from thousands of paper cuts of well-intentioned exceptions designed to maintain social harmony."[1]

In an era when words and images can be transmitted around the world instantaneously by anyone with a cell phone, even some American academics argue that an absolutist view of First Amendment protections couldn't be expected to prevail. Several made that case after protests broke out in several Muslim countries last

September over an American-made video uploaded to YouTube defamed the Prophet Muhammad.

Even the administration of President Obama, who defended the nation's free-speech traditions at the United Nations in the wake of video backlash, supports a proposed U.N. resolution to create an international standard to restrict some anti-religious speech. And, under Obama, the Justice Department has prosecuted a record number of government employees who have leaked sensitive documents, discouraging potential whistleblowers from exposing government waste, fraud or abuse.[2]

"Wherever you look, you see legislation or other measures seeking to reassert state control over speech and the means of speech," says John Kampfner, author of the 2010 book *Freedom for Sale.*

In the United Kingdom and Australia, government ministers last month proposed that media outlets be governed by new regulatory bodies with statutory authority, although they ran into opposition. Two years ago, a new media law in Hungary created a regulatory council with wide-ranging powers to grant licenses to media outlets and assess content in a way that Human Rights Watch says compromises press freedom.[3]

"Not only is legislation such as this bad in and of itself, but it is crucial in sending a green light to authoritarians who use these kind of measures by Western states to say, whenever they are criticized by the West, 'Hey, you guys do the same,'" says Kampfner, former CEO of Index on Censorship, a London-based nonprofit group that fights censorship.

Some observers have hoped the growth of social media and other technologies that spread information faster and more widely than previously thought possible could act as an automatic bulwark protecting freedom of expression. "The best example of the impact of technology on free speech is to look at the Arab Spring," says Dan Wallach, a computer scientist at Rice University, referring to the series of upheavals starting in 2011 that led to the fall of autocratic leaders in Tunisia, Egypt, Yemen and Libya.[4]

But as studies by Wallach and many others show, countries such as China and Iran are building new firewalls to block sensitive information and track dissidents. "The pattern seems to be that governments that fear mass movements on the street have realized that they might want to be able to shut off all Internet communications in the country and have started building the infrastructure that enables them to do that," said Andrew McLaughlin, a former White House adviser on technology.[5]

In January, a French court ordered Twitter to help identify people who had tweeted racist or anti-Semitic remarks, or face fines of 1,000 euros (about $1,300) per day. The San Francisco-based company refused to comply, citing First Amendment protections for free speech.[6]

But even as Twitter appeals the French court order, the microblogging site in October blocked the account of a neo-Nazi group called Besseres Hannover, or Better Hanover, which had been charged with inciting racial hatred. Twitter said it was the first time it had used technology to monitor and withhold content based on a given country's concerns and laws.

Meanwhile, government arrests of journalists and mob attacks against them are on the rise. Journalists are being arrested more often than in previous years in countries such as Russia and Turkey, and in 2012, mobs attacked journalists in Mali and Canada — among other countries — for what the protesters perceived as their blasphemous coverage of Islam. Blasphemy prosecutions have become more common, especially in predominantly Islamic countries such as Pakistan, where blasphemy laws apply only to comments about Islam or Muhammad, not to derogatory comments about Christianity, Judaism or other world religions.[7]

"There have been attempts to pass so-called religious-sensibility laws, which are, in fact, a way of curbing press freedom and expression," says Robert Mahoney, director of the Committee to Protect Journalists, a New York-based nonprofit group that promotes press freedom.

In one widely covered case, three members of the Russian punk rock band Pussy Riot were found guilty of hooliganism motivated by religious hatred last year. They had been arrested in March after a performance in Moscow's main cathedral, in which they profanely called for the Virgin Mary to protect Russia against Vladimir Putin, who was returned to the presidency soon after the performance. The three were sentenced to two years in a prison colony, but one member was released on probation before being sent to prison.[8] In more open societies, laws meant to protect against hate speech, Holocaust denial and offenses against religious sensibilities also can end up limiting what people can talk and write about.

Free-speech laws traditionally have been about the protection of unpopular and provocative expression. Popular and uncontroversial opinions usually need no protection. But in recent years, free-speech protections have been fading away.

"The new restrictions are forcing people to meet the demands of the lowest common denominator of accepted speech," Turley contends.

Number of Journalists Killed on the Rise

Seventy journalists were killed in 2012, nearly half of them murdered, a 43 percent increase from 2011. A total of 232 journalists were imprisoned in 2012, the highest number since the Committee to Protect Journalists began keeping track in 1990. Experts say a select group of countries has fueled the increase by cracking down on criticism of government policies.

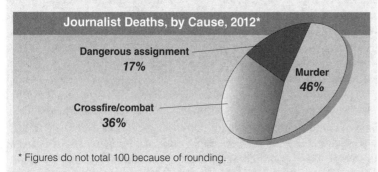

Journalist Deaths, by Cause, 2012*

Dangerous assignment
17%

Crossfire/combat
36%

Murder
46%

* Figures do not total 100 because of rounding.

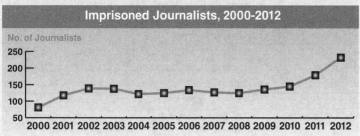

Imprisoned Journalists, 2000-2012

No. of Journalists

2000 2001 2002 2003 2004 2005 2006 2007 2008 2009 2010 2011 2012

Source: "Attacks on the Press," Committee to Protect Journalists, 2013, www.cpj.org/attacks/

As people monitor the health of free expression around the globe, here are some of the questions they're debating:

Has technology made speech freer?

As Arab protesters took to the streets — and the Internet — in 2011 in countries such as Tunisia and Egypt, everyone from commentators for serious foreign-policy journals to "The Daily Show" asked whether the world was witnessing a "Twitter revolution."

Social-media sites such as Twitter and Facebook were used by activists both as organizing tools and as a means of communication with the outside world.

"Tunisians got an alternative picture from Facebook, which remained uncensored through the protests, and they communicated events to the rest of the world by posting videos to YouTube and Daily-motion," Ethan Zuckerman, a researcher at Harvard University's Berkman Center for Internet and Society, wrote in 2011. "It's likely that news of demonstrations in other parts of the country disseminated online helped others conclude that it was time to take to the streets."[9]

Unquestionably, new-media tools make it easier for activists to spread their messages farther and faster than was conceivable during the days of the mimeograph machine, or even the fax. "What's happening with new technology is that it's making publication of these stories easier, and they're reaching a bigger audience," says Mahoney, the Committee to Protect Journalists deputy director.

"Twenty years ago, you'd struggle to get published in a local newspaper," Mahoney says. "Now, as a journalist, you've got far more platforms open to you, and you can get it out."

And not just journalists. From Libya and Iran to Syria and Myanmar, activists and average citizens are able to disseminate text, images and video all over the world, ensuring that their voices can be heard even at moments when regimes are violently cracking down on them.

Social media and other technological tools have become so omnipresent that former Rep. Tom Perriello, D-Va., worries that people become addicted to the online dialogue rather than reaching out to broader populations. "My pet peeve is that people think that social media can replace traditional organizing," says Perriello, President of the Center for American Progress Action Fund, part of a liberal think tank in Washington.

And even free-speech advocates readily admit that, in a broader sense, technology can be a two-edged sword. "Suddenly, you have the ability to reach people all over the world and communicate in ways that you never could before, and that's wonderful," says Eva Galperin, global policy analyst with the Electronic Frontier Foundation (EFF), a San Francisco-based group that promotes an unrestricted Internet. "But it also allows government surveillance on a scale that was never before possible."

Journalists find that their e-mail accounts have been hacked by "state-sponsored attackers" in countries such as China and Myanmar.[10] Mobile phones become surveillance devices.

"Modern information technologies such as the Internet and mobile phones . . . magnify the uniqueness of individuals, further enhancing the traditional challenges to privacy," according to a recent study by researchers from MIT and other universities that exposed the ease of tracking individual cellphone users. "Mobility data contains the approximate whereabouts of individuals and can be used to reconstruct individuals' movements across space and time."[11]

Authoritarian regimes also use technology to access dissidents' computers, installing malware that tracks their movements online, according to Galperin. "It records all of their keystrokes and can use the microphones and cameras on the computers, circumventing all attempts to use encryption," she says.

It's not just dictatorships. Galperin notes that EFF's longstanding lawsuit against the National Security Agency for using warrantless wiretaps in the United States is "now old enough to go to school." And many of the surveillance tools used by authoritarian regimes are made by U.S. companies, she points out.

In the United Kingdom, in response to a phone-hacking scandal that has led to government investigations and a national debate about press abuses, a communications data bill has been proposed by Home Secretary Theresa May to require Internet service providers and mobile phone services to collect and retain data on user activity. The measure is "designed to give the state blanket rights to look at e-mails and IMs [instant messages] and requires all companies to retain the data for a year and hand it over [to the government]," says Kampfner, the former editor of *New Statesman* magazine. "It was halted a few months ago, but will be reintroduced this year."

Iran, which saw its own "Twitter revolution" during a spasm of postelection protests in 2009, has attempted to

AFP/Getty Images/Attila Kisbenedek

A free-speech activist in Budapest, Hungary, protests against a new media law on March 15, 2011. The law set up a regulatory council with wide control over media outlets and content, a power that Human Rights Watch says compromises press freedom. Pictured on the poster is the revered poet of Hungary's 1848-1849 revolution, Sandor Petofi.

keep a "Halal Internet," free of unclean influences and information from the outside world.

In March, Iran's Ministry of Information and Communications Technology blocked software used by millions of Iranians to bypass the state's elaborate Internet filtering system. "A collection of illegal virtual private networks, or VPNs, was successfully closed off by the ministry, making visits to websites deemed immoral or politically dangerous — like Facebook and Whitehouse .gov — nearly impossible," *The New York Times* reported.[12]

Governments and Internet users are engaged in an unending game of cat and mouse, Kampfner says, with each trying to advance technology in ways that gives its side the upper hand.

"There's something called Tor, an open-source project that aims to break through all those barriers, whether in China or Iran or anywhere else," says Wallach, the computer scientist at Rice University. "Tor keeps getting more and more clever about hiding what they're doing, and regimes like Iran get more and more clever about blocking them regardless."

But as many commentators have noted, free speech online depends not only on government policies and court rulings, but on private companies such as Twitter, Facebook and Google. Increasingly, these companies are being called on to block posts by terrorists and unpopular or banned political parties.

"At the end of the day, the private networks are not in any way accountable if they choose to censor or prevent individuals from accessing services," says Katherine Maher, director of strategy and communications for Access, a New York-based digital-rights group.

"The Internet is not something different," Maher says. "It is just an extension of the area in which we live."

Should religious sensibilities be allowed to limit free expression?

When an assassin's bullet narrowly missed the head of Lars Hedegaard, suspicion immediately fell on Muslims, since Hedegaard, a former newspaper editor in Denmark, has been an anti-Islam polemicist.

But a number of Danish Muslims condemned the February attack and rose to defend Hedegaard. "We Muslims have to find a new way of reacting," said Qaiser Najeeb, a Dane whose father had emigrated from Afghanistan. "We don't defend Hedegaard's views but do defend his right to speak. He can say what he wants."[13]

For free-speech advocates, it was a refreshing reaction — particularly in a country where Muslim sensitivities have run high since the 2006 publication of cartoons caricaturing the Prophet Muhammad in a Danish newspaper.

"For those, like me, who look upon free speech as a fundamental good, no degree of cultural or religious discomfort can be reason for censorship," writes British journalist and author Kenan Malik. "There is no free speech without the ability to offend religious and cultural sensibilities."[14]

In recent years, a growing number of people around the globe have been prosecuted on charges of blasphemy

or offending cultural sensibilities through hate speech. According to the International Humanist and Ethical Union (IHEU), only three people were arrested for committing blasphemy via social media between 2007 and 2011, but more than a dozen such arrests occurred in 10 countries last year.[15]

Turkish pianist Fazil Say, for instance, was given a suspended sentence of 10 months in jail on April 15 for posting tweets considered blasphemous, while Gamal Abdou Massoud, a 17-year-old Egyptian, was sentenced to three years for posting blasphemous cartoons on Facebook.

"When 21st-century technology collides with medieval blasphemy laws, it seems to be atheists who are getting hurt, as more of them go to prison for sharing their personal beliefs via social media," says Matt Cherry, editor of the IHEU report.

In Pakistan, those accused of blasphemy often fall victim to violence — before they even get their day in court. Dozens have been killed after being charged with blasphemy over the past 20 years. Last November, a mob burned Farooqi Girls' High School in Lahore after a teacher assigned homework that supposedly contained derogatory references to Muhammad.

"Repeating the blasphemy under Pakistan law is seen as blasphemy in itself," says Padraig Reidy, news editor for the Index on Censorship. "You have these bizarre cases where evidence is barely given but people are sentenced to death."

Even criticizing Pakistan's blasphemy law can be dangerous. Sherry Rehman, the Pakistani ambassador to the United States, has received death threats since calling for changes in the law, while two like-minded politicians have been assassinated.[16]

In Pakistan, free speech is pretty much limited to those hanging around cafes and literary festivals, says Huma Yusuf, a columnist for the Pakistani newspaper *Dawn*. "The threat of blasphemy —a crime that carries the death penalty — has stifled public discourse," she writes.[17]

YouTube has been blocked throughout Pakistan since September, when an anti-Muslim video was uploaded to the site. Thousands of other websites also have been blocked, allegedly for containing pornographic or blasphemous content. "In truth, most had published material criticizing the state," according to Yusuf.

In countries such as Pakistan and Egypt, the line between blasphemy laws designed to protect against religious offense and those meant to punish minorities and stifle dissent is highly porous. "There have been attempts to protect religious sensibility which are in fact a way of curbing press freedom and expression," says Mahoney, of the Committee to Protect Journalists.

In the West, worries about offending religious and cultural sensibilities have sometimes trumped free-speech concerns. "Denigration of religious beliefs is never acceptable," Australian Prime Minister Julia Gillard stated before the United Nations in September. "Our tolerance must never extend to tolerating religious hatred."[18]

Gillard emphasized her disdain for speech that incites hatred and violence, which has become a common concern among Western politicians. "Western governments seem to be sending the message that free-speech rights will not protect you" when it comes to hate speech, writes Turley, the George Washington University law professor.[19]

Hate speech is intended to incite discrimination or violence against members of a particular national, racial or ethnic group, writes Aryeh Neier, a former top official with the American Civil Liberties Union, Human Rights Watch and the Open Society Institute.

Blasphemy Laws Proliferate

Videos and cartoons mocking the Muslim Prophet Muhammad have prompted many countries to enact strict anti-blasphemy laws. Christians and Muslims have used the laws to prosecute people seen as insulting religion. Blasphemy laws in Muslim countries usually refer only to defaming Islam, and punishments can include the death penalty. Many cases involve comments or videos posted on social media such as Twitter and YouTube.

Examples of Recent Blasphemy Cases

Country	Law
Austria	Prohibits disparaging a religious object, society or doctrine.

On Dec. 11, 2010, Helmut Griese, 63, was convicted for offending his Muslim neighbor by yodeling while mowing his lawn; the neighbor claimed Griese was imitating the Muslim call to prayer. On Jan. 22, 2009, politician Susanne Winter was fined $24,000 for saying Muhammad was a pedophile because he had a 9-year-old wife.

India	Allows up to three years in prison for insulting religion or religious beliefs.

On April 21, 2012, the Catholic Church filed a complaint against Sanal Edamaruku, the founder of the reason-based organization Rationalist International, after he exposed a "miracle" by showing water from a statue of Jesus was coming from a leaky drain. On Nov. 19, 2012, college student Shaheen Dhada and a friend were arrested for complaining on Facebook that Mumbai had been shut down for the funeral of the leader of the Hindu nationalist party.

Iran	Bars criticism of Islam or deviation from the ruling Islamic standards.

Web designer Saeed Malekpour, 35, a Canadian, served four years on death row in Iran for "insulting Islam." He was arrested while visiting his dying father in Iran in 2008 because a photo-sharing program he created while in Canada was used by others to download pornography. The death sentence was suspended in 2012 after Malekpour "repented."

Netherlands	Penalizes "scornful blasphemy" that insults religious feelings.

On March 19, 2008, Dutch cartoonist Gregorius Nekschot was arrested for insulting Muslims in his drawings. On Jan. 21, 2009, politician Geert Wilders was put on trial because his film "Fitna" compared Islam and Nazism. He was acquitted.

Pakistan	Bans blasphemy, including defiling the Quran and making remarks against the Prophet Muhammad.

In 2011 the governor of Punjab and the minister for minority affairs were assassinated because they opposed the country's blasphemy laws. On June 22, 2011, 29-year-old Larkana resident Abdul Sattar was sentenced to death and fined $1,000 for sending text messages and blaspheming the Quran, Muhammad and other Islamic figures during a phone conversation.

United Kingdom	Prohibits "hate speech" against religious groups.

On March 4, 2010, philosophy tutor Harry Taylor was sentenced to six months in prison, 100 hours of community service and fined €250 ($337 at the time) for leaving anti-Christian and anti-Islam cartoons in an airport prayer room.

Source: International Humanist and Ethical Union, December 2012

Indians protest against the American-made anti-Muslim video "Innocence of Muslims" in Kolkata on Oct. 5, 2012. The film incited a wave of anti-U.S. violence in Libya, Egypt and other countries across the Muslim world. Speaking at the United Nations after the protests, President Obama explained that such films could not be banned in the United States because of the U.S. Constitution's free-speech rights.

But, Neier notes, "It is important to differentiate blasphemy from hate speech. The proclivity of some elsewhere to react violently to what they consider blasphemous cannot be the criterion for imposing limits on free expression in the U.S., the United Kingdom, Denmark or the Netherlands (or anywhere else)."[20]

In recent months, the human rights group American Freedom Defense Initiative (AFDI) has been running anti-Muslim ads on public transportation systems around the United States. Posters that appeared on San Francisco buses last month, for example, included a picture of Osama bin Laden and a made-up quote from "Hamas MTV" that said, "Killing Jews is worship that brings us closer to Allah."

After New York's Metropolitan Transit Authority tried to block the ads last summer, Federal District Judge Paul A. Engelmayer ruled that the agency had violated AFDI's First Amendment rights.

"Not only did [he] rule that the ads should be 'afforded the highest level of protection under the First Amendment,' he went on to offer some eye-opening examples," writes *San Francisco Chronicle* columnist C. W. Nevius. "Engelmayer said an ad could accuse a private citizen of being a child abuser. Or, he suggested, it could say, 'Fat people are slobs' or 'Blondes are bimbos' and still be protected."[21]

Rather than put up a legal fight, San Francisco's Municipal Railway decided to put up peace posters of its own and donate the AFDI's advertising fee to the city's Human Rights Commission.

Should the United States promote free speech abroad?

Because of the First Amendment and the history of its interpretation, the United States has what comes closest to absolute protection of free speech of any country on Earth. And many believe free expression is not only essential to democracy but a value Americans should help export to other countries.

At a 2011 Internet freedom conference in The Hague, then-Secretary of State Hillary Rodham Clinton said, "The United States will be making the case for an open Internet in our work worldwide.

"The right to express one's views, practice one's faith, peacefully assemble with others to pursue political or social change — these are all rights to which all human beings are entitled, whether they choose to exercise them in a city square or an Internet chat room," Clinton said. "And just as we have worked together since the last century to secure these rights in the material world, we must work together in this century to secure them in cyberspace."[22]

But the right to free expression that is taken for granted in the United States is not shared around the world. Some people — including some Americans — worry that the United States risks offending governments and citizens in other nations by preserving free-speech rights — including the right to racist and blasphemous speech — above nearly every other consideration.

Such voices have been prominent when Americans have exercised their free-speech rights in ways that offend others. Threats to burn the Quran — as well as actual Quran burnings — by Florida pastor Terry Jones led to deadly riots in the Muslim world in 2010 and 2011. Last fall, video portions from an anti-Muslim film called "Innocence of Muslims" triggered riots in several predominantly Muslim nations.

Speaking to the United Nations two weeks later, President Obama explained that the U.S. government could not ban such a video because of free-speech rights enshrined in the U.S. Constitution.

"Americans have fought and died around the globe to protect the right of all people to express their views, even views that we profoundly disagree with," Obama said. "We do not do so because we support hateful speech, but because our founders understood that without such protections, the capacity of each individual to express their own views and practice their own faith may be threatened."[23]

But Obama noted that modern technology means "anyone with a cellphone can spread offensive views around the world with the click of a button."

While reality, some commentators said it was foolish to expect other nations to understand the American right to unbridled speech. "While the First Amendment right to free expression is important, it is also important to remember that other countries and cultures do not have to understand or respect our right," Anthea Butler, a University of Pennsylvania religious studies professor, wrote in *USA Today.*[24]

Americans must remember that "our First Amendment values are not universal," cautioned Eric Posner, a University of Chicago law professor.

"Americans need to learn that the rest of the world — and not just Muslims — see no sense in the First Amendment," Posner wrote in *Slate*. "Even other Western nations take a more circumspect position on freedom of expression than we do, realizing that often free speech must yield to other values and the need for order. Our own history suggests that they might have a point."[25]

Access' Maher, who has consulted on technology issues with the World Bank and UNICEF, notes that even other Western nations tend to hold free-speech rights less dear, viewing them within a context not of personal liberty but a framework where they risk infringing on the rights of others. "This often leads to robust debates about incitement, hate speech, blasphemy and their role in the political discourse, often in a manner more open to possible circumscription than would be acceptable in the United States," she says.

Even some who promote free expression worry about the United States taking a leading role in its promotion, because of the risk of it being seen elsewhere as an American value being imposed from without.

"The problem is freedom of expression has come to be seen as either an American or Anglo-Saxon construct, whereas we would all like to see it as a universal principle,"

says Kampfner, the British journalist. "There is a danger that if this value is seen as proselytized primarily by the United States, it will reinforce those who are suspicious of it."

But it may be that America's staunch adherence to free speech makes the United States uniquely well-suited to promote and defend the idea.

"The United States values a free press and should promote those values abroad," says Robert Mahoney, deputy director of the Committee to Protect Journalists.

"No Western country wants to appear to be lecturing other countries to uphold its values, but it's not an American construct," he says. "We have a duty to remind them of that, and we expect international bodies like the U.N. and countries like the United Kingdom and the European Union to do the same thing."

During his first trip abroad as secretary of State, John Kerry in February defended free speech — including the "right to be stupid" — as a virtue "worth fighting for."[26]

It's important that individuals and groups in foreign countries take the lead in explaining free-speech rights, "so it's not seen as a Western concept," says Reidy, the Index on Censorship editor.

"Certain human rights are not Western," he says, "they're universal. That's the whole point of human rights."

BACKGROUND

Refusal to *"Revoco"*

The struggle for free speech has been a long story about testing limits. Many of the most famous moments in the development of free speech in the Western world involved notable figures such as the French philosopher Voltaire, the Biblical translator William Tyndale and the Italian astronomer Galileo, who were variously exiled, executed or forced to recant things they had said or written.

"Governments in all places in all times have succumbed to the impulse to exert control over speech and conscience," writes Rodney A. Smolla, president of Furman University.[27]

The first great flowering of democracy and free speech occurred 500 years before the birth of Christ in the Greek city-state of Athens. The city pioneered the idea of government by consent, allowing the people the freedom to choose their own rules.

"Free speech was an inseparable part of the new Athenian order," Robert Hargreaves, who was a British broadcaster, writes in his 2002 book *The First Freedom.* "Never before had ordinary citizens been given the right to debate such vital matters as war and peace, public finance or crime and punishment."[28]

But although Athens embraced, off and on, the concept of government by consent, it did not yet accept the idea of individual free speech that might upset the prevailing order. Athens now may be remembered less for pioneering free speech than for trying and executing the great philosopher Socrates in 399 B.C., after he refused to recant his teachings.

Demanding that critics and heretics recant has been a persistent theme throughout history. After Martin Luther printed his *Ninety-Five Theses* in 1517, which criticized clerical abuses, Cardinal Thomas Cajetan, the papal legate in Rome, asked him to say *revoco,* or "I recant," and all would be well. Luther refused.

Cajetan wanted to turn Luther over to Rome on charges of heresy, but Frederick III, the elector of Saxony, allowed him to stay. Luther's works became bestsellers. Not only was he a celebrity, but his writings helped spark the Protestant Reformation.

Eventually, Pope Leo X and the Holy Roman Emperor Charles V also asked Luther to recant his writings. He argued that he was defending works about the teachings of Christ and therefore was not free to retract them. He offered this famous defense: "Here I stand; God help me; I can do no other."[29] As a result, the pope excommunicated him, and the emperor condemned him as an outlaw.

Controlling the Press

Luther's writings were spread thanks to the advent of the printing press, a new technology that governments sought to control. The Star Chamber of the British Parliament in 1586 strictly limited the number of master printers, apprentices and printing presses that could operate in London. All books were required to be licensed by the archbishop of Canterbury or the bishop of London.

A few decades later, members of Parliament won the ability to speak and vote without royal restraint. This led to a freer press, as London printers began publishing journals that were largely accounts of Parliament but also contained news. By 1645, the printers were putting out an average of 14 separate weekly titles.[30]

A year earlier, the English poet John Milton had published his *Aereopagitica,* remembered as one of the most eloquent pleas for a free press ever penned. "Truth is strong next to the Almighty, she needs no policies, no stratagems nor licensing to make her victorious," Milton wrote in the treatise. "Give her but room, and do not bind her."

Although it grew out of ongoing debates about press licensing and limiting free speech, the *Aereopagitica* had little influence in its day. The press remained heavily regulated both in the United Kingdom and in its American colonies.

In 1734, a German-born printer in New York named John Peter Zenger published criticism of royalist Gov. William Cosby, calling him "a governor turned rogue" who was undermining the colony's laws. At Zenger's trial the following year, attorney Andrew Hamilton argued that the judge and jury should not separately consider the questions of whether he had published the material and whether it was libelous, as was the practice at the time, but rather simply determine whether it could not be libel because it was true.

The jury's verdict of not guilty was considered an important precedent, but it would be 70 years before New York changed its libels laws so the question of truth could be entered into evidence.

William Blackstone, in his *Commentaries on the Laws of England* of 1769, laid the groundwork for the idea that there should be no licensing or prior restraint of the press, but that publishers could still face punishment after publication. This formed the basis for the thinking of the American Founders, who remained skeptical about a completely free press.

"License of the press is no proof of liberty," John Adams wrote in his *Novanglus Letters* of 1774. "When a people are corrupted, the press may be made an engine to complete their ruin . . . and the freedom of the press, instead of promoting the cause of liberty, will but hasten its destruction."

As U.S. president, Adams signed the Alien and Sedition Acts, which led to multiple arrests and convictions of printers and publicists (all Republicans, or political opponents of Adams). The law was overturned under Thomas Jefferson, who had been skeptical about the

CHRONOLOGY

1940s-1980s *New laws, international entities and court decisions expand free-speech rights.*

1946 French constitution upholds principle that "free communication of thought and of opinion is one of the most precious rights of man."

1948 United Nations adopts Universal Declaration of Human Rights, declaring "the right to freedom of opinion and expression" for all.

1952 U.S. Supreme Court extends First Amendment protections to movies.

1954 Congress effectively criminalizes the Communist Party.

1961 British jury allows Penguin to publish the novel *Lady Chatterly's Lover,* which had been on a list of obscene material.

1964 In landmark *New York Times v. Sullivan* decision, U.S. Supreme Court rules that public officials must prove "actual malice" on the part of journalists in order to sue for libel. . . . Free Speech Movement at University of California, Berkeley, insists that administrators allow campus protests.

1968 U.K. abolishes 400-year-old laws allowing for government censorship of theater performances.

1971 In the first instance of prior restraint on the press in U.S. history, a court blocks *The New York Times* from publishing the Pentagon Papers, but the Supreme Court OKs publication of the classified Vietnam War history.

1989 Iran's Islamic government issues a fatwa, or kill order, against *Satanic Verses* author Salman Rushdie forcing him into hiding for years. . . . Supreme Court upholds the right to burn the U.S. flag in protest.

2000s *In response to terrorist attacks, many Western countries limit civil liberties.*

2000 At the first meeting of the post-Cold War Community of Democracies, 106 countries pledge to uphold democratic principles, including freedom of expression

2005 George W. Bush administration ultimately fails in its year-long campaign to pressure *New York Times* not to publish a story about warrantless wiretaps.

2006 More than 200 people die in violent protests across the Muslim world after the Danish newspaper *Jyllands-Posten* publishes cartoons satirizing the Prophet Muhammad. . . . United Kingdom bans language intended "to stir up religious hatred." . . . In response to July 2005 terrorist bombings of bus and subway system that killed more than 50 people,

U.K. enacts Prevention of Terrorism Act, which curtails speech in the name of security. . . . Crusading Russian journalist Anna Politkovskaya, known for her coverage of the Chechen conflict, is assassinated.

2010s *In an age of new media, both rich and developing countries restrict speech that may offend.*

2010 WikiLeaks publishes thousands of sensitive documents related to U.S. diplomatic efforts in Iraq, Afghanistan and elsewhere. . . . Google announces it is pulling out of China due to government censorship of its service.

2012 U.S. Supreme Court finds the Stolen Valor Act unconstitutional; the 2006 law made it a crime to falsely claim to have won military decorations. . . . Members of the Russian punk band Pussy Riot are convicted of hooliganism for protesting President Vladimir Putin's policies in a Moscow church. . . . "Innocence of Muslims," an anti-Muslim video posted on YouTube, triggers riots in several Middle Eastern and North African countries. . . . Twitter blocks German access to posts by a banned neo-Nazi party, its first bow to "country-withheld content" regulations. . . . Inquiry on press abuses in Britain spurred by telephone-hacking scandal by media outlets calls for greater regulation. . . . Egyptian court sentences to death in absentia Florida pastor Terry Jones, who had offended Muslims through Quran burnings and promotion of an anti-Muslim film.

2013 Pfc. Bradley Manning pleads guilty to 10 charges of giving government secrets to WikiLeaks (Feb. 28). . . . Due to lack of support, Australia's ruling party withdraws a proposal to regulate the press (March 21). . . . Privately owned newspapers are distributed in Myanmar for the first time in 50 years (April 1). . . . Egyptian court drops charges against popular comedian Bassem Youssef, who had been accused of insulting the president (April 6).

Free Speech Can Be Deadly in Russia

"Many journalists end up dead, assaulted or threatened."

Aleksei A. Navalny expects to go to jail. Last month, a Russian court announced it would schedule a trial against Navalny, who is accused of embezzling from a timber company, even though the case was dismissed last year for lack of evidence. Still, Navalny said, "Honestly, I am almost certain I am going to prison."[1]

Many of Navalny's supporters believe his real crimes were organizing protests in Moscow in 2011 and 2012, blogging and running a nonprofit group that operates websites that allow citizens to report incidents of government corruption.

Navalny, who announced on April 4 that he will run for president, is not the only activist to come under pressure from Russia's government. Since Vladimir Putin returned to the presidency last May, new restrictions have been imposed on Internet content, and fines of up to $32,000 have been imposed for participating in protests deemed illegal.

International nonprofit groups such as Amnesty International, Human Rights Watch and Transparency International have been ordered to register as foreign agents. All have refused, and their offices recently have been raided by government investigators.

Last month, Dmitry Gudkov, an opposition politician and one of only two members of the Russian parliament to support public protests such as those organized by Navalny, was accused of treason by some of his colleagues after he visited the United States in March. Gudkov's father was stripped of his seat in parliament last fall.

While cracking down on opposition voices, Putin's government has been able to rely on friendly state-run media coverage, including from Channel One, the nation's most widely watched television station. During his U.S. visit, Gudkov noted that Russian state-controlled media had accused him of treason and selling secrets.

While some countries try to crack down on independent media outlets through intimidation, Russia for the most part controls communications directly, with the state or its friends owning most of the major newspapers and broadcasters.

Arch Puddington, vice president for research at Freedom House, a Washington-based watchdog group, says what he calls the "Putin model" is widely practiced. "They buy television stations and turn them into mouthpieces of the government," he says.

It's a case of, "If you can't beat them, buy them," says Anthony Mills, deputy director of the International Press Institute in Austria.

Russia is not alone. In some Central Asian and Latin American countries, government-owned media are commonly used for propaganda and to negate foreign criticism.

In Turkey, most of the media are controlled by a few private companies, which leads more to collusion than intimidation, says former Rep. Tom Perriello, D-Va. "In Turkey, you have less of the situation of people being shaken down [or threatened] if they print this story," he says. "Instead, many of the TV companies are doing contracts with the government, so there's a financial interest in not wanting to irritate people in the . . . government."

In other countries, antagonism is the norm. According to Freedom House, Ecuadoran President Rafael Correa has called the press his "greatest political enemy," which he says is "ignorant," "mediocre," "primitive," "bloodthirsty" and "deceitful."[2]

need for unbridled press but embraced it in his second inaugural, stating that the press needed no other legal restraint than the truth.

The principle that there was a right to disseminate facts in a democracy was crystallized in British philosopher John Stuart Mill's *On Liberty* of 1859. "News, independently gathered and impartially conveyed, was seen to be an indispensable commodity in a society where the people ruled themselves," Mill wrote.

Expanding Rights

The U.S. Supreme Court seldom examined the question of free speech during the 19th century, but justices began to expand its sense in the 20th century.

"Ecuador under its president of the last five years, Rafael Correa, has become one of the world's leading oppressors of free speech," Peter Hartcher, international editor for *The Sydney Morning Herald,* wrote last summer. "Correa has appropriated, closed and intimidated many media outlets critical of his government. He has sued journalists for crippling damages."[3]

Analysts say the Venezuelan government tries to own or control nearly all media, while vilifying and jailing independent journalists.

And in Russia, government harassment of independent voices is common. Only a few independent outlets operate, such as *Novaya Gazeta,* a newspaper co-owned by former Soviet President Mikhail Gorbachev, but they aren't widely read or heard except by law enforcement agencies that often arrest, beat and — according to watchdog groups — even kill journalists.[4]

The 2006 killing of Anna Politkovskaya, a *Novaya Gazeta* reporter noted for her coverage of the Chechen conflict, drew international attention, although no one has been convicted of her murder. "Russia is among the most dangerous countries in which to be a journalist," says Rajan Menon, a political scientist at City College of New York. "Many journalists end up dead, assaulted or threatened for looking into hot-button issues, especially corruption."

In some countries, state-owned media criticize their own governments, says Robert Mahoney, deputy director of the Committee to Protect Journalists, citing the example of the BBC. But when nearly all media are owned by a few individuals or companies, it's not "good in the long term for a diverse and vibrant free press," he says.

Nor is it good when journalists fear they might be killed for digging into stories. In Russia, for instance, journalists are routinely killed with impunity. "There are 17 cases where journalists were killed in the last dozen years or so," Mahoney says, "and there have been no prosecutions."

— *Alan Greenblatt*

AFP/Getty Images/Olga Maltseva

Rnssian activist Aleksei Navalny, a leading critic of President Vladimir Putin, addresses an anti-Putin rally in St. Petersburg on Feb. 12, 2012.

[1] Andrew E. Kramer, "With Trial Suddenly Looming, Russian Activist Expects the Worst," The New York Times, March 28, 2013, p. A4, www .nytimes.com/2013/03/28/world/europe/with-case-reopened-the-russian-activist-aleksei-navalny-expects-the-worst.html.

[2] "Freedom of the Press 2011: Ecuador," Freedom House, Sept. 1, 2011, www.freedomhouse.org/report/freedom-press/2011/ecuador.

[3] Peter Hartcher, "Hypocrisy Ends Hero's Freedom to Preach," The Sydney Morning Herald, Aug. 21,2012, www.smh.com.au/opinion/politics/hypocrisy-ends-heros-freedom-to-preach-20120820-24ijx.html.

[4] Peter Preston, "Putin's win is a hollow victory for a Russian free press," The Guardian, March 10, 2012, www.guardian.co.uk/media/2012/mar/11/putin-win-russian-free-press.

During World War I, more than 1,900 Americans were prosecuted under the Espionage Act of 1917 and the Sedition Act of 1918, which banned printing, writing and uttering of statements deemed disloyal or abusive of the U.S. government.

One case led to the famous formulation of Justice Oliver Wendell Holmes. "The most stringent protection of free speech would not protect a man in falsely shouting 'fire' in a crowded theater and creating a panic," Holmes wrote in his dissent in *Schenck v. U.S.* in 1919. "The question in every case is whether the words used are used in such circumstances and are of such a nature to create a clear and present danger that they will bring about the substantive evils that Congress has a right to prevent."

China Opens Up — But Just a Crack

Journalists' and dissenters' activities are still monitored.

It's been decades now since China opened up to the West. But it's still not completely open, especially with regard to freedom of speech and the press.

In recent months, angered by coverage it viewed as hostile, such as reports that the families of top government officials have enriched themselves while the officials have been in power, China has denied entry visas to reporters from media organizations such as *The New York Times*, Al-Jazeera English and Reuters.

Since October, it has blocked access within China to *The Times*' website, while Chinese hackers have broken into email accounts belonging to reporters from *The Times* and *The Wall Street Journal*, possibly to determine the sources of stories critical of government officials.

China has long maintained a "Great Firewall," blocking its citizens from accessing critical content from foreign sources. But the Chinese government is also at pains to block internal criticism from its own citizens and media, as well.

In any given year, China typically ranks in the world's top two or three countries in terms of how many journalists it imprisons.[1] "There's a certain level of very localized dissent allowed, but it can never be expressed directly at the regime," says Padraig Reidy, news editor for Index on Censorship, a free-speech advocacy group.

"You can say a local official is corrupt — maybe," Reidy says. "But you can't say the party is corrupt. That's the end of you."

Besides tracking journalists' activities, China's government also monitors activists' online postings. A recent study by computer scientist Dan Wallach of Rice University and several colleagues found that China could be employing more than 4,000 censors to monitor the 70,000 posts per minute uploaded to Weibo, the Chinese version of Twitter.[2]

The censors tend to track known activists and use automated programs to hunt for forbidden phrases. "Certain words you know are never going to get out of the gate," Wallach says. "Falun Gong" — a spiritual practice China has sought to ban — "those three characters you can't utter on any Chinese website anywhere in the country."

Weibo users are "incredibly clever" at coming up with misspellings and neologisms to sneak past the censors, Wallach says. For instance, a colloquial phrase for China, the Celestial Temple, is sometimes rewritten as "celestial bastard," using similar-looking characters.

But once such usage becomes widespread, the censors are quick to catch on and such terms also are quickly eradicated from websites. "China is definitely the market leader in technical tools for clamping down on free expression," says British journalist John Kampfner.

Aside from imprisonment and hacking attacks, China uses self-censorship to suppress criticism of the state, says Robert Mahoney, deputy director of the New York-based Committee to Protect Journalists. Reporters and others constantly worry about what sort of statements could trigger a crackdown.

"With self-censoring, journalists tend to be more conservative," Mahoney says. Such sensitivity to what censors will think extends even to Hollywood movies. Given the growing

Although fewer dissenters were prosecuted during World War II there were still dozens. "The Roosevelt administration investigated suspects for their 'un-American' associations and employed a variety of legal devices to harass the dissenters and suppress the dissent," writes historian Richard W. Steele.[31]

During the 1940s and '50s, Congress did what it could to ban Communist Party activities in the United States, but after World War II, the sense that free speech was an inalienable right took deep hold in the country and the courts. It was even included in Article 19 of the Universal Declaration of Human Rights, adopted by the United Nations in 1948, which says: "Everyone has the right to freedom of opinion and expression; this right includes freedom to hold opinions without interference and to seek, receive and impart information and ideas through any media and regardless of frontiers."[32]

A series of lectures by American free-speech advocate Alexander Meiklejohn published in 1948 was hugely influential as a defense of the notion that free speech and democracy are intertwined. "The phrase 'Congress shall make no law . . . abridging the freedom of speech,' is importance of the Chinese film market, the country's censors now review scripts and inspect sets of movies filmed in China to make sure that nothing offends their sensibilities.

"There were points where we were shooting with a crew of 500 people," said Rob Cohen, director of "The Mummy: Tomb of the Dragon Emperor," which kicked off a recent wave of co-productions between Chinese companies and American studios. "I'm not sure who was who or what, but knowing the way the system works, it's completely clear that had we deviated from the script, it would not have gone unnoticed."[3] The Academy Award-winning "Django Unchained" was initially cut to delete scenes of extreme violence, but censors blocked its scheduled April 12 release due to shots of full-frontal nudity.

In addition to carefully inspecting Western content coming into the country, China is seeking to export its model for rigid media control to other countries. "It's fascinating to look at Chinese investment in Africa," says Anthony Mills, deputy director of the Austria-based International Press Institute. "They've bought into a variety of media outlets in Africa."

While China can't impose censorship in Africa, its control of media outlets there helps ensure favorable coverage. Beijing is actively promoting its image abroad through news-content deals with state-owned media in countries including Zimbabwe, Nigeria, Cuba, Malaysia and Turkey, according to the South African Institute of International Affairs. "Countries that need Chinese trade, aid and recognition, and those with tense relations with the U.S., are more likely to be influenced by China's soft power," the institute concluded in a report last year.[4]

"China has this model in which the economic welfare and the perceived welfare of the state as a whole trump individual freedoms," Mills says.

Some Western observers, such as Reidy, believe China will eventually have to become more open, because capitalist investment demands a free flow of information.

But others wonder whether China's more authoritarian approach represents a challenge to the transatlantic model that has been fairly dominant around the globe since World War II, with freedom of expression seen as essential to democracy and economic growth.

Already, says former Rep. Tom Perriello, D-Va., residents of countries such as Turkey complain less about individual freedoms while the economy is growing.

"If you actually get to a point where China is associated with economic prosperity more than Western countries are, then people look differently at democracy and human rights," he says. "I wish they didn't, but that's part of the fear, that we can't assume there's this natural march toward more liberalism."

— *Alan Greenblatt*

[1] Madeline Earp, "Disdain for Foreign Press Undercuts China's Global Ambition," Committee to Protect Journalists, March 11, 2013, www.cpj.org/2013/02/attacks-on-the-press-china-tightens-control.php.

[2] "Computer Scientists Measure the Speed of Censorship on China's Twitter," *The Physics arXiv Blog*, March 6, 2013, www.technologyreview.com/view/512231/computer-scientists-measure-the-speed-of-censorship-on-chinas-twitter.

[3] Michael Cieply and Brooks Barnes, "To Get Movies Into China, Hollywood Gives Censors a Preview," *The New York Times*, Jan. 15, 2013, p. A1, www.nytimes.com/2013/01/15/business/media/in-hollywood-movies-for-china-bureaucrats-want-a-say.html.

[4] Yu-Shan Wu, "The Rise of China's State-Led Media Dynasty in Africa," South African Institute of International Affairs, June 2012, p. 11, www.saiia.org.za/images/stories/pubs/occasional_papers_above_100/saia_sop_%20117_wu_20120618.pdf.

unqualified," Meiklejohn wrote. "It admits of no exceptions. . . . That prohibition holds good in war and peace, in danger as in security."[33]

In the 1960s, the U.S. Supreme Court protected racist speech, as well as speech by advocates of integration. "A decision protecting speech by a Ku Klux Klan member cited a decision that protected an African-American antiwar state legislator, and the case of the klansman was, in turn, cited [in 1989] to protect a radical who burned the American flag as a political protest," writes Wake Forest law professor Michael Kent Curtis.[34]

In 1964, the Supreme Court limited libel suits brought by public officials, finding that the First Amendment required "actual malice" — that is, knowledge that information published was false.[35] Seven years later, a lower court blocked *The New York Times* from publish further portions of the Pentagon Papers, a government history of the Vietnam War — the first example in U.S. history of prior restraint.

Ku Klux Klan members in Pulaski, Tenn., participate in a march honoring Nathan Bedford Forrest, a Confederate general who helped found the Klan, on July 11, 2009. The U.S. Supreme Court has ruled that even hate groups like the Klan have a constitutional right to express their racist views publicly.

The Supreme Court lifted the injunction. Justice Hugo Black wrote, "In revealing the workings of government that led to the Vietnam War, the newspapers nobly did precisely that which the Founders hoped and trusted they would do."[36]

After a long period of expansion, press freedoms and other civil liberties were challenged following the terrorist attacks of Sept. 11, 2001. Once again, free speech was seen as possibly undermining the government at a time when security concerns had become paramount. "Press freedoms are positively correlated with greater transnational terrorism," write University of Chicago law professor Posner and Harvard University law professor Adrian Vermeule. "Nations with a free press are more likely to be targets of such terrorism."[37]

For example, they cited a 2005 *New York Times* story on the so-called warrantless wiretapping program at the National Security Agency, which they argue alerted terrorists that the United States was monitoring communications the terrorists believed were secure.[38] The Bush administration made similar arguments to *The Times*, which held the story until after the 2004 presidential election.

Worried that the administration would seek a federal court injunction to block publication, *The Times* first published the story on its website. "In the new digital world of publishing, there were no printing presses to stop," notes Samuel Walker, a University of Nebraska law professor.[39]

CURRENT SITUATION
Government Secrets

With so much speech, commerce — and terrorist activity — taking place online, Congress is struggling to find an appropriate balance between security on the one hand and privacy and free-speech concerns on the other.

On April 18, the House passed the Cyber Intelligence Sharing and Protection Act, known by the acryonym CISPA. The bill would give military and security agencies greater access to Americans' online activity by making it easier for private companies to share cyberthreat information with the government, allowing government and businesses to help each other out when they get hacked.

The nation's networks are already under attack from countries such as Iran and Russia, Texas GOP Rep. Michael McCaul, chair of the House Homeland Security Committee, told his colleagues during floor debate.[40]

"I think if anything, the recent events in Boston demonstrate that we have to come together to get this done," McCaul said, referring to the bombs that exploded near the finish line of the Boston Marathon three days earlier. "In the case of Boston, they were real bombs. In this case, they're digital bombs."[41]

But the bill's opponents said it represented a violation of privacy and free-speech rights, giving government agencies such as the FBI and CIA easy access to online accounts without warrants, chilling free expression. On April 16, the Obama administration threatened to veto the bill, if it were to reach the president's desk.[42]

The bill would allow Internet companies "to ship the whole kit and caboodle" of personal information to the government, including that which does not pertain directly to cyberthreats and "is none of the government's business," said California Rep. Nancy Pelosi, Democratic leader of the House.[43]

"I am disappointed . . . we did not address the concerns of the White House about personal information," Pelosi said. "It offers no policies and did not allow any amendments and no real solutions to uphold Americans' right to privacy."

Should journalists be regulated?

YES
STEVEN BARNETT
Professor of Communications,
University of Westminster, London, England

Written for *CQ Researcher*, April 2013

In an ideal world, a free press should not be constrained any more than free speech. Unfortunately, this is not an ideal world. Would-be terrorists seek to recruit supporters, grossly offensive material can reap huge financial rewards and some publications try to boost circulation and scoop competitors using immoral and even downright malicious methods.

Some methods, such as hacking into voicemails, are illegal in Britain. Others are not. Public outrage was sparked by atrocious behaviour that some British newspapers have sanctioned in the name of "journalism," such as splashing on the front page the private and intimate diaries of Kate McCann after the disappearance of her daughter Madeleine. Although Mrs. McCann begged the *News of the World* not to publish the diaries, the newspaper ignored her pleas. Such callous indifference to people's feelings had become institutionalized in some of Britain's best-selling newspapers.

What is required is not state control or statutory regulation. But the press must be held accountable for egregious abuses of its own privileged position within a democracy.

In the United Kingdom, Sir Brian Leveson, who chaired a judicial inquiry into press practices and ethics as a result of the phone-hacking scandal, recommended the moderate solution of voluntary self-regulation overseen by an autonomous body that would assess whether self-regulation was effective and independent. If so, news organizations choosing to belong would be entitled to financial incentives such as lower court costs and exemption from exemplary damages if sued. It is, I repeat, a voluntary incentive-based system, which is needed to protect ordinary people from amoral and sometimes vindictive practices that have no place in journalism.

Such proposals might feel uncomfortable in the land of the First Amendment, but it is exceptionally mild by European standards. In Finland, a Freedom of Expression Act mandates, among other things, that aggrieved parties have a right of reply or correction without undue delay. In Germany, newspapers are required to print corrections with the same prominence as the original report. Scandinavian countries have passed legislation on press ethics.

These countries are not rampant dictatorships. But they all, as will Britain, find a proper balance between unconstrained journalism and the rights of ordinary people not to have their misery peddled for corporate profit.

NO
ANTHONY MILLS
Deputy Director, International Press Institute,
Vienna, Austria

Written for *CQ Researcher*, April 2013

In any healthy democracy, the media play a watchdog role, holding elected officials accountable and serving the public interest by satisfying citizens' right to know what is being done in their name in the often not-so-transparent corridors of power. In the United States, for instance, the Watergate scandal was unearthed and covered, at not inconsiderable risk, by two young *Washington Post* reporters.

Not surprisingly, there are those in office for whom such media scrutiny is, to put it mildly, unwelcome. And, lo and behold, they become advocates for state regulation of the media. They may very well point to one or more examples of egregious, even criminal, journalist behavior as evidence of the need to exert greater control.

No one suggests that journalists are above the law. But when they engage in criminal behavior, they should be held accountable in criminal courts. The profession must not be overseen by the very elected officials whom it is supposed to hold to account. Surely, from the perspective of the politicians, that would be a conflict of interest.

The answer is self-regulation. That could be accomplished through independent regulatory bodies with the teeth to hold journalists ethically accountable or through ethical standards rigorously and systematically imposed by media outlets themselves as is the case in the United States, where the First Amendment right to freedom of the press is fiercely guarded. Professional peers must lead by example.

In the absence of self-regulation, or where it is not effectively implemented, the path is easily paved for statutory regulation, whether direct, or roundabout, in form. The aftermath of the *News of the World* phone-hacking scandal in the U.K., and the ensuing inquiry by Lord Justice Leveson, have amply demonstrated this. The U.K. press is set to be bound by statutory legislation for the first time in hundreds of years. That cannot be healthy for democracy, and other countries tend to follow the lead of their democratic "peers."

So it is incumbent upon everyone in the profession to resist any efforts to impose statutory regulation of the press by those upon whom the press is supposed to be keeping its watchful eye. But it falls upon the press to ensure that the standards it embraces are of the highest order of professionalism and integrity. Anything less offers cannon fodder for those targeting a free media.

The measure now goes to the U.S. Senate. A similar bill was unable to muster enough Senate votes last year to overcome a filibuster, and this year's outcome is uncertain.

Information Explosion

The explosion of information on the Internet and in online databases has made legal concerns about free speech more complicated, says Randall Bezanson, a law professor at the University of Iowa. For most of U.S. history, such concerns turned largely on the question of whether the government had the power to censor speech. Now, he says, regulating speech involves the government not just quashing the speech of individuals but in protecting documents and databases — its own, and others — from disclosure.

The Obama administration has learned that lesson well, he says, and is doing its best to keep state secrets secret. "Eric Holder, attorney general under President Barack Obama, has prosecuted more government officials for alleged leaks under the World War I-era Espionage Act than all his predecessors combined," Bloomberg News reported last fall.[44]

The administration was disturbed by the leak of thousands of diplomatic cables, which were published in 2010 by the whistleblower website WikiLeaks, founded by former Australian computer hacker Julian Assange.[45]

"The Julian Assange episode and those disclosures of pretty well unfiltered information, I think, scared people in government and raised a whole different specter of what could be done and what the consequences are, and that has probably triggered a more aggressive approach in the Justice Department," Bezanson says.

On Feb. 28, Army Pfc. Bradley Manning, who leaked thousands of diplomatic, military and intelligence cables to WikiLeaks, pleaded guilty to 10 charges of illegally acquiring and transferring government secrets, agreeing to spend 20 years in prison. Manning pleaded not guilty, however, to 12 additional counts — including espionage — and faces a general court-martial in June.

Manning's case has made him a cause célèbre among some on the left who see him as being unduly persecuted. A similar dynamic is playing out in memory of American online activist and pioneer Aaron Swartz, who committed suicide in January while facing charges that could carry a 35-year prison sentence in a case involving his downloading of copyrighted academic journals.

In March, the entire editorial board of the *Journal of Library Administration* resigned over what one member described as "a crisis of conscience" over the 26-year-old Swartz's death.[46] The librarians were concerned not only about the Swartz case but the larger issue of access to journal articles, feeling that publishers were becoming entirely too restrictive in their terms of use.

In general, Bezanson says, courts are becoming less accepting of the idea that "information wants to be free," as the Internet-era slogan has it. The courts are not only more supportive of copyright holders but seemingly more skeptical about free speech in general, with the Supreme Court in recent cases having curbed some of the free-speech rights it had afforded to students and hate groups in previous decisions.

"The doctrine of the First Amendment is going to be more forgiving of regulated speech," Bezanson says.

Regulating the Press?

In other countries, concern is growing that freedom of speech and of the press have been badly abused in recent years. A phone-hacking scandal involving the *News of the World*, a British tabloid, shocked the United Kingdom in 2011 and has led to more than 30 arrests, as well as a high-profile inquiry chaired by Sir Brian Leveson, then Britain's senior appeals judge. Leveson's report, released in November, called for a new, independent body to replace the Press Complaints Commission, the news industry's self-regulating agency. The recommendations triggered difficult negotiations among leaders of the United Kingdom's coalition government, which announced a compromise deal in March.

"While Lord Leveson was quite correct to call for a regulator with more muscle that can impose substantial fines for future misconduct, [Prime Minister] David Cameron pledged that he would resist the clamor for such measures to be backed by law," the *Yorkshire Post* editorialized. "Given that to do so would be to take the first step on the slippery slope toward censorship of the press, a weapon that has been employed by many a corrupt dictatorship around the globe, he was right to do so."[47]

The U.K. is not the only country considering new media regulations. In March, Australia's government proposed tighter regulation of media ownership and a new media overseer with statutory authority. "Australians want the press to be as accountable as they want politicians, sports people and business people," said Stephen Conroy, Australia's communications minister.[48]

Media executives argued that the proposals were draconian and amounted to the government's revenge for hostile coverage. "For the first time in Australian history outside wartime, there will be political oversight over the conduct of journalism in this country," said Greg Hywood, the CEO of Fairfax Media.[49]

In response to such criticisms, Australia's government quickly withdrew the proposals.

Reporters Under Attack

If journalists, commentators, artists and writers are feeling embattled in the English-speaking world, they face worse fates elsewhere. According to the Committee to Protect Journalists, 232 journalists around the world were imprisoned as of Dec. 1 — the highest total since the group began its survey work in 1990. And 70 journalists were killed while doing their jobs in 2012 — a 43 percent increase from the year before.[50]

According to the group, 49 journalists were imprisoned in Turkey alone in 2012, a record high, and more than were in jail in either Iran or China. Francis J. Ricciardone, the U.S. ambassador to Turkey, has been openly critical about the country's approach to free speech. "The responsibility of Turkey's friends and allies is to. . . to point out, with due respect, the importance of progress in the protection of freedom of expression for journalists and blog writers," State Department spokeswoman Victoria Nuland said at a news conference in February.[51]

In India freedom of expression is enshrined in the constitution, but with many provisos. And lately, India's judiciary has appeared to show little concern when the government has arrested people over their Facebook posts and remarks made at literary festivals. "Writers and artists of all kinds are being harassed, sued and arrested for what they say or write or create," writes Suketu Mehta, a journalism professor at New York University. "The government either stands by and does nothing to protect freedom of speech, or it actively abets its suppression."[52]

India — the world's most populous democracy — has slipped below Qatar and Afghanistan in Reporters Without Borders' press freedom index.[53]

In emerging economic powerhouses such as Turkey and India, along with Brazil, Mexico, South Africa and Indonesia, governments are "kind of floating" between two different models, says Kampfner, the *Freedom for Sale* author: the open-society approach favored by transatlantic democracies and a more authoritarian approach.

"I slightly fear it's going in the wrong direction in all of them," Kampfner says.

But there also have been signs recently that things may be improving in places for free-speech advocates. On April 1, for the first time in half a century, privately owned daily newspapers hit newsstands in Myanmar.[54]

In Syria, new newspapers have emerged to cover the civil war, countering bias from both government-controlled media and opposition-friendly satellite channels based in Qatar and Saudi Arabia.

"We need to get out of this Facebook phase, where all we do is whine and complain about the regime," said Absi Smesem, editor-in-chief of *Sham,* a new weekly newspaper.[55]

OUTLOOK
Shame, Not Laws?

It's always impossible to predict the future, but it's especially difficult when discussing free speech, which is now inextricably bound up with constantly changing technologies.

"I don't know what's next," says Reidy, the Index on Censorship news editor. "None of us five years ago thought we would be spending our lives on Twitter." Still, Reidy says, the fact that so many people are conversing online makes them likely to equate blocking the Internet with more venerable forms of censorship, such as book burning.

"Within the next five years, you will have a lot of adults in the Western world who literally don't know what life is like without the Internet," he says. "That is bound to change attitudes and cultures."

Information technology is penetrating deeper into the developing world, says Kampfner, the British journalist and author. For instance, thanks to mobile technology African farmers can access more information they need about crop yields and prices. And with cell phones, everyone has better access to information on disasters.

However, "In terms of changing the political discourse, the jury is out," Kampfner says. "Every new technology, by its nature, is open to both use and abuse."

Activists wanting to use technology to spread information and governments trying to stop them play an ongoing "cat and mouse game," says Galperin, of the Electronic Frontier Foundation.

Given how easily commercial applications can track individuals' specific interests and movements online, it's not difficult to imagine that political speech will be tracked as well, Belarus-born writer and researcher Evgeny Morozov, a contributing editor at *The New Republic* and a columnist for *Slate,* contends in his 2011 book *The Net Delusion.* It's not the case, as some have argued, he says, that the need to keep the Internet open for commercial purposes will prevent regimes from stamping out other forms of online discourse.

"In the not so distant future, a banker perusing nothing but Reuters and *Financial Times,* and with other bankers as her online friends, would be left alone to do anything she wants, even browse Wikipedia pages about human-rights violations," he writes. "In contrast, a person of unknown occupation, who is occasionally reading *Financial Times* but is also connected to five well-known political activists through Facebook and who has written blog comments that included words like 'democracy' and 'freedom,' would only be allowed to visit government-run websites, or. . . to surf but be carefully monitored."[56]

In democratic nations, concerns about security and offending religious believers could lead to more restrictions — although not necessarily in terms of new laws, says Arch Puddington, vice president for research at Freedom House, but through shaming and "other informal methods" of disciplining unpopular ways of speaking.

"What you could have over the next 10 years in the U.S. and abroad is a distinction between rights and norms," says former Rep. Perriello, at the Center for American Progress Action Fund. "Having a legal right to say certain things does not actually mean one should say certain things."

Anthony Mills, the deputy director of the International Press Institute in Austria, suggests that the more things change, the more they will stay recognizably the same. "Unfortunately, in 10 years we'll still be having similar conversations about efforts by everyone from criminals to militants and government operatives to target the media and silence them," Mills says.

"But at the same time, . . . a variety of media platforms — of journalists and of media practitioners — will continue to defy that trend," he says. "I have no doubt that in the grand scheme of things, the truth will always come out. The dynamic of the flow of information is unstoppable."

Wallach, the Rice University computer scientist, is equally certain that despite all legal, political and technological ferment, the basic underlying tension between free expression and repressive tendencies will remain firmly in place.

"There will always be people with something to say and ways for them to say it," Wallach says. Likewise, "There will also always be people who want to stop them."

NOTES

1. Jonathan Turley, "Shut Up and Play Nice," *The Washington Post,* Oct. 14, 2012, p. B1, http://articles.washingtonpost.com/2012-10-12/opinions/35499274_1_free-speech-defeat-jihad-muslim-man.

2. For background, see Peter Katel, "Protecting Whistleblowers," *CQ Researcher,* March 31, 2006, pp. 265-288.

3. "Memorandum to the European Union on Media Freedom in Hungary," Human Rights Watch, Feb. 16, 2012, www.hrw.org/node/105200.

4. For background, see Kenneth Jost, "Unrest in the Arab World," *CQ Researcher*, Feb. 1, 2013, pp. 105-132; and Roland Flamini, "Turmoil in the Arab World," *CQ Global Researcher,* May 3, 2011, pp. 209-236.

5. Tom Gjelten, "Shutdowns Counter the Idea of a World-Wide Web," NPR, Dec. 1, 2012, www.npr.org/2012/12/01/166286596/shutdowns-raise-issue-of-who-controls-the-internet.

6. Jessica Chasmar, "French Jewish Group Sues Twitter Over Racist, Anti-Semitic Tweets," *The Washington Times,* March 24, 2013, www.washingtontimes.com/news/2013/mar/24/french-jewish-group-sues-twitter-over-racist-anti-.

7. Jean-Paul Marthoz, "Extremists Are Censoring the Story of Religion," Committee to Protect Journalists, Feb. 14, 2013, www.cpj.org/2013/02/attacks-on-the-press-journalism-and-religion.php. See also, Frank Greve, "Combat Journalism," *CQ Researcher,* April 12, 2013, pp. 329-352.

8. Chris York, "Pussy Riot Member Yekaterina Samutsevich Freed on Probation by Moscow Court," *The Huffington Post UK,* Oct. 10, 2012, www.huffingtonpost.co.uk/2012/10/10/pussy-riot-member-yekaterina-samutsevich-frees-probation-moscow-court_n_1953725.html.

9. Ethan Zuckerman, "The First Twitter Revolution?" *Foreign Policy,* Jan. 14, 2011, www.foreignpolicy.com/articles/2011/01/14/the_first_twitter_revolution.

10. Thomas Fuller, "E-mails of Reporters in Myanmar Are Hacked," *The New York Times,* Feb. 10, 2013, www.nytimes.com/2013/02/11/world/asia/journalists-e-mail-accounts-targeted-in-myanmar.html.

11. Yves Alexandre de Mountjoye, *et al.,* "Unique in the Crowd: The Privacy Bounds of Human Mobility," *Nature,* March 25, 2013, www.nature.com/srep/2013/130325/srep01376/full/srep01376.html.

12. Thomas Erdbrink, "Iran Blocks Way to Bypass Internet Filtering System," *The New York Times,* March 11, 2013, www.nytimes.com/2013/03/12/world/middleeast/iran-blocks-software-used-to-bypass-internet-filtering-system.html.

13. Andrew Higgins, "Danish Opponent of Islam Is Attacked, and Muslims Defend His Right to Speak," *The New York Times*, Feb. 28, 2013, p. A8, www.nytimes.com/2013/02/28/world/europe/lars-hedegaard-anti-islamic-provocateur-receives-support-from-danish-muslims.html.

14. Kenan Malik and Nada Shabout, "Should Religious or Cultural Sensibilities Ever Limit Free Expression?" Index on Censorship, March 25, 2013, www.indexoncensorship.org/2013/03/should-religious-or-cultural-sensibilities-ever-limit-free-expression/.

15. "Freedom of Thought 2012: A Global Report on Discrimination Against Humanists, Atheists and the Nonreligious," International Humanist and Ethical Union, Dec. 10, 2012, p. 11, http://iheu.org/files/IHEU%20Freedom%20of%20Thought%202012.pdf.

16. Asim Tanveer, "Pakistani Man Accuses Ambassador to U.S. of Blasphemy," Reuters, Feb. 21, 2013, http://news.yahoo.com/pakistan-accuses-ambassador-u-blasphemy-124213305.html.

17. Huma Yusuf, "The Censors' Salon," *Latitude,* March 14, 2013, http://latitude.blogs.nytimes.com/2013/03/14/in-lahore-pakistan-the-censors-salon/.

18. See "Speech to the United Nations General Assembly — Practical progress towards realising those ideals in the world," Sept. 26, 2012, www.pm.gov.au/press-office/speech-united-nations-general-assembly-%E2%80%9Cpractical-progress-towards-realising-those-idea.

19. Turley, *op. cit.*

20. Aryeh Neier, "Freedom, Blasphemy and Violence," Project Syndicate, Sept. 16, 2012, www.project-syndicate.org/commentary/freedom—blasphemy-and-violence-by-aryeh-neier.

21. C. W. Nevius, "Free Speech Protects Offensive Ads on Muni," *The San Francisco Chronicle,* March 14, 2013, p. D1, www.sfgate.com/bayarea/nevius/article/Offensive-ads-on-Muni-protected-speech-4352829.php.

22. Clinton's remarks are available at www.state.gov/secretary/rm/2011/12/178511.htm.

23. Obama's remarks are available at www.whitehouse.gov/the-press-office/2012/09/25/remarks-president-un-general-assembly.

24. Anthea Butler, "Opposing View: Why 'Sam Bacile' Deserves Arrest," *USA Today,* Sept. 13, 2012, http://usatoday30.usatoday.com/news/opinion/story/2012-09-12/Sam-Bacile-Anthea-Butler/57769732/1.

25. Eric Posner, "The World Doesn't Love the First Amendment," *Slate,* Sept. 25, 2012, www.slate.com/articles/news_and_politics/jurisprudence/2012/09/the_vile_anti_muslim_video_and_the_first_amendment_does_the_u_s_overvalue_free_speech_.single.html.

26. Eyder Peralta, "John Kerry to German Students: Americans Have 'Right to Be Stupid,'" NPR, Feb. 26, 2013, www.npr.org/blogs/thetwo-way/2013/02/26/172980860/john-kerry-to-german-students-americans-have-right-to-be-stupid.

27. Rodney A. Smolla, *Free Speech in an Open Society* (1992), p. 4.

28. Robert Hargreaves, *The First Freedom* (2002), p. 5.

29. *Ibid.* p. 51.

30. *Ibid.* p. 95.

31. Richard W. Steele, *Free Speech in the Good War* (1999), p. 1.

32. See "The Universal Declaration of Human Rights," United Nations, www.un.org/en/documents/udhr/index.shtml#a19.

33. Alexander Meiklejohn, *Free Speech and Its Relation to Self-Government* (1948), p. 17.

34. Michael Kent Curtis, *Free Speech, 'The People's Darling Privilege': Struggles for Freedom of Expression in American History* (2000), p. 406.

35. David W. Rabban, *Free Speech in Its Forgotten Years* (1997), p. 372.

36. "Supreme Court, 6-3, Upholds Newspapers on Publication of Pentagon Report," *The New York Times,* July 1, 1971, www.nytimes.com/books/97/04/13/reviews/papers-final.html.

37. Eric A. Posner and Adrian Vermeule, *Terror in the Balance: Security, Liberty and the Courts* (2007), p. 26.

38. James Risen and Eric Lichtblau, "Bush Lets U.S. Spy on Callers Without Courts," *The New York Times,* Dec. 16, 2005, www.nytimes.com/2005/12/16/politics/16program.html.

39. Samuel Walker, *Presidents and Civil Liberties From Wilson to Obama: A Story of Poor Custodians* (2012), p. 468.

40. For background, see Roland Flamini, "Improving Cybersecurity," *CQ Researcher,* Feb. 15, 2013, pp. 157-180.

41. Karen McVeigh and Dominic Rushe, "House Passes CISPA Cybersecurity Bill Despite Warnings From White House," *The Guardian*, April 18, 2013, www.guardian.co.uk/technology/2013/apr/18/house-representatives-cispa-cyber-security-white-house-warning.

42. See the "Statement of Administration Policy" at www.whitehouse.gov/sites/default/files/omb/legislative/sap/113/saphr624r_20130416.pdf.

43. McVeigh and Rushe, *op. cit.*

44. Phil Mattingly and Hans Nichols, "Obama Pursuing Leakers Sends Warning to WhistleBlowers," Bloomberg News, Oct. 17, 2012, www.bloomberg.com/news/2012-10-18/obama-pursuing-leakers-sends-warning-to-whistle-blowers.html.

45. For background, see Alex Kingsbury, "Government Secrecy," *CQ Researcher,* Feb. 11, 2011, pp. 121-144.

46. Russell Brandom, "Entire Library Journal Editorial Board Resigns," *The Verge*, March 26, 2013, www.theverge.com/2013/3/26/4149752/library-journal-resigns-for-open-access-citing-aaron-swartz.

47. "A Vital Test for Democracy," *Yorkshire Press*, March 19, 2013, www.yorkshirepost.co.uk/news/debate/yp-comment/a-vital-test-for-our-democracy-1-5505331.

48. Sabra Lane, "Stephen Conroy Defends Media Change Package," Australian Broadcasting Company, March 13, 2013, www.abc.net.au/am/content/2013/s3714163.htm.

49. Nick Bryant, "Storm Over Australia's Press Reform Proposals," BBC, March 19, 2013, www.bbc.co.uk/news/world-asia-21840076.

50. Rick Gladstone, "Report Sees Journalists Increasingly Under Attack," *The New York Times,* Feb. 15, 2013, p. A10, www.nytimes.com/2013/02/15/world/attacks-on-journalists-rose-in-2012-group-finds.html.

51. "U.S.: American Ambassador to Turkey Reiterating What Clinton Previously Said," *Today's Zaman,* Feb. 7, 2013, www.todayszaman.com/news-306435-us-american-ambassador-to-turkey-reiterating-what-clinton-previously-said.html.

52. Suketu Mehta, "India's Speech Impediments," *The New York Times*, Feb. 6, 2013, www.nytimes.com/2013/02/06/opinion/indias-limited-freedom-of-speech.html.

53. "Press Freedom Index 2013," Reporters Without Borders, fr.rsf.org/IMG/pdf/classe-ment_2013_gb-bd.pdf.

54. Aye Aye Win, "Privately Owned Daily Newspapers Return to Myanmar," The Associated Press, April 1, 2013, www.huffingtonpost.com/huff-wires/20130401/as-myanmar-new-newspapers/.

55. Neil MacFarquhar, "Syrian Newspapers Emerge to Fill Out War Reporting," *The New York Times*, April 2, 2013, p. A4, www.nytimes.com/2013/04/02/world/middleeast/syrian-newspapers-emerge-to-fill-out-war-reporting.html.

56. Eugeny Morozov, *The Net Delusion* (2011), p. 97.

BIBLIOGRAPHY

Selected Sources

Books

Ghonim, Wael, *Revolution 2.0: The Power of the People Is Greater Than the People in Power,* Houghton Mifflin Harcourt, 2012.
A Google employee who became a leader in using social media to organize protests against the government in Egypt during the so-called Arab Spring of 2011 writes a memoir about those tumultuous times.

Hargreaves, Robert, *The First Freedom: A History of Free Speech,* Sutton Publishing, 2002.
The late British broadcaster surveys the long history of speech, from Socrates to modern times, highlighting the personalities and legal cases that eventually led to greater liberties.

Kampfner, John, *Freedom for Sale: Why the World Is Trading Democracy for Security,* Basic Books, 2010.
Visiting countries such as Russia, China, Italy and the United States, a British journalist examines how citizens in recent years have been willing to sacrifice personal freedoms in exchange for promises of prosperity and security.

Articles

Erdbrink, Thomas, "Iran Blocks Way to Bypass Internet Filtering System," *The New York Times,* March 11, 2013, www.nytimes.com/2013/03/12/world/middleeast/iran-blocks-software-used-to-bypass-internet-filtering-system.html.
Iran's Ministry of Information and Communications Technology has begun blocking the most popular software used by millions of Iranians to bypass the official Internet censoring system.

Malik, Kenan, and Nada Shabout, "Should Religious or Cultural Sensibilities Ever Limit Free Expression?" *Index on Censorship*, **March 25, 2013, www.indexoncensorship.org/2013/03/should-religious-or-cultural-sensibilities-ever-limit-free-expression/.**
An Indian-born British broadcaster (Malik) and an Iraqi art historian debate whether even the most offensive and blasphemous speech should be protected.

Mattingly, Phil, and Hans Nichols, "Obama Pursuing Leakers Sends Warning to Whistle-Blowers," Bloomberg News, Oct. 17, 2012, www.bloomberg.com/news/2012-10-18/obama-pursuing-leakers-sends-warning-to-whistle-blowers.html.
Attorney General Eric Holder has prosecuted more government officials for leaking documents than all his predecessors combined.

Posner, Eric, "The World Doesn't Love the First Amendment," *Slate*, **Sept. 25, 2012, www.slate.com/articles/news_and_politics/jurisprudence/2012/09/the_vile_anti_muslim_video_and_the_first_amendment_does_the_u_s_overvalue_free_speech_.single.html.**
In the wake of violent protests across the globe triggered by an anti-Muslim video that was produced in the United States, a University of Chicago law professor argues that freedom of expression must give way at times to other values.

Turley, Jonathan, "Shut Up and Play Nice," *The Washington Post*, **Oct. 14, 2012, http://articles.washingtonpost.com/2012-10-12/opinions/35499274_1_free-speech-defeat-jihad-muslim-man.**
A George Washington University law professor argues that freedom of speech is being eroded around the world as efforts to protect various groups against being offended become enshrined in law.

Reports and Studies

"Attacks on the Press: Journalism on the Front Lines in 2012," Committee to Protect Journalists, February 2013, www.cpj.org/2013/02/attacks-on-the-press-in-2012.php.
The latest edition of this annual report documents how more journalists are disappearing or being imprisoned in countries ranging from Mexico to Russia.

"Freedom of Thought 2012: A Global Report on Discrimination Against Humanists, Atheists and the

Nonreligious," International Humanist and Ethical Union, Dec. 10, 2012, http://iheu.org/files/IHEU%20 Freedom%20of%20Thought% 202012.pdf.
The number of prosecutions for blasphemy is sharply on the rise, according to a global survey of laws regulating religious beliefs and expression.

Leveson, Lord Justice Brian, "An Inquiry Into the Culture, Practices and Ethics of the Press," The Stationary Office, Nov. 29, 2012, www.official-docu ments.gov.uk/document/ hc1213/hc07/0780/0780.asp.
A judge appointed by the British prime minister to examine press abuses calls for greater regulation.

"There is no organized profession, trade or industry in which the serious failings of the few are overlooked because of the good done by the many," Leveson writes.

Zhu, Tao, *et al.,* "The Velocity of Censorship: High-Fidelity Detection of Microblog Post Deletions," March 4, 2013, http://arxiv.org/abs/1303.0597.
A team of computer scientists examined the accounts of 3,500 users of Weibo, China's microblogging site, to see if it was being censored. The scientists found that thousands of Weibo employees were deleting forbidden phrases and characters.

For More Information

Access, P.O. Box 115, New York, NY 10113; 888-414-0100; www.accessnow.org. A digital-rights group, founded after protests against Iran's disputed 2009 presidential election, that fosters open communications.

Article 19, Free Word Centre, 60 Farringdon Road, London, United Kingdom, EC1R 3GA; +44 20 7324 2500; www .article19.org. A group named for a section of the Universal Declaration of Human Rights that designs laws and policies promoting freedom of expression.

Committee to Protect Journalists, 330 7th Ave., 11th Floor, New York, NY 10001; 212-465-1004; www.cpj.org. Documents attacks on journalists; publishes its findings and works to promote press freedom.

Freedom House, 1301 Connecticut Ave., N.W., 6th Floor, Washington, DC 20036; 202-296-5101; www.freedomhouse

.org. An independent watchdog group founded in 1941 that advocates greater political and civil liberties.

Index on Censorship, Free Word Centre, 60 Farringdon Rd., London, United Kingdom, EC1R 3GA; +44 20 7324 2522; www.indexoncensorship.org. Founded in 1972 to publish stories of communist dissidents in Eastern Europe; promotes global free speech through journalistic reports and advocacy.

International Press Institute, Spielgasse 2, A-1010, Vienna, Austria; +43 1 412 90 11; www.freemedia.at. A global network of media executives and journalists founded in 1950, dedicated to promoting and safeguarding press freedoms.

Reporters Committee for Freedom of the Press, 1101 Wilson Blvd., Suite 1100, Arlington, VA 22209; 703-807-2100; www .rcfp.org. Provides free legal advice and other resources to journalists on First Amendment issues.

Press Freedom

*Can governments control
the press in the internet age?*

Jennifer Koons

Freed U.S. journalist Euna Lee is reunited with her husband and daughter upon her arrival in the United States on Aug. 5, 2009. She and fellow journalist Laura Ling were arrested in North Korea in March and sentenced to 12 years of hard labor for allegedly entering the country illegally. Released after former U.S. President Bill Clinton pleaded their case in North Korea, the two were among the 136 journalists jailed worldwide in 2009.

From *CQ Researcher*,
November 2010

A s the editor of Ciudad Juárez's leading daily newspaper, Pedro Torres had seen enough. After a second journalist at the paper was murdered recently, Torres published a startling open letter to the drug cartels ravaging the Mexican city just across the border from El Paso, Texas. "Tell us what we should try to publish or not publish, so we know what to expect," he pleaded in a frontpage editorial.[1]

In September, suspected cartel gunmen had killed 21-year-old photographer Luis Carlos Santiago in the parking lot of a shopping mall where he planned to attend a photography workshop.[2] In November 2008, hitmen shot the paper's crime reporter, José Armando Rodríguez, outside his home.[3]

Mexico overall has experienced the greatest decline in press freedom in Latin America during the last five years, according to the press freedom watchdog groups Freedom House and the Committee to Protect Journalists (CPJ). More than 30 reporters investigating crime, drug trafficking and official corruption have been murdered or gone missing since Mexican President Felipe Calderón took office in 2006 and cracked down on the cartels. Many other journalists have been kidnapped or threatened, making Mexico one of the world's most dangerous places for journalists, according to CPJ.[4]

Moreover, rampant corruption within law enforcement and the judiciary has left most of the murderers unpunished.[5] The growing danger has led to increased self-censorship, and many Mexican newspapers no longer publish bylines on stories involving organized crime. "You love journalism, you love the pursuit of truth,

Western Countries Have the Most Press Freedom

Media freedom worldwide has declined for the eighth year in a row, according to the pro-democracy watchdog group Freedom House. The United States, Canada, Australia, Japan and the European Union had the most media freedom in 2009, while the Middle East, Russia and much of Asia had the least.

Global Press Freedom Rankings, 2009

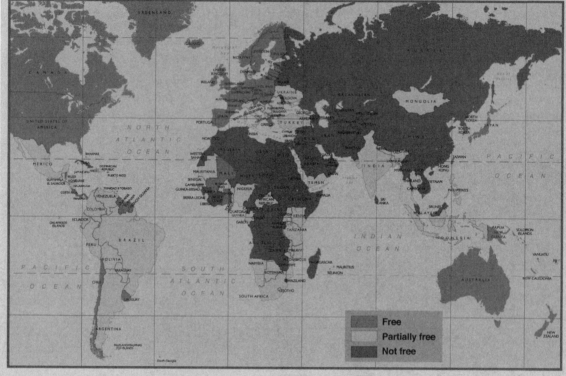

Free
Partially free
Not free

Source: "Freedom of the press 2010," Freedom house, WWW.freedomhouse.org/template.cfm?page=363&year=2010

you love to perform a civic service and inform your community. But you love your life more," an editor in Reynosa, a city just across the Rio Grande from McAllen, Texas, told the *Los Angeles Times* recently. "We don't like the silence. But it's survival."[6]

The lack of accountability for the murders encourages further bloodshed, according to a CPJ report released in September.[7] "It is not a lack of valor on the part of the journalists. It is a lack of backing," TV reporter Jaime Aguirre told the *Times*. "If they kill me, nothing happens."[8]

The dire conditions for Mexican journalists are reflected worldwide. According to Freedom House, 72 journalists died last year in the line of duty — 52 of them murdered. Of those, 33 were killed in the Philippines in the run-up to the presidential election, 32 of them gunned down in a premeditated massacre by more than 60 heavily armed gunmen on Mindanao Island in the southern Philippines. Besides the Philippines, the other deadliest places for journalists in 2009 were countries in conflict, such as Somalia — where nine reporters died while doing their jobs — and

Iraq and Pakistan, where four died in each country.[9] This year also promises to be bloody: As of October 29, 37 journalists have been killed in the line of duty in 2010.[10]

In addition to violence, journalists also face imprisonment for reporting on unpopular subjects. A total of 136 reporters, editors and photojournalists were imprisoned worldwide in 2009, including 24 in China and 23 in Iran, many jailed during Iran's crackdown on dissent following the disputed 2009 election.[11] Governments in Belarus, Myanmar, China, Cuba, Eritrea, North Korea, Tunisia, Uzbekistan and Venezuela also imprisoned journalists for publishing stories critical of governments.

"The numbers of journalists killed and jailed are both up, which is very alarming," says CPJ Executive Director Joel Simon. "You will typically see the killings of journalists along with the killings [of dissidents], and the common factor is impunity or systemic violence without consequence."

In Russia, journalists know exactly what topics will put them in danger— organized crime, government corruption and the conflict in Chechnya — the subjects covered by nearly all of the 52 journalists killed in Russia since 1992.[12] Two of the journalists killed in 2009 had worked for Moscow's independent *Novaya Gazeta* (New Newspaper), including Natalya Estemirova, 50, an award-winning human rights activist who was kidnapped and shot execution-style.[13]

But violent retribution and imprisonment aren't the only threats limiting media freedom. The globalization of censorship and restrictions on the Internet also constrain press freedom, especially for journalists working in countries engulfed in political conflict.

Criminal defamation laws, for instance, frighten journalists into self-censorship. Such laws make it illegal — punishable by imprisonment and fines — to defame or

Philippines Was Deadliest Country for Journalists

Fifty-two journalists were murdered in 2009 — 32 of them in the Philippines during a bloody massacre allegedly ordered by provincial officials during the presidential campaign. Killers of journalists were convicted in only 6 percent of the murder cases in 2009. Politics was the most dangerous beat for reporters: That was the subject covered by 67 percent of the 72 journalists killed in the line of duty worldwide in 2009.

No. of Journalists Killed in Eight Deadliest Countries, 2009		Beats Covered by Journalists Killed in 2009*	
Philippines	33	Corruption	11%
Somalia	9	Crime	8%
Iraq	4	Culture	8%
Pakistan	4	Human rights	10%
Mexico	3	Politics	67%
Russia	3	Sports	1%
Afghanistan	2	War	25%
Sri Lanka	2		

Impunity in Journalist Murder Cases

No Convictions 94%

Partial justice** 6%

* Totals more than 100 percent because some reporters covered more than one beat.

** Some, but not all, of those responsible have been convicted; typically, assassins are convicted but not masterminds.

Source: Committee to Protect Journalists

libel private citizens, public officials or even countries. In Turkey, for instance, it is illegal to "insult Turkishness." In industrialized countries, defamation and libel cases are litigated in civil courts, punishable only by fines.

Criminal libel or defamation laws, popular among the 57-member Organisation of the Islamic Conference, are punishable by both imprisonment and fines. "If you look at the more than 20 countries from Morocco to Turkey and Iran . . . every single one of [them] has criminal defamation laws on the books," says Mohamed Abdel Dayem, CPJ program coordinator for the Middle East and North Africa. "When journalists are charged

Journalists enact a mock murder during a protest in Mexico City on Aug. 1, 2010, against violence toward journalists in Mexico. More than 30 reporters have been murdered or gone missing since Mexican President Felipe Calderon took office in 2006 and began cracking down on the nation's powerful drug cartels. Many others have been kidnapped or threatened — mostly by drug traffickers — making Mexico one of the world's most dangerous places for journalists.

with libel, they go before a criminal court. If they are found guilty, they are fined and/or imprisoned — with an emphasis on the imprisonment. This should really be a matter for civil courts, but it's not."

Also, in some Muslim countries any expression that can be interpreted as an insult to Islam — and therefore blasphemous — is widely criminalized and punishable by death, powerful motivations for self-censorship.

When Yemen established a special press and publications court in 2009 to examine media-related disputes, more than 150 cases — some from as far back as 2006 — were brought before the judicial body.[14] In one of its first rulings, the court banned a U.S.-based reporter from ever practicing journalism in Yemen. Munir Mawari, a contributor to the independent weekly *Al-Masdar,* had described President Ali Abdullah Saleh's leadership style as a "weapon of mass destruction."[15]

Also in 2009, the Yemeni government shuttered eight newspapers it said were inciting separatism in the southern part of the country, charging the editors with instigating violence and upsetting national unity.[16] "All kinds of semantic cat-and-mouse business takes place in this part of the world, which doesn't change the fact that journalists have to operate under a climate of fear," CPJ's Dayem says.

The advent of the Internet and the growing popularity of social networking sites have created a countervailing trend that is helping to offset government censorship. With reporters and editors blogging and posting to Facebook and Twitter and online media outlets posting stories around the clock, governments are having a harder and harder time suppressing negative stories. "The current 24/7 news cycle is way too fast for most governments anyway, and their voices get drowned in the general noise," said Wilfried Ruetten, director of the European Journalism Centre in Maastricht, the Netherlands. "If Paris Hilton's dog dies and, on the same day, Obama speaks on U.S. relations with, say, Syria, you know what Google News will look like."

As journalists around the world face violent attacks and government censorship, here are some of the questions being asked:

Can governments control media coverage?

Journalists and press-freedom advocates spent the summer battling the creation of a proposed media tribunal in South Africa, which currently enjoys one of Africa's freest press climates. Warning the tribunal would restrict press coverage, Raymond Louw, chairman of South Africa's Press Council, said the country is headed toward becoming "the kind of state where we want to criminalize information and. . . put editors behind bars."[17] Louw and fellow South African journalists have launched a campaign against what they say amounts to reinstating apartheid-era press laws. During the apartheid era, the now-ruling African National Congress (ANC) strongly defended media freedom. But after 16 years in power, it has lobbied for creation of the tribunal.[18]

"We need stronger measures where . . . people have been defamed, where . . . malicious intents have driven reporting by media houses or reporters," ANC spokesman Jackson Mthembu told reporters in August.[19]

South Africa's proposed tribunal and Yemen's new special press and publications court both represent overt government attempts to influence media coverage. And the persistent threat of prosecution in one of those media courts triggers self-censorship.

"Governments are becoming increasingly more sophisticated at dictating the terms and the content of media coverage," says Byron Scott, a professor emeritus at the University of Missouri School of Journalism. And governments are aided in those efforts by such journalistic practices as "professional laziness, the blurring of the line between significant news and entertaining and, in many nations under stress, the most important of all, self-censorship."

Self-censorship often reaches its peak during wartime. Prominent American media outlets self-censored their reporting during the first year and a half of the Iraq War, largely due to concerns about public reaction to graphic images and content, according to a 2005 survey of more than 200 journalists by American University's School of Communications.[20]

"Mixed with patriotism, self-censorship becomes the easiest, cheapest and most pernicious of all," Scott says. "It tends to take root during times of national stress and distort news values for some time afterward."

The growing popularity of social media websites has changed how journalists work in the countries with repressive regimes, such as Malaysia, which falls near the bottom of most international rankings on press freedom. While the government-controlled mainstream media previously screened out criticism in newspapers and on TV and radio programs, opposing views increasingly are appearing on blogs and mobile phone messages.

"All our reporters have BlackBerrys and use them to follow these tweets. The social media [have] changed the way journalists work in fundamental ways," said Premesh Chandran, founder of the online news source Malaysiakini.[21] The prevalence of real-time updates from critics and opposition sources inhibited officials from controlling the flow of information, he said.

In fact, legislators today "are forced to engage and debate their counterparts across the aisle in social media like Twitter and Facebook, allowing us to report on the opposition and avoid much censorship," said a veteran reporter at one of Malaysia's leading newspapers, who spoke on condition of anonymity. "Although the restrictions and controls are still in place, it's become much harder to censor what the opposition or rights groups say in the media."[22]

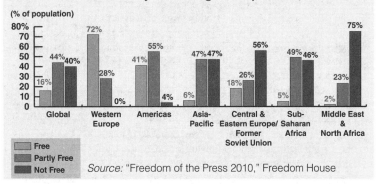

Press Freedom Is Limited in Most of the World

Only 16 percent of the world's population — mainly in Western Europe or the Americas — enjoys a free press. More than three-quarters of the people on Earth live in countries where the press is not free or only partly free. The Middle East and North Africa have the least freedom of the press.

Press Freedom by Percentage of Population, 2009

Source: "Freedom of the Press 2010," Freedom House

In 2009, Reporters Without Borders (Reporters Sans Frontiéres, or RSF) — a Paris-based group that promotes press freedom around the world — ranked Malaysia 131st out of 175 countries on press freedoms.[23] The low ranking reflected Malaysia's implementation in 2009 of a publishing-permit system that made it easier to censor publications, according to RSF.[24]

Still, the situation is better than it used to be. To promote its information-technology sector, Malaysian officials pledged in 1996 to limit online censorship, which has significantly opened up the country's reporting landscape.

RSF regional correspondent Patrice Victor said Malaysia's experience could be recreated in other nations where authoritarian regimes allow reasonable Internet access.[25]

"We are seeing social media free the way journalists report in this region, and the trend in Malaysia can also be seen happening in Singapore, Thailand and Burma," she said. "Governments here are slowly realizing that it is very hard to censor and restrict information once people have access to the Net, and this trend of using social media to break down censorship looks like it is here to stay."[26]

Freelance Journalists Have Few Protections

A handful of press-freedom organizations offer help.

After police in Kasensero, Uganda, arrested Sengooba Eddie in September in connection with the murder and robbery of a motorcycle taxi driver, a group of angry fellow drivers gathered at Eddie's home. In an act of vigilantism recorded by freelance radio reporter Paul Kiggundu, the bikers burned Eddie's house to the ground.

Assuming Kiggundu was a spy for the police, the mob turned on him, kicking and beating him until he was unconscious, ignoring his screams that he was only a journalist, according to witnesses. He later died of internal bleeding at nearby Kalisizo hospital.[1]

Shocked by the incident, the chairman of Uganda's Human Rights Network for Journalists, Robert Ssempala, said: "Injustice cannot be used to obtain justice."[2] The Committee to Protect Journalists (CPJ) called on the Ugandan police to bring the perpetrators to justice. "No journalist should be killed simply for carrying out their profession," said CPJ East Africa Consultant Tom Rhodes.[3]

Kiggundu's death reflects the dangers faced by freelancers and journalists who work for small, independent media outlets around the world. They report on critical issues but often lack the support provided to staff reporters employed by larger news organizations. Furthermore, in an era of shrinking foreign and domestic news bureaus, struggling media organizations increasingly are relying on freelance journalists. Nine freelancers were among the 72 journalists killed in 2009.[4]

The CPJ said impunity is the greatest threat to local journalists because it leads potential murderers to believe they will never be held accountable. "The perpetrators assumed, based on precedent, that they would never be punished," said CPJ. "Whether the killings are in Iraq or the Philippines, in Russia or Mexico, changing this assumption is the key to reducing the death toll."[5] Several international press-freedom organizations help journalists and freelancers cope with threats, injuries and other obstacles. For instance, when Mikhail Beketov, editor of a suburban Moscow newspaper, was viciously attacked for his coverage of local government policies, he suffered a skull fracture, concussion and leg and finger injuries that required partial

Will new government cyber controls effectively censor journalists?

Free-press advocates say the most troubling press censorship trend centers around government efforts to restrict communication online, according to Simon of the Committee to Protect Journalists.

"Nowadays, more and more newsgathering and dissemination is being done on the Web," he says. "It doesn't matter if it's print or broadcast or nonprofit or for-profit. . . . It's all online. And governments recognize that."

During a crackdown on months-long demonstrations last spring, Thai officials expanded Internet controls to further restrict a wide range of online speech, including commentary and newsgathering. To protect national security, said Prime Minister Abhisit Vejjajiva, the government ordered security forces to block access to at least 36 websites and broadcasts of the People's Channel satellite news station, which had been supporting antigovernment protests.[27]

Political protests moved online as more Thai citizens have gained access to the Internet. By 2009, nearly a quarter of the population (or 16.1 million people) had Internet access.[28] Even exiled former Prime Minister Thaksin Shinawatra and Prime Minister Abhisit's spokesman post competing messages to Twitter.[29]

The Thai government is not the only government instituting cyber controls. Iran, China, Russia and Venezuela — among others — have developed highly advanced techniques to monitor citizens' online activities and block critical websites.

"At first, the perception was that the Internet could not be controlled and was highly resistant to regulation," Simon says. "No one believes that anymore. Governments have taken effective measures to curtail free speech online." Some countries are more heavy-handed than others, he says. "Cuba and Burma do it in a very unsophisticated way — they simply block people from going online."

amputations. CPJ's Journalist Assistance Program provided ongoing financial support to Beketov during his long rehabilitation.

Similarly, during the Iranian government's post-election crackdown on journalists in 2009, photojournalist Ehsan Maleki was forced to flee his home in the face of likely imprisonment. CPJ helped him resettle in another country.[6]

Other journalist assistance programs include:

- **International Federation of Journalists** — Based in Brussels, Belgium; promotes international action to defend press freedom and social justice through independent journalist trade unions. (www.ifj.org/en/splash)
- **International Freedom of Expression Exchange** — A clearinghouse based in Toronto, Canada, providing accurate, timely information on freedom of expression issues and abuses worldwide. (www.ifex.org)
- **Media Legal Defence Initiative** — A nongovernmental organization based in London that provides legal support to journalists and media outlets around the world. (www.mediadefence.org/index.html)
- **The Rory Peck Trust** — Supports freelancers around the world from its base in London; promotes good practices on behalf of freelancers, supports their right to work safely and provides them with assistance when needed. (www.rorypecktrust.org)
- **World Press Freedom Committee** — An international umbrella organization of press-freedom groups; fights against press restrictions such as the licensing of journalists and imposition of mandatory codes of conduct. (www.wpfc.org)

—Jennifer Koons

[1] Nangayi Guyson, "Uganda: Journalist Beaten to Death," AfricaNews.com, Sept. 14, 2010, www.africanews.com/site/list_message/30344PdatalsourcePrss.

[2] "Radio reporter beaten to death," IFEX, Sept. 13, 2010, www.ifex.org/uganda/ 2010/09/13/kiggundu_killed/.

[3] "Freelance journalist beaten to death in Uganda," Committee to Protect Journalists, Sept. 13, 2010, http://cpj.org/2010/09/freelance-journalist-beaten-to-death-in-uganda.php.

[4] "72 Journalists Killed in 2009/Motive Confirmed," Committee to Protect Journalists, http://cpj.org/killed/2009/.

[5] *Ibid.*

[6] "Making an Impact; CPJ aids dozens of journalists worldwide in 2009," Journalist Assistance Program, Committee to Protect Journalists, www.cpj.org/campaigns/assistance.

Simon is encouraged that the Internet is dominated by a handful of fairly large companies, some of which "have demonstrated a commitment to — at least in principle — privacy and freedom of expression," he says. The companies generally "understand that they are in the business of providing information and guaranteeing that this information will be protected," he added, despite some glaring shortcomings. Yahoo! Inc., for example, on four occasions was accused of helping the Chinese government track down dissidents that were using its search engine, triggering outcries from Internet users around the world concerned about growing U.S. corporate acceptance of repressive Chinese media laws. The last incident, in 2005, enabled the government to identify online journalist Shi Tao, who was subsequently arrested and jailed. Since then, Google and Microsoft also have been criticized for censoring their content within China.[30]

But the European Journalism Centre's Ruetten says that even the most restrictive government controls can be skirted. "China in particular shows how to turn the Web into a controlled intranet," he said. "But there is always a way around censorship if you are somewhat tech-savvy."

David Bandurski, a researcher at the University of Hong Kong's China Media Project, says "Internet controls are not, in fact, the core issue facing journalists in terms of what they can and cannot report." Rather, government censorship of print and broadcast news sources, which is much easier, directly impacts what's available on the Internet, he says. "In China, Internet sites are still prevented from doing their own news reporting, which means they rely on the reporting done by traditional media." Thus, he explains, restricting traditional investigative reporting or examinations of the deeper causes behind news stories will "directly impact the Web."

In Syria, where the state controls most print publications, the government began restricting digital speech when Syrians began using the Internet in large numbers.

By 2008, with more than 2 million Syrians online, the Web had emerged as a platform for dissent, so authorities began to beef up online monitoring and censorship.

Although no Syrian laws specifically regulate online content, reporters and bloggers face prosecution under the nation's emergency laws, penal code and press law, which lists topics or lines of inquiry journalists are forbidden to discuss and the punishments for violating those restrictions.[31] "The Internet represents the final frontier in the Middle East, and a lot of governments are really uncomfortable," says CPJ's Dayem. "Satellite TV felt like something they couldn't control, but a blog is even worse."

In 2008 the Syrian Ministry of Communications ordered Internet cafe owners to keep records of their customers' personal information along with the exact time they accessed the Web.[32]

In March 2009, authorities sentenced online journalist Habib Saleh to three years in prison for writing articles that "weakened national feeling" and "incited civil and religious warfare."[33] In May 2009, Syrian officials set out to expand the existing press law to cover Internet users.

Many governments, especially in the Gulf states, monitor and limit Internet access by retaining monopoly ownership of local Internet service providers (ISPs). But Abdul Rahman al-Rashed, general manager of the Dubai-based satellite TV channel Al-Arabiya, said governments are wrong to think they can control the spread of information online.

"A lot of information is getting through to the average person, in Cairo, in Jeddah and Dubai. Censorship will not stop the free flow of information, in my opinion," he said.[34]

Al-Rashed cited the rising influence of the telecommunications sector, including the critical role played by the Internet in growing economies and businesses and the increasing demand for new technology tools from the middle class. Remote areas of the world that still lack basic access to the Web could be the last refuge for strict government control, he said.[35]

Iran is the Middle East's poster child for repression of online activity, combining old-school detention and harassment with newer techniques such as blocking and monitoring Internet behavior. The theocratic government has also moved aggressively to extend the longstanding legal restrictions on print and broadcast journalism to online media.

As in Iran, officials in Egypt, Saudi Arabia, Syria and elsewhere are experimenting with old press statutes and new strategies like blocking and monitoring bloggers from disseminating information, according to a 2009 CPJ survey.[36]

"As Internet connectivity mushrooms in the region, the popularity of blogs has rivaled that of traditional news media," Dayem says. "This is especially true with sensitive topics such as sexual harassment, torture and HIV/AIDS. On topics such as these, bloggers have pushed boundaries and provided cover for traditional journalists."

Governments are pushing back, hard. They're expanding existing legal restrictions, writing new Web-specific laws and requiring service providers to police customers, according to CPJ. In addition, officials are using technology to monitor and block online content and employing old-school tactics such as harassment and detention against bloggers, most of whom are isolated and vulnerable.

"The tactics of authorities may vary, but the goal is often the same: Convince a blogger that the cost of doing battle with the state far outweighs any benefit," Dayem says.

In Cuba, however, bloggers are finding ways to share news and views online, despite widespread legal and technical restrictions. "A lively blogging culture has emerged over the last three years, despite Havana's attempts to control the Internet," says CPJ's Simon. "Some bloggers are examining controversial subjects considered off-limits by the mainstream media, like official corruption and human rights abuses — a risky enterprise considering that the majority of imprisoned Cuban journalists were targeted for work distributed online."[37]

The bloggers, mainly young professionals, have opened a new space for free expression in Cuba. "I am heartened by the rise of a new generation of blogger/journalists," says Scott, of Missouri's journalism school. "They are getting an audience."

In November 2009, President Barack Obama took the unusual step of answering questions submitted by Cuban blogger Yoani Sánchez, who has gained international acclaim for criticizing Cuba online, despite government harassment.[38]

"Your blog provides the world a unique window into the realities of daily life in Cuba," Obama wrote. "It is telling that the Internet has provided you and other courageous Cuban bloggers with an outlet to express yourself so freely. The government and people of the United States join all of you in looking forward to the day all Cubans can freely express themselves in public without fear and without reprisals."[39]

Is press freedom a prerequisite for economic development?

Indian Nobel laureate Amartya Sen and other economists say a free press is a central condition for the development and maintenance of transparent and honest government and lasting economic growth.[40] It is no coincidence, they say, that repression of information and opinion is most severe in the poorest, least-developed countries, where journalists are persecuted, murdered, beaten, arrested and imprisoned, often for reporting on corruption.

Yet many autocratic and repressive governments — notably China — say a free press hampers economic and social development. The free flow of information and expression should be postponed, they argue, until a satisfactory level of economic development has been achieved.

Media experts from 100 countries gathered in Jordan in October 2005 for the Global Forum for Media Development, which explored the link between media development and economic, political and overall development.[41] The World Bank Institute presented empirical evidence to show that independent, financially stable media are essential to good governance and that they succeed when the business environment in which they operate is strengthened.[42]

"Unstable economies invariably breed irresponsible journalism. Studies by Freedom House, Transparency International and others clearly show that the more stable a nation is economically, the better the public perception of the press," says Missouri's Scott. "A press that cannot afford to live cannot thrive."

But oil-rich Gulf nations such as Oman and Qatar would appear to buck that trend: They continued to prosper while keeping a firm hold on the media. Qatar's government-owned Al Jazeera, which has become one of the most popular Arabic satellite television channels in the Middle East, generally does not cover Qatari politics, focusing instead on regional issues, such as the situation in Iraq and the Arab-Israeli conflict.

"There are countries in the region that are entirely closed, politically and economically speaking, or underdeveloped economically and have a media landscape that is nearly the most repressive in the region," says Dayem, CPJ's Middle East program coordinator.

"Others are open [but] have virtually a nonexistent media landscape. Look at Saudi Arabia and Kuwait or Saudi Arabia and the United Arab Emirates," he continues. "Economically, neither is lagging behind the other. Saudi Arabia is a much bigger country, but the media landscape is completely different" in the three countries.

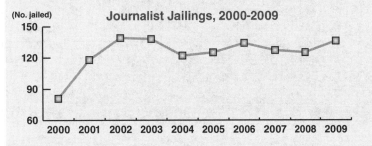

China Leads Way in Jailing Journalists

More than 130 journalists were jailed worldwide in 2009 — the highest number since 2003 and a 68-percent increase over 2000. China jailed the most journalists, followed by Iran and Cuba (list).

Journalist Jailings, 2000-2009

(No. jailed)

Countries that Jailed the Most Journalists, 2009

China	24	Uzbekistan	7
Iran	23	Azerbaijan	6
Cuba	22	Ethiopia	4
Eritrea	19	Egypt	3
Burma (Myanmar)	9		

Source: Committee to Protect Journalists

AFP/Getty Images/Hazem Bader

Palestinian photojournalist Nasser Shiyuki's camera goes flying as Israeli soldiers try to stop him from photographing a protest against Jewish settlements in the West Bank village of Beit Omar, near Hebron, on Sept 25, 2010.

Al Jazeera Director General Wadah Khanfar summed up the situation in the Middle East: "As long as our governments are not convinced that free media could help in developing society, and as long as they see us [as] potential recruits for their propaganda, and as long as there are journalists around who will seek grants from governments to act on their behalf and to deceive and to disinform, I think we are going to have a problem."[43]

China also provides a counterargument to those who contend a free press precedes economic prosperity, according to Ruetten, of the European Journalism Centre.

"The theory was, once you get middle classes, they will want more freedoms and that, again, can lead to more economic development," Ruetten says. "But looking at China seems to prove the opposite. Substantial economic development happens even though there is no free press. The same goes for Singapore and the Gulf states. And how free is 'the press' anyway in countries like yours [in the United States] when its [media] institutions have to generate quarterly profits for shareholders?"

BACKGROUND

Fall of the Wall

After World War II, most of Eastern Europe disappeared behind an "Iron Curtain" of Soviet communist authoritarian rule, which barred press freedom. Berlin was sliced

in half by an 11-foot wall, erected in 1961 to keep East Berliners away from the influences — and freedoms — enjoyed by West Berliners. By the early 1980s, military dictators ruled throughout Latin America, and Cold War-fueled conflicts raged across Africa and Asia. Press freedom was largely unknown outside the United States, Western Europe and Japan.

In the late 1980s and early '90s, press freedom began to expand greatly, after a wave of democratization swept the globe — first in Latin America where military juntas were replaced by democratic governments and then in the former Soviet Union and its satellite states. Later, some parts of Africa and Asia saw some relaxation of media restraints.

Beginning in 1989, popular discontent toppled communist governments in rapid succession. "Ironically, I was playing poker with a bunch of journalists and journalism professors the night the Berlin Wall fell," remembers Missouri's Scott. "Sadly, none of us paused to exclaim what a seminal event it would prove to be; probably because none of us anticipated those consequences. The subsequent rapid collapse of the Soviet Union rewrote the rules for all of us, not just those behind the Iron Curtain. Suddenly, we all had access, each to the other. We could talk, question and report on an equal basis. At least, that was the naive theory.

"The reality was that there were virtually no journalists in the former Communist bloc trained . . . in the principles of press freedom, at least as we in the West considered it," Scott says. "The subsequent couple of decades have been about mutual adjustment."

The fall of the wall mainly benefited younger journalists, since so many older journalists in Eastern Europe had pledged allegiance to the communist regimes or suffered in silence.

"Those reporters and editors lost their jobs, since they were all totally discredited," the European Journalism Centre's Ruetten says. "This is especially true for public broadcasting operations. That is why you find only very few journalists in Eastern Europe who are above age 50 or so. So it did benefit all the younger guys. As for [Western] publishers, they all went east with their papers and magazines, trying to establish new ventures in the new countries," he says. "Some worked, some failed: The jury is still out on whether this has been a success or not."

With Eastern Europe opening up, Western governments and agencies, such as the U.S. Agency for International Development, sent visiting journalists to train local news organizations in how to operate in a free society.

But unforeseen problems quickly emerged. "Neither journalists nor their governments had much prior experience with press freedom, so they changed their constitutions but not their practices," Scott says. "Laws were adopted but never followed. In many nations, press freedom was a Potemkin Village erected for foreign visitors and their funding agencies.

"As computer technology spread, benefits and abuses have walked side-by-side," he said. "Hacking, copyright abuse and Internet fraud emanate from many computer cafes and newsrooms" in the former Eastern bloc countries. "No longer supported by the state, journalists have taken second and third jobs, some with the very news sources on which they report."

As Eastern Europeans fell into old patterns, press freedom suffered. "If you look at the annual rankings of Freedom House, Reporters Without Borders and IREX [a Washington-based nonprofit specializing in media development], for example, not much has changed in recent years. However, we know from looking at post-Salazar Portugal and post-Franco Spain that true change comes more slowly, with the passing of generations," he added, citing the repressive regimes of former Portuguese Prime Minister Antônio de Oliveira Salazar and Spanish dictator Francisco Franco.

"We have begun to see this in the nations of Central Europe that got a head start under *perestroika* and *glasnost,*" he continued, referring to the economic reform and government transparency, respectively, instituted by Soviet leader Mikhail Gorbachev in the mid-1980s. "That process also is progressing in the Balkans with the influence of the European Union and Europeanization" — the process whereby former Soviet bloc countries must liberalize their press-freedom laws to qualify for EU membership. But such media reforms have "hardly begun in Central Asia and the Caucasus region, although there are some heartening examples of success."

Latin America Cracks Down

As communist governments were collapsing in Eastern Europe, authoritarian regimes in Latin America were disappearing as well. Over the past 30 years, all of Latin America's military juntas, except in Cuba, have been replaced by democratically elected governments that adopted more liberal press policies.

Then, as the 20th century drew to a close, "a veritable left-wing tsunami" appeared ready to hit the region, observed former Mexican Foreign Minister Jorge Castañeda. And, indeed, beginning with Hugo Chávez's victory in Venezuela in 1998, "a wave of leaders, parties and movements generically labeled 'leftist' swept into power in one Latin American country after another."[44]

But the news media have not always benefited from the new leftist governments. Despite widespread protests by Bolivian journalists, President Evo Morales recently signed into law a controversial measure allowing news outlets to be shut down and journalists jailed for publishing or writing about statements or acts deemed racist. Several Bolivian papers published blank front pages protesting, "There is no democracy without freedom of expression."[45]

Since taking office, Chávez has frequently vilified the press, while using politicized administrative procedures to force critical broadcasters off the air. Last year, authorities arrested Guillermo Zoloaga, president of the 24-hour opposition television news network Globovision, and his son. Media watchdog organizations called the move part of a systematic campaign of harassment of the private media that also resulted in the closure of Radio Caracas Televisión Internacional (RCTV), Venezuela's main critical cable television network, and dozens of private radio stations.[46] Chávez has also worked to closely align his country with Iran and Cuba, two nations with similarly restrictive press laws and policies.

With 22 reporters and editors in prison, Cuba is the third-biggest jailer of journalists in the world, after Iran and China.[47] Most of the Cuban journalists were imprisoned in March 2003, when 75 dissidents — including 29 journalists — were arrested in the so-called Black Spring roundup. After summary trials held within weeks, the journalists were sentenced to up to 28 years in prison on vague antistate charges connected to their reporting.[48]

Over the past seven years, Cuba has freed a small number of journalists in exchange for international political concessions, according to the Committee to Protect Journalists.[49] But in a country where the government has complete control of the media, independent journalists working for foreign-based news websites are routinely threatened and harassed by security police. Laws and regulations restricting Internet access continue to be among the most repressive in the world.[50]

Chinese 'Schizophrenia'

As China continues to make its mark on the global economy, leaders in Beijing are struggling to balance the need for more information while controlling content and maintaining power. The balancing act makes the government appear to be in a state of "schizophrenia" about media policy, said Council on Foreign Relations Senior Fellow Elizabeth C. Economy. It "goes back and forth, testing the line, knowing they need press freedom — and the information it provides — but worried about opening the door to the type of freedoms that could lead to the regime's downfall."[51]

As a result, the past few years have been rocky for press freedom in China, where the government operates what is widely regarded as the world's most extensive system of Web monitoring and filtering, blocking both pornographic sites and those seen as subversive to communist rule. The controls were relaxed temporarily before and during the 2008 Olympic Games in Beijing, but as soon as the international spotlight faded, authorities clamped down again.

"The issue of press freedom and the Beijing Olympics was decided when China was awarded host status years earlier," the University of Hong Kong's Bandurski says. "In fact, China never promised press freedom for the Beijing Olympics." China only committed to allowing foreign journalists to have access to the Olympics. "The core issue for press freedom in China is the environment that faces China's own journalists, and Chinese journalists understood from the beginning that an international event of this scale would mean only tighter controls."

The temporary loosening of controls on both local and foreign media leading up to the Olympics — and then the welcome announcement that the less restrictive regulations for foreign media would remain in force past October 2008 — generated hope for positive change on the press-freedom front. But the optimism quickly faded early in 2009, as authorities sought to reexert control, focusing in particular on the rising power of the Internet as a means for social expression and organizing.[52]

According to Bandurski, "2009 was a year of intensified control of the Internet and new media in China. These controls had a devastating effect on many small and medium-sized websites in China and sent a general chill through China's Internet sector."

Then, last January, Google executives suddenly announced that the company would end its four-year practice of blocking search results that the Chinese government considered subversive or pornographic. Google reached the decision, it said, after Chinese computer hackers tried to steal the company's technology and e-mail information from Chinese human rights activists.[53] Eventually, Google won permission to continue operating in the country after agreeing to eliminate an automatic detour around China's online censorship requirements.

Starting in March, Google began automatically rerouting search requests from the Google.cn site on the mainland to its Hong Kong service, which isn't subject to Beijing's censorship rules.* After Chinese officials threatened not to renew the company's operating license, Google compromised. Search requests from within mainland China now require an extra click to get to the Hong Kong site.[54] Since Google must renew its license with China on an annual basis, the issue could arise again if the authorities become displeased with the current arrangement.

Some observers have pointed out that because all companies must comply with China's censorship demands as a condition of doing business in China, "Google knew, or should have known, what kind of environment it was dealing with when it entered the country," Bandurski notes. "But 2009 demonstrated just how capricious China's Internet sector is as a result of political controls, and that undoubtedly forms some of the background for Google's confrontation."

President Hu Jintao at first seemed flexible. Shortly after assuming office in 2003, Hu told Chinese lawmakers, "The removal of restrictions on the press, and the opening up of public opinion positions, is a mainstream view and demand held by society; it is natural,

---

* Chinese censorship rules don't apply to Hong Kong, which is recognized by international treaty as being vested with independent judicial power.

C H R O N O L O G Y

1980s *Press freedom reaches great heights and even greater lows as the Cold War comes to an end.*

1986 Colombian journalist Guillermo Cano Isaza is assassinated in front of his newspaper's offices in Bogotá on Dec. 17, after his writings offend Colombia's powerful drug barons. Since then the U.N. has marked World Press Freedom Day each year by conferring the UNESCO/Guillermo Cano World Press Freedom Prize.

1987 U.N. General Assembly adopts Article 19 of the Universal Declaration of Human Rights, declaring: "Everyone has the right to freedom of opinion and expression; . . . to hold opinions without interference and to seek, receive and impart information and ideas through any media and regardless of frontiers."

1989 Press freedom expands in former Soviet bloc after Berlin Wall falls.

Early 2000s *After the Sept. 11 terrorist attacks in the United States, journalists covering the wars in Afghanistan and Iraq encounter increased violence.*

2002 *Wall Street Journal* reporter Daniel Pearl is kidnapped and murdered in Pakistan by Muslim extremists. . . . More than 200 people die in riots in the Nigerian capital of Abuja after fashion writer Isioma Daniel, in an article about the Abuja Miss World beauty contest, writes that the Prophet Mohammed probably would have married one of the contestants.

2003 U.S. invasion of Iraq begins in March; more than 220 journalists and media assistants die during the six-and-a-half-year war.

Late 2000s *Olympic Games in Beijing and the Iranian presidential election draw the world's attention back to press censorship.*

2006 U.N. Security Council unanimously adopts Resolution 1738, which calls for war correspondents and associated personnel to be protected as civilians under the Geneva Conventions. . . . Russian Journalist Anna Politkovskaya is shot dead at her Moscow apartment,

provoking international outrage. Politkovskaya had written frequently about human rights abuses in Chechnya for the *Novaya Gazeta* newspaper. In February 2009, three men were acquitted in her murder, but the Russian Supreme Court later ordered a new trial.

2008 Olympic Games in China shine international spotlight on limited press freedom in the communist country. Some official concessions are made toward foreign correspondents covering the Games, but Chinese journalists still face wide-ranging restrictions.

2009 On March 24 American TV journalists Euna Lee and Laura Ling are taken into custody by North Korean officials after "illegal intruding" from across the border with China. Both are pardoned on August 4 after former U.S. President Bill Clinton intercedes. . . . Disputed reelection of Iranian President Mahmoud Ahmadinejad on June 12 triggers a wave of antigovernment protests and the arrests of more than 170 journalists and bloggers. . . . In November, 32 journalists are murdered in a massacre during the run-up to the presidential election by gunmen linked to municipal leaders in a southern Philippine province. . . . Fourth World Electronic Media Forum in Mexico calls "for sustained and concrete international action to address the murder of journalists and media support staff . . . in peacetime and war."

2010 President Barack Obama in May directs U.S. State Department to cover press freedom in its annual global human rights reports. . . . About 60-70 of the journalists arrested after the 2009 Iranian election are still awaiting trial. The others are either in prison or were fined; many are forbidden from ever practicing journalism in Iran again. . . . Trial begins in the Philippines of accused murderers of 32 journalists. . . . In October, World Association of Newspapers and News Publishers awards its annual press freedom prize to Iranian journalist/political analyst Ahmad Zeid-Abadi, sentenced to six years in prison and banned from journalism on charges that he plotted to overthrow the government during his coverage of the 2009 election protests in Iran. . . . Twenty-three Chinese Communist Party elders release an open letter calling for an end to restrictions on free speech and the media in China.

Journalism Proves Lethal in the Philippines

Will the alleged murderers of 32 journalists be convicted?

L uis Teodoro, director of the Manila-based Center for Media Freedom and Responsibility, discusses the ongoing challenges facing journalists in the Philippines following the massacre on Nov. 23, 2009, of 57 unarmed civilians — including 32 journalists. They were shot to death in broad daylight by a group of gunmen allegedly hired by the politically powerful Ampatuan family of Maguindanao Province. Teodoro, who answered reporter Jennifer Koons' questions via e-mail, teaches journalism at the University of the Philippines' College of Mass Communication, where he was dean from 1994 until 2000. He is also editor of the Philippine Journalism Review.

Has journalism in the Philippines changed since the massacre?

Journalism hasn't changed since Nov. 23, 2009. Many journalists assume that what happened to others won't happen to them, which I suppose is a cultural trait. Filipinos are basically optimistic despite their historical and current experience. So they persist in writing their usual stories.

Do you believe those responsible for the Maguindanao massacre will be found guilty?

Because there are 197 accused of planning and participating in the massacre, and more than 200 prosecution witnesses, the trial will take at least five years, during which anything can happen, including the witnesses' being killed or bought off. I am not optimistic that anyone will be punished, but some people say the Ampatuans are prepared to sacrifice Andal Ampatuan Jr., since the evidence against him at this point is overwhelming.

What are the biggest obstacles faced by journalists in your country?

One of the reasons the killing of journalists persists — 117 have been murdered since 1986 — is the failure to punish

the killers. Only nine of these murders have led to the trial and imprisonment of the guilty, and no mastermind has ever been arrested and tried.

How much do Filipino journalists rely on the Internet and social networking sites like Twitter for stories?

Few of the several thousand journalists in the country, especially those in the provinces, rely on the Internet and social networking sites, but that's slowly starting to change as we get better access to these technologies.

Reuters/Erik de Castro

Bodies mark the grisly scene of a politically motivated massacre on Mindanao Island in the southern Philippines on Nov. 23, 2009. Of the 57 victims, 32 were journalists. Members of a powerful local clan were charged with masterminding the murders and are being held in Manila, where their trial is expected to last several years.

and should be resolved through the legislative process. If the Communist Party does not reform itself, if it does not transform, it will lose its vitality and move toward natural and inevitable extinction."[55] In the past seven years, however, Hu has taken a tougher stance than

some expected in regulating content and prosecuting journalists.

Nevertheless, some of China's state-run media have been allowed to pursue some level of commercialization — to profit from selling ads while remaining tied to the state structure. According to a government report, there are more than 2,000 privately owned newspapers, 8,000 magazines and 374 TV stations.[56]

"Journalists in China face a host of struggles — social, economic, political and personal. But the most important restrictions are still political, and these are many-faceted," Bandurski says. "Media receive daily directives from propaganda authorities about what they can and cannot report, or what they must.

"However, controls are much less ideologically driven today than in the past," he explains. "They are no longer about violations of Marxist ideology or the party line but more often about protecting the vested interests of entrenched party leaders."

As a result, many of today's press restrictions are carried out "to protect commercial and political interests, which are often one and the same. So the protection of journalists and their professional work must be dealt with ultimately through political reforms."

CURRENT SITUATION

Press Freedom Today

After two decades of progress, mostly in former Soviet bloc countries, press freedom recently has begun declining in almost every part of the world, according to Freedom House's most recent annual report.

"Only 16 percent of the world's citizens live in countries that enjoy a free press," the report said. "In the rest of the world, governments as well as non-state actors control the viewpoints that reach citizens and brutally repress independent voices who aim to promote accountability, good governance, and economic development."[57]

As fast as reporters in repressive societies adopt new technologies — like cell phones, the Internet, Facebook and Twitter — to connect to the outside world, governments like China, Iran and Venezuela devise sophisticated new tools to control the flow of online information. Or regimes take the easier route: Using heavy-handed, old-school methods such as intimidation and violence to control the media.

The 10 nations that made Freedom House's "worst of the worst" list were Belarus, Burma (or Myanmar), Cuba, Equatorial Guinea, Eritrea, Iran, Libya, North

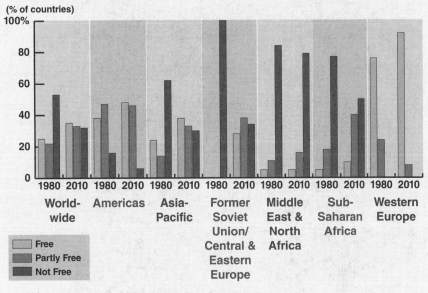

More Countries Now Have a Free Press

The percentage of countries with a free press has risen from 25 percent in 1980 to 35 percent in 2010, while the percentage without a free press has dwindled from 53 percent to 32 percent. The biggest improvement occurred in Russia and the former Soviet bloc countries, which went from having no press freedom in 1980 to 66 percent enjoying a free or partly free press in 2010. The Middle East and North Africa saw the least improvement: Only 5 percent of the countries had a free press in 1980 — a figure that has not changed in three decades.

Press Freedom Status, 1980-2010, by Region

Free
Partly Free
Not Free

Source: "Freedom of the Press 2010," Freedom House

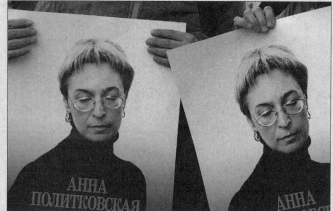

Murdered Journalists

Prominent Iraqi TV anchorman Riad al-Saray (top) is shown anchoring an Al-Iraqiya news broadcast before he was shot while driving his car on Sept. 7 in Baghdad, bringing to 15 the number of Al-Iraqiya reporters murdered since the Iraq War began. Not considered a controversial journalist, al-Saray sought to reconcile Shiites and Sunnis in his broadcasts. Of the 735 journalists killed worldwide in the past decade because of their jobs, 170 died in Iraq — many during war coverage — making it the most dangerous country in the world for journalists over the 10-year period. Russian human rights activists (bottom) rally in Moscow on Oct. 7 to mark the fourth anniversary of the assassination of celebrated Russian investigative journalist Anna Politkovskaya, known for her critical coverage of the war in Chechnya.

crushed through imprisonment, torture and other forms of repression," according to the report. Despite hope that the advent of the Internet and other new media would lead to improvements in these countries, most of their scores have remained stagnant.

In one notable development, however, Iran replaced Zimbabwe in the worst-performing group. Zimbabwe's score improved slightly after the new "government of national unity" led to "small openings in media coverage and editorial bias, as well as less stringent application of harsh media laws," while press freedom in Iran "suffered a dramatic deterioration, as both official and unofficial avenues for news and information sharing were severely curtailed" after the disputed presidential election. Journalists were arrested, imprisoned and tortured.

Here is the situation elsewhere around the globe, according to Freedom House:

Sub-Saharan Africa — The steepest overall drop in press freedom occurred in this vast region. South Africa's ongoing battle over a proposed media tribunal pushed the country's press freedom ranking from "free" to "partly free," leaving southern Africa with no "free" countries for the first time in 20 years. Last year, incidents of violence, prosecutions, imprisonment and censorship occurred in Angola, Burundi, Cameroon, Democratic Republic of Congo, Ethiopia, Eritrea, Ghana, Nigeria, Somalia, Sudan and Uganda.[58] Press freedom in Kenya increased slightly after the post-election violence in 2008. In August 2010, Kenyans approved a new constitution, which ensures the right to freedom of expression and information.[59] Meanwhile, Nigerian officials sponsored a three-day national conference on promoting press freedom across the country.[60]

Korea, Turkmenistan and Uzbekistan. In these countries — scattered across the globe —"independent media are either nonexistent or barely able to operate, the press acts as a mouthpiece for the regime, citizens' access to unbiased information is severely limited and dissent is

Is the climate for Chinese journalists worsening?

YES MADELINE EARP
Senior Asia Program Researcher,
Committee to Protect Journalists

Written for *CQ Global Researcher*, October 2010

The climate for journalists in China is worsening in some ways, even as many Chinese journalists have more freedom than in the past. Foreign journalists operate more easily since regulations were relaxed during the 2008 Beijing Olympics, although local authorities still try to obstruct them, and their local news assistants and sources are often questioned or monitored.

Many Chinese journalists say the press-freedom climate has improved immeasurably over the last 30 years, partly because of the Internet and partly because more commercial news outlets exist. Yet, as distribution methods become more sophisticated, so do the state's information authorities. Censorship regulations have increased around sensitive events, including the Olympics, in the past three years, handed down to newsrooms (and increasingly to Internet portals) answerable to state sponsors. So while the Committee to Protect Journalists (CPJ) is finding professional journalists less likely to be imprisoned than a decade ago, that's partly because the system to stifle aggressive reporting in-house is strengthening.

When editors and journalists cross the line, they may be reprimanded, demoted or fired — punitive actions that are less visible to the outside world. Banned news stories circulate online, but censors work to erase them. When the story is too big — like imprisoned Chinese dissident Liu Xiaobo winning the Nobel Peace Prize — propaganda to undermine it ("Nobel win criticized") appears in the mainstream media. So the version that remains on record is the one selected to favor the Communist Party.

Journalists who work independently online are especially vulnerable. The CPJ counted 24 journalists in Chinese prisons in 2009, many of them activists or minorities who published online. Gheyret Niyaz, a Uighur website editor, was sentenced last summer to 15 years for endangering state security after he wrote about 2009 ethnic unrest in the Xinjiang Uighur Autonomous Region.

In an October report, the CPJ found a debate raging in the Chinese media on "press rights." The government has pledged to protect journalists — and many media outlets are publicizing cases in which reporters are harassed by local police or security guards. This is a positive development. CPJ also found that while the state continues to repress the media, it remains a superficial development.

Journalists in China are energetically overcoming many restrictions. But that will not amount to an improved climate until the state allows a genuinely independent media.

NO DAVID BANDURSKI
Researcher, China Media Project,
University of Hong Kong

Written for *CQ Global Researcher*, October 2010

China's media environment is a very complicated terrain. It doesn't lend itself to simplistic characterizations of tightening vs. opening. To really understand the situation facing journalists in China, one must balance a very complex equation involving many factors, not just state controls.

For example, media commercialization – allowing commercial spin-offs of state-run newspapers that survive by selling advertising, but are still formally tied into the state structure — is changing the relationship between media and society in China. The Chinese media consumer now has greater power than ever before: Journalistic professionalism is increasing, and technology is advancing, enabling the growth of the Internet and new tools such as Twitter-like microblogs. And while the Chinese Communist Party (CCP) has remained determined to control the media to maintain party rule, which leaders call "public opinion guidance," broader social and economic change in China has complicated this goal and opened up interesting new spaces for journalism.

Nevertheless, Chinese journalists face new hurdles. The Chinese government has imposed new curbs on investigative reporting, which enjoyed rather strong growth from the late 1990s to 2004. In 2004, the CCP officially curbed the practice of what it calls "extra-territorial reporting" *(yidi jiandu)*, which refers to journalists from one city or province reporting hard news or exposés in another region. In a country where media are still controlled directly by party officials in their jurisdiction, "extraterritorial reporting" has been an important tool of professional journalists, allowing them to report harder-hitting stories without fear of reprisals from their immediate party superiors.

But provincial party leaders complained that the practice was hindering their work. The government has not banned extraterritorial reporting, but it has given officials extra leverage in fighting back against tough news stories. Secondly, Chinese media and journalists are facing much greater resistance from both local governments and corporations.

The resistance reflects the development and entrenchment of special-power interests during the country's economic boom in the absence of substantial political reforms — what some have characterized as "market-Leninism." Vested party, government and commercial entities now work aggressively to contain news and information that contravenes their interests. As a result, officials now restrict reporting on corporations, and some companies now intimidate or even attack journalists. Thus, say some Chinese journalists, while the space for reporting on certain issues such as corporate corruption has formally expanded in China, in other instances reporting has become more hazardous.

AFP/Getty Images/Sabah Arar

Iraqi journalists protest attempts to muzzle journalists on Aug. 14, 2009, after an influential Shiite political leader reportedly threatened violence against a local journalist for reporting that the cleric was linked to a deadly July 28, 2009, bank robbery. The cartoon reads "Don't kill the truth."

The Americas — In Latin America, where a deep-rooted culture of impunity prevails and authoritarian and populist regimes tolerate minimal scrutiny or criticism, reporting on organized crime, drug cartels and high-level corruption is fraught with danger. With chilling regularity, Mexican journalists are murdered, threatened, assaulted and harassed. Five journalists were killed in Honduras last year,[61] and Venezuelan radio journalist Orel Sambrano was shot in the back of the head on his way home from work in January 2010.[62] The United States continues to have a free press, but it faces several challenges, including the lack of a federal shield law to protect confidential sources, an economic threat from the nation's poor economic conditions and the increased polarization of news content.

Central and Eastern Europe/Former Soviet Union — Russia remains one of the world's more repressive and dangerous media environments. In April, an antiterrorism measure was proposed that would broaden the definition of "extremism" to include criticism of officials, punishable by fines and jail terms.[63] In Bulgaria, journalists are threatened by pervasive organized crime, assaults and death threats.[64] And six newspapers in Estonia published blank pages in March to protest a proposed law reducing protections for journalists' confidential

sources.[65] On the other hand, the National Assembly of Armenia decriminalized defamation, including libel. If the legislation is signed into law, journalists could no longer be imprisoned for defamation.[66]

Middle East and North Africa — In the aftermath of the crackdown on protests following its disputed 2009 election, Iran remains one of the world's most inhospitable countries for journalists. Hundreds of local journalists have been arrested, and Iranian newspapers have been explicitly warned to stay away from touchy subjects. The rapidity with which the press-freedom situation deteriorated in Iran has been shocking, says CPJ's Simon. "Imprisoned journalists are held incommunicado, abused, tortured, some die in custody, . . . it's a very, very alarming situation," he says. "While Iran was never an open society, there was a certain level of tolerance for critical journalism and some thriving independent media outlets. Those are gone, many leading journalists are in jail, and the future for freedom of expression in Iran looks very bleak indeed."

Neighboring Iraq is also a dangerous place to practice journalism; two local TV anchors were murdered in September.[67] Harassment, defamation suits and other measures are commonly used in Bahrain, Yemen, the Palestinian Territories, Egypt and Tunisia to control the press and limit freedom of information.

Asia-Pacific — As China continues to closely monitor journalists, 23 Communist Party elders, in a surprising development, released an open letter in October calling for an end to restrictions on free speech and the media. "If the Communist Party does not reform itself, does not transform, it will lose its vitality and die a natural death," warned the letter, which was posted on the Internet. The signers included a former secretary to Mao Zedong and a former publisher of the *People's Daily*, the official Communist Party newspaper.[68]

Meanwhile, other governments across Asia continue to impose various press restrictions, including state interference in day-to-day newsgathering and impunity for violent retribution against journalists. Kidnapping and the deliberate targeting of journalists make Pakistan — where six journalists have been killed so far this year — one of the more dangerous countries for media professionals in 2010.[69] North Korea continued its tight control over the media and even arrested two U.S. journalists, Euna Lee and Laura Ling, caught near the North Korean-Chinese border region where they were reporting on the trafficking of North Korean women into China's sex trade industry. They were found guilty and sentenced to 12 years of hard labor for allegedly entering the country illegally. But after 140 days in custody, the reporters were freed on humanitarian grounds after former President Bill Clinton flew to Pyongyang and met with North Korean leader Kim Jong Il on their behalf.[70]

Deadliest Country

But the most dangerous place on Earth for journalists in 2009 was the Philippines, where in September the first trial began in Manila against some of the nearly 200 suspects charged in connection with the 2009 slaughter of 57 people, including 32 journalists.[71]

The gruesome, premeditated massacre was "a shocking display of barbarism apparently motivated by political clan rivalries," said the Committee to Protect Journalists. It was the bloodiest attack on journalists since CPJ began documenting violence against the press 18 years ago.[72] The journalists were apparently caught up in a long-running feud between powerful rival political clans in a lawless region of Muslim-dominated Mindanao, one of the poorest islands in the Southeast Asian archipeligo.

On Nov. 23, 2009, the reporters were traveling in an eight-car convoy with family members and relatives of mayoral candidate Esmael Mangudadatu to watch him file papers to run for governor of

AP Photo/Anjum Naveed

Reuters/Fayaz Aziz

Targeted in Pakistan

Eight years after American journalist Daniel Pearl — being remembered in a musical tribute in Islamabad in October (top) — was kidnapped and beheaded by Muslim extremists in Pakistan, the country is still a dangerous place for journalists. A Pakistani journalist calls for help (bottom) after a suicide bomb attack at the gate of the Peshawar Press Club last Dec. 22 killed three people and wounded 17.

Cameroonian journalists continue their demonstration on May 3, 2010, in another part of the capital city of Yaoundé after police forcefully prevented several hundred of them from staging a sit-in at the prime minister's office. The journalists are marking World Press Freedom Day and protesting the death in prison earlier in the year of popular newspaper editor Bibi Ngota.

Maguindanao Province. The convoy was stopped at a checkpoint, said a farmer who lives nearby, when nearly a dozen vehicles — including police cars and a Hummer outfitted with a .50-caliber sniper rifle — with more than 60 heavily armed, camouflage-wearing men arrived and ordered the reporters and others out of their cars.

According to the witness, the local mayor, Andal Ampatuan, Jr., his uncle and the police chief were among those who slapped, kicked and punched the 57 victims before forcing them at gunpoint to an isolated field where pits had been dug by backhoes.[73] The victims — 15 of whom were women, including the candidate's wife — were then shot dead, he told the court, and most were buried in the mass graves.[74]

Another witness — former Ampatuan employee Lakmudin Salio — told the court that six days before the massacre he overheard the Ampatuans planning the murders at dinner. Later, he said, family patriarch Andal Sr. — the mayor's father and former Maguindanao governor — tried to bribe national and local officials in an effort to keep his family from being prosecuted. However, both Andal Jr. and Sr. have been charged in connection with the murders, as were the uncle, 16 policemen and more than 170 others. At least

100 people who have been indicted are still at large. Five potential witnesses have been murdered.[75]

But those weren't the only journalists killed in the Philippines recently. In June, seven months after the Maguindanao massacre, two outspoken radio broadcasters who had criticized corruption among local officials were killed in separate attacks at opposite ends of the country during a 24-hour period.[76] Police found no suspects, but Filipino media groups pointed out that the attacks appeared to follow a typical pattern in which journalists are targeted for exposing corruption, and their murderers are rarely prosecuted.

The Filipino journalists killed this past year are just the latest of 145 to die in the line of duty in the 25 years since the late dictator Ferdinand Marcos left office and press freedom was restored to the country, according to Journalists of the Philippines (NUJP) Vice Chairman Nonoy Espina.[77] There is scant accountability in a nation where journalists — like human rights attorneys and advocates — often face violence and intimidation, says Luis Teodoro, director of the Philippines-based Center for Media Freedom and Responsibility.

"The conditions which make these killings possible must be removed," Teodoro told Agence France-Presse in June 2010. "That means you are going to have to punish the guilty and show that the justice system works. You must show that one cannot just kill anybody and get away with it."[78]

To fight the deep-seated climate of impunity in the Philippines, CPJ has worked for three years with local Filipino partners in its Global Campaign Against Impunity. The program presses government officials for greater resolve, provides legal support and assistance to victims' families and pursues legal tactics that improve the odds for arrests and convictions.[79]

OUTLOOK
'Critical Juncture'

As the beleaguered news business struggles to survive in the Internet age, media organizations are expected to rely increasingly on local journalists, particularly freelancers and bloggers — the very people who are least protected by big media institutions.

"We're at a very critical juncture right now," says Simon of the Committee to Protect Journalists. "You're seeing several trends simultaneously.

"First, media institutions in most developed countries around the world are facing the deepest threat to their business model in a generation [so] they are cutting resources. And one of the resources they are cutting is international coverage. Those who step into the breach are freelancers and local journalists."

While international journalists are often well-protected — with flak jackets, armored cars and armed guards, not to mention lawyers — local journalists usually do not have the means to protect themselves sufficiently, either from gunshots or from government action. Thus, they have traditionally been the easiest targets for censorship, harassment — and even murder. In 2009, more than 90 percent of the unsolved murders of journalists were local reporters killed in their home countries, according to CPJ.[80]

That is especially true in conflict zones. "In Afghanistan, Iraq and now Pakistan . . . those being killed are almost exclusively local journalists," says Sherry Ricchiardi, a senior writer specializing in international affairs for the *American Journalism Review* and a professor of journalism at Indiana University. "They are targeted by all sides." While several foreign correspondents were killed at the beginning of the Iraq War in 2003 and 2004, Iraqi journalists are now the primary targets, especially photographers and TV journalists who are easier to spot. And in Pakistan and Afghanistan local journalists who have consistently provided much of the frontline coverage have been exposed to greater risk.

Moreover, according to Simon, nine out of 10 journalist murders show signs of premeditation — such as careful planning, groups of assailants and gang-style executions. Journalists can be targeted by rebel groups, militias, drug traffickers, extremists or corrupt politicians — both in conflict zones and in countries where press freedom is not sufficiently valued.

Government officials realize that local reporters, who speak the language and are known in their communities, can uncover damaging information, so "they're taking steps to limit this kind of information," he adds. But in repressive societies, he adds, "institutions that would normally protect journalists are not there. So when governments take steps against bloggers and freelancers in their own countries, they are vulnerable. There will be an increase in the number of journalists in jail in places like Iran."

As a result, he predicts, "Five years from now we could have a Balkanized world confined to certain spheres where information does not reach the vast majority of society."

Jennifer Windsor, executive director of Freedom House, describes the declining press freedom around the world as inherently troubling but also emblematic of more serious problems.[81]

"Freedom of expression is fundamental to all other freedoms. Rule of law, fair elections, minority rights, freedom of association and accountable government all depend on an independent press, which can fulfill its watchdog function," she says. "When the Iranian Revolutionary Guards torture a journalist, or communist authorities in China imprison a blogger or criminal elements in Russia assassinate yet another investigative reporter, it sends a clear message that every person fighting for basic rights is vulnerable to a similar fate."[82]

NOTES

1. Katherine Corcoran, "Juarez editorial ignites a beleaguered Mexico," The Associated Press, Sept. 25, 2010, www.google.com/hosted-news/ap/article/ALeqM5jm93hjH5nQsBSdR19AJyiQSmfV8gD9IDQVC82; and '¿Que quieren de nosotros?" *ElDiario de Juarez,* Sept. 18, 2010, www.diario.commx/notas.php?f=2010/09/18&i d=6b124801376ce134c7d6ce2c7fb8fe2f.

2. "Luis Carlos Santiago," Committee to Protect Journalists, Sept. 16, 2010, http://cpj.org/killed/2010/luis-carlos-santiago.php.

3. "Journalist Murdered by Drug Gang in Cuidad Juarez," Reporters Without Borders, Nov. 14, 2008, http://en.rsf.org/mexico-journalist-murdered-by-drug-gang-14-11-2008,29293.

4. "Silence or Death in Mexico's Press," Committee to Protect Journalists, Sept. 8, 2010, http://cpj.org/reports/2010/09/silence-or-death-in-mexicos-press.php.

5. *Ibid.*

6. Tracy Wilkinson, "Under Threat From Mexican Drug Cartels, Reporters Go Silent," *Los Angeles Times,* Aug. 16, 2010, http://articles.latimes.com/

2010/aug/16/world/la-fg-mexico-narco-censorship-20100816.

7. "Silence or Death in Mexico's Press," *op. cit.*

8. Wilkinson, *op. cit.*

9. "Freedom of the Press 2010," Freedom House, www.freedomhouse.org/template.cfm?page=251&year=2010.

10. "37 Journalists Killed in 2010/Motive Confirmed," Committee to Protect Journalists, 2010, www.cpj.org/killed/2010/.

11. "CPJ's 2009 Prison Census: Freelance Journalists Under Fire," Committee to Protect Journalists, Dec. 8, 2009, www.cpj.org/reports/2009/12/freelance-journalists-in-prison-cpj-2009-census.php.

12. "52 Journalists Killed in Russia Since 1992," Committee to Protect Journalists, www.cpj.org/killed/europe/russia/.

13. "Getting Away With Murder," Committee to Protect Journalists, http://cpj.org/killed/europe/russia/murder.php.

14. For background, see "Attacks on the Press 2009: Yemen," Committee to Protect Journalists, www.cpj.org/2010/02/attacks-on-the-press-2009-yemen.php.

15. *Ibid.*

16. *Ibid.*

17. Andrew Geoghegan, "Journalists Fear Return to Apartheid-Era Laws," ABC News Online, Aug. 18, 2010, www.abc.net.au/news/sto-ries/2010/08/18/2986773.htm.

18. *Ibid.*

19. *Ibid.*

20. M. J. Bear and Jane Hall, "Media coverage of the War in Iraq," American University School of Communication, March 17, 2005, http://ics.leeds.ac.uk/papers/vp01.cfmloutffcpmt&folder=193&paper=2246.

21. "Malaysians Use Social Media to Bypass Censorship," Agence France-Presse, Aug. 18, 2010, www.asiaone.com/News/Latest%2BNews/Digital One/Story/A1Story20100818-232717.html.

22. *Ibid.*

23. "Press Freedom Index 2009," Reporters Without Borders, http://en.rsf.org/press-freedom-index-2009,1001.html.

24. "Authoritarianism Prevents Press Freedom Progress in Much of Asia," Reporters Without Borders, Oct. 20, 2009, http://en.rsf.org/asia-authoritarianism-prevents-press-20-10-2009,34788.html.

25. *Ibid.*

26. *Ibid.*

27. "Government Uses State of Emergency to Escalate Censorship," Reporters Without Borders, April 8, 2010, http://en.rsf.org/thailand-government-uses-state-of-emergency-08-04-2010,36968. For background, see Barbara Mantel, "Democracy in Southeast Asia," *CQ Global Researcher,* June 1, 2010, pp. 131-156.

28. Danny O'Brien, "In Censoring Web, Thailand Could Worsen Crisis," Committee to Protect Journalists, April 12, 2010, http://cpj.org/blog/2010/04/in-censoring-Web-thailand-could-worsen-crisis.php.

29. *Ibid.*

30. Robert Marquand, "Yahoo, Chinese police, and a jailed journalist," *The Christian Science Monitor,* Sept. 9, 2005, www.csmonitor.com/2005/0909/p01s03-woap.html. Also see Ilya Garger, "Yahoo China is under fire again," Marketwatch, Wall Street Journal Digital Network, April 28, 2006, www.marketwatch.com/story/yahoo-helps-china-jail-dissidents-says-rights-group.

31. Anthony Mills, "World Press Freedom Review: Syria," International Press Institute, Feb. 9, 2010, www.freemedia.at/publications/world-press-freedom-review/singleview/4749/.

32. *Ibid.*

33. "Cyber Dissident Sentenced Habib Saleh To Three Years Jail," Reporters Without Borders, March 16, 2009, http://en.rsf.org/syria-cyber-dissident-habib-saleh-16-03-2009,30591.html.

34. Joe Sterling, "Report: Mideast, North African Countries Censor, Control Media," CNN.com, Feb. 12, 2010, http://insidethemiddleeast.blogs

.cnn.com/2010/02/12/report-mideast-north-african-countries-censor-control-media/.

35. *Ibid.*

36. Mohamed Abdel Dayem, "Middle East Bloggers: The Street Leads Online," Committee to Protect Journalists, Oct. 14, 2009, www.cpj.org/reports/2009/10/middle-east-bloggers-the-street-leads-online.php.

37. For background, see "Press Freedom in the Americas," Committee to Protect Journalists' Executive Director Joel Simon's Testimony before the House Subcommittee on the Western Hemisphere, June 16, 2010, http://foreignaffairs.house.gov/111/sim061610. pdf.

38. Sara Miller Llana, "Obama Grants Interview to Cuban Blogger Yoani Sanchez," *The Christian Science Monitor*, Nov. 20, 2009, www.csmonitor.com/World/Global-News/2009/1120/obama-grants-interview-to-cuba-blogger-yoani-sanchez.

39. "Obama Responses Stun Cuban Blogger Yoani Sanchez," Carlos Lauria, Committee to Protect Journalists, Nov. 19, 2009, http://cpj.org/blog/2009/11/obama-responses-stun-cuban-blogger-yoani-sanchez.php.

40. For background, see Amartya Sen, *Development as Freedom* (1999).

41. For background, see the Global Forum for Media Development, October 2005, http://70.87.64.34/~intint/gfmd_info/index.php?option=com_content&task=view&id=40&Itemid=93.

42. See *Right to Tell: The Role of Mass Media In Economic Development* (2002).

43. Claire Ferris-Lay, "No Progress on Press Freedom, Al Jazeera Chief," *ArabianBusiness.com* July 4, 2010, www.arabianbusiness.com/591970-no-progress-on-mideast-press-freedom---al-jazeera-chief.

44. Jorge G. Casteñada, "Latin America's Left Turn," *Foreign Affairs*, May/June 2006, www.foreignaffairs.com/articles/61702/jorge-g-castaneda/latin-americas-left-turn. For background, see Roland Flamini, "The New Latin America," *CQ Global Researcher*, March 1, 2008, pp. 57-84.

45. Carlos A. Quiroga, "Bolivia's Morales signs racism law as media fret," Reuters, Oct. 8, 2010, www.reuters.com/article/idUSN0822976220101008.

46. "Press Freedom in the Americas," *op. cit.*

47. *Ibid.*

48. Sara Miller Llana, "Cuba Prisoner Release: Seven 'Black Spring' Dissidents are Freed in Spain," *The Christian Science Monitor*, July 13, 2010, www.csmonitor.com/World/Americas/2010/0713/Cuba-prisoner-release-Seven-Black-Spring-dissidents-are-freed-in-Spain.

49. "Newly Freed, Six Cuban Journalists Arrive in Spain," Committee to Protect Journalists, July 13, 2010, http://cpj.org/2010/07/newly-freed-six-cuban-journalists-arrive-in-spain.php.

50. *Ibid.*

51. Carin Zissis, Corinne Baldwin and Preeti Bhattacharji, "Media Censorship in China," Council on Foreign Relations, May 27, 2010, www.cfr.org/publication/11515/media_censorship_in_china.html.

52. "China: New Restrictions Target Media," Human Rights Watch, March 18, 2009, www.hrw.org/en/news/2009/03/18/china-new-restrictions-target-media.

53. Ellen Nakashima, Steven Mufson and John Pomfret, "Google Threatens to Leave China After Attacks on Activists' E-Mail," *The Washington Post,* Jan. 13, 2010, www.washingtonpost.com/wp-dyn/content/article/2010/01/12/AR 2010011203024.html.

54. Michael Liedtke, "Google Wins Permission to Keep Website in China," The Associated Press, July 9, http://abcnews.go.com/Technology/wireStory?id=11123889.

55. Li Rui, *et al.,* "China Must Abandon Censorship," *Guardian,* Oct. 13, 2010, www.guardian.co.uk/commentisfree/2010/oct/13/china-censorship-freedom-speech.

56. *Ibid.*

57. "Freedom of the Press, 2010," *op. cit.*

58. *Ibid.*

59. Dennis Itumbi, "Kenya's new constitution good news for media," *Journalism.co.za*, August 2010,

www.journalism.co.za/index.php?option=com_content&Itemid=51&catid=168&id=3367&view=article.

60. "National Conference Could Herald Start of New Era for Niger's Media," Reporters Without Borders, April 1, 2010, http://en.rsf.org/niger-national-conference-could-herald-01-04-2010,36931.html.

61. Roy Greenslade, "Two More Journalists Killed in Honduras," *Guardian,* March 29, 2010, www.guardian.co.uk/media/greenslade/2010/mar/29/honduras-press-freedom.

62. "Orel Sambrano," Committee to Protect Journalists, Jan. 16, 2009, http://cpj.org/killed/2009/orel-sambrano.php.

63. "Freedom House Calls on Medvedev to Veto FSB Legislation," Freedom House, July 16, 2020, www.freedomhouse.org/template.cfm?page=70&release=1210.

64. Clive Leviev-Sawyer, "Bulgaria Has Lowest Press Rankings in EU," *Sofia Echo,* Oct. 20, 2009, http://sofiaecho.com/2009/10/20/802401_bulgaria-has-lowest-press-freedom-ranking-in-eu-reporters-without-borders.

65. "Estonian Press Protests Against the Source Protection Act," Estonian Free Press, March 2010, www.estonianfreepress.com/2010/03/estonian-press-protests-against-the-source-protection-act/.

66. "CPJ Welcomes Armenian Vote to Decriminalize Defamation," Committee to Protect Journalists, May 19, 2010, http://cpj.org/2010/05/cpj-welcomes-armenian-vote-to-de criminalize-defama.php.

67. "Second TV Anchor Gunned Down in Two Days in Iraq," Committee to Protect Journalists, Sept. 8, 2010, http://cpj.org/2010/09/second-tv-anchor-gunned-down-in-two-days-in-iraq.php.

68. "Open Letter from Party Elders Calls for Free Speech," China Media Project, Oct. 13, 2010, http://cmp.hku.hk/2010/10/13/8035/.

69. "Abducted British Journalist Freed in Pakistan," Committee to Protect Journalists, Sept. 9, 2010, http://cpj.org/2010/09/abducted-british-journalist-freed-in-pakistan.php.

70. Laura Ling and Euna Lee, "Hostages of the Hermit Kingdom," *Los Angeles Times,* Sept. 1, 2009, www.latimes.com/news/opinion/la-oe-lingleeweb2-2009sep02,0,7489638.story.

71. Oliver Teves, "Nearly 200 People Indicted in Philippine Massacre," The Associated Press, Feb. 9, 2010, http://news.yahoo.com/s/afp/20100908/wl_asia_afp/philippinespoliticsmassacretrial.

72. "Attacks on the Press 2009: Philippines," Committee to Protect Journalists, www.cpj.org/2010/02/attacks-on-the-press-2009-philippines.php.

73. "Philippine massacre victims 'begged for mercy,'" Agence France-Presse, Sept. 7, 2010, http://news.yahoo.com/s/afp/20100908/wl_asia_afp/philippinespoliticsmassacretrial.

74. Simon Montlake, "Philippines massacre trial: a test for justice and accountability," *The Christian Science Monitor*, Sept. 29, 2010; www.csmonitor.com/World/Asia-Pacific/2010/0929/Philippines-massacre-trial-a-test-for-justice-and-accountability. See also "2nd prosecution witness in Maguindanao massacre trial resumes testimony," Philippines News Agency, Oct. 6, 2010.

75. Montlake, *op. cit.*

76. Roy Greenslade, "Filipino Radio Journalists Murdered," *Guardian,* June 18, 2010, www.guardian.co.uk/media/greenslade/2010/jun/18/press-freedom-philippines.

77. Cecil Morella, "Outrage as Two More Journalists Killed in Philippines," Agence France-Presse, June 15, 2010, www.google.com/hostednews/afp/article/ALeqM5hiJCKV53HtMJgAwi8pylquJFi8uA.

78. *Ibid.*

79. "Attacks on the Press 2009: Philippines," *op. cit.*

80. "Getting Away With Murder," Committee to Protect Journalists, April 20, 2010, www.cpj.org/reports/2010/04/cpj-2010-impunity-index-getting-away-with-murder.php.

81. "Restrictions on Press Freedom Intensifying," Freedom House, April 29, 2010, www.freedomhouse.org/template.cfm?page=70&release=1177.

82. *Ibid.*

BIBLIOGRAPHY

Selected Sources

Books

Bollinger, Lee C., *Uninhibited, Robust, and Wide-Open: A Free Press for a New Century,* Oxford University Press, 2010.
The president of Columbia University argues for spreading freedom of the press around the world.

Heinemann, Arnim, Olfa Lamloum and Anne Francoise Weber, eds., *The Middle East in the Media: Conflicts, Censorship and Public Opinion,* Saqi Books, 2010.
The rise of satellite television and the Internet have forced Middle Eastern governments to adapt their censorship methods. The editors are a researcher at the Orient-Institut (Heinemann), a researcher at the Institut Français du Proche-Orient (Lamloum) and a program manager at the Friedrich Ebert Foundation — all in Beirut.

Shirk, Susan L., ed., *Changing Media, Changing China,* Oxford University Press, 2010.
A leading authority on contemporary China edited this collection of essays.

Articles

"'Blogfather,' columnist get heavy prison terms in Iran," Committee to Protect Journalists, Sept. 28, 2010, http://cpj.org/2010/09/iranian-journalist-and-blogfather-receive-heavy-pr.php.
Two prominent journalists were jailed for comments about leading Iranian clerics.

"Philippine massacre victims 'begged for mercy,'" Agence France-Presse, Sept. 7, 2010, http://news.yahoo.com/s/afp/20100908/wl_asia_afp/philippinespoliticsmassacretrial.
During the first trial in the killings of more than 30 journalists in the Philippines, a witness said the victims begged for mercy before being shot.

Aumente, Jerome, "Lessons in Teaching Foreign Journalists," Nieman Reports, summer 2005, www.nieman.harvard.edu/ reportsitem.aspx?id=101136.
A professor emeritus at the School of Communication, Information and Library Studies at Rutgers University reflects on his experience teaching foreign journalists how to avoid the party line and deal with threats of reprisals and kidnappings.

Baldauf, Scott, "Global News Agencies Uneasy over South Africa's Press Freedom," *The Christian Science Monitor,* Sept. 7, 2010, www.csmonitor.com/World/Africa/Africa-Monitor/2010/0907/Global-news-agencies-uneasy-over-South-Africa-s-press-freedom.
In a letter to South African President Jacob Zuma, four syndicated news services express concern over South Africa's plan to create a media tribunal to punish inaccurate reporting and limit scrutiny on much of the government's activities.

Bhattacharji, Preeti, *et al.,* "Media Censorship in China," Council on Foreign Relations, May 27, 2010, www.cfr.org/publication/11515/media_censorship_in_china.html.
A study of China's media climate finds growing demand for information is testing the regime's media controls.

Dehghan, Saeed Kamali, "Iran's Fight for Press Freedom," *Guardian,* Feb. 26, 2010, www.guardian.co.uk/commentisfree/2010/feb/26/iran-press-freedom-fight.
An Iranian reporter examines the crackdown on journalists in Iran, where more than 100 journalists and bloggers have been imprisoned since last year's disputed election.

Londoño, Ernesto, "Iraqi Journalist Sees Threats to Press Freedom," *The Washington Post,* Feb. 26, 2010, www.washingtonpost.com/wp-dyn/content/article/2010/02/25/AR2010022505730.html?sid=ST2010022506210.
Iraqi journalists continue to struggle with government restrictions and targeted violence.

Reports and Studies

"Freedom of the Press 2010," Freedom House, April 29, 2010, www.freedomhouse.org/template.cfm?page=533.
In its 2010 annual report, the pro-democracy watchdog organization found that global media freedom has declined for the eighth year in a row.

"World Press Freedom Index 2010," Reporters Without Borders, Oct. 20, 2010, http://en.rsf.org/press-freedom-index-2010,1034.html.
The press freedom watchdog organization's ninth annual report listed the 10 worst countries for journalists: Rwanda, Yemen, China, Sudan, Syria, Burma, Iran, Turkmenistan, North Korea and Eritrea. These countries were selected because of their "persecution of the media and a complete lack of news and information."

Lauria, Carlos, and Mike O'Connor, "Silence or Death in Mexico's Press," Committee to Protect Journalists, Sept. 8, 2010, http://cpj.org/reports/2010/09/silence-or-death-in-mexicos-press.php.
A special report on the impact of crime, violence and corruption on Mexican journalism concludes that systemic failures, if left unaddressed, will further erode freedom of expression and the rule of law.

For More Information

Access, P.O. Box 115, New York, NY 10113; 888-414-0100; www.accessnow.org. A digital-rights group, founded after protests against Iran's disputed 2009 presidential election, that fosters open communications.

Article 19, Free Word Centre, 60 Farringdon Road, London, United Kingdom, EC1R 3GA; +44 20 7324 2500; www.article19.org. A group named for a section of the Universal Declaration of Human Rights that designs laws and policies promoting freedom of expression.

Committee to Protect Journalists, 330 7th Ave., 11th Floor, New York, NY 10001; 212-465-1004; www.cpj.org. Documents attacks on journalists; publishes its findings and works to promote press freedom.

Freedom House, 1301 Connecticut Ave., N.W., 6th Floor, Washington, DC 20036; 202-296-5101; www.freedomhouse.org. An independent watchdog group founded in 1941 that advocates greater political and civil liberties.

Index on Censorship, Free Word Centre, 60 Farringdon Rd., London, United Kingdom, EC1R 3GA; +44 20 7324 2522; www.indexoncensorship.org. Founded in 1972 to publish stories of communist dissidents in Eastern Europe; promotes global free speech through journalistic reports and advocacy.

International Press Institute, Spielgasse 2, A-1010, Vienna, Austria; +43 1 412 90 11; www.freemedia.at. A global network of media executives and journalists founded in 1950, dedicated to promoting and safeguarding press freedoms.

Reporters Committee for Freedom of the Press, 1101 Wilson Blvd., Suite 1100, Arlington, VA 22209; 703-807-2100; www.rcfp.org. Provides free legal advice and other resources to journalists on First Amendment issues.

5

Journalism Standards in the Internet Age

Are the news media sacrificing ethics online?

Tom Price

Yahoo News produces a growing amount of original news content that is created by experienced journalists following traditional standards, with third-party content on the site produced by responsible news organizations. Many Internet sites, however, do not have the same standards as "legacy" news organizations. Moreover, the Internet culture of speed and interactivity challenges accuracy and invites objectionable reader comments.

CQ Press/Screenshot

From *CQ Researcher*,
Ocotober 8, 2010

In early 2007, reporter Nick Budnick of Oregon's *Portland Tribune* received a tip that former Vice President Al Gore had been accused of sexually assaulting a local masseuse the previous October. On and off for nearly two years, Budnick chased the story.

He studied police reports. He conducted dozens of interviews with the accuser. He examined her phone records. He placed a Craigslist ad that sought other masseuses who had experienced a political figure "cross the line." And, he contemplated with his editors the relevance of the accuser having failed a lie detector exam.

In November 2008, the newspaper's former managing editor, Todd Murphy, later wrote, "the *Tribune* was contemplating an article about highly serious allegations by an unnamed woman who had flunked a polygraph and whose best ally able to vouch for her talking about the assault shortly after it happened was a local homeless man."[1]

The *Tribune* never ran the story.

Was Gore a sex criminal or the innocent victim of an unsubstantiated charge? There were too many unanswered questions for the *Tribune*. According to traditional journalism standards, spiking the story was the proper course. But those standards are not universally followed.

Last June, the *National Enquirer* ran with the story, and news media around the world followed suit. Even then, Murphy said, he still grappled with the same question: "When [is] such a charge 'news'? When are such allegations — white-hot, controversial and

105

Many Web Users Contribute to News

About one-third of Internet users have actively contributed to the creation, commentary or dissemination of news. Commenting has been the most frequent contribution, with one-quarter of all Internet users having commented on an online news story or blog.

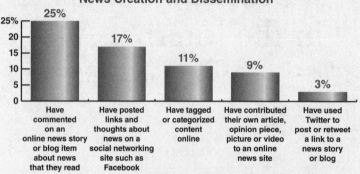

Contributions of Internet Users to News Creation and Dissemination*

* *Note:* Percentages add to more than 33% because some respondents are counted in more than one category.

Source: "How Internet and Cell Phone Users Have Turned News Into a Social Experience," Project for Excellence in Journalism, Pew Research Center, March 2010

potentially containing evidence of real violence — ready for the larger world to judge?"[2]

The sensationalist supermarket tabloid decided the accusation alone was enough to support a breathless cover story headlined "Al Gore Sex Attack!" Other publishers in the Internet Age don't need even that much fact on which to hang a story. Rumor is enough, as the *TechCrunch* website demonstrated on May 5.

"Rumors popped up that Apple may be looking to buy Twitter," *TechCrunch* founder Michael Arrington wrote, quoting a "normally reliable source" as saying that the purchase was "in late-stage negotiations" for a $700-million deal.

Arrington himself doubted the rumor, writing in the same story that "we've checked with other sources who claim to know nothing about any Apple negotiations."[3]

Arrington offered no apologies when the rumor proved false. "It was interesting, and it didn't hurt anyone to write about it," he said. "I don't ever want to lose the rawness of blogging."

One of *TechCrunch's* missions is to report "the scuttlebutt around Silicon Valley," he explained. He doesn't have major media's fact-checking resources, he added. "Getting it right is expensive. Getting it first is cheap."[4]

But "getting it right" is the news media's top responsibility, according to traditional journalism standards.

"You have to want to get it right," University of California journalism Professor Cynthia Gorney wrote in an open letter to journalism students. "Getting it right has to matter to you so much that, if you're going to lie awake at night worrying, getting it right is what you worry about."[5]

Another key standard is verifying information before reporting an unsubstantiated accusation, especially when the allegation is criminal behavior. That "is what separates journalism from other modes of communication," according to Tom Rosenstiel, director of the Project for Excellence in Journalism, and Bill Kovach, former editor of the *Atlanta Journal-Constitution* and chief of *The New York Times* Washington Bureau.[6]

Supermarket tabloids never have held themselves to the Society of Professional Journalists' Code of Ethics. But, with the growth of online news media and 24/7 cable TV news channels, traditional journalism standards are under fire as never before. Many new media journalists argue, like Arrington, that at least some of the traditional standards are out of date. Many mainstream media are loosening standards in their online operations. Even old-school defenders of traditional standards acknowledge that the online world may require some revisions, including creation of new standards to address issues that don't exist in print and broadcast news operations. And severe financial challenges make it more difficult for print and broadcast media to hold onto traditional standards while grappling with the new technologies.

New Yorker press critic A. J. Liebling wrote in 1960 that "freedom of the press is guaranteed only to those who own one."[7] Now, everyone with an Internet connection owns a virtual press that publishes worldwide. And therein lies much of the problem.

"We're making the difficult transition from ethics of a very powerful profession toward an open ethics for a multiplatform journalism that is global in scope and where the practice of journalism is open to citizens," says Stephen Ward, director of the University of Wisconsin's Center for Journalism Ethics.

The transition raises questions about who are journalists, what journalists should be doing and what their standards should be, Ward explains. "We have even more radical questioning [by some online journalists] about whether journalism should have ethics in the first place," he says.

The Internet poses "a lot of challenges to the classical journalism mindset," says Vikki Porter, director of the Knight Digital Media Center at the University of Southern California. "There's not a guidebook out there besides the core value of the integrity of the product itself."

The Internet's hallmarks of speed and interactivity wreak havoc with traditional journalism practices. The always-on nature of the Internet and cable news channels pressures traditional print and broadcast newsrooms — the so-called "legacy media" — to forgo the delays that can be caused by fact-checking. Internet users' expectations that they can comment on the news strains the media's ability to hold all their online content to traditional standards of accuracy and decency. So does the expectation that websites will provide links to outside sources of information.

Moreover, the informal, chatty nature of much online communication pushes reporters to throw off the time-honored cloak of objectivity and reveal more about their personal values and opinions than they traditionally have been allowed to do. And the success of Fox News Channel's conservative programming has led MSNBC to offer counter-programming from the left, in a weakening of the American news media's traditional

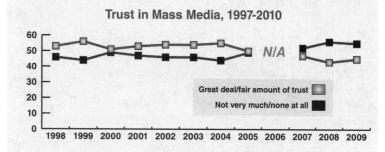

Distrust in U.S. Media Higher Than Ever

For the third year in a row, a majority of Americans — 57 percent — say they have little or no trust in the mainstream media. Conversely, trust in the media dropped from 53 percent in 1998 to 43 percent. In polls taken in the 1970s (not shown), about 70 percent of Americans said they trusted the media.

How much trust and confidence do you have in the mass media — such as newspapers, TV and radio — when it comes to reporting the news fully, accurately and fairly — a great deal, a fair amount, not very much, or none at all?

Trust in Mass Media, 1997-2010

Great deal/fair amount of trust

Not very much/none at all

Source: "Media Use and Evaluation," Gallup Poll, September 2010

commitment to nonpartisan, disinterested, independent and balanced journalism.

"I'm not saying that form of journalism shouldn't exist," Ward says. "But I worry whether this is becoming the dominant mode of journalism because people think that's what people want to watch. I don't think the answer to unbalanced media is to say 50 percent are Fox and 50 percent are liberal."

Some mainstream journalists also worry that opinion's growth online and on cable is infecting the printed news media as well.

When *Forbes* magazine gave its Sept. 27 cover to a heavily criticized, speculative "explanation" of "How Obama Thinks" by conservative writer Dinesh D'Souza,[8] *New York Times* media reporter Tim Arango called it "a cautionary tale for the new media age." *Forbes* published the piece shortly after Internet entrepreneur Lewis D'Vorkin began to oversee content for the magazine and its website, Arango noted. He pictured the business magazine "responding both to the economic imperatives of the digital age by cutting staff and to the editorial imperatives by bringing in more outside voices — Mr. D'Souza

Should Online Comments Be Anonymous?

Newspaper readers see both "the product of sick, angry minds" and "real thinking."

Online commenters themselves disagree about whether comments should be anonymous and if they should be reviewed before publication. Below is a wide range of comments about commenting posted on *The Washington Post* website, which publishes readers' submissions anonymously and does not review them before publication.

— *I never, ever read comments — many are disgusting and the product of sick, angry minds on both the left and the right. In contrast, I love letters to the editor. What's the difference? Letters are SIGNED. Vicious anonymous comments are made by cowards, who are owed shunning, not attention.*

— *Anonymity makes the comments section a cross section of readers' gut reactions and real thinking, however messy that might be. I would miss that.*

— *If The Post wishes to remain credible, you must "take back" the discourse and enforce standards of civility. You would be doing our American society and democracy a huge favor.*

— *Freedom of speech means not just hearing things that we like, but allowing that which we very much dislike.*

— *Posting under one's real name might cut down on the ability to share useful information. I've seen people provide useful insights on their professions and industries, which they might not be able to do under their own names.*

— *I would have had no problem if the WP had forced people to use their real names. It would reduce the amount of garbage that people fling simply because anonymity reduces self-restraint. I realize that there are cases where genuine anonymity is needed, but that can't be more than 1 post in 1,000.*

— *Enduring abusive comments comes with the privilege of the bully pulpit.*

— *We'd all be divorced and/or fired from our jobs if we interacted with each other the way some people do on comment boards — but there is something about the boards that makes people lose sight of how respect and a good hearing are gained in the outside world.*

— *Internet anonymity does not just free people to express hate without fear, but to express the legitimate opinions our society does not treat with the respect it should.*

is not a staff writer — and sometimes elevating opinion above rigorous reporting."[9]

In a Project for Excellence in Journalism survey last year, online journalists — most of whom worked for legacy media websites — said the Internet was changing journalism values for the worse, especially because an emphasis on speed was causing carelessness and inaccuracy.[10]

Slippage in quality is likely when a journalist is given a tight deadline to report a story, then has to write for the newspaper, the website and Twitter, says Jeffrey Dvorkin, executive director of the Organization of News Ombudsmen.

Quality also suffers from staff reductions — especially buyouts of veterans — which leave fewer experienced journalists to report and oversee the reporting,

— *A humble suggestion: limit commenting to actual subscribers. I suspect that the most objectionable comments come from those far, far from the area, and that the best come from the folks who actually take the time to read the physical paper and have a stake in the community.*

— *I also sometimes become angry at abusive posts. But these people are not going to go away as a result of censorship. All these kinds of posters do is discredit the point of view they claim to support in the eyes of most reasonable people.*

— *All I can say is that it's about time that* The Post *did something to deter the endless stream of hate-filled, anonymous comments, which inevitably ruin any chance of having a serious discussion of political issues. Personally, I wish* The Post *would require the same standards here as they do for their letters section — full name and home town to accompany all commentary.*

— *An open forum gives the reader a notion of actually how many loons there are out there and what they believe.*

— *I have pretty much given up reading comments because they are generally so nasty, vindictive or off topic. The issue is about civility and courteous discourse.*

— *While the columnists and reporters at* The Post *may find it inconvenient and unsettling to read criticism of their work, these message boards provide a necessary check and balance to ensure quality.*

— *If WaPo did not permit anonymous postings, the quality of commentary content and nature of discourse would improve overnight.*

— *The WP message boards provide a place for spirited debate, and can provide balance to stories that can sometimes be blatantly biased. They make* The Post *interesting, and on a personal level, they provide me the opportunity to add facts to a story (usually editorials) that either subvert the truth or "conveniently" leave out a key fact in a story.*

— *Like pretty much everyone I know, I've found the overwhelming bulk of those "Comments" to be completely devoid of substance, full of bile, and accomplishing little more than driving these discussions down to the lowest common denominator. At the very least, everyone who posts should have a verifiable home address and phone number, even if it's not posted along with the message. You hold to this standard for letters in the print edition. Is there any reason not to do this for online Comments?*

— *In today's world of political correctness and employers who look for your trail on the internet, being able to comment anonymously is ESSENTIAL.*

— ***Compiled and excerpted by Tom Price***

---

says Jane Kirtley, director of the University of Minnesota's Silha Center for the Study of Media Ethics and Law. "Copy editors used to catch factual errors, spelling errors and other errors that aren't being caught now," she explains. *Washington Post* Ombudsman Andrew Alexander attributes his newspaper's "uneven" enforcement of standards online to managers' preoccupation with "issues of survival."

Despite the challenges, Online News Association Executive Director Jane McDonnell thinks the traditional media are doing a pretty good job on the Internet. "When you think about the sheer volume of information that's going out now from every single platform into every single distribution system," she says, "the level of professionalism is really high."

As journalists grapple with these new ethical challenges, here are some of the questions they are asking:

Should journalistic websites permit anonymous comments?

Connie Schultz's approach to journalism changed the day Cleveland's *Plain Dealer* published her 2009 column about a factory worker who killed himself in depression after losing his job. The man's 30-year-old daughter, the source for the column, had left a voice-mail message that was nearly unintelligible because she was sobbing so hard.

"You never told me people would say those things about my father," Schultz remembers the woman crying. "My mother says she'll never talk to me again" for sharing the family's tragedy with the world.

Those "people" were *Plain Dealer* readers who posted anonymous comments about the father on the newspaper's website.

The daughter, a nurse, had described her father's reluctance to work in a Wal-Mart distribution center, where he felt the team-building chants were demeaning. She described him curled in the fetal position, bemoaning his inability to support his family, which she viewed as a symptom of depression. The commenters wondered what kind of Christian kills himself, what kind of man would not work at Wal-Mart, Schultz recalls.

"It changed me," Schultz says of the experience. "Over the years, I've done a lot of columns about hourly wage-earners, servers who get their tips skimmed, factory workers. Now I really hesitate in naming them because the comments section becomes so ugly so quickly. I very seldom do personal columns because they go after my family and my friends." Other columns don't get written because subjects refuse to cooperate out of fear of what might be said about them.

The Plain Dealer is hardly unique. A few news organizations review comments before they're published online. But most do not, and vile comments are common on those sites. At *WashingtonPost.com,* for example, politicians' deaths inspire a special brand of venom.

After former Sen. Ted Stevens died in a plane crash, one commenter noted that the Alaska Republican perished "on a free junket with a defense contractor. Who says God doesn't have a sense of humor?" West Virginia Sen. Robert Byrd's death brought the comment that he

was "a scumbag, racist KKKer, hood wearing poster child of the left."[11] When former Vice President Dick Cheney was hospitalized, a commenter asked: "Why tell us when this neanderthal is ill . . . just tell us when he is dead."

Reporters across the country complain that vile comments create reluctant sources. Some, like Schultz, monitor comments about their stories so the worst can be deleted. Others simply avoid reading them at all.

"Like a lot of reporters here, I stopped worrying about (or even reading, to be honest) the commenters long, long ago," *Post* reporter Paul Duggan wrote during an online chat. *Post* sports writer Tracee Hamilton avoids comments because "the vitriol is remarkable."[12]

The worst comments appear on websites that allow unedited, anonymous postings, which most news media sites allow. Such comments would not be found in print editions because almost all newspapers require letters to the editor to be signed and civil.

Editors defend anonymous commenting on the Web as popular with readers and in the tradition of anonymous political commentary that stretches back to the American Revolution. At a time of declining revenues, they add, they can't afford to hire the staff necessary to review all comments ahead of time or even to monitor them shortly after they're published.

The Post receives more than 320,000 comments a month, up a third from last year, and they arrive round the clock, according to *Post* Ombudsman Alexander, "so someone enjoys it." Many readers have told him they hold sensitive jobs that would prevent them from signing their names to comments, he says. Acknowledging that comments can be "brutal" and "devastating," he remains "just very hesitant to limit that type of speech."

Other journalists refuse to accept the practice.

The New York Times is among the handful of news media that review comments before they're published online, as does *The Roanoke Times,* which allows commenting on only a limited number of stories.

"I'm a strong advocate for comments on websites," *Roanoke Times* Editor Carole Tarrant says, "but if you open that door you have to take the responsibility to moderate them. The kind of garbage you see out there, I think the public sees that as reflecting on you, your newspaper and journalism."

Many news organizations allow readers to flag objectionable comments that editors then review and possibly remove. But that's not good enough for Robert Steele, director of the Prindle Institute for Ethics at DePauw University.

"It's like letting someone drive drunk and cause an accident and then bring them in," Steele says. "If somebody posts racist or homophobic words, and then you take the post down, there's been harm caused in the meantime. In the digital arena, stuff is passed along rapidly and it's cached. If it's expunged from your website, that doesn't mean it isn't still out there. And you can't take away the wounds from those who have been hurt."

Anonymous postings also can deceive the public, in violation of the most basic journalism standard for accuracy, according to Howard Owens, publisher of *TheBatavian.com,* an online news site in upstate New York.

"Newspapers set themselves up for a horrendous ethical dilemma when they create a situation whereby public officials, who have obvious conflicts of interest, can support their own agenda, or oppose another's, through anonymous, unfiltered and unvetted commenting," he wrote in his blog. "The public, for example, has a right to know if the person pushing cuts to local bus routes is the politician who wrote the legislation or just some well-informed citizen."[13]

Should news media be held legally responsible for all material on their own websites?

News media aren't legally liable for scurrilous, anonymous comments because of the Communications Decency Act of 1996. The law was intended to shield minors from "indecent" online content. It also exempted Internet service providers from liability for content posted by other parties, the way telephone companies aren't held responsible for what people say over phone lines.

Courts later held that online news organizations were covered by that protection.[14] Ironically, the Supreme Court struck down the act's indecency provisions,

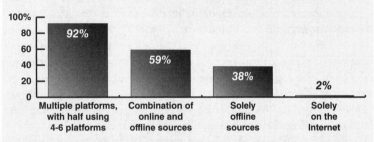

Most Get News From Multiple Platforms

More than 90 percent of Americans rely on a variety of sources — print, online and broadcast — to get their news on a typical day. About 40 percent still rely exclusively on newspapers and other offline sources. Only 2 percent rely exclusively on the Internet.

How Americans Access News on a Typical Day

- Multiple platforms, with half using 4-6 platforms: 92%
- Combination of online and offline sources: 59%
- Solely offline sources: 38%
- Solely on the Internet: 2%

Source: "How Internet and Cell Phone Users Have Turned News Into a Social Experience," Project for Excellence in Journalism, Pew Research Center, March 2010

finding them in violation of First Amendment free-speech protections. But the court let the liability protection stand. As a result, when obscene and other objectionable materials are posted online, Internet service providers and website operators can't be sued or prosecuted successfully.[15]

Many free-speech advocates argue that legitimate online expression would be inhibited if providers and website operators had to worry about what their users post. Others contend that news media shouldn't be given such a free pass.

"It would be a dangerous precedent to say everything that's ever posted on their site, even if it's just up for 30 seconds, would be legally actionable," says Craig Silverman, managing editor of PBS's "MediaShift" and a *Columbia Journalism Review* columnist. "That would probably end up being a chill on free speech. You would have organizations walking back their websites to the point there is no interaction."

Every news organization would shut down its comments and stop taking any user-generated content, predicts Jim Brady, general manager of *TBD*, an online and cable news organization in the Washington, D.C., area. "It would make the sites far less interesting than they need to be."

DePauw University's Steele, however, finds the avoidance of responsibility "ethically bankrupt. It is just asinine that news organizations throw up their hands in a Pontius Pilate fashion by saying 'It's not our problem.'"

The law "doesn't remove ethical responsibility," agrees Al Tompkins, group leader for broadcasting and online at the Poynter Institute, a journalism education organization in St. Petersburg, Fla.

The ethical debate about responsibility extends to all of a news organization's online content. There's little argument that the organizations are responsible for what their staffs produce. But what about content that's supplied by outside organizations, or the content on websites that news organization's link to?

A news organization diminishes its brand when it links to a site that doesn't adhere to the same standards, *Washington Post* Ombudsman Alexander says. "We have a responsibility to make sure what we link to is credible and balanced."

The Online News Association's McDonnell suggests that editors examine sites before linking, to make sure they're appropriate and helpful to readers. Editors then should "continually vet over and over again," the University of Wisconsin's Ward says. Because a news organization can't review every piece of content on every site it links to, it should warn readers when they are about to leave its site, Kirtley at the University of Minnesota advises.

It can be appropriate to link to a site with offensive content if the link enhances a story, Steele says. "But there has to be a significant journalistic purpose at a very high threshold." And readers must be clearly informed of what lies at the other end of the link, he adds.

During a Poynter Institute attempt to create guidelines for online journalism ethics, journalists disagreed about whether news organizations should allow readers to post links with their comments.

"It's a crucial part of the debate," *MSNBC.com* Executive Editor Thomas Brew said. "If someone abuses such a policy (or any policy), delete him/her." Someone — perhaps readers — would need to check the appropriateness of the links, *St. Petersburg Times* Media and TV critic Eric Deggans said.[16]

Media Bloggers Association President Robert Cox opposes such links, warning that "allowing commenters to place links into a site is an invitation to finding vile,

outrageous images and video on your site. What I do know from personal experience is that there are two kinds of websites: those that have been infested with vile, foulmouthed, disgusting trolls and those that will be."

Even if news organizations aren't held responsible for objectionable content posted by others, they should be held accountable for how they address the material after it appears on their sites, Silverman and Tompkins contend.

"I lean toward enabling them to have people participate in discussions, but to have a mechanism in place to remove things that are libelous or contravene the law," Silverman says.

"I think we can accept that when things move fast there are going to be more troublesome things that go up," Tompkins explains. "If [an objectionable] comment gets posted, how quickly do we remove it and what actions do we take against the violator?"

Should news media allow their reporters to express opinions?

It seemed appropriate that Raju Narisetti, *The Washington Post's* managing editor for online operations, would be active on Twitter. Some of his tweets turned out to be inappropriate, however, according to the traditional journalism standards that still hold sway at *The Post.*

"We can incur all sorts of federal deficits for wars and what not," he tweeted last year. "But we have to promise not to increase it by $1 for healthcare reform? Sad." Shortly thereafter, when 91-year-old Democratic Sen. Robert Byrd of West Virginia was hospitalized following a September fall, Narisetti wrote: "How about term limits. Or retirement age. Or common-sense to prevail."

After some *Post* staffers questioned the propriety of the tweets, Narisetti tweeted again: "For flagbearers of free speech, some newsroom execs have the weirdest double standards when it comes to censoring personal views."

Then, following a meeting with *Post* Executive Editor Marcus Brauchli, Narisetti changed his tune. He realized that expressing his opinion, even though he intended to reach just a small, private audience, created "a clear perception problem."[17]

In the wake of Narisetti's tweeting, *The Post* issued guidelines for online social networks that warned reporters: "What you do on social networks should be presumed to be publicly available to anyone, even if you have created a private account." And: *"Post* journalists must refrain from writing, tweeting or posting anything . . . that could be perceived as reflecting political, racial, sexist, religious or other bias or favoritism that could be used to tarnish our journalistic credibility."[18]

Such guidelines — which reflect longtime, widespread bans on reporters and news editors expressing opinions — are under attack as out-of-date in the Internet Age.

"Attempting to pretend that you have no opinions or views is to pretend that you are not human," charged Amy Gahran, a communications consultant, blogger and freelance journalist. "This is fundamentally not credible."[19]

David Weinberger, a senior researcher at Harvard University's Berkman Center for Internet & Society, argues that "transparency is the new objectivity." Objective journalists act as if they have no opinions, he said. They'd gain more credibility by acknowledging their points of view and showing how they go about their work, he argued.

He recalled an exchange he had with longtime Associated Press political writer Walter Mears. After Weinberger asked whom Mears was supporting in the 2004 presidential campaign, Mears responded, in effect, "If I tell you, how can you trust what I write?" Weinberger then asked Mears: "If you don't tell us, how can we trust what you blog?"

"The problem with objectivity," Weinberger argued, "is that it tries to show what the world looks like from no particular point of view, which is like wondering what something looks like in the dark."[20]

Journalists need to reveal a point of view in order to succeed on the Internet, according to Robert Niles, a Web editor and consultant who previously worked as a newspaper reporter and editorial writer. "If you want to attract an audience in the competitive, online information market, I think you need to choose some values to believe in, and to express them, defend them and practice them before your audience. Readers know that they have more choices [and] want to know whose side you are on."[21]

That's precisely the problem, say supporters of traditional standards.

"They want to know the point of view of the journalists so they can dismiss them," Dvorkin at the Organization of News Ombudsmen says.

When critics argue a reader needs to know a journalist's point of view in order to evaluate his work, they are assuming the reporter can't set aside his personal opinions when doing his job, Minnesota's Kirtley argues. "But that's not a view I share. Part of being a professional is being able to do that."

DePauw's Steele likens a reporter's skills to those of a jurist. "Judges have opinions," he says, "but they function professionally in a role in which they subjugate their personal beliefs in their duty to the judicial process." Reporters can do the same, he insists.

Some journalists even give up voting so they never have to answer, refuse to answer or dodge the question: "Who did you vote for?" Former *Washington Post* Executive Editor Leonard Downie Jr. was among them, as is current *Post* politics writer and editor Chris Cillizza.

"I think, unfortunately, that people would interpret any vote I made as some sort of indication of my political leanings," Cillizza explained. "The desire to 'prove' a political reporter's 'real' partisanship is just so toxic that, for me, it's not worth it."[22]

Cillizza's position is "extreme" in the eyes of Porter at the University of Southern California's Knight Digital Media Center. She would like to know something about reporters' personal opinions, and she's following with interest the *Patch.com* news site's experiment in putting that information in reporters' and editors' online biographies.

"It becomes a plus-minus" for the reporter who reveals his or her opinions, she says. "He's going to attract some people and repel some people. In his work, he's got to show that those positions aren't influencing how he does what he does."

Revealing or concealing reporters' opinions is "not hard and fast anymore," says Porter. "It would be crazy for *The Washington Post,* because [disinterested political coverage] is their franchise."

BACKGROUND
In the Beginning

The University of Wisconsin's Ward, author of *The Invention of Journalism Ethics,* traces 20th-century American journalism standards to 17th-century England and the very beginning of periodical news media.[23]

There were no codes of journalism standards, but publishers proclaimed their allegiance to accuracy and impartiality. Some publications separated news from commentary. Some journalists focused on facts, others on opinion.

Their motivation to a great extent was to avoid conflict with a government that controlled publishing through licensing and censorship, and the standards often were honored in the breach. The result, Ward said, was a "mix of puffery, opportunism, toadying to authority and concern for truth."

Opinion and inaccuracy were common. Newspapers played partisan roles as England went through civil war in mid-century. The end of licensing in 1695 ushered in a new era of greater independence.

In 1702, London's *Daily Courant* announced that it would "relate only Matter of Fact, supposing other people to have Sense enough to make reflections for themselves."[24] That statement anticipated the quintessential motto of 20th-century American journalism, which was adopted by the Scripps Howard newspapers in the 1920s: "Give light and the people will find their own way."[25]

Also foreshadowed in the 18th century were today's worries that the speed of Internet communication degrades journalism. French writer Benjamin Constant complained in 1797 that "the necessity of writing everyday is the tomb of talent."[26]

As the 1700s progressed, the press grew in influence until philosopher and political leader Edmund Burke raised it above Britain's traditional three estates — clergy, nobility and commons — in the latter part of the century. "Burke said there were Three Estates in Parliament," British historian and essayist Thomas Carlyle wrote, "but in the Reporters' Gallery yonder, there sat a Fourth Estate more important than they all."[27]

Despite proclamations to the contrary, partisanship and opinion defined the newspapers of the time. And in Britain's American colonies, journalists agitated for revolution.

"The Business of Printing has chiefly to do with Men's Opinions," Benjamin Franklin wrote in 1731. Another 18th-century journalist declared: "Professions of impartiality I shall make none. They are always useless, and are besides perfect nonsense."[28]

Rise of Standards

Following the American Revolution, U.S. publishers turned on each other, often financed by the political parties they supported. During the first third of the 19th century, historian Frank Luther Mott wrote, editors filled American newspapers with "scurrility," "vulgar attack on personal character," "vituperative political attack," "vile innuendo" and "corruption." It was, Mott declared, "a kind of Dark Ages of American journalism."[29]

It was also a time of diversity, as different publications practiced reporting, opinion and nonpartisan analysis. Some publishers embraced impartiality as a means of appealing to the largest number of readers. But only 5 percent of American newspapers were considered "neutral and independent" in 1850.

The march toward the commonly accepted standards of the late-20th century accelerated with the demand for accurate news about the Civil War and the development of wire services that supplied news to many clients.

A variety of newspapers organized The Associated Press in 1848 to supply news they all could use. Their journalistic styles ranged from elite to sensational, and their editors held conflicting positions on the major issues of the day, such as slavery and party politics. Lawrence Gobright, AP's first Washington correspondent, described how writing for that diverse audience affected his job. "My instructions do not allow me to make any comments upon the facts which I communicate. I try to write without regard to men or politics."[30]

By mid-century, journalism standards began to be codified, at first in the form of instructions by publishers to their staffs. In 1860, the future of journalism standards was laid out by *The New York Times,* which said it planned to "publish facts, in such a form and temper as to lead men of all parties to rely upon its statements of facts."[31] In 1896, *Times* Publisher Adolph S. Ochs added that his newspaper would "give the news impartially, without fear or favor, regardless of party, sect or interests involved." The statement resonated with newspaper editors around the country, who reprinted it.[32]

In the 1870s, state press associations began to draft codes of standards. By 1880, 25 percent of U.S. newspapers were dropping partisan affiliations and calling themselves independent, neutral or just local. By 1890, that rose to a third. Other papers began calling themselves Republican Independent or Democrat Independent, indicating they leaned toward a particular party but wouldn't necessarily support it all the time.

CHRONOLOGY

1848-1911 *Newspapers move toward accuracy, independence. Journalism becomes a profession; journalism schools are established.*

1848 Newspapers with varied political views create Associated Press to provide even-handed news reporting.

1850 Just 5 percent of U.S. newspapers are "neutral and independent."

1860 *The New York Times* declares its "proper business is to publish facts."

1861 Great interest in Civil War creates increasing demand for accurate reporting.

1870s State press associations begin to draft ethics codes.

1878 University of Missouri offers first college journalism courses.

1880 A quarter of U.S. newspapers say they are independent, neutral or just local.

1890 A third of U.S. newspapers declare their independence.

1893 University of Pennsylvania's Wharton School of Business develops a journalism curriculum.

1894 First comprehensive journalism textbook declares: "The mission of the reporter (is) to reproduce facts and the opinions of others, not to express his own."

1896 *New York Times* Publisher Adolph S. Ochs pledges to "give the news impartially, without fear or favor, regardless of party, sect or interests involved."

1904 University of Illinois offers four-year journalism curriculum.

1908 University of Missouri opens first journalism school.

1911 *The Writing of News* declares that "news writing is objective."

1923-1967 *Objectivity, independence and social responsibility become major newspaper watchwords.*

1923 American Society of Newspaper Editors advocates objectivity, responsibility, independence, truthfulness, impartiality and decency.

1926 Truth and objectivity called top goals for journalists in ethics code of Sigma Delta Chi, a predecessor of the Society of Professional Journalists.

1950s-60s Newspapers embrace social responsibility, accept obligation to air diverse views and probe serious issues.

1967 Defense Department studies how to create a computer network, eventually spawning the Internet.

1990-Present *The Internet revolutionizes journalism, challenges traditional industry standards.*

1991 Restrictions on commercial Internet activities rescinded. . . . World Wide Web is invented.

1993 First graphical Internet browser invented, opening door for comprehensive online journalism. . . . *The New York Times* goes online.

1998 Cybergossip Matt Drudge reveals *Newsweek* investigation of Clinton-Lewinsky affair before the magazine is ready to publish, launching a trend toward online publication without thorough verification.

1999 All but two of 100 largest newspapers publish online editions.

2008 More Americans get news from Internet than from newspapers, but newspapers top Internet as local news source.

2009 American Society of Newspaper Editors becomes American Society of News Editors; Radio and Television News Directors Association becomes Radio Television Digital News Association.

2010 Apple exempts political cartoonists from its ban on iPhone applications that are "offensive or mean-spirited," a sign that electronic devices and online businesses are performing like publishers.

Many Media Mistakes, But Few Corrections

Pressure to deliver news faster digitally erodes accuracy.

Newspaper corrections can be amusing, such as this one from the *Dallas Morning News*. "An Oct. 19 article on songwriter John Bucchino incorrectly stated that he doesn't read. The sentence should have said he doesn't read music."[1]

The errors that produce corrections are not funny at all, however, and some research indicates that news media make mistakes more often than they realize and that they correct a smaller proportion of their errors than they think they do. With the speed demands of the Internet and the cutbacks in many news staffs, the situation is getting worse, in the public's view.

According to a Gallup Poll released on Sept. 29, 57 percent of Americans say they have little or no confidence that the mass media report the news fully, accurately and fairly, up from 46 percent in 1997.[2] A survey by the Pew Research Center for the People and the Press last July found that 63 percent said news stories often are inaccurate, up 10 percentage points in just two years.[3]

Several recent studies indicate the public is right.

Research shows that between 40 and 60 percent of newspaper news stories contain some type of error, according to Craig Silverman, a Canadian journalist who collects information about errors and corrections for his website, *www.RegretTheError.com*. Research published in 2007 by Scott Maier, an associate professor at the University of Oregon School of Journalism and Communication, found that newspapers correct only 2 percent of their mistakes.[4]

Silverman acknowledges that those figures may be exaggerated. Researchers asked sources in news stories if the story was correct, then checked for corrections. The statistics don't tell whether the alleged error was major or minor, whether the claim of error was legitimate or whether the source notified the news organization of the alleged mistake. Nevertheless, Silverman believes that the news media make too many mistakes and that research shows the error rate is growing.

A *Columbia Journalism Review* study this year found that magazines do not edit their websites as carefully as they edit their print editions.[5] Interviews with magazine staffers revealed that half of website content is not edited at all or is edited less rigorously than print content. A third of staffers interviewed said their magazines applied a lower standard for fact-checking online content, and 8 percent said no online fact-checking is done.

"There's great pressure on news organizations to deliver more news faster digitally, and those pressures often erode the standards of accuracy, fairness and completeness," says Robert Steele, a professor of journalism ethics and director of the Prindle Institute for Ethics at DePauw University. "The cutbacks in staffing mean diminishing expertise and fewer journalists to cover even more stories than ever before."

Online journalists also are tempted to publish incomplete and possibly inaccurate stories because corrections and updates can be published quickly, Steele adds. "That's a weak argument," he says, "because it can diminish

In the late-19th century the need for ethics codes seemed to grow greater as newspapers grew larger and more powerful, and their owners built influential newspaper chains.

"Journalists themselves are sitting in newsrooms and they're starting to worry about their own ability to be accurate informers, because advertisers, business interests and the publishers themselves are threatening [the journalists'] independence," Ward explains.

As a mark of journalism's growing professionalism, the University of Missouri offered the first college journalism courses in 1878. Other colleges began to teach journalism in English departments and schools of

commerce. The University of Pennsylvania's Wharton School of Business developed a journalism curriculum in 1893. Students could study a four-year curriculum at the University of Illinois in 1904. Missouri opened the first journalism school in 1908.

Accuracy and Objectivity

Journalists and journalism educators wrote textbooks that stressed objectivity and accuracy. In the first comprehensive journalism textbook, published in 1894, *Chicago Tribune* Literary Editor Edwin Shuman advised students that "the mission of the reporter (is) to substantive reporting that truly informs the public and because incomplete, erroneous and unfair information can cause great harm."

Some websites unabashedly publish unverified information, which puts additional pressure on competitors to cut corners.

That's a perilous path for mainstream news organizations to follow, according to Jane Kirtley, director of the Silha Center for the Study of Media Ethics and Law at the University of Minnesota.

"It seems to me the main thing the legacy [traditional] media have to offer is context and verification," Kirtley explains. "If they aren't doing that, you have to ask what they have to offer that the neighborhood blogger doesn't."

Corrections can be as important as accuracy, because they set the erroneous record straight. "Surveys show people feel better when they see corrections because they can see an accountability process going on," Silverman says.

Newspapers have followed *The New York Times* in publishing corrections prominently in the same place every day, where readers know to look for them, Silverman says. Many news organizations attach corrections to online stories. But, in most cases, readers of an erroneous story won't see the correction unless they look at the story again.

In a study this year of 28 San Francisco-area websites, most made it difficult for readers to report mistakes and to find published corrections. The study was conducted by MediaBugs, a nonprofit organization funded by the Knight Foundation to help readers get corrections in local news media.[6]

The foundation's Knight News Challenge funded MediaBugs as a pilot project to promote corrections and to recognize organizations that admit and fix their errors.

Requests for corrections will be tracked to see if the mistakes are corrected and if the requests lead to a conversation between the person requesting the correction and the journalist alleged to have made the mistake.[7]

The online magazine *Slate* has adopted perhaps the most comprehensive correction policy online. In addition to attaching a correction to an erroneous article, *Slate* — which is owned by *The Washington Post* — publishes a corrections page, puts all corrections on its home page once a week, and allows readers to register for an RSS feed that sends them all corrections.[8]

— *Tom Price*

---

[1] Chip Scanlan, "We Stand Corrected: When Good Journalists Make Stupid Mistakes," PoynterOnline, Dec. 12, 2007, www.poynter.org/column.asp?id=52&aid=134345.

[2] Lymari Morales, "Distrust in U.S. Media Edges Up to Record High," Gallup Poll, Sept. 29, 2010, www.gallup.com/poll/143267/Distrust-Media-Edges-Record-High.aspx?utm_source=alert&utm_medium=email&utm_campaign=syndication&utm_content=morelink&utm_term=Politics.

[3] "Press Accuracy Rating Hits Two Decade Low," Pew Research Center for the People and the Press, Sept. 13, 2009, http://people-press.org/report/543/.

[4] Scanlan, *op. cit.*

[5] Craig Silverman, "CJR report highlights how magazine websites handle online corrections, fact checking," March 1, 2010, www.regrettheerror.com.

[6] "Hard to get a fix," MediaBugs, July 2010, http://mediabugs.org/pages/hard-to-get-a-fix-state-of-bay-area-corrections-july-2010.

[7] "MediaBugs," Knight News Challenge, June 17, 2009, www.newschallenge.org/winner/2009/mediabugs.

[8] Scanlan, *op. cit.*

---

reproduce facts and the opinions of others, not to express his own."[33] In *The Writing of News in 1911,* Charles G. Ross declared that "news writing is objective."[34]

Objectivity claimed a prominent spot in the codes of the American Society of Newspaper Editors, in 1923, and Sigma Delta Chi, a precursor to the Society of Professional Journalists, in 1926. The editors' code also called for responsibility, independence, truthfulness, impartiality and decency. The professional fraternity declared truth to be a journalist's ultimate goal and objectivity to be "a standard of performance toward which we strive."[35]

By the 1930s, mainstream newspapers gave widespread support to objectivity and other tenets of the codes. News and opinion were to be separated. Reporters should be balanced, fair, disinterested, accurate and independent. Even editorial writers and columnists should arrive at their opinions independent of political parties or other interests.

But 20th-century tabloids produced a great deal of sensationalism, and independence from political parties didn't always apply to those who owned the presses. The 1920 presidential election gave Americans the all-Ohio-newspaper-publisher campaign. Republican Warren

Anonymous Comments Traced to Judge's Computer

"Not to disclose this would be a violation of our mission," paper's editor says.

The anonymous comments on the Cleveland *Plain Dealers* website revealed an insider's knowledge of Cuyahoga County Common Pleas Judge Shirley Strickland Saffold's courtroom. The postings, under the screen name "lawmiss," also could be quite offensive.

"Rufus Sims did a disservice to his client," lawmiss wrote about the attorney for a vehicular homicide defendant in Saffold's court. "If only he could shut his Amos and Andy style mouth. There are so many lawyers that could've done a much better job. Amos and Andy, shuffling around did not do it."[1]

Another lawmiss posting criticized a jury in Saffold's court for sentencing a man to life in prison, instead of execution, for committing multiple murders.

"If a black guy had massacred five people then he would've received the death penalty," lawmiss wrote. "A white guy does it and he gets pat on the hand. The jury didn't care about the victims. They were set to cut him loose from day one. All of them ought to be ashamed."[2]

But it was lawmiss' comment about the mental state of a relative of *Plain Dealer* reporter Jim Ewinger that led the newspaper to wonder who this commenter really was.

Reporters checked records at *cleveland.com*, the newspaper's website, to find the email address that was used to create the lawmiss account. They traced the address to Saffold and, using public records law, traced many of lawmiss' postings to a computer in Saffold's office. They also discovered the computer had been used to post comments to at least 10 other websites. Some of the comments disparaged Arabs, Asians, white men, homosexuals and police.[3]

Saffold denied posting the comments, and her 23-year-old daughter claimed responsibility for posting some. Legal experts told *The Plain Dealer* that the judge could be disciplined if it is established that she did post comments about cases in her court.[4] She already has been removed from at least one case.[5]

Saffold has clashed with *The Plain Dealer* repeatedly during her 16 years on the bench, especially with Ewinger, who was the Common Pleas court beat reporter until about a decade ago.[6] And, after *The Plain Dealer* published its findings in March, the judge filed a $50-million breach-of-privacy lawsuit against the newspaper. She charged *The Plain Dealer* with violating a pledge of privacy made to its website users, even though the site reserves the right to "use

G. Harding, publisher of *The Marion Star,* defeated Democrat James Cox, publisher of the *Dayton Daily News.*

Broadcast media developed their own codes in the 1940s and '50s. As newspapers became richer and more powerful — and monopolistic — in the second half of the 20th century they embraced the need to be socially responsible. In addition to providing accurate and objective reporting, they were to provide a forum for diverse views and to probe serious issues that might not grab large readership.

To underscore their independence, major papers and broadcast news media forbade reporters from accepting gifts from sources and insisted on paying the costs when reporters traveled with politicians or sports teams or ate while on the job. Strict conflict of interest policies were

adopted. Business reporters were restricted in how they could invest. Some news organizations even prevented their sports reporters from voting for hall-of-fame inductees or player-of-the-year awards. When major college football conferences created the Bowl Championship Series in the early 1990s, The Associated Press wouldn't allow the AP Poll to be used in determining which teams would play. These all were seen as conflicts of interest.

The fact that codes exist doesn't mean all news organizations always use them, however. News media ombudsmen frequently complain that their organization's codes are well-written but not well-obeyed. And the Poynter Institute's Tompkins warns journalists not to paint too rosy a picture of the past.

the information we collect about your computer, which may at times be able to identify you, for any lawful business purpose."[7]

Identifying lawmiss could have a chilling effect on conversations at the newspaper's website, Rebecca Jeschke, the Electronic Frontier Foundation's media relations director, charged. But others came to *The Plain Dealers* defense.[8]

"Ordinarily, if you encourage anonymity, it should remain that way," Case Western Reserve University Law Professor Lewis Katz said. "But if a person is abusing the process, and the person's identity is available, I don't see why [the newspaper] should not identify the person," especially a judge.[9]

Plain Dealer Editor Susan Goldberg has been a defender of anonymous comments that aren't edited before publication. "We all want to promote a freewheeling conversation in the medium increasingly at the center of how we disseminate news and information," she wrote in a 2009 column that acknowledged the objectionable nature of much anonymous commentary. Her newspaper doesn't have enough staff to review comments before publication, she said, and she worried that requiring signed comments would "bring online conversation to a halt."[10]

In the lawmiss case, however, Goldberg argued that *The Plain Dealer* had an obligation to identify the judge because a potential miscarriage of justice in a capital case was at stake.

"What if it ever came to light that someone using the email of a sitting judge made comments on a public website about cases she was hearing, and we did not disclose it?" she asked. "These are capital crimes and life-and-death issues for these defendants. I think not to disclose this would be a violation of our mission and damaging to our credibility as a news organization."[11]

— *Tom Price*

[1] James F. McCarty, "Anonymous online comments are linked to the personal e-mail account of Cuyahoga County Common Pleas Judge Shirley Strickland Saffold," *The Plain Dealer of Cleveland*, March 26, 2010, http://blog.cleveland.com/metro/2010/03/post_258.html.

[2] *Ibid.*

[3] Gabriel Baird, "'Lawmiss' left comments on other websites; Some of the postings take aim at Arabs, Asians, other groups," *The Plain Dealer*, May 9, 2010, p. A1, http://blog.cleveland.com/metro/2010/05/lawmiss_comments_found_on_othe.html.

[4] McCarty, *op. cit.*

[5] Baird, *op. cit.* p. A1.

[6] McCarty, *op. cit.*

[7] Leila Atassi, "Judge sues PD, says it breached privacy; Saffold, daughter seek $50 million," *The Plain Dealer*, April 8, 2010, p. A1, http://blog.cleveland.com/metro/2010/04/cuyahoga_county_judge_shirley.html.

[8] Henry J. Gomez, "Plain Dealer sparks ethical debate by unmasking anonymous Cleveland.com poster," *The Plain Dealer*, March 26, 2010, http://blog.cleveland.com/metro/2010/03/plain_dealer_sparks_ethical_de.html.

[9] *Ibid.*

[10] Susan Goldberg, "Anonymity of the Internet attracts anger's poster children," *The Plain Dealer*, May 12, 2009, www.cleveland.com/opinion/index.ssf/2009/05/anonymity_of_the_internet_attr.html.

[11] Gomez, *op. cit.*

"I've worked for enough news organizations to know that we shouldn't give advertisers preferential treatment, but I know it goes on," Tompkins says. "We shouldn't treat sources favorably because they're good to us, but it happens. It's almost folklore that there was a time when everyone was fair and we all had professional standards that everyone adhered to. It's never been as tidy as 'everybody plays by the same rules.'"

CURRENT SITUATION
New Challenges

Florida minister Terry Jones' plan to burn copies of the Koran illustrates the challenge mainstream media face whenever new media, operating under different standards, publish materials the old media normally would not.

Before the Internet, Jones' threat would not have become a global sensation. Newspapers and broadcast news media would have ignored the obscure pastor with fewer than 50 members in his congregation. No one beyond the reach of his unamplified voice would ever hear of his plan.

With the Internet, news media no longer serve as "gatekeepers" who sort the wheat from the chaff before publishing their newspapers and magazines or airing their broadcasts. Now, the chaff can grab public attention on its own.

It took a while, but what Jones began with a few anti-Islamic Twitter and Facebook posts on July 12 exploded into a heated worldwide controversy that led to protests, riots and deaths. Information about Jones' plan was publicized first by Islamic websites. CNN interviewed him in late July. In early August, condemnation of the planned burning circulated among Islamic Facebook users. In early September, news media in Muslim countries replayed the CNN interview (which was circulating on the Internet), a large protest was held in Indonesia, Muslim outrage escalated, high-ranking government officials around the world urged the preacher to back off, and soon all the world's media were covering the story.[36]

Most mainstream media did not cover Jones until the protests, riots and comments by prominent public officials created a story too big to be ignored.

"In the past, you were competing against people who had very similar standards to you," Kirtley at the University of Minnesota's Silha Center for the Study of Media Ethics and Law says. "Now you're competing against people who can speak to the world but who don't have the same standards." Challenges also are posed by what has become the Internet culture of speed and interactivity.

A growing number of news media are attempting to minimize objectionable reader comments without incurring the expense of pre-publication editing. Efforts include automatically feeding the comments through software filters that reject posts containing profanity or other objectionable language. Other software automatically highlights posts that are praised by other commenters in an attempt to elevate worthwhile commentary over the objectionable. Readers who frequently post worthwhile comments are labeled "trusted commenters" by some sites, and their posts get more prominent display. Some sites don't allow comments about stories that editors think are likely to inspire objectionable posts. Others assign staff to watch comments about such stories. Some encourage reporters and editors to engage in the online conversation with readers.

"When you have the editor or the author of a piece in the comments, you're sending a message that there's someone listening with the authority to police bad actors," says Brian Farnham, editor-inchief of *Patch .com,* a nationwide chain of local online news operations. "I think if people feel they can jump into a conversation and no one's watching, they might be a little more malicious."

Discussions are civil at *Shine,* a Yahoo website for women, because editors and users have built a true community, according to Dave Morgan, executive editor for Yahoo's North American audience.

Indeed, civil discourse is the central mission of *Civil Beat*, an Internet news organization in Hawaii that went online in May. "If we're going to have a society that we want to live in, we have to have a forum where people who disagree with each other can engage without being disagreeable," *Civil Beat* Editor John Temple says.

Civil Beat has not found it difficult to keep its online discussions civil, probably because of its policies, explains Temple, former editor of the *Rocky Mountain News*. Reporters are called reporter-hosts, and they lead discussions around the topics they cover. While some of the site's content is free, users must pay (starting at 99 cents a month) to participate at various levels, including commenting. While they don't have to use their real names online, *Civil Beat* knows who they are.

Patch, Shine and *Civil Beat* are examples of new media that follow traditional journalism standards, or most of them.

Although *Civil Beat* reporters lead discussions, and much of their writing is analytical, they are restricted in expressing opinion. "Do not take a position on an issue that would compromise your ability to cover that issue fairly or to be perceived as covering that issue fairly," Temple tells his staff.

As with other search engines, readers can use Yahoo's search function to enter "an echo chamber of unfactual information" that feeds the readers' biases, Morgan acknowledges. But Yahoo also produces a growing amount of original news content that is created by experienced journalists who follow traditional standards, Morgan, a 21-year veteran of the *Los Angeles Times,* says. "We are willing to take the extra time to make sure we're doing things properly," he explains. Third-party content on the *Yahoo News* pages is from news organizations that "have the highest journalism standards," Morgan says.

Patch abides by traditional standards, for the most part, but is experimenting with requiring reporters and editors to reveal some of their personal beliefs. In the *Mill Valley Patch* editor's biography, for instance, longtime California journalist Nancy Isles Nation tells readers that "my political leanings are to the left and, while I was raised Catholic, my family left the church when I was a teen, and I do not have any religious beliefs."

Farnham, who worked for several magazines before becoming an online journalist, describes the effort at transparency as an experiment in "going beyond the cold guise of the objective reporter. We want to try to engage readers and have personalities. I think you can have a personality and a voice without crossing a journalistic line. We're online asking people to share a lot about themselves. It seems only fair for us to make a gesture in the same way." According to the theory *Patch* is testing, going public with their beliefs will cause reporters to take extra care to be balanced in their writing, Farnham explains. If readers accuse reporters of bias, the reporters can jump into the conversation and defend themselves, he adds.

New Models

TBD, the new online and cable news organization in Washington, also is following traditional standards, with some twists, in its online and cable news operations.

"You have to be faster, give up some control on the Web, interact with the audience," Brady, a former *Washington Post* reporter and executive, explains. "There are other people on the Web that are producing things that have value and that you should be pointing to. But you can't abandon the principles."

TBD links to a large number of blogs in the Washington area, all of which were carefully vetted, Brady says. He allows his writers "more room for voice," which means that "you can write with a little bit of edge — a little snark — without necessarily expressing a clear opinion on something."

Patch.com and Shine are examples of new media that, with significant exceptions, follow traditional media standards. Patch.com is a nationwide chain of local online news operations that is experimenting with requiring reporters and editors to reveal some of their personal beliefs in an effort to foster transparency. Shine, a Yahoo website for women, fosters civil reader comments by creating a community of readers.

CQ Press/Screenshot (both)

Is transparency the new objectivity?

YES David Weinberger
Senior Researcher, Berkman Center for Internet & Society, Harvard University; Co-Director, Harvard Library Innovation Lab

Written for *CQ Researcher*, October 2010

Transparency is the new objectivity. It's about time. We used to think objectivity is how knowledge works. It turns out it's just how paper works. The physics and economics of print required writers to try to encapsulate in the printed article everything essential the reader needed to know about a topic or story, because finding out more was so difficult.

The article had to claim (implicitly, usually) to be free of bias to give readers confidence that they need not jump on the next library-bound bus to get the other side of the story. Objectivity was about providing the reader with a stopping point because the paper medium made it so hard to continue.

But in our new, profoundly connective media ecology, there is no need to encapsulate when you can link out to your sources, data and other points of view. The fact that an article exists in an accessible web of ideas frees writers from having to attempt to construct the one, sole version, especially when doing so requires them to attempt the impossible: to write from no particular point of view, as if one were free of one's history, culture and personal values. The "situatedness" of human life is not a bug, but a feature.

Our new medium allows writers to acknowledge that. If it is true that humans cannot fully escape their own experience and values, then readers are served better (although they need "new literacies") when the inevitably subjective stance of writers is open to inspection.

This transparency of self can be trumpeted in manifestly subjective writing when appropriate, but it can also be acknowledged and manifested through links even when the writer is trying to be more objective rather than less. Not every news article should be a confessional, but just about all of them should contain links to more information about the topic (transparency of argument) and to more information about the stance of the person responsible for it (transparency of self).

In the new connective ecology of media superabundance, objectivity without transparency looks like arrogance. Why should we trust what one person — with the best of intentions — insists is true when we instead could have a web of evidence, ideas and argument?

NO Andy Schotz
Past Chairman, Society of Professional Journalists Ethics Committee

Written for *CQ Researcher*, October 2010

I used to think objectivity was concrete and attainable. I no longer do, but I haven't given up on the ideal. Journalists can't be free of all biases as long as they live on this planet. We come to our work from different places, families, friends and experiences. These shape who we are and how and what we think.

But if we give up and profess to being hopelessly slanted, we give up on neutrality and impartiality. This takes us back to the days of the Republican newspaper in town competing against the Democratic paper, with no attempt to be anything but relentlessly partisan toward the side we favor.

Some cable TV news networks seem to have adopted this approach, and perhaps a few newspapers.

But it's harmful for people to turn only to the news organization with a like political view. The world is so much more complicated and gray. We journalists can admit that we have biases and do our best to set them aside.

An editor once told me she struggled while she was a reporter because she had an opinion about everything she covered.

I told her, truthfully, that it was very much the opposite for me. As a reporter, I had practically no personal opinions — I was too focused on the best way to gather and present the best obtainable version of the truth.

Did I consider all of the angles? Was the main point clear? Did I check my facts and quotes? Were names spelled correctly?

Right up until deadline — was there one more call I could make to glean one more helpful detail? (Sometimes, that last call changed the story 180 degrees, challenging what I thought I knew.)

Journalists should be open-minded and inquisitive, understanding that "truth" sometimes comes in layers and shades, and often is not perfectly presented in any one account. Always, we keep trying.

While there is no true objectivity, I believe in the pursuit of it. I do my best to avoid actual and perceived conflicts, which carry as much weight and which I cannot control in the eyes of my readers.

I've been a professional journalist for 18 years. I've been a reader almost twice as long. I respect and am more likely to trust reporters who try as best as they can to stay free from entanglements, and disclose the ones that are unavoidable. To me, that's a serious commitment to an impartial pursuit of truth.

That approach has caused a few double-takes among readers used to more traditional writing. In one story, *TBD* Editor Eric Wimple quoted himself under the heading "Weatherman, editor disagree on heat trends." Another story carried the headline "*TBD* compiles early voting guide, not-so-secretly hopes for early voting problems."

"We're trying to be a little bit more transparent, tongue-in-cheek, a little more edgy," Brady says. But he acknowledges that it probably wasn't a good idea to publicly hope for trouble at the polls, even if it would be journalistically more interesting for both writers and readers.

The name itself is a bit tongue-in-cheek. *TBD* (To Be Determined) was used as a place-holding name while the site was being developed. Later, executives decided to keep it. "*TBD* will never be a finished product," *TBD* Director of Community Engagement Steve Buttry said.[37]

New media also are adopting traditional standards in partnerships with legacy media. On Oct. 5, ABC News announced it will join with Facebook for some 2010 general election coverage, for example. ABC plans to broadcast election-night reports in November from Facebook's headquarters in Palo Alto, Calif., and stream ABC's coverage live on Facebook, on the network's website and through ABC's iPod application.[38]

Another development that challenges traditional journalism standards is the advent of organizations that engage in journalism-like practices while having no background in journalism. When Apple approves certain applications for its iPhone, for example, it acts like an editor, and it has stumbled into controversy because of some of those decisions.

Late last year, Apple rejected an application that would play Mark Fiore's animated political cartoons. The reason: "It contains content that ridicules public figures."[39] As Fiore noted: "Ridiculing public figures is what I do and is an essential part of journalism. A blanket ban on ridicule is, um, ridiculous."

Apple changed its mind after Fiore won the Pulitzer Prize, the first online cartoonist to do so. It also formally exempted "professional political satirists and humorists" from the iPhone ban on "offensive or mean-spirited commentary."[40]

"Apple IS a private company," Fiore said, acknowledging the firm's right to ban anything it wants to. "But

I think it goes farther than that now, because they're becoming a media company. And as a media company, they're the '4.0 Estate.'"[41]

OUTLOOK
New Codes

Chinese Communist Party Chairman Mao Zedong once declared, "let a hundred flowers blossom [and] let a hundred schools of thought contend." In a sense, the future of journalism standards is just as open-ended.

Journalists and journalism scholars think it's unlikely that one code of standards will be adopted by all who practice journalism in the future. They expect that mainstream journalists — in print, broadcasting and online — will adhere to a core set of standards similar to what they followed in the latter half of the 20th century. There may be some variations — about allowing readers to post anonymous, unvetted comments on news media websites, for instance. And there likely will be a wide variety of standards followed online and in cable news, with some Internet sites adhering to no standards at all.

"We don't know in any way what the economic model is going to be, and that will have a lot to do with how journalism is practiced and who's practicing it," DePauw University's Steele says. "It's reasonable to presume we'll have a lot more players, and that means we'll likely have fewer standards accepted across the board."

Washington Post Ombudsman Alexander expects "the marketplace will sort itself out. There may be different standards for different types of so-called news organizations, and the public will come to recognize the differences in those standards."

And getting the standards right won't be easy, *TBD's* Brady says. "We will fix hundreds of things, and there will be another hundred to take on. There will be new standards we have to come up with every year." Legislative solutions may be required for some issues, such as Apple denying access for iPhone applications, and Internet service providers playing favorites among websites, he adds.

The Poynter Institute's Tompkins worries about temptations to blur the line between news content and advertising, especially when readers access news media on cell phones' small screens. "Are we going to allow politicians to buy ads adjacent to news stories when the politician has something to say about that issue" addressed in the story? he asks. "My suspicion is we'll say you can buy whatever you want wherever you want, and looking at a three-inch screen it's going to be difficult to figure out which is the paid content."

The University of Wisconsin's Ward says journalists need to educate citizens about acting responsibly when posting online. The public "can't get off the hook," he insists.

At least some journalists will become more engaged in the communities they cover, instead of following the traditional disinterested and independent posture, Porter at the Knight Digital Media Center at the University of Southern California predicts.

Schultz and Dvorkin are optimistic because of the journalism students they encounter.

"The young people are telling me that the basics will remain," *Plain Dealer* columnist Schultz says, describing recent meetings with students at Ohio University, DePauw, Penn State and the University of Kansas.

"The students that I'm meeting understand what they need to do," the Organization of News Ombudsmen's Dvorkin says. "They're trying to figure out a way to [practice journalism] that doesn't compromise their own values."

Many of today's professional journalists "care deeply about what they do, and they want to make it right," McDonnell at the Online News Association says. "That's why I'm so confident."

Others see business incentives for news organizations to maintain traditional standards.

"There are opportunities for some news organizations to set themselves apart from others that have lesser standards," Alexander says.

"The brand of credibility in this chaos is going to be one of the winning cards," according to Porter.

Yahoo Executive Editor Morgan argues that "best practices and best principles will always elevate themselves. There always will be a home for quality and independently verifiable work. In the online world, where people can share what they like and don't like, that is the kind of work that will always be valued." If a news organization expects to sell ads beside its news content, he says, "it better be credible."

NOTES

1. Todd Murphy, "Gore Chase Had no Finish," *Portland Tribune,* July 15, 2010, www.portland tribune.com/news/story.php?story_id=127913967 087475000.

2. *Ibid.*

3. Michael Arrington, "Twitter Mania: Google Got Shot Down. Apple Rumors Heat Up," *TechCrunch,* May 5, 2009, http://techcrunch.com/2009/05/05/ twitter-mania-google-got-shut-down-apple-rumors-heat-up.

4. Damon Darlin, "Get the Tech Scuttlebutt! (It Might Even Be True)," *The New York Times,* June 7, 2009, p. BU3, www.nytimes.com/2009/06/07/ business/media/07ping.html?_r=1&scp=1&sq=%2 2a+headline+flashed+on+Gawker% 22&st=nyt.

5. Cynthia Gorney, "Getting It Right," *American Journalism Review,* March 2001, www.entre preneur.com/tradejournals/article/71962141.html.

6. Bill Kovach and Tom Rosenstiel, "The Elements of Journalism," Committee of Concerned Journalists, www.concernedjournalists.org/tools/principles/ele ments. For background see the following *CQ Researcher* reports: Tom Price, "Future of Journalism," March 27, 2009, pp. 273-296 (updated Sept. 3, 2010); Marcia Clemmitt, "Internet Accuracy," Aug. 1, 2008, pp. 625-648; and Kenneth Jost and Melissa J. Hipolit, "Blog Explosion," June 9, 2006, pp. 505-528 (updated Sept. 14, 2010).

7. "Voices from the Underground," University of Connecticut Libraries, Oct. 26, 2005, doddcenter .uconn.edu/exhibits/voices/press.htm.

8. Dinesh D'Souza, "How Obama Thinks," *Forbes,* Sept. 27, 2010, www.forbes.com/forbes/ 2010/0927/politics-socialism-capitalism-private-enterprises-obama-business-problem.html.

9. Tim Arango, "Forbes Article Spurs Media Soul Searching," *The New York Times,* Sept. 24, 2010, www.nytimes.com/2010/09/25/business/media /25forbes.html?_r=1&emc=eta1&pagewanted= print.

10. "Online Journalists Optimistic About Revenue, Concerned About Quality," Project for Excellence

in Journalism, March 30, 2009, http://pewresearch .org/pubs/1172/online-journalists-optimistic-about-revenues-worried-about-news-quality.

11. Philip Rucker, "West Virginia's coal country pays tribute to Byrd, who never forgot it," *The Washington Post,* June 29, 2010, www.washingtonpost.com/wp-dyn/content/article/2010/06/28/AR2010062802 392_Comments.html#.

12. http://live.washingtonpost.com/tracee-hamilton-0909.html.

13. Howard Owens, "The why and how of a real names policy on comments," *My PersonalBlog,* April 2, 2010, www.howardowens.com/node/7349.

14. Jeffrey D. Neuburger, "CDA Protects Newspapers from Liability for Libelous Comments," PBS "MediaShift," May 12, 2010, www.pbs.org/ mediashift/2010/05/cda-protects-newspapers-from-liability-for-libelous-comments132.html.

15. Courtney Macavinta, "The CDA: Case closed," *CNET News,* June 26, 1997, http://news.cnet.com/ The-CDA-Case-closed/2009-1023_3-200971 .html?tag=lia;rcol.

16. "Online Journalism Ethics: Guidelines from the Conference," *PoynterOnline,* Feb. 11, 2007, www .poynter.org/content/content_view.asp?id=117350.

17. Andy Alexander, "Post Editor Ends Tweets as New Guidelines Are Issued," *Washington Post.com,* Sept. 25, 2009, http://voices.washingtonpost.com/ ombudsman-blog/2009/09/post_editor_ends_ tweets_as_new.html.

18. *Ibid.*

19. Michele McClellan, "Washington Post guidelines cast social media as a minefield and that's bad," Knight Digital Media Center, Sept. 29, 2009, www .knightdigitalmediacenter,org/leadership_blog/ comments/washington_post_guidelines_cast_ social_media_as_a_mine field_and_thats_bad/.

20. David Weinberger, "Transparency is the new objectivity," *JOHO The Blog,* July 19, 2009, www.hyper org.com/blogger/2009/07/19/transparency-is-the-new-objectivity.

21. Robert Niles, "You've got to know what you stand for to survive in journalism online," *Online*

Journalism Review, April 3, 2009, www.ojr.org/ojr/ people/robert/200904/1688.

22. Chris Cillizza, "The Live Fix with Chris Cillizza," *WashingtonPost.com,* Sept. 24, 2010, http://live .washingtonpost.com/live-fix-0917.html.

23. Unless otherwise noted, this historical section draws from the following sources: Stephen J.A. Ward, *The Invention of Journalism Ethics* (2008); Ward, "Researching Ethics: History of Journalism Ethics," Center for Journalism Ethics, School of Journalism & Mass Communication, University of Wisconsin-Madison, 2009, www.journalismethics.ca/research_ ethics/history.htm; Ward, "Researching Ethics: Codes of Journalism Ethics," Center for Journalism Ethics, School of Journalism & Mass Communication, University of Wisconsin-Madison, 2009, www.journalismethics.ca/research_ ethics/codes.htm; Frank Luther Mott, *American Journalism: A History* (1962); Mitchell Stephens, "History of Newspapers," written for *Collier's Encyclopedia,* www.nyu.edu/classes/stephens/ Collier%27s%20page.htm; Roger Streitmatter, *Mightier than the Sword: How the News Media Have Shaped American History* (1997); Jean Folkerts, Dwight L. Teeter Jr. and Edward Caudill, *Voices of a Nation: A History of Mass Media in the United States* (2009).

24. *The Invention of Journalism Ethics, op. cit.,* p. 148.

25. "Our Motto," E.W. Scripps Company, www .scripps.com/heritage/our-motto.

26. *The Invention of Journalism Ethics, op. cit.* p. 131.

27. *Ibid.* p. 170.

28. Jill Lepore, "The Day the Newspaper Died," *The New Yorker,* Jan. 26, 2009, www.newyorker.com/ arts/critics/atlarge/2009/01/26/090126crat_ atlarge_lepore?currentPage=all.

29. Mott, *op. cit.* pp. 168-169.

30. Calvin Woodward, "The AP: Playing it straight for 150 years," American Society of Newspaper Editors, Aug. 19, 1998, www.asne.org/kiosk/editor/98.july/ woodward1.htm.

31. William H. Rentschler, "The Most Illustrious Journalist No One Ever Heard of," *USA Today*

Magazine, Society for the Advancement of Education, July 1998, findarticles.com/p/articles/mi_m1272/is_n2638_v127/ai_20954323.

32. *The Invention of Journalism Ethics, op. cit,* p. 200.

33. *Ibid,* p. 210.

34. *Ibid,* p. 214.

35. *Ibid,* p. 215.

36. Ann Gerhart and Ernesto Londono, "Fla. pastor's Koran-burning threat started with a tweet," *The Washington Post,* Sept. 11, 2010, www.washington post.com/wp-dyn/content/article/2010/09/10/AR2010091007033.html.

37. Michael Malone, "Allbritton Plots 'Real-Time' D.C. Web Launch," *Broadcasting & Cable,* May 10, 2010, www.broadcastingcable.com/article/452438-Allbritton_Plots_Real_Time_D_C_Web_Launch.php.

38. "ABC News Partnering With Facebook For Midterms," *The Huffington Post,* Oct. 5, 2010, www.huffingtonpost.com/2010/10/05/abc-news-facebook-midterms_n_751485.html.

39. Rob Pegoraro, "Apple rejects Pulitzer winner's iPhone app because it 'ridicules public figures,'" *The Washington Post,* April 16, 2010, http://voices.washingtonpost.com/fasterforward/2010/04/apple_refuses_pulitzer_winners.html?hpid=topnews.

40. Rob Pegoraro, "The one App Store rule that matters: It's up to Apple," *The Washington Post,* Sept. 10, 2010, p. A18, wwwwashingtonpost.com/wp-dyn/content/article/2010/09/09/AR2010090906328.html.

41. Michael Cavna, "Now is the time for all cartoonists to satirize Steve Jobs," *The Washington Post,* June 30, 2010, http//voices.washingtonpost.com/comic-riffs/2010/06/the_rant_now_is_the_time_for_a.html.

BIBLIOGRAPHY

Selected Sources

Books

Christians, Clifford G., *et al., An Ethics Trajectory: Visions of Media Past, Present and Yet to Come,* Institute of Communications Research, University of Illinois, 2008.

Based primarily on the U.S. Media Ethics Summit of 2007, about 40 scholars and practitioners address a variety of journalism challenges, such as privacy, fairness, accuracy, diversity and the Internet's impact on ethical journalism.

Kovach, Bill, and Tom Rosenstiel, *The Elements of Journalism: What Newspeople Should Know and the Public Should Expect,* Three Rivers Press, 2007.

Kovach, former *Atlanta Journal-Constitution* editor and *New York Times* Washington Bureau chief, along with Project for Excellence in Journalism Director Rosenstiel, explain what they say are core principles that should be shared by journalists around the world. Originally based on an extensive study, including a survey of journalists, a decade ago, this updated edition also addresses the rights and responsibilities of citizens who are able to practice journalism on the Internet.

Patterson, Philip, and Lee Wilkins, *Media Ethics: Issues and Cases*, 7th edition, McGraw-Hill Humanities/Social Sciences/Languages, 2010.

This widely used college text by two journalism professors teaches media ethics through actual and hypothetical case studies.

Ward, Stephen J.A., *The Invention of Journalism Ethics,* McGill-Queen's University Press, 2008.

The director of the University of Wisconsin's Center for Journalism Ethics traces the evolution of journalism ethics from the 17th century and explores its philosophical underpinnings.

Articles

Chittum, Ryan, "Forbes' Shameful Piece on Obama as the 'Other,'" *Columbia Journalism Review,* Sept. 13, 2010, www.cjr.org/the_audit/forbes_shameful_obama_dinesh_dsouza.php.

CJR's media critic attacks *Forbes'* cover story (see D'Souza, below) as a "gross piece of innuendo," a "fact-twisting, errorladen piece of paranoia," the "worst kind of smear journalism" and a "singularly disgusting work."

D'Souza, Dinesh, "How Obama Thinks," *Forbes,* Sept. 27, 2010, www.forbes.com/forbes/20i0/0927/politics-socialismcapitalism-private-enterprises-obama-business-problem.html.

This conservative writer's essay touched off media debate about the propriety of a business magazine giving its cover story to speculation. Among its gems: "The President's actions are so bizarre that they mystify his critics and supporters alike."

Murphy, Todd, "Gore Chase Had no Finish," *Portland Tribune,* July 15, 2010, www.portlandtribune.com/news/story.php?story_id=12791396708747500.
The paper's former managing editor explains how and why it did not report sexual-assault allegations against former Vice President Al Gore after the newspaper couldn't confirm the charge.

Niles, Robert, "You've got to know what you stand for to survive in journalism online," *Online Journalism Review,* April 3, 2009, www.ojr.org/ojr/people/robert/200904/1688.
A Web editor and consultant argues that journalists must reveal their values if they're to succeed on the Internet.

Reports and Studies

"Online Journalism Ethics: Guidelines from the Conference," *PoynterOnline,* Feb. 11, 2007, www.poynter.org/content/content_view.asp?id=117350.
At a 2006 conference, online journalists — most from mainstream media websites — attempt to write guidelines for practicing ethical journalism on the Internet.

"The Roanoke Times News Standards and Policies," *roanoke.com, The Roanoke Times website,* updated Dec. 9, 2009, www.roanoke.com/newsservices/wb/xp-59614#37.
The Virginia newspaper's standards code includes a section of "Online Policies," which begins: "All our standards for accuracy, sourcing, taste and avoidance of conflict of interest apply to work posted on *roanoke.com.*"

Christians, Clifford, and Vernon Jensen, "Books in Media Ethics," Silha Center for the Study of Media Ethics and Law, University of Minnesota, www.silha.umn.edu/assets/pdf/bib1998.pdf.
This annotated bibliography of media ethics books begins with Nelson Crawford's *The Ethics of Journalism* (Alfred A. Knopf, 1924).

Navasky, Victor, with Evan Lerner, "Magazines and Their Web Sites," *Columbia Journalism Review,* March 2010, www.cjr.org/resources/magazines_and_their_websites.
Magazines don't pay as much attention to accuracy online as they do in print, according to a freestanding report from CJR.

For More Information

American Society of News Editors, 11690B Sunrise Valley Dr., Reston, VA 20191; (703) 453-1122; www.asne.org. Founded in 1922 as the American Society of Newspaper Editors, issued first ethics code in 2003, changed name and admitted online journalists to membership in 2009. Promotes ethical journalism, supports First Amendment rights, defends freedom of information and open government.

Center for Journalism Ethics, 821 University Ave., Madison, WI 53706; (608) 262-3690; www.journalismethics.ca. Based at the University of Wisconsin School of Journalism and Mass Communication, with links to the University of British Columbia Graduate School of Journalism in Vancouver, looks at journalism ethics as a global topic.

Among its website content: news, analysis, book reviews, links to ethics experts.

The Poynter Institute for Media Studies, 801 Third St. South, St. Petersburg, FL 33701; (888) 769-6837; www.poynter.org. A journalism education and research organization; ethics section of its website includes articles, discussions, tip sheets, case studies and a toll-free number for journalists who need ethics advice on deadline.

Radio Television Digital News Association, 529 14th St., N.W., Suite 425, Washington, DC 20045; (202) 659-6510; www.rtdna.org. Membership organization that sets standards for reporting on television, radio and the Internet. Ethics section of its website contains the organization's ethics code plus guidelines for addressing specific challenges such as blogging, using social media, covering bomb threats, airing 911 calls.

Silha Center for the Study of Media Ethics and Law, 206 Church St., S.E., Minneapolis, MN 55455; (612) 625-3421; wwwsilha.umn.edu. Part of the University of Minnesota's School of Journalism and Mass Communication, studies the ethical responsibilities and legal rights of the mass media; produces publications, sponsors forums and supports graduate student research. Website contains links to other organizations that address communications ethics.

Society of Professional Journalists Ethics Committee, 3909 N. Meridian St., Indianapolis, IN 46208; (317) 927-8000; www.spj.org/ethics.asp. Advises journalists on ethical matters; website contains many ethics resources and a continuing online discussion through the committee's blog.

Press Freedom

Should partisan bloggers get free-press protections?

Peter Katel

Courtesy Christopher Elliott

Travel blogger Christopher Elliott refused to comply with a Department of Homeland Security subpoena prompted by his posting of a confidential security directive that followed the attempted bombing of a U.S. jetliner on Christmas day. Journalism experts worry about the beleaguered news industry's ability to protect press freedom amid questions about who qualifies as a legitimate journalist.

From *CQ Researcher,*
February 5, 2010

Journalist Christopher Elliott and his wife had just started giving their children their baths one evening a few days after Christmas when there was an unexpected knock at the door of their home in Washington. The early-evening visit was from a Department of Homeland Security (DHS) investigator bearing a subpoena for Elliott, who runs an independent, consumer-oriented Web site about travel.

DHS was demanding that Elliott turn over "all documents, e-mails, and/or faxsimile [sic] transmissions" involving his receipt and posting of a restricted Transportation Security Administration (TSA) security order.[1]

Elliott had posted the directive on his blog on Dec. 27, two days before the agent arrived. The document showed that, in response to the attempted Christmas Day bombing of a Northwest Airlines flight, TSA was stepping up security on United States-bound flights from abroad. News articles citing passengers and TSA personnel had already reported additional pre-boarding searches and a requirement that passengers remain in their seats for the last hour of a flight.[2]

Now, thanks to Elliott and another Web-based writer, the new measures weren't being paraphrased or interpreted but spelled out directly by TSA. "I broke no laws," Elliott says, noting that the directive carried no secrecy classification, though he acknowledges that airline employees and other direct recipients are prohibited from disclosing the document. "DHS didn't even tell me to take it off my Web site; they just wanted my source."

Traffic Increases on News Web Sites

The number of visitors to the nation's top 10 news Web sites increased an average of 23 percent from 2007 to 2008. Yahoo! News had the highest number of visitors; CBS News saw its viewership increase more than 50 percent.

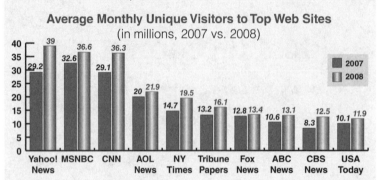

Average Monthly Unique Visitors to Top Web Sites
(in millions, 2007 vs. 2008)

Source: Project for Excellence in Journalism analysis of comScore, Inc., data.

Elliott wasn't the only subpoena target. That same December evening, DHS agents called at the home of another travel blogger, Steven Frischling, who had posted the TSA directive on his "Flying With Fish" blog. Frischling, a commercial photographer, complied the next day, turning over his computer. With that, TSA dropped its subpoena for Elliott and notified Frischling that no more information was sought from him.[3]

Law-enforcement demands that journalists name confidential sources, or supply other information gathered in reporting, raise questions about how much freedom the Constitution's free-press guarantee requires. The Supreme Court ruled in 1972 that journalists don't enjoy a special privilege against testifying, though judges have ruled for reporters in many such cases — at least until the past decade. "Shield" laws in 37 states and Washington, D.C., give journalists some protection against supplying evidence, and a federal shield bill passed the House last year and is pending in the Senate.[4]

The congressional legislation largely was prompted by a 2007 case in which reporter Judith Miller of *The New York Times* spent 85 days in jail for refusing to disclose intelligence information. She finally complied after saying her confidential source released her from her pledge to protect his identity.[5]

If Miller's eventual testimony gave other prosecutors hopes of success in forcing information from journalists, the rise of independent blogging has also expanded the field of potential subpoena targets, many of whom may not have the legal backing that news-organization employees typically enjoy.

The ever-expanding universe of the Web is home to old-line media organizations and news-oriented start-ups of both the nonpartisan and highly partisan kind, as well as individuals — specialists and amateurs alike — who offer news, commentary, documents and more.

On the one hand, the migration of media to the Internet is threatening to extinguish news on paper and on television — hitting old-line media companies in the pocketbook and weakening their ability to wage free-press fights. Yet these same companies have jumped to the Web, benefiting news consumers, who can also dive into the limitless outpouring of news from all over the world collected and disseminated by means that didn't even exist in recent memory — cellphone cameras, Twitter and social-networking sites.

Indeed, "citizen journalists" almost instantly reached the Web from earthquake-ravaged Haiti. And President Obama made it known that he followed on-the-ground Twitter reports on the upsurge of protests that followed Iran's presidential election last year that were disseminated on the *Atlantic* magazine's Web site by blogger Andrew Sullivan, one of the first paper-based journalists to turn to full-time blogging.[6]

Travel blogger Elliott also boasts old-school journalism credentials: reader advocate for *National Geographic Traveler* and columnist for *The Washington Post* and MSNBC. In keeping with his journalism training, Elliott refused to turn over anything and immediately called his own lawyer and The Reporters Committee for the Freedom of the Press. He says the *Post* and his other outlets said they'd stand behind him.

A smaller news organization might have abandoned him. "There might be a circumstance in which we would refuse to comply with a court order, but we are a small company and could not afford a protracted legal action," an anonymous editor wrote to a media-law specialist tracking the volume of subpoenas at newsrooms nationwide.[7]

The study, based on a detailed survey, counted 3,062 subpoenas — 332 of them in federal cases — issued to the 761 respondents in 2006 alone, reported study author RonNell Andersen Jones, a law professor at Brigham Young University Law School in Provo, Utah. In 2001, the Reporters Committee made a similar survey and counted 823 subpoenas, 9 percent of them in federal proceedings. The data aren't strictly comparable, but Jones concluded they show a marked increase in subpoenas demanding confidential information.[8]

Added to the financial burdens weighing down newspapers and other traditional media, the legal pressure is giving rise to a mood approaching despair. "I've been going to media law conferences for a long time," says Jones, a onetime newspaper reporter and law clerk for former Supreme Court Justice Sandra Day O'Connor. "In the last year or so there's been a lot of dialogue about how we sustain some of the most important things we do in the face of widespread bankruptcy and collapse."

Since the early 2000s, traditional news media have been engulfed in a business crisis whose end seems nowhere in sight. As newspapers and TV news lose readers and viewers, advertisers (now also suffering from the recession) are leaving as well. For example, newspaper ad revenue plummeted by 26 percent — from $46.7 billion to $34.7 billion — from 2005 to 2008 alone and continued falling last year.[9]

Long-established regional newspapers that closed in the last two years include the *Seattle Post-Intelligencer*, which now exists in much reduced form online; the *Albuquerque Tribune*; and the *Rocky Mountain News* of Denver. And the year ended with rounds of substantial news cuts at major news organizations including The Associated Press and *New York Times*. Early this year,

Decline in Print Circulation Continues

Daily and Sunday newspaper circulation declined by 7.1 percent and 5.4 percent, respectively, between September 2008 and March 2009, reflecting accelerating circulation declines since 2003.

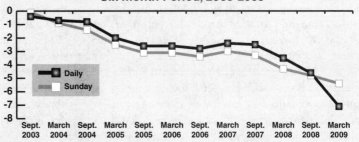

Decline in Daily and Sunday Newspaper Circulation by Six-month Period, 2003-2009

Source: "State of the News Media," Pew Project for Excellence in Journalism, 2009

CBS News began layoffs of about 90 people, including star producers.[10]

Big media companies, meanwhile, are enjoying vastly expanded Web audiences, but they're haunted by an inescapable reality. "The advertising model has collapsed," says Edward Wasserman, a journalism professor at Washington and Lee University in Lexington, Va., and former executive business editor of *The Miami Herald*. Newspaper and TV executives widely agree that news companies will never earn from Web advertising what they used to make in print and broadcast ad revenue.

Among journalists whose jobs have disappeared, some have joined the Web-based start-ups, usually nonprofit and donor-funded, that have cropped up around the country, such as *ProPublica* and the *Texas Tribune*. Others have launched their own online enterprises. As for young people starting out, the old model of graduating from journalism school and finding a job at a news organization may be dying.

Alan Mutter, an adjunct journalism professor at the University of California, Berkeley, often advises job-searching recent graduates. "I tell them, 'You can be a journalist by saying you're a journalist and starting to commit journalism.' It's utterly gratifying when you find people who do. One started a blog penetrating the intricacies of the university's financing."

In any case, add new J-school graduates with blogs to the ranks of those who might benefit from a federal shield law, depending on how it defines "journalist." Some lawmakers are complaining that the legislation's present definition is too broad. "For those of us who have been around for a while and have watched the change in journalism, there's always been a standard for legitimacy — that's the future of journalism," Sen. Dianne Feinstein, D-Calif., said at a December session of the Senate Judiciary Committee. "Here there is no standard for legitimacy."[11]

Few would disagree that old journalistic norms are under siege. But travel journalist Elliott has no doubt about the standards that led him to seek out and post the TSA security order. "It was a directive that TSA should have told everybody about — what to expect on an inbound flight," he says. "But they didn't. The document had been widely disseminated; every airline had it, every airport had it. It was information that the public needed to know."

Here are some of the key questions about press freedom being asked:

Can media companies afford free-press battles?

Fear and uncertainty grip traditional media companies large and small. News of layoffs, bankruptcies and debates over how to rebuild a new business model have been constant in recent years. In this climate, the once-powerful news industry is now seen by many as too burdened by its own problems to actively defend press freedom. To be sure, notes Lucy Dalglish, executive director of The Reporters Committee for Freedom of the Press, major media companies still leap to the legal barricades on important cases, such as subpoenas involving journalism students at Northwestern University's Medill School investigating a possible miscarriage of justice.

But the layoffs have been extensive. From November 2009 to early January alone, major developments included: Layoffs of 90 employees by The Associated Press; a cutback of 100 news staffers at *The New York Times;* a bankruptcy reorganization by MediaNews Group, a chain with 54 daily newspapers in 11 states, plus TV and radio stations; planned layoffs of at least 400 news division employees from several magazines at Time Inc., whose publications include *Sports Illustrated*

and *Fortune.* Overall, an estimated 15,000 newspaper employees (not all of them journalists) lost jobs last year.[12]

Somewhat more encouraging, major Web news sites launched or announced during the same period included the not-for-profit *Texas Tribune,* which said it raised nearly $4 million in start-up money; *Peer News,* founded by eBay founder and chairman Pierre Omidyar to cover news in Hawaii; and the *Connecticut Mirror,* a foundation-funded site focusing on government and policy.[13]

But as old media fight to stay afloat and new ventures try to find their way, freedom-of-the-press efforts seem to be diminishing.

"To the extent that press and government are at odds with each other, it seems there is an endless supply of government lawyers now, and fewer media lawyers, and fewer causes that the media can afford to champion," says Michael A. Giudicessi, a lawyer for the *Des Moines Register,* one of the Midwest's leading papers. "If there's a meeting [of public officials] being closed, if a document is being withheld, the government understands it can turn to staff lawyers and say, 'Find us an excuse to keep it confidential,'" says Giudicessi. "But news executives have to ask themselves, 'Do I keep a reporter on staff for another year, or fight an access case?'" In fact, Giudicessi was formerly a staff lawyer for the paper.

However, says conservative activist and publisher Andrew Breitbart, of *Breitbart.com,* the news media — which he views as a left-liberal political group — isn't coming to the aid of right-leaning entrepreneurs like him.

Breitbart was sued after posting a video shot by conservative political activists James O'Keefe and a female associate, posing as a pimp and a prostitute in a sting aimed at the liberal Association of Community Organizations for Reform Now (ACORN). The two were pretending to solicit advice on how to set up a prostitution business. "The lawsuit against me, as a publisher, was a stab in the heart of press freedom," Breitbart says. "But there has yet to be a MSM [mainstream media] entity to come to our defense, to say that ACORN is wrong to sue the journalists or me."

Breitbart argues that traditional news organizations don't consider him to be a journalist because, unlike them, he's open about his political agenda. "Maybe the media can pretend that nobody noticed" the ACORN lawsuit, he says.

Dalglish says Breitbart might well have been able to avail himself of the group's pro-bono assistance. "He hasn't called. If he's out there trying to independently present information," says Dalglish, a former journalist and media lawyer, "and has no financial interaction with political candidates of any type, then he probably is committing journalism."

Former business editor Wasserman of Washington and Lee University says the media have been complaining of reduced resources for decades. "I've been in the media since the early '70s, and they've always complained about inadequate resources even when they were absolutely minting money and had unchallenged monopolies in broadcasting," he says.

In the present climate, though, Wasserman agrees that a weakened press means a more timid journalism. "There's less money for reporting, certainly less for litigation and less to go after those more adventurous and expensive stories that require litigation to get documents freed up," he says.

But the University of California's Mutter, a former top editor at the *Chicago Sun-Times* and the *San Francisco Chronicle* and ex-CEO of three Silicon Valley firms, argues that the digital technology that helped explode the news media's old business model also creates entirely new avenues for making information public. "One reason I believe there is going to be a lot of press freedom is that it's impossible to suppress people, even in totalitarian countries," he says.

Wide availability of cell-phone videos showing Iranian security forces repressing demonstrators is one example, Mutter says. "Even in China, people can route around government censorship," he says.

Are independent bloggers entitled to free-press protections?

In journalism's ancient past — say, 20 years ago — a working journalist by definition was affiliated with a

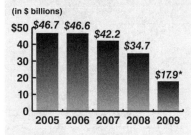

Newspaper Ad Revenue in Free Fall

Total newspaper advertising revenue dropped 26 percent from 2005 to 2008, and early figures indicate an even more dramatic decline for 2009.

Newspaper Advertising Revenue, 2005-2009

(in $ billions)

$50 $46.7 $46.6 $42.2 $34.7 $17.9*

2005 2006 2007 2008 2009

* Through Sept. 30, 2009

Source: Newspaper Association of America

newspaper or magazine or a radio or TV station, or perhaps a specialized newsletter. Virtually everyone in the business had formally or informally learned the basics — get all sides of a controversy, attribute quotes to the people who made them, verify information and don't allow yourself to be used as a platform for libel.

At least one veteran of old-school training argues that the instant quality of Web publishing makes some long-established journalism standards obsolete — even the one about not spreading rumors. In late January, journalist and Web entrepreneur Michael Wolff bragged on his *Newser* site that he had posted on Twitter.com — a new, much-discussed short-form message site for social networks — the unverified rumor that media mogul Rupert Murdoch might be preparing to sell two of his London newspapers. "A very short while ago, this would have been unpublishable," he said. But in the instant-news world, "We'll know together" if the rumor is true.[14]

The late David Shaw, the *Los Angeles Times'* influential media critic, deplored such conduct. "Many bloggers — not all, perhaps not even most — don't seem to worry much about being accurate," Shaw wrote. "They just want to get their opinions — and their 'scoops' — out there as fast as they pop into their brains. . . . The knowledge that you can correct errors quickly, combined with the absence of editors or filters, encourages laziness, carelessness and inaccuracy."[15]

Commenting on a lawsuit filed against two Web publications by Apple Computers, Shaw argued that bloggers weren't entitled to constitutional free-press privileges, such as protection by a "shield" law against having to reveal sources. Such protections — on the books in 37 states — were designed for "the media as an institution," Shaw wrote.

Anticipating Shaw's arguments by a few months, Garrett Graff, now editor of *Washingtonian* magazine, countered some of them. Most bloggers don't even

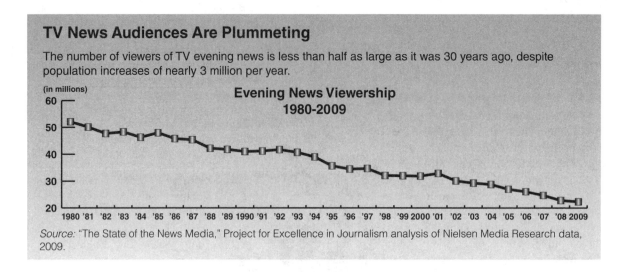

TV News Audiences Are Plummeting

The number of viewers of TV evening news is less than half as large as it was 30 years ago, despite population increases of nearly 3 million per year.

Evening News Viewership 1980-2009

(in millions)

Source: "The State of the News Media," Project for Excellence in Journalism analysis of Nielsen Media Research data, 2009.

consider themselves journalists, Graff wrote, but added, "Over the coming months and years there will be an ever-increasing number of bloggers who are doing reporting and news gathering, and there will be many times when a blogger breaks news simply because there are 8 million of them writing — far more than there are journalists in the U.S."[16]

And Graff wrote, "As a society we have to err on the side of giving out journalism's protections of free speech and a free press more widely than not. . . . As soon as someone, whether it's a judge or the White House or a panel of 'real' journalists, becomes the arbiter of 'journalism' we're all in trouble."[17] In 2005, at age 23, Graff became the first blogger admitted to a White House press briefing.[18]

The Apple case centered on the firm's demand for the sources used by two Web publications that disclosed details about a new Apple product. A trial judge ruled in Apple's favor on the grounds that the sites had disclosed trade secrets. But an appeals court rejected Apple's claim that the sites weren't practicing bona fide journalism and said the state shield law — enacted in 1974, before the Web existed — protected them against naming sources.[19]

In effect, the appeals court was applying what media-law specialists call a "function test." By that standard, anyone who does what journalists do — find information, analyze and perhaps comment on it and disseminate their work — is performing the work of the free press and should be treated accordingly when authorities

demand sources' identities. But Dalglish of the Reporters Committee says that not everyone with a Web site can meet that standard.

She asks, "Do you as a citizen, or as a journalist, want anybody at all who's been subpoenaed to testify to a grand jury to go home and write something on their home computer and then say they can't be subpoenaed?"

People untrained in journalism who make an effort to practice the craft on their sites can easily run afoul of problems that have also bedeviled experienced reporters, argues Wasserman of Washington and Lee University. Although he supports a functional definition of journalism, he adds, "You'd like to think that people doing this are exercising a measure of care."

For instance, Wasserman notes that journalists often have to negotiate situations in which their sources attempt to manipulate them. He posits a plausible scenario for a business writer: "A short-seller approaches you with nasty information about a CEO's divorce, and it's just wonderful stuff and it's solid, and you know they want to discredit the guy and make lots of money" by selling the company's stock short when it declines. The reporter's dilemma: write the piece, knowing he is being used as part of a business strategy, or walk away from a hot story.

Ethical pitfalls aside, thousands of people with no background on how to deal with sources' agendas, and no editors to guide them, arguably are practicing some form of journalism on the Web. As "citizen journalism" grows, its practitioners include people posting information about zoning issues to a neighborhood site, or rescue workers providing information on the Web about disaster victims after hurricanes and earthquakes.

With the citizen journalist trend unlikely to slow down, argues Mary-Rose Papandrea, a professor at Boston College Law School, the idea of limiting free-press protection only to journalists — however defined — is obsolete. "Americans increasingly obtain their information and insights into important issues through the Internet and through bloggers in particular," she writes.[20]

With virtually everyone empowered to transmit news, information and opinion, Papandrea writes, everyone who does so should have a limited right to refuse to testify about their sources. Eyewitness testimony about a crime, or evidence of an imminent national security threat, wouldn't be shielded, she says. "Given that the institutional press no longer has a monopoly over the dissemination of information to the public, all those who disseminate information to the public must be presumptively entitled to invoke the privilege's protections."[21]

Is the era of mass-market objective journalism coming to an end?

In late January, not long after his undercover sting at ACORN offices, videographer O'Keefe was arrested at the New Orleans office of Democratic Sen. Mary Landrieu. O'Keefe and two of his three companions, both dressed as phone repairmen, were charged with entering a federal building for the purpose of "interfering" with the senatorial office's phone system.[22]

O'Keefe later wrote that "as an investigative journalist" he'd been trying to check on whether the senator's office phones were working. Constituents critical of her support for the administration's health care bill had reported trouble getting their calls through, he said. "On reflection, I could have used a different approach," he acknowledged.[23]

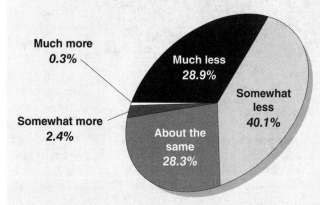

Journalists Say Protection of Sources Declined

Nearly 70 percent of the journalists surveyed felt they had less support from the courts in protecting their sources in 2006 than in 2001. Less than 3 percent said more protection was provided.

Perceived Protection of Media Sources by Courts, 2006
(compared to 2001)

Much more 0.3%
Much less 28.9%
Somewhat less 40.1%
Somewhat more 2.4%
About the same 28.3%

Source: RonNell Andersen Jones, "Media Subpoenas: Impact, Perception, and Legal Protection in the Changing World of American Journalism," *Washington Law Review*, September 2009

The conservative activist may be an extreme case. But provocateurs, on both the left and the right, have long existed on the margins of traditional, nonpartisan journalism.

Today, the opening up of the media universe has also provided a platform for press critics of all stripes to decry errors or bias in news organizations that proclaim adherence to objective journalism.

Among the major examples of the fury that media faults can whip up, veteran anchorman Dan Rather's premature departure from CBS News in 2004 followed discoveries made by conservative Web sites.[24]

That same year, *The New York Times* came under scathing criticism from the left — criticism to which the paper eventually bowed. In a front-page 1,200-word explanation — a tacit apology — the paper conceded fundamental weaknesses in a series of pre-Iraq War articles that made a strong case for the existence of weapons of mass destruction in Iraq. The weapons — which turned out not to exist — became the official justification for the U.S.-led invasion. "Accounts of

Senate Judiciary Committee members Charles Schumer, D-N.Y., left, and Dick Durbin, D-Ill., disagree over proposed legislation to create a journalists' "shield" law. Durbin says the bill's definition of a journalist is so broad as to be meaningless, but Schumer and others who support the legislation contend the courts would weed out those undeserving of being shielded.

Iraqi defectors were not always weighed against their strong desire to have Saddam Hussein ousted," *The Times* said of principal sources.[25] Many of those articles had been written by Judith Miller.

Yet for all the outrage directed at mainstream media by critics on the right and the left, the most-visited news sites on the Web provide reporting of the standard, objective kind. Yahoo! News, MSNBC, CNN and AOL ranked at the top in 2008, the Pew Research Center's Project for Excellence in Journalism found. They were followed by *The New York Times,* which got 19.5 million unique visitors a month in 2008 (and 15.4 million in December 2009).[26]

The non-newspaper sites ranked ahead of *The Times* —Yahoo! News, MSNBC, CNN and AOL News — all provided news in the nonpartisan, mainstream mode. "The majority of news that is produced with the largest audience, in traditional platforms and online, is still produced by institutions that adhere to traditional values of reportorial verification and independence," says Tom Rosenstiel, director of the Pew journalism center.

Rosenstiel acknowledges that the appeal of partisan journalism is growing. "There is no doubt that there is more of that content than there was," he says. "But the role of the growing partisan media appears at the moment to get a news institution that is somewhat friendly — like a cable news outlet — to grab a story and have it leap into the mainstream."

Breitbart, the right-of-center Web publisher, used that launch process to publicize O'Keefe's covert ACORN videos. Breitbart immediately alerted star Fox News commentator Glenn Beck, who ran excerpts. Fox News then covered the story heavily, with the mainstream media following days later.[27]

"My sites are trying to go from simply acting as media critic and saying, 'Let's report stories, let's get rid of the middleman,'" Breitbart says. "You can be 'Deep Throat' and you can be Woodward and Bernstein." (Breitbart, however, says he didn't know in advance about the Landrieu office attempt.)

Breitbart's main site, a news aggregation service, includes many links to dispatches by The Associated Press and other wire services that follow strict rules of nonpartisan coverage. "For those who aspire to it, [objectivity] is an admirable goal," he says. "But those adherents are few and far between. The left media, such as *The New York Times,* used objective journalism as a front for pushing the media to the left."

What Breitbart sees as a purely ideological contest may owe more to business imperatives that favor sites which draw identifiable demographic groups.

"Highly targeted advertisers want editorial content that's already tagged for the buyers they want to get," says Wasserman of Washington and Lee University, contrasting the Web model to old-style newspaper advertising aimed at the public in general. "A lot of people are tearing their hair out over that issue."

Nevertheless, Wasserman argues that a strong market still remains for reporting that strives for political neutrality. "You still have tremendous strength in these national franchises — *The Times,* the *Wall Street Journal, USA Today,*" he says. "These are publications people go to because they trust them to get the facts basically right and to have pretty good judgment about what's important and what's not."

Still, even resolutely nonpartisan news sites can be driven into trends they would once have resisted by the Web's business imperatives: to draw as many "unique users" as possible to a site. "We are seeing an enormous tilt in what is defined as news — an enormous tilt towards entertainment," says editor-turned-tech entrepreneur Mutter, citing major news organizations' attention to the Jay Leno-Conan O'Brien uproar at NBC, and earlier wall-to-wall coverage of pop star Michael Jackson's death.

Moreover, Mutter says, the Web-enabled habits of readers are hitting hard at the old model of neutral coverage that people of all persuasions can read. "We are seeing more and more people subscribing only to things that comport with their interests. If you're anti-Israel, you only want to read anti-Israel blogs. That's quite terrifying. In a day when there was a comparatively limited number of media outlets, most were sort of balanced and ecumenical, especially in the modern era."

BACKGROUND

Shifting Boundaries

Attempts to restrict press freedom began soon after the 1791 ratification of the Bill of Rights.[28]

In 1798, Congress passed the Sedition Act, which defined as criminal "any false, scandalous, and malicious" writing about the president (but not the vice president), Congress or the U.S. government.

Officially, justification for the law was an imminent war with France (which never went beyond undeclared hostilities). In reality, the Federalist-controlled Congress aimed to crack down on its Democratic-Republican opponents, including Thomas Jefferson, the vice president.

Of the 10 people arrested under the Sedition Act, at least three were journalists. The law expired in 1801, ending any chance of a Supreme Court decision on its constitutionality.

In a larger sense, passage of the controversial act reflected a postindependence view of the press. Before the American Revolution, pamphlets and newspapers that attacked colonial authorities earned applause from the future Founding Fathers. That attitude changed once they were in power.

Jefferson, before he became president, wrote, "Were it left to me to decide whether we should have a government without newspapers, or newspapers without a government, I should not hesitate to prefer the latter." His perspective changed in the White House. "The man who reads nothing at all," he wrote after taking office, "is better educated than the man who reads nothing but newspapers."[29]

The impulse to restrict newspapers when they criticized the government arose again during the Civil War. As the conflict raged, Union generals, but not President Abraham Lincoln, halted publication of about 300 newspapers on grounds that they'd published antiwar or antiadministration writings.

But the next major war saw another president, Woodrow Wilson, call for systematic repression of the speech and writings of radicals and pacifists who opposed U.S. entrance into World War I. Congress obliged with the Espionage Act of 1917, which made it a crime to "promote the success of" enemy forces or to "willfully obstruct the recruiting or enlistment service."[30]

A year later, Congress went even further with the Sedition Act of 1918, which made it a crime to criticize the U.S. government, Constitution or military.

After the war, courts began to hear challenges to convictions under the sedition law and similar state statutes, as well as other laws designed to curb dissident writings. Two landmark U.S. Supreme Court decisions proved critical in setting new press-freedom standards.

In 1925, *Gitlow v. New York* established that the First Amendment applied in states as well as to the federal government. For that reason, press-freedom scholars call the decision an advance. But it did uphold the conviction under state law of a Communist Party founder who wrote a pamphlet advocating revolution. "A State may punish utterances endangering the foundations of organized government and threatening its overthrow by unlawful means," the court said.[31]

Six years later, the high court took a bigger step toward protecting freedom to publish. In a case arising from political accusations — freighted with anti-Semitism — leveled against a Minneapolis police chief, the court rejected a state prohibition on "malicious, scandalous or defamatory" publications.[32]

Chief Justice Charles Evans Hughes, author of the 5-4 majority opinion in *Near v. Minnesota,* swept aside the state's argument that it banned only publications that couldn't prove their allegations. Decisions on whether allegations or comments were illegally defamatory should be made after publication, the court said.

Changing Profession

In the Republic's early days, newspapers and magazines were used as political weapons. But the rise of technology helped the development of fact-based journalism. In 1846, newspapers began using the newly invented telegraph to receive news and helped organize a cooperative news service, The Associated Press. Telegraph transmission was costly, and member newspapers had differing political orientations, so AP reporters sent stripped-down, factual dispatches.[33]

In the early 20th century, magazine journalists took fact-based reporting in a new direction: investigative journalism. *McClure's* magazine led the charge, running exposés on topics such as the anti-competitive business tactics of John D. Rockefeller's Standard Oil Co., corruption in city and state governments and child labor. President Theodore Roosevelt derisively called the crusading reporters "muckrakers," which they took as a badge of honor.

During this period, some newspaper industry leaders sought to raise reporting standards. Journalism should attain the "rank of a learned profession," newspaper magnate Joseph Pulitzer said in endowing the Columbia University School of Journalism, which began operating in 1912.[34]

In the early 1920s, the newly formed American Society of Newspaper Editors (ASNE) continued the trend toward professionalism, adopting a code that demanded impartiality: "News reports should be free from opinion or bias of any kind."[35]

As efforts to separate objective newspaper reporting from opinion-mongering and sensationalism continued, a new source of information emerged. In the late 1920s, radio networks began delivering news along with the entertainment they'd been featuring since earlier in the decade.

The professional rivalry may have mattered less to newspaper publishers than the appearance of their first major competitor for advertising dollars. By 1939 radio had 27 percent of advertisers' dollars — up from only 4 percent in 1927. Newspapers accounted for 38 percent — down from 54 percent. Magazines — 35 percent in 1939, down from 42 percent in 1929.

Nevertheless, advertising was so massive, especially during the post-World War II economic expansion, that the market proved big enough for most players. After a sharp drop-off during the war, the number of mass-market daily newspapers remained basically stable from 1945 to 1976, barely increasing from 1,744 to 1,756.

Journalistically, "objectivity" had established itself firmly by the 1950s. During the war, however, journalists and the government worked as comrades-in-arms, with censorship essentially voluntary. And the media ran dispatches from the government's Office of War Information without challenging their accuracy.

That history may have fostered an atmosphere of acceptance in reporting public officials' statements, especially on the most politically explosive issue of the day, communism. Notably, many news organizations covered Sen. Joseph R. McCarthy's campaign to unmask alleged Communists in government by merely reporting his allegations, even as he announced wildly varying numbers of alleged infiltrators.[36]

Some journalists worried at the time that they were backing down. "We are all very much more careful about what we write, what we say, what we join, than we used to be because we all start from the premise that whatever we do may be subject to damaging criticism from the extreme right," *New York Times* editorial writer John B. Oakes wrote to a colleague in 1953.[37]

Adversarial Journalism

While newspapers generally held back, the star of the newest medium — television — took on McCarthy. In 1954, as host of the news program "See It Now," Edward R. Murrow declared that McCarthy was promoting a climate of suspicion that gave "considerable comfort to our enemies."[38]

Murrow said privately that he was only following the lead of the handful of forthright print reporters. But he contributed to McCarthy's political decline, demonstrating TV's mass-communication power.

In 1950, only 13 percent of households had televisions. By 1960, televisions sat in 87 percent of American households.[39]

But for all the power of TV broadcasts — such as the dramatic, round-the-clock live coverage following the assassination of President John F. Kennedy — most TV news reports gave only the basics. Newspapers remained essential reading for detail and background.

In the early 1960s, sustained coverage of the violence directed at civil rights activists played a crucial part in building support for anti-discrimination and voting rights legislation. Not surprisingly, segregationists depicted the press (including some crusading Southern papers, such as the *Atlanta Constitution* and the *Delta Times-Democrat* of Greenville, Miss.) as an ally of the movement it was covering.

Overseas, another conflict was developing over news reports from Vietnam. In the early 1960s, Kennedy

CHRONOLOGY

1950s-1980 *Television grows in influence as U.S. confronts major challenges.*

1954 TV newsman Edward R. Murrow challenges red-baiting Sen. Joseph R. McCarthy, R-Wis., contributing to McCarthy's downfall.

1963 Press coverage of violence against civil rights protesters arouses widespread indignation, support for legislation. . . . President John F. Kennedy demands that *The New York Times* withdraw a Vietnam correspondent whose reporting challenges Pentagon's inflated success stories.

1968 News reports of North Vietnam's failed but powerful Tet Offensive help turn public opinion against war.

1971 *New York Times* begins publishing "Pentagon Papers." . . . Supreme Court refuses to block articles, ruling government hadn't proved national security threat.

1972 Supreme Court rules that reporters are required to obey subpoenas for information, including confidential sources. . . . Justice Lewis F. Powell writes separately that courts should balance need for testimony against free-press rights.

1973 *Washington Post* and other papers uncover Watergate scandal, building new respect for news media.

1980 Supreme Court rules that the press and public must have access to criminal trials except under limited circumstances.

1981-1990s *News media fall in opinion polls as talk radio hosts step up criticism, and Internet sites begin to offer news alternatives.*

1981 In a harbinger of scandals at other papers, *Washington Post* loses Pulitzer Prize awarded for a bogus story about an 8-year-old heroin addict.

1987 Federal Communications Commission repeals "Fairness Doctrine," allowing the emergence of talk radio, which becomes a largely conservative alternative to the mainstream media.

1996 Fox News begins building audience by nurturing conservative hosts.

1998 Pioneer Internet news entrepreneur Matt Drudge shows new Web's power by breaking news of President Bill Clinton-Monica Lewinsky scandal.

2000s *Old media revenues decline dramatically as news consumption on the Web skyrockets, and court decisions turn against journalists.*

2002 Senate Republican Leader Trent Lott of Mississippi loses his leadership post after a liberal news Web site reports his praise for the segregationist policies once championed by Sen. Strom Thurmond, R-S.C.

2003 Influential federal Judge Richard Posner cites 1972 Supreme Court decision in ruling that reporters enjoy no shield against subpoenas.

2004 Conservative bloggers uncover flaws in a report by longtime CBS News anchor Dan Rather about President George W. Bush's youthful military service; Rather is later forced out.

2005 Garrett Graff becomes first blogger accredited to White House news briefing.

2006 Newsroom executives report that subpoenas for reporters have risen substantially.

2007 *New York Times* reporter Judith Miller testifies in federal court after spending 85 days in jail for refusing to name source. . . . Videographer Joshua Wolf is freed after a record 226 days in jail for refusing to hand over video of San Francisco anti-war protest.

2008 Newspaper ad revenue drops 26 percent from 2005.

2009 Newspaper industry cuts 50,000 jobs since mid-2008. . . . House passes federal shield bill for journalists facing subpoenas; Senate Judiciary Committee approves another version of bill but continues debating who should be covered. . . . Homeland Security Department issues subpoenas for two travel bloggers; subpoenas withdrawn after blogger complies.

2010 Conservative media activist James O'Keefe is arrested with three others at Democratic Sen. Mary Landrieu's New Orleans office as they attempt an undercover video operation.

'Citizen Journalists' Spread News About Quake

In Iran, savvy protesters use Bluetooth, Twitter.

Citizen journalists using social-media technology sprang into action after the earthquake in Haiti and amidst savage political repression in Iran.

Hotel Oloffson manager Richard Morse sent what almost certainly was the first "citizen journalist" report from Port-au-Prince after the earthquake: "were ok at the oloffson. internet is on !! no phones ! hope all are okay.. alot of big building in PAP are down," Morse wrote on his Twitter.com account.[1]

He sent it at 5:23 p.m. on Jan. 12, noted Shashi Bellamkonda, a social-media expert for Network Solutions. The U.S. Geological Survey registered the earthquake began at 4:53 p.m.[2] The Associated Press correspondent in Port-au-Prince sent his first urgent "NewsAlert" only minutes before Morse, at 5:11 p.m.: "A strong earthquake has hit the impoverished country of Haiti where a hospital has collapsed."[3]

Cell-phone calls were going through only intermittently, but tweets — which use less bandwidth on wireless networks — turned into one of the major sources of information in the immediate aftermath of the catastrophe.

"People are praying in groups . . . others are looking for relatives . . . no phone service . . . no electricity," Morse wrote. "I'm told that parts of the Palace have collapsed . . . the UNIBANK here on Rue Capois has collapsed . . . people are bringing people by on stretchers . . . two helicopters have flown over head an hour ago but nothing since then. . . . "

The evocative details had journalists pressing for more: "Mainstream reporters were relying on social media for details," the *Columbia Journalism Review* reported on Jan. 13. The magazine noted that *The New York Times'* news blog put out a call to people with digital connections to or from the island nation: "Any readers who are in Haiti or in touch with people there are encouraged to . . . share first-hand accounts with us."[4]

Twittering, Facebook messaging and texting reinforced traditional media rather than replacing it. "I needed the media; I was glued to CNN," says Valda Valbrun, principal of Walkersville Middle School in Frederick, Md., whose 82-year-old Haitian-born father had moved back to Haiti after retiring. "The coverage they did was spectacular. Then I did go to Twitter, because I saw that people were able to do that."

But as days passed with no word from her father, Valbrun started using Facebook to communicate with friends who had their own connections to Haiti. "And I used CNN to post my father's picture," she said, praising the network's Web page of missing people. As it turned out, he survived the disaster and was able to return to the United States.

In the holy city of Qum last December, Iranian journalist Nazila Fathi of *The New York Times* reported from her home in exile in Toronto, demonstrators at the funeral of anti-government leader Grand Ayatollah Hossain Ali

summoned *New York Times* publisher Arthur Ochs Sulzberger to the White House to demand that he withdraw correspondent David Halberstam, whose reporting challenged official reports of progress.

Sulzberger ignored Kennedy's demand, and subsequent events vindicated the skeptical reporters, whose key sources were junior officers and officials. However, some press critics still argue that distorted reporting, notably of the 1968 Tet Offensive, turned public opinion against the war.[40]

The seeming disconnect between official optimism and reality in Vietnam drove domestic journalists to scrutinize government ever more rigorously. What some called "adversarial" coverage reached a high point in 1973 with the uncovering of the Watergate scandal, led by *Washington Post* reporters Bob Woodward and Carl Bernstein. After the unprecedented resignation of President Richard M. Nixon, journalists grew in public and judicial esteem as watchdogs over government.

Montazeri deployed a tool that many Americans may not know about. "Long ago, Iranian dissidents discovered that Bluetooth can link cellphones to each other in a crowd," Fathi wrote. "And that made 'Bluetooth' a verb in Iran: a way to turn citizen reportage instantly viral. A protester Bluetooths a video clip to others nearby, and they do the same. Suddenly, if the authorities want to keep the image from escaping the scene, they must confiscate hundreds or thousands of phones and cameras."[5]

Ever since protests began during the election of President Mahmoud Ahmadinejad, videos and Twitter feeds from Iran have been retransmitted abroad via blogs and social networks. "By following blogs and the cellphone videos seeping out of Iran," Fathi wrote, "in some ways I could report more productively than when I had to fear and outwit the government."[6]

But citizen journalism has its limits, especially in Iran. The government's security services show plenty of technological savvy as well. Exiles' social networks are heavily penetrated by government agents, *The Wall Street Journal* reports, leaving democracy activists abroad open to emailed threats.

Some exiles visiting the homeland have encountered unpleasant surprises. "One 28-year-old physician who lives in Dubai said that in July he was asked to log on to his Facebook account by a security guard upon arrival in Tehran's airport," *The Journal's* Farnaz Fassihi reported. "At first, he says, he lied and said he didn't have one. So the guard took him to a small room with a laptop and did a Google search for his name. His Facebook account turned up, he says, and his passport was confiscated. After a month and several rounds of interrogations, he says, he was allowed to exit the country."[7]

— *Peter Katel*

Iranians take pictures with cameras and cellphones in Tehran during the August 2007 hanging of two men convicted of killing a prominent judge.

AP Photo/Vahid Salemi

[1] Redistributed on "Corbett," listserv on Haitian affairs maintained by Bob Corbett of St. Louis, Mo.

[2] Shashi Bellamkonda, "Haiti Earthquake: Twitter reports on the ground from Haiti give early picture of calamity," Jan. 17, 2010, www.examiner.com/x-33257-DC-Social-Media-Marketing-Examiner-y2010m1d17-Twitter-reports-on-the-ground-from-Haiti-give-early-picture-of-calamity.

[3] The Associated Press, APNewsAlert,0020,www.breitbart.com/article.php?id=D9D6F7A00&show_article=1.

[4] Quoted in Curtis Brainard, "'New' Media Crucial in Aftermath of Haitian Earthquake," *Columbia Journalism Review*, Jan. 13, 2010, www.cjr.org/the_observatory/new_media_crucial_in_aftermath.php.

[5] Nazila Fathi, "The Exile's Eye," *The New York Times*, Jan. 17, 2010, "Week in Review," p. 1.

[6] *Ibid.*

[7] Farnaz Fassihi, "Iranian Crackdown Goes Global," *The Wall Street Journal*, Dec. 3, 2009, http://online.wsj.com/article/SB125978649644673331.html.

"A skyrocketing reputational status . . . led some judges and scholars to suggest that daily newspapers and television news operations should be revered as a fourth branch of government," writes press-law scholar Jones of Brigham Young University Law School.[41]

Judicial respect had been building for some time. The Supreme Court's landmark 1964 *New York Times v. Sullivan* decision shielded the press from libel suits by public officials. Only in cases of "actual malice," in which a news organization published a statement knowing it was untrue, or with "reckless disregard of whether it was false," could justify a libel claim against a news organization.[42]

Subsequently, the high court extended the *Sullivan* standard to public figures who don't hold public office. A modified version of the rule was applied to libel suits by private individuals.

The Supreme Court's next major press-freedom decision protected publication of secret government information. In 1971, *The New York Times* began publishing a series of articles based on the leaked "Pentagon Papers," a massive, secret Defense Department history of the Vietnam War.

Lower courts granted the Nixon administration's demand to halt publication. But the Supreme Court reversed the ruling, saying the government hadn't proved the articles harmed national security, which could justify prior restraint.[43]

Tide Turns

After the Pentagon Papers, however, another case muddied the press-freedom issue. The high court ruled 5-4 in 1972 that journalists weren't shielded from subpoenas seeking their notes and testimony in criminal cases.

But Justice Lewis F. Powell softened the blow. In a separate concurring opinion, Powell agreed that in the case at hand, journalists who had reported information from anonymous sources enjoyed no privilege against testifying. But in future cases, he concluded, courts should strike "a proper balance between freedom of the press and the obligation of all citizens to give relevant testimony with respect to criminal conduct."[44]

Powell didn't specify how to balance those interests. But at a time of high esteem for the press, his opinion gave media lawyers a tool to persuade judges to block subpoenas.[45]

For many years thereafter, the press enjoyed de facto protection, but Judge Richard A. Posner, an influential member of the 7th U.S. Circuit Court of Appeals in Chicago, brought the long spell to an end in 2003. Relying on the Supreme Court's full 1972 decision — not on Powell's concurrence — Posner pointed out that no precedent existed for applying "special criteria" to journalists trying to resist subpoenas.[46]

Thereafter, reporters challenging orders to testify endured major defeats. The most prominent case involved subpoenas for reporters in the 2007 trial of Lewis "Scooter" Libby, a top aide to Vice President Richard B. Cheney who was eventually convicted of perjury in a case that grew out of leaked intelligence secrets. *Times* reporter Miller spent 85 days in jail for defying a subpoena to testify. She gave in, she said, because her source, Libby, released her from a confidentiality agreement.[47]

Other reporters summoned in the Libby trial gave evidence after they or their companies made deals with prosecutors to limit their testimony. Elsewhere, in San Francisco, prosecutors demanded that two *San Francisco Chronicle* reporters name their source for a major story

about steroids in baseball. (They refused, but the source finally came forward.) The same year, freelance videographer Joshua Wolf was released after a record 226 days in federal custody for refusing to turn over all his video of violence at a street demonstration in San Francisco. He was freed after agreeing to post the material on the Web.[48]

The change in the legal climate coincided with declining regard for journalists and the media industry's sinking fortunes. By 2009, public opinion had hit a 24-year low, with 63 percent of Americans finding a pattern of media inaccuracy and 60 percent claiming political bias in news reports.[49]

Some pinpoint the decline's beginning to 1987, when the Federal Communications Commission (FCC) dropped the Fairness Doctrine, established in 1949, which required broadcasters to present controversial issues of public importance and to do so fairly.*[50]

Repeal of the Fairness Doctrine enabled political talk radio to emerge as an important political force. Rush Limbaugh, a pioneer of the format, made biting criticism of the "mainstream media" a major part of his conservative take on issues. When media tycoon Rupert Murdoch's News Corp. founded Fox News Channel in 1996, directed by former Republican political strategist Roger Ailes, its mostly conservative lineup of commentators echoed Limbaugh's denunciations of so-called liberal media.[51]

As a cable channel, Fox didn't come under FCC jurisdiction. But its overall approach makes clear its debt to Limbaugh and — some observers say — to the end of the Fairness Doctrine. "TV's Fox could not get away with its shameless shilling for the [Bush] White House if the Fairness Doctrine were still in place," liberal radio commentator Ian Masters of KPFK in Los Angeles argued in 2003.[52]

Liberal talk radio, however, draws smaller audiences. Some conservatives saw the recent collapse of Air America — a liberal talk-radio syndication service — as a major development. Bill O'Reilly, a popular, conservative Fox News commentator, called Air America's closing evidence of "the collapse of the far-left media." Air America veterans cited bad business management and noted that some of its stars have gone on to successful radio careers on their own, and in the case of comedian and former host Al Franken, to the U.S. Senate.[53]

---

* The Fairness Doctrine differs from the Equal Time rule, which deals only with political candidates.

Journalism Schools Adapting to Changing Times

But teaching the basics still gets top billing.

In the fast-changing world of journalism, reporters and editors have no choice but to change with the times. The same goes for journalism schools.

With the industry increasingly embracing more personal forms of journalism — not to mention shifting from print to the Web — journalism schools are changing their curricula as well. While traditional news reporting still dominates the curricula, J-schools are putting more emphasis on new media and advocacy and opinion journalism.

Journalism should "have a greater ambition than simply reporting facts without analysis or context," Nicholas Lemann, dean of the Columbia University Graduate School of Journalism, wrote in *The Chronicle of Higher Education.*[1] Ironically, amid the shrinking news industry, journalism schools are thriving. The question is, how are they changing to accommodate the professionally dynamic but financially beleaguered field?

Susanne Shaw, a professor of journalism at the University of Kansas and executive director of The Accrediting Council on Education in Journalism and Mass Communications, says the numerous changes in the journalism industry are causing many schools to consider changing their curriculum. However, she thinks the focus is more on multimedia — including Web-based video and audio — than on advocacy journalism. The university currently has just one class dedicated solely to commentary and opinion writing, as does the University of Kentucky, though it covers such writing in other classes too, Shaw says.

"Most schools, I think, are trying to include courses to prepare students to do it all," Shaw says, instead of focusing

J-School Grads Heading for Web Jobs

The percentage of journalism graduates writing and editing for the Web increased by 35 percent from 2006 to 2007 and nearly tripled from 2004 to 2007. Overall, about 56 percent of J-school grads were doing Web editing and writing; more than a quarter of the graduates were designing Web pages.

Percentage of Journalism Graduates in Web-Related Journalism Jobs (2004-2007)

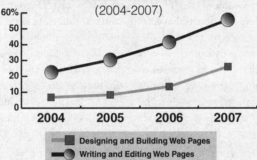

Source: "Annual Survey of Journalism & Mass Communication Graduates," Project for Excellence in Journalism, Cox Center at the University of Georgia

more on just advocacy journalism.

Tom Warhover, chairman of the print and digital news faculty at the University of Missouri School of Journalism — the nation's first J-school — says that despite the emergence of blogs and other new electronic opportunities for citizen journalists, the journalism industry as a whole is not abandoning old-fashioned, straight-news journalism for advocacy.

Nonetheless, Warhover deems advocacy and opinion writing important and says Missouri also offers an editorial-writing class. Moreover, Missouri is considering a new curriculum track dedicated to opinion and advocacy journalism, he says. Students need those skills in order to have the flexibility to go down any journalistic path they choose, especially if it leads to the "open range of the Internet," or to the increasingly popular world of nonprofit organizations.

"Teaching advocacy in that realm is a really interesting and burgeoning possibility," he says.

Above all, Shaw says, students must acquire solid journalism skills. "The bottom line is you've got to be a good writer, and know how to ask the right questions," she says.

—Julia Russell

[1] Nicholas Lemann, "Opinion and Ideas," *The Chronicle of Higher Education,* Nov. 15, 2009, www.lexisnexis.com.proxy-um.researchport .umd.edu/us/lnacademic/results/docview/docview.do?doc LinkInd=true&risb=21_T8456847691&format=GNBFI&sort=BOOL EAN&startDocNo=1&resultsUrlKey=29T8456847699&cisb=22_ T8456847696&treeMax=true&treeWidth=0&csi=171267&docNo=1.

In any event, the appearance of the Web and its repercussions for the news business have proved far more consequential than the talk-radio surge. The first event to make that point also showed that the Internet could extend the reach of one individual worldwide. That individual, Matt Drudge, runs the *Drudge Report*, a constantly updated page of news links and occasional reporting. In 1998, he reported that *Newsweek* had killed a detailed story on President Clinton's affair with a former White House intern, soon identified as Monica Lewinsky. Drudge's report touched off the political firestorm that led to Clinton's impeachment.

"This story has done for the Internet what the Gulf War did for CNN and what the Kennedy assassination did for television in general," said Michael Kinsley, then editor of *Slate,* a pioneering Web-based magazine. (When it started up in 1996 *Slate* occasionally reached 10,000 readers a day; now it gets about 1.3 million a day.)[54]

By 2000, news organizations had concluded that having a Web presence was indispensable. But the disconnect between a Web site's power to vastly expand a news organization's reach, and its inability to build revenues to match, was already plain. "Except in a few cases, the idea that anyone will make money from selling news on the Web is laughable," Barry Parr, a business analyst with International Data Corp., told the *Los Angeles Times.*[55]

But independent sites, especially those with clear political identities, did build readership — and showed their power. In 2002, Josh Marshall's then one-man Web operation, the Democratic-oriented *TalkingPointsMemo,* scooped the mainstream press by reporting the significance of a comment by then-Senate Majority Leader Trent Lott of Mississippi praising the Jim Crow-era policies once chanpioned by Sen. Strom Thurmond. (Lott lost his Republican leadership post.)[56]

Two years later, conservative blog sites set the stage for veteran anchor Dan Rather's premature departure from CBS News in 2004. Contributors to *Free Republic, Power Line* and *Little Green Footballs* (whose political orientation has since shifted), highlighted suspicious features of documents that Rather cited to back up a story that young George W. Bush had used family political connections to land a safe spot in the Texas Air National Guard to avoid serving in Vietnam. The documents later turned out to have been created years after they were dated, as the bloggers had argued.[57]

CURRENT SITUATION

Shielding Everyone?

A bill recently approved by the Senate Judiciary Committee would create the first federal shield law for journalists facing demands to testify in court or turn over material to law enforcement agencies.

Backers of the Senate legislation say their bill wouldn't extend the privilege to just anybody who, in today's Web-enabled world, blogs, tweets, or uploads video to YouTube and finds him or herself facing a federal subpoena.

But some committee members criticize the bill as it now reads, arguing it would cover everybody, even a leafleter in a Senate office building hallway. "This definition is no definition at all," Sen. Richard Durbin, D-Ill., said during a Dec. 10, 2009, meeting of the panel. "It is so broad as to be meaningless."[58]

But fellow Democrats who support the legislation contend that the courts would weed out those undeserving of being shielded.

"We're talking really about bloggers here," Sen. Arlen Specter, D-Pa., the bill's main sponsor, said during a debate that included mention of the liberal *Huffington Post* Web site, which includes posts by dozens of bloggers. "I would give them the benefit of the coverage."

Specter and other bill supporters won the argument, passing the bill after voting down an amendment to restrict the bill's coverage proposed by Sen. Dianne Feinstein, D-Calif., with support from Durbin.

Whatever definition committee members finally settle on, the bill wouldn't automatically confer immunity from subpoenas. A judge could order that a potential witness give evidence that was ruled to be necessary to prevent or lessen threats to national security. Nor would protection be granted for eyewitness evidence of a crime.

Arguments on those issues have been resolved.

But staffers and outside experts say that given Durbin's position as assistant majority leader, the bill will not come to the floor until he's satisfied with the definition of who would be covered. "He wants a sense of professionalism," says Dalglish of The Reporters Committee for Freedom of the Press, who is active in the crafting of a modified definition. The committee is concerned that reporters covering news via the Internet not be excluded.

The definition issue was expected to be resolved as early as the first week in February. Shield backers were

AT ISSUE

Should the proposed "shield" bill protect independent bloggers and all freelance journalists?

YES — Sen. Charles E. Schumer, D-N.Y.
Chairman, Committee on Rules and Administration
From Remarks Before Senate
Judiciary Committee Meeting and Afterward, Dec. 10, 2009

Journalism is changing. But I do not believe we should define [who merits protection] by the medium. People can do bad things on paper and good things on paper, bad things electronically and good things electronically. I've been subject to the brickbats of bloggers, but what they say shouldn't matter. We shouldn't look at whether people are saying bad things. That doesn't change what kind of privilege they have if they are protecting information.

Maybe it will happen — maybe once every three years — that the press secretary of one of us gets confidential information and then disseminates it. But the idea that every press secretary or every leafleter is going to invoke the [shield] privilege — it's not going to happen. It's only in a rare instance that you're disseminating confidential information and someone wants you to disclose it.

We've struck the right balance between national security concerns and the public's right to know. And it's important to remember that even if someone is a covered person, they don't automatically get protection. There is a [court] balancing test. Certainly a leafleter would not meet the balancing test. This bill does not give a huge privilege to everyone.

The [defeated] amendment proposed by Sen. [Dianne] Feinstein [D-Calif.] and Sen. [Richard] Durbin [D-Ill.] would require that a freelance journalist be able to demonstrate they've been under contract for six months of the past two years, and that a covered person gather information by direct interviews or by making direct observations of events.

Legitimate people who deserve this protection wouldn't even be allowed in. The definition excludes those who comment on public events, but who don't necessarily go into the field; mainstream columnists for established newspapers would be excluded. Journalists whose story results from a review of Freedom of Information Act documents would not be covered. Freelance journalists — in today's economy it is less and less likely that a freelance journalist would be able to demonstrate they've been under contract for six months of the past two years. If I am a journalist and I write a column, but don't have a contract for it, why in God's name should I be excluded? It makes no sense whatsoever.

This bill will ensure a free press, which is a cornerstone of our democracy.

NO — Sen. Dianne Feinstein, D-Calif.
Chairwoman, Senate Select Committee On Intelligence
From Remarks Before Senate
Judiciary Committee Meeting, Dec. 10, 2009

I've always believed that being a journalist carries with it certain responsibilities. Journalists are trained to at least try to cover an issue objectively and to search for truth. Established newspapers and broadcasters set journalistic standards for the reporters. They have editors, directors or producers who review the reporters' work and hold them to account. Under the new definition in this bill, none of these safeguards exist.

Under the definition that we proposed, the journalist worked as a salaried employee or independent contractor of an entity that disseminates information.

The current language makes anyone a journalist no matter how crazy, hateful or false the information they post.

Or let's say, hypothetically, that a neo-Nazi blogger obtained information from [another neo-Nazi] at an anti-immigration demonstration, and the authorities sought the identity of that [person] so they could identify the perpetrators of violent crimes. This neo-Nazi blogger would qualify as a journalist under this bill, and federal authorities would have to exhaust all reasonable alternatives [to a subpoena]. And the court would have to engage in analysis, applying a balancing test. . . . In my view, hatemongers do not deserve the protection.

I'm concerned that if we keep the wide-open definition in the bill we will create a mechanism for a disgruntled person to leak slanted, incomplete or even deliberately false information to an ideologically sympathetic person, knowing that the person could then invoke the shield created by this bill to protect this ill-spirited source.

Even worse, we could create a regime where somebody could just make up a piece of information, and make up a source for it and then invoke the shield to cover up their own deception.

For those of us who have been around for a while and watched the change in journalism — a lot of it is very good. But there has always been a standard for legitimacy. Here, there is no standard for legitimacy. It's a hard one to come up with; I'm the first to admit it. But as I read the definition, it virtually applies to most of us. I could consider myself a journalist under this, and I'm not. I hope that this is a work in progress.

counting heads in the Senate in early February. With backers having included a prominent Republican, Sen. Lindsey Graham of South Carolina, Dalglish was not expecting a partisan fight.

Senate passage would likely guarantee enactment. The House passed a version of the bill on a voice vote last March, and the bills are seen as relatively easy to reconcile. The Obama administration has endorsed the Senate bill.

"This legislation provides robust judicial protection for journalists' confidential sources," National Intelligence Director Dennis C. Blair and Attorney General Eric H. Holder Jr. wrote in a Nov. 4, 2009, letter to Senate Judiciary Committee Chairman Patrick J. Leahy, D-Vt., "while also enabling the Government to take measures necessary to protect national security and enforce our criminal laws."[59]

On the state front, Republican Texas Gov. Rick Perry signed a new state shield law last May. And shield legislation passed the Wisconsin Assembly and is pending in the state Senate.[60]

Subpoenaing Students

An unusual media-subpoena case under way in Chicago centers on a group of journalism students who are fighting subpoenas not for their sources — which are public — but for their grades.

The matter might sound relatively trivial, but it grows out of a homicide conviction and life sentence and the students' reinvestigation of the case.

The students were part of the Innocence Project at Northwestern University's Medill School. Since 1999, students in the program have conducted investigations that helped free 11 men from prison, five of them on death row.[61]

Last year, the students' digging succeeded in reopening the case of Anthony McKinney, convicted in 1981 in the killing of a security guard and imprisoned ever since. But the Cook County state attorney's office, which has cooperated with the Innocence Project in other cases, balked at cooperating in the McKinney case.[62]

State Attorney Anita Alvarez subpoenaed all of the students' notes and electronic communications in the case plus the grades they'd received and the grading criteria set by Project Director David Protess, a veteran journalist and criminal-justice researcher. As the case has developed,

Alvarez and her colleagues have argued in court filings that in an effort to win good grades students paid two witnesses for their statements, and that a female student flirted with another witness to encourage him to talk.[63]

The alleged bribe centered on an alleged overpayment of $60 for a cab ride. And Protess and one of his woman students denied any use of flirting as a tactic. As to the suggestion that students' grades depend on acquiring evidence of innocence, a 2008 graduate said she'd gotten an A for work that proved one man's guilt.[64]

Beyond the factual issues is a link to the question that's preoccupying journalism-watchers and lawmakers elsewhere. "When I was a law student, I wasn't a lawyer," Alvarez said in an interview with *Chicago Magazine,* arguing that the journalism students aren't journalists — and hence ineligible for protection under the Illinois shield law.[65]

But, a coalition of 18 media companies and organizations countered in a friend of the court brief on behalf of the students, their work was clearly journalistic. And, a motion filed with the brief adds, "The use of student journalists is only likely to increase as news organizations face declining advertising revenues and shrinking newsroom staffs."

Freedom of Information

Press freedom involves more than protection from subpoenas. For decades, media organizations have been in the vanguard of campaigns for access to government documents and meetings and trials.

These guarantees, where they exist, apply to ordinary citizens, not just reporters. In practice, though, reporters make the greatest use of that access.

At a time when the media are short of time and money, some media-law experts worry that government officials are feeling less obliged to comply with reporters demanding access to meetings and records.

In Iowa, Democratic Gov. Chet Culver and the *Des Moines Register,* the state's leading newspaper, have been sparring for about a year over the paper's efforts to obtain internal documents concerning state supervision of facilities for disabled people.

State officials "may get sued yet," says Giudicessi, an attorney for the paper. "The statute of limitations hasn't run."

Culver's office argued a year ago that 50 e-mails between members of his staff concerning the 2008 death of a 26-year-old resident of the Glenwood Resource Center were exempt from disclosure under the state's open-records law because they are "draft documents."[66]

The newspaper reported that the law doesn't protect draft documents from public release. But the governor relies on an opinion by the state attorney general's office that the legislature never meant to include draft documents in the open-records law.[67]

Later in 2009, Culver's office began charging for document requests — not for standard photocopying costs but for the expense of staff analyzing the documents to decide if they could be released. For one set of documents involving state care for mentally retarded workers at another facility, the fee was $630. The newspaper turned down the arrangement on the grounds that it might be paying for documents it wasn't allowed to have.[68]

With both sides dug in, only courts can determine who is interpreting open-records law correctly. But, first, a news organization would have to bring the matter to court. And media lawyers worry that such lawsuits are becoming less common, as struggling news organizations tighten their belts.

"A lot of these acts — sunshine laws, public meetings laws, the Freedom of Information Act — are not self-executing," says Jones of Brigham Young University. "Without the mainstream media to act as the enforcement arm, some of these laws I really worry will be dead on the books."

OUTLOOK

Limited Resources

In late January *The New York Times* announced a fee system (to begin in 2011) for non-subscribers who want full Web access to the paper. "It was clear when consumer [circulation] revenues surpassed advertising revenues last year that *The New York Times* was going to come up with some kind of pay model," *Times* media columnist David Carr wrote."[69]

But, Carr acknowledged, "Every plan that could be conceived of heads into a large headwind, built up over years, that consumers do not expect to pay for content no matter where it comes from."

Meanwhile, think tanks are striving to develop plans to ensure that public-interest journalism survives, in some form.

At the University of Southern California, the Annenberg School's Center on Communication Leadership & Policy is proposing indirect public subsidies of the news media. "The government has always supported the commercial news business. It does so today," argues a report by the center's director, Geoffrey Cowan, and David Westphal, a senior fellow, citing subsidized postal rates for mailed publications and special tax treatment for news businesses. "Unless the government takes affirmative action, though, the level of support is almost certain to decline at this important time in the history of journalism."[70]

The Pew Research Center's Project for Excellence in Journalism, meanwhile, devotes itself to analyzing trends rather than devising solutions to the business crisis. Where those trends are headed, acknowledges project director Rosenstiel, isn't exactly clear. "The analogy may be the early '20s and radio, when you're at the beginning of something, and the actual direction of the storm can be hard to determine."

One possible form the news universe may take is "a handful of national newspapers and a smaller number of metro newspapers, and an increase in the number of niche neighborhood sites," Rosenstiel says. "It may be that we have an ecosystem that is partly citizen- or amateur-based at a very local level, and more conventional and professional at a national level."

But will either model provide the resources for journalists — professional or amateur — to take on government officials who close off access or subpoena reporters' notes?

"My concern is that the only people who will be able to afford to wage those kinds of fights are people underwritten in one form or another by government subsidies," says *Des Moines Register* attorney Giudicessi. "If we go to a digital model, an iPod-Kindle model, I don't know where the money is going to come from to afford that watchdog element."

Web-based journalism operations funded by foundations and private donors offer a potential approach. The best-known of these is *ProPublica,* which was started two years ago with a three-year $30 million grant from husband-and-wife philanthropists Herbert and Marion Sandler and dedicated to nonpartisan, investigative journalism.[71]

Wasserman of Washington and Lee University argues the money might have been better spent in grants for investigative reporting by local newspapers, which is diminishing. "We are going to reap a year's worth of local and state corruption, because that's where the news cutbacks have been most numerous," he says. "God only knows what's happening in zoning and the provision of public works."

Jones of Brigham Young University Law School shares his grim outlook. She doubts that a legal battle for courtroom access that led to a 1980 Supreme Court victory by a Richmond, Va., newspaper company would happen today.[72] "That holding is not limited to newspapers," she says. "All of us as citizens are guaranteed access to criminal trials because newspapers had the resolve and dollars to litigate."

But at least in the near future, Jones continues, "unless some very creative solutions come into being quite quickly, I predict that at least initially we'll have a fairly significant void in this kind of democracy-enhancing litigation that newspapers have provided to us."

Still, Dalglish of the Reporters Committee says her organization and some big media companies remain capable of fighting free-press battles. As to the future, "I think the hemorrhaging of the mainstream media will have stabilized. I'm hoping that someone comes forward and figures out how to make journalism pay on the Internet."

NOTES

1. Christopher Elliott, "Full text of my subpoena from the Department of Homeland Security," *Elliott.org,* Dec. 29, 2009, www.elliott.org/blog/full-text-of-my-subpoena-from-the-department-of-homeland-security.

2. Larry Margasak and Corey Williams, "Search for answers, tighter security after attack," The Associated Press, Dec. 27, 2009; Richard Sisk *et al.,* "In An Upright Position," *Daily News* (New York), Dec. 27, 2009, p. 6.

3. Steven Frischling, "The Fallout From SD 1544-09-06: The Feds At My Door," Dec. 30, 2009, http://boardingarea.com/blogs/flyingwithfish/2009/12/30/the-fallout-from-sd-1544-09-06-the-feds-at-my-door/; Larry Margasak, "US ends journalist subpoenas over leaked memo," The Associated Press, Jan. 1, 2010, http://news.yahoo.com/s/ap_travel/20100101/ap_tr_ge/us_travel_brief_airliner_attack_tsa_sub poenas_1.

4. RonNell Andersen Jones, "Avalanche or Undue Alarm? An Empirical Study of Subpoenas Received by the News Media," *Minnesota Law Review,* 2008, p. 113, http://papers.ssrn.com/sol3/papers.cfm?abstract_id=1125500.

5. Neil A. Lewis and Scott Shane, "Reporter Who Was Jailed Testifies in Libby Case," *The New York Times,* Jan. 31, 2007, p. A1.

6. Anne E. Kornblut and Michael A. Fletcher, "In Obama's decision-making, a wide range of influences," *The Washington Post,* Jan. 25, 2010, www.washingtonpost.com/wp-dyn/content/article/2010/01/24/AR2010012403014.html? hpid=topnews.

7. RonNell Andersen Jones, "Media Subpoenas: Impact, Perception, and Legal Protection in the Changing World of American Journalism," *Washington Law Review,* August 2009, p. 363, http://papers.ssrn.com/sol3/papers.cfm?abstract_id=1407105.

8. *Ibid.,* p. 144; and Jones, "Avalanche or Undue Alarm . . . ," *op. cit.* p. 142.

9. David Westphal, "News Media in Crisis," in "Public Policy and Funding the News," University of Southern California, Annenberg Center on Communication Leadership & Policy, 2010, p. 5, www.fundingthenews.org/pdf/public_policy_report.pdf.

10. David Lieberman, "Newspaper closings raise fear about industry," *USA Today,* March 19, 2009, www.usatoday.com/money/media/2009-03-17-newspapers-downturn_N.htm; Matea Gold, "CBS News staffers fret that layoffs will hamper newsgathering," *Los Angeles Times,* Company Town (blog), Feb. 2, 2010, http://latimesblogs.latimes.com/entertainmentnewsbuzz/2010/02/cbs-news-staffers-fret-that-layoffs-will-hurt-newsgathering.html.

11. Video of Senate Judiciary Committee debate over the bill on Dec. 10, 2009, is available at "Full Committee, Executive Business Meeting," http://judiciary.senate.gov/resources/webcasts/index.cfm?t=m&d=12-2009&p=all.

12. "'New York Times' Begins Round of Newsroom Layoffs," The Associated Press (*Editor & Publisher),* Dec. 17, 2009, www.editorandpublisher.com/ eandp/news/article_display.jsp?vnu_content_ id=1004054338; Emma Heald, "Associated Press confirms total of 90 layoffs this week," editorswe blog.org, *World Editors Forum,* Nov. 20, 2009, www.editorsweblog.org/newspaper/2009/11/associ ated_press_confirms_total_of_90_la.php; Paul Beebe, "Salt Lake Tribune owner files Chapter 11 reorganization," *Salt Lake Tribune,* Jan. 22, 2010, www.sltrib.com/business/ci_14248521; Stephanie Clifford, "Time Inc. Layoffs Begin at Sports Illustrated," *The New York Times*, Media Decoder blog, Nov. 3, 2009, http://mediadecoder.blogs .nytimes.com/2009/11/03/time-inc-layoffs-begin- at-sports-illustrated/; Jeff Pijanowsky, "More than 15,000 People Have Lost Their Jobs in 2009 in the Newspaper Industry," *New Cycle* (blog), Dec. 14, 2009, http://news-cycle.blogspot.com/2009/12/ more-than-15000-people-have-lost-their.html.

13. John Thornton, "A Note from Our Chairman," *The Texas Tribune,* Jan. 24, 2010, www.texastribune.org/ stories/2010/jan/25/note-chairman/; John Temple, "I'm moving to Honolulu to become the first editor of Peer News," *Temple Talk* (blog), Jan. 21, 2010, www.johntemple.net/2010/01/im-moving-to- honolulu-to-become-first.html; Bill Mitchell, "Nonprofit Connecticut Mirror Targets Gaps in Political Coverage and Data," *NewsPay* (blog), *Poynter Online,* Jan. 25, 2010, www.poynter.org/ column.asp?id=131&aid=176435.

14. Michael Wolff, "Is a Tweet News?" *Off the Grid,* Jan. 25, 2010, www.newser.com/off-the-grid/post/382/ is-a-tweet-news-and-is-murdoch-selling-his-papers .html.

15. David Shaw, "Do bloggers deserve basic journalistic pro- tections?" *Los Angeles Times*, March 27, 2005, p. E14.

16. Garrett Graff, "Bloggers and Journalism," *echoditto*, March 23, 2005, www.echoditto.com/node/619.

17. *Ibid.*

18. Adam Cohen, "The Latest Rumbling in the Blogosphere: Questions About Ethics," *The New York Times*, May 8, 2005, Sect. 4, p. 11.

19. Court decisions summarized in Mary-Rose Papandrea, "Citizen Journalism and the Reporter's Privilege," *Minnesota Law Review*, 2007, pp. 517- 518, http://lsr.nellco.org/cgi/viewcontent.cgi? article=1168&context=bc_lsfp.

20. *Ibid.*, p. 590.

21. *Ibid.*, p. 591.

22. Campbell Robertson and Bernie Becker, "Tampering at Senator's Office was 'Stunt,' Lawyer Says," *The New York Times,* Jan. 29, 2010, p. A16.

23. Statement from James O'Keefe, Jan. 29, 2010, http://bigjournalism.com/jokeefe/2010/01/29/state ment-from-james-okeefe/#more-14542.

24. Josh Levin, "Rather Serious," *Slate,* Sept. 10, 2004, www.slate.com/id/2106553/.

25. "The Times and Iraq," *The New York Times,* May 26, 2004, p. A1.

26. Zachary M. Seward, "Top 15 newspaper sites of 2008," Nieman Journalism Lab, Feb. 17, 2009; "The State of the News Media 2009," *op. cit.* p. 12. "Site profile, nytimes.com," as of Feb. 1, 2010, http://siteanalytics.compete.com/nytimes.com/.

27. Perry Bacon Jr., "ACORN video creates new conser- vative star," *The Washington Post,* Oct. 31, 2009, www.washingtonpost.com/wp-dyn/content/article/ 2009/10/30/AR2009103003737_p.html.

28. Except where otherwise indicated, this subsec- tion draws on Alex S. Jones, *Losing the News: The Future of the News That Feeds Democracy* (2009). For background, see Kenneth Jost, "Free-Press Disputes," *CQ Researcher*, April 8, 2005, pp. 293-316.

29. Both quoted in Jones, *ibid.*

30. "U.S. Espionage Act, 15 June 1917," firstworldwar .com, www.firstworldwar.com/source/espionageact .htm.

31. *Gitlow v. New York*, 268 U.S. 652 (1925).

32. *Near v. Minnesota,* 283 U.S. 697 (1931).

33. Except where otherwise indicated, this subsection is drawn from Michael Emery and Edwin Emery, *The Press and America: An Interpretive History of the Mass Media* (6th ed., 1988), pp. 216-217.

34. Quoted in Michael Schudson, "The objectivity norm in American journalism," *Journalism,* 2001, jou.sagepub.com/cgi/content/abstract/2/2/149.

35. Quoted in *ibid.*

36. Edwin R. Bayley, *Joe McCarthy and the Press* (1981).

37. Quoted in *ibid.*, p. 216.

38. Except where otherwise indicated, this subsection is drawn from Emery and Emery, *op. cit.*

39. For 1960 statistic, "Facts for Features," U.S. Census Bureau, March 11, 2004, www.census.gov/Press-Release/www/releases/archives/facts_for_features_special_editions/001702.html.

40. Peter Braestrup, *The Big Story: How the American Press and Television Reported and Interpreted the Crisis of Tet 1968 in Vietnam and Washington* (1994).

41. Jones, "Media Subpoenas," *op. cit.* p. 319.

42. *New York Times Co. v. Sullivan,* 376 U.S. 254 (1964).

43. The case is *New York Times v. United States,* 403 U.S. 713 (1971).

44. *Branzburg v. Hayes,* 408 U.S. 665 (1972).

45. Jones, "Media Subpoenas," *op. cit.* p. 346.

46. *McKevitt v. Pallasch,* 339 F.3d 530 (7th Cir. 2003), quoted in Jones, "Media Subpoenas," *op. cit.* p. 347 (footnote 118). For the legal ambiguity of Powell's opinion, see Adam Liptak, "Courts Grow Increasingly Skeptical of Any Special Protections for the Press," *The New York Times,* June 28, 2005, p. A1.

47. Carol D. Leonnig and Amy Goldstein, "Libby Given 2-1/2-Year Prison Term," *The Washington Post,* June 6, 2007, www.washingtonpost.com/wp-dyn/content/article/2007/06/05/AR 2007060500150.html; Neil A. Lewis and Scott Shane, "Reporter Who Was Jailed Testifies in Libby Case," *The New York Times,* Jan. 31, 2007, p. A1.

48. David Kravetz, "Freelance journalist is freed after spending record time in jail," The Associated Press, April 4, 2007.

49. "Press Accuracy Rating Hits Two Decade Low," Pew Research Center for People and the Press, Sept. 13, 2009, http://people-press.org/report/543/.

50. Jim Puzzanghera, "Democrats speak out for Fairness Doctrine," *Los Angeles Times,* July 23, 2007, p. C1.

51. David Carr and Tim Arango, "A Fox Chief at the Pinnacle of Media and Politics," *The New York Times,* Jan. 9, 2010, www.nytimes.com/2010/01/10/business/media/10ailes.html?scp=1&sq=Roger Ailes&st=cse.

52. Ian Masters, "Media Monopolies Have Muzzled Dissent," *Los Angeles Times*, May 1, 2003, Part 2, p. 15.

53. Steve Carney, "The message of Air America's end," *Los Angeles Times,* Jan. 23, 2010, www.latimes.com/entertainment/news/la-et-air-america 23-2010jan23,0,1604003.story.

54. Quoted in Marlene Cimons, "Some See Internet Coming of Age During Clinton Troubles," *Los Angeles Times,* Feb. 2, 1998, p. A5; "Newsweek Kills Story on White House Intern," Jan. 17, 1998, www.drudgereportarchives.com/data/2002/01/17/20020117_175502_ml.htm; David Plotz, "A Slate Timeline," June 19, 2006, www.slate.com/id/2143235/; Site profile: slate.com, siteanalytics.compete.com/slate.com.

55. Quoted in Charles Piller, "Web News Sites Fail to Click," *Los Angeles Times,* Aug. 18, 2000, p. A1.

56. Matthew Klam, "Fear and Laptops on the Campaign Trail," *The New York Times Magazine,* Sept. 26, 2004, p. 43.

57. Josh Levin, "Rather Serious," *Slate,* Sept. 10, 2004, www.slate.com/id/2106553/.

58. "Full Committee, Executive Business Meeting," webcast, *op. cit.* O'Reilly quoted in Brian Stelter, "Liberal Radio, Even Without Air America," *The New York Times,* Jan. 24, 2010, www.nytimes.com/2010/01/25/arts/25radio.html?scp=1&sq=airamerica&st=cse.

59. Blair and Holder to Leahy, Nov. 4, 2009, www.rcfp.org/newsitems/docs/20091105_1551 25_letter.pdf.

60. Kelly Shannon, "Texas Governor Signs Shield Law to Protect Journos," The Associated Press (*Editor and Publisher*) May 14, 2009, www.editorandpublisher.com/eandp/news/article_display.jsp?vnu_content_id=1003973183; Stacy Forster and Patrick Marley, "Shield law for reporters gets OK," *Milwaukee Journal Sentinel,* Sept. 23, 2009, p. B3.

61. "Medill Innocence Project" Web site, www.medillinnocenceproject.org.

62. Bryan Smith, "The Professor and the Prosecutor: Anita Alvarez's office turns up the heat on David Protess' Medill Innocence Project," *Chicago Magazine,* February 2010, www.chicagomag.com/Chicago-Magazine/February-2010/Anita-Alvarez-turns-up-the-heat-in-her-battle-with-Northwesterns-David-Protess-and-his-Medill-Innocence-Project/.

63. *Ibid.;* Karen Hawkins, "Prosecutors claim students paid 2 witnesses," The Associated Press, Nov. 11, 2009.

64. Smith, *ibid.*

65. Quoted in *ibid.*

66. Quoted in Clark Kauffman, "E-mail 'drafts' on Glenwood death kept secret," *Des Moines Register,* Jan. 8, 2009, p. B1.

67. *Ibid.*

68. Clark Kauffman, "Consultant's report not ready for public, governor's office says," *Des Moines Register,* Sept. 4, 2009.

69. David Carr, "Dialing in a Plan: The Times Installs a Meter on its Future," *Media Decoder* (blog), Jan. 20, 2010, http://mediadecoder.blogs.nytimes.com/2010/01/20/dialing-in-a-plan-the-times-installs-a-meter-on-its-future/.

70. Geoffrey Cowan and David Westphal, "Public Policy and Funding the News," Center on Communication Leadership and Policy, Jan. 28, 2010, p. 14.

71. Joe Nocera, "Self-Made Philanthropists," *The New York Times Magazine,* March 9, 2008, p. 58.

72. *Richmond Newspapers, Inc. v. Virginia,* 448 U.S. 555 (1980). For background, see Jost, *op. cit.*

BIBLIOGRAPHY
Selected Sources
Books

Bollinger, Lee C., *Uninhibited, Robust, and Wide-Open: A Free Press for a New Century,* Oxford University Press, 2010.
The president of Columbia University calls for making press freedom a priority in domestic and international affairs.

Jones, Alex S., *Losing the News: The Future of the News That Feeds Democracy,* Oxford University Press, 2009.
Combining personal memories with recent history, a veteran journalist who directs the Joan Shorenstein Center for the Press, Politics and Public Policy at Harvard University's Kennedy School of Government analyzes the collapse of the old business model and explores possible new directions.

Sanford, Bruce W., *Don't Shoot the Messenger: How Our Growing Hatred of the Media Threatens Free Speech For All of Us,* Rowman & Littlefield, 2001.
A veteran First Amendment lawyer examines the reasons why public esteem for the media began plummeting.

Articles

"Nonprofits and Journalism: An Interview with Mark Jurkowitz," *The Nonprofit Quarterly*, Sept. 21, 2009, www.nonprofitquarterly.org/index.php?option=com_content&view=article&id=1611:nonprofits-and-journalism-an-interview-with-mark-jurkowitz&catid=154:current-issue.
The associate director of the Project for Excellence in Journalism discusses the growth of foundation-financed journalism.

Breitbart, Andrew, "Media does matter for America," *The Daily Caller*, Jan. 11, 2010, http://dailycaller.com/2010/01/11/media-does-matter-for-america/.
A conservative Web publisher hails Internet-enabled competition with what he calls the false objectivity of the mainstream media.

Kauffman, Clark, "State withholds another Glenwood document," *Des Moines Register*, Dec. 5, 2009, p. B1.
Iowa's leading newspaper reports on its latest attempt to access state documents concerning state institutions for disabled people.

Mutter, Alan D., "Putting bite back in newspapers," *Reflections of a Newsosaur* (blog), Dec. 15, 2009, http://newsosaur.blogspot.com/2009/12/putting-bite-back-in-newspapers.html.
An adjunct journalism professor at the University of California says more point of view in newspaper articles might bring back readers.

Yusuf, Huma, "Rise in lawsuits against bloggers," *The Christian Science Monitor*, **July 16, 2008, www .csmonitor.com/Innovation/Tech-Culture/2008/0716/ rise-in-lawsuits-against-bloggers.**
The potential legal pitfalls of blog journalism got early attention in an old-line newspaper that switched entirely to the Web in 2009.

Reports and Studies

"Press Accuracy Rating Hits Two Decade Low," Pew Research Center for the People & the Press, Sept. 13, 2009, http://people-press.org/report/543/.
A nonpartisan survey finds continued diminution of public confidence in the media.

"The State of the News Media: An Annual Report on American Journalism," Project for Excellence in Journalism, 2009, www.stateofthemedia.org/2009/index.htm.
An in-depth analysis shows the extent of crisis in traditional news organizations.

Cowan, Geoffrey, and David Westphal, "Public Policy and Funding the News," Center on Communication Leadership & Policy, USC Annenberg School for Communication & Journalism, January 2010, http:// fundingthenews.org/.
Leaders of a journalism think tank argue for increasing indirect public financing of the media.

Downie, Leonard Jr., and Michael Schudson, "The Reconstruction of American Journalism," *Columbia Journalism Review*, **Oct. 19, 2009, www.cjr.org/ reconstruction/the_ reconstruction_of_american.php.**
Universities, foundations and other institutions should help fill the gap left by the continuing collapse of traditional news media, a former Washington Post editor and longtime journalism professor conclude.

Gajda, Amy, "Judging Journalism: The Turn Toward Privacy and Judicial Regulation of the Press," *California Law Review*, **August 2009, http://papers .ssrn.com/sol3/papers.cfm?abstract_id=1103248##.**
A journalist-turned-lawyer points to perils for reporters in public and judicial reactions to privacy erosion in the Internet Age.

Jones, RonNell Andersen, "Media Subpoenas: Impact, Perception, and Legal Protection in the Changing World of American Journalism," *Washington Law Review,* **August 2009, http://papers.ssrn.com/sol3/ papers.cfm? abstract_id=1407105.**
A nationwide survey shows editors feel under siege legally as well as financially.

For More Information

Big Journalism, http://bigjournalism.com. Site founded by conservative Web publisher Andrew Breitbart for criticism of mainstream media; published the undercover ACORN videos of James O'Keefe.

Citizen Media Law Project, Berkman Center for Internet & Society, Harvard Law School, 23 Everett St., Second Floor, Cambridge, MA 02138; (617) 495-7547; www .citmedialaw.org/about/citizen-media-law-project. Also affiliated with Arizona State University-based Center for Citizen Media, the Project focuses on promoting and defending citizen journalism and related activities.

Joan Shorenstein Center on the Press, Politics, and Public Policy, John F. Kennedy School of Government, Harvard University, 79 JFK St., Cambridge, MA 02138; (617) 495-8269; www.hks.harvard.edu/presspo. Fosters contact between journalists and academic experts.

The Poynter Institute, 801 Third St South, St. Petersburg, FL 33701; (888) 769-6837; www.poynter.org. Nonprofit journalism-training organization whose Web site includes Jim Romenesko's popular industry-news site.

Project for Excellence in Journalism, 1615 L St., N.W., Washington, DC 20036; (202) 419-3650; www.journalism .org. Researches trends in the news business, including the rise of Web-based media.

The Reporters Committee for Freedom of the Press, 1101 Wilson Blvd., Suite 1100, Arlington, VA 22209; (703) 807-2100; www.rcfp.org/. Provides free legal representation for reporters, researches free-press issues and advocates free-press legislation.

7

Polarization in America

Does partisan conflict threaten democracy?

Tom Price

Police arrest a protester during an Occupy Wall Street demonstration in New York City on Sept. 17, 2012. The Occupy movement drew worldwide attention to the growing divide between the rich and the poor, or what Harvard University government professor Michael Sandel called the "skyboxification" of American life, where wealthy football fans sit in warm skyboxes while others shiver in outdoor seats.

From *CQ Researcher,*
February 5, 2010

For decades, Dick Metcalf wrote columns for *Guns & Ammo* magazine, starred in a television show about guns and was considered one of America's top firearms journalists. Then, late last year, he wrote a piece titled "Let's Talk Limits."

"All constitutional rights are regulated," he told his readers, and some gun regulations are justified.[1]

Reaction from gun enthusiasts and the gun industry was swift, heated and devastatingly effective.

Gun manufacturers threatened to pull their ads unless Metcalf was fired. Readers canceled subscriptions while leaving comments such as "I refuse to support/read a magazine that espouses views that are contrary to the 2nd Amendment." Richard Venola, a former *Guns & Ammo* editor, said Metcalf needed to recognize that "we are locked in a struggle with powerful forces in this country who will do anything to destroy the Second Amendment [and that] the time for ceding some rational points is gone."[2]

Metcalf was fired. The editor who approved the column resigned. And anti-gun-control absolutists carved another notch into their firearms.

"Compromise is a bad word these days," Metcalf laments. "People think it means giving up your principles."[3]

On a wide range of issues — not just gun control — more and more Americans seem to be separated by an unbridgeable chasm of beliefs, values and habits, from politics and religion to culture and entertainment.

In the political arena polarization is tearing at the fabric of national unity and even the country's democratic traditions, many social scientists contend.

Partisan Divisions on Values Have Widened

Americans' values and basic beliefs are more polarized along partisan lines than at any time in the past 25 years, according to the Pew Research Center's Values Survey. The gap between Republicans and Democrats on issues such as the social safety net, equal opportunity and the environment has grown over the past quarter-century, with the widest occurring in attitudes on the environment and government.

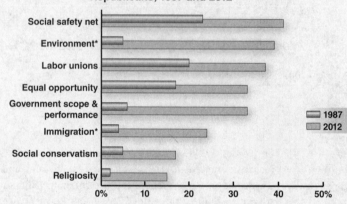

Average Percentage-Point Difference Between Democrats and Republicans, 1987 and 2012

* Attitudes on the environment were measured starting in 1992, on immigration since 2002.

Source: "2012 American Values Survey," Pew Research Center, 2012, http://bit.ly/1gWA28M

"That's the type of questions people pose."

Within the GOP, traditional conservatives fend off attacks from far more conservative activists while moderates are pushed to the side. The great divide has shut down the federal government and taken the nation to the brink of defaulting on its national debt. Congress finds it nearly impossible to legislate on any complicated issue.

The breakdown in Washington is especially troubling because "we have no precedent — we're operating in uncharted territory," says Smith College government professor Howard Gold." There have been divided governments in the past in the United States that have been fairly productive. The problem is divided government coupled with severe polarization."

Outside of Washington, so-called red (conservative) states and blue (liberal) states move in opposite directions on such hot-button issues as abortion, gay marriage and voting rights. And beyond the government, Americans live increasingly divergent lives. Liberals tend to live among liberals and conservatives among conservatives. Some communities are becoming more white as others become more diverse.

As a result, "we have fewer and fewer civic spaces where citizens from different walks of life encounter one another," said Harvard University government professor Michael Sandel.[5] And that isolation, according to Washington-based political analyst Charlie Cook, "makes opposing points of view seem more alien, suspicious, even threatening."[6]

The divide can be cultural as well as political. Market researchers, pollsters and political scientists have found that liberals and conservatives differ in what they drink, where they shop and what they choose for entertainment. Democrats like vodka, Republicans whiskey — or so the research suggests. Republicans drink Kendall-Jackson wines, Democrats Columbia Crest. Democrats

And a monsoon of independent spending — allowed by several Supreme Court rulings that toppled spending restrictions — exacerbates the conflicts by supporting candidates and causes that would not have found the financial wherewithal to dominate public debate in the past.

"America is splitting apart without going through all the trouble of a civil war," said Robert Reich, a public policy professor at the University of California-Berkeley and former Labor secretary in the Democratic Clinton administration.[4]

Indeed, today's compromise-free government gridlock leads some to worry about the future of American democracy, according to former Maine Republican Sen. Olympia Snowe, who retired from the Senate last year in frustration over the rise of obstructionism in Congress. "One man said to me: 'What's going to become of the country?'" she recalls from recent travels to promote bipartisanship.

shop at Whole Foods, Republicans at Walmart. Republicans watched Leno. Democrats prefer Letterman.[7]

Even love and parenting have acquired a political dimension, which has intensified over the past 50 years. In a 2010 YouGov Poll, about half of Republicans and one-third of Democrats said they would be unhappy if their child married someone from the opposite party. Fifty years earlier, only 5 percent of Republicans and 4 percent of Democrats responding to a Gallup Poll expressed such feelings.[8]

Some divisions, such as where to live, can be wealth-based and drive ever-thicker wedges between the affluent and poor. Heather Kimmel, a neuropharmacologist for the Environmental Protection Agency, worries her children could grow up not understanding how most of the world lives. "We talk to them a lot about it," she said, "that not everyone has a college degree and a big house."

Kimmel's husband is a nuclear physicist for the Defense Department. Their neighbors tend to be well-educated professionals, many with degrees from prestigious universities. They live in a Northern Virginia suburb of Washington, D.C., that qualifies as a "super zip" neighborhood, according to calculations by *The Washington Post*. Super zips — a term coined by Charles Murray, a scholar at the American Enterprise Institute, a conservative-leaning think tank in Washington — are the 5 percent of U.S. zip codes with the highest median household income and highest percentage of adults with college degrees. Nationwide, super zips average more than $120,000 in annual household income, and two-thirds of their adult residents are college graduates. In the rest of the country, median income is just under $54,000, and only about a quarter of adults have college degrees.[9]

Most U.S. neighborhoods are predominantly middle class or contain families with varied incomes. But the rich and poor increasingly are congregating in separate communities that make interaction among the different economic classes unlikely. The percentage of wealthy

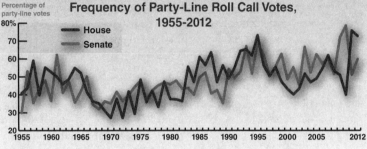

Party Opposition Reaches Record High

Congressional polarization is often measured by how often the two main parties oppose each other in roll call votes. Such party unity broke modern-day records in 2011 in the House, when the parties opposed each other in 76 percent of the votes, and in 2010 in the Senate, in 79 percent of the votes. Members of Congress tended to cross party lines more often in the 1960s and '70s.

Frequency of Party-Line Roll Call Votes, 1955-2012

Percentage of party-line votes

— House
— Senate

Source: "Party Unity History," *CQ Almanac*, 2012, p. B-19

families living in upper-income neighborhoods doubled to 18 percent between 1980 and 2010, according to the Pew Research Center. The percentage of lower-income families living in poorer neighborhoods increased to 28 from 23.[10]

Sandel calls this divide the "sky-boxification" of American life, referring to the rich sitting in warm skyboxes during December professional football games while most fans shiver in the outdoor seats below.[11]

And the rich-poor divide is growing. From 1979 to 2007, for instance, the inflation-adjusted after-tax income of the top 1 percent of Americans increased 275 percent, but only by 18 percent for the lowest fifth, according to the Congressional Budget Office.[12] Income is closely related to education, and studies show that the children of the well-educated are the most likely to become well-educated themselves.[13]

"People increasingly are moving into places where they are surrounded by like-minded individuals," says Norman Ornstein, a prominent political analyst at the American Enterprise Institute.

A glance at an election map underscores his point. In Democratic President Barack Obama's 2012 re-election bid, he carried the Northeast and upper Midwest from

Maine to Minnesota (except Indiana), along with Virginia, Florida, Nevada and the West Coast. The rest of the country, except for New Mexico and Colorado, voted for Republican challenger Mitt Romney (Hawaiians voted for Obama, Alaskans for Romney.) County-by-county results showed Democrats concentrated in urban areas and Republicans spread across the more rural parts of the country.

Romney won 59 percent of the votes cast by whites in 2012, Obama 93 percent of the votes by blacks and 71 percent by Latinos.[14] And more whites are migrating to Republican-dominated states. While the white population declined in the Northeast and Midwest between the 2000 and 2010 censuses, it rose in the South and West, increasing most steeply in six states that went for Romney — Arizona, Idaho, North Carolina, South Carolina, Utah and Wyoming — as well as in two that voted for Obama: Hawaii and Nevada.[15]

People don't choose where to live because of their politics, says Gary Jacobson, who studies polarization as a political science professor at the University of California, San Diego. Rather, "there are cultural divisions that map onto political divisions these days. People are making lifestyle choices that are based on what kinds of places they want to live in, their jobs, their activities, and it turns out there are political manifestations as well."

As liberal and conservative Americans continue to drift apart, here are some questions that political activists and scholars are pondering:

Will political polarization inevitably increase across America?

The extent and intensity of polarization around the country indicate that U.S. political life won't get more peaceful anytime soon, many political activists and scholars have concluded.

In fact, Smith College's Gold says, "essentially, it needs to get worse before it gets better. I think we're very likely to have a status quo [midterm] election in 2014. Beyond 2014, I'm not very optimistic."

Similarly, Jacobson of UC-San Diego predicts that "you'll get rid of partisan polarization when partisans in Congress start to lose elections." But that doesn't seem likely anytime soon, he says, because "as long as they see political advantages in taking strongly ideological positions, they're going to take them."

Gold also points to the "segregated bubbles" in which a growing number of Americans live. "If they are less exposed to other points of view, that may work to create more polarization," he says. If children grow up in those bubbles, "we're imparting polarization to the next generation."

When she retired in 2013, Sen. Snowe expressed deep frustration at what she saw as Congress's inability to act. She says she worries about "the institutionalization of this culture" in Washington. "You have more than half the Senate and the House having served less than six years," she says. "Ultimately, that creates a generation of lawmakers who know no legislative environment other than the current one."

Snowe's pessimism about changing the culture stems in part from the dearth of competitive congressional and state legislative districts and the growing polarization between liberal and conservative states. Most House members face serious competition only in primaries, which ideological voters tend to dominate. That has driven Democrats to the left and Republicans to the right. And Senate and gubernatorial general elections have become less competitive as the country polarizes geographically.

Only 62 of 435 U.S. House general elections were decided by less than a 10 percent margin in 2012, and political analyst Stuart Rothenberg puts the number of truly competitive House districts at just 51. In two-thirds, the margin was 20 percent or more. Thirty-one winners ran without a major party opponent or with no opposition at all.[16]

Competition has declined substantially, according to Cook, who created the Cook Political Report Partisan Voter Index to distinguish between safe and competitive districts. Following the 2012 elections, he identified 90 "swing districts," where neither party would be entering the 2014 campaign with more than a 5 percent advantage. In 1998, there were 164.[17]

Presidential election results reveal declining competition at the state level as well. In 20 states in 1976, the margin between Democrat Jimmy Carter and Republican incumbent Gerald Ford was less than 5 percent, but only five states were that close in 2012.[18]

In all but 14 states, one party controls both legislative houses and the governor's mansion. "A lot of states are going to have one-party government for a long time," predicts Rob Richie, executive director of the Takoma Park, Md.-based Center for Voting and Democracy, which advocates election reforms to boost competition.[19] Once called "laboratories of democracy" for their willingness to try new governing ideas that might later spread across the country, states now can more accurately be called "laboratories of polarization," he says.

Because of one-party rule, states are rapidly pushing further apart from one another. In the last few years, Democratic-run states have enthusiastically marketed "Obamacare" through state-run insurance exchanges; expanded Medicaid roles; legalized gay marriage and the use of marijuana for medicinal and recreational purposes; made union organizing easier; eased access to abortion; stiffened gun-control laws; allowed illegal immigrants to pay in-state tuition at public colleges and obtain driver's licenses; raised taxes; increased government spending; and adopted tougher environmental regulations.

Meanwhile, Republican-governed states have refused to open "Obamacare" exchanges or to expand Medicaid; opposed gay marriage; made it harder for unions to organize; trimmed the powers of public-employee unions; increased the number of places where guns can be carried; cut taxes and spending; and stiffened abortion restrictions beyond what the Supreme Court has permitted in past rulings in hopes the court will reverse *Roe v. Wade*.[20]

Both parties are moving to lock in their supremacy by changing voting laws to favor their candidates: In many states, Republican-controlled governments, vowing to prevent fraud, are requiring voters to show identification before they can cast a ballot. But Democratic officials are trying to make it easier to vote by extending hours and allowing simpler registration.[21]

The widening rift between the parties' leaders contributes to polarization of all Americans, some political analysts say. "It's easier to figure out which side you belong to" when the Senate has no liberal Republicans or conservative Democrats, says Matthew Levendusky, associate professor of political science at the University of Pennsylvania and author of *The Partisan Sort* and *How Partisan Media Polarize America*. "Once people are sorted onto the correct team, they are much more likely to vote for their party and less likely to split a ticket. They are more likely to become devoted cheerleaders."

Republicans also complain that Democrats are uncompromising.

Getty Images (both)

Critics say that commentators like conservative Ann Coulter and liberal Rachel Maddow foster polarization by reinforcing their audiences' biases. Fox and MSNBC revolutionized the tone of cable news when they went on the air in 1996. Fox's conservative orientation attracted the largest cable audience, and MSNBC attempted to copy that success by becoming the liberal alternative.

Perpetual polarization is not inevitable, however, some contend. Congress's recent passage of the 2014 budget was "a nice moment," says Jason Grumet, president of the Bipartisan Policy Center, a Washington-based think tank that advocates consensus building among lawmakers.

"We've heard from some members who went home after that agreement who felt some palpable change in the mood" of their constituents, he says. "I remain bullish on the basic arc of our democracy — this notion that what makes the United States unique is the capacity to repair mistakes."

"In the long term," Levendusky says, reduced polarization "almost necessarily has to happen. We know that no party system will last forever, so something will happen to change the nature of the political debate. We don't have Federalists and anti-Federalists and Whigs any longer, because new dimensions were introduced into the political debate, new parties formed and new alliances came into existence."

Does a no-compromise stance threaten U.S. democracy?

Michael Gerson, a senior White House adviser during Republican George W. Bush's presidency, finds it preposterous that political activists who call themselves "constitutional conservatives" refuse to compromise.

"The Constitution itself resulted from an extraordinary series of compromises," Gerson, now a *Washington*

Post columnist, noted, adding that the government it created can't function without compromise.[22]

The Constitution's checks and balances were designed to limit the power of the central government, said Jonathan Rauch, a fellow at the Brookings Institution, a centrist Washington think tank, but not to prevent government from acting at all. The Constitution "does not require or desire that individuals should all be moderates," he said. But it does require compromise by "creating competing power centers and depriving any of them of the power to impose its will on the others."[23]

Tea Party activists — and the lawmakers and organizations supporting them — contend that compromise is what produced the problems they perceive in the government.

"Congress worked really well for decades, and it got our nation $17 trillion in debt," says Dan Holler, communications director at Heritage Action for America, the activist arm of the conservative Heritage Foundation think tank. "People could say it was wrong that we didn't compromise" on the bipartisan budget agreement that avoided another government shutdown in December. "But the facts are it was a spending increase and a deficit increase, not something a conservative political organization will ever support."

South Carolina Republican Jim DeMint — who left the Senate last year to become Heritage's president — explained his no-compromise stance while still a senator in 2010 by saying that "I cannot recall any bipartisan bill that did not increase spending, expand government and increase our debt."[24]

Ornstein, of the American Enterprise Institute, argues that conservatives' nocompromise posture makes it "extremely difficult to enact policies responsive to the country's most pressing challenges." Democrats, also, have become less willing to compromise. Obama refused to negotiate concessions in return for Republican votes to lift the debt ceiling, a battle he won when the ceiling was suspended earlier this month, for example. And he recently has been promoting policies designed to mobilize the Democratic base rather than to strike deals with the GOP — proposing a minimum-wage increase and abandoning plans to cut Social Security benefits in order to reduce the deficit, for instance.

Chris Van Hollen of Maryland, top Democrat on the House Budget Committee, attributed the president's posture to "Republicans' refusal to work with the president and move the country forward." But Michael Steele, House Speaker John Boehner's spokesman, charged that Obama is "unwilling to show leadership and take on his party on any issue of substance."[25]

Snowe laments that the federal government has "become all about ideology and absolutes rather than trying to develop practical solutions to the problems. It's abundantly evident how we have lost years that could have contributed to the prosperity of the country if we had concentrated on the issues that matter. If we have perpetual ideological warfare, how are we going to advance the interests of the country?"

Political scientists Richard Fox and Jennifer Lawless warn that polarization and gridlock threaten democracy's future by turning young people away from serving in government. Fox, chair of the Loyola Marymount University Political Science Department, and Lawless, an American University government professor, surveyed 4,200 high school and college students in 2012 and found that 85 percent didn't think elected officials want to help people, 79 percent didn't consider politicians smart or hard-working and nearly 60 percent believed politicians are dishonest. Only 11 percent said they might consider running for political office some day.

"This political profile of the next generation should sound alarm bells about the long-term, deeply embedded damage contemporary politics has wrought on U.S. democracy and its youngest citizens," Fox and Lawless wrote. "But if the best and brightest of future generations neither hear nor heed the call to public service, then the quality of U.S. democracy may be compromised."[26]

Smith College's Gold finds it "hard to imagine a crisis of legitimacy such that our entire system of government would unravel." But he notes that Latin American democracies have fallen to military coups and that recurring political crises led France to trade its parliamentary system for a hybrid parliamentary-presidential structure and elected Charles de Gaulle as president in 1958.

If polarization and dysfunctional government aren't dealt with soon, Ornstein warns, "the nature of the tribal media [his term for highly partisan cable and social media] and the amplification of divisions by social media could create a much greater gulf in the country as a whole. If, say, 40 percent of Americans on either side believe the other side is evil and is trying to undermine our way of life — not people who simply feel a different way — you could end up with a kind of sectarianism that would be deeply dangerous."

Others expect the country to muddle through.

"Things that have to get done will get done because the consequences of not doing them for everybody involved are just too politically awful," says Jacobson of the University of California at San Diego. "It's very ugly and it's very contentious, and then eventually they get around to cutting a deal."

Democratic Sen. Richard Durbin of Illinois said he hoped Congress' recent passage of the 2014 budget and suspending of the federal debt ceiling indicate "a new bipartisan spirit."[27] But House GOP leaders subsequently announced that passing major legislation — such as comprehensive immigration or tax reform — was unlikely before next fall's midterm elections.[28]

"It is an acknowledgment of where they stand, where nothing can happen in divided government," said Frank Luntz, a leading Republican pollster, "so we may essentially have the status quo."[29]

"I don't think it's the end of the world yet," says Dan Glickman, a former U.S. representative and Agriculture secretary and current executive director of the congressional education program at the Aspen Institute, a Washington think tank. "We have great resilience in our society. We're like a person who has some chronic illnesses and ought to deal with them, but we haven't reached a point where they're terminal."

Similarly, Lawrence Summers, a former Treasury secretary in the Democratic Clinton administration and current professor of business and government at Harvard, said that "anyone prone to pessimism about the United States would do well to ponder the alarm with which it

Decline in Swing Seats Erodes Bipartisanship

In the last 15 years, the number of House congressional districts up for grabs by either party — called swing or competitive districts — has plummeted, reducing the number of districts in which the incumbents have an incentive to work on a bipartisan basis. In 1998, there were 164 swing districts, representing a third of the House membership. By 2014, the number had fallen to 90.

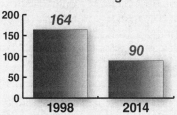

Number of Swing Seats

Source: David Wasserman, "Introducing the 2014 Cook Political Report Partisan Voter Index," *The Cook Political Report*, April 4, 2013, http://bit.ly/1fnqKCV

viewed the Soviet Union after the launch of the *Sputnik* satellite or Japan's economic rise in the 1980s and the early 1990s.

"One of America's greatest strengths is its ability to defy its own prophecies of doom," said Summers.[30]

Should the United States shift to a parliamentary system of government?

One thing America's warring politicians seem to agree on is their reverence for the Constitution.

"It's often noted that the United States is governed by the world's oldest written constitution that is still in use," legal analyst Jeffrey Toobin wrote recently. "This is usually stated as praise, though most other products of the 18th century, like horse-borne travel and leech-based medical treatment, have been replaced by improved models."[31]

Now — as polarization-fueled gridlock has forced government shutdowns and carried America to the brink of defaulting on its national debt — proposals for some 21st-century constitutional updates are commanding increasing attention.

The most radical suggestion for a complete overhaul would mean replacing the nation's checks-and-balances system, in which Congress, the president and Supreme Court share equal power, with a parliamentary structure used by nearly all other advanced democracies. In that system, voters choose the legislature, which in turn picks the prime minister, who is both the chief executive and a legislator. If the legislature and executive disagree, the legislators can pick a new prime minister.

The American system creates a "vetocracy," that "empowers a wide variety of political players representing minority positions to block action by the majority and prevent the government from doing anything," according to Stanford University political scientist

Francis Fukuyama. The president, the high court and both houses of Congress — even the minority in the Senate — can thwart the majority's will, he wrote. When they fail to get their way, he added, minorities still can wreak havoc, as Republicans did last fall by shutting down the government and threatening default in futile attempts to repeal or alter the Affordable Care Act, President Obama's signature legislative achievement.[32]

In less wealthy and less stable countries, presidential government has produced worse outcomes, according Bruce Ackerman, a professor of political science and law at Yale. "There are about 30 countries, mostly in Latin America, that have adopted American-style systems," he said. "All of them, without exception," eventually collapsed.[33]

Even Americans, when helping to establish democratic governments in Japan and West Germany after World War II, turned to European parliamentary models, not their own presidential system.[34] Arend Lijphart, political science professor emeritus at the University of California-San Diego, and a specialist on democratic institutions, says parliamentary systems are superior.

"In a parliamentary system, you don't have [gridlock] because the executive and cabinet are creatures of parliament, and they have to see eye to eye," he says. When they don't, parliament can replace the executive or call an election to select a new government. In America's system, legislators and the president answer to different constituencies, he says. "They reach a conflict, and you get to deadlock and both sides can claim to represent the people."

In addition, Lijphart says, America's two-party system promotes polarization by limiting voters' access to more options on the ideological spectrum. If he could design a new U.S. government, Lijphart would choose a parliamentary system. Five to 10 legislators would be elected in each district, with members chosen according to their parties' proportion of the vote. He thinks four main parties and several smaller ones would evolve. Centrists usually would form the governing coalitions, eliminating or limiting polarization and gridlock, he says.

Critics raise ideological and practical objections to such a plan.

Conservatives say liberals object to the current U.S. system because they want a more activist government.

But a slow-moving government is a good thing, according to Rich Mitchell, senior managing editor of *Conservative Daily News.*

"Checks and balances are mechanisms to prevent tyranny," he writes. "Imagine if we'd had a parliamentary system in 2009. The health care law would certainly have been single payer, destroying an entire segment of the U.S. economy."[35]

Gene Healy, vice president of the libertarian Cato Institute, acknowledges the shortcomings of presidential government demonstrated in many Latin American countries, but he still prefers the U.S. system. "American-style separation of powers has its advantages, after all," he said. "Without it, for example, there's little doubt we'd have had socialized medicine long ago."[36]

A parliamentary system might make sense "if we could start from scratch, but we're not building from scratch," says Richie of the Center for Voting and Democracy, which also calls itself FairVote. "No state has a parliamentary system," he says. "Very few cities have one. Every state has a directly elected governor. The trend of cities is to go to directly elected mayors."

Polarization and gridlock are not inevitable in the American system, nor is the parliamentary system perfect, says John Fortier, director of the Democracy Project at the Bipartisan Policy Center.

"When President Obama took office in 2009, he came on the heels of [Democratic congressional victories in] 2006, and the Democrats had significant power," Fortier says. Before Republicans retook control of the House in 2010, the Democrats passed the Affordable Care Act and other Democratic priorities.

Noting that parliamentary elections usually produce a governing coalition or outright party majority that can begin enacting its priorities upon taking office, Fortier asks if Americans really want "a majority that is the one-day snap-judgment of the people." In the American system, "if you win a couple of elections you're going to have a lot of power. But if you win just one election, you're not necessarily going to have a real consensus of the American people."

In addition, he says, even in a multiparty parliament, parties usually group in left and right coalitions. And, many times, "parliaments won't do difficult things. It's the nature of politics that it's not easy to do hard things."

BACKGROUND

Bickering and Brawling

The Founding Fathers decried factions, then founded parties and set the stage for today's polarization and gridlock.

During the first half of the 19th century, partisan tempers sometimes turned into physical confrontations. Members of Congress threw punches at each other on the House floor. South Carolina Democratic Rep. Preston Brooks invaded the Senate chamber and beat Massachusetts Sen. Charles Sumner, a Republican, with a cane. In 1804 Vice President Aaron Burr killed Alexander Hamilton, America's first Treasury secretary, in a duel. And, of course, Americans fought a Civil War over slavery and states' rights that resulted in more than 750,000 deaths.[37]

Partisan bickering and complaints about do-nothing Congresses aren't new, either.

In 1822, a *Saturday Evening Post* editorial described the 17th Congress' accomplishments as "Procrastination. Debate. . . . New committees. New Reports. New speeches . . . and, finally, indefinite postponements."[38]

Fourteen decades later, the magazine's political writer, Stewart Alsop, said Congress was inspiring public "indifference, amusement, and contempt," as Southern Democrats and some Republicans stalled President John F. Kennedy's proposed civil rights legislation in 1963.[39] "Never before in history has Congress talked so long to accomplish so little," Alsop wrote.[40]

Alsop was echoing Democratic President Harry S. Truman, who successfully ran for re-election in 1948 while bashing the "Republican, 80th do-nothing Congress" for rejecting his calls for price controls and a federal housing program.[41]

Political polarization has waxed and waned throughout U.S. history. Measured by differences in parties' congressional roll call votes, polarization was high in the late 19th and early 20th centuries, dipped to a low during the Great Depression and World War II, then slowly rose again to current levels.[42]

Gulfs on basic values have widened among the rank and file as well. Differences in Democratic and Republican views on 48 values ranged from 2 to 23 percent in 1987, then jumped to between 5 and 41 percent in 2012, according to Pew Research Center surveys.[43]

Partisans' attitudes toward the president also have changed drastically since the administration of Republican President Dwight D. Eisenhower in the 1950s. Since 1953, nine of the 10 most polarized years occurred during the last two administrations.[44]

States and legislative districts also are becoming more polarized in their voting habits. In the 1976 presidential race, the margin between Democrat Jimmy Carter and Republican incumbent Gerald Ford was less than 5 percent in 20 states. Only five states were that close in 2012. More than 180 U.S. House races were decided by less than five percentage points in 1976, compared with fewer than 60 in 2012.[45]

"The parties became more cohesive and consistent in their beliefs," says Jacobson of the University of California, San Diego. "So we have a Congress composed primarily of people who are elected by their own party stalwarts and not by people in the middle or people from the other party. It used to be Democrats could win Republican-leaning districts with Blue Dogs," he says, using the nickname for fiscally conservative Democrats. "That's no longer the case."

Despite the diminished competition within states and districts, enough House and Senate seats are competitive to put control of the government at stake in most elections. That, too, contributes to polarization, according to University of Maryland politics professor Frances Lee. "Competition fuels party conflict by raising the political stakes of every policy dispute," Lee said. "During the long years of Democratic dominance following the New Deal, politics was less contentious in part because the national political stakes were so much lower."

Democrats didn't worry about losing control of Congress, she said, and Republicans were willing to cooperate to achieve at least some legislative goals.[46]

Battles over civil rights played a key role in sorting Americans into the highly polarized factions witnessed today. During the century after the Civil War, white Southerners had formed the most dependable pillar of the Democratic Party. That began to change in 1948, when South Carolina Gov. Strom Thurmond led a walkout from the Democratic National Convention to protest Truman's support for civil rights measures. Thurmond became the presidential nominee of the rump States Rights' Democratic Party (nicknamed the Dixiecrats) and carried Louisiana, Mississippi, Alabama and his home state in the general election.[47]

The South's flip toward the GOP accelerated after the Democratic-controlled Congress passed civil rights legislation in 1964. While losing in a landslide to Lyndon B. Johnson in that year's presidential election, conservative Republican Barry Goldwater carried five Deep South states plus his home state of Arizona. Since then, the only Democratic presidential nominee to win a majority of Southern states was Georgian Jimmy Carter in 1976.[48]

The Supreme Court's 1973 *Roe v. Wade* decision legalizing most abortions spurred more polarization, Smith College's Gold says, because it energized religious conservatives and pushed them into the Republican Party, where candidates were more likely than Democrats to support abortion restrictions.

"Another really important factor was that the right wing became livid over [Republican President George] H. W. Bush's violation [in 1990] of his pledge about no new taxes," Gold says. "They then took the position that we can't compromise on these issues anymore."

The demonization of Congress by Rep. Newt Gingrich, R-Ga., also was a key factor, according to the American Enterprise Institute's Ornstein. "What Newt wanted to do was to nationalize the [1994 House] election and to make it all about the disgusting, awful, horrible, could-not-be-worse Congress, and get people to say 'Anything would be better than this,'" Ornstein says.

Gingrich, who became House minority whip in 1989, first attacked Republican congressional leaders for being too subservient to Democrats, then turned his rhetorical guns on the opposite party. Gingrich organized highly negative campaigns against Democratic incumbents in 1994, helping the GOP take the House majority for the first time since Eisenhower's landslide in 1952 and for only the second time since 1928. His colleagues then made him House speaker in 1995, a post held until 1999.

The personal attacks launched in the 1994 election helped to erode a tradition of friendship across party lines and a search for common ground. In the 1970s, for instance, liberal South Dakota Democrat George McGovern and conservative Kansas Republican Bob Dole had worked together in the Senate to create the Special Supplemental Food Program for Women, Infants and Children (commonly called WIC), and to expand availability of food stamps and school lunches.

When World Food Program USA last December presented Dole the "George McGovern and Bob Dole Leadership Award" for fighting hunger, Dole said of the late South Dakotan, "I used to argue [with him] about Vietnam all day, and then in the evening we would talk about food for poor people."[49]

The decline of such friendships — as lawmakers began to spend less time socializing and more time raising funds and campaigning back home — has exacerbated polarization, many say. "Members spent more time together, and I think it was easier to find somebody from the other party to join with you in your legislative initiatives," says former Agriculture secretary Glickman, a House member from 1977 to 1995. "If you do that now, the fringe groups attack you for abandoning your principles or collaborating with the enemy."

Despite growing polarization in the 1980s and '90s — with multiple government shutdowns during the Reagan and Clinton administrations — Republicans and Democrats cooperated with one another more than they do today. In 1986, for example, Congress passed and Reagan signed the biggest reforms in federal tax policy in more than four decades. Two years of negotiations had produced significant concessions from the administration and both parties in Congress, where Democrats held the House majority and Republicans led the Senate.[50] Similarly — even as he was savaging Democrats and leading the House to impeach Clinton — Gingrich worked with the president to pass welfare-reform legislation in 1996 and to balance the budget three times at the end of the '90s.[51]

Bipartisanship was particularly noticeable at the state level during the '80s, according to David Osborne, whose book, *Laboratories of Democracy*, describes the innovative work of governors at that time. "They would communicate with each other across party lines, and when you'd go interview them, they would say things like, 'Governors from the different parties have more in common with each other than they do with colleagues from the same party in Washington,'" Osborne said.

Republican Tommy Thompson, Wisconsin governor from 1987 to 2001, said government officials now are "much more doctrinaire with our philosophies and much more locked into our positions," in part because many governors contemplate running for president. They know they can't get nominated if they stray too far from party orthodoxy, Thompson said.[52]

C H R O N O L O G Y

1800s *Growing polarization culminates in Civil War.*

1806 Filibuster created accidently when Senate drops rule to limit debate.

1837 First filibuster conducted.

1843 "Nativist" movements opposing immigration of Catholics accelerate.

1848 Feminist convention in Seneca Falls, N.Y., sparks campaign for women's suffrage and equal rights.

1861-1865 Civil War fought over slavery and states' rights.

1876 Post Civil War Reconstruction ends. Southern Jim Crow laws sustain white supremacy and segregation.

1900-1947 *Depression, wars inspire national unity.*

1904 Almost no one in U.S. House compiles a moderate voting record.

1907 Annual immigration from Europe peaks at more than 1 million.

1924 Legislation restricts immigration from Southern, Eastern Europe.

1939 Great Depression and threat of war produce near-record levels of congressional bipartisanship.

1948-2000 *Battles emerge over civil rights, social issues and taxes.*

1948 South Carolina Gov. Strom Thurmond leads walkout from Democratic National Convention to oppose civil rights.

1964 Democratic support for civil rights leads white Southerners to back conservative GOP presidential nominee Barry Goldwater.

1973 *Roe v. Wade* decision legalizing most abortions pushes religious conservatives toward GOP.

1976 Jimmy Carter becomes last Democratic presidential nominee to win majority of Southern states.

1986 Democrats and Republicans cooperate in adopting federal tax reform.

1990 Antitax conservatives blast Republican President George H. W. Bush for reneging on no-new-taxes campaign pledge.

1994 Following GOP House whip Newt Gingrich into negative campaigns, Republicans capture U.S. House majority for first time since 1952.

1996 Gingrich and Democratic President Bill Clinton cooperate on welfare reform, then pass three balanced budgets. . . . Fox News and MSNBC begin cablecasting, contributing to polarization as MSNBC moves to become liberal alternative to conservative Fox.

2000-Present *Controversies during Bush, Obama administrations heighten polarization.*

2004 Largest gap ever emerges between Democrats and Republicans in approval ratings of a president (George W. Bush), until Barack Obama spurs identical 76-percentage-point chasm in 2012.

2007 Former Senate majority leaders form Bipartisan Policy Center to fight disruptive partisanship in Congress.

2010 Lockstep party voting sets record in U.S. Senate; House sets record two years later. . . . YouGov poll finds sharp increase in parents who oppose their children marrying member of different political party.

2012 Margin between presidential candidates is below 5 percent in only five states, down from 20 states in 1976.

2013 Market researchers report liberal/conservative divides over what to drink, where to shop, how to be entertained. . . . Senate Democrats seek to stop 56 filibusters through Nov. 21, then change the rules to end filibusters with majority vote for most presidential nominees.

2014 Moderate and establishment Republicans organize to combat continuing right-wing efforts to oust less-conservative GOP office holders. Left-wing Democrats begin efforts to move their party more in their direction.

California Election Reforms Have Unintended Consequences

New rules meant to reduce polarization diminish state's clout in Congress.

In 2012 California implemented a revolutionary change in the state's election laws, a bid to spur electoral competition, empower more moderate candidates and reduce polarization and gridlock.

The reforms replaced party primaries with a single wide-open contest that sends the top two vote-getters to the general election. In the Eighth Congressional District, a Republican stronghold along the Nevada border, the primary's top vote-getter in 2012 was Tea Party conservative Gregg Imus, but the second-place finisher — the less-conservative Republican Paul Cook — went on to win the November general election.[1]

Along with the new nonpartisan primaries, the changes include legislative redistricting by a nonpartisan panel to reduce gerrymandering — political line-drawing for purely partisan purposes.

Political analysts say it's too early to evaluate the effectiveness of the state's reforms, which California voters approved in a 2010 ballot initiative over the objections of many political leaders. But the changes clearly have shaken up California politics.

During the previous decade, after Democratic legislators drew district maps to protect their incumbents, none of the state's 53 congressional districts was truly competitive and only one changed party hands. The gerrymandering legislation was so effective that David Wasserman, an analyst for the Washington-based *Cook Political Report,* dubbed it the "incumbent protection act."

Members of Congress and the state legislature knew "they would never lose a general election to a candidate from the other party," said Dan Schnur, director of the University of Southern California's Jesse M. Unruh Institute of Politics. So, to protect themselves from challenges from the more ideological candidates in their own party primaries, they "retreated from the middle . . . toward their respective ideological end zones," Schnur said.[2]

As a result, in the 2011-12 Congress, of the 19 members tied for the most liberal voting record in the U.S. House, seven were California Democrats, according to the *National Journal.*[3]

After the election reforms were implemented, no congressional incumbent was defeated in the state's 2012 primaries. But a fourth of the state's delegation did not return to Congress in 2013, either because they lost in the general election or because they retired.[4] Among those defeated were 80-year-old Democrat Pete Stark — a volatile partisan who spent half his life in the House and was among the 19 most liberal members — and 71-year-old Democrat Howard Berman, a three-decade House veteran.

Stark won his three-way primary but lost the general election to a 31-year-old suburban city council member who targeted Stark's combative style.[5]

After redistricting threw them into the same race, Berman lost to fellow Democratic Rep. Brad Sherman, 59.[6] The Berman-Sherman combat between two veteran

Impact of the Filibuster

The filibuster — unlimited debate used by a minority faction or an individual to tie up the Senate — was created by accident, according to George Washington University political science professor Sarah Binder. Cleaning up its rulebook in 1806, the Senate dropped a procedure by which a majority could cut off debate. For decades, no one noticed the implication.[53]

Beginning in 1841, various senators proposed rules for ending debate, but none passed until 1917, when a

Republican filibuster blocked Democratic President Woodrow Wilson's plan to arm U.S. merchant ships to protect against German submarines in World War I. With backing from the press and the public on national security grounds, Wilson demanded a provision to break filibusters, and the Senate created "cloture." The process allowed two-thirds of senators voting to end debate on some measures.[54]

In 1949, the Senate expanded the circumstances under which cloture could be invoked and required votes incumbents of the same party highlighted some of the reforms' unintended consequences. The candidates spent millions in what *Politico* termed one of the "five ugliest member vs. member battles" of 2012.[7] Berman's loss cost California a highly respected legislator whom the *Los Angeles Times* termed a "Democratic lion" and *National Journal* described as "one of the most creative members of the House and one of the most clear-sighted operators in American politics."[8]

The new rules created "a great number of competitive districts" but also "a level of nastiness in campaigns that I have not seen before — and some of the most expensive races ever," according to University of Southern California political scientist Sherry Bebitch Jeffe.[9]

Probably the most devastating unintended consequence was the loss of senior legislators of both parties, which diminished California's clout in Washington. The state's power stemmed from both the size of the delegation and its seniority.

"The problem with a [nonpartisan redistricting] commission in one state and not the others is that the House of Representatives still relies to a great deal on a seniority system," said Democrat Henry Waxman, another senior representative from California, who won re-election in 2012 but is retiring after this year.[10]

The reforms did produce nonpartisan redistricting that was indifferent to incumbents' interests, says Gary Jacobson, a political science professor at the University of California, San Diego. Primary turnout remained low, however. And independent and third-party candidates had no impact on the general election. Moreover, polarization did not decline significantly.

A statewide survey found that "voters can't tell a moderate Republican from a conservative Republican or a moderate Democrat from a liberal Democrat in bottom-of-the-ticket races, including in the state legislature," says Thad Kousser, associate professor of political science at UC-San Diego.

Candidates still have to raise money, and "funds generally come from strongly partisan ideological sources," Jacobson notes.

Despite the skepticism about the California reforms, *Los Angeles Times* editors have declared them a success because "the political parties no longer pick their voters."[11]

— *Tom Price*

[1] Jean Merl, "New rules make it a new game," *Los Angeles Times,* July 8, 2012, p. A-21.

[2] Dan Schnur, "Good news from Tuesday's vote," *Los Angeles Times,* June 7, 2012, p. A-23.

[3] Ryan Morris and Peter Bell, "Searchable Vote Ratings Tables: House," *National Journal,* Feb. 23, 2012, http://bit.ly/Nfq9bO.

[4] Michael B. Marois, "California Nonpartisan Districting Ousts Life Incumbents," Bloomberg, March 19, 2013, http://bloom.bg/1gmjcOI.

[5] "Pete Stark, veteran Calif. congressman, defeated by 31-year-old," *Los Angeles Times,* Nov. 7, 2012, http://lat.ms/1cvoBno.

[6] Jean Merl, "Democratic lion Howard Berman is leaving Congress, a casualty of California's new political landscape," *Los Angeles Times,* Nov. 7, 2012, p. AA-9.

[7] "Congress 2012: The 5 ugliest member vs. member battles," *Politico,* Feb. 27, 2012, www.politico.com/news/stories/0212/73347.html.

[8] Merl, "Democratic lion Howard Berman is leaving Congress . . .," *op. cit.*

[9] Jean Merl and Patrick McGreevy, "Democrats gain big in Legislature," *Los Angeles Times,* Nov. 7, 2012, p. 1.

[10] Adam Nagourney, "California Set to Send Many New Faces to Washington," *The New York Times,* Feb. 13, 2012, http://nyti.ms/1jNQMzp.

[11] "Lines of contention," *Los Angeles Times,* Aug. 22, 2011, p. A-10.

from two-thirds of the entire Senate for passage. The supermajority was lowered to three-fifths in 1975.[55]

Filibusters were rare until the 1970s, with entire congresses going by without a single cloture motion. During the 1971-72 term, 24 cloture motions were filed. But the practice soared during President George W. Bush's last two years in office, when 139 motions were filed. During the first five years of Obama's presidency, 329 were filed.[56]

Conservative Democrats fueled the 1970s uptick, when they expanded their filibustering from civil rights legislation to measures unpopular with Republicans in order to discourage GOP opposition, according to Steven Smith, professor of social and political science at Washington University. Later, interest groups and party activists pressured lawmakers to use every available tool to advance their positions, he said. Then, as the parties became more homogeneous, "no longer is there that moderate Republican or moderate Democrat telling their own leaders, 'do not obstruct . . . I am going to get hurt.'"[57]

Bipartisan Policy Center Seeks to Bridge Partisan Divide

"Most people want the government to work."

Traveling the country in 2012, Maine Republican Sen. Olympia Snowe noted Americans' increasing alienation from the partisan warfare in Washington. They were observing at long distance what she was witnessing first-hand, and she found them as appalled as she was.

"Most people are in the middle," she concluded, "and they want the government to work." But Snowe says "policymaking has been virtually abandoned" in Congress, and debates are "all about ideology and absolutes, rather than trying to develop practical solutions to problems."

Figuring she could "serve the country more effectively from outside than within," Snowe announced in early 2012 that she would not run for another term. She wrote a book entitled *Fighting for Common Ground,* established "Olympia's List" to raise money and encourage grassroots support for centrist candidates, urged citizens to demand an end to government gridlock and became a senior fellow at the Bipartisan Policy Center, a Washington think tank that promotes bipartisanship.

The center was established in 2007 by four former Senate majority leaders: Democrats Tom Daschle and George Mitchell and Republicans Bob Dole and Howard Baker. Partisan debate had "grown so hostile, . . . so raucous, that it has now had a corrosive effect on our ability to govern," Baker said at the time.[1] Snowe and others say damaging partisanship is worse today.

Begun with a staff of 20 and a $7 million annual budget — primarily from philanthropies such as the William and Flora Hewlett Foundation and the Pew Charitable Trusts — the center proposes bipartisan solutions to major policy problems by culling the ideas of political leaders, scholars, business executives, union officials and others from across the political spectrum.

While the center hasn't ended the polarization and gridlock that spurred its creation, it does get audiences on Capitol Hill and among policy advocates.

Republican Sen. Lamar Alexander of Tennessee said he turns to it for "competent, disinterested advice and specific information" about complex issues, such as how to reduce the national debt. Democratic Sen. Mark Warner of Virginia describes it as a "support network for those of us up here in the Senate who [believe] that the best policy solutions are found when you can find common ground."[2]

The center focuses on about 20 projects addressing such red-hot topics as immigration reform, Iran's nuclear ambitions and the partisan political divide. And it attracts prominent national figures to lead its endeavors.

Its immigration task force, for instance, is co-chaired by two Republicans — former Mississippi governor and GOP chairman Haley Barbour and former Secretary of State Condoleezza Rice — and two Democrats: former Pennsylvania Gov. Edward Rendell and Henry Cisneros, a former San Antonio mayor who served as secretary of Housing and Urban Development. The center's debt-reduction task force was led by former Senate Budget Committee Chairman Pete Domenici, a Republican, and Alice Rivlin, the founding director of the Congressional Budget Office and head of the White House Office of Management and Budget for Democratic President Bill Clinton.

Center President Jason Grumet says it is "delightfully easy" to land big-name participants because most "have had profound careers solving big problems, and a lot of them miss that opportunity." They also "are pretty disgusted with what's happening in both parties and eager to be part of something that harkens back to the more productive experiences they've had in their careers."

Much of the center's work occurs behind closed doors, Grumet says, including with lawmakers who eschew bipartisanship in public. "It won't shock you that there's a tremendous amount of posturing in our nation's capital," Grumet says, "and we often have very productive experiences working privately to understand where people's bottom lines are. Often the gulf between those bottom lines is much smaller in private than one would see in public."

Center staff members have briefed lawmakers privately, for example, on several occasions when the need to raise the federal debt ceiling loomed, Grumet says. "Our analysis hasn't told people what they should do," he says, "but has very carefully walked through what the world would look like if we were to default. We have yet to meet somebody who has told us [in private] that they think that would be an appropriate strategy for the United States."

Not everyone is enamored of the center's bipartisan posture. Some liberal critics question its ties to corporate donors, which include oil companies BP America and Chevron, pharmaceutical giant Eli Lilly and conglomerate General Electric. Still, philanthropic foundations contributed four times as much to the center as corporations did in 2012.[3]

Writing in the environmental publication *Grist,* liberal activist David Halperin said the center "often seems more like a voice for corporate interests in Washington."[4] And when a center task force released a health care plan in 2009, opponents of the proposal questioned the organization's donations from a pharmaceutical company and its other health care industry ties. Daschle and Dole, for example, have worked for legal and consulting firms with health care clients.[5]

Conversely, some conservatives say the center is too tolerant of big government. And Erick Erickson, editor of the conservative website *Red State,* described the organization as "left-of-center" because its task force reports support comprehensive immigration reform with a path to citizenship for illegal immigrants.[6]

When Snowe appeared on ABC's "This Week" last year to describe the center's goal of drawing more Americans into political action so they can hold government "accountable for reaching agreement," conservative columnist George Will said he wasn't sure he agreed with that goal.

Republican Sen. Olympia Snowe of Maine retired in 2013 over deep frustration at what she saw as Congress's inability to act. She is now a senior fellow at the Bipartisan Policy Center, a Washington think tank.

"I think Sen. Snowe wishes the American people were less cynical about Washington and more trusting," Will said. "I wish Americans were less trusting of government than we are. We wouldn't have the largest, sprawling government, which by its very size guarantees the kind of [gridlock] that Sen. Snowe dislikes."[7]

— *Tom Price*

[1] David S. Broder, "Wily Senate veterans chart a path to common ground," *The Seattle Times,* March 8, 2007, http://bit.ly/1d6KINU.

[2] See "A Sense of Common Purpose," Bipartisan Policy Center, a video at http://bit.ly/1fe2gxi.

[3] Bipartisan Policy Center, "Annual Report," 2012, http://bit.ly/1jTjVfV.

[4] David Halperin, "Keystone Pipeline Not a Big Deal — Say Interests Supported By Oil and Gas Industry," *Grist,* May 12, 2013, http://bit.ly/1gmfULq.

[5] Sam Stein, "Daschle's Firm and Group Have Ties to Private Health Care Industry," *The Huffington Post,* July 19, 2009, http://huff.to/1jhG1FW.

[6] Erick Erickson, "The Fix Is In," Red State, Dec. 5, 2013, http://bit.ly/1fl0KYO.

[7] "Martha Raddatz Hosts ABC's This Week," *Political Transcript Wire,* May 13, 2013, http://abcn.ws/Og1Zir.

Getty Images/T. J. Kirkpatrick

In a rare instance of compromise, Senate Budget Committee Chairman Patty Murray, D-Wash., and House Budget Committee Chairman Paul Ryan, R-Wis., announce last Dec. 10 that they had reached agreement on the Bipartisan Budget Act of 2013. Some optimists hoped congressional budget approval would lead to future cooperation between the two parties. But House GOP leaders subsequently announced that passing major legislation was unlikely before next fall's midterm elections.

Recently, filibusters have been used most notably to block judicial nominees. Democrats filibustered 10 of Republican President George W. Bush's circuit court nominees. Eventually several were confirmed after a group of Democrats and Republicans in 2005 arranged to break the logjam in exchange for a GOP pledge not to "go nuclear" by changing Senate rules to confirm judges by majority vote rather than the two-thirds traditionally required for major changes.[58]

Democrats finally did go nuclear, however, in November 2013 after repeated GOP filibusters of nominations ranging from secretary of Defense to relatively low-level posts. A Senate majority now can end filibusters of all presidential nominees except Supreme Court justices.[59]

Polarizing Media

Partisan media have savaged their political opponents since before the founding of the republic. During the first third of the 19th century, American newspapers published "scurrility," "vulgar attack on personal character," "vituperative political attack" and "vile innuendo," according to journalism historian Frank Luther Mott.[60]

Because of modern technology, however, what the American Enterprise Institute's Ornstein calls the tribal media exert much more influence today. "The immediacy of talk radio and cable TV, amplified by social media, gives them reach and powers significantly beyond what we had seen before," he says.

When Fox News Channel and MSNBC went on the air in 1996, they revolutionized the tone of cable news, which previously had been dominated by the traditional journalism of CNN. Fox's conservative orientation attracted the largest cable news audience, and MSNBC eventually attempted to copy that success by becoming the liberal alternative. Critics say that together they foster polarization by reinforcing their audiences' biases.

"People now can engage in selective exposure to leftwing and rightwing media," as Levendusky, of the University of Pennsylvania, puts it. Thus, "they are not exposed to debate to the extent they used to be," Smith College's Gold says. This results, Ornstein says, in "sets of people who do not share common sets of facts."

According to a Pew survey, 54 percent of staunch conservatives watch Fox regularly, while just 44 percent read a newspaper and 30 percent watch network broadcast news.[61] Staunch conservatives' reliance on partisan media is unusual, according to Pew Research Center founding director Andrew Kohut, because other Americans — whether on the right, left or center — tend to rely primarily on newspapers and broadcast television networks.[62] Only 19 percent of the staunchest liberals turn to MSNBC regularly, for instance, while 69 percent rely on newspapers and 38 percent on network news.[63]

Polarized news consumers may be intensely partisan and highly interested in politics, but they also are few in number, Levendusky says. "It's not the normal person who watches Fox or MSNBC."

Cable news programs exert out-sized influence by reaching political activists and frequent voters. They're also influential, researchers say, because of people's tendency to believe what they want to believe and to cling to their beliefs despite powerful evidence to the contrary.

Fox, for instance, is both the most and least trusted news source, according to a poll published Jan. 30. MSNBC was second as least trusted.

Polarization has created "belief communities," said Steven Strauss, a public policy lecturer at Harvard's Kennedy School, "where people who want to believe patently untrue things (e.g., that President Obama was born in Kenya) are never challenged in their beliefs, and may even be encouraged in their fantasies."[64]

Some striking scientific experiments provide evidence that goes beyond observing the behavior of cable news fans. In one, Yale researchers asked mathematically skilled liberals and conservatives to conduct a mathematical analysis of fake data from a fake study of the effectiveness of a law banning private citizens from carrying concealed handguns in public. One data set showed that crime increased as a result of the law, the other that crime decreased.

Liberal Democrats were much more likely to solve the problem correctly when the correct answer indicated that crime was decreasing than they were when the right answer was that crime was increasing. The opposite was true for conservative Republicans.[65]

And the "belief communities" are strengthened by unlimited independent political spending that reinforces polarized beliefs through advertising and support of candidates who would have fallen by the wayside in the past. Wealthy casino operator Sheldon Adelson, for instance, spent between $98 million and $150 million in the last presidential election cycle, including at least $10 million to help keep former House Speaker Newt Gingrich's run for the 2012 GOP presidential nomination alive. Wealthy financier Tom Steyer plans to spend $50 million — and raise another $50 million — for candidates who support action on climate change. And Charles and David Koch — principal owners of the multibillion-dollar Koch Industries conglomerate — have donated hundreds of millions to conservative causes.[66]

And political scientists say the independent spending also has contributed to polarization by weakening the influence of parties.

Parties leaders want to procure "the broadest electoral appeal of the party brand," said constitutional law professor Richard Pilde of New York University. Conversely, said Richard Hasen, a law and political science professor at the University of California at Irvine, "ads funded by outside spending tend to be more inflammatory than party or candidate ads, because outside groups don't have to worry about their long-term reputations."[67]

CURRENT SITUATION

Intraparty Conflicts

As candidates run their 2014 campaigns and many activists look ahead to the 2016 presidential race, both parties face internal struggles over whether they should be shifting more to the left or the right. Moderates and traditional conservatives are trying to beat back more extreme conservatives who have pulled the Republican Party far to the right, and some liberals are seeking to exercise more influence in a Democratic Party they believe has slipped too much toward the center.

In a late-January action that highlighted the GOP's party-shattering polarization, the Arizona Republican Party censured John McCain — the state's senior U.S. senator and the 2008 GOP presidential nominee — for insufficient conservatism.

"Only in times of great crisis or betrayal is it necessary to publicly censure our leaders," the GOP state committee said in a resolution adopted by voice vote Jan. 25. "Today we are faced with both." The party leaders accused McCain of having "amassed a long and terrible record of drafting, cosponsoring and voting for legislation best associated with liberal Democrats," such as immigration reform and confirmation of the president's "liberal nominees." At the same time, the committee praised conservative GOP senators and Tea Party favorites Ted Cruz of Texas and Mike Lee of Utah, who led last year's government shutdown and threat to default on the national debt.[68]

In Texas, conservative Sen. John Cornyn is being challenged in the GOP primary by even more conservative Rep. Steve Stockman. Even though *National Journal* ranked Cornyn the second-most-conservative senator in the 2011-12 Congress and the 14th-most conservative last year, Stockman has attacked him as a "compromising liberal" and Democratic Senate Majority Leader "Harry Reid's Republican."[69]

Cornyn and Minority Leader Mitch McConnell of Kentucky are among seven GOP Senate incumbents — of 12 running for re-election — who face primary challenges from the right this year.[70]

However, unlike in recent years — when insurgent conservatives won GOP primaries, then lost general elections that Republicans had been favored to win — moderate, business-oriented and more-traditional Republicans are organizing to fight back.

Would a parliamentary system reduce political polarization?

YES — Arend Lijphart
Research Professor Emeritus of Political Science, University of California, San Diego

Written for *CQ Researcher*, February 2014

My proposals for reducing the negative effects of polarization in the United States will sound radical to many Americans, but they are commonplace among modern industrial democracies. America would be better off in a parliamentary system with proportional representation and competition among several parties.

Systems with a separated president and legislature contain flaws that are contributing to America's gridlocked government. The first problem is what the late Yale University political scientist Juan J. Linz called "dual democratic legitimacy."

In parliamentary systems, only the legislature is popularly elected and is the clear and legitimate representative of the people. But in presidential systems both president and legislature are popularly elected and can claim legitimacy. It is quite possible — even likely — that the president and the majority of legislators will have divergent political preferences. There is no democratic principle to resolve such disagreements. The result tends to be stalemate, as seen now in the United States.

The second problem is rigidity. Presidents are elected for fixed terms, which cannot be extended due to term limits even if a president is successful, and cannot be shortened even if a president proves incompetent. Impeachment is almost always time-consuming and unsuccessful because extraordinary majorities are required to impeach a president. If parliamentary systems run into major problems or crises, they can be resolved much more easily by calling new elections and forming a new government.

The third problem is the winner-take-all nature of presidential elections. The winner wins all executive power, leaving losing viewpoints with no voice in the executive office. As Linz noted, parliamentary elections can produce an absolute majority for a single party, but power-sharing, coalition-forming and attention to the interests of smaller parties are more common.

The United States likely would end up with four main parties — representing liberal Democrats, moderate Democrats, moderate Republicans and very conservative Republicans — and a few small parties. Governing coalitions probably would be formed by the centrists most of the time, eliminating gridlock and reducing the impact of extremists.

Some will say that parliamentary government would be impossible in the United States because of America's strong tradition of presidentialism. By that logic, should we tell nondemocratic countries to refrain from introducing democracy because of their nondemocratic traditions?

Presidentialist traditions may be a big obstacle to the adoption of parliamentarism, but they are not a valid argument against a switch to the healthier parliamentary system of government.

NO — Jason Grumet
President, Bipartisan Policy Center

Written for *CQ Researcher*, February 2014

Frustrated with gridlock? Get in line. Congress' inability to overcome differences is causing real damage today and saddling our kids with tremendous debt, a crumbling infrastructure and broadly diminished opportunities. Still, suggesting that we jettison a system that has served us well for 225 years is more a commentary on our desire for instant gratification than a reflection of fundamental flaws in our nation's Constitution.

Parliamentary systems may seem more efficient, but their outcomes are often neither stable nor resilient. For example, Australia enacted, repealed and re-enacted universal health care within a decade.

In contrast, while our Constitutional "checks and balances" and inclination toward divided government can be maddening, they're also the foundation of America's historic cohesion, stability and economic strength. Leaders with disparate constituencies and varying views are compelled to engage one another. The resulting policy outcomes are more thoughtful, measured and broadly accepted than in a majority-driven system, where the ruling party or coalition has no obligation to engage the opposition. In the current closely divided and polarized environment, does anyone really want Republicans or Democrats empowered to govern with no constraints?

And therein lies the real problem: Today's highly polarized atmosphere discourages the interaction our system needs to flourish. Instead of clamoring for an unlikely "do-over" of the Constitution, let's commit ourselves to pragmatic measures that restore engagement across party lines.

For example, greater transparency in political donations would loosen the grip of divisive activists. Wider primary participation would ensure more appealing — and reasonable — general-election candidates. Devolving power from Senate and House leadership back to congressional committees would hand the hard work of legislating back to members with greater incentive for substance than sound bites. And turning the cameras off for a few hours each week would allow frank and energetic exchanges of views free of anxiety that considering new ideas would unleash attacks from the far right or far left.

America has been here before. We have enjoyed periods of great legislative accomplishment and suffered through years of devastating dysfunction. People are mad. This is good. Public outrage is an essential driver of political change — but it needs to be directed toward practical solutions.

There is value to contemplating disruptive ideas — even bad ones. But when it comes to repairing our democracy, the best thinking will be found "inside the box."

The U.S. Chamber of Commerce — which had tended to stay out of party primaries — spent more than $200,000 to help Bradley Byrne win a special election to fill an Alabama congressional seat late last year. The chamber backed Byrne in the November GOP primary runoff against Dean Young, who questioned President Obama's birthplace and advocated closing the government again to fight the Affordable Care Act. Byrne then easily won the December general election in the heavily Republican district.

The Chamber is making independent expenditures on behalf of McConnell as well.[71] The Main Street Advocacy Fund is also raising funds to support establishment Republicans. Led by moderate Ohio Republican Steve LaTourette, who left the U.S. House last year because he was frustrated by the extreme partisanship, the group aims to raise $8 million to defend moderates or oust extreme conservatives in eight to 10 races this year.

"We want our party back," LaTourette said. But he acknowledged that "we are behind the curve with our more conservative counterparts," referring to organizations such as the Club for Growth, Freedom Works and the Senate Conservatives Fund, which have been supporting staunchly conservative candidates for years.[72]

In addition to attacking the rightwing groups' policies and polarizing strategies, Main Street Advocacy accuses them of damaging the GOP. "If not for [those groups], the Republicans would control the Senate today," says David Hobson, a moderate former representative from Ohio and a Main Street member. "Because of nominating these narrow people in primaries, they give advantage to Democrats in general elections."

Tom Borelli, a senior fellow at Freedom Works, dismissed LaTourette's organization as a "RINO (Republican in Name Only) protection fund."[73] And Club for Growth spokesman Barney Keller said Main Street contributors are wasting their money. "We look forward to adding to the ranks of pro-growth conservatives in Congress," Keller said.[74]

Things are more peaceful among Democrats, but more liberal party members increasingly are complaining that both the Obama and Clinton administrations made too many concessions to the right, and they are talking about changing things in the 2014 and 2016 elections.

Some tout liberal Democrat Bill de Blasio's triumph in last year's New York mayoral race as a harbinger of a left-wing revival to come. Some promote Massachusetts Sen. Elizabeth Warren as a more liberal alternative to Hillary Rodham Clinton, who is widely expected to run for president in 2016.

As Obama embraced the need to rein in entitlement spending, Warren and some allies have proposed increasing Social Security benefits. They also want tougher regulation of large financial institutions. "The first Obama administration was focused too much on saving the banks and Wall Street," said liberal Democratic Sen. Tom Harkin of Iowa, who is retiring after this year. "There's going to be a big populist push on whoever's running for office to espouse these kinds of progressive policies."[75]

Redistricting Reforms

Outside of party conflicts, election-law reformers are promoting changes they say would reduce polarization, ease government gridlock, remove barriers to voting and cause more citizens to feel they have a real voice in running the country.

For instance, say reformers, recent election-law changes in California are making elections there less conducive to polarization. In 2012, California elected all of its federal and state legislators in nonpartisan elections conducted in districts designed by a nonpartisan citizens' commission.

One of the most ambitious reform plans comes from FairVote, which advocates multimember legislative districts and rank-order voting. Under the plan, three to five legislators would be chosen from each district. Voters would select their first choice, as well as their second, third and additional picks. To be elected in a three-member district, for instance, a candidate would have to receive more than a quarter of the votes. If fewer than three candidates reached that goal, the secondary-choice votes would be counted until three candidates were chosen.

In a multimember district with rank-order voting, victory likely would go to candidates who reach out to the broadest range of voters, and a larger proportion of voters would feel they had helped to select their public officials, FairVote's Richie says. In singlemember districts, supporters of losing candidates get no representation, he says, even if they comprise nearly half the electorate.

Movements are underway in several states to combat polarization by establishing nonpartisan or bipartisan redistricting commissions that would not try to create uncompetitive districts.

Fortier, of the Bipartisan Policy Center, says that while he's intrigued by many of the proposals, researchers question how much polarization can be attributed to gerrymandering, or drawing districts to benefit the party in power. For instance, he points out, many statewide elections are polarized even though they can't be gerrymandered.

However, much evidence shows that gerrymandering can determine the outcome of many elections. After the 2010 census, for instance, Republicans redrew most congressional districts. Then, although Democratic House candidates outpolled GOP candidates by 1.4 million votes in 2012, Republicans won 234 seats to Democrats' 201.[76]

But the American Enterprise Institute's Ornstein warns that redistricting reforms alone won't end polarization and restore civility. To get a broader swath of the electorate voting, Ornstein advocates adopting Australia's requirement that citizens show up at the polls. Turnout has been 90 percent or greater since the measure was enacted. "Australian politicians will tell you that, if you know both sides' base will be there, you focus more on voters in the middle," he says. "You change the issues you talk about, the rhetoric you use."

In addition, "We have to do some things that change culture," he says. "If we can create a culture with a sense that, when you say outrageous things that divide people there's going to be a sense of shame, that would be helpful."

OUTLOOK
Proposed Solutions

FairVote's Richie says he's confident that his group's presidential reform proposal — that states cast their electoral votes for the winner of the national popular vote — will become reality in 2016 or 2020.

Already, the plan has been adopted by nine states that represent 25 percent of the electoral votes needed to win the presidency, he says. When states with 270 votes approve the plan, it will take effect because their votes would be enough to win, "so it's halfway to enactment."

He's optimistic about FairVote's other proposals, as well, because the country is "at such a level of crisis and dysfunction that some changes that need to happen are going to start happening," he says. "Reforms tend to come in bunches. The last big wave of constitutional change was direct election of senators in 1913, women's suffrage in 1920 and the income tax in 1913." Bipartisan Policy Center President Grumet suggests voters will solve the problem eventually by rejecting polarizing candidates. "It's a question of time-frame, and it's not going to be geologic," he says.

The University of California at San Diego's Lijphart acknowledges that the United States is unlikely to shift to parliamentary government. Adoption of proportional representation is more likely, he says, because "it does not require a constitutional amendment."

"The positive news is the public is not satisfied," former Agriculture Secretary Glickman says. However, he warns, "if we can't solve basic problems like the national debt or repairing our national infrastructure or creating an educational system that works at high levels, we are in deep trouble as a society."

In addition, former Rep. Hobson says, "as long as anonymous people are able to fund these (polarizing campaigns) on both sides, in my opinion, it's only going to get worse."

Gridlock will end when one party seizes control of both congressional chambers and the White House at the same time, Heritage Action's Holler says. "You have two parties who should be offering very distinct visions for the proper role of the government. With the way the political parties are right now — and if they become increasingly clear about what they stand for and the direction they want to move — one of them eventually will have a mandate from the American people to move forward in that direction.

"Until one party does," Holler says, "we'll be stuck in the situation we are now, where there's not a lot of clarity about what direction to go."

NOTES

1. Ravi Somaiya, "Banished for Questioning the Gospel of Guns," *The New York Times,* Jan. 4, 2014, http://nyti.ms/1jSc52R.

2. Paul Erhardt, "Between The Berms: Paging Uncle Ted," *The Shooting Wire,* Nov. 6, 2013, http://bit.ly/1nUhZBd.

3. Somaiya, *op. cit.*

4. Robert Reich, "Red States Get More Extreme," AlterNet, June 10, 2013, http://bit.ly/OkaWY6.

5. Katie Koch, "'Skyboxification' of American life at issue in Sandel's latest book," *Harvard Gazette,* July 18, 2012, http://bit.ly/1jVFRH7.

6. Charlie Cook, "Whole Foods versus Cracker Barrel: How Americans Are Self-Sorting," *National Journal,* Aug. 5, 2011, http://bit.ly/1fnVeEV.

7. Reid Wilson, "What your favorite drink says about your politics, in one chart," *The Washington Post,* Dec. 31, 2013, http://wapo.st/1islhNv; Reid Wilson, "You are where you shop," *The Washington Post,* Dec. 9, 2013, http://wapo.st/1jVFnkp; Reid Wilson, "Red America, blue America and reality TV," *The Washington Post,* Aug. 22, 2013, http://wapo.st/1miVQgM.

8. Shanto Iyengar, Gaurav Sood and Yphtach Lelkes, "Affect, Not Ideology: A Social Identity Perspective on Polarization," *Public Opinion Quarterly,* Fall 2012, http://stanford.io/1fi4snC.

9. Carol Morello and Ted Mellnik, "Washington: A world apart," *The Washington Post,* Nov. 9, 2013, http://wapo.st/1l6GDRS.

10. Carol Morello, "Study: Rich, poor Americans increasingly likely to live in separate neighborhoods," *The Washington Post,* Aug. 1, 2013, http://wapo.st/1jSfsXG.

11. Koch, *op. cit.*

12. Carlos Lozada, "The deal with rich people," *The Washington Post,* Nov. 27, 2013, http://wapo.st/1fGfGxc.

13. Ronald Brownstein, "College Used to Be a Path to Success. Now It Divides Us," *National Journal,* Dec. 10, 2013, http://bit.ly/1gV8HUb.

14. "President: Full Results," CNN, http://cnn.it/1blqn9N.

15. Carol Morello, "Census count finds decreasing white population in 15 states," *The Washington Post,* Sept. 29, 2011, CNN, http://cnn.it/1blqn9N.

16. Drew DeSilver, "Only 1 in 7 House districts were competitive in 2012," Pew Research Center, Nov. 5, 2013, http://bit.ly/Okezx7.

17. David Wasserman, "Introducing the 2014 Cook Political Report Partisan Voter Index," *The Cook Political Report,* April 4, 2013, http://bit.ly/1fnqKCV.

18. Chris Cillizza, "The political middle is dying. But it's not redistricting's fault," *The Washington Post,* Oct. 29, 2013, http://wapo.st/1fi4RGs.

19. Reich, *op. cit.*

20. *Ibid.;* Fred Hiatt, "A red state/blue state chasm," *The Washington Post,* April 21, 2013, http://wapo.st/1p3eJXp; Ronald Brownstein, "Colorado Is America, Writ Small," *National Journal,* Oct. 31, 2013, http://bit.ly/1fnPHht; Lawrence R. Jacobs, "Right vs. Left in the Midwest," *The New York Times,* Nov. 23, 2013, http://nyti.ms/1eeyOkQ.

21. Reid Wilson, "New laws coming in elections and social issues," *The Washington Post,* Dec. 26, 2013, http://wapo.st/MJu2G1; also see for background, Kenneth Jost, "Voting Controversies," *CQ Researcher,* Feb. 21, 2014, pp. 169-192.

22. Michael Gerson, "A compromised reputation among the GOP," *The Washington Post,* Sept. 26, 2013, http://wapo.st/1bSTMeD.

23. Jonathan Rauch, "Rescuing Compromise," *National Affairs,* Fall 2013, http://bit.ly/1bmNnb8.

24. Stephen Dinan, "Bipartisanship' in Congress: Good or bad?" *The Washington Times,* March 1, 2010, http://bit.ly/1myQ8ef.

25. Karen Tumulty, "Obama seeks to defuse tensions among Democrats," *The Washington Post,* Feb. 22, 2014, www.washingtonpost.com/politics/obama-seeks-to-defuse-tensions-among-democrats/2014/02/22/92e472fc-9b1b-11e3-ad71-e03637a299c0_story.html.

26. Richard L. Fox and Jennifer L. Lawless, "Turning off the next generation of politicians," *The Washington Post,* Nov. 22, 2013, http://wapo.st/1e0nsW0.

27. "David Gregory Hosts NBC's Meet The Press," *Political Transcript Wire,* Jan. 26, 2014.

28. Robert Costa, "Hill GOP is focused on calm in its ranks," *The Washington Post,* Feb. 18, 2014, p. 1.

29. *Ibid.*

30. Lawrence Summers, "When gridlock is good," *The Washington Post,* April 14, 2013, http://wapo.st/Mhi6dG.

31. Jeffrey Toobin, "Our Broken Constitution," *The New Yorker,* Dec. 9, 2013, http://nyr.kr/Iy1U6D.

32. Francis Fukuyama, "Why are we still fighting over Obamacare?" *The Washington Post,* Oct. 6, 2013, p. B-1, http://wapo.st/1fi5GPK.

33. Alex Seitz-Wald, "A How-To Guide to Blowing Up the Constitution," *National Journal,* Oct. 31, 2013, http://bit.ly/Mhihpg.

34. *Ibid.*

35. Rich Mitchell, "CNN's Fareed Zakaria Does Not Think Highly of America," *Conservative Daily News,* Aug. 21, 2011, http://bit.ly/1l6U4RX.

36. Gene Healy, "South of the Border, the Cult of the Presidency," *DC Examiner,* Feb. 2, 2010, http://bit.ly/1h6XAIf.

37. Ray Smock, "Dysfunction in Congress a National Crisis," *LA Progressive,* Oct. 24, 2011, www.laprogressive.com/elections/dysfunction-congress/?utm_source=feedburner&utm_medium=feed&utm_campaign=Feed%3A+laprogressive+%28The+LA+Progressive%29; "Alexander Hamilton and Aaron Burr's Duel," PBS, www.pbs.org/wgbh/amex/duel/peopleevents/pande17.html.

38. Jeff Nilsson, "Your Government Inaction," *The Saturday Evening Post,* Sept. 5, 2013, www.saturdayeveningpost.com/2013/09/05/archives/post-perspective/your-government-inaction-the-do-nothing-congress-of-50-years-ago.html.

39. *Ibid.*

40. *Ibid.*

41. Harry S. Truman, "Know Nothing, Do Nothing Congress," speech in Elizabeth, N.J., Oct. 7, 1948, www.speeches-usa.com/Transcripts/053_truman.html.

42. Greg Marx, "Polar Opposites," *Columbia Journalism Review,* June 21, 2010, www.cjr.org/campaign_desk/polar_opposites.php.

43. "American Values Survey 2012," Pew Research Center, www.people-press.org/2012/06/04/partisan-polarization-surges-in-bush-obama-years/6-4-12-v-4.

44. Chris Cillizza, "What George W. Bush meant for politics," *The Washington Post,* April 25, 2013, www.washingtonpost.com/blogs/the-fix/wp/2013/04/25/what-george-w-bush-meant-for-politics/?hpid=z.

45. Chris Cillizza, "The political middle is dying. But it's not redistricting's fault," *The Washington Post,* Oct. 29, 2013, www.washingtonpost.com/blogs/the-fix/wp/2013/10/29/the-political-middle-is-dying-but-its-not-redistrictings-fault/?tid=hp Module_f8335a3c-868c-11e2-9d71-f0feafdd1394.

46. Frances Lee, "American politics is more competitive than ever," *The Washington Post,* Jan. 9 2014, www.washingtonpost.com/blogs/monkey-cage/wp/2014/01/09/american-politics-is-more-competitive-than-ever-thats-making-partisanship-worse.

47. For background, see Tom Price, "Political Conventions," *CQ Researcher,* Aug. 8, 2008; "Historical Presidential Elections," 270 to Win, www.270towin.com/historical-presidential-elections.

48. Messick, *op. cit.*

49. Melinda Henneberger, "Bob Dole honored for work in helping to feed the poor," *The Washington Post,* Dec, 12, 2013, http://tinyurl.com/jwzsw56.

50. David E. Rosenbaum, "The Tax Reform of 1986," *The New York Times,* Oct. 23, 1986, www.nytimes.com/1986/10/23/business/the-tax-reform-of-1986-political-implications-president-signs-new-tax-bill.html.

51. Adam B. Kushner and Michael Hirsh, "How Bill Clinton and Newt Gingrich Set the Stage for the Shutdown," *National Journal,* Oct. 1, 2013, http://tinyurl.com/lycpbw6.

52. Ronald Brownstein and Stephanie Czekalinski, "How Washington Ruined Governors," *NationalJournal,* April 11, 2013, www.nationaljournal.com/magazine/how-washington-ruined-governors-20130411.

53. Sarah A. Binder, statement to the U.S. Senate Committee on Rules and Administration, April 22,

2010, p. 16, www.rules.senate.gov/public/?a=Files.Serve&File_id=ac170e75-5bb8-404e-9cb1-3c5018cccb50.

54. *Ibid.*

55. Donald R. Wolfensberger, "A Brief History of Congressional Reform Efforts," Bipartisan Policy Center, Feb. 22, 2013, http://bipartisanpolicy.org/sites/default/files/History%20of%20Congressional%20Reform.pdf.

56. Donald R. Wolfensberger, "Getting Back to Legislating," Bipartisan Policy Center and The Woodrow Wilson Center. Nov. 27, 2012, http://bipartisanpolicy.org/sites/default/files/BPC%20Congress%20Report-6.pdf. Also see "Senate Action on Cloture Motions," www.senate.gov/pagelayout/reference/cloture_motions/clotureCounts.htm.

57. Steven S. Smith, statement to the U.S. Senate Committee on Rules and Administration, April 22, 2010, p. 483, www.rules.senate.gov/public/?a=Files.Serve&File_id=ac170e75-5bb8-404e-9cb1-3c5018cccb50.

58. Paul Kane, "GOP blocks Obama court nominee, but parties' confirmation wars aren't new," *The Washington Post,* Nov. 12 2013, http://tinyurl.com/k63aszf.

59. Paul Kane, "Reid, Democrats trigger 'nuclear' option," *The Washington Post,* Nov. 21, 2013, www.washingtonpost.com/politics/senate-poised-to-limit-filibusters-in-party-line-vote-that-would-alter-centuries-of-precedent/2013/11/21/d065cfe8-52b6-11e3-9fe0-fd2ca728e67c_story.html.

60. Tom Price, "Journalism Standards in the Internet Age," *CQ Researcher,* Oct. 8, 2010, pp. 821-844.

61. Andrew Kohut, "The numbers prove it: The GOP is estranged from America," *The Washington Post,* March 22, 2013, www.washingtonpost.com/opinions/the-numbers-prove-it-the-republican-party-is-estranged-from-america/2013/03/22/3050734c-900a-11e2-9abd-e4c5c9dc5e90_story.html?hpid=z1.

62. *Ibid.*

63. "Beyond Red vs. Blue: The Political Typology: Section 3: Demographics and News Sources," Pew Research Center for the People & the Press, May 4, 2011, www.people-press.org/2011/05/04/section-3-demographics-and-news-sources/.

64. Steven Strauss, "Six Reasons American Political Polarization Will Only Get Worse," *The Huffington Post,* Oct. 14, 2012, www.huffingtonpost.com/steven-strauss/megatrend-six-reasons-ame_b_1965182.html.

65. Chris Mooney, "Science Confirms: Politics Wrecks Your Ability to Do Math," *Mother Jones,* Sept. 4, 2013.

66. See Richard L. Hasen, "How 'the next Citizens United' could bring more corruption — but less gridlock," *The Washington Post,* Feb. 21, 2014, http://wapo.st/1fs27R2; Rachel Weiner and James Grimaldi, "Sheldon Adelson reportedly betting $10 million more on Newt Gingrich," *The Washington Post,* Feb. 17, 2012, http://wapo.st/1cQTGlG; Andrew Restuccia, "Tom Steyer planning $100 million campaign push," *Politico,* Feb. 18, 2014, http://politi.co/1c94Zb6; and Kenneth P. Vogel, "Koch World reboots," *Politico,* Feb. 20, 2013, http://politi.co/1fs2paA.

67. Hasen, *ibid.*

68. Ashley Killough, "Arizona GOP rebukes McCain for not being conservative enough," CNN, Jan. 26, 2014, www.ksbw.com/news/politics/Arizona-GOP-rebukes-McCain-for-not-being-conservative-enough/24127380.

69. Brian McGill, "How Liberal Is Your Senator?" *National Journal,* Feb. 21, 2013, http://bit.ly/1cz7Pnq. Stockman's comments are from a fundraising email, Jan. 25, 2014.

70. Paul Steinhauser, "Will challenges from right hurt GOP chances to retake Senate?" CNN, Dec. 10, 2013, http://cnn.it/1hD1mfP.

71. Julie Hirschfeld Davis, "Chamber Taking on Tea Party in Kentucky Senate Primary," *Bloomberg-Businessweek,* Nov. 27, 2013, http://buswk.co/1l6UXKj.

72. Eric Lipton, "In G.O.P. a Campaign Takes Aim at Tea Party," *The New York Times,* Nov. 6, 2013, p. A-14, http://nyti.ms/1goOTa7.

73. Tom Borelli, "Steve LaTourette's "Main Street" Advocacy Project Reeks of Hypocrisy," *Red-State,* Nov. 19, 2013, http://bit.ly/1myVarg.

74. Lipton, *op. cit.*

75. Jane White, "New Year's Resolution: Help Sen. Warren Preserve Social Security," *The Huffington Post,* Dec. 31, 2013, www.huffingtonpost.com/jane-white/new-years-resolution-help-sen-warren-preserve-social-security_b_4520884.html.

76. Sam Wang, "The Great Gerrymander Of 2012," *The New York Times,* Feb. 3, 2013, p. SR-1.

BIBLIOGRAPHY

Selected Sources

Books

Abramowitz, Alan I., *The Polarized Public? Why American Government Is So Dysfunctional,* Pearson, 2013.
An Emory University political science professor argues that America's checks and balances — in an era defined by ultra-polarized political activists — almost guarantee a dysfunctional government.

Levendusky, Matthew, *How Partisan Media Polarize America,* University of Chicago Press, 2013.
A University of Pennsylvania political scientist concludes that cable news channels such as MSNBC and Fox harden their audiences' partisan views rather than creating them.

Mann, Thomas E., and Norman J. Ornstein, *It's Even Worse Than It Looks: How the American Constitutional System Collided with the New Politics of Extremism,* Basic Books, 2013.
Two longtime political analysts blame the Republican Party's right wing for nearly destroying the federal government's ability to function.

Matthews, Chris, *Tip and the Gipper: When Politics Worked,* Simon & Schuster, 2013.
An MSNBC host writes about his years as an aide to Democratic House Speaker Tip O'Neill during Republican Ronald Reagan's administration, when political opposites forged compromises.

Articles

Brownstein, Ronald, and Stephanie Czekalinski, "How Washington Ruined Governors," *National Journal,* April 11, 2013, http://bit.ly/1kYF3Bv.
The authors outline the sharp differences in how today's Democratic and Republican governors approach problems compared to the past, when governors of both parties worked together to attack challenges.

Carr, David, "It's Not Just Political Districts. Our News Is Gerrymandered, Too," *The New York Times,* Oct. 11, 2013, http://nyti.ms/ObsvcV.
A columnist laments how the rise of polarized media enables even a Supreme Court justice to be exposed only to opinions he agrees with.

Kohut, Andrew, "The numbers prove it: The GOP is estranged from America," *The Washington Post,* March 22, 2013, http://wapo.st/NbXrIU.
The founding director of the Pew Research Center contends that only once in his career as a pollster has he seen a political party as estranged from the American mainstream as the current GOP: In the late 1960s and early '70s, when left-wing activists pushed the Democratic Party away from the center over a variety of issues.

Rauch, Jonathan, "Rescuing Compromise," *National Affairs,* Fall 2013, http://bit.ly/1bmNnb8.
A senior fellow at the Brookings Institution, a Washington think tank, contends that compromise is a conservative value and an essential component of the American system of government.

Strauss, Steven, "Six Reasons American Political Polarization Will Only Get Worse," *The Huffington Post,* Oct. 14, 2012, http://huff.to/1maWoFC.
A public policy lecturer at Harvard University's Kennedy School of Government blames growing polarization on partisan media, people's tendency to ignore information that contradicts their beliefs, gerrymandered congressional districts, the rise of single-issue interest groups and the lack of common perspectives.

Reports and Studies

"The American Voting Experience: Report and Recommendations of the Presidential Commission on Election Administration," Presidential Commission on Election Administration, January 2014, http://bit.ly/1g3EZN6.
A bipartisan presidential commission created by President Obama recommends reforms to make it easier for more Americans to vote.

"Partisan Polarization Surges in Bush, Obama Years," Pew Research Center, http://bit.ly/1eTsY8m.
A series of Pew surveys shows that Republicans' and Democrats' disagreements about basic values have been growing since 1987.

Olmstead, Kenneth, Mark Jurkowitz, Amy Mitchell and Jodi Enda, "How Americans Get TV News at Home," Pew Research Center, Oct. 11, 2013, http:// bit.ly/1eTt282.
Broadcast news programs draw far more viewers than cable news, but cable viewers are more politically engaged than broadcast viewers.

Wolfensberger, Donald R., "Getting Back to Legislating," Bipartisan Policy Center and The Woodrow Wilson Center, Nov. 27, 2012, http://bit .ly/1bMT1nh.
A scholar at two Washington-based think tanks summarizes recommendations from scholars and former lawmakers and congressional aides on how to make Congress work better. The solutions include: Have legislators spend more time together in Washington, restore authority to congressional committees and give minorities a greater voice.

For More Information

Bipartisan Policy Center, 1225 I St. N.W., Suite 1000, Washington, DC 20005; 202-204-2400; www.bipartisanpolicy.org. Forms taskforces of political, business, labor and academic figures to develop bipartisan solutions to major national challenges.

Brookings Institution Governance Studies Program, 1775 Massachusetts Ave., N.W., Washington, DC 20036; 202-797-6000; www.brookings.edu/about/programs/governance. Section of the centrist think tank that supports research into such topics as elections, partisanship, budgeting, presidential appointments and improving government performance.

Center for Voting and Democracy, 6930 Carroll Ave., Suite 610, Takoma Park, MD 20912; 301-270-4616; www

.fairvote.org. Nonpartisan organization that researches elections and voting and advocates reforms, including multi-member legislative districts and presidential election by popular vote.

Gallup Organization, 901 F St., N.W., Washington, DC 20004; 202-715-3030; www.gallup.com. Conducts surveys on a wide range of public issues.

Heritage Action for America, 214 Massachusetts Ave., N.E., Suite 400, Washington, DC 20002; 202-548-5280; http://heritageaction.com. Advocacy arm of the conservative Heritage Foundation think tank; rates members of Congress according to their support for the organization's positions and is a key player in the effort to pull the Republican Party to the right.

Privacy and the Internet

Should Americans have a "right to be forgotten"?

Sarah Glazer

8

Max Schrems, a 28-year-old Austrian law student, argued in the European Union's highest court that Facebook should not be allowed to transfer his and other European users' data to its American servers because the information would be subject to U.S. government spying. In October, the court agreed, declaring an international agreement on data transfer invalid on the grounds that the United States does not sufficiently protect citizens' personal information.

From *CQ Researcher*, December 4, 2015

I n 2010, Spanish lawyer Mario Costeja González was disturbed to find that when he Googled his name, a 12-year-old newspaper item appeared at the top of the search results announcing that his house was for sale to pay his unpaid taxes. The debt had been settled long ago. When Costeja González asked Google to eliminate the links from the search engine's Spanish domain, the company refused.

He took Google to court, arguing that, under a European legal principle known as "the right to be forgotten," he could demand the removal of data that besmirched his reputation. Last year, the European Union's (EU) highest court agreed.

The Court of Justice in May 2014 upheld an order from the Spanish data-protection agency saying that Google must eliminate the links. The court went on to say that for individuals in the EU, the rights to privacy and to control of their personal data "override" the public's interest in finding out the information by searching a name.[1]

The ruling has had far-reaching consequences and is at the heart of a growing debate spanning multiple countries about how much of an individual's personal information should remain private — and for how long. The debate pits bedrock free-speech protections against privacy rights and increasingly is being played out in the courts and across federal and state governments trying to determine how Google and other technology companies should operate.

Many legal experts say a European-style right to be forgotten will never take hold in the United States because it would violate

France Leads in Link-Removal Requests

Google has removed 42 percent of links that European Union Internet users have asked to be deleted from the company's search results (top). Google began accepting such requests in May 2014, after the EU's highest court ruled that Internet users have the right to ask search engines to remove links with personal information about them under certain conditions. More than 175,000 removal requests have originated in France, Germany and the United Kingdom, with most coming from France (middle). Links from Facebook were the most removed (bottom).

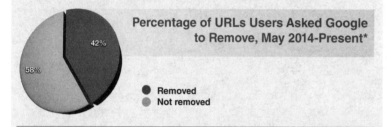

Percentage of URLs Users Asked Google to Remove, May 2014-Present*

- Removed
- Not removed

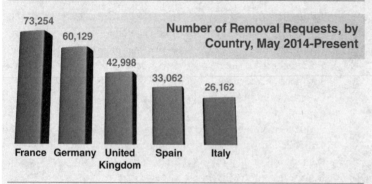

Number of Removal Requests, by Country, May 2014-Present

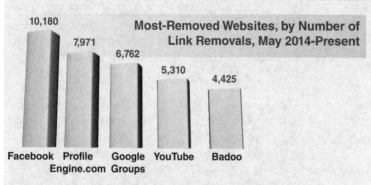

Most-Removed Websites, by Number of Link Removals, May 2014-Present

* Excludes removal requests Google is still reviewing.

Source: "European privacy requests for search removals," Google, updated Nov. 24, 2015, http://tinyurl.com/ptypu56

the Constitution's free-speech protections. But in a digitally linked world, it is drawing increasing attention in this country. Some U.S. privacy advocates who favor the idea claim public sentiment is with them: 69 percent of Americans who use the Internet think they should have the right to delete personal information online, according to a recent poll by the market-research firm Ipsos.[2]

"If we are to have an Internet that protects the freedom of its users, we must place fundamental rights of users before the commercial interests of companies," wrote Marc Rotenberg, president of the Electronic Privacy Information Center, a nonprofit research group in Washington.[3]

Under the EU court decision, Google, and all other search engines doing business in Europe, must remove links from an Internet user's name search upon request if the information is "inadequate," "irrelevant," "excessive" or out of date. Google said it had received requests to remove more than 1 million links and deleted 42 percent of them. Most requests originated in France, and Facebook was the most affected website.[4]

Google did not respond to a request for comment on this story.

Journalists and civil libertarians both here and in Europe have criticized the EU court decision as an infringement of free speech. Search engines "must censor their own references to publicly available information in the name of privacy, with little guidance or obligation to balance the needs of free expression," said Danny O'Brien, international director of the Electronic Frontier Foundation, a San Francisco-based nonprofit defending digital civil liberties.[5]

Defenders of the ruling say the court defended freedom of expression when it affirmed that the Spanish newspaper in question, *La Vanguardia,* was not obliged to erase the original announcement of the house sale from its archives, as Costeja González had originally requested. The court also said search engines should not remove links if the general public has a clear public interest in retaining access to the information, such as when public figures request removal of information about themselves that would inherently be of public concern.

Further heating up the issue, France's data-protection regulatory agency (CNIL) this past June interpreted the Google Spain ruling as applying to all country domains in Europe and to Google's global network. The agency ordered Google to eliminate requested links not only on its French search page but also on its Google.com search engine which the company considers its American site.[6] Most Europeans using Google access search results through their country's Google domain, such as Google.fr in France. But one click on that Google page can instantly bring up Google.com.

Google has complied with delisting requests on its European domains but has refused to extend this service to Google.com. If implemented, the CNIL order also would limit search results that American Internet users could view on Google.com, potentially forcing the company to violate the U.S. Constitution's free-speech guarantees.

The French agency's order "creates an ominous new precedent for Internet censorship that jeopardizes speech and press freedoms worldwide," the Washington, D.C.-based Reporters Committee for Freedom of the Press wrote in a Sept. 14 letter to CNIL signed by 29 other major news organizations including *The New York Times* and Reuters.[7]

Most in U.S. Back 'Right to Be Forgotten'

Nearly seven in 10 American adults who use the Internet say the freedom to remove links containing certain personal data from search engine results should be a human right.

Percentage of American Adults Who Say the Right to be Forgotten . . .

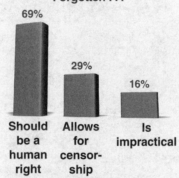

Source: "Majority of Americans Think It Should be a Human Right to be Able to Delete or Remove Personal Information Online," press release, TRUSTe and Ipsos, Aug. 26, 2015, http://tinyurl.com/nvejtt8

It's unclear how this standoff with French regulators will be resolved. Many legal experts believe the order violates First Amendment free-expression rights as well as principles of territorial sovereignty. Moreover, the conflict is likely to heat up even more when the EU unveils sweeping new legislation, currently being drafted, establishing new rights for Internet users to erase content about themselves.

For American consumers, the differences are stark in terms of how the United States and Europe approach the issue. After false claims popped up in the Google search for New York City hedge-fund manager Jeffrey Ervine in 2009, it took a $2 million court judgment to persuade Google to remove the links. Costeja González, in contrast, got a negative link removed even though the information was true.

In America, it's much harder to get information removed if it is accurate, as Californian Christos Catsouras discovered when he tried to remove gory photos of a fatal car crash in which his daughter Nikki, 18, was decapitated. The photos showed up on thousands of websites after California Highway Patrol employees emailed them to family and friends. The family asked that the photos be removed, and many websites did, but the photos remain easy to find on Google. With no right to be forgotten in American law, the family had no way to force Google to remove the photos.[8]

Consumer Watchdog, a consumer advocacy group based in Santa Monica, Calif., filed a complaint with the Federal Trade Commission (FTC) arguing that Google's failure to extend its European delisting right to U.S. consumers is an "unfair and deceptive" practice.[9]

Before the Internet existed, embarrassing acts, such as being photographed drunk at a party, could be forgotten over time unless one searched through old newspaper clippings or photo albums, observes John M. Simpson,

Executive Wages a Painful Fight to Erase a Slur

"Everything I'd worked for, my reputation, was destroyed."

The seeds of Jeffrey Ervine's digital nightmare go back to 2005, when the New York hedge fund manager was asked to manage the family fortune of a 21-year-old Turkish college student who claimed to be running another hedge fund.

"Something didn't smell right," Ervine says. So he did a deep background check and discovered evidence of a Ponzi scheme, which he turned over to the FBI. He never managed the student's money, he says.

Later that year, the student, Hakan Yalincak, was arrested on charges of bilking investors out of more than $7 million for a fake hedge fund and passing $45 million in bad checks. He pleaded guilty to bank and wire fraud in 2006 and spent nearly three years in federal prison before being deported to Turkey in 2009.[1]

That should have been the end of the story. But around that same time, Ervine suddenly discovered a mysterious headline, "Con v. Con," appearing at the top of his search page when he Googled himself. It linked to a website, www.hakanyalincak.com, that court documents have identified as being operated by four Bulgarian nationals. The website claimed Ervine had sought to "con" the young man and implied that Ervine had committed fraud. It also claimed Ervine's financial situation had deteriorated badly and that he could not manage money.[2]

---

[*]A Ponzi scheme is a fraudulent investment operation that pays quick returns to initial investors using money from subsequent investors rather than from profit. Named for Charles Ponzi, who perpetrated such a scheme in the United States (1919-1920).

Each time Ervine met with prospective investors, he was forced to spend the first 15 minutes explaining the accusatory search result, he says. "But it didn't matter because people weren't going to take any career risk by investing with you," he says, especially at a time when the headlines were filled with news about New York investor Bernard Madoff, who had defrauded thousands of investors out of billions of dollars with a giant Ponzi scheme.[3]

"I felt hopeless at 42," Ervine says. "What could I do? Everything I'd worked for, my reputation, which was now primarily digital, was destroyed."

Ervine asked Google to take down the search result. But Google responded that it would eliminate the link only if it had been the subject of a court order determining the content to be defamatory or unlawful — part of its standard policy, according to Charles Lee Mudd Jr., a Chicago lawyer specializing in Internet law, who represented Ervine.

It took Ervine three years to track down the operators of the website and thousands of dollars in legal fees to sue them for defamation over the course of 13 months, he says. He finally won a $2 million judgment in 2012 in federal court in Chicago against the operators, whom the court found responsible for publishing "false and defamatory" accusations.[4]

The court ordered the operators to take down the Web page and request that Google, Bing, Yahoo! "and all other search engines" remove the page from their search and cached results.[5]

"The most important part was getting the search engines to pull it," since most people wouldn't have found an obscure website like that otherwise, says Mudd.

Consumer Watchdog's Privacy Project director. "This right to be forgotten would restore that natural privacy-by-obscurity," he says, noting that today such records are likely to come up every time a prospective employer searches for someone's name.

Unlike Europe, the United States does not have an explicit constitutional right to privacy. So, the Constitution's right to freedom of expression probably would trump

privacy rights in a court challenge, many legal experts say. Laws in selected areas of American life parallel the right to be forgotten, but they tend to involve personal data — such as an individual's credit information.

Constitutionally, the press "has a nearly absolute right to publish accurate, lawful information," *New Yorker* legal writer Jeffrey Toobin has noted.[10] And, says Paul Alan Levy, an attorney with the legal arm of the

Under American law, search engines are legally protected from lawsuits for hosting content created by someone else. Seeking to allow young Internet services to flourish, Congress in 1996 added Section 230 to the Communications Decency Act, providing search engines and other intermediaries, such as Facebook, immunity from civil suits for hosting bloggers' or others' information.[6]

Ervine's court order doesn't compel the search engines to remove the links — but it "strongly encourages" them to do so.[7]

That's a sharp contrast from European law, which requires search engines to remove someone's search results upon request unless the information is in the public interest or meets some other legal exception.

If a similar right had existed in the United States, Ervine says, it would have saved him years of time, money and personal stress when his name, and by extension his family's, was defamed.

During those difficult years, Ervine started reading about other cases of cyberbullying, particularly those targeting children and teens. He says he was shocked to learn of cases where children were driven to cutting themselves in despair or to suicide.

Like Ervine, parents of a child who is being harassed must track down the Internet service provider where the material originates and be prepared to sue to get the material taken down.

That takes time and money. "If you're rich, you get it done faster than if you're poor," Ervine says. That's an inequity he says he would like to fix.

Ervine went on to found a for-profit company, Bridg-it, aimed at helping schools, parents and children fight bullying, including persecution online. His program is now being used in 10 New York City public schools.[8] For children, bullying often starts off face-to-face. But, as Ervine says he learned from his own painful experience, "The Internet is the largest megaphone of prejudice in the world."

— *Sarah Glazer*

New York City hedge fund manager Jeffrey Ervine needed a $2 million court judgment to persuade Google to remove false and defamatory links about him that popped up in a Google search on his name.

[1] Alison Leigh Cowan, "An Inmate and a Scholar," *The New York Times*, Feb. 7, 2014, http://tinyurl.com/ok47ac9. Also see, Lisa W. Foderaro, "Former NYU Student Pleads Guilty to Fraud," *The New York Times*, June 7, 2006, http://tinyurl.com/pja78wk.

[2] United States District Court, Northern District of Illinois Eastern Division, *Jeffrey Ervine v. S. B. et al.*, Findings of Fact, Conclusions of Law, Default Judgment and Permanent Injunction, March 9, 2012.

[3] "Bernard Madoff Fast Facts," CNN, April 24, 2015, http://tinyurl.com/nlbemdh.

[4] United States District Court, *op. cit.*

[5] *Ibid.*

[6] "Section 230 of the Communications Decency Act," Electronic Frontier Foundation, http://tinyurl.com/ka6gkjj, and "CDA 230 Legislative History," http://tinyurl.com/o2y8nvx, both undated.

[7] United States District Court, *op. cit.*

[8] See "Building a Bridge to Better Behavior," Bridg-it, undated, www.bridgit.com.

consumer advocacy group Public Citizen, "Our system gives much greater countervailing weight to the right to speak about other people."

In California, a new Internet "eraser button" law gives children under 18 the right to request removal of information they have posted about themselves, such as an embarrassing social media post, but it does not affect what others write about them. Similar measures have been introduced in other states and in Congress to extend to children the right to delete their online personal information.[11]

It's unclear how the clash of free speech vs. privacy values will be resolved between Europe and the United States. The most likely compromise, some experts predict, will be technological: Under pressure from French regulators, Google could block French users from seeing the search results on Google.com. That, some critics say, would mean a "balkanized" Internet — a far cry from the original vision of a World Wide Web in which information would be "free" and available to everyone on the planet. Already, civil liberties groups have expressed alarm at governments — including Russia and Brazil — that have cited the European right to be forgotten in considering legislation that could further censor the press.[12]

As consumers, regulators and tech companies weigh the implications of the European decisions, here are some of the questions being debated:

Does the "right to be forgotten" violate free-speech principles?

Journalists and free-speech advocates in the United States and Europe say the EU court's ruling allowing the removal of personal data suppresses free expression.

By limiting a search engine's ability to select the most vital news stories and blog postings out of billions of websites and bring them to public attention, the European court "has strait-jacketed the librarian," declared Peter Noorlander, CEO of the London-based Media Legal Defense Initiative, which helps journalists and bloggers worldwide defend their rights.[13]

However, defenders of the ruling have disputed the idea that Google's search function acts like a neutral "library" or a "card catalogue," as Google has maintained.[14] Although Google's algorithm for its search results is a trade secret, EU antitrust investigators have accused the company of giving preference to its own products in shopping search results.[15] And Google already removes millions of links a year after being told they violate copyrights, notes Paul Bernal, a lecturer in information technology, intellectual property and media law at England's University of East Anglia Law School.

"This is not about free speech; it's about privacy and dignity," Michael Fertik, the founder of Reputation.com, a Redwood City, Calif., company that helps people improve their search results, told *The New Yorker*. "If Sony or Disney wants 50,000 videos removed from YouTube, Google removes them with no questions asked. If your daughter is caught kissing someone on a cell-phone home video, you have no option of getting it down. That's wrong. The priorities are backward."[16]

Much of the debate reflects the different values Europeans and Americans have historically placed on freedom of expression versus privacy. In Europe, the right to privacy is considered a fundamental right and "is co-equal with your right to freedom of expression," notes First Amendment lawyer Marc Randazza, who practices in Las Vegas. By contrast, the European Convention requires freedom of expression to be balanced against "the reputation or rights of others."[17]

To Europeans, says Bernal, "Privacy underpins freedom of speech. If you know that the stuff you do on the Internet will come back to bite you, you'll feel less free to act on the Internet. If you know that every move is watched by the government, you will be less likely to act freely on the Internet."

In the Costeja Gonzalez ruling, the court said search engines, in deciding whether to grant a delisting request, should consider the public's right to know the information, especially if the person involved was a public figure, such as a politician.

But some critics say the court emphasized an individual's right to privacy as the overriding right.[18] The court "did not undertake any kind of balancing between privacy and data protection on the one hand, and freedom of expression and access to information on the other," the Reporters Committee for Freedom of the Press said.[19]

In contrast, in the United States, the First Amendment guarantee of freedom of speech generally trumps privacy rights, many legal experts agree.[20] If challenged in an American court, "It's hard to see how the Google Spain ruling could possibly proceed in the United States given the First Amendment," says Public Citizen attorney Levy.

But Randazza sees the Google Spain ruling as protecting free speech. "The EU says the original article about Costeja González is sacred and you can't get rid of it," he says. "But the links can and should be removed from search results, because he was in a foreclosure 16 years ago, and there's more to him than that."

Ironically, Costeja Gonzalez and his past debts have become more famous than ever as a result of the publicity surrounding the court's ruling. Links to news stories and blogs about the case now show up at the top of his search results.

Costeja González recently asked Spanish regulatory authorities to remove a link to negative comments about his case that show up in his name search. The Spanish

Data Protection Authority refused, saying the Google Spain ruling creates a "preponderant interest of the public" in the now-famous case.[21]

That decision demonstrates that European regulators are protecting the right of free expression and the public's right to know, once someone such as Costeja Gonzalez becomes a public figure, argues Randazza.

Following the Google Spain court ruling, Google released examples of requests it had received that troubled free-speech advocates — ranging from removing mentions of past criminal activities to a pianist's bad reviews to a past scandal involving a sports referee. Some links were later reinstated after reporting on the deletions by the British newspaper *The Guardian* caused a furor.[22]

However, *The Guardian* later found that fewer than 5 percent of removal requests involved public figures, politicians or convicted criminals, and Google was far less likely to grant requests involving politicians, public figures or serious crimes. Of the 218,000 requests Google had received up to March 2015, the paper reported, more than 95 percent were made by individuals who were not famous but wanted their private data removed, and almost half of those requests were granted.[23]

Nevertheless, critics and journalists say the system established by the European court neglects any kind of role for reporters or their publishers to protest the removal of links to their work. Journalists, if informed, can try to influence a search engine's removal decision, but they don't have a recognized role in the decision-making process.

That is likely to be a continuing problem under new EU-wide data-protection legislation expected to be approved later this year or early next year, says Daphne Keller, director of intermediary liability at Stanford Law School's Center for Internet and Society, who has been studying the draft legislation. The legislation (known as the General Data Protection Regulation) would replace the EU's existing data-protection rules and give Internet users broader rights to erase content posted about them, according to Keller and others who have seen the drafts.

If Google rejects a request for removal of a link, the requestor can appeal to his or her country's regulators or the courts, Keller says. "But there's no role for the publisher, who put the speech up in the first place and is being silenced" to protest, Keller says. "In terms of due process, it's extremely lopsided."

Google chairman Eric Schmidt, left, and chief legal officer David Drummond visited Spain and other European countries last year to discuss Web privacy issues after a landmark ruling by the European Union's Court of Justice. The court upheld an order from Spain's data-protection agency saying that Google must eliminate personal Web links that sullied the reputation of Spanish lawyer Mario Costeja González.

Getty Images/Bloomberg/Antonio Heredia

Should nations regulate Internet privacy beyond their borders?

When Danish-born lawyer Dan Shefet, who practices in Paris, became the subject of defamatory articles accusing him of professional malpractice and fraud, he asked Google to remove the links from searches for his name. Google took down the links, but only from its French domain, Google.fr.

That didn't solve the problem, Shefet says, because his clientele is international, and prospective clients elsewhere could still see the defamatory links. Then last year, after the Google Spain ruling, Shefet took the case to a Paris court, arguing that the links should be removed not just from Google.fr but from all the company's domains, including Google.com. He cited a little-noticed phrase of the EU high court's ruling, saying that Google, Inc. and its Spanish subsidiary Google Spain were "inextricably linked." In a precedentsetting decision, the French judge interpreted that to mean that Google's local subsidiary in one country — in this case France — could be liable for the activities of its parent.

The Paris court's decision was the first to interpret the Google Spain ruling as having a worldwide scope. It concluded that because Internet users in France could still access the information through Google.com, Google's delisting should have global reach. In September 2014, it ordered the company to pay daily fines of 1,000 euros ($1,073) unless links to a defamatory article were removed from Google's entire global network.[24]

Then, last June, the French data-protection agency, CNIL, went further: Every time Google responds to a delisting request in France, the company also must remove the link from its global search network including Google.com, the regulators ordered. Although someone doing a Google search in France is automatically directed to Google's French search engine, it takes merely one click on the bottom right corner of the page to reach Google.com.

Google so far has acceded to removal requests only on its EU domains, such as Google.fr and Google.uk, but not on Google.com.

"If the CNIL's proposed approach were to be embraced as the standard for Internet regulation, we would find ourselves in a race to the bottom," Google global's privacy counsel, Peter Fleischer, wrote in a July 30 blog post. "In the end, the Internet would only be as free as the world's least-free place."[25]

He cited instances where content that is illegal in one country is legal in another: Russia outlaws speech that government officials deem "gay propaganda," while Thailand criminalizes speech the government considers critical of the king.[26] If the French regulator's order extended to the Google.com searches that Americans typically use on U.S. soil, it would prevent Americans from seeing content that is legal in the United States.

"That is extremely worrisome to me," said Jonathan Zittrain, who teaches digital law at Harvard Law School. "France is asking for Google to do something that if the U.S. government asked for, it would be against the First Amendment."[27]

The order "sends a cue to repressive and autocratic regimes around the world to impose their own local restraints on free expression extraterritorially," the Reporters Committee on Freedom of the Press said.[28]

Jules Polonetsky, who heads the Future of Privacy Forum, a Washington, D.C., think tank, agrees. "Imagine China telling Google that Google.com shouldn't have this disparaging stuff about Tiananmen Square globally . . . truly a scary notion," says Polonetsky.

Opponents also raise concerns that rulings such as CNIL's violate legal standards of territorial sovereignty.

An advisory council of outside technology and legal experts appointed by Google endorsed the company's decision to remove links only from domains in Europe, citing the EU Court's limited "authority across Europe as its guidance."[29]

In a dissenting opinion to the Google Advisory Council report, Germany's former minister of justice, Sabine Leutheusser-Schnarrenberger, said, "Since EU residents are able to research globally the EU is authorized to decide that the search engine has to delete all the links globally."[30]

Legal experts are divided, however, over whether French regulators can legally order an American company to edit its searches globally. Viktor Mayer-Schönberger, a professor of Internet governance and regulation at Oxford University and an early champion of the right to be forgotten in his 2009 book *Delete: The Virtue of Forgetting in the Digital Age,* thinks the regulators can do so.

"It is not just the stupid crazy French" who have attempted to stretch the long arm of jurisdiction outside its borders, he says. The United States has prosecuted overseas gambling websites that have U.S.-based customers, he points out. An obvious compromise would be technological, Mayer-Schönberger and other experts say: Google could block Internet users sitting in France from accessing the .com search page by sensing their location — a technology known as "geo-blocking."

But others say the answer is not so simple. As the Electronic Frontier Foundation's O'Brien observes, "The history of geolocation on the Internet is all about people getting around it." For example, an Internet user in Europe can circumvent geo-blocking by using a "proxy" server in the United States to watch an American TV show that is blocked in Europe by copyright law.

Trying to enforce virtual geographic walls just makes governments more repressive, O'Brien suggests: "What courts are effectively demanding is that the Internet develop its own set of international borders. Not only is that defeating the purpose of the Internet as a global communication system, the more you try to enforce that, the more restricted and balkanized the Internet becomes."

With countries so divided in their views on privacy and free speech, and with their courts likely to come up with clashing decisions, the result will be "legal chaos," says Shefet, the Paris lawyer. As founder of the newly formed Association for Accountability and Internet Democracy, he advocates an international treaty to require search engines and servers to swiftly remove false and defamatory content.

International data experts are skeptical, however, that consensus could be reached on a treaty anytime soon, given cultural and historical divides. For example, the intergovernmental Council of Europe, a human rights organization including 47 member countries, promulgated a data-protection convention in 1981 that all EU member states have signed and that is open to signature from other countries. But the United States has never signed it.[31]

"Even that very loose law — with no teeth in terms of what to do if a country doesn't implement it — has almost no ratifiers from outside Europe," says David Erdos, who teaches data-protection law at England's University of Cambridge.

Should the United States adopt a "right to be forgotten"?

Before the Internet, finding the records of a teenager's arrest for selling drugs or a divorcing couple's accusations in court of infidelity involved tediously digging through paper files in a courthouse basement.

If a right to be forgotten were introduced into the United States, it simply would restore the situation Americans had in the pre-Internet era, when those deeds faded into oblivion, University of Chicago law professor Eric Posner has argued.

"You can beg people to take down offending images and text. If you really work at it and spend money on a lawyer, you might be able to get a court order. But all of the effort will be wasted if the telltale content has already been copied and pasted elsewhere and then swept into Google's servers," according to Posner. "Shouldn't new laws and rulings" — such as the one in the Google Spain case — "give people back the privacy that technology has taken away?"[32]

Consumer Watchdog echoes Posner's argument in its complaint asking the Federal Trade Commission (FTC) to make Google extend the right to be forgotten to American consumers. The group said that in the pre-Internet era, "people tended to forget whatever embarrassing things someone did in their youth." In a formal complaint, it argued that Google is engaging in "deceptive behavior" by describing itself as "championing users' privacy while not offering a key privacy tool," namely the right to be forgotten, that it is implementing in Europe.[33]

But other public-interest advocates say a European-style right to erasure would hamper consumers' ability to make an informed choice. Take the case of Costeja Gonzalez, the Spanish lawyer. Shouldn't the prospective client know "that 10 years ago, this guy was so irresponsible with his money that he had to have his house sold to pay unpaid taxes?" asks Levy of the Public Citizen Litigation Group.

"The danger of the right to be forgotten is it hides negative information," Levy says. "Why should Costeja González get to hide his past problems when his competitors in the bar have been squeaky clean for the past 20 years?"

The Association of National Advertisers, a marketers' trade group representing 670 companies including Google, has urged the FTC to dismiss Consumer Watchdog's complaint. The hundreds of thousands of delisting requests Google is receiving from Europeans "clearly show that expanding this type of program to the United States would be time-consuming, expensive, burdensome and difficult for Google or any other company," the association said in a July 31 letter to the FTC.[34]

Google's position as judge and jury — operating behind closed doors determining whether information people ask to be erased is relevant, excessive or inadequate — also provokes criticism from American privacy experts. "Those are decisions that ought to be made by courts, not by companies," says Polonetsky of the Future of Privacy Forum.

Moreover, he says, this kind of law puts pressure on Google to block links when in doubt, simply to avoid future legal challenges. As evidence, critics cite copyright law, which is America's closest parallel to Google's European personal-data takedown orders. It exempts search engines from liability if they swiftly take down material after being told it violates copyright.[35]

As a result, the law has led to excessive removal of content from the Internet on spurious grounds, according to several studies, and has been abused to suppress speech.[36] In a famous 2002 case, the Church of Scientology succeeded in getting Google to remove search links to Web pages criticizing the church by claiming that they violated the church's copyright.[37]

Such instances are "absolutely a warning sign" of what could happen in Europe under the right to be forgotten, says Stanford's Keller, who worked as a lawyer for Google and is a specialist in liability issues faced by Google, Facebook and similar Web hosting companies. "By far the easiest thing for these companies is to say, "We'll remove it. Because if we don't, we might face liability and an expensive process."

Under American law, an important distinction is made between personal "data," such as health or credit information already protected by privacy laws, and "expressive content," such as an article someone else writes about someone, which is protected by the First Amendment.

"It's hard to imagine" importing a right to be forgotten to the United States, Posner has conceded. "The First Amendment will protect Google, or any other company, that resurfaces or publishes information that's already public."[38]

In two lower-court cases, Google has argued successfully that its search results are First Amendment-protected speech.[39] However, Google's argument has never been tested in an appellate court or the Supreme Court. Randazza, the lawyer who favors a U.S. right to be forgotten, says he is "not 100 percent convinced" that such courts would say Google's practice of putting search results in a certain order rises to the level of protected speech. "That's a new theory."

In the United States, tentative steps have been taken toward an erasure right, but only for minors, such as California's eraser button law, which took effect Jan. 1.[40] However, the California law is "very different from the right to be forgotten because it doesn't give you any right to take down something your friend has reposted" or anything that someone posts about you, explains Ariel Fox Johnson, policy counsel for Common Sense Media, a San Francisco advocacy group that pushed for the legislation.

That may explain why no First Amendment challenges have been filed against the law. However, the law would let someone delete their postings of public interest, such as a teenager writing online about a

newsworthy event, according to David Greene, who teaches First Amendment law at the University of San Francisco School of Law.

"Any law that requires speech to be removed, without an exception for speech that is a matter of public interest, is going to be problematic" from a First Amendment viewpoint, he says.

BACKGROUND
Legacy of Fascism

The two sides of the Atlantic feature "two different cultures of privacy, which are home to different intuitive sensibilities, and which have produced two significantly different laws of privacy," wrote James Q. Whitman, a Yale University professor of comparative and foreign law.[41]

Whitman explains that in Europe privacy means the protection of one's dignity, dating back to 19th-century "laws of insult" governing duels over honor. In the United States, where the laws of insult never took hold, privacy means the protection of liberty from the government, with a constant wariness of restrictions on speaking freely.

While Europe has developed comprehensive laws protecting privacy, the United States has developed a far more piecemeal approach but with a particularly high value on press freedom.

In the 1930s, the Dutch government compiled a comprehensive registry of its population, which included the names, addresses and religions of all citizens. At the time, the registry was praised as helping the government with its welfare planning. But when the Nazis invaded the Netherlands, they used the registry to track down Jews and Gypsies.[42]

Author Mayer-Schonberger cites that example to explain why Europeans are so protective of their private data. "We may feel safe living in democratic republics, but so did the Dutch," he writes.[43]

The European experience, with the Nazis' obsessive — often fatal — recordkeeping and later with communist secret police spying in Eastern Europe, helps to explain why protecting privacy is seen as such a fundamental right on the continent.

In 1948, following World War II, the United Nations adopted the Universal Declaration of Human

CHRONOLOGY

1890-1950s *Right to privacy fails to gain recognition as constitutional right in the United States, but Europe recognizes it as a fundamental human right.*

1890 Louis D. Brandeis argues for a right to privacy in landmark law review article.

1928 Brandeis, as a Supreme Court justice, argues for a constitutional right to privacy in dissent in *Olmstead v. United States.*

1948 U.N. Universal Declaration of Human Rights establishes privacy as fundamental human right.

1950 European Convention on Human Rights adopted; protects right to "private and family life."

1960s-1970s *Supreme Court recognizes right to privacy in some areas, but First Amendment trumps privacy in landmark broadcasting case.*

1967 In *Griswold v. Connecticut,* justices strike down Connecticut law against contraception as invasion of privacy.

1970 Congress passes Fair Credit Reporting Act, preventing old bankruptcies from appearing in credit reports.

1973 In *Roe v. Wade,* Supreme Court recognizes right to privacy in a woman's decision to have an abortion.

1974 Federal Privacy Act bars federal agencies from disclosing personal information without the person's consent.

1975 Supreme Court rejects invasion-of-privacy suit against Cox Broadcasting Corp. for disclosing name of rape victim, saying First Amendment protects true information.

1980s-1990s *After collapse of communism, Europe adopts sweeping privacy laws, while United States protects privacy in specific areas.*

1989 Fall of Berlin Wall marks collapse of East Germany and leads to revelations about how its secret police spied on individuals.

1990 Virtually all U.S. states recognize a right to privacy in civil suits.

1995 European Union (EU) adopts Data Protection Directive, a framework for EU countries' privacy laws, including right to erase personal data.

1996 Section 230 of Communications Decency Act grants websites and search engines immunity from lawsuits for information they host. . . . President Bill Clinton signs Health Insurance Portability and Accountability Act, protecting personal health information.

1998 Congress passes Children's Online Privacy Protection Act giving parents control over information websites can collect from their children.

2000s *EU strengthens "right to be forgotten" online; "eraser" rights allowing children to delete material they post online passes in California.*

2003 Supreme Court recognizes privacy right in homosexual relations in *Lawrence v. Texas.*

2009 EU Treaty of Lisbon grants constitutional stature to right to data protection.

2011 Sen. Edward Markey, D-Mass, and Rep. Joe Barton, R-Texas, introduce "eraser button" bill for children's online data, but Congress does not act on it; similar bill dies in 2013.

2012 EU introduces new legislation to supersede 1995 personal-data directive, to be approved in 2015 or early 2016.

2013 California passes children's "eraser" bill.

2014 In landmark ruling in *Google Spain v. Mario Costeja González,* EU court declares search engines must remove results on request. . . . EU regulators say Google must remove search links from Google.com.

2015 California children's "eraser" bill goes into effect. . . . French regulator orders Google to extend search-result removals requested by French beyond its French search page to include Google.com. . . . French regulator denies Google's appeal. . . . EU "Safe Harbor" decision blocks transfer of personal data from Europeans to U.S.-based servers.

'Revenge Porn' Victims Seek to Be Forgotten

"3,000 people know where I live and what I look like."

In 2011, Annmarie Chiarini, an English professor at a Maryland community college, Googled her name and found herself on a pornography site. "Hot for Teacher? Well, Come Get It!" said her profile, which featured naked images of her, along with her address and the name of her employer.

An ex-boyfriend had posted the information and nude photos he had taken of her, according to Chiarini.[1]

In a genre known as "revenge porn," at least 3,000 websites specialize in purveying sexually explicit photos of women (and sometimes men) without their consent, typically posted by vengeful ex-lovers or ex-husbands.[2]

Images of a typical victim can be posted on up to 2,000 websites, according to Chiarini, who went public with her experience and now serves as victim services director of the Cyber Civil Rights Initiative (CCRI), which advocates criminalizing revenge porn. Removed from one site, the images often reappear on another, reposted by avid revenge-porn aficionados.

Many victims worry most about their search results, says Carrie Goldberg, a Brooklyn attorney and CCRI board member, because that's how prospective employers, landlords or romantic interests are most likely to discover the link to a pornography site.

"If the first three pages of your Google results are monopolized by links to porn sites, you just won't get the job" you're applying for, Goldberg says. "You won't even get asked to the interview. The same is true if you're dating or searching for an apartment."

When Google announced on June 19 that it would honor requests to remove search results involving revenge porn, CCRI rejoiced, having worked with the technology giant to set up a request-and-removal system.[3] Other big online companies — Twitter, Reddit, Facebook and Microsoft's Bing search engine — have followed suit.[4]

"People are saying now there's a 'right to be forgotten' for revenge-porn victims," says Goldberg, referencing Europeans' legal right to request the removal of objectionable results from one's name search.

Chiarini says she never thought to contact Google when she found her photo on a porn site. By then, her profile had been up for 14 days and viewed 3,000 times. It was "absolutely terrifying," she says, to realize that "3,000 people know where I live and what I look like and think I'm open for casual sex." In several horrific cases, online harassment has stepped off the screen into a person's home.

In 2009 a Craigslist ad featured a woman's picture next to her "interest" in "a real aggressive man with no concern for women." Her ex-boyfriend, Jebidiah James Stipe, who had posted the ad, according to prosecutors, masqueraded as his former girlfriend and sent Ty Oliver McDowell her home address. McDowell broke into the house and raped her at knifepoint, later insisting he was responding to the ad.[5] McDowell and Stipe were convicted of sexual assault, aggravated kidnapping and aggravated burglary and received identical sentences of 60 years to life.[6]

Chiarini eventually got her profile removed by contacting the porn site's Web host and server operators. She also contacted police about an earlier posting in 2010 and again in 2011, but each time officers told her there was no law under which they could prosecute her ex-boyfriend. The experience turned her into an advocate for a Maryland law to criminalize revenge porn.

Today, 26 states, including Maryland and the District of Columbia, have such laws. Rep. Jackie Speier, D-Calif., said she would introduce legislation to make the posting of revenge porn a federal crime. "With our patchwork of current laws, people victimized by 'revenge porn' often have no recourse, and their images can continue to circulate on the Internet indefinitely," Speier says. "The only sufficient solution is to criminalize these destructive acts at the national level."

Civil liberties advocates have opposed some state revenge-porn laws. The American Civil Liberties Union

(ACLU) sued Arizona last year on behalf of booksellers and publishers, claiming a just-passed state law, which would have made it a felony to post a nude photo of someone without the person's consent, violated the First Amendment. A court settlement blocked the law from going into effect.[7]

"In many states this is a new felony that targets the sharing of nudity — something that is frankly a very common American pastime," says Lee Rowland, senior staff attorney at the ACLU. "And whatever you think of sharing pornography or nudity, it's fully protected by the First Amendment."

The ACLU says such laws should be narrowly drawn to apply only to someone who "knowingly and maliciously" posts a revenge-porn photo.

Moreover, Rowland says, some revenge porn already violates existing civil and criminal laws. Indeed, in what experts believe is the first case involving a revenge porn website operator, Kevin Bollaert, was convicted in April under California's identity theft and extortion laws. Bollaert, who was sentenced to 18 years in prison, was convicted of uploading 10,000 photos of women without their consent, then redirecting women to another site where he charged them $300 to $350 to have a photo removed from his website.[8]

Mary Anne Franks, a professor at the University of Miami School of Law who has been helping Speier draft her legislation, says a federal law would eliminate one of the biggest obstacles to shutting down the revenge-porn industry. The federal Communications Decency Act exempts website owners from civil suits and state criminal prosecution for hosting revenge-porn photos posted by others, but it does not prevent prosecution under a federal criminal statute.

Franks says proposed legislative language she drafted for Rep. Speier "would allow for prosecution of websites and other platforms that actively and knowingly engage in the promotion and solicitation" of revenge porn.

— *Sarah Glazer*

Annmarie Chiarini, an English professor at a Maryland community college, Googled her name in 2011 and found herself on a pornography site. She got her profile removed by contacting the porn site's Web host and server operators.

[2] "Misery Merchants," *The Economist*, July 5, 2014, http://tinyurl.com/lvakqqc.

[3] Amit Singhal, " 'Revenge Porn' and Search," Google Public Policy Blog, June 19, 2014, http://tinyurl.com/oe4syb7.

[4] Ruth Reader, "Microsoft Joins Facebook, Google, Twitter, and Reddit in Fight Against Revenge Porn," *VB* (VentureBeat.com), July 22, 2015, http://tinyurl.com/qhlhbne.

[5] Danielle Keats Citron, *Hate Crimes in Cyberspace* (2009), p. 6.

[6] Caroline Black, "Ex-marine Jebidiah James Stipe Gets 60 Years for Craigslist Rape Plot," CBS News, June 29, 2010, http://tinyurl.com/p3us2hg; Ben Neary, "Second Man Gets 60 Years in Wyo. Internet Rape Case," *Ventura County Star*, June 29, 2010, http://tinyurl.com/olxl7wg.

[7] "Federal Judge Blocks Enforcement of Arizona's 'Revenge Porn' Law," *The Range, Tucson Weekly*, July 10, 2015, http://tinyurl.com/na87ykk.

[8] Liberty Zabala and R. Stickney, "'Revenge porn' Defendant Sentenced to 18 Years," NBC San Diego, April 3, 2015, http://tinyurl.com/o35ezsz.

[1] Annmarie Chiarini, "I was a victim of revenge porn," *The Guardian*, Nov. 19, 2013, http://tinyurl.com/nadwv5z.

Future Supreme Court justice Louis D. Brandeis, shown in about 1900 when he was a young lawyer, argued in a landmark law review article in 1890 that Americans had a right to privacy. In 1928, when he was on the court, he argued for a constitutional right to privacy, becoming the first Supreme Court justice to recognize the threat that technology posed to citizens.

Rights, which established privacy as a fundamental human right, a model widely adopted in constitutions around the world but never ratified by the United States Senate.[44]

In 1950, the Council of Europe adopted the European Convention on Human Rights, which has since been embraced by all 28 members of the European Union. Article 8 protects the right to "private and family life." The European Court of Human Rights — an international court that rules on allegations of human rights violations — has interpreted that right to include the protection of personal data. The convention requires member states to ensure their national laws adhere to its principles.[45]

In 1989, with the fall of the Berlin Wall, East German citizens learned that the secret police had compiled extensive files on them, often fed by spying from their neighbors. The new democracies that replaced the communist governments rewrote their laws to prevent the return of such privacy invasions.

In subsequent years, the EU has promulgated a detailed series of laws designed to protect privacy, most significantly under the EU's umbrella regulation known as the Data Protection Directive. It was adopted by the EU in 1995 and became effective in 1998.[46]

Right to Be Forgotten

Traditionally, some European countries, including France and Italy, had a form of the right to be forgotten in statutes aimed at expunging criminal records after a certain number of years. In the United States, state "expungement" laws may permit minor crimes to be removed from a criminal record after a period of years or if the crime was committed by someone under age 18.[47]

The EU's Data Protection Directive contained a "right to erasure" of one's personal online data and the "right to object" to a website publishing or storing it. Together those provisions became popularly known as the right to be forgotten, explains Jef Ausloos, a legal researcher in information technology at the University of Leuven in Belgium.

Technically, the directive allowed Europeans to demand that the publisher of a website remove their personal data if it did not comply with strict data-protection rules. But Cambridge University's Erdos, who has studied data regulation across Europe, says, "There's quite a gap between what the law says and what often goes on."

For example, the directive required member states to make some exceptions for news published by journalists — a form of protection for the press. But, in laws adopted by EU member countries, Erdos says, "That's been implemented totally differently across Europe, ranging from making no explicit provision at all to the complete exemption of journalists."

In 2009, the Treaty of Lisbon, which granted constitutional stature to the EU Charter, came into force. It recognized the right to data protection as a separate fundamental right along with the right to respect for one's private and family life.

The concept of a right to be forgotten gained prominence in 2010, when Vivian Reding, the European commissioner responsible for justice and fundamental rights, pushed for a right to remove unwanted information on social media sites such as Facebook. "With more and more private data floating around on the Web — especially on social networking site[s] — people should have the right to have their data completely removed," she said in a speech.[48]

In May 2014, the EU Court of Justice issued its landmark ruling in *Google Spain v. Mario Costeja Gonzalez,* declaring that Google, and all other search engines, were considered data "controllers" subject to the 1995 Data Protection Directive and were obliged to act on requests to have links deleted from the requestor's name search.

In November 2014, an EU advisory body of data-protection officials from member countries issued recommendations on how the Google Spain ruling should be carried out by each country's data-protection regulatory authority. Any delisting of search links must be made not just on EU search sites but "on all relevant domains," including .com, for the ruling to be effective, the group said.[49]

The group also said search engines should not routinely inform publishers that links to their material were being deleted. Doing so, according to several commissioners, would encourage republication of the material.[50]

The group's statements, intended only as advisory guidelines, were widely interpreted as predicting how data-protection agencies would implement the new ruling.

U.S. Privacy Rights

In an 1890 *Harvard Law Review* article, 34-year-old Boston lawyer Louis Brandeis lamented how new portable cameras and the spread of yellow journalism* were invading individuals' privacy.

"Recent inventions . . . call attention to the next step which must be taken for the protection of the person, and for securing to the individual . . . the right 'to be let alone,'" he wrote. "[N]umerous mechanical devices threaten to make good the prediction that 'what is whispered in the closet shall be proclaimed from the house-tops.'"[51]

Brandeis and co-author Samuel D. Warren proposed that invasions of privacy be classified as a tort — a social wrong for which someone can sue and obtain economic damages in court.

In 1928, the growing popularity of other new technology — the telephone and wiretapping — led Brandeis, who by then was a Supreme Court justice, to argue for a constitutional right to privacy in a dissenting opinion in *Olmstead v. United States*. Brandeis became

---

* Yellow Journalism, popular during the 19th century, was practiced by newspapers that emphasized sensationalism over factual reporting. The term derived from a popular New York newspaper comic strip that featured a character known as the Yellow Kid.

the first Supreme Court justice to recognize such a right under the Fourth Amendment's prohibition against "unreasonable searches and seizures" and to recognize the threat that technology posed to citizens.[52]

Nevertheless, Brandeis' view of privacy received a "cold reception" in American law, since it drew on aristocratic European ideas of the law of insult, wrote Yale's Whitman.[53] In the years following the Brandeis-Warren article, some lower-court judges recognized a right to privacy while "others refused to recognize such a right merely because two disgruntled legal scholars had written about it," privacy law expert Robert Ellis Smith wrote in *The Law of Privacy Explained.*[54]

In the early 1900s several states, starting with New York and continuing with Virginia and Utah, recognized a right to privacy by statute when someone's image or persona was misappropriated without consent for commercial purposes. By 1990, all states except Minnesota recognized, either by statute or common law, a right to privacy in a tort action.[55]

The right to privacy has been among the most controversial areas of constitutional law during the past half century, according to Erwin Chemerinsky, a University of California-Irvine law professor.[56] The Supreme Court cited a right to privacy in decisions establishing a right to use contraception (*Griswold v. Connecticut,* 1965), to have an abortion (*Roe v. Wade,* 1973) and to engage in private homosexual relations (*Lawrence v. Texas,* 2003).[57]

While a right to privacy is not mentioned explicitly in the Constitution, Justice William O. Douglas, writing for the majority in *Griswold v. Connecticut,* found that privacy was a "penumbral right," meaning it was implicit in the Bill of Rights. For example, he wrote, the Fourth Amendment, protecting against "unreasonable searches and seizures," created a zone of privacy in the bedroom.

"Would we allow the police to search the sacred precincts of marital bedrooms for telltale signs of the use of contraceptives?" he asked.[58]

Free Speech Versus Privacy

Despite these Supreme Court rulings upholding a right to privacy, Chemerinsky said, there has been little judicial protection for "informational privacy," the right to prevent one's private information from public dissemination when that information is true.

"[A]lthough there is a strong argument that the Constitution should be interpreted to protect the right to control information, there has been little support for such a right from the Supreme Court," he writes.[59]

In a string of landmark cases, the court consistently has ruled against a right to informational privacy in First Amendment challenges to lawsuits over the public disclosure of private, personal facts.[60] For example, in *Cox Broadcasting Corp. v. Cohn* (1975), a television reporter disclosed the name of a rape and murder victim. The victim's father sued for invasion of privacy, but the Supreme Court ruled against him, saying the information had been obtained from court records and truthfully reported and that the First Amendment protects the publication of such information.[61]

While interpretations of a constitutional right to privacy remain controversial, the United States has mandated privacy rights in specific areas of law. For example:

- The 1970 Fair Credit Reporting Act, which regulates information included in credit reports, stipulated that after seven years — and 10 years for bankruptcy — information about debt collections, civil lawsuits, tax liens and arrests for criminal offenses must be taken out of such reports.[62]
- The 1974 Privacy Act prohibits federal agencies from disclosing personal information about an individual without the person's consent, except for purposes such as law enforcement, census statistics and congressional investigations.[63]
- The 1996 Health Insurance Portability and Accountability Act protects personal health information and established standards for the security of electronic health records.[64]

Congress protected children's privacy rights in 1998, when it passed the Children's Online Privacy Protection Act giving parents control over information that websites collect from children under age 13. Websites and online services must give parents the choice of consenting to the collection of their children's personal information — such as name, address, phone number and screen name — and also provide parents with the opportunity to have the information deleted.[65]

Updated Federal Trade Commission rules in 2013 widened the definition of children's personal information to include geolocation data that could identify a child's street address; photos, videos, audio recordings that contain the child's image or voice; and "persistent identifiers" such as Internet cookies that track a child's activity online.[66]

CURRENT SITUATION
Conflict Ahead

No one is sure how the current standoff between French regulators and Google will turn out.

Google appealed the French regulator's order to erase worldwide the links requested by French consumers, including on Google.com. But in September, when the French data-protection agency, CNIL, denied that appeal, it said Google "must now comply with the formal notice" or it would consider sanctions against the company.[67]

It remains unclear whether Google will try to fight that order in court.

The current dispute "is just a skirmish" in preparation for "the real endgame" — sweeping new data-protection legislation the European Union is expected to enact later this year or early next year, according to Oxford's Mayer-Schönberger. Google's stance is partly aimed at influencing the EU's drafting of that new right-to-be-forgotten legislation, known as the General Data Protection Regulation, he says.[68] With numerous drafts floating around, it's unclear how strict the final provisions will be. Moreover, EU member states themselves are divided, and some European media conglomerates share Google's views, Mayer-Schönberger says. However, some American experts are already sounding the alarm about the wide-ranging consequences the new legislation could have on American companies.

As Stanford's Keller interprets the current drafts, removal requestors will be able to ask not only for removal of a link from a search engine but also for the erasure of underlying content — such as a post on Facebook, a tweet on Twitter or possibly a news article that someone else has posted about them.

Moreover, the legislation appears to "apply to tons of Internet companies that are small and never even heard of it," she says. Noting the conflict with American-style free-speech rights, she adds, "it's not something Americans are going to like at all." And since American companies will be reluctant to fight requests in court or face steep fines for disobeying regulators, the new right to be forgotten "will be the easiest tool at hand for someone who would like some online content to disappear," Keller predicts.

American businesses are nervously eyeing Europe's data-protection stance, ever since October, when the European Union Court of Justice said American companies could no longer transfer data from Europe to America under the long-standing Safe Harbor agreement, a U.S.-EU accord regulating how U.S. companies handle European citizens' data. EU privacy law forbids the transfer of European citizens' data outside the European Union unless the receiving country has rules in line with EU privacy-protection laws.[69]

Recognizing that the United States lacks such laws, the Safe Harbor pact allowed U.S. companies like Facebook to self-certify that they would protect Europeans' data transferred to and stored in U.S. data centers.

Max Schrems, a 28-year-old Facebook user and Austrian law student, went to the EU's highest court to argue that the social networking site should not be allowed to transfer his and other European Facebook users' data to its American servers. Schrems argued that the transfer would subject his data to the risk of U.S. government snooping revealed in 2013 by former National Security Agency contractor Edward Snowden.[70]

In October, the court agreed, declaring the agreement invalid on the grounds that the United States does not sufficiently protect citizens' data from government spying.[71]

U.S. Privacy Legislation

Some privacy advocates hope the European Court's Safe Harbor decision will nudge the United States towards strengthening data privacy, but they're also realistic about the lack of political momentum. The decision is "a reminder that American privacy law needs to be updated," privacy advocate Rotenberg told a November hearing of a House Energy and Commerce subcommittee, citing "skyrocketing identity theft, data breaches and financial fraud."[72] In an interview with *CQ Researcher*, Rotenberg says the EU court's recent rulings, including Google Spain, show that, "The EU is moving forward with new protections, and the United States is

Getty Images/*Los Angeles Times*/Allen J. Schaben

Californian Christos Catsouras, shown with family, tried to remove gory photos of a fatal car crash in which his daughter Nikki, 18, was killed. The photos showed up on thousands of websites after California Highway Patrol employees emailed them to family and friends. At the family's request, many websites removed the photos, but they remain easy to find on Google. With no "right to be forgotten" in American law, the family had no way to force Google to remove the photos.

still stuck in the mud; and there's no meaningful progress in the United States."

"Now it's easy for other countries to say to the United States, 'You're wild, lawless actors. . . because you have no privacy legislation," says Polonetsky of the Future of Privacy Forum. "It will be helpful if the U.S. does pass its own privacy legislation."

The most comprehensive recent privacy legislation, President Obama's Consumer Privacy Bill of Rights, unveiled Feb. 27 in draft form, was "dead on arrival," according to Jeff Chester, executive director of the Center for Digital Democracy, a Washington advocacy group for greater consumer Internet privacy. The draft bill was opposed by Internet services companies as well as consumer-privacy activists such as Chester.

The draft called for companies to let consumers see, correct and delete personal information held about them — like credit card numbers, passwords and Social Security numbers.[73] Chester's group said it would weaken privacy by allowing the industry to self-regulate, while industry groups condemned it as too onerous.[74]

The draft has no congressional sponsor, and no congressional action is scheduled. To overcome congressional inaction and to find common ground, U.S. and

AT ISSUE

Should the United States adopt Europe's "right to be forgotten"?

YES John M. Simpson
Privacy Project Director,
Consumer Watchdog

Written for *CQ Researcher*, December 2015

The failure of Internet search engines such as Google, Yahoo and Bing to honor the so-called "right to be forgotten" in the United States is not an abstract issue. Their callous decision hurts real people.

Consider the case of Nikki Catsouras, the 18-year-old daughter of Christos and Lesli Catsouras. Nine years ago she died in a horrific automobile wreck in California. Graphic police photos of her remains were leaked and posted on the Internet. Today those gruesome images are still linked to her name and the names of other Catsouras family members in Internet search results.

"The right to be forgotten is the only chance for my family to find closure and to finally grieve," says Christos Catsouras.

In Europe, the right to be forgotten — perhaps more accurately called the right of relevancy — allows individuals to request the removal of search-engine links to personal information that is "inadequate, irrelevant or no longer relevant, or excessive."

It is not censorship. The original published item is not removed or altered. The link to a person's name may be removed, but the original item can still be accessed using other search terms.

Google's announcement this year that it would honor requests to remove links to "revenge porn" — nude or explicit photos posted without the subject's consent — makes it clear that Google could also easily honor right-to-be-forgotten requests in the United States.

Indeed, U.S. law already recognizes that certain information should become irrelevant after the passage of time has demonstrated that an individual is unlikely to repeat the mistake. The Fair Credit Reporting Act says that debt collections, civil lawsuits, tax liens and even arrests for criminal offenses in most cases should be considered obsolete after seven years and must be excluded from credit reports. The government should extend the same principle to the online world.

Before the Internet, personal privacy was largely protected by the difficulty of gathering information as well as the tendency of humans to forget. Search-engine algorithms don't allow that now. We need to focus on what this sea change means to society and how we can deal with it.

The right to be forgotten offers a clear path forward to help protect our privacy in the digital age. Companies like Google that claim to care about users' privacy should be ashamed that they are not treating people on both sides of the Atlantic the same way.

NO Samantha Bates
Research Associate, Berkman Center for
Internet & Society, Harvard University

Written for *CQ Researcher*, December 2015

Imagine that 10 years after graduating from college you are still explaining to potential employers why the first Google search result under your name is a photo of you passed out drunk at a party. What if you could ask that this photo be permanently removed from Google search results after explaining why it's both embarrassing and not something the public particularly needs to know?

European regulators have granted their citizens the "right to be forgotten," which allows them to request that Google and other search engines remove links from their search results in these types of circumstances.

If Europeans have the power to shape their online reputations, shouldn't Americans be accorded the same right? Although a noble cause in theory, an American version of the right to be forgotten is a bad idea.

First, the right to be forgotten raises genuine First Amendment concerns. In comparison to European nations, the U.S. Constitution places stricter limitations on what the government can order a company to say or not say. Europe's right-to-be-forgotten decision, which orders Google to evaluate removal requests and remove links to content deemed "inadequate, irrelevant or no longer relevant, or excessive," would likely violate the First Amendment by allowing governments to determine what links appear on a Google search-results page. This isn't merely limiting Google's speech. Europeans can request the removal not only of content they personally have posted but also links to content posted by a third party.

Second, the European Court of Justice has left it to Google to judge whether search results should be removed, pressuring Google to abandon neutrality and alter its search results. Worse, Google faces legal action and a fine if it fails to comply with a removal request that the court deems sufficient — but no one can challenge a removal that is in fact in the public interest. With such vague guidelines to follow, Google is likely to remove results in ambiguous cases rather than risk fines.

In a time when people rely on search engines as one of their main sources of information, do we want Google to control the searchability of online content? What will prevent Google from manipulating the search algorithm to suit its own purposes? The United States has a strong tradition of charting its own course — and in this case, doing so is amply justified.

European data experts have formed the "Privacy Bridges Project," recommending that regulators and industry representatives from both continents try to agree on basic values and policies relating to privacy without changing laws.

"I spent a lot of the last six years trying to get Congress to pass a consumer-privacy bill, and I still hope that will happen, but I don't want to wait around and just hope that will happen," explains Daniel J. Weitzner, former deputy chief technology officer in the Obama White House, who co-chaired the trans-Atlantic Privacy Bridges Project.[75]

Weitzner, who now directs the Internet Policy Research Initiative at the Massachusetts Institute of Technology, would like to see U.S. and European regulators draft privacy notices that are easier to understand than the dense privacy language that Internet users often agree to without reading. In its report describing possible areas of compromise, the Bridges Project does not mention a right to be forgotten. However, Weitzner says, "had our 'bridges' been in place, perhaps the right to be forgotten discussion might have turned out differently."

Eraser Buttons

In Congress, Sen. Edward J. Markey, D-Mass., and Rep. Joe Barton, R-Texas, have proposed the Do Not Track Kids Act, which would give parents and children nationwide an "eraser button" similar to California's but would apply it to a more limited age range and category of personal information. Markey and Barton say the current federal children's online protection law should be updated to recognize that data-collection companies are tracking children's locations and creating detailed profiles about them for marketing purposes.[76]

While existing law requires parental consent for collection of personal information for children up to age 13, the Markey-Barton bill would extend protection to age 15. It also would allow children, as well as parents, to request deletion of publicly available personal information.

"Industry sees teens as a digital gold mine," says Chester, whose Center for Digital Democracy supports the measure. He is concerned about the vast amount of data that marketing companies collect about teens. "The Markey bill is a major step forward in making sure America's youth don't daily confront a wholesale invasion of their personal information," he says.

A woman identified in court as "Chantal," shown with her lawyer at a courthouse in Amsterdam, Netherlands, sued Facebook last year after a video was posted on the social-networking site showing her in a sex act with her boyfriend; both were minors at the time. A Dutch court ordered Facebook on June 26, 2015, to reveal the identity of the person who posted the so-called revenge porn video on the site or face having its servers opened to outside investigators.

However, Facebook and other large online companies argued when California's eraser button law was being debated that it was unnecessary because they already provide deletion options. And according to Barton's communications director Daniel Rhea, "some large industry stakeholders" oppose the Markey-Barton proposal because, they say, "they are able to self-regulate." The Markey-Barton bill has been introduced twice before — in 2011 and 2013 — but failed to gain legislative momentum either time. "We are hopeful it will move this Congress," says Rhea. As of mid-November, the measure had only three co-sponsors in the Senate and 14 in the House.[77]

With Congress currently gridlocked, children's advocates say, states may be more receptive to protecting children's privacy. Several states including New York are considering legislation similar to the California bill, according to the advocacy group Common Sense Media. "Congress doesn't have the appetite for addressing difficult privacy rules at the leadership level," says Danny Weiss, vice president for national policy at Common Sense Media, which pushed for the California bill.

OUTLOOK

Fragmented Internet?

Some privacy advocates argue that Americans and Europeans may not be as far apart as their legal systems currently suggest. For example, a Pew Research Center poll earlier this year found that 74 percent of Americans believe control over personal information is "very important," yet only 9 percent believe they have such control.[78]

Even so, says former White House adviser Weitzner, "The likelihood is [that] over time EU law will evolve on the trajectory it's on, and U.S. law will evolve on the trajectory it's on, but they won't magically converge." He doubts that "there will be some grand interglobal treaty on privacy and all these problems will be solved" anytime soon.

Meanwhile, he argues, the United States and Europe can take practical steps to devise common privacy policies by having informal discussions between regulators and industries on both sides of the Atlantic. American corporations that do business in Europe often adopt European privacy guidelines voluntarily, he points out, simply because the Internet works better when common practices cross national borders.

The pressure on U.S. companies operating in Europe to comply with EU laws is likely to increase as the world's information system becomes increasingly global. And that leaves companies like Google in a bind when ordered to do something by the French government that would violate the U.S. constitution.

"All of these businesses [Google, Twitter, Facebook] have a major part of their business in Europe, and they have employees who could be arrested and assets that could be seized," points out Stanford's Keller, a former Google lawyer. "The need to comply with the law of European countries where they operate is significant."

The result could be an increasingly fragmented Internet, or "splinternet," divided by national laws, she warns.

That day is already here, maintains author Mayer-Schönberger, who, in his book *Delete,* extolled the virtues of "oblivion" as preferable to the online world's tendency toward eternal remembering. With its right to be forgotten, the EU has succeeded in putting up "speed bumps" to casual surfers doing name searches of someone who has successfully delisted disparaging links, he says — even if computer geeks can find ways around them. "This speed-bump approach gives people a chance to grow and get beyond these incidents in their pasts."[79]

In *Delete*, Mayer-Schönberger proposed expiration dates for online personal information. Already some apps address the concern that everything will be preserved online. The mobile phone app Snapchat, hugely popular with teens, lets users take photos that last only a few seconds after they're sent to a friend.[80] However, Snapchat last year admitted that the photos don't "disappear forever" after a Federal Trade Commission investigation found the claim deceptive. The app has introduced a new feature this year to let recipients keep the photos long-term, which could surprise some senders who are still counting on Snapchat to make their embarrassing photos disappear quickly.[81]

So-called ephemeral applications — those that are intended to expire — show that technology is evolving to reflect "more nuanced" responses to how we communicate, says Polonetsky of the Future of Privacy Forum. "Why should I expect that yakking to my friends should be enshrined forevermore?"

As online storage has become cheaper and more spacious in the cloud, online platforms have tended to retain more and more information. But Polonetsky says, "Why shouldn't the default shift to: 'Hey, this is really old; do you want to keep it?' Technology should empower me to live better. I think that's the phase that we're going to enter now."

NOTES

1. "Judgment of the Court, Google Spain SL and Google Inc. v AEPD and Mario Costeja Gonzalez," Court of Justice of the European Union, May 13, 2014, http://tinyurl.com/mjd6hru. The court upheld the order of the Spanish Data Protection Agency (AEPD) saying that the newspaper *La Vanguardia* could leave the items about Costeja González on its website, but that Google must remove the links.

2. "Majority of Americans Think it Should be Human Right to Delete or Remove Personal Information Online," PR Newswire, Aug. 27, 2015, http://tinyurl.com/okroxo2.

3. Marc Rotenberg, "EU Strikes a Blow for Privacy, Opposing View" *USA Today,* May 14, 2014, http://tinyurl.com/qhvsqaf.

4. "Google Transparency Report," Google, updated Nov. 20, 2015, http://tinyurl.com/oghquhn.

5. Danny O'Brien and Jillian York, "Rights That Are Being Forgotten," Electronic Frontier Foundation, July 8, 2014, http://tinyurl.com/qams66g.

6. "CNIL orders Google to apply delisting on all domain names of the search engine," CNIL, June 12, 2015, http://tinyurl.com/o6e2wvh. Also see "Right to delisting: Google informal appeal rejected," CNIL, Sept. 21, 2015, http://tinyurl.com/ohettz6.

7. "Letter to Commission nationale de l'infor-matique et des libertés (CNIL)," Reporters Committee for Freedom of the Press, Sept. 14, 2015, http://tinyurl.com/pbgxp2a. Text of letter: http://tinyurl.com/qdloddb.

8. Jeffrey Toobin, "The Solace of Oblivion," *The New Yorker,* Sept. 29, 2014, http://tinyurl.com/neo4qyu.

9. Letter of complaint to FTC, Consumer Watchdog, July 7, 2015, http://tinyurl.com/nkarduu.

10. Toobin, *op. cit.*

11. Ronnie Cohen, "California Law allows kids to erase digital indiscretions," Reuters, Sept. 26, 2013, http://tinyurl.com/pg5jffq.

12. See Danny O'Brien, "Brazil's Politicians Aim to Add Mandatory Real Names and a Right to Erase History to the Marco Civil," Electronic Frontier Foundation, Oct. 14, 2015, http://tinyurl.com/o688pek. For Russia, see Tarun Krishnakumar, "Russian Roulette and the Right to be Forgotten," Chilling Effects, Lumen, June 16, 2015, http://tinyurl.com/o5myt35.

13. Peter Noorlander, "Google Spain Case," LSE Media Policy Project Blog, May 14, 2014, http://tinyurl.com/pu9v4bb.

14. Toobin, *op. cit.*

15. European Commission press release: "Antitrust," April 15, 2015, http://tinyurl.com/oxusos8.

16. Toobin, *op. cit.*

17. Section 1 Rights and Freedoms, Article 10, European Convention on Human Rights, Council of Europe, undated, http://tinyurl.com/qywhyns.

18. David Erdos, "Mind the Gap," Open Democracy, May 15, 2014, http://tinyurl.com/nff2fc7.

19. "Reporters Committee leads Coalition urging French data regulator to reconsider "right to be forgotten" delisting order," Reporters Committee for Freedom of the Press, Sept. 15, 2014, http://tinyurl.com/pkbku2d. Also see text of Sept. 14, 2015 letter at: http://tinyurl.com/qjykmp8.

20. Toobin, *op. cit.* The First Amendment states, "Congress shall make no law . . . abridging the freedom of speech or of the press."

21. Miquel Peguera, "No More Right to be Forgotten for Mr. Costeja," CIS blog, Oct. 3, 2015, http://tinyurl.com/olc8drw. Note: The court papers did not reveal which article link Costeja Gonzalez was protesting.

22. Marc Scott, "Google Reinstates European Links to Articles from *The Guardian,"* *The New York Times,* July 4, 2014, http://tinyurl.com/n3enf4w,

23. Sylvia Tippmann and Julia Powles, "Google accidentally reveals data on 'right to be forgotten' requests," *The Guardian,* July 14, 20015, http://tinyurl.com/ne8ns9o.

24. Owen Bowcott and Kim Willsher, "Google's French arm faces €1,000 daily fines over links to defamatory article," *The Guardian,* Nov. 13, 2014, http://tinyurl.com/owyljur.

25. Peter Fleischer, "Implementing a European, not global, right to be forgotten," Google Europe blog, July 30, 2015, http://tinyurl.com/pfl7rvr. Also see "Russian Parliament Approves 'right to be forgotten' law," *Deutsche Welle,* July 3, 2015, http://tinyurl.com/pzpmmtc.

26. *Ibid.*

27. Farhad Manjoo, "Right to be Forgotten' Online Could Spread," *The New York Times,* Aug. 5, 2015, http://tinyurl.com/o8yasrf.

28. "Reporters Committee leads Coalition urging French data regulator to reconsider "right to be forgotten" delisting order," *op. cit.*

29. "The Advisory Council to Google on the Right to be Forgotten," Google.com, Feb. 6, 2015, http://tinyurl.com/p8jjcov.

30. Natasha Lomas, "Google faces fight in Europe on search delisting," *Tech Crunch*, Feb. 6, 2015, http://tinyurl.com/q8fyc6l.

31. "Convention for the Protection of Individuals with regard to Automatic Processing of Personal Data," Council of Europe, http://tinyurl.com/ng7cmqf.

32. Eric Posner, "We all have the right to be forgotten," *Slate*, May 14, 2014, http://tinyurl.com/mc6ttwx.

33. Consumer Watchdog letter to FTC, *op. cit.*

34. ANA letter to FTC, July 31, 2015, http://tinyurl.com/q8qhmly.

35. "Digital Millennium Copyright Act," Summary, U.S. Copyright Office, 1998, http://tinyurl.com/6u7hf.

36. Daphne Keller, "Empirical Evidence of 'OverRemoval' by Internet Companies under Intermediary Liability Laws," CIS blog, Oct. 12, 2015, http://tinyurl.com/q4r7oxy.

37. Evan Hansen, "Google pulls anti-Scientology links," CNET, April 22, 2002, http://tinyurl.com/pzd6z72.

38. Posner, *op. cit.*

39. Greg Sterling, "Another Court Affirms Google's First Amendment Control of Search Results," *Search Engine Land*, Nov. 17, 2014, http://tinyurl.com/npcrbea.

40. Cohen, *op. cit.*

41. James Q. Whitman, "The Two Western Cultures of Privacy: Dignity versus Liberty," *Yale Law Journal*, Jan. 1, 2004, pp. 1151-see p. 1160, http://tinyurl.com/q4gd9nu.

42. Viktor Mayer-Schonberger, *Delete* (2009), p. 141.

43. *Ibid.*

44. The Universal Declaration was absorbed into the International Bill of Rights, consisting of four treaties, only one of which the United States has ratified. See University of Minnesota Human Rights Library, "Ratification of International Human Rights Treaties-USA," http://tinyurl.com/opk937y. Also see United Nations, "Fact Sheet No. 2,

International Bill of Human Rights," http://tinyurl.com/nu6uk7g.

45. European Convention on Human Rights, *op. cit.*

46. See "EU Data Protection Directive," search security, co.uk, http://tinyurl.com/9p4xka5.

47. Sharon Dietrich, "New Ruling Highlights Why We Need REDEEM Act," *Talk Poverty*, June 3, 2015, http://tinyurl.com/qxeeqer.

48. Vivian Reding, "Privacy Matters," European Union, Nov. 30, 2010, http://tinyurl.com/qgyumag.

49. Article 29 Data Protection Working Party, European Commission, press release, Nov. 26, 2014, http://tinyurl.com/ocwgbec.

50. Toobin, *op. cit.*

51. Samuel D. Warren and Louis D. Brandeis, "The Right to Privacy," *Harvard Law Review*, Dec. 15, 1890, pp. 193-220, p. 195, http://tinyurl.com/qavzf2b.

52. Leah Burrows, "To Be Let Alone: Brandeis foresaw privacy problems," *Brandeis Now*, July 24, 2013, http://tinyurl.com/pyhcqgg.

53. Whitman, *op. cit.*

54. Robert Ellis Smith, *The Law of Privacy Explained* (1993), pp. 5-8, http://tinyurl.com/pgr9n5g.

55. *Ibid.*

56. Erwin Chemerinsky, "Rediscovering Brandeis's Right to Privacy," *Brandeis Law Journal*, vol. 45, 2006-2007, pp. 643-657, http://tinyurl.com/pyg5slp.

57. *Ibid.*

58. *Griswold v. Connecticut* (1965) opinion, *Justia*, U.S. Supreme Court, http://tinyurl.com/orrrxc4.

59. Chemerinsky, *op. cit.* p. 653.

60. *Ibid.*

61. *Ibid*, p. 654.

62. "A Summary of your Rights under the Fair Credit Reporting Act," Federal Trade Commission, 2014, http://tinyurl.com/narqyf8.

63. "Privacy Act of 1974," Department of Justice, updated July 17, 2015, http://tinyurl.com/nox2xpf.

64. Health Information Privacy, U.S. Department of Health and Human Services, updated, http://tinyurl.com/pydcvt.

65. "Complying with COPPA," Federal Trade Commission, http://tinyurl.com/okd9e5k.

66. Kristin Cohen and Christina Yeung, "Kids apps disclosures revisited," Federal Trade Commission, Sept. 3, 2015, http://tinyurl.com/pb6k586.

67. "Right to delisting: Google informal appeal rejected," CNIL, Sept. 21, 2015, http://tinyurl.com/ohettz6.

68. See "Reform of the Data Protection legal framework in the EU," *op. cit.*

69. For background see Julia Powles, "Tech companies like Facebook not above the law, says Max Schrems," *The Guardian,* Oct. 9, 2015, http://tinyurl.com/oy5crtn.

70. Mark Scott, "Data Transfer Pact Between U.S. and Europe is Ruled Invalid," *The New York Times,* Oct. 6, 2015, http://tinyurl.com/o469wa4. For background, see Chuck McCutcheon, "Government Surveillance," *CQ Researcher,* Aug. 30, 2013, pp. 717-740.

71. "Max Schrems: the lawyer who took on Facebook," Reuters, Oct. 7, 2015, http://tinyurl.com/qg9gesc.

72. Testimony of Marc Rotenberg, hearing on "Examining the EU Safe Harbor Decision and Impacts for Transatlantic Data Flows," United States House of Representatives Energy & Commerce Subcommittees on Commerce, Manufacturing, and Trade and Communications and Technology, Nov. 3, 2015.

73. "Administration Discussion Draft: Consumer Privacy Bill of Rights Act of 2015," White House, undated, http://tinyurl.com/oydmctk.

74. Elizabeth Dwoskin, "White House Proposes Consumer Privacy Bill of Rights," "Digits," *The WallStreetJournal,* Feb. 27, 2015, http://tinyurl.com/m9mflja. The Information Technology Industry Council, a group supported by Microsoft, Facebook and Google, said, "The U.S. has a robust legal framework of privacy protections" that permits the industry to innovate and that "any efforts to modify this framework must be carefully considered."

75. See "EU-US Privacy Bridges," report released Oct. 21, 2015, http://tinyurl.com/o5jwvcu.

76. Sen. Edward J. Markey, press release, "Markey, Barton . . . Reintroduce Bipartisan, Bicameral Legislation to Protect Children's Online Privacy," June 11, 2015, http://tinyurl.com/ q3juroo.

77. Do Not Track Kids Act of 2015, "S1563," Congress.gov, http://tinyurl.com/p8cxyhq; Congress.gov, "H.R. 2734," http://tinyurlcom/np56avl.

78. Mary Madden and Lee Rainie, "Americans' Views About Data Collection and Security," Pew Research Center, May 20, 2015, http://tinyurl.com/oj83fb9.

79. Toobin, *op. cit.*

80. "FTC Approves Final Order Settling Charges against Snapchat," Federal Trade Commission, Dec. 31, 2014, http://tinyurl.com/o6w3cln.

81. Helena Horton, "Will Snapchat's New Update stop people from sexting using the app?" *The Telegraph,* Sept. 16, 2015, http://tinyurl.com/pft6ayr.

BIBLIOGRAPHY
Selected Sources
Books

Bamberger, Kenneth A., and Deirdre K. Mulligan, *Privacy on the Ground: Driving Corporate Behavior in the United States and Europe,* **MIT Press, 2015.**
U.S. privacy law remains more fragmented than in Europe, but American corporations often have more robust privacy practices than their European counterparts, according to two professors at the University of California's Berkeley Center for Law and Technology.

Citron, Danielle Keats, *Hate Crimes in Cyberspace,* **Harvard University Press, 2014.**
A University of Maryland professor reviews the state of the law for cyber-harassment victims and argues that those who engage in "revenge porn" should be criminally prosecuted.

Mayer-Schönberger, Viktor, *Delete: The Virtue of Forgetting in the Digital Age,* **Princeton University Press, 2009.**
A person's online information should have an expiration date, a professor of Internet governance and regulation says in this seminal book.

Articles

Ausloos, Jef, and Aleksandra Kuczeraway, "From Notice-and-Takedown to Notice-and-Delist: Implementing the Google Spain Ruling," ICRI Research Paper 24, forthcoming in *Colorado Technology Law Journal,* Oct. 5, 2015, http://tinyurl.com/qhyanmm.
Two researchers at the University of Leuven, Belgium, analyze legal controversies over the recent Google Spain ruling in the European Union saying search engines have a duty to remove someone's search results upon request.

Chemerinsky, Erwin, "Rediscovering Brandeis' Right to Privacy," *Brandeis Law Journal,* 2006-07, pp. 643-657, http://tinyurl.com/pyg5slp.
Tracing Supreme Court decisions on privacy, a University of California-Irvine law professor concludes that there is little judicial protection for individuals trying to prevent their private information from being publicly disseminated.

Keller, Daphne, "The GDPR's Notice and Takedown Rules: Bad for Free Expression, but Not Beyond Repair," Center for Internet and Society, Oct. 29, 2015, http://tinyurl.com/nko8vzt.
Pending European Union legislation could hamper free expression by imposing new erasure requirements, an Internet expert warns.

O'Brien, Danny, and Jillian York, "Rights That Are Being Forgotten: Google, the ECJ, and Free Expression," Electronic Frontier Foundation, July 8, 2014, http://tinyurl.com/pq5gvsm.
Two members of a civil liberties advocacy group criticize the Google Spain ruling as forcing search engines to "censor publicly available information" without properly balancing free expression.

Posner, Eric, "We all have the right to be forgotten," *Slate,* May 14, 2014, http://tinyurl.com/mc6ttwx.
A University of Chicago law professor says adopting a "right to be forgotten" in the United States would simply return individuals' privacy to the way it was before the Internet.

Rosen, Jeffrey, "The Right to be Forgotten," Feb. 13, 2012, *Stanford Law Review,* http://tinyurl.com/7cwjwvn.
In this widely quoted article, a George Washington University law professor called pending EU data-protection legislation the "biggest threat to free speech on the Internet in the coming decade."

Tippmann, Sylvia, and Julia Powles, "Google accidentally reveals data on 'right to be forgotten' requests," *The Guardian*, July 14, 2015, http://tinyurl.com/ne8ns9o.
The vast majority of requests to Google to remove search results came from people who were not famous.

Toobin, Jeffrey, "The Solace of Oblivion," *The New Yorker*, Sept. 29, 2014, http://tinyurl.com/neo4qyu.
A New Yorker writer and lawyer presents a sympathetic portrayal of a family that tried to remove gory photos of their daughter's fatal car crash from the Internet, but says Europe's right to be forgotten would "never pass muster under U.S. law."

Reports and Studies

"The Advisory Council to Google on the Right to be Forgotten," Google, Feb. 6, 2015, http://tinyurl.com/qg4uhuu.
Experts appointed by Google to advise it on how to implement the "right to be forgotten" agreed with the company that it should not remove search results outside of Europe.

"Google Transparency Report: European Privacy Requests for Removals," Google, updated Nov. 11, 2015, http://tiny url.com/ptypu56.
In this report, updated periodically, Google provides information about requests it has received for search removals in Europe by country, and examples of its decisions about whether to remove search results.

Humphries, Daniel, "U.S. Attitudes towards the 'Right to be Forgotten,' IndustryView 2014," Software Advice, Sept. 5, 2014, http://tinyurl.com/pjrkkhp.
A software industry poll of 500 Americans found 61 percent want some version of the right to be forgotten.

For More Information

Association of National Advertisers, 2020 K St., N.W., Washington, DC 20006; 202-296-1883; www.ana.net. Industry group representing 670 companies that opposes implementing a "right to be forgotten" in the United States.

Center for Digital Democracy, 1621 Connecticut Ave., N.W., #500, Washington, DC 20009; 202-986-2220; www .democraticmedia.org. Consumer group advocating online consumer privacy.

Common Sense Media, 650 Townsend, Suite 435, San Francisco, CA 94103; 415-863-0600, www.commonsense media.org. Research and advocacy group that works to protect children's online privacy.

Consumer Watchdog, 2701 Ocean Park Blvd., Suite 112, Santa Monica, CA 90405; 310-392-8874; www.consumer watchdog.org. Consumer advocacy group that favors implementing a "right to be forgotten" in the United States.

Court of Justice of the European Union, Palais de la Cour de Justice, Boulevard Konrad Adenauer, Kirchberg, L-2925 Luxembourg, Luxembourg; +352-4303-1; http://curia .europa.eu. The European Union's high court that interprets E.U. law to make sure it is applied the same way in all countries.

Electronic Frontier Foundation, 815 Eddy St., San Francisco, CA 94109; 415-436-9333; www.eff.org. Membership organization that defends civil liberties in the digital world.

Electronic Privacy Information Center, 1718 Connecticut Ave., N.W., Suite 200, Washington, DC 20009; 202-483-1140; www.epic.org. Research center that works to protect privacy and provide a public voice in decisions concerning the future of the Internet.

Federal Trade Commission, 600 Pennsylvania Ave., N.W., Washington, DC 20580; 202-326-2222; www.ftc.gov. Federal consumer protection agency.

Future of Privacy Forum, 1400 Eye St., N.W., Suite 450, Washington, DC 20005; 202-642-9142; https://fpf .org. Think tank that seeks to advance responsible data practices.

Digital Journalism

Is news quality better or worse online?

Kenneth Jost

Former *Washington Post* star reporter Ezra Klein is one of several top journalists who have jumped from traditional print publications to explore new frontiers in digital journalism. Klein, who launched the *Post*'s popular site *Wonkblog*, started *Vox* – "a general news site for the 21st century" – with the main goal of explaining the news.

From *CQ Researcher*,
May 30, 2014

Many news junkies who logged onto their computers Sunday night, April 6, went straight to a site with a fullscreen image of the U.S. Capitol under ominously gray clouds. A headline superimposed over the scene declared: "How politics makes us stupid."

The foreboding tableau marked the eagerly awaited launch of the newest of a growing number of digital-only news sites: *Vox*, the brainchild of journalistic wunderkind Ezra Klein, who turned 30 on May 9. For the debut, Klein wrote a 4,000-word essay built around research suggesting that political partisanship makes people impervious to new information contradictory to their views.[1]

Klein had launched *Vox* after a storied, five-year run at *The Washington Post* as the founder and main writer for the newspaper's political site, *Wonkblog*. After *The Post* refused Klein's request for a multimillion-dollar expansion of the must-read site, he left in January to practice what he calls a new kind of journalism. Its mission would be "to explain the news" and to move readers "from curiosity to understanding."

In years past, would-be Clark Kents and Lois Lanes aspired to work at nationally recognized newspapers such as *The Washington Post* or *The New York Times*. Today, however, newspapers are often dismissed as "legacy media," and stars such as Klein are jumping ship to explore new frontiers in digital journalism. Their sites are drawing mixed reviews for design, even as they attract attention and traffic for their content and their role as experiments in how to present news and run a successful news business today. They join other digital-only general news sites

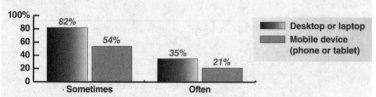

Most Americans Get Their News Online

Percentage who say they get their news sometimes or often from a digital source.

Desktop or laptop

Mobile device (phone or tablet)

Source: Kenneth Olmstead, "5 key findings about digital news audiences," Pew Research Center, March 17, 2014, http://tinyurl.com/lr7tqb9.

that over the past decade have been luring news consumers onto the Web.

"The vast majority of Americans now get news in some digital format," the Pew Research Center's Journalism Project notes in its most recent report "State of the News Media 2014."[2]

Others, who like Klein are making closely watched transitions, include Nate Silver, who built a name for himself as a data-crunching political handicapper at *The New York Times'* blog *FiveThirtyEight*, and veteran technology reporters Walt Mossberg and Kara Swisher, who founded the closely watched tech blog *AllThingsD* at Dow Jones, publisher of *The Wall Street Journal.* Silver left *The Times* last year and launched a data-journalism site, also called *FiveThirtyEight,* on March 17 under sponsorship of the sports network ESPN. Mossberg and Swisher launched their technology news site *Re/code* on Jan. 2 with financial backing from NBCUniversal and the investment operation of former Yahoo chief executive Terry Semel.

In another high-profile startup, Glenn Greenwald is editor of *The Intercept,* launched on Feb. 2 and funded by Pierre Omidyar, the billionaire founder of eBay, the Internet auction site. Greenwald, who previously worked with the U.S. website of the British newspaper *The Guardian,* made international headlines over the past year with Pulitzer Prize-winning disclosures of U.S. and British global surveillance based on documents leaked by former National Security Agency (NSA) contractor Edward Snowden.

"It seems like not a week goes by without an announcement of a new project online headed by a prominent journalist," says Jim Romenesko, a veteran

newspaperman who tracks media on the eponymous website *jimromenesko .com.* "A lot of legacy journalists want to try something new, something that's maybe a little bit edgy and experimental."

Among the best known of the older so-called digital natives, *The Huffington Post* mimics conventional newspapers in format and tone, while the virally popular *BuzzFeed* traffics in irreverent entertainment even while adding serious journalism. Other popular sites include what are known as news aggregators — sites that republish stories from other news media. Two of the most widely viewed are maintained by the established Internet search engine companies, *Google News* and *Yahoo News.* By contrast, two newer aggregators — *Mashable* and *Flipboard* — are the built-from-scratch creations of entrepreneurially minded techies, both tied to the explosion in social media. *Mashable* says it "covers top social media news," meaning both news about social media and news popular on social media; *Flipboard* self-identifies as "Your social magazine for iPad, iPhone and Android."[3]

Meanwhile, traditional print and broadcast media are putting more energy, effort and resources into their websites amid declining news readership and viewership.[4] "There's no stopping the migration from print to digital," says Tom Rosenstiel, executive director of the newspaper industry-affiliated American Press Institute and a former reporter with the *Los Angeles Times* and *Newsweek.*

These trends amount to "a virtual digital revolution," according to Tim McGuire, a longtime newspaperman and now a professor at Arizona State University's Walter Cronkite School of Journalism in Phoenix. "There is no choice," he explains. "It's the set of tools we have today. We didn't keep driving horses and buggies when cars came along."

The digital revolution has changed the economics of the newspaper, magazine and television industries. Classified advertising in print newspapers has shriveled, while retail and national advertising have shrunk as well, though less dramatically. Newspapers and other media have shed thousands of jobs, but the losses have not been offset by employment at digital publications.

The developments have prompted alarmed hand-wringing. The total number of newspaper reporters, editors and other journalists fell to 38,000 in 2012 — down nearly one-third from a peak of 56,400 in 2000, according to the American Society of News Editors' annual census.[5] Nearly 60 percent of journalists surveyed recently by Indiana University's School of Journalism say journalism is headed in the wrong direction. Slightly more than 60 percent say their newsrooms have shrunk in the past few years. Those interviewed worked for online media as well as traditional print, television, radio and news services.[6]

Some journalism experts see a bright side even while acknowledging the wrenching changes. "News for the most part is in fine shape," writes Mitchell Stephens, a professor at New York University's Arthur L. Carter Journalism Institute, in his new book *Beyond News*.[7]

Technology has been "a boon for news," Stephens explains in his book. Despite the job losses, he writes, technology has allowed fewer hands to gather more information on "an extraordinarily wide variety of events" from "an extraordinarily wide variety of sources" and to disseminate the information "in a wide variety of formats fast and far."

Others agree. "Digital has made it possible for people to do different things that they were not able to do before," says Pablo Boczkowski, director of the Program in Media, Technology and Society at Northwestern University in Evanston, Ill. Among other changes, Boczkowski notes that people can now access news around the clock — at work, at home or on the go — and can comment on articles without being filtered by editors. Digital "has broadened the possibility of public engagement," he says.

At the same time, some experts and critics say the new digital-only news sites have some less attractive features — in particular, a higher degree of political partisanship. Mark Jurkowitz, associate director of the Pew Research Center's Journalism Project and a former

Digital Sites Debut to Mixed Reviews

New digital-only news sites include several launched by prominent journalists that debuted with great fanfare and high expectations for their content. But the sites drew mixed reviews from design experts surveyed by Digiday, a site for digital media, marketing and advertising professionals.

Name	Founder(s)	Review of Design
Vox	Ezra Klein	"Accessible;" "best job" of creating brand identity
FiveThirtyEight	Nate Silver	"Straightforward" look, but "a lot of scrolling" required
The Intercept	Glenn Greenwald	"Looks . . . like a bare-bones blog"
Re/code	Walt Mossberg, Kara Swisher	"Hard to read," but good information

Source: Lucia Moses, "Which new digital news publisher designed it best?" *Digiday*, April 9, 2014, http://tinyurl.com/om2r5ms.

ombudsman for *The Boston Globe*, complains of the "proliferation of argumentative ideological media" in the digital world.

For instance, *The Huffington Post* is widely seen as having a left-liberal tilt, although founder Arianna Huffington minimizes the importance of any political slant.[8] Other sites, however, are overtly partisan, such as the progressive *Think Progress Memo* or its conservative counterpart *Red State*.

McGuire agrees on the increase in partisanship, but sees market demand as driving the trend. "You've got people seeking affirmation, not information," he says.

As traditional news organizations still strive to find their place in the new digital world, some of the older digital-only publications have shown signs of health. *The Huffington Post* was acquired by the Internet service provider AOL in February 2011 in a $315 million deal. AOL chief executive Tim Armstrong has said the publication may be profitable in 2014, taking into account the conferences it organizes and other associated businesses.[9] *BuzzFeed* has expanded its editorial staff to 170 since hiring the rising journalistic star Ben Smith as editor late in 2011. Jurkowitz says he asked Smith in a telephone interview to explain the phenomenal growth. Smith's answer: "The business staff has overperformed."

The newer sites — *Vox, FiveThirtyEight* and others — are works in progress at this point. Experts differ on

Magazine Industry
Tries to Adjust to Digital Age

Going all-digital is "like life support — before we pull the plug."

For millions of African-Americans, *Jet* has been essential reading for the past six decades — a weekly chronicle of events and issues that were barely covered, if at all, in the nation's predominantly white news media. Starting in July, however, *Jet* will no longer be delivered in the mail or available at newsstands and grocery store checkout lines.

Instead, *Jet* will switch from print to an all-digital format. In announcing the move on May 7, Johnson Publishing Co., which also publishes the black-oriented magazine *Ebony*, called the step a "proactive decision to adapt to the changing needs of its readers" as they increasingly want information quickly and easily.[1]

Jet, launched in 1951, was an invaluable source of information for black Americans during the most tumultuous decades of the civil rights revolution. The pocket-sized magazine was a weekly until it cut back to every three weeks last year.

Jet's move is evidence that the magazine industry, like the newspaper industry, is trying to adjust to the digital age. The magazine industry's trade association changed its name in 2010 to recognize the change: the Magazine Publishers Association became instead MPA — the Association of Magazine Media.

"The industry can no longer by judged by print alone," says Meredith Wagner, the association's executive vice president for communications. "Magazine media is an evolving industry that is not tied to any one single format or medium."

Jet's move does not sit as well, however, with one expert on the industry. "It's very bad news," says Samir Husni, director of the Magazine Innovation Center at the University of Mississippi in Oxford and a consultant to magazine companies. "Instead of investing in the magazine, they say, 'We are going to be cutting the magazine.'"

For Husni, print remains an essential part of what he calls the "total experience" of subscribing to a magazine, even as readers also want immediate access to continually

their financial prospects. "Some will win, and some will lose," Arizona State's McGuire says. In the meantime, however, news and information consumers are able to choose from among an ever-expanding number of news sources. "The more, the merrier," says media tracker Romenesko.

As the news industry continues to adapt to change, here are some of the questions being debated:

Do digital-only publications benefit readers?

The digital media site *Mashable* scored a coup of sorts last fall by hiring Jim Roberts, a longtime editor at *The New York Times*, as executive editor and chief content officer. Roberts announced his arrival in an open letter posted on *Mashable* on Oct. 30 that extolled the benefits of digital technology in reporting news faster, combining text and video and allowing the site's users to help tell and spread stories via interactions with the site and social media.

"In other words," Roberts wrote, "as disruptive as certain technologies have been to the news business, they have created much greater benefits for those of us who make a living as communicators — and for our audience."[10]

Mashable's "community" — as Roberts termed the site's users — are greeted daily by a kaleidoscopic display of changing headlines and images on stories both weighty and light. The home page sorts stories under conventional headings such as U.S. & World, Tech, Business and Entertainment and newer usages such as Must Reads and Water Cooler.

The home pages of other digital sites offer users similarly wide arrays of options. *The Huffington Post* divides topics into 44 general news and nine local categories, or "verticals" — to use the current news jargon. Users who click on "Sports," for example, find not just daily scores, standings and highlights, but also a wealth of features, commentaries and the like — many with updated content online. The digital-only route, he says, "has been like life support — before we pull the plug."

Like newspapers, magazines have been in a challenging environment for decades. The weekly editions of such general-interest magazines as *Saturday Evening Post* and *Life* are distant memories from the 1960s and '70s. *Time* is a shrunken relic of its former self; *Newsweek*, which once had a circulation of 3.3 million, dropped its print edition at the end of 2012, only to return in March with a limited print run of only about 70,000 copies.[2] Monthly titles have also churned, with launches and closures as publishers feel out the changing environment.

Overall industry figures show that magazine circulation revenue peaked at $10.5 billion in 2005 and declined to $8.3 billion in 2011.[3] Total ad pages have fallen for the past two years, according to an MPA press release, but the decline slowed in 2013 to 4 percent from an 8 percent drop in 2012. Print ad revenue overall rose 1 percent, to $19.7 billion — presumably thanks to rate increases. But the trade association called 2013 a "growth year," primarily because of a 16 percent increase in tablet advertising revenue.[4]

Despite economic uncertainties, Husni says the magazine industry overall has a positive future, but only if it takes care of its print legacy. "The future of digital begins with print," he says. "The rumors of our demise," he adds, "have been greatly exaggerated."

— ***Kenneth Jost***

Courtesy Johnson Publishing Co

The pocket-size print version of Jet was once a staple for millions of African-American readers, but starting in July the magazine will switch from print to an all-digital format.

[1] "Johnson Publishing Company Announces Transition of JET Magazine to Digital Magazine," press release, Johnson Publishing, May 7, 2014, http://tinyurl.com/q2xtuwb; and Rem Reider, "'Jet' comes in for a digital landing," *USA Today*, May 8, 2014, p. 2B, http://tinyurl.com/nqgweh2.

[2] Leslie Kaufman, "Newsweek to Restart Printing Process," *The New York Times*, March 3, 2014, p. B1, http://tinyurl.com/k6y28up.

[3] "Top Statistics about Magazine Industry in the U.S. — Statista Dossier 2013," *Statista*, http://tinyurl.com/ms9f978.

[4] "2013 a Growth Year for Magazine Media Across Platforms," MPA — The Association of Magazine Media, Jan. 9, 2014, http://tinyurl.com/q737v3v.

reader comments numbering into the hundreds or beyond. In contrast to print newspapers or magazines, digital readers can never really "finish" exploring a site because there is always more to read, view, link to or share.

"There are obviously some real advantages to producing content in the digital space, which is infinite," says Pew's Jurkowitz. "It allows news consumers to do a much deeper dive into news content than they could in traditional platforms. You can click on links that can take you to original documents, links to everything that's been written about on that subject for the last three to four years, links to related issues or timelines."

Other veterans of print media also wax ecstatic. "Digital news is richer, more convenient," says Rosenstiel at the American Press Institute. "It's in my pocket when I want it. It's not confined to one medium."

At the same time, the wealth of news, information and commentary threatens overload, according to

Jurkowitz. "It's obviously more difficult to be a news consumer in this digital age because there are so many choices," he explains.

"There are so many outlets now, so many information gatherers and distributors," says Jane McDonnell, executive director of the Online News Association, an organization for online journalists founded in 1999. "How do you know where your accurate journalism is coming from?"

The change reduces the agendasetting and educational roles that news media have played for decades. "People consume more of what they're interested in and less of what they're not interested in," says Northwestern professor Boczkowski. "That exacerbates the gap between what the public wants to know and what the media considers they should know about." McGuire, the Arizona State professor, agrees. "You are no longer talking about the kind of mass publications that you and I are familiar with," he says. "The idea of mass has largely evaporated." Social media tools contribute to the phenomenon. Computer-generated algorithms funnel stories on particular subjects or from particular viewpoints to users based on profiles developed from stories they followed in the past. Increasingly, people are referred to news via their friends on Facebook, Twitter, Instagram or other services rather than seeking out news sites on their own.[11] "Another question looming over developments in social media," the Pew report says, "is whether the self-selective process combined with algorithmic feeds are narrowing the kinds of information Americans are exposed to."[12]

Roberts voiced none of these concerns, however, as he assumed his new post at *Mashable,* where news is inextricably linked to social media. In his vision, the site's users are an essential part of newsgathering and reporting in the 21st century.

"[T]he *Mashable* community is not just a bunch of passive consumers, but are also active and thoughtful participants in the conversation, creators and contributors of unique content, and an essential part of the distribution chain," Roberts wrote. "The members of *Mashable's* community are smart and voracious; they like to share, and it's *Mashable's* mission to create smart material for them to do so."

Do digital-only publications have drawbacks for readers?

Visitors to *BuzzFeed* are greeted on the home page's left side by such conventional section headings as "News," "Entertainment" and "Life." On the right side, however, are headings such as "cute," "trashy" and "fail." Others are acronyms — "OMG" (for "Oh, my God"), "LOL" (for "laughing out loud") and "WTF," which uses a common obscenity to express surprise and disappointment.

The headings hark to *BuzzFeed's* birth in 2006 as a social media site specializing in creating posts that would go viral and leave "buzz" in their wake. *BuzzFeed's* most distinctive contribution to 21st-century journalism is the creation of the "listicle" — numbered combinations of images and text such as "43 Things That Will Make You Feel Old." But even as *BuzzFeed* has increased its editorial staff and moved into serious reporting and analysis, editor-in-chief Smith makes no apologies for relying on the whimsical to draw traffic.

"The fabric of politics has always been gossip and jokes and crazy personality stuff and memes," Smith, who came to *BuzzFeed* from the hyperpolitical website *Politico,* snapped at a *New York Times* interviewer in February 2013. "Political coverage that wants to be solely high-minded," he continued, "is missing huge chunks of the actual interplay of personality and power that is what actually drives things."[13]

The approach produces mixed reactions from media watchers. "Cat videos don't do anything for me," Pew's Jurkowitz remarks, referring to another common BuzzFeed feature. But he adds that traditional newspapers also offered less-than-serious fare, including comics, crossword puzzles and horoscopes. "There's always been part of American media that's been trivial and light," he says. "There's enough substantive content out there."

Arizona State's McGuire agrees. "*BuzzFeed* does some things that make journalistic traditionalists squint a lot, but they are talking about doing more serious journalism," he says. "Us [sic] grand pooh-bahs have worried about the trivialization of the news for the past 30 years," he adds. "With every tool you can do bad things."

Media watchers raise concerns about more serious downsides of digital journalism — most notably, inaccuracies and ideological biases. As Jurkowitz notes, digital journalism's emphasis on speed increases the possibility that some information will prove inaccurate.

"The newspaper newsroom, the television newsroom — editors had time to think about what they had, what they didn't have, what they needed to fill holes," Jurkowitz says. With digital publications, "there's a built-in error rate," he says.

McDonnell, with the Online News Association, acknowledges the increased risk of errors in digital journalism's emphasis on speed. But she notes that some of the mistakes are spread online by nonjournalists. "It's a journalist's job to figure out what's real and what's not," she says. Digital also has an offsetting advantage: the possibility of instantaneous corrections, unlike in print publications or scheduled radio or television newscasts.

Jurkowitz also complains about what he calls "the hybrid mix of fact and opinion" found in some digital sites. "You get a lot of ideology in digital news," he says. News sites on both sides of the ideological spectrum "play loose with the facts because they are in service to a particular idea."

Stephens, the NYU professor, also sees more ideology in digital journalism, but views the trend more favorably. "There's great opinionated analysis that appears all over in this news ecology," he says. In his book, Stephens argues that journalism in the 20th century became too wedded to "the religion of objectivity." He calls instead for "wisdom journalism" — journalism that" includes and even emphasizes informed, interpretive, explanatory, even opinionated takes on current events."[14]

Stephens is also untroubled by the cat videos and the like. "Newsstands were and are still filled with a lot of very dumb magazines which are mostly concerned with celebrities and other trivialities," he says. "Obviously, we're going to get a lot of that on line."

For his part, *BuzzFeed*'s Smith believes that humor, done well, is one of the keys to the success of digital journalism. To reach people these days, he wrote in an essay in *Playboy*, "you have to write an article so funny, so revelatory or so trenchant that they will actively share it with their friends. To go viral, you have to do something excellent."[15]

Will the new digital news sites succeed financially?

Swisher and Mossberg created a money-making business under Dow Jones's auspices with their "All Things Digital" technology conferences, which began in 2003 and gave birth to the *AllThingsD* blog four years later. Now that they have gone out on their own with a digital tech news site, *Re/code,* Swisher acknowledges that the financial prospects are uncertain.

In every year they were with Dow Jones, *"AllThingsD* was profitable," Swisher told an interviewer with *San Francisco* magazine in April. "We'll probably lose money this year, and that will be upsetting. I'm focused on getting to a place where we can prove that journalism can make good money on the web. So we'll see about that."[16]

Klein was similarly reluctant to make financial predictions one week after the launch of his brainchild *Vox.*

Newspaper Ad Revenue Plummeted

Revenue for newspaper print and online advertising fell 57 percent from 2004 to 2013.

Newspaper Advertising Revenue

Total revenue (in $ millions)

Source: Newspaper Association of America, "Archived Advertising & Circulation Revenue Data," undated, http://tinyurl.com/d83po24; 2013 figures from "Business Model Evolving, Circulation Revenue Rising," Newspaper Association of America, April 18, 2014, http://tinyurl.com/kljkoj7.

"You've gotta give this stuff some time to play out," he told an interviewer for *New York* magazine. "People are just constantly pronouncing on business strategies or content strategies. We're all going to be different organizations a year from now than we are today."[17]

The four most buzz-producing new sites — Vox, *FiveThirtyEight, Re/code* and the Intercept — all start with solid financial backing, but most media watchers are hesitating to make specific forecasts about their long-term viability. "Some will win, some will lose," says McGuire, the Arizona State professor. "You're at a high stage of experimentation."

Among those more skeptical is media watcher Michael Wolff, who writes for, among other publications, *GQ.* In a chat with Hearst Magazines president David Carey in early April just as *Vox* was being launched, Wolff was openly contemptuous of the likely fortunes of journalists-turned-entrepreneurs such as Klein and others.

"There is not a chance in the world," said Wolff, who wrote a 1998 book, *Burn Rate*, about the failure of his own Internet media company. "It's just preposterous. I don't know what they're thinking, what they're smoking. Nobody knows anything about selling an ad, nobody knows anything about aggregating an audience. So I think this is, to put it kindly, a bubble."[18]

Kara Swisher is among the print journalists making closely watched transitions to digital news. Along with Walt Mossberg, also a veteran technology reporter at *The Wall Street Journal*, she founded the much-heralded tech blog *AllThingsD* at Dow Jones, publisher of *The Journal*. Swisher and Mossberg left Dow Jones to start tech news site Re/code.

Fellow media watcher Romenesko, for one, dismisses Wolff's forecast. "I think he's a kind of negative Nancy," Romenesko says. "They're smart people. I don't think they're going to throw buckets of money out the window."

The new sites follow in the steps of older publications that have made money with digital journalism. "*Buzz Feed* says they're profitable now," Romenesko notes. "The secret is to stay lean and be cautious."

Boczkowski, the Northwestern professor, also emphasizes the need to be cautious and keep expectations low. "Sure, there is a way to make money — the question is how much money," he says. "Making money involves having costs less than the income. The question is how to keep the costs low and how to get revenue."

Vox, FiveThirtyEight, Re/code and *The Intercept* are all starting out as free sites seeking revenue from advertising and other sources. An exception to that pattern is *The Information*, a tech industry news site launched in December by former *Wall Street Journal* reporter Jessica Lessin, with an annual subscription cost of $399. "Instead of chasing the highest number of eyeballs," Lessin explained in a blog post, "we will chase and deliver the most valuable news."[19]

Digital advertising revenue could prove disappointing for digital sites, as it has so far for legacy media. A recent survey notes that companies are spending a relatively small portion of their digital marketing budgets — only 12.5 percent — on digital advertising. A much bigger portion — around 40 percent — was spent on social networks, email marketing, mobile marketing and company websites and blogs.[20]

Romenesko notes, however, that digital sites do not need to rely solely on advertising. "The conference business is very lucrative for them, too," he notes, citing All Things Digital as an example. "They're finding ways to get revenue beyond advertising."

The new sites are not alone in trying to figure out the new economics of the journalism business, according to the experts. "All of these startups — have they figured out some kind of business model?" Jurkowitz asks rhetorically. "Frankly, the consensus is no. They have not figured out what the legacy organizations haven't figured out either."

BACKGROUND
Changing Technologies

The technology now transforming journalism may seem revolutionary, but it is only the latest in a succession of innovations since the invention of the printing press that have helped disseminate news ever faster and ever wider. Newspapers became a daily, household commodity in the United States by the turn of the 20th century thanks to the steam-powered cylindrical press. Radio brought the sound of history into the living room by the 1920s and '30s; television added pictures in the 1940s and '50s. And with the launch of the World Wide Web in 1990, people around the world gained a tool for nearly instantaneous access to the events of the day.[21]

The German blacksmith Johannes Gutenberg made handwritten manuscripts and woodblock prints obsolete when, sometime around 1439, he combined the essential elements of what was once "modern" printing: movable type, oil-based inks and a screw-driven press. The printers of 18th-century colonial America, such as Benjamin Franklin and John Peter Zenger, used much the same technology to print the often highly partisan newspapers that played an important part in unifying colonists around the cause of independence.

The 19th-century invention of the steam-driven cylindrical press made newspapers widely accessible and the newspaper business reliably profitable, according to NYU professor Stephens. Printer Benjamin Day, in 1835, was first in the United States to use a steam-driven press to mass-produce his newspaper, the *New York Sun,* and sell copies for a penny each. The great turn-of-the-century publishers — William Randolph Hearst and Joseph Pulitzer, among others — showed that the so-called penny press could bring news to the masses at a healthy profit. Those newspapers depended on another 19th-century advance, the telegraph, for news accounts written by far-flung reporters and published not after months, weeks or even days, but the very next day.

In the 20th century, radio and then television erased even that delay. Americans listened in their living rooms to President Franklin D. Roosevelt's fireside chats delivered from the White House in the 1930s. Beginning with Harry S. Truman in 1949, Americans grew accustomed to watching their president take the oath of office via live television — first in black and white and then, in the 1960s, in "living color." In 1969, millions around the world viewed the first man to step onto the moon via televised images delayed only by the time required for radio waves to travel 240,000 miles across space.

Newspapers and the news divisions of what were then the three commercial TV networks built profitable businesses by selling news written and edited for mass audiences. Americans had more information about events of the day than ever before, but Stephens rues what was missing. "They're mostly recounting the facts," he says of mid- and late 20th-century U.S. journalists. "They didn't provide anywhere near the ability to understand the facts."

The World Wide Web, which allows users to link easily to information via the global network of computer systems, created new opportunities for journalists to disseminate news farther and faster. The transformation now so apparent materialized only slowly. Credit for inventing the Web goes to the British computer scientist Tim Berners-Lee, now Sir Timothy. Working as an independent contractor at the European Organization for Nuclear Research, known as CERN, Berners-Lee developed the now-familiar hypertext transfer protocol (HTTP), hypertext markup language (HTML) and Web browser to facilitate communication among the center's

Traditional newspapers, such as *The Dallas Morning News*, above, have seen their popularity dwindle as digital media have become increasingly popular. "There's no stopping the migration from print to digital," says Tom Rosenstiel, executive director of the American Press Institute. As a result, so-called "legacy media" are putting more effort and resources into developing their websites.

dispersed facilities. The first site outside CERN was brought online in January 1991.[22]

The "handful" of newspapers publishing on the Web before 1995 grew to 175 that year and more than quadrupled to 702 by mid-1997, according to Northwestern professor Boczkowski.[23] *USA Today* boasted 2.5 million Web visitors in December 1998 — pitifully small in comparison to the newspaper's current figure of 35 million unique visitors a month. And the "online newspapers" of the period differed little from the print editions.

"They had not really figured out what was native to the digital space," Pew's Jurkowitz recalls. "They weren't doing any special thinking about the digital world."

Exploiting the Web

Within a few years of its launch, the World Wide Web was drawing interest from a growing array of companies, organizations and computer-savvy individuals. Over time, the number of websites worldwide grew into the hundreds of millions and the number of users to more than 2 billion by 2010.[24] The growing popularity of the Web hurt other media, especially newspapers, by diverting both advertising revenue and readers' time and attention.

The economic impact of Web advertising on newspapers began to materialize early in the 21st century. Print retail advertising peaked at $22.2 billion in 2005 and fell by nearly half by 2011, according to the Newspaper Association of America, while print national advertising crested at $8.1 billion in 2004 and fell by more than half by 2011. Classified ad revenue was siphoned off by Web innovations such as Craigslist, a free online marketplace, and the Web auction site eBay. Print revenue from classifieds, which peaked at $19.6 billion in 2000, had plummeted by more than 70 percent by 2011. Online ad revenue gains offset less than 10 percent of the print revenue losses.[25] At the same time, to attract as many viewers as possible to those ads, almost all sites offered their news content for free.

The rapidly multiplying number of websites also contributed to the continuing decline in newspaper circulation and readership, which had begun in the 1970s. Free Web-based news aggregators — such as *Yahoo News,* launched in 2001, and *Google News,* launched in 2002 — gave audiences continually updated access to multiple news sources with no need for print copies. Government websites provided official information at the federal, state and local levels. Professional sports leagues created websites — such as *NFL.com* and *MLB .com* — as early as the mid-1990s for fans to follow games in real time and keep track of standings, scores, statistics and much more than any sports section could provide.

Special-interest blogs became essential reading for specific audiences. For example, two legal blogs launched in 2002 — *SCOTUSblog* on the Supreme Court and *How Appealing* on appellate litigation — provide news and analysis that judges, lawyers and legal affairs journalists depend upon today. For health policy news, the Kaiser Family Foundation launched a free health-news site in 2009 that is similarly invaluable for people in and around the nation's largest industry sector.

Gawker was founded in 2003 as a Manhattan-oriented celebrity gossip site; Gawker Media developed seven other blogs, including the sports site *Deadspin.* Another popular sports site is *Grantland,* created by sports journalist Bill Simmons in 2011 and named in honor of one of the great sports-writers of the print era, Grantland Rice, whose daily column was syndicated across the country. For business audiences, the *Business Insider* is now a popular site with some original content after having been launched in 2009 as a blog and financial and tech news aggregator.

Newspapers were challenged more directly by new digital-only general news publications even as they tried to innovate online and simultaneously tend to the print editions that yielded roughly 80 percent of their revenue. In the clearest head-to-head matchup, the author and syndicated columnist Arianna Huffington launched *The Huffington Post* in May 2005 with financial backing from venture capitalist Kenneth Lehrer. The site's design mimicked to some extent the various sections of print newspapers. The site grew to become a 24/7 operation, with local and international editions, before the legacy Internet service provider AOL bought it in 2011 for $315 million.[26]

Within a year after *HuffPost*'s debut, two more of today's most popular sites were launched, both more as social media than the general news sites that they were to become. *Mashable* was the brainchild of Pete Cashmore, a college dropout in Aberdeen, Scotland. Three months shy of his 20th birthday, Cashmore launched *Mashable* in July 2005 as a tool for collecting news about social media and about what users were sharing. By 2009, *The Huffington Post* hailed Cashmore as one of the globe's "top game changers," crediting him with taking social media mainstream and "translating geek-speak for the curious and converted."[27]

BuzzFeed debuted in November 2006, created as "the Internet popularity contest" by Jonah Peretti, a graduate of the MIT Media Lab and cofounder of *The Huffington Post* along with Huffington and Lehrer. Peretti developed technologies for searching out items being posted and shared — creating "buzz," that is. He left *The Huffington Post* after the AOL purchase in 2011 to devote full time to *BuzzFeed.* His decision to hire political journalist Smith as editor in December 2011 marked the site's evolution into a serious news site with its buzz-creating features still intact.[28]

Flipboard came along in 2010, designed by creators Mike McCue and Evan Doll to bring magazine-like graphics to a social media aggregator, which pulls together feeds from a user's various social networks.[29] McCue had been head of a voice-recognition company, Tell Me, which was acquired by Microsoft in 2007; Doll was an Apple iPhone engineer McCue met after leaving Microsoft in 2009. Their app was released first for Apple's iPad in 2010 and then for iPhone late in 2011. *The New York Times* marked the iPhone debut of the app

C H R O N O L O G Y

Early 1990s *The World Wide Web is invented; online news publications are born.*

1990-1991 British computer scientist Tim Berners-Lee develops World Wide Web so his colleagues can collaborate; first site outside his institution comes online January 1991.

Mid-1990s Newspapers with online editions grow from 175 in 1995 to more than 700 by mid-1997. . . . Professional sports leagues establish websites for fans.

1999 Online News Association is founded.

2000s *More news goes online. . . . Classified ad revenue for print newspapers reaches peak and then declines by more than 70 percent over the decade.*

2001 Yahoo launches *Yahoo News* as news aggregator. . . . Annual classified ad revenue for print newspapers peaks at $19.6 billion and begins to decline; retail, national advertising begin less drastic declines in 2004, 2005.

2002 Google launches *Google News* as news aggregator. . . . *How Appealing* and *SCOTUSblog* launched as legal news websites.

2003 *Gawker.com* launches as Manhattan-based celebrity gossip site (January).

2005 *Huffington Post* launches as digital-only, national news source (May 9). . . . *Mashable* is founded as social media news aggregator (July).

2006 *BuzzFeed* launches as site to chronicle events, trends "on the rise and worth your time" (Nov. 17).

2007 Walt Mossberg and Kara Swisher launch *AllThingsD* blog at *The Wall Street Journal* (April 18).

2008 *The Wall Street Journal* adds reader comment section; *The New York Times* allows users to share stories from site (September).

2009 Ezra Klein hired as economics and domestic policy blogger at *The Washington Post* (June); develops *Wonkblog.* . . . Kaiser Family Foundation launches online health news website.

2010s *Star journalists launch online news sites.*

2010 Nate Silver moves political forecasting blog *FiveThirtyEight.com* to *The New York Times* under three-year licensing agreement (June 3). . . . Flipboard debuts as news aggregator app for iPad (July 21).

2011 AOL acquires *Huffington Post* for $315 million (Feb. 7). . . . Sports-writer Bill Simmons launches sports website *Grantland* (June 8). . . . *BuzzFeed* hires political reporter Ben Smith as editor; news staff begins expansion (Dec. 11).

2012 Upworthy launches as website for viral content (March). . . . *Huffington Post's* military correspondent David Wood wins Pulitzer Prize for national reporting (April 16). . . . *Newsweek* announces plan to end print edition at end of year (Oct. 18).

2013 Gadfly journalist Glenn Greenwald breaks news of U.S., U.K. global surveillance with leaked documents from National Security Agency contractor Edward Snowden (June 5). . . . Silver's plan to leave *The New York Times* becomes public (July 19). . . . eBay founder Pierre Omidyar announces plans to bankroll Greenwald, others in new online publication, eventually named *The Intercept* (Oct. 17). . . . Veteran newspaperman Jim Roberts hired as *Mashable* executive editor (Oct. 31). . . . Mossberg, Swisher leave Dow Jones (Dec. 31).

2014 Mossberg and Swisher launch *Re/code* (Jan. 2). . . . Klein's departure from *The Washington Post* is announced (Jan. 21). . . . Greenwald's team launches *The Intercept* (Feb. 10). . . . *Newsweek* announces plan to resume print edition, with limited run (March 3). . . . Silver launches *FiveThirtyEight* (March 17). . . . Study finds vast majority of news consumers get news in digital format "sometimes," roughly one-third "often" (March 26). . . . Klein launches *Vox.com* (March 9). . . . Newspaper industry group releases figures showing revenue losses are slowing, digital-only subscription revenue is up (April 18). . . . Poll by Indiana University finds 60 percent of journalists say profession is headed "in wrong direction" (May 5). . . . *Jet* magazine announces it will end print edition (May 7).

Hyperlocal News Sites Cover What Others Don't

"Mark every death. Remember every victim. Follow every case."

Laura Amico broke into journalism in her home state of California and put in two years on the crime beat at the Santa Rosa *Press Democrat*. But when she moved to Washington, D.C., in 2009 with her husband, Chris, for his new job at PBS's "NewsHour," she could not find a journalism position that she wanted.

Five years later, however, Amico is founder and publisher of an award-winning local digital news site that covers every homicide in the District of Columbia from the killing through the end of legal proceedings. *Homicide Watch D.C.* greets visitors with a promise of unremitting thoroughness: "Mark every death. Remember every victim. Follow every case."[1]

The combined effects of electronic commerce and online journalism have been hard on coverage of local news. Advertisers and readers alike have been drawn away from local newspapers that previously were the principal source for coverage of local news, whether it be crime and justice, business and real estate or local government.[2]

At the same time, however, technology reduces the barriers to entry for start-up local news operations, like the one Amico and her web-developer husband began in 2010 and relaunched in 2011. The site provides coverage and a searchable database of D.C. homicides based on original reporting, court documents and social media.

Start-up operations practicing what has come to be called "hyperlocal journalism" are an antidote to the long-term decline in local reporting that has concerned journalists, community activists and others who follow local government. "Many of them are covering statehouses, city halls or local neighborhoods at a very granular level, compensating for the decline in reporting from legacy media," says Mark Jurkowitz, associate director of the Pew Research Center's Journalism Project.

Columbia Journalism Review's Guide to Online News Startups lists around 60 "hyperlocal" sites from *ARLNow.com* (Arlington, Va.) to *West Seattle Blog*. That number does not count *Homicide Watch* and affiliated sites in Chicago and Trenton, N.J., which are listed in other categories, as are most of the numerous sites devoted to local high school sports.[3]

Two dozen of the hyperlocal listings are state entries for *Patch,* described in Feb. 24, 2012, postings as "AOL's fast-growing hyperlocal network." AOL sold the financially troubled operation in January to Hale Global, an investment firm that specializes in turning around ailing businesses. Hundreds of *Patch* employees were laid off, but those who remained were told that all 900 *Patch* sites would be continued.[4]

Community newspapers have long provided some of the hyperlocal coverage of neighborhoods, schools, zoning boards and the like that metropolitan dailies do not cover. But most of the community papers are weekly and

with a headline describing it as useful "for killing time standing in line."[30]

Yet another entrant in the attentiongrabbing competition was born in 2012: *Upworthy,* launched by Eli Pariser, a liberal political activist, and Peter Koechley, former managing editor of the satirical newspaper *The Onion*. With financial backing from one of Facebook's founders, Chris Hughes, the site announced its mission of becoming "the place to find awesome, meaningful, visual things to share." By deft use of virally appealing headlines, it grew with phenomenal speed.[31]

Gaining Respect

Digital publications such as *The Huffington Post* and *BuzzFeed* slowly gained respect and proved their worth, editorially and financially, as the 21st century moved into its second decade. Meanwhile, major newspapers discovered that they could increase their audience by expanding their digital products, including some digital-only content. Meanwhile, some journalists who had become stars on the newspapers' platforms outgrew their employers and decided to venture into the digital world on their own.

have limited space, at least in their print editions. Digital sites offer the advantage of continual updating and unlimited space.

The Amicos had been financing *Homicide Watch* themselves, but they raised $47,450 in 2012 through a Kickstarter online crowd-funding campaign, allowing the site to hire student interns to take over some of the reporting.[5] Amico prides herself on thoroughness. In a recent story on a mistrial in a homicide case, she noted that local news media had covered the killing but only *Homicide Watch* reported on the no-verdict trial.

The site's home page also makes an unmistakable allusion to the widespread feeling in Washington's African-American and Latino communities that the District's major news media devote more time, attention and space to homicides in predominantly white neighborhoods than in their communities. "If we are to understand violent crime in our community, the losses of every family, in every neighborhood must be recognized," the introductory statement reads.

Digital technology is what makes the operation work, as Laura and Chris Amico explained to an interviewer in 2013.[6] "Having the platform speeds up my workflow by creating a pattern out of my work," Laura Amico said. By checking the database regularly, she continued, she is able to fill in holes as new information becomes available.

"Some of what makes the site work is really fundamental to the web," Chris Amico added. The site allows links to profile pages, he explained, eliminating the need to include background in each story. He also built a database application that creates maps showing where each homicide occurred.

Laura Amico saw a concrete advantage to that database recently when the District recorded three homicides in one night. With a quick check, she determined that it had been

The hyperlocal news site Homicide Watch D.C. covers every homicide in the city from the killing through the end of legal proceedings.

the deadliest week of the year for Washington. "I haven't seen any other reporter with a database robust and agile enough to do that," she said.

— Kenneth Jost

[1] *Homicide Watch D.C.,* http://homicidewatch.org.

[2] Some background drawn from Paul Farhi, "Is local reporting in a death spiral?" *The Washington Post,* March 27, 2014, p. C1, http://tinyurl.com/mmx8zcg.

[3] "CJR's Guide to Online News Startups," accessed May 2014, http://tinyurl.com/7oebz3d.

[4] Leslie Kaufman, "New Owner of Patch Lays Off Hundreds," *The New York Times,* Jan. 30, 2014, p. B7, http://tinyurl.com/mqpywdb.

[5] "A One-Year Student Reporting Lab within Homicide Watch DC," Kick-starter, http://tinyurl.com/kg72l6q.

[6] Erin Kissane, "Homicide Watch: An Interview," *Contents,* Issue 4 (2013), http://tinyurl.com/kbpcqem.

In their early years, *The Huffington Post* and *BuzzFeed* were held in low regard by some in the traditional media. In retrospective pieces, leading media writers have recalled *The Huffington Post* in its early days as "a viral aggregation factory and unpaid-blogger's paradise" and *BuzzFeed* as "something like *The Huffington Post* without the pretension of producing news and commentary."[32]

Not long after *BuzzFeed* got a new editor and a $15.5 million infusion of new capital late in 2011, it turned heads in the world of political journalism with a good scoop: Arizona Republican Sen. John McCain's endorsement of Mitt Romney for the GOP presidential nomination. A few months later, *The Huffington Post* gained new stature when its senior military correspondent David Wood won the Pulitzer Prize — the first ever for work by a for-profit, digital-only publication. The prize, for national reporting, was for a 10-part series on the plight of wounded veterans from the Afghanistan and Iraq wars.

In the meantime, major U.S. newspapers were expanding their digital presence, adding some features and content that appeared only online and not in their

Digital Newcomers

New digital news sites such as *Re/code*, Vox and *FiveThirtyEight* were launched by high-profile print reporters with high expectations for their content, but they have drawn mixed reviews from design experts. *FiveThirtyEight* is the brainchild of Nate Silver, who built a name for himself as a data-crunching political handicapper at *The New York Times. The Washington Post's* Ezra Klein started *Vox* when *The Post* refused his request to invest more in *Wonkblog*, his *Post* digital site. *Wall Street Journal* tech reporters Kara Swisher and Walt Mossberg started *Re/code* on Jan. 2 with backing from NBCUniversal and the investment operation of former Yahoo chief executive Terry Semel. How they will do financially remains to be seen.

print editions. At Dow Jones, Mossberg and Swisher launched the *AllThingsD* blog on April 18, 2007, as an extension of the tech conferences that they had begun hosting in 2003.[33] Klein, who had blogged for the liberal magazine *The American Prospect,* came on board at *The Washington Post* in 2009. He was introduced to *The Post's* readers in June as writing a blog about domestic and economic policy.[34] A year later, *The New York Times* announced plans to host the political blog that statistician Silver had created in 2008, *FiveThirty Eight.com. The Times* announcement on June 3, 2010, noted that under a three-year licensing agreement, Silver will retain all rights to the blog and will run it himself.[35]

Greenwald, a political gadfly blogger and columnist for the British-based newspaper *The Guardian*, made worldwide headlines beginning in June 2013 with sensational disclosures about U.S. and British global surveillance. Greenwald and his colleague documentary filmmaker Laura Poitras were recipients — along with *The Washington Post's* Barton Gellman — of classified documents leaked by Snowden, the whistle-blowing one-time NSA contractor. Four months after the first of the stories was published, eBay founder Omidyar announced that he would bankroll Greenwald and others, to the tune of $250 million, in a new digital-only venture into serious journalism.[36]

Silver's plan to leave *The Times* leaked on July 19, 2013, in the form of a post by its then-media reporter Brian Stelter on another of the newspaper's branded blogs, *Media Decoder.*[37] Stelter, who later left the newspaper for

CNN, noted that Silver's affiliation with ESPN would allow him to return to sports and statistics, the area where he had first gained prominence, and to cover politics in election years for ABC. ESPN and ABC are both owned by the Disney Company.

Mossberg and Swisher left Dow Jones at the end of the year. In a final jointly bylined post on *AllThingsD* on Dec. 31, they took credit for writing more than 40,000 posts, testing "hundreds" of new products and services and drawing "millions" of readers. But they closed — "taking a page from the industry we cover" — by saying, "It's once again time to refresh, reimagine, remake and reinvent." They launched *Re/code* on Jan. 2, as principal owners of the newly formed company Revere Digital, and took all of the *AllThingsD* staff along with them.[38]

Klein's departure from *The Post* was confirmed on Jan. 21, 2014, in a memo distributed to the newspaper's staff and reported in *The New York Times* and elsewhere.[39] Klein was quoted as expressing gratitude to *The Post*, but it was later disclosed that he had unsuccessfully pitched to the newspaper's editors and its new owner, Amazon.com founder Jeffrey Bezos, a plan for an expanded *Wonkblog* that he would run as a stand-alone site still with *The Post*. Instead, Klein started his new policy-oriented site under the aegis of Vox Media, parent of digital-only sports site *SB Nation* and tech site *The Verge*.[40]

"We are just at the beginning of how journalism should be done on the web," Klein told *New York Times* media writer David Carr. "We really wanted to build something from the ground up that helps people understand the news better. We are not just trying to scale *Wonkblog*, we want to improve the technology of news, and *Vox* has a vision of how to solve some of that."[41]

CURRENT SITUATION

Starting Up

The new stars of digital news are filling their sites with lots of content, but keeping mum on how much traffic they are getting and generally steering clear of broad pronouncements about how they are doing.

Of the high-profile sites that launched this year — *Re/code, The Intercept, FiveThirtyEight* and *Vox*

One of the newest entrants into the digital news field is Glenn Greenwald, an investigative reporter for *The Guardian* who won a Pulitzer Prize for his disclosures of U.S. and British global surveillance, based on documents leaked by former National Security Agency consultant Edward Snowden. Greenwald, here with colleague Laura Poitras, a documentary filmmaker, launched *The Intercept* on Feb. 2. The national security publication was funded by the billionaire founder of eBay, Pierre Omidyar.

.com — none responded to requests for figures on visitors to the sites. Mossberg, cofounder of *Re/code*, was the only one of the principals to agree to an interview to discuss the post-launch output and impact. And media watchers appear to be slow so far in offering detailed reviews of the sites.

At *Vox.com,* the most recent of the four to launch, Klein oversees an editorial staff of roughly 20 reporters who write stories or conduct interviews that could just as easily appear in a conventional newspaper or news website.[42] But in the interest of what he calls "persistent explanatory journalism," Klein has created two distinctive features: numbered yellow "card stacks" that explain a subject step-by-step, in primer-like terms; and Vox-Explains videos, such as a two-minute piece on income inequality narrated by Klein.

One week after launch, Klein told an interviewer he was "really, really happy with week one," but hoped that week two would be better and week three better still.[43] Most of the stories are on serious, policy-oriented subjects, but *Vox's* readers are not necessarily wedded to the high-brow. One afternoon early in May, the top three "most read" stories dealt with sex, beer and the NFL draft.

Nate Silver, 36, who ran his political data blog *FiveThirtyEight* at *The New York Times*, left the paper to relaunch the site in March under the same name at the sports network ESPN.

At *FiveThirtyEight,* Silver used a launch-day "manifesto" to announce the hiring of more than 20 people described as skilled not only in "statistical analysis" but also in "data visualization, computer programming and data-literate reporting." Silver said the site would apply data-journalism techniques to five areas: politics, economics, science, life and sports.[44]

In the two months since, *FiveThirty Eight* has explored such issues as whether white Republicans are more racist than white Democrats (yes, but only a little); whether children born to older fathers are at greater risk of attention deficit disorder (unclear); and whether cheerleading is unsafe compared with other high school and college sports (in the middle).[45]

Mossberg says he and Swisher named their new product *Re/code* to combine an abstract word with tech connotations and the importance of "reinvention," which he says characterizes the tech and media industries the site covers. "We're off to an excellent start," Mossberg says four-and-a-half months after launch. Mossberg and Swisher have majority control of the new company, Revere Digital, but financing from NBC and Semel's company, Windsor Media, has allowed an expanded editorial staff. Reporters cover such beats as Washington tech policy and tech and society. The total staff count, including Web developers, is 30.

Along with *Re/code,* Revere will be sponsoring what Mossberg says will be "lucrative" conferences about tech issues. The first is being held at the end of May in

Rancho Palos Verdes, Calif. "The conference sold out in hours," Mossberg says. Advertising, however, is slow so far. "We haven't built out the business staff," he explains.

At *The Intercept,* Greenwald and his co-founders — documentary filmmaker Poitras and investigative reporter Jeremy Scahill — have assembled a team of 13 others to carry on what the trio described at launch as a "central mission . . . to hold the most powerful governmental and corporate factions accountable." Two months after the launch, however, the newly appointed editor-in-chief John Cook acknowledged the site had been slow to gear up and so far had published only more material from Snowden's leaked documents.[46]

Cook, former *Gawker* editor in chief, acknowledged organizational start-up problems in his message, published the same day the liberal blog *Daily Kos* suggested the site was "stalled."[47] The site had published three dozen stories as of mid-April and also cached a trove of national security-related documents. A month later, only three new stories had appeared.

Going Mobile

Major newspapers are redesigning their websites to tailor them for mobile devices, just as the industry is reporting an increase in digital revenue that is helping to slow the bottom-line slide of the past decade.

The *Los Angeles Times* is touting a website redesign announced on May 6 that promises to be user-friendly on all devices: desktop, tablet or smartphone. Meanwhile, top editors at *The New York Times* are studying a specially commissioned internal report that sets out a five-step plan to what the report's authors call a "digital-first transition" — a report that surfaced only days before the tumultuous firing of executive editor Jill Abramson and the appointment of her deputy, Dean Baquet, to succeed her.

The latest figures from the Newspaper Association of America show a 2.6 percent decrease in total revenue in 2013 — the smallest decrease since 2006. Even though advertising fell by 6.5 percent, the decrease was offset somewhat by a 3.7 percent increase in circulation revenue. That increase came mostly from digital-only subscriptions as more newspapers instituted so-called "paywall plans" that require users to pay for access to websites.[48]

Instead of bemoaning the demise of print, industry spokesman Jim Conaghan touts the revenue potential

Are print publications adapting to online journalism?

YES
Caroline Little
President and Ceo,
Newspaper Association of America

Written for *CQ Researcher*, May 2014

When I joined the Newspaper Association of America in 2011, I said that newspapers were going to transform. As we survey the industry in 2014, it is clear that this transformation has taken place, and the numbers bear this out.

According to comScore, a company that measures Internet use, digital newspaper content was accessed by 161 million Americans in March 2014. That is an increase of 19 percent from April 2013. It shows that print publications have put an emphasis on digital content, and that emphasis is being rewarded with growing audiences.

When you look at newspaper financials, you see that circulation revenue has increased the past two years and that this was driven largely by digital subscriptions. This is another example of print publications adapting to a changing landscape and how it is paying off.

Our members are no longer looking at their newspapers as "print publications," because that is now just one part of the larger business model. That is why I like to discuss "newspaper media" instead of simply "newspapers" because a successful newspaper media company will focus on both print and digital, which includes the website, social media channels and mobile capability.

The younger generation remains engaged with newspaper content; they are simply doing so in a different way. We see that a majority of young adults, ages 18 to 24, access newspaper content exclusively through mobile devices. This is obviously a drastic change from how content was accessed even five years ago, when it was all on the desktop.

There are now more than 450 newspapers that offer digital subscriptions, and that number is increasing every day. We are seeing that readers will pay for good, trusted content, which is exactly what newspapers deliver.

Additionally, digital platforms have provided newspapers a better way to tell stories. When I look at the future of journalism, I see journalists who have an eye for telling stories in the best possible manner. That can be a written article and a video. Or it can be in a long-form package with accompanying infographics. At the Newspaper Association of America, our members no longer focus solely on print. To continue our recent success, print publications must continue to balance between print, digital and mobile. So far, so good — and I expect even more good things in the future.

NO
Mitchell Stephens
Author, Beyond News: The Future of Journalism,
Journalism Professor at New York University

Written for *CQ Researcher*, May 2014

Newspapers and magazines have two problems as they attempt to survive in a world where information can move fast and far digitally.

The first and least interesting is practical. These publications are going to have to complete their "migration," to use the jargon, to the new "platform." It is hard to imagine much justification for continuing to go to the expense and trouble of printing on and schlepping around paper, when it is possible to distribute equally attractive publications more or less for free, more or less instantly, online.

As the printing press was first being used in Europe, there were those who insisted that there would always be a place in libraries for handwritten books. They were wrong. Those who — succumbing to a similar nostalgia — think there will always be a place for journalism in print are similarly wrong.

The more interesting question is how journalism originally designed for print will change as it completes this inevitable journey into a new form. Here the issue is mindset, not technology. And mindsets usually change more slowly than technologies.

For a century after the arrival of the printing press in Europe, books were still being printed with typefaces that imitated the thick, black letters of handwritten manuscripts and with illuminations that were hand painted on each page. Online journalism sites are similarly stuck. Their "pages," story formats and "headlines" haven't changed much — even in magazines, where more creativity might be expected. They make little use of the fluidity of the Web. The content of their articles has stayed mostly true to the print model, too.

Newspapers today, even online, still announce the day's events as if there weren't numerous other places — Twitter, Facebook, blogs, dozens of other easily available websites — that are announcing those events at the same time. They persist in the assumption that they are selling news, although in a world where information is available fast and free that is about as good a business as selling encyclopedias. They are figuring out only slowly that they need to sell something else — interpretations of the news, what I call "wisdom journalism."

New forms — the novel, the newspaper — were eventually invented to take best advantage of the printing press, but it took a century and a half. New approaches to journalism will have to be invented to take best advantage of digital communication. That process is just getting started.

Former *New York Times* executive editor Jill Abramson makes the commencement address at Wake Forest University on May 19, 2014, in Winston-Salem, N.C. Days earlier, *Times* Publisher Arthur Sulzberger fired Abramson, the paper's first female executive editor, and replaced her with Dean Baquet, who became the first African-American to hold the post. Sulzberger attributed the firing to "newsroom management issues," but one source of friction between Abramson and Baquet was said to be Abramson's attempt to recruit a new managing editor for digital content who would have equal standing with Baquet.

from digital and the benefits to newspapers' audiences. "We are really a multiplatform business," says Conaghan, the Newspaper Association of America's vice president for industry research and analysis. "The distribution system has gotten much wider for newspaper media companies, which certainly is an advantage to the public."

Digital-only advertising for the industry — that is, ads that are not sold in combination with print advertising — now accounts for about one-fourth of digital advertising. Conaghan acknowledges that digital advertising growth has been "slower than we would like." A new challenge, he says, is "how to monetize the growing mobile audience." The statistics show a growing reliance on mobile devices to read newspaper content: Among online readers age 34 or younger, the number who rely exclusively on mobile devices more than doubled over the past year.[49]

The *Los Angeles Times*, the fourth-largest U.S. newspaper by circulation, had the mobile device readership in mind as it redesigned its website. Visitors touring the site are greeted by the slogan, "designed to fit your life > as it happens," and later are promised that the website is "smart enough for all your devices." A laptop, tablet and

smart phone are used to illustrate. The site tour shows that users can "share effortlessly," "explore further," "join the conversation" and "find news near you." The result is described as "a completely reinvented latimes.com."

The redesign draws warm praise from Mario Garcia, a renowned newspaper designer who is president of a Tampa-based media consulting company, as "clean" and "easy to navigate."

Newspapers need to "stop regretting print," he says, and instead "learn to cope with storytelling."[50]

Closer to home, however, a writer for *L.A. Weekly* was less impressed with the redesign. Denis Romero complained of what he called the residue of "print DNA," pointing to the list of newspaper-style sections on the left side of the desktop version of the home page. He called the redesign "formulaic."[51]

The Los Angeles newspaper's online redesign comes about 20 months after a similar revamping by *USA Today,* another of the nation's biggest newspapers. In announcing the change on Sept. 18, publisher Larry Kramer said the "bold redesign" amounted to "an evolution" of the newspaper's brand "in print and across all our digital platforms."[52] Today, the newspaper says it has reclaimed its status as the nation's largest-circulation newspaper, based on a new industry standard of including digital-only readers in subscription figures.[53]

The New York Times, third-largest in circulation after *USA Today* and *The Wall Street Journal,* needs to do more to transition to the digital world, according to the 11-page internal report submitted by a team of editors and reporters in early May. The task force was headed by Arthur Gregg Sulzberger, a metro reporter and son of publisher Arthur Sulzberger Jr.[54]

The report recalls that *The Times* print and digital news staffs were once housed in separate buildings but have since been partly consolidated. But it calls for a more complete transition and a determined focus on spreading its journalistic content through social media with the creation of, among others, a "newsroom audience development team."

In a jointly signed memo to the staff, executive editor Abramson and managing editor Baquet said the report represented "another milestone in our digital transformation. They indicated changes were likely, but set no timetable.

Only a few days later, however, publisher Sulzberger summarily fired Abramson, the newspaper's first female executive editor, and replaced her with Baquet, who became the first African-American to hold the post. Sulzberger attributed the dismissal to a "newsroom management issue," but news accounts said that one source of friction between Abramson and Baquet was the attempted recruitment of a new managing editor for digital content, who was to have equal standing with Baquet.[55]

OUTLOOK
"Golden Age"?

Many baby boomer journalists are known to recall their days as youngsters delivering newspapers by saying that they "started out in circulation." Today, millions of newspaper readers still pick up a print edition. But the vast majority also read the news sometimes on screens: laptop, tablet or smartphone. And a growing number of younger news readers are "mobile-exclusive" — weaned completely off print and accustomed to news and information in their pockets.

Print-era veterans acknowledge or even embrace the change. "I've pretty much abandoned print," says media watcher Romenesko. At NYU, Stephens says, "I teach journalism students. I've stopped asking them whether they read the print version of *The New York Times.*"

Stephens professes not to be discouraged. "There's tremendous hope for journalism," he says. Another print veteran agrees that news is faring well in the digital age. "People are consuming news differently," says the American Press Institute's Rosenstiel, "but consuming more."

For much of the second half of the 20th century, news audiences were in fact disadvantaged by consolidation in the newspaper industry — the fading away of the two-newspaper town — and by the limited number of radio and television outlets until the rise of cable in the 1980s and '90s.

In the digital age, however, the barriers to entry have come down. A digital news organization needs no printing press, warehouse or fleet of delivery trucks, only a computer infrastructure and a team of good Web developers to work with so-called content producers. "The news ecosystem has increased," says the Pew Center's Jurkowitz. "There are a lot of new players."

"The largest legacy media have the advantage of having a brand," says Boczkowski, the Northwestern professor. "They have the disadvantage of being associated with traditional ideas and the disadvantage of having very high fixed costs."

With lower fixed costs, *The Huffington Post* has eclipsed *The New York Times* in total readership "in just a few years," according to *The Times* innovation study completed in April. The report warns that all of *The Times'* competitors — traditional newspaper rivals, social media such as Facebook and LinkedIn and start-ups such as *Vox* and *First Look Media* — are becoming more "digitally sophisticated."

The impact on legacy media of the newest digital-only news sites — *Vox, FiveThirtyEight, Re/code* and *The Intercept* — has yet to be seen. Nate Silver's prediction in March that Republicans were favorites to gain control of the Senate in the November elections — a reversal of his previous forecast — created instantaneous waves among politicians and political junkies.[56] Otherwise, however, none of the four new sites appears to have launched a story yet that went on to become a major item of water-cooler conversations or public policy debate.

"All of these things are young and still in experimental form," says Stephens. "It's going to take a while."

With the digital age barely in its third decade, news organizations that invested time, energy and resources in websites are already being forced to adapt to the new formatting requirements of mobile devices. "Certainly mobile is going to present a whole new set of challenges," says McGuire, the Arizona State professor. "With that smaller screen, there is so much going on. We need to develop mobile-only designs that communicate with audiences more effectively." And Conaghan, of the newspaper industry association, acknowledges that advertisers are yet to be persuaded that mobile is such a great venue for their messages.

Of the new ventures, Boczkowski thinks most will fail — just as most business startups do. Jurkowitz, too, thinks the odds of survival for any particular one are not necessarily high. "There's going to be churn," he says. For his part, though, McGuire shies away from a bearish forecast. "People are trying new things," he says.

"It's a golden age of media experimentation," McGuire concludes. "I think that's cool."

NOTES

1. Ezra Klein, "How politics makes us stupid," *Vox,* April 6, 2014, http://tinyurl.com/ocdwzru.

2. Amy Mitchell, "State of the News Media 2014," Pew Research Center Journalism Project, March 28, 2014, http://tinyurl.com/kk2opwy.

3. For background, see Marcia Clemmitt, "Social Media Explosion," *CQ Researcher,* Jan. 25, 2013, pp. 81-104.

4. For background, see these *CQ Researcher* reports: Peter Katel, "Future of TV," April 18, 2014, pp. 313-336; Tom Price, "Future of Journalism," March 27, 2009, pp. 273-296; Kenneth Jost, "The Future of Newspapers," Jan. 20, 2006, pp. 49-72.

5. Rick Edmonds, "ASNE census finds 2,600 newsroom jobs were lost in 2012," Poynter.org, June 25, 2013, http://tinyurl.com/pymo9fx.

6. Lars Willnat and David H. Weaver, "The American Journalist in the Digital Age," Indiana University School of Journalism, May 5, 2014, http://tinyurl.com/q5fjk85.

7. Mitchell Stephens, *Beyond News: The Future of Journalism* (2014), p. xii.

8. Dana Milbank, "Arianna Huffington's ideological transformation," *The Washington Post,* Feb. 9, 2011, http://tinyurl.com/p2wjtg7.

9. See Joe Pompeo, "The Huffington Post, nine years on," *Capital,* May 8, 2014, http://tinyurl.com/n7spoh6.

10. "Jim Roberts Is Mashable's Executive Editor and Chief Content Officer," *Mashable,* Oct. 31, 2013, http://tinyurl.com/qxc63xl.

11. Derek Thompson, "The Facebook Effect on News," *The Atlantic,* Feb. 12, 2014, http://tinyurl.com/o7ev4jv.

12. "State of the News Media 2014," *op. cit.*

13. Douglas Quenqua, "The Boy Wonder of BuzzFeed," *The New York Times,* Feb. 17, 2013, p. ST1, http://tinyurl.com/bhprs3c.

14. Stephens, *op. cit.* p. xxvi.

15. Ben Smith, "Tweet Victory: How Twitter and Facebook will save journalism (mostly)," *Playboy,* January 2014, http://tinyurl.com/oxmxpah.

16. Ellen Cushing, "I Think Google's Pretty Dangerous and Thuggish. I've Always Said That," *San Francisco* (magazine), April 29, 2014, http://tinyurl.com/kbua2g9.

17. Joe Coscarelli, "Ezra Klein on Vox's Launch, Media Condescension, and Competing With Wikipedia," *Daily Intelligencer, New York* magazine, April 11, 2014, http://tinyurl.com/onw8plt.

18. Lucia Moses, "Michael Wolff: 'Online journalism can't pay for itself,'" *Digiday,* April 7, 2014, http://tinyurl.com/nh2nfpp. Wolff's appearance with Carey was part of Hearst's Master Class series; others who have recently appeared include Arianna Huffington of *The Huffington Post* and Jonah Peretti of *BuzzFeed.*

19. Jessica Lessin, "Introducing The Information!" Dec. 4, 2013, http://tinyurl.com/qyluqxq; and Jenna Wortham, "A Missing Revenue Stream From Mobile Apps," *The New York Times,* Dec. 15, 2013, p. BU3, http://tinyurl.com/nn7ksm7.

20. "Key Findings From U.S. Digital Marketing Survey 2013," Gartner for Marketing Leaders, March 6, 2013, http://tinyurl.com/d4tqjfd.

21. Background drawn in part from Stephens, *A History of News* (3d. ed.), 2007; Pablo J. Boczkowski, *Digitizing the News: Innovation in Online Newspapers* (2004).

22. Tim Berners-Lee, "Frequently asked questions," undated, http://tinyurl.com/b4zy79 (accessed May 2014). See also Tim Berners-Lee, *Weaving the Web: The Original Design and Ultimate Destiny of the World Wide Web* (2000).

23. Boczkowski, *op. cit.* p. 8.

24. Estimate by the International Telecommunications Union, a United Nations agency, quoted by Jonathan Lynn, "Internet users expected to exceed 2 billion this year," Reuters, Oct. 19, 2010, http://tinyurl.com/o37q7dz.

25. "State of the News Media 2012," Pew Research Center Project for Excellence in Journalism, http://tinyurl.com/6rjxylx.

26. David Carr and Jeremy W. Peters, "Big Personality and Behind-the-Scenes Executive Prove a Top

Media Team," *The New York Times*, Feb. 8, 2011, p. B1, http://tinyurl.com/oxmq9rm.

27. Arianna Huffington, "HuffPost Game Changers: Your Picks for the Ultimate 10," *The Huffington Post,* Nov. 19, 2009, http://tinyurl.com/ndx6on9.

28. David Carr, "Significant and Silly at BuzzFeed," The New York Times, Feb. 6, 2012, p. B1, http://tinyurl.com/7utu8pb.

29. Michael Liedtke, "New iPad app mines Web links for 'social magazine,'" The Associated Press, July 21, 2010, http://tinyurl.com/nu922ma. See also Richard McManus, "How Flipboard Was Created and its Plans beyond iPad," *readwrite,* Oct. 6, 2010, http://tinyurl.com/nocht4l.

30. Claire Cain Miller, "Flipboard Introduces an iPhone App for Killing Time Standing in Line," Bits *(New York Times* blog), Dec. 7, 2011, http://tinyurl.com/ph8wgo8.

31. Ed Pilkington, "New media gurus launch Upworthy — their 'super basic' internet startup," *The Guardian,* March 26, 2012, http://tinyurl.com/o3pzylx.

32. Pompeo, *op. cit.;* Carr, "Significant and Silly at Buzzfeed," *op. cit.*

33. Walt Mossberg and Kara Swisher, "You Say Goodbye and We Say Hello," *AllThingsD.com,* Dec. 31, 2013, http://tinyurl.com/lxbpd4a.

34. "Economy Department with Ezra Klein," *The Washington Post,* June 11, 2009, http://tinyurl.com/medwqn.

35. Brian Stelter, "Times to Host Blog on Politics and Polls," *The New York Times*, June 4, 2010, p. B2, http://tinyurl.com/oqhcbjl.

36. Noam Cohen and Quentin Hardy, "Snowden Journalist's New Venture to Be Bankrolled by eBay Founder," *The New York Times,* Oct. 17, 2013, p. B1, http://tinyurl.com/q9etmuw.

37. Brian Stelter, "Blogger for Times Is to Join ESPN Staff," *The New York Times,* July 20, 2013, p. B6, http://tinyurl.com/nympltn.

38. Mossberg and Swisher, *op. cit.;* and Brian Stelter, "Re/code: new site launched by All ThingsD founders," CNNMoney, Jan. 2, 2014, http://tinyurl.com/lakbw9d.

39. Ravi Somaiya, "Top Wonkblog Columnist to Leave Washington Post," *The New York Times,* Jan. 22, 2014, p. B6, http://tinyurl.com/plhq4ar.

40. David Carr, "A Big Hire Signals Web News Is Thriving," *The New York Times,* Jan. 27, 2014, p. B1, http://tinyurl.com/k58kx3k.

41. *Ibid.*

42. Leslie Kaufman, "Vox Takes Melding of Journalism and Technology to New Level," *The New York Times*, April 7, 2014, p. B1, http://tinyurl.com/ms97rhe.

43. Joe Coscarelli, "Ezra Klein on Vox's Launch, Media Condescension, and Competing With Wikipedia," *New York Magazine,* http://tinyurl.com/onw8plt.

44. Nate Silver, "What the Fox Knows," *Five ThirtyEight.com,* March 17, 2014, http://tinyurl.com/q6cduqb.

45. Nate Silver, "Are White Republicans More Racist Than White Democrats?" *FiveThirty Eight.com,* April 24, 2014, http://tinyurl.com/k35qs6a; Emily Oster, "Are Older Men's Sperm Really Any Worse?" *FiveThirtyEight.com,* April 24, 2014, http://tinyurl.com/k9m8exp; and Walt Hickey, "Where Cheerleading Ranks in Safety Among High School Sports," *Five ThirtyEight.com,* May 11, 2014, http://tinyurl.com/kjg7bxp.

46. Glenn Greenwald, Laura Poitras and Jeremy Scahill, "Welcome to The Intercept," *The Intercept,* Feb. 10, 2014, http://tinyurl.com/m9bt2u5; and John Cook, "Passover Greetings from the Editor," *The Intercept,* April 14, 2014, http://tinyurl.com/puykfzf.

47. Richard Lyon, "First Look Media/The Intercept Appears to Be Stalled," *dailykos,* April 14, 2014, http://tinyurl.com/ntnehxo.

48. "Business Model Evolving, Circulation Revenue Rising," Newspaper Association of America, April 18, 2014, http://tinyurl.com/kljkoj7; and Rick Edmonds, "Newspaper industry narrowed revenue loss in 2013 as paywall plans increased," Poynter, April 18, 2014, http://tinyurl.com/mtj7vnv.

49. Jim Conaghan, "Mobile-Exclusive Surges Among Young Adults," Newspaper Association of America, April 28, 2014, http://tinyurl.com/o3t5w23.

50. Mario R. Garcia, "New Los Angeles Times website: innovative, inspiring," Garcia Media, May 7, 2014, http://tinyurl.com/qfjam6w.

51. Dennis Romero, "Los Angeles Times Website Redesign Is Meh," *L.A. Weekly,* May 6, 2014, http://tinyurl.com/qcvm7xx.

52. "Welcome to USA Today — again," *USA Today,* Sept. 14, 2012, p. 1A.

53. "USA Today regains national circulation lead," *USA Today,* Oct. 21, 2013, http://tinyurl.com/qzd5cj5.

54. Joe Pompeo, "New York Times Completes 'Innovation Report' by Sulzberger Scion," *Capital,* May 8, 2014, http://tinyurl.com/l2z5bds. Pompeo's story includes this link to the report itself: http://tinyurl.com/q39y9wz ("Innovation Study").

55. David Carr, "Abramson's Exit at The Times Puts Tensions on Display," *The New York Times,* May 18, 2014, http://tinyurl.com/odc557x.

56. Nate Silver, "FiveThirtyEight Senate Forecast: GOP Is Slight Favorite in Race for Senate Control," *FiveThirtyEight.com,* March 23, 2014, http://tinyurl.com/lskyb92; and Catalina Camia, "Senate Democrats Debunk Nate Silver's GOP-favored Forecast," *On Politics* (*USA Today*), March 24, 2014, http://tinyurl.com/ommef5s.

BIBLIOGRAPHY

Selected Sources

Books

Boczkowski, Pablo, *Digitizing the News: Innovation in Online Newspapers,* **MIT Press, 2004.**
A professor and director of the Program in Media, Technology and Society at Northwestern University examines the early days of electronic newspaper publishing. Includes detailed notes, bibliography.

Boler, Megan, ed., *Digital Media and Democracy: Tactics in Hard Times,* **MIT Press, 2008.**
A professor of the history and philosophy of education at the University of Toronto examines, via essays by scholars, journalists and activists, the role of digital media in creating new avenues for exploring truth and practicing media activism.

Palfrey, John, and Urs Gasser, *Born Digital: Understanding the First Generation of Digital Natives,* **Basic Books, 2008.**
The authors explore philosophical and practical issues about "digital natives," children born into and raised in a digital world. Palfrey, head of school at Phillips Academy in Andover, Mass., was formerly executive director of Harvard University's Beekman Center on Internet and Society; Gasser is a professor at Harvard Law School and current executive director of the Beekman Center.

Stephens, Mitchell, *Beyond News: The Future of Journalism,* **Columbia University Press, 2014.**
A professor at New York University's Arthur L. Carter Institute argues that in the digital age there is a need for what he calls "wisdom journalism" – providing analysis and opinion along with fact-based reporting. Stephens also wrote *A History of News* (3d. ed., Oxford University Press, 2007).

Usher, Nikki, *Making News at* **The New York Times, University of Michigan Press, 2014.**
An assistant professor at George Washington University's School of Media and Public Affairs examines the inner workings of *The New York Times,* including the tension between print and digital content, based on unique access to the Times' newsroom from January to June 2010.

Articles

Gapper, John, "Silicon Valley gets excited about a small story," *Financial Times,* **April 9, 2014, http://tinyurl.com/l9uval8.**
Columnist Gapper questions the potential profitability of digital start-ups Vox.com and FiveThirtyEight.com.

Grabowicz, Paul, "The Transition to Digital Journalism," **Knight Digital Media Center, University of California-Berkeley Graduate School of Journalism, updated March 2014, http://tinyurl.com/kd5gnun.**
This comprehensive tutorial on digital journalism covers major digital tools and trends; it includes embedded links to a vast number of resources from a variety of research organizations, news media and scholars and experts.

Packer, George, "Telling Stories About the Future of Journalism," *The New Yorker*, Jan. 28, 2014, http://tinyurl.com/lqy682c.
The article discusses Ezra Klein's plan to launch a new digital news site, Vox.com.

Scott, Ben, "A Contemporary History of Digital Journalism," *Television and New Media*, February 2005, pp. 89-126.
The article traces the history of online journalism from its birth in the mid-1990s to a period of relative stabilization early in the 21st century.

Reports and Studies

"State of the News Media 2014," Pew Research Journalism Project, March 26, 2014, http://tinyurl.com/kk2opwy.
The annual report by the Washington-based research center examines the growth and growing importance of digital news media.

Grueskin, Bill, Ava Seaves, and Lucas Graves, "The Story So Far: What We Know About the Business of Digital Journalism," Tow Center for Digital Journalism, Columbia University Graduate School of Journalism, May 2011, http://tinyurl.com/6aumlu3.
The 140-page comprehensive report examines the economics of digital journalism at for-profit news organizations.

Stencel, Mark, Bill Adair, and Prashanth Kamalakanthan, "The Goat Must Be Fed: Why digital tools are missing in most newsrooms: A report of the Duke Reporters' Lab," May 2014, http://tinyurl.com/o8qkwd7.
The 21-page report finds that newsrooms are slow in using digital tools to find and sift government information, analyze social media and crunch data.

On the Web

"CJR's Guide to Online News Startups," *Columbia Journalism Review*, http://tinyurl.com/l8b3xg7 (accessed May 2014).
The site features a continually updated database of digital news outlets across the country.

For More Information

American Press Institute, 4401 Wilson Blvd., Suite 900, Arlington, VA 22203; 571-366-1200; www.americanpressinstitute.org. Journalism research and training organization founded in 1946 and affiliated with Newspaper Association of America since 2012.

Arthur L. Carter Journalism Institute, New York University, 20 Cooper Square, 6th floor, New York, NY 10003; 212-998-7980; www.journalism.nyu.edu. Graduate program in journalism.

MPA — The Association of Magazine Media, 757 Third Ave., 11th Floor, New York, NY 10017; 212-872-3700; www.magazine.org. Trade association for the magazine industry, formerly known as Magazine Publishers Association.

Newspaper Association of America, 4401 Wilson Blvd., Suite 900, Arlington, VA 22203; 571-366-1000; www.newspapers.org. Trade association for the newspaper industry.

Online News Association; *http://journalists.org. Membership organization for digital journalists.*

Pew Research Center Journalism Project, 1615 L St., N.W., Suite 700, Washington, DC 20036; 202-419-4300; www.journalism.org. Publishes annual reports — "State of the News Media."

Tow Center for Digital Journalism, Columbia University Graduate School of Journalism, Pulitzer Hall, 6th floor, 116th St. and Broadway, New York, NY 10027; 212-854-1945; www.towcenter.org. Institute established in 2012 to foster development of digital journalism.

10

Conspiracy Theories

Do they threaten democracy?

Peter Katel

Radio-show host Alex Jones warns listeners that Americans could be taken to detention camps by the government and tortured and murdered. Actor Charlie Sheen, a so-called "truther," recently declared on Jones' show, "The official 9/11 story is an absolute fairy tale, a work of fiction." Jones' popularity reflects the enduring appeal of conspiracy theories throughout U.S. history.

From *CQ Researcher,*
October 23, 2009

R adio-show host Alex Jones says Americans should be scared — really scared. Pretty soon, he warned listeners earlier this year, trucks will be pulling up in front of their houses to take them to Federal Emergency Management Agency (FEMA) detention camps.

Televised government propaganda will assure people the camps are for their safety, says Jones, and to outward appearances everything will be fine — "except for those being . . . put in an acid bath or killed or flown to a black site. You've got to ask [yourself] when the truck pulls up, 'Are you going to go to the camp? . . . That's the point where it's lock-and-load time. I'm not going to a camp where some piece of filth guard is going to break my family up and take me off for interrogation where they can torture me for two years."[1]

Until recently, Jones was largely unknown outside the circle of conspiracy-theory fans of his Austin, Texas-based show. Over the past several months, however, his over-the-top claims have landed him on Fox News and brought celebrity guests to his own program, such as actor Charlie Sheen, a supporter of the so-called "truther" movement, which claims that airborne terrorists couldn't have inflicted the damage done by the Sept. 11 attacks and that, consequently, there must have been some degree of government involvement. "The official 9/11 story is an absolute fairy tale, a work of fiction," he said.[2]

Jones' own views about the Sept. 11, 2001, terror attacks run along the same lines. "I see this whole cover-up collapsing," he told Sheen.

From UFOs to Secret Societies

The popular conspiracy theory Web sites below are among hundreds of sites that present alternative theories on everything from 9/11 to environmental policies. They use the Internet to question mainstream ideas and have acquired a large following in recent years.

1   **Above Top Secret**   www.abovetopsecret.com/
With nearly 176,000 members, the site is the Internet's largest and most popular community dedicated to a wide range of conspiracy topics, including UFOs, paranormal activity, secret societies, political scandals, "new world order" and terrorism.

2   **Prison Planet**   www.prisonplanet.com/
Affiliated with radio host Alex Jones, the site features forums where members can discuss alternative theories on everything from 9/11 to swine flu vaccinations.

3   **Infowars**   www.infowars.com
Radio broadcaster Alex Jones examines numerous topics and presents interviews with fellow "9/11 Truthers," such as country singer Willie Nelson.

4   **911 Truth**   www.911truth.org
Calls into question the U.S. government's account of the events of 9/11/2001 and discusses alternative theories. The site wtc7.net features similar content.

5   **Centre for Research on Globalization**   http://globalresearch.ca/
Based in Canada, the site promotes the "unspoken truth" on issues ranging from the U.S. invasion of Iraq to environmental policies.

6   **What Really Happened**   www.whatreallyhappened.com
Presents alternative theories focusing on the War on Terror and accuses the U.S. government of hiding information.

7   **The Zeitgeist Movement**   www.thezeitgeistmovement.com
Promotes the idea that nations, governments, races, religions, creeds and social classes are false distinctions. Seeks to achieve unity among people through a common conception of nature.

8   **The Jeff Rense Program**   www.rense.com
Radio broadcaster Rense positions himself as an opponent to mainstream news coverage. His Web site and radio broadcasts cover the daily news from an alternative perspective.

9   **YouTube**   www.youtube.com
Most conspiracy theorists are putting their content here now in order to gain a wide audience.

10   **David Icke**   www.davidicke.com/index.php/
Icke is popular with people who want to ridicule conspiracy theorists because he presents radical conspiracy theories, but he does not have a significant following among conspiracy theorists themselves.

Source: Edward L. Winston, conspiracyscience.com, Oct. 15, 2009

Jones maintains a Web site that gets roughly as much traffic as those of either conservative talk-show host Rush Limbaugh or the liberal news site Talking Points Memo.[3]

The popularity of Jones' Web site points to the widespread appeal today of conspiracy theories and the corresponding emergence of hundreds of conspiracy-oriented Web sites, videos and books. Among their recent claims: President Barack Obama isn't a U.S. citizen, and the "truth" about 9/11 remains hidden from most Americans.

Such theories represent only the latest variations on a conspiracy theme that traces its origin to the nation's earliest days. The early conspiracists believed that American presidents headed criminal or treasonous conspiracies, some of them linked to longtime "villains," such as international bankers and Jews. Indeed, presidential conspiracy theories run in an unbroken chain since President George H. W. Bush proposed a New World Order and, conspiracists believed, plotted the takeover of the United States.

The 2007 documentary-style movie "Zeitgeist," for example, links 9/11 to an alleged plot that drew the United States into both world wars as well as the Vietnam War. An earlier, Web-distributed movie, "Loose Change," played a key role in fostering the conspiracist view of the Sept. 11 attacks. More recently, bestselling author Dan Brown draws on conspiracy notions about the Freemasons in his new novel, *The Lost Symbol,* much as his phenomenally popular *DaVinci Code* involved an ancient conspiracy within the Roman Catholic Church.

Oliver Stone's 1991 film "JFK" presented one of the most persistent conspiracy subjects — President John F. Kennedy's assassination — including the purported involvement of U.S. intelligence and military agencies. "The X-Files," a hit TV series in the '90s, merged Kennedy assassination and space-alien theories.

The view of events as stage-managed affairs designed to fool the public runs deep enough that an estimated 6 percent of the American people believe that the 1969 moon landing was a hoax. "A model of the moon is used for the *Apollo 11* descent footage," wrote Bart Sibrel, a Nashville filmmaker who made a movie to argue his theory. "Anyone with basic knowledge of motion pictures can see it's a fake moon." The National Aeronautics and Space Administration is concerned enough about the doubters to post detailed rebuttals on its Web site.[4]

Underlying many conspiracy theories is distrust of government, says John E. Moser, a history professor at Ohio's Ashland University. "We don't trust leaders anymore," says Moser, a specialist in 20th-century conspiracism. "Maybe that's a good thing, but it certainly leaves the door open to kookery. At various points in history, conspiracy theories captured a great part of the population, but they fizzled out as the sense of crisis passed. Now, conspiracy theories tend to stick around. I'm wondering if we're not in a permanent crisis mode."

Some experts even worry that the cynicism reflected in conspiracy theories today endangers U.S. democracy, not to mention Americans' health: Conspiracy theorists even have stoked the widespread opposition to swine flu vaccine.

One thing is certain: Thanks to the ever-expanding Internet, disclosures of genuine government misdeeds have intensified the public's suspicions. Moreover,

Most Regard Obama as American-Born

More than half of Americans believe that President Obama was born in the United States, not Kenya, including more than three-fourths of Democrats. But more than 60 percent of Republicans are skeptical. Nearly a quarter of Americans believe President George W. Bush knew about the Sept. 11 attacks before they occurred.

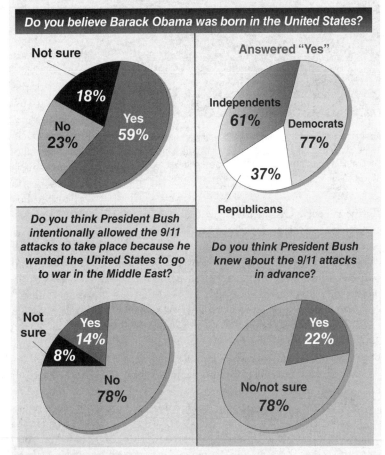

Sources: Public Policy Polling; Rasmussen Reports

today's unsettled climate — dominated by scandal, economic turmoil, war and intense partisan conflict — stimulates a search for explanations that often reach extremes.

A Public Policy Polling survey in September showed that 41 percent of Americans — and 64 percent of Republicans — didn't believe or weren't sure President Obama was born in the United States. Indeed, many

National Aeronautics and Space Administration

Apollo 11 astronaut Buzz Aldrin walks on the Moon on July 20, 1969. Six percent of Americans think the historic landing was a government hoax, prompting NASA to post detailed rebuttals on its Web site.

"birthers" believe Obama has engaged in a decades-long deception about his place of birth. And 22 percent of all voters — and 37 percent of Democrats — either believed or questioned whether former President George W. Bush purposely allowed the 9/11 attacks to occur to provide a pretext for war in the Middle East.[5]

Although the sample size was a relatively small 621 respondents, the results were consistent with a broader 2007 poll showing 22 percent of respondents thought Bush knew of the 9/11 attacks in advance.[6]

The "birther" movement is raising enough jitters in the political mainstream that the Senate and House passed resolutions last July stating that Obama was born in Hawaii.[7]

The resolutions followed the introduction of "birther"-influenced legislation proposed by Rep. Bill Posey, R-Fla., that would require presidential candidates to provide birth certificates; 11 House Republicans signed the bill. Limbaugh and Michael Savage, another conservative commentator, last year joined the chorus of those deriding Obama's citizenship credentials.[8]

Administration officials, however, touch conspiracy matters at their peril. In September, Van Jones, an Obama environmental adviser, resigned after disclosure that he had signed a 2004 petition, popular with some on the left, calling for "immediate inquiry into evidence that suggests high-level government officials may have deliberately allowed the Sept. 11 attacks to occur."[9]

Those who've tried arguing with "truthers" often find themselves accused of being in on the plot — a classic feature of conspiracy theories. For example, after an exhaustive investigation by *Popular Mechanics* debunked 9/11 conspiracy theories, the magazine was accused of being a CIA front and a friend of Israeli intelligence.[10]

"A common refrain in conspiracy circles is the claim that, 'We're just asking questions,'" wrote editor-in-chief James B. Meigs. "One would think that at least some quarters of the conspiracy movement might welcome a mainstream publication's serious, nonideological attempt to answer those questions. One would be wrong."

Conspiracists such as the late W. Cleon Skousen insist that major public figures can generate smoke screens that obscure conspiracies in action. A former Brigham Young University professor and FBI agent, Skousen heavily influenced Fox TV talk-show host Glenn Beck, whose introduction to one of Skousen's books describes his writing as "divinely inspired."[11]

Skousen envisioned a plot by banker David Rockefeller and others in the financial elite to establish "ruler's law" — as opposed to God's law — in the U.S. "Rockefeller . . . has a plan," Skousen once said. "He wants to restore ruler's law and force the stupid masses — those are Lenin's words — to do what's good for them."[12]

Beck hasn't explicitly endorsed that view. But in September he hinted at a connection between the Rockefeller family, radical politics and Obama appointee Van Jones. The takeoff point was Beck's interpretations of the artwork at Rockefeller Center by early-20th-century fascist and communist-inspired artists. "It makes sense that you feel a little uneasy, and everything seems to be a little hidden," Beck said. "Progressives, fascists, communists — now what do they all have in common today? That's something you're going to have to figure out." But he added, "The Rockefeller Foundation, they gave a big award and an awful lot of credibility to — oh, Van Jones, our new green jobs czar."[13]

Beck had flirted with the idea that FEMA was setting up detention camps, but he eventually said evidence was lacking, telling CBS News anchor Katie Couric that the camps theory was "easy to debunk." He also told her he is not a conspiracy theorist.[14] Jerome R. Corsi, a frequent guest on Alex Jones' program, also rejects the conspiracist label.[15] "I don't think the term has any meaning," he says. "It's an intentionally politically charged term that's used to demonize work somebody doesn't agree with politically." He describes himself as an investigative reporter and is active in the network of Obama-citizenship challengers.

But conspiracist or not, Corsi readily evokes the specter of Nazi Germany in describing a House bill introduced in January by Rep. Alcee Hastings, D-Fla. The bill would create six National Emergency Centers on military bases for use by communities hit by natural disasters.[16] Corsi wrote that the legislation "appears designed to create the type of detention center that those concerned about use of the military in domestic affairs fear could be used as concentration camps for political dissidents, as in Nazi Germany."[17]

Jones also depicts those he sees as the country's enemies in the most sinister terms, along with the mainstream media that he accuses of serving the conspiracy. Jones' Web site said the H1N1 flu originated with "powerful industrialists operating a crime ring [who] are behind the pandemic's creation, media persuasions, vaccination preparations and health official promotions."[18]

The "globalists" who run the conspiracy have to be fought, Jones preaches. "I just want to get my hands around their throats. . . . And you know they feel the same about us."[19]

As conspiracy theories proliferate, here are some of the questions being debated:

Are conspiracy theories becoming part of mainstream politics?

Conspiracy theories are woven into the fabric of U.S. history. Some have become national issues, such as those involving a real secret society — but one that never left Europe — known as the Illuminati, whose supposed goal was subverting the nation.

The Illuminati theory was transplanted to the newly founded United States by defenders of the old European order that was overthrown by the French Revolution. Anti-Masonic theories, also transplanted from Europe, typically were adopted by con-spiracists who argued that the Masons were out to destroy Christianity.

Past generations of conspiracists, however, didn't enjoy the global electronic megaphone — the Internet — that their political descendants now command. Radio and cable TV talk shows also have helped conspiracists reach wider audiences.

One of the day's hottest issues concerns Obama's birthplace. "Where's the birth certificate?" asked a placard-carrying demonstrator at the "09.12.09 March on Washington."[20] Other signs at the rally depicted the president as, variously, a Nazi, a socialist and a communist.

While the embrace of the "birthers" by some radio and cable-TV talk-show hosts demonstrates the reach of conspiracy theories, experts disagree whether their appeal imbues them with political relevance. (Some conservative Obama foes vigorously reject the birthers.)

Political analyst Chip Berlet, a longtime chronicler of conspiracy movements, argues that conspiracy theories are on the upswing both in volume and influence.[21] "The government lacks transparency, which encourages a sense of delegitimization," says Berlet, of Political Research Associates, a liberal consultancy in Cambridge, Mass. "And for a lot of conservative people, to have a black boss whom they see as a bully is quite unsettling. Proxies for that attitude are seen in claims Obama is a Muslim, or was not born in the United States or plans to socialize the economy through health-care reform."

Berlet argues that conspiracy theories can help knit together groups that fundamentally have little use for each other — the Christian right, economic libertarians and white nationalists, to name a few. "All these sectors are pushing the idea that Obama is conspiring against the well-being of America."

Not all conspiracy experts see an immediate danger. The fact that conspiracy theories are widely disseminated doesn't in itself constitute a threat, says Daniel Pipes, director of the Philadelphia-based Middle East Forum, which advocates for U.S. interests in the Middle East. "Ultimately, it's the impact that's more important than volume," says Pipes, who has written about conspiracy theories in U.S., Middle Eastern and European settings. "I see them more than I did 15 years ago, but their impact is still limited. You don't see them really having an impact on the policies of government and the actions of Americans."

Pipes cites the long-lived constellation of conspiracy theories about JFK's death that has spread throughout popular culture to little political effect. "Kennedy assassination theories are voluminous, but irrelevant," he says.

Other scholars argue that conspiracy theories challenging Obama's legitimacy as president have the potential to be influential. "It seems that the election of an African-American president has triggered the anxieties of a big segment of the white population," says Kathryn S. Olmsted, a professor of history at the University of California, Davis, and author of the new book *Real Enemies: Conspiracy Theories and American Democracy, World War I to 9/11.*[22]

The racial factor, she says, adds a dimension that was absent in the conspiracy theories centering on President Bill Clinton. They reflected the fear and suspicion of growing federal power — as seen in violent confrontations between federal agents and armed government opponents. Whether the anti-Obama theories reach that level of intensity remains to be seen, Olmsted acknowledges. But, she says, "I think we're in new territory."

The communications revolution alone ensures that conspiracy theorists can reach millions more people, says Ashland University's Moser. "Back in the 1930s, what we call today the mainstream media was pretty much *the* source of information," says Moser, author of a biography of Pearl Harbor conspiracy theorist John T. Flynn.[23] "In the archives, you find conspiracy theories back then were expressed in very amateurish-looking newsletters, created on typewriter and circulated by mimeograph. Today they're in very slick online formats."

Still, presentation and audience don't automatically confer influence, Moser adds. In fact, the easy accessibility of platforms may encourage some media figures to latch on to conspiracy theories — the more attention-grabbing the better — simply to get or keep audiences. For instance, "If you have a radio show, and you're going to be on for three or four hours a day," he says, "you have to say things that are going to get peoples' attention. There's no place for wonkishness in the talk-radio format."

Do conspiracy theories appeal more to the right than the left?

A long tradition among historians and political scientists links conspiracy theories with the far right. Historian Richard Hofstadter's classic 1963 essay, "The Paranoid Style in American Politics," focused exclusively on right-wing conspiracism. "The modern right wing . . . feels dispossessed: America has been largely taken away from them and their kind," he wrote. "The old national security and independence have been destroyed by treasonous plots, having as their most powerful agents not merely outsiders and foreigners but major statesmen seated at the very centers of American power."[24]

Increasingly, however, conspiracy theory-watchers are concluding that conspiracism's appeal goes beyond ideology. For instance, the "truther" theories about the 9/11 attacks have attracted both left- and right-wingers. Indeed, some scholars have argued in recent years that theories once closely associated with the right have been attracting followers from the left. Anti-Semitism is the classic case, in the form of left-wing attacks on Israel that challenge its right to exist.

Shortly before the war in Iraq began in 2003, a conflict erupted in the antiwar left after Rabbi Michael Lerner of Berkeley, Calif., was blocked from speaking at a peace rally in San Francisco. Lerner had criticized one of the organizations sponsoring the event for planning to use it for anti-Israel propaganda purposes. "Fellow progressive Jews, some anxious to speak at these rallies, have urged me to keep quiet about anti-Semitism on the left," Lerner wrote in *The Wall Street Journal.*[25]

Since then, however, the furor over anti-Jewish prejudice on the left has quieted along with the anti-war movement. And some conspiracy theory opponents view the major conspiracist current of the moment as a right-wing trend. "Of all the conspiracy theorists, 90 percent are on the far right," says Edward L. Winston, a St. Louis software engineer who runs a conspiracy-debunking Web site (conspiracyscience.com).

But Winston adds that the widespread and growing skepticism about government favors the expansion of conspiracism beyond what he considers its natural right-wing constituency. Media productions such as the first "Zeitgeist" movie — which mixes classical conspiracy theories about "international bankers" and new ones about Sept. 11 — may be broadening the ranks of conspiracy believers, he says. "I was surprised how popular 'Zeitgeist' was and how many people believed it," he says.

Conspiracy scholar Pipes argues that linking conspiracy theories exclusively to the right is a long-standing and erroneous response. "It's as much a left phenomenon as it is right," he says. "I would argue that the whole premise of communist ideology is a conspiracy theory — that the bosses are stealing your money."

Vladimir I. Lenin — founder of the Soviet state — in effect confirmed the vision of those who denounced communist conspiracies, Pipes has argued. Lenin had concluded the countries that embraced capitalism took that path because the big-business class had covertly seized government power. Communists should follow that example, Lenin argued, and greet charges of conspiratorial methods as "flattering."[26]

The University of California's Olmsted argues that right-wing conspiracy theories tend to gain more traction, though she acknowledges that conspiracy theories appeal to the extremes on both right and left. "They feel they know the truth, yet the majority of the country votes against them," she says. "Most people don't share their beliefs — or they think evil people in power are manipulating things."

Still, conspiracy theories that appeal to those on the right usually become more prominent, Olmsted says, "because they're backed generally by people with more power." Contrasting the attention that Limbaugh and other radio and TV talk-show hosts have given the "birther" theories, Olmsted notes that comparably popular supporters can't be found for the "truther" conspiracists. "Is there anyone really significant out there" among the 9/11 conspiracists "who has a real platform?" The "truther" movement generated no congressional legislation along the lines of the recent bill on birth certificates for presidential candidates.

Even so, the economic crisis may favor a resurgence of conspiracy theories that appeal to the left, says Michael Barkun, a professor of political science at Syracuse University who has studied conspiracies throughout his career. But that holds true for right-oriented theories as well, he adds. "Going well back into the 19th century, American conspiracists had almost a stylistic preference for conspiracy theories that emphasize financial power or financial manipulation," he says. That preference applies on the left and right.

In general, conspiracy theories draw their strength from deep-seated needs and emotions, not from ideology, Barkun says. "Conspiracy theories have the psychological benefit of taking a complex reality and simplifying it. Whatever these things that bother you, they all are the result of some single cause."

Do conspiracy theories threaten democracy?

The American system of government has survived more than 250 years of conspiracy theories, but the global picture is far grimmer.

In the 20th century alone, Nazi leader Adolf Hitler convinced millions of Germans that Jews were an evil force that had to be exterminated. Josef Stalin persuaded communists and sympathizers around the world that the millions of revolutionaries — and ordinary citizens — executed in the "Great Terror" of 1937-1938 had been plotting the destruction of the Soviet state.

But conspiracy theories cooked up abroad also have proved dangerous to Americans. The 19 men who carried out the Sept. 11 attacks on the United States had been deeply influenced by a conspiratorial ideology that saw Muslims in general and Arabs in particular as the objects of manipulation by Western powers and Jews.[27]

Mohammed Atta, the terrorists' onscene commander, believed the Jews were behind wars against Muslims in the former Yugoslavia and Chechnya (now a Russian province). Even the White House sex scandal involving President Clinton fit into Atta's conspiratorial worldview, writes Lawrence Wright in his Pulitzer Prize-winning chronicle of the roots of the 2001 attacks. "He believed that Monica Lewinsky was a Jewish agent sent to undermine Clinton, who had become too sympathetic to the Palestinian cause."[28]

Made-in-the-U.S.A. conspiracy theories generally have generated passion and activism — and violence — without producing major alterations in the course of events, even when believers have tried to exert influence. Timothy McVeigh, who detonated the powerful fertilizer bomb that destroyed the federal building in Oklahoma City in 1995, apparently believed he would spark a revolution against the Jewish-dominated system he perceived.[29]

McVeigh killed 168 people, including 19 children, but no revolution occurred. Other conspiracists also were involved in conflicts that ended in multiple deaths, notably the 1993 showdown near Waco, Texas, at the Branch Davidian compound, in which about 80 sect members and four federal agents died. Church leader David Koresh had expounded "new world order" conspiracy theories in the 1990s. And earlier this year, a man in Pittsburgh, Richard Poplawski, was charged with killing three police officers in a confrontation apparently sparked by his beliefs in a coming social collapse engineered by "elite Jewish powers."[30]

Those deaths, and others, bolster the argument by some conspiracy scholars that conspiracism represents a danger not to be taken lightly. "They can be a threat to democracy in the sense that conspiracy theories are premised on the idea that nothing is as it seems, that appearances can never be trusted," says Barkun of Syracuse University." If you take that seriously, as many conspiracy believers do, then the work of democratic institutions is deemed fraudulent or a charade."

If large numbers of people believe the real work of government is carried out by people pulling strings behind the scenes, Barkun says, "that delegitimizes the political process."

The Middle East Forum's Pipes agrees, in principle, that conspiracy theories could threaten democracy. In practice, though, he thinks their appeal to Americans is limited. "I don't see a surge" in conspiracy believers, he says. For example, Pipes notes, the fringe views of Obama's former minister in Chicago, the Rev. Jeremiah Wright — who believed HIV was a government-invented tool of genocide — proved unacceptable in mainstream politics.[31]

"He was marginalized and repudiated," Pipes says.

Conspiracy-watchers who have direct contact with conspiracy theory believers tend to be more likely to sense danger. "They don't care about the republic," debunker Winston says of people who post comments on his Facebook page. "Anyone who disagrees is an enemy. Conspiracy theorists claim that I really work for the government, that I'm getting paid to do this. Since I mounted a Web site, the consensus is that if I'm smart enough to do that, I must be getting paid."

Winston has heard worse. "When I had my e-mail address posted, probably 50 percent of the e-mails I got were death threats or threats in general," he says. "So I didn't have it up for long."

Even John Hawkins, who edits the "Right Wing News" Web site — slogan: "kneecapping Barack Obama at every opportunity" — has attracted hate mail for his scornful treatment of Obama-birthplace challenges, which he calls groundless. But that response hasn't persuaded him that conspiracism represents a threat. "It would have to cross into the mainstream, and so many people who knew better would have to say nothing."

Conspiracy theories do exert a strong appeal, given the natural urge to find explanations for events and trends, Hawkins says. But the theories, he argues, tend to be so intricate and dependent on leaps of faith that

they're easily punctured. "Everybody wants to believe that everything is not random and that somebody has control," he says. "But I'm a conservative, I believe that government is too dumb to carry out these conspiracies. If you had enough people addressing a lot of these conspiracy theories, they would die down."

BACKGROUND
Witch Hysteria

In 1692, nearly a century before American independence, 20 men and women were executed in Salem, Mass. Their crime: They were thought to be witches plotting evil in the service of the devil. Historian Jeffrey L. Pasley of the University of Missouri calls the witch hysteria that briefly swept New England "the very first American conspiracy theories."[32]

As Americans were fighting for independence in 1776, a law professor in Bavaria (now a German state) founded Illuminism, a political philosophy that sought to create a world ruled by reason, not clerics — a blasphemous notion in a Roman Catholic state.[33]

In 1784, the Society of the Illuminati, which had joined forces with the anti-clerical Freemasons, was outlawed in Bavaria amid a series of lurid confessions and supposed instructions on poisoning and counterfeiting. Defenders of the old order that was being shaken by the winds of change said the evidence proved the Illuminati had survived repression and were behind the French Revolution and ensuing Jacobin Reign of Terror and ultimately sought world domination.

Two books, one by a University of Glasgow scientist and the other by a French Jesuit priest, soon brought the Illuminati conspiracy theory to the United States. They claimed to have proved that the Illuminists aimed at world domination and the destruction of religion and morality. The Federalists, headed by President John Adams, feared that American acolytes of the radical Jacobin wing of the French revolutionaries were planning a wave of anti-religious destruction. However, after Thomas Jefferson — a French Revolution supporter whom some Federalists considered an Illuminist — became president in 1801, Illuminist conspiracy fears faded.

But a wave of accusations against the Freemasons followed. Masonry, a conspiracy theorist claimed, was "an engine of Satan . . . blasphemous, murderous, anti-republican and anti-Christian."[34]

Denunciations of Masonry were followed by a more influential conspiracy theory centered on the Catholic Church. "A conspiracy exists . . . its plans are already in operation," wrote Samuel Morse, inventor of the telegraph, in the 1830s. Its agents, he said, included "Jesuit missionaries traveling through the land."[35]

As in other countries, U.S. conspiracy theories flourished during conflicts leading to war. Before the Civil War, abolitionists feared that Southern conspiracists were plotting to take over the federal government to ensure slavery's survival.[36]

Southerners and others indeed wanted to ensure slavery's future, and its extension to newly created states, such as Kansas and California. While no proof of a federal takeover conspiracy surfaced, the so-called "slave power" plot set the stage for 20th-century conspiracy theories that built on established fact.

Conspiracy American-Style

Americans in the 19th century began shaping their own conspiracy theories. But unlike their Old World models, which reflected threats to an ethnic homogeneity unknown in the U.S. melting pot, American conspiracy theories tended to focus on powerful and evil men acting in secret.

"A small, unelected minority representing un-American interests . . . takes over the federal government and uses it against the people," writes conspiracy scholar Pipes at the Middle East Forum.[37] Even U.S. conspiracism focusing on Jews and Catholics typically centered on alleged manipulation rather than on threats to racial purity. Europe's Rothschild banking family typically was cited to signify alleged Jewish control of world finances. As for Catholics in the late 19th century, they were "suspect as the pawns of a foreign power."[38]

By the mid-20th century, fear of foreign powers had morphed into fear that U.S. leaders were selling out the country's interests to foreigners. Following the devastating Japanese surprise attack on Pearl Harbor on Dec. 7, 1941, some U.S. isolationists claimed President Franklin D. Roosevelt had known about — and allowed — the attack because it would plunge the United States into the war in Europe.

In a 1944 article — "The Truth About Pearl Harbor" — *The Chicago Tribune* argued that Roosevelt had deliberately incited Japanese hostility, learned of the impending attack, failed to warn commanders at Pearl Harbor — and then blamed them for the absence of preparation.[39] In fact, Roosevelt and his aides did believe that U.S. entry into the war was inevitable and did conclude — days before Pearl Harbor — that American attempts to mitigate hostilities with Japan had failed. No one, however, expected Pearl Harbor to be a target.

A postwar disclosure during congressional hearings (1945-1946) added fuel to the conspiracists' fire: Before the war began, the United States had broken the Japanese diplomatic code, which provided major evidence of U.S. awareness of pre-war Japanese intentions. The majority report said no evidence supported the claim that the FDR administration had schemed to get America into the war. But two Republicans signed a minority report claiming the administration withheld warnings from Pearl Harbor commanders in furtherance of "some long-range plan which was never disclosed to Congress or the American people."[40]

However, the conspiracists didn't produce what would later be called a "smoking gun." The decrypted Japanese cables — code named "Magic" — did reveal the Japanese saw war as imminent — but no cables mentioned an attack on Pearl Harbor.

Cold War Conspiracies

Threats of communist subversion dominated the conspiracy landscape following the war. The era's rabid anti-communism — known as McCarthyism — was spawned by Sen. Joseph McCarthy, R-Wis., who depicted himself as a crusader against communist infiltration of the government.

In 1951, McCarthy accused Secretary of State Dean Acheson and Defense Secretary George C. Marshall of being Soviet agents. The false accusations were followed by news that Americans spying for the Soviet Union — Julius and Ethel Rosenberg, executed in 1953 — had been charged with stealing U.S. atomic bomb secrets. At the same time, American troops were fighting Soviet- and Chinese communist-backed forces in Korea. In this atmosphere, McCarthy's sensational allegations of a "vast conspiracy. . . on a scale so immense as to dwarf any previous venture in the history of man" polarized the country.

Notwithstanding McCarthy's demagoguery and disregard for fact, Soviet spies had, in fact, penetrated the U.S. government and defense contractors — but in the 1930s and '40s. By the time McCarthy launched his campaign, the spies who had transmitted nuclear, high-tech and diplomatic information had been arrested, fled the country or gone to ground.[41]

Even before McCarthy surged to prominence, investigators and loyalty boards in federal and state governments had begun probing thousands of public employees who might have participated in communist political activities in the 1930s and '40s; some lost their jobs. When McCarthy's Permanent Investigations Subcommittee took up the cause, alleged — and in a few cases actual — communists or excommunists in government, entertainment and higher education were interrogated, sometimes in highly theatrical, televised public hearings.[42]

While the injustice of the McCarthy "witch hunts" is widely acknowledged, some on the communist-influenced left hyped the McCarthy era into the equivalent of early Nazi Germany. "It seemed to us that America was veering toward fascism, a fascism that would be much the same as that of Nazi Germany," Morton Sobell, an associate of the Rosenbergs who served 19 years for espionage, wrote in a 2001 memoir, recounting what he and his comrades had forecast as imminent in the early 1950s. "We saw mass roundups, concentration camps and death ovens." Sobell confessed in 2008 that he had been a Soviet spy.[43]

McCarthy himself ended in political disgrace. After Republican President Dwight D. Eisenhower was elected in 1952, McCarthy stayed on the attack, and his Republican allies abandoned him.

Despite his political collapse, McCarthy helped spur an important development in conspiracism. His targeting of Acheson, an esteemed member of the East Coast foreign policy establishment, led other conspiracists to scrutinize the liberal Council on Foreign Relations (CFR), an influential think tank in New York whose members are high-profile scholars and former and future diplomats.[44] For the new generation of right-wing conspiracists, the CFR figured prominently — along with the Rockefeller family — in alleged takeover plots. David Rockefeller, the senior member of the oil-and-banking dynasty, is now the council's honorary chairman.

"The ultimate aim of the Council on Foreign Relations (however well-intentioned its prominent and powerful members may be) is the same as the ultimate aim of international communism: to create a one-world socialist system and make the United States an official part of it," Dan Smoot, a former FBI agent and far-right activist and author, wrote in his influential 1962 book, *The Invisible Government.*[45]

But scholars scoff at such efforts to link the CFR to conspiracy. "Finding a hierarchy where none exists, reading discipline into a voluntary organization, the Right fingers the CFR as the 'invisible government' that really runs the United States," writes conspiracism scholar Pipes.[46] The Trilateral Commission, a similar group founded in 1973, also prompts conspiracist suspicions.

Members of the far right have gone even farther back in time in tracing the roots of plotting against the United States. "The John Birch Society has long held that the conspiracy of the Illuminati . . . is the predecessor of a modern-day conspiracy warring against our country and civilization," John F. McManus, president of the right-wing organization, wrote in 2007. Long centered in Massachusetts, it is now based in Appleton, Wis., McCarthy's hometown.

JFK and Beyond

The assassination of President Kennedy in 1963 launched the modern era of conspiracism. Ordinary citizens by the thousands embraced conspiracy theories about "what really happened," and terms such as "grassy knoll" and "lone gunman" became staples of popular culture."[47]

Citizen interest in the assassination got a major boost when the murder of Kennedy's assassin, Lee Harvey Oswald, was broadcast live to millions of homes. Similarly, an 8 mm movie of the assassination — shot by Abraham Zapruder, a bystander along Kennedy's limousine route — became a staple piece of evidence for assassination buffs, historians and conspiracists.[48]

The conclusion of the government commission headed by Chief Justice of the United States Earl Warren — that Oswald conceived and carried out the assassination by himself — was greeted skeptically by many. The most widely circulated theories said that U.S. military and business interests had had Kennedy killed because he opposed their plans to escalate the Vietnam War; or

CHRONOLOGY

1700s-1850s *European-inspired conspiracy theories evolve into American-style conspiracism.*

1776 Bavarian law professor founds "Illuminism" movement, a secret society devoted to creating a world ruled by reason instead of clerics.

1798 Anti-"Illuminati" propaganda reaches U.S., sparking fear that Thomas Jefferson seeks to destroy religion.

1830s Anti-Catholic conspiracy theory flourishes.

1840s-1850s "Slave Power" conspiracists see a federal takeover by slaveholding interests.

1940s-1950s *World War II and Cold War prompt fear of takeover of U.S.*

1944 *Chicago Tribune* alleges President Franklin D. Roosevelt provoked 1941 Pearl Harbor attack.

1945-46 Congressional hearings conclude Roosevelt didn't purposely prompt Pearl Harbor attack.

1951 Sen. Joseph McCarthy, R-Wis., falsely accuses secretaries of state and defense of being Soviet agents.

1958 John Birch Society founded to promote theory that Illuminati conspirators have penetrated government.

1960s-1970s *Kennedy assassination opens era of disbelief in government explanations.*

1962 Joint Chiefs of Staff chairman secretly proposes faked Cuban attacks to create pretext for U.S. military intervention in Cuba.

1963 Assassination of President John F. Kennedy provokes conspiracy theories still in circulation today.

1972 Revelations that government doctors injected black farmers with syphilis — the "Tuskegee Experiment" — fuel later suspicion that government invented AIDS.

1975 Church Committee produces evidence of secret drug tests on U.S. citizens.

1980s-1990s *Conspiracy theories based on actual and imagined government misdeeds build a following.*

1982 CIA ignores reports that Nicaraguan guerrillas are trafficking drugs — sparking conspiracy theory on the origin of crack cocaine epidemic.

1986 "Iran-Contra" scandal reveals secret U.S. plan to sell arms to Iran.

1987 Soviet-bloc scientists spread rumor that U.S. military created AIDS.

1991 Televangelist Pat Robertson warns of global takeover plot.

1993 Suicide of White House aide Vincent Foster prompts theories that President Bill Clinton and/or his wife, Hillary, had Foster killed. . . .

Branch Davidian confrontation near Waco, Texas, spurs growth of con-spiracist-influenced militia movement.

1997 Militia movement leader Linda Thompson calls "black helicopters" — a frequent element of conspiracy theories — part of a CIA-sponsored government takeover plot.

2000s *Sept. 11 attacks involve President George W. Bush in conspiracy theories; later theories target President Barack Obama.*

2004 "Truther" conspiracy theorists demand investigation of government's "deliberate" failure to prevent 9/11 attacks.

2005 *Popular Mechanics* debunks conspiracy theories of the attacks.

2007 Poll shows 22 percent of respondents believe Bush knew about attack.

2008 Presidential campaign spurs theories that Obama is Muslim. . . . Rev. Jeremiah Wright, Obama's former minister, endorses conspiracy theory on AIDS origin.

2009 "Birther" activists take their arguments to federal court. . . . Obama appointee Van Jones resigns after disclosure he signed "truther" petition. . . . Conspiracists help spur resistance to flu shots.

Critics Skewer Conspiracy Theories

"They have no clue what they're talking about."

Noam Chomsky, intellectual superstar of the international left, has been harshly analyzing U.S policies since the Vietnam War. As *The New Yorker's* Larissa MacFarquahar wrote, his works are a "catalogue of crimes committed by America, terrible crimes, and many of them . . . but it is not they that produce the sensation of blows: it is Chomsky's rage as he describes them."[1]

No wonder, then, that people certain the George W. Bush administration connived in the Sept. 11 attacks have been trying to recruit Chomsky, an emeritus professor of linguistics at the Massachusetts Institute of Technology (MIT). "I am bombarded with letters about this subject," he said in a 2007 interview.

Many commentators shy away from tackling conspiracy theories, given the passion or fanaticism they inspire. But Chomsky subjected the 9/11 conspiracy theories to the same unsparing scrutiny that he focuses on government. "With regard to the physical evidence, can you become a highly qualified civil and mechanical engineer and expert in the structure of buildings by spending a couple of hours on the Internet?" he asked in 2007. "If you can, we can get rid of the civil and mechanical engineering departments at MIT."[2]

Another critic is Edward L. Winston, a 31-year-old software engineer in St. Louis who runs a Web site, "ConspiracyScience.com," devoted to his merciless analyses of popular conspiracy themes.

In one of his responses to the most common Obama-birthplace theories, Winston took on the notion advanced by some "birthers" that a "natural born citizen" of the United States — an eligibility standard for the presidency — must be the child of two U.S. citizens. (Obama's Kenya-born father was a British subject.)[3]

"They have no clue what they're talking about," Winston writes. "Anyone born within the borders of the United States or within the territories of the United States is a natural born citizen. That even includes individuals born to two illegal immigrants on U.S. soil."[4]

Winston's site also includes some of the messages he receives on his Facebook page from conspiracy believers. "With a last name like Winston, I'm sorry but you've got Jew in your blood," one e-mailer wrote him. "So don't say you're not Jewish just because you don't practice it. Jew is blood. Jew is usury."[5]

"Little Green Footballs," an influential blog by Web designer Charles Johnson — once known for attacking radical Islamists and defending Israel — has in recent years been ridiculing far-right conspiracists. "Unbelievable," Johnson wrote in September. "Now the Christian far right is promoting the mind-bogglingly dim 'birther' conspiracy theory, with an IQ-destroying infomercial. . . . (The site pictures President Obama with the caption 'God's Enemy.')"[6]

Conservative blogger John Hawkins combined mockery with textual analysis in a 2006 debate with the author of a theory that President George W. Bush was planning to erode U.S. sovereignty. Jerome R. Corsi had written: "President Bush is pursuing a globalist agenda to create a

that the Cuban government and/or its Soviet patron were responsible, in retaliation for U.S. plans to have Cuban leader Fidel Castro killed.

Mistrust of government in general grew even more in the late 1960s and early 1970s, as the Vietnam War ended in U.S. defeat in 1975, after years of optimistic official reports that the war was being won. Two years earlier, the Watergate scandal began coming to light, with its revelations of systematic official deceit and law-breaking and, ultimately, President Richard M. Nixon's resignation.

Reports of questionable government activities continued during the Gerald R. Ford administration. In 1975, a commission headed by Vice President Nelson Rockefeller reported on a massive pattern of illegal CIA activities within the United States during the 1960s. And the Senate conducted a larger investigation headed by Sen. Frank Church, D-Idaho, that revealed the attempted FBI blackmail of the Rev. Martin Luther King Jr., the CIA's attempt to use Mafia members to assassinate Castro, assassination plots against other foreign leaders and a host of other actions

North American Union, effectively erasing our borders with both Mexico and Canada. This was the hidden agenda behind the Bush administration's true open-borders policy. . . . President Bush intends to abrogate U.S. sovereignty to the North American Union, a new economic and political entity which the President is quietly forming."[7]

Debating Corsi, Hawkins, editor of the "Right Wing News" Web site, wrote, "There's no real evidence . . . anywhere except in Jerome's fevered imagination. . . . The misleading trash you're cranking out on a weekly basis is duping people who would normally know better."[8]

Of course, the U.S.-Mexico-Canada borders remained intact after Bush's term ended. But Corsi, who rejects the conspiracy theorist label, maintains that North American integration plans remain in place. "Certainly the writing that I and others did brought the agenda to light," he says. "Largely, that was my goal."

Whatever the precise goals of those who embrace theories about Sept. 11 and other events, anti-conspiracists from the left argue that the theories do serious damage to the left-liberal side even when presented under its banner. Chomsky, in fact, argued that the "power centers" preferred to see activists obsessing about conspiracy theories. "It's a terrible drain of energy away from much more serious problems," he said.[9]

David Corn, Washington bureau chief for the leftist magazine *Mother Jones* and a harsh critic both of the Bush administration and the "truthers," pointed to the latter as largely responsible for the resignation under pressure of Obama administration environmental appointee Van Jones, who had signed a 2004 "truther" petition.

"The American taxpayers have lost a public servant who was uniquely qualified to help move the country in the right direction," Corn wrote in September. "Jones is

responsible for his own actions, but the 9/11 truthers are also responsible for concocting and spreading the poison that he drank."[10]

— Peter Katel

[1] Larissa MacFarquahar, "The Devil's Accountant," *The New Yorker,* March 31, 2003.

[2] Noam Chomsky, *What We Say Goes: Conversations on U.S. Power in a Changing World,* interviews with David Barsamian (2007), pp. 35-37; excerpted in: "Noam Chomsky on the 9/11 Conspiracy Kooks," harmonicminor (blog), Sept. 21, 2009, http://harmonicminor .com/2009/09/21/noam-chomsky-on-the-911-conspiracy-kooks/.

[3] "Does Barack Obama have Kenyan citizenship?" Factcheck.org, Aug. 29, 2008, www.factcheck.org/askfactcheck/does_barack_obama_have_ kenyan_citizenship.html.

[4] "Barack Obama — Obama was not born in the United States," *Conspiracy Science,* undated, http://conspiracyscience.com/articles/ obama/obama-was-not-born-in-the-united-states/#obama_cannot_be_ president_because_both_ parents_must_be_citizens_for_one_to_be_ eligible.

[5] "Anti-Semite Comedy Goldmine," *Conspiracy Science* blog, Sept. 27, 2009, http://conspiracyscience.com/blog/2009/09/27/anti-semite-comedy-goldmine.

[6] "Nirthers on Television," Little Green Footballs, Sept. 26, 2009, http:// littlegreen footballs.com/article/34760_Nirthers_on_Television.

[7] Jerome R. Corsi, "North American Union to Replace USA?" Human Events.com, May 19, 2006, www.humanevents.com/article.php? id=14965.

[8] "John Hawkins vs. Jery Corsi: Round 4," July 6, 2009, www .humanevents.com/right angle/index.php?1=1&title=john_hawkins_vs_ jerry_corsi_round_1.

[9] Chomsky, *op. cit.*

[10] David Corn, "How 9/11 Conspiracy Poison Did In Van Jones," *Inside Politics Daily,* Sept. 7, 2009, www.politicsdaily.com/2009/09/07/how-9-11-conspiracy-poison-did-in-van-jones/.

that might once have been dubbed the ravings of conspiracy theorists.

During President Ronald Reagan's two terms (1981-1989), White House officials were revealed to have been involved in a scheme to sell arms to the Islamic revolutionary government of Iran — a hostile power — in an effort to secretly raise money for weapons for U.S.-supported guerrillas fighting the Soviet-backed Nicaraguan government.

The chain of scandals contributed to a sense that the real actions of government were so secretive they were only rarely revealed.

Against that backdrop, President George H. W. Bush described the geopolitical scene as the Soviet Union neared collapse — and as a U.S.-assembled alliance was preparing to oust Iraqi dictator Saddam Hussein's army from Kuwait in 1990 — as the hoped-for beginning of a "new world order." Conspiracists seized on the term as a kind of admission that the global elite — an updated version of the Illuminati — were bent on submitting the United States to internationalist rule.

In 1991, TV evangelist and onetime Republican presidential primary candidate Pat Robertson promoted this

Secret Files Shed Light on Real Conspiracies

"Operation Northwoods" fed suspicions about government plots.

Some conspiracy theories sound unbelievable, and they are. Others sound just as wild, but the paper trails they have left erase any doubts.

In 1962, soon after the Cuban Missile Crisis, Gen. Lyman L. Lemnitzer, chairman of the Joint Chiefs of Staff, proposed a series of fake Cuban attacks on the United States or its allies designed to provide a pretext for U.S. military intervention in Cuba.

"Operation Northwoods," which was never approved, is one of a series of secret plans that, once revealed, provided supporting evidence for conspiracists who believe in secret plots by government agents.

The government's penchant for keeping secrets confers some value on conspiracy theories, says historian Kathryn Olmsted of the University of California, Davis. "They get people skeptical and demanding answers," she says. "And you get big investigations that, at times, produce a lot of information."

For example, Olmsted writes, a controversial *San Jose Mercury-News* investigation of an alleged CIA partnership with Central American drug dealers prompted a CIA internal investigation. That probe effectively confirmed that agency officials had worked closely with traffickers because they were part of a campaign to destabilize the communist-supported Nicaraguan government.[1] However, the newspaper's probe veered into conspiracism when it blamed the CIA, through its trafficker allies, of playing a key role in sparking the crack cocaine boom of the 1980s and '90s.

"Operation Northwoods" took far longer to come to light. The scheme included a shootdown — elaborately engineered to look like Cuban action — of a pilotless drone aircraft designed as an exact replica of a plane carrying passengers, shootings of Cuban exiles in Miami and the blowing up of a ship off the U.S. Naval Base at Guantanamo.[2]

Kennedy administration Defense Secretary Robert McNamara threw out the entire proposal, wrote author James L. Bamford, who discovered the "Northwoods" memo in 2001, months before the Sept. 11 attacks.[3]

In the years that followed, the "Northwoods" documents took on new life as support material for 9/11 "truther" theories.

"Some of the ideas, such as the proposal to 'blow up a U.S. ship in Guantanamo Bay and blame Cuba,' would have required killing Americans," wrote James Ray Griffin, a retired professor of philosophy and religion at Claremont School of Theology and a "truther" activist, suggesting that the government wasn't beyond manufacturing the 9/11 attack.[4]

Ten years after the "Northwoods" proposal, The Associated Press reported that the U.S. Public Health Service had for decades been injecting syphilis germs into illiterate black sharecroppers in Alabama without telling them what they were receiving. The justification was that the disease's effects could be studied. The so-called "Tuskegee Experiment" was named after Tuskegee Institute (now Tuskegee University) Hospital, where the project was carried out.[5]

The experiment helped sustain a strong belief today among black Americans — hit hard by HIV — that AIDS was produced in a government laboratory. About 50 percent of African-Americans share that view, according to a 2002-2003 survey by the RAND Corp. think tank and Oregon State University.[6] "The government lied about inventing the HIV virus as a means of genocide against people of color," the Rev. Jeremiah Wright of Chicago said during one of the sermons that caused then-presidential candidate Barack Obama to back away from his ex-pastor.[7]

Wright later cited the Tuskegee experiment in defending his statement. "I believe our government is capable of doing anything," Wright said at the National Press Club.[8]

No credible scientific evidence exists to support the notion that the government developed AIDS. But an AIDS-origin conspiracy did exist in the Soviet intelligence establishment. In the mid-1980s, when the AIDS epidemic was generating global alarm, the Soviet Union heavily promoted the notion that the U.S. military invented AIDS.

"The AIDS virus is the unfortunate product of work in preparation for waging bacteriological war," a Soviet-bloc scientist, Jakob Segal of East Germany, wrote in the English-language *Moscow News* in 1987.[9]

Distributed by a Soviet press agency, versions of the conspiracy theory appeared in newspapers in 50 countries, a Reagan administration official wrote in 1987. "Obviously the United States is technically capable of almost anything," a government official in Africa told Deputy Assistant Secretary of State Kathleen Bailey. "Also, why would such a story be in so many newspapers if it's not true?"[10]

Further instigating suspicion about U.S. government activities, an American spy agency waited until 1995 to release documentary evidence of spying by hundreds of Americans for the Soviet Union before and during World War II.

The "Venona Papers" were a series of decryptions by American and British decoding experts of messages between spy-handlers in the United States and their bosses in Moscow.

Venona was so secret that even President Harry S Truman was kept in the dark — though Moscow knew about the project by 1949. "The president thus saw little proof of a real espionage conspiracy but heard many tales told by self-interested and alarmist conspiracists," historian Olmsted writes. As a result, Truman remained highly skeptical of reports of Soviet spying.[11] A few years later, Sen. Joseph McCarthy, R-Wis., made his wild accusations of a government completely penetrated by Soviet spies. The charge flourished because only a handful of people were aware about how much the government actually knew. "Had we learned about the Venona Project in the late 1940s, had the FBI revealed it was following Soviet spies, that would have shut up McCarthy," argues historian John E. Moser of Ohio's Ashland University,

In the end, Moser says, excessive government secrecy can provide fertile soil for conspiracy theories. "So many theories from the 18th and 19th centuries focused on monasteries and convents, because they were closed institutions. A fevered imagination can come up with all kinds of ideas."

Indeed, some Kennedy assassination experts say that the CIA — to this day — is giving conspiracists plenty of grounds for suspicion. The spy agency is still fighting against releasing documents concerning a CIA officer's ties to an anti-Castro group that clashed with Lee Harvey Oswald, who later killed Kennedy, *The New York Times* reported on Oct. 16.[12]

Gerald Posner, author of a book rebutting conspiracy theories of the assassination, says of the CIA's conduct: "It feeds the conspiracy theorists who say, 'You're hiding something.'"[13]

— *Peter Katel*

[1] Kathryn Olmsted, Real Enemies: *Conspiracy Theories and American Democracy, World I to 9/11* (2009), pp. 188-192.

[2] "Pentagon Proposed Pretexts for Cuba Invasion in 1962," National Security Archive, April 30, 2001, www.gwu.edu/~nsarchiv/news/20010430.

[3] James L. Bamford, "Bush wrong to use pretext as excuse to invade Iraq," *USA Today*, Aug. 29, 2002, p. A13.

[4] David Ray Griffin, "The American Empire and 9/11," 2007, www.journalof911studies.com/volume/200704/DavidRayGriffin911Empire.pdf.

[5] Borgna Brunner, "The Tuskegee Syphilis Experiment," undated, Tuskegee University, www.tuskegee.edu/global/story.asp?s=1207586

[6] Jeffrey Weiss, "Obama pastor Jeremiah Wright's incendiary quotes illuminate chasm between races," Dallasnews.com, April 8, 2008, www.dallasnews.com/sharedcontent/dws/dn/religion/stories/040808dnmetwrightchasm.442a11fb.html.

[7] "Best of Jeremiah Wright's Sermons Pt. 1," YouTube, March 15, 2008 (posting date), www.youtube.com/watch?v=617eK2XIaLk.

[8] "The Full Wright Transcript," Marc Ambinder blog, April 28, 2008, http://marcambinder.theatlantic.com/archives/2008/04/the_full_wright_transcript.php.

[9] "AIDS Virus Product of Genetic Manipulation," BBC Summary of World Broadcasts, April 29, 1987.

[10] Kathleen Bailey, "Soviets Sponsor Spread of AIDS Disinformation," *Los Angeles Times* (op-ed), April 19, 1987, Part 5, p. 2.

[11] Olmsted, *ibid.*, pp. 91-92; Steven T. Usdin, *Engineering Communism: How Two Americans Spied for Stalin and Founded the Soviet Silicon Valley* (2005), pp. 122-125.

[12] Scott Shane, "C.I.A. Is Still Cagey About Oswald Mystery," *The New York Times*, Oct. 16, 2009, www.nytimes.com/2009/10/17/us/17inquire.htmkhpw.

[13] Quoted in *ibid.*

conspiratorial vision in a best-selling book, *New World Order*. He wrote of "a single thread (that) runs from the White House to the State Department to the Council on Foreign Relations to the Trilateral Commission to secret societies to extreme New Agers." Robertson also invoked the specter of the Illuminati, the purported villains in the oldest conspiracy theory in U.S. history: "The New Age religions, the beliefs of the Illuminati, and Illuminated Freemasonry all seem to move along parallel tracks with world communism and world finance."[49]

The flames of conspiracism that Robertson helped fan reached new heights during Bill Clinton's two terms (1993-2001). Clinton and his wife, Hillary, were targeted by a series of allegations about their real estate dealings and commodities trades that grew progressively more conspiratorial, especially after the 1993 suicide of lawyer Vincent Foster, a senior White House aide.

Hardcore anti-Clinton activists developed a wealth of evidence that showed, they said, that Foster had been murdered, possibly on the Clintons' orders — contrary to what police and an independent counsel reported.[50]

In addition to Foster's death, Clinton conspiracists also zeroed in on Clinton's supposed involvement in drug-smuggling and the training of Nicaraguan guerrillas while he had been Arkansas governor.[51]

Meanwhile, two deadly events sparked a wave of far-right conspiratorial thinking. In 1992, a mother and son were killed by federal agents during the siege of a right-wing survivalist family at Ruby Ridge, in northern Idaho. A year later came the botched confrontation and lethal fire at the Branch Davidian compound near Waco, Texas.[52]

In far-right circles, the deaths were interpreted in light of a conspiracist belief that black helicopters were constantly sweeping through the U.S.-Canadian border area in preparation for military occupation by U.N. troops that would rule the United States as part of the "New World Order."[53] However, another leading conspiracist, Linda Thompson, who headed the Indianapolis-based America Justice Federation, took a more limited view of the black helicopters. Holding that the government murdered the Waco cult members, she claimed the choppers were part of a CIA-sponsored "private mafia" aiming at "a military takeover of the United States through a combination of drug running, gun running, lobbying, blackmailing congressmen and terrorism."[54]

Thompson's was a prominent voice of the militia movement, a loosely organized group that included far-right extremists and apolitical survivalists, many given to conspiracism. The movement virtually disappeared after the 1995 bombing of the federal building in Oklahoma City by Army veteran McVeigh, who had traveled in militia circles.

CURRENT SITUATION
Swine Flu Plot?

Medical professionals are battling a host of conspiracy theories and other scares about the swine flu pandemic and the vaccine against it.

"We have the right vaccine for this virus," Health and Human Services Secretary Kathleen Sebelius told ABC News in early October. "We also have years of clinical data on seasonal flu vaccine and a great safety record."[55]

Yet 41 percent of adults told pollsters for the Harvard School of Public Health they won't get vaccinated. And only 51 percent said they definitely would vaccinate their children.[56]

Forty-eight percent of those not getting vaccinated said lack of trust in public officials' information on the vaccine played a role in their decision.[57] The survey didn't ask about the sources of that mistrust, but flu-related conspiracy theories have been flying around the Web since news of the new flu strain broke last spring.

Dr. Paul A. Offitt, chief of infectious diseases at the Children's Hospital of Philadelphia, sees two major schools of conspiracism — the belief the U.S. Centers for Disease Control and Prevention is misrepresenting or falsifying data, and that profit-obsessed pharmaceutical companies are indifferent to vaccine quality.

"As far as the most extreme theories — that they're making products to kill us — that is so outlandish that I have trouble commenting on it," Offitt says.

Yet such over-the-top theories are plentiful. Mike Adams, editor of a "natural health" Web site, asked readers in April: "Could world governments, spooked by the prospect of radical climate change caused by overpopulation of the planet, have assembled a super-secret task force to engineer and distribute a supervirulent strain of influenza designed to 'correct' the human population (and institute global Martial Law)?"[58]

Are conspiracy theories now a threat to democracy?

YES Chip Berlet
Senior Analyst
Political Research Associates

Written for *CQ Researcher*, Oct. 15, 2009

Conspiracy theories are not harmless. They are exaggerated stories falsely portraying a scapegoated group as plotting against the common good. Throughout the history of our country, mass movements have been built around conspiracy theories targeting witches, Freemasons, Catholics, Jews, immigrants and "Reds."

In the 1800s, an angry mob near Boston was so enraged by conspiracy stories about Catholic priests and nuns that it burned a convent school to the ground. Between 1919 and 1921, thousands of Italian and Russian immigrants were rounded up and deported by our government based on conspiracy fearmongering falsely targeting them as subversives and terrorists. The McCarthy period illustrated the damage conspiracy theories can do to a society.

The administration of President Bill Clinton was sidetracked by waves of conspiracy theories claiming he had ordered the assassination of a key aide or was plotting a U.N. takeover of America with jackbooted troops arriving in black helicopters.

Now the "birthers" and other conspiracy theorists circulate false allegations that President Obama is not really a U.S. citizen; is planning to merge the U.S., Canada and Mexico into a North American Union or that he is a secret Muslim plotting more terror attacks. The xenophobic and racist subtext here is clear. Some people have acted on these base and baseless claims. Since Obama's inauguration there have been nine murders where the alleged killers have been entangled in white supremacist or anti-Semitic conspiracy theories.

James W. von Brunn, accused of killing a guard at the U.S. Holocaust Memorial Museum in Washington, D.C., feared a conspiracy of Jews and Freemasons to control the world and keep white Christians subjugated while at the same time elevating blacks to undeserved positions of power. Other conspiracists blame Muslims, immigrants, Mexicans, feminists and gay people.

The recent "Tea Party" protests and town hall disruptions are awash in conspiracy claims and false and misleading information. Democracy is based on informed consent — not myths and lies woven into conspiracy theories.

It is unlikely that conspiracy theorists will overthrow the government. They can, however, poison the body politic; distort and derail public policy debates; spread bigotry and paranoia and wind up some people so tightly that they commit acts of violence against targeted scapegoats. Conspiracy theories are toxic tap democracy.

NO John E. Moser
Professor of History
Ashland University

Written for *CQ Researcher*, Oct. 15, 2009

Angry right-wing talk radio hosts suggest that financier/philanthropist George Soros is secretly pulling the strings of the Obama White House, while equally angry "birthers" deny that the president was born in the United States. A few years ago, we heard from the left that the election of 2000 had been "stolen," that 9/11 was an "inside job" and that Halliburton, the global oil field services company once headed by Dick Cheney, was secretly behind the war in Iraq.

Conspiracy theories do seem to be everywhere in today's society, although, like body odor, they are generally things that other people have. Are they a threat to our democracy? One might be tempted to say so, until one recognizes that conspiracy theories have an old and distinguished place in American political history. It is hard to imagine that the War of Independence would have been fought had Britain's American colonists in 1775 not been convinced that George III was actively plotting to enslave them. New Englanders were convinced in the late 1790s that the country had been infiltrated by members of a secret organization known as the Bavarian Illuminati, and Thomas Jefferson, it was claimed, was one of their agents.

Nor is it likely that there would have been a Civil War — or the subsequent destruction of slavery — had it not been for Northern claims of a "slave power conspiracy," matched only by the Southern notion that their neighbors to the North were intent on destroying their way of life. Fears of communist subversion shaped the 1950s as surely as theories over who shot President Kennedy influenced the 1960s.

Some may claim, however, that conspiracy theories pose a greater danger today because they seem to circulate so quickly. This is certainly the case, thanks largely to so-called "new media" such as talk radio, the Internet and 24-hour news networks. Moreover, thanks to the Watergate scandal, Americans today understand that major conspiracies can, and do, exist.

Yet what is striking about so many of the conspiracy theories that have found adherents throughout American history is that they all purport to identify threats to our form of government. In addition, they represent a deep distrust of traditional authority, whether it be the government, corporations, the mainstream media or "the experts." In other words, far from being a danger, the presence of such theories — as silly as most of them are — might actually be seen as a sign of a healthy democracy.

A writer for the respected British magazine *New Scientist* dismissed such speculation. "Deliberately engineering a virus of this kind would be a huge challenge," wrote Michael Le Page, though he conceded a laboratory mistake could conceivably have a played a role.[59]

Extreme conspiracism that sees the H1N1 flu and/or the vaccine as deliberately fatal coexists with generalized suspicion. Right-wing radio and TV hosts Glenn Beck and Rush Limbaugh have been skeptical and belligerently suspicious, respectively. "Screw you, Mrs. Sebelius! I'm not going to take it precisely because you're telling me I must," Limbaugh shouted on his show.[60]

But Limbaugh's response was mild compared with some of the flu conspiracies taking shape on the Web. "In the next few months, we are about to face our own American soldiers who have killed and maimed indiscriminately in Iraq and Afghanistan," wrote Ilya Sandra Perlingieri, who writes frequently on health matters from an antimedical establishment viewpoint. "These soldiers will now probably be deployed to accompany FEMA to come door-to-door into our homes to force us to take these poisonous injections. . . . We are at the brink of even the loss of our very own lives all under the guise of protecting us from a non-existent 'pandemic.' [They will] genetically engineer the flu in some bioweapons lab, and then create debilitating and deathly vaccines that will do further harm to everyone."[61]

Perlingieri's denunciation was posted on rense.com, a site with a heavy interest in Holocaust denial and so-called anti-Zionism. One graphic on the site shows a baby about to be stabbed to death on an altar bearing a Star of David overlaid with a "Z" as Obama and other world leaders, dressed in black robes, look on.

Outside that wing of the conspiracist community, the focus is on pharmaceutical companies. Paul Joseph Watson, a writer on Alex Jones' "Prison Planet" site blames a "mammoth level of fear-mongering" on drug firms' appetite for profits during a recession. The high level of public resistance to the vaccine is anti-corporate victory in the face "of such a huge effort on behalf of the pharmaceutical industry and their soapbox, the mass media."[62]

"Birthers" Challenged

U.S. District Judge David O. Carter of Orange County, Calif., is weighing dismissal of a lawsuit challenging President Obama's citizenship and, consequently, his eligibility for office. If the recent actions of other federal judges in similar suits are any guide, the suit's chances are slender.

All of the legal action has centered on what the "birther" movement insists is lack of definitive official proof that Obama was born in the United States — evidence to the contrary notwithstanding. Orly Taitz, the Southern California lawyer who has filed the most recent of these cases, takes that claim of a non-U.S. birthplace several steps further.

Taitz told *The Washington Post* she thought Obama had been born in Kenya — his father's native country — then brought to Hawaii by his mother, who persuaded state workers to falsify his birth record. She also entertained the idea — a common one among "birthers" — that Obama was also a citizen of Indonesia, where he lived for several years as a child while his mother was married to her second husband, who was Indonesian. "He is lying about his identity, he is hiding his whole identity, this is dangerous!" Taitz told the newspaper.[63]

Weeks earlier, U.S. District Judge Clay D. Land of Columbus, Ga., had dismissed a similar case, ruling that it was based on "sheer conjecture and speculation." The judge also remarked that Taitz "is a self-proclaimed leader in what has become known as 'the birther movement.'"[64]

Taitz fired back with a motion to remove Land from the case. In it, she called "birther" a "pejorative appellation (often coupled with even more colorful epithets such as batshit crazy')."[65]

The preferred designation among Obama birth-certificate challengers is "eligibility movement."[66]

Even before Obama was elected, some of them questioned why his original birth certificate wasn't on file in the Hawaii public records system. Hawaii had stored all original birth certificates, making them available only to people with "a tangible interest" in the documents. The state does make available a "certification of live birth" — as opposed to a "certificate" — which states that Obama was born in Hawaii.[67]

Then, in early August, *WorldNet Daily,* a Web site that has made the theme a specialty, posted a story reporting that Taitz's discovery of an alleged Kenyan birth certificate for Obama could be "the smoking gun" of the entire subject.[68]

But *Politifact,* a fact-checking arm of the *St. Petersburg Times,* reported persuasive evidence that the "Kenyan" certificate was a digitally altered Australian birth certificate that its owner had posted on a genealogy Web site. "Same format," *Politifact* said. "Same book and page number in the birth registry. Some of the officials' last names were even the same." Factcheck.org, owned by the University of Pennsylvania's Annenberg Public Policy Center, has also concluded that challenges to Obama's citizenship are groundless.[69]

By the time *Politifact* posted its report, *WorldNet Daily's* editor and CEO, Joseph Farah, had backed away from the story. "No one here has made a judgment that it is real," he wrote.[70]

Farah went on to question the "Certification of Live Birth" that *Politifact* posted. "Anyone could march into a Hawaii Public Health Department office and say he or she had a baby, fill out a form with the pertinent details, sign it and there would be no questions asked," he wrote.[71]

But even before the election, Chiyome Fukino, Hawaii Health Department director, said that she and the registrar of vital statistics "have personally seen and verified that the Hawaii State Department of Health has Sen. Obama's original birth certificate on record."[72]

Robert Farley of *Politifact* acknowledged that Obama hasn't posted his original birth certificate. "Maybe the original would identify the hospital where Obama was born, but that's irrelevant," he wrote. "The issue is in what city, and therefore country, was he born. The document posted by the campaign proves Obama was born in Honolulu, according to Health Department officials. And that's really the central issue here."[73]

Even outside the *WorldNet Daily* orbit, not everyone agrees Obama has resolved the issue satisfactorily. "There are legitimate questions about the documentation of Obama's birth certificate," Camille Paglia, a political iconoclast who largely supports Obama, said on National Public Radio's "Fresh Air" in September. "I'm sorry, I've been following this closely from the start."[74]

Others argue that those challenging Obama's eligibility are operating outside the world of fact and evidence. "If the long-form birth certificate were released, with its unequivocal identification of Hawaii as Obama's place of birth, the cycle would almost certainly continue," Alex Koppleman, a staff writer for the online magazine *Salon,* wrote before Obama was sworn in. He noted that talk-show hosts

Limbaugh and Savage, as well as author Corsi, had questioned Obama's midcampaign trip to Hawaii to see his dying grandmother. "It's got to do with his birth certificate," Savage said of the trip.[75]

Obama may well have concluded that releasing his original birth certificate would never quiet the attackers. "As long as he doesn't, the 'birthers' are going to keep going, and as long as they do, they're going to look ridiculous," suggests Ashland University historian Moser. "The people who believe in the theory, they're never going to go for him. So why not keep it alive?"

OUTLOOK
Looking for Answers

Conspiracy theories will be part of the national conversation over the next decade, Moser says. "This is a side effect of America losing its unquestioned position of dominance in the world that it has enjoyed since World War II," he explains. "We're not going to become a Third World country, but we're not going to be on top, as many Americans are used to seeing the United States. People are going to look for conspiracy theories to explain that."

At the same time, he's skeptical that conspiracism will come to dominate the political landscape. "You can be a listener to talk radio and enjoy it, but that doesn't mean you're going to buy into the whole master theory," he says, likening talk radio to pro wrestling.

But the political system may be vulnerable in ways that an entertainment spectacle is not, argues Berlet of Political Research Associates. "Conspiracism is a threat because democracy is not a stable system," he says. "It's constantly being buffeted by people who want to subdue subversives or an external threat. Constant waves of scapegoating and bigotry have to be pushed back."

Moreover, Berlet says, the so-called mainstream media have effectively relinquished their monitoring role — "watchdogs on Valium," he calls them. "There are no stories about maybe something is wrong in society if people are this unhappy. There is almost no analytical presence in the media that most people consume — no coverage of ideas."

However, conservative blogger John Hawkins says fact-based Web media can react more quickly when conspiracy theories appear. "In the old world, media didn't have to address these," he says. "In the new world, people will address them and kill them in their cradle."

Speed is important, Hawkins says, because of the Web's oft-noted role in propagating conspiracy theories. "I think it's very important to turn these things around before people get them in their heads," he says. "If you do a Google search on a conspiracy theory, you'll find 50 articles all borrowing from each other, each saying there's a conspiracy. Joe Average will say, 'Maybe it's true; I don't see anything going in the other direction.'"

Historian Olmsted at the University of California is uncertain if conspiracism will gather strength over the next decade, noting that the "truther" theories lost momentum once Bush left office. For now, "There is always a surge in conspiracy theories when there's an economic crisis," she says. "Also, it seems that the election of an African-American president has triggered the anxieties of a significant segment of the white population."

Along the same lines, anti-conspiracist Web writer Winston of St. Louis also notes an Obama effect. "If he's reelected, I would say that conspiracy theories definitely will not die down."

Winston adds, "A minority of them are dangerous enough to warrant people being a little worried about them."

Still, conspiracy expert Pipes hasn't seen present-day theories rise to the level they sometimes reached in the early and middle 19th century.

Further, some well-known conspiracy theories center on the facts of past events, Pipes notes. So, by definition, these theories look backward instead of forward. As a result, "Something like the 'truther' phenomenon looks pretty impactless," he says.

But radio host Jones is looking to the future. And it's a grim one. "You're in locked-down prison cities," he said, in a message that he says is aimed at people living 20 or 30 years from now. "Your mother, your father, your children are dying from the bioweapons, you're dying from the engineered cancers."[76]

The only positive feature of this horrific universe, Jones said, is that people would know who their enemies are. "If you're listening to me 20-30 years in the future," he said, "just please fight against the new world order." As for present-day listeners who laugh at Jones' forecast, he called them "buffoons."[77]

Clearly, Jones has a perspective on the future. But even conspiracy theories that don't focus on what's ahead may build constituencies for forward-looking theories. "My guess is that people who believe in the 'birther' theory have probably folded it into other conspiracy theories," says Syracuse University's Barkun.

Whether conspiracy theories maintain their present momentum or not, Barkun says one facet of conspiracist thinking seems unlikely to change: adherents' resistance to argument. "Some months ago I got an e-mail from someone teaching at a university in Montana," he says. "All her neighbors were listening to Alex Jones. What could she do about it? How could she convince them they were mistaken? I told her, I don't think you can do anything."

NOTES

1. "FEMA Concentration Camps, Rant (Part 1)," "Alex Jones Show," Feb. 9, 2009, www.youtube .com/watch?v=qecd5d-fySc&feature=related.

2. "Alex Jones Interviews Charlie Sheen," In-fowars. com, Sept. 8, 2009, www.infowars.com/twenty-minutes-with-the-president/; Lee Fang, "Gohmert Trades Ideas With Conspiracy Theorist," ThinkProgress, July 27, 2009 (audio clip), http:// thinkprogress.org/2009/07/27/gohmert.conspiracies .alexjones.

3. Alexa, the Web Information Company, Oct. 7, 2009, www.alexa.com/siteinfo/infowars.com.

4. "Top 10 Reasons Why No Man Has Ever Set Foot on the Moon," Moonmovie.com, undated, www .moonmovie.com/moonmovie/default.asp; Christina Caron, "Refuting the Most Popular Apollo Moon Landing Hoax Theories," ABC News, July 19, 2009, http://abcnews.go.com/Technology/ Apollo11MoonLanding/story? id=8104410&page= 1&page=1; "The Great Moon Hoax," NASA, Feb. 23, 2001, http://science.nasa.gov/headlines/y2001/ ast23Feb_2.htm.

5. "Obama's approval steady," Public Policy Polling, Sept. 23, 2009, www.publicpolicypolling.com/pdf/ PPP_Release_National_819513.pdf.

6. "22% Believe Bush Knew About 9/11 Attacks in Advance," Rasmussen Reports, May 4, 2007,

www.rasmussenreports.com/public_content/pol itics/current_events/bush_administration/22_ believe_bush_knew_about_9_11_attacks_in_ advance.

7. Kathleen Hunter and Jonathan Allen, "Senate Affirms Obama's U.S. Citizenship," *CQ Today,* July 28, 2009.

8. *Ibid.,* and "Conservative media figures alleged Obama's Hawaii trip is about discredited birth-certificate rumors, not his ailing grandmother," Media Matters for America, Oct. 23, 2008, http:// mediamatters.org/research/200810230020.

9. "Respected Leaders and Families Launch 9/11 Truth Statement Demanding Deeper Investigation Into Events of 9/11," 911Truth.org, Oct. 26, 2004, www.911truth.org/article.php?story=200410260 93059633.

10. David Dunbar and Brad Reagan, eds., *Debunking 9/11 Myths: Why Conspiracy Theories Can't Stand Up to the Facts* (2006).

11. Quoted in Sharon Haddock, "Beck's backing bumps Skousen book to top," *Deseret News,* March 20, 2009, www.deseretnews.com/article/1,5143,70529 2222,00.html?pg=1.

12. "The History of Secret Combinations, Part 3," W. Cleon Skousen, 1976, YouTube, www.youtube .com/watch?v=I8fo6bdudVI&feature=related.

13. "Glenn Beck analyzes fascist and communist symbolism in artwork at Rockefeller Center," YouTube, Sept. 2, 2009, /www.youtube.com/watch?v=xWL-pfCao-U.

14. Glenn Beck interview, @katiecouric, CBS News, Sept. 22, 2009, www.cbsnews.com/video/watch/?id =5330485n&tag=cbsnewsSec tionsArea.0.

15. "Alex Jones — Corsi Pt2," "Alex Jones Show," May 4, 2009, www.youtube.com/watch?v=j2qKUhdj Hj8&feature=related.

16. "Hastings Reintroduces National Emergency Centers Establishment Act," Hastings Web site, Jan. 22, 2009, http://alceehastings.house.gov/index .php?option=com_content&task=view&id=243 &Itemid=98; H.R. 645, http://thomas.loc.gov/cgi-bin/query/z?c111:H.R.645.

17. Jerome R. Corsi, "Bill creates detention camps in U.S. for 'emergencies,'" *WorldNet Daily,* Feb. 1, 2009, www.wnd.com/index.php?pageId=87757.

18. "The Drug Cartel and Pandemic H1N1 Swine Flu Viruses and Vaccines," *Infowars,* Sept. 21, 2009, www.infowars.com/the-drug-cartel-and-pandemic-h1n1swine-flu-viruses-and-vaccines/; Leonard G. Horowitz, "Introgenocide: The Biotechnology, Politics, and Economics of Emerging Pandemics," Tetrahedron Publishing Group, undated, www.tetra hedron.org.

19. "Alex Jones TV," July 21, 2009, www.youtube.com/ watch?v=KkoHZ4DylH4.

20. "09.12.09 March on Washington: The Tea Party Movement Goes to Capitol Hill," http://912dc.org; Talking Points Memo, www.talkingpointsmemo .com/gallery/2009/09/hearses-nazi-dogs-and-crucified-liberty-scenes-from-the-912-march.php? img=24.

21. Chip Berlet, "Toxic to Democracy: Conspiracy Theories, Demonization & Scapegoating," Political Research Associates, 2009, www.publiceye.org/ conspire/toxic2democracy/Toxic-2D-all-rev-04.pdf.

22. Kathryn S. Olmsted, *Real Enemies: Conspiracy Theories and American Democracy, World War I to 9/11* (2009).

23. John E. Moser, *Right Turn: John T. Flynn and the Transformation of American Liberalism* (2005).

24. Richard Hofstadter, *The Paranoid Style in American Politics* (2008 edition), pp. 23-24. For a view of Hofstadter as ahead of his time, see Thomas Frank, "From John Birchers to Birthers," *The Wall Street Journal,* Oct. 21, 2009, p. A21.

25. Michael Lerner, "The Antiwar Anti-Semites," *The Wall Street Journal,* Feb. 12, 2003, www.opinion journal.com/editorial/feature.htm1?id=11 0003061.

26. Quoted in Daniel Pipes, *Conspiracy: How the Paranoid Style Flourishes and Where It Comes From* (1997), p. 175.

27. Among numerous books on the subject, see Lawrence Wright, *The Looming Tower: Al-Qaeda and the Road to 9/11* (2006).

28. *Ibid.*, p. 346.

29. For background, see Peter Katel, "Hate Groups," *CQ Researcher,* May 8, 2009, pp. 421-448.

30. *Ibid.*

31. Juliet Lapidos, "The AIDS Conspiracy Handbook," *Slate,* March 19, 2008, www.slate.com/id/2186860/

32. Jeffrey L. Pasley, "Conspiracy Theory and American Exceptionalism from the Revolution to Roswell," paper for symposium, May 13, 2000, http://pasley brothers.com/conspiracy/CT_and_American_ Exceptionalism_web_version.htm.

33. Unless otherwise indicated, this subsection is drawn from Jeffrey L. Pasley, "Illuminati," chapter in Peter Knight, ed. *Conspiracy Theories in American History: An Encyclopedia* (2003); chapter published separately online at http://pasleybrothers.com/ conspiracy/readings/Pasley_CTAHE_articles.pdf; and Hofstadter, *op. cit.*

34. Quoted in *ibid.*, p. 17.

35. *Ibid.*, pp. 19-20.

36. James C. Foley, "Slave Power," in Knight, *op. cit,* pp. 658-662.

37. Pipes, *op. cit,* p. 91.

38. Michael Barkun, *A Culture of Conspiracy: Apocalyptic Visions in Contemporary America* (2003), pp. 51, 128.

39. Except where otherwise noted, material on Pearl Harbor and subsequent events are drawn from Kathryn S. Olmsted, *Real Enemies: Conspiracy Theories and American Democracy, World War I to 9/11* (2009).

40. Quoted in *ibid.*, p. 79.

41. Quoted in Steven T. Usdin, *Engineering Communism: How Two Americans Spied for Stalin and Founded the Soviet Silicon Valley* (2005); Sam Tanenhaus, *Whittaker Chambers: A Biography* (1998).

42. Pipes, *op. cit.*, p. 116; the subcommittee's closed sessions are now online, "Historic Senate Hearings Published," United States Senate, www.senate.gov/ artandhistory/history/common/generic/McCarthy_ Transcripts.htm.

43. Quoted in Usdin, *op. cit.,* p. 151. See also Sam Roberts, "57 Years Later, Figure in Rosenberg Case Says He Spied for Soviets," *The New York Times,* Sept. 12, 2008, p. A1.

44. Peter Grose, "Continuing the Inquiry: The Council on Foreign Relations From 1921 to 1996," Council on Foreign Relations, undated, www.cfr.org/about/ history/cfr/.

45. Dan Smoot, *The Invisible Government* (1962), available online, www.gutenberg.org/files/20224/20224-h/20224-h.htm.

46. Pipes, *op. cit.,* p. 116.

47. Except where otherwise indicated, material for this subsection is drawn from Olmsted, *op. cit.*

48. The film is now viewable on the Web; "The Zapruder Film," www.youtube.com/watch?v=E66 vymfPA.

49. Quoted in Paul Feldman, "Conspiracy Talk a U.S. Tradition," *Los Angeles Times,* May 29, 1995, p. A3.

50. Philip Weiss, "The Clinton Haters," *The New York Times Magazine,* Feb. 23, 1997, p. 35.

51. *Ibid.*, Micah Morrison, "Mysterious Mena," *News & Record* (Greensboro, N.C.), July 31, 1994, p. F1.

52. Katel, *op. cit.*

53. Barkun, *op. cit.*, pp. 69-71.

54. Quoted in *ibid.*

55. "Fear of Swine Flu Vaccine? Why Are Parents Saying No?" "Good Morning America," ABC News, Oct. 7, 2009.

56. "Survey Finds Just 40% of Adults 'Absolutely Certain' They Will Get H1N1 Vaccine," Harvard School of Public Health, Oct. 2, 2009, www.hsph .harvard.edu/news/press-releases/2009-releases/ survey-40-adults-absolutely-certain-h1n1-vaccine .html.

57. *Ibid.*

58. Mike Adams, "As Swine Flu Spreads, Conspiracy Theories of Laboratory Origins Abound," Natural News.com, April 27, 2009, www.naturalnews .com/026141.html.

59. Michael Le Page, "Is swine flue a bioterrorist virus?" *Short Sharp Science* (blog), April 27, 2009,

www.newscientist.com/blogs/shortsharpscience/2009/04/is-swine-flu-a-bioterrorist-vi.html.

60. "PMSNBC Doctor Rips Rush for Refusing to Take Sebelius Flu Shot," "Rush Limbaugh Show," Oct. 8, 2009, www.rushlimbaugh.com/home/daily/site_100809/content/01125108.guest.html. Also, Christopher Beam, "Pig Pile: the bizarre alliance of the far left and far right against swine flu vaccinations," *Slate*, Oct. 12, 2009, www.slate.com/id/2232187/.

61. Ilya Sandra Perlingieri, "Dangers In The Shots," *rense.com*, Aug. 4, 2009, www.rense.com/general86/dngers.htm.

62. Paul Joseph Watson, "Swine Flu Shot Propaganda Goes Into Overdrive," *PrisonPlanet*, Oct. 14, 2009, www.prisonplanet.com/swine-flu-shot-propaganda-goes-into-overdrive.html.

63. Quoted in Liza Mundy, "Burden of Proof on Obama's Origins," *The Washington Post,* Oct. 6, 2009, www.washingtonpost.com/wp-dyn/content/article/2009/10/05/AR2009100503819_pf.html.

64. *Rhodes v. MacDonald*, Case No. 4:09-CV-106 (CDL), U.S. District Court for the Middle District of Georgia, Columbus Division, 9/16/09, pp. 1, 12, http://ftpcontent.worldnow.com/wtvm/ConnieRhodesvsArmy.pdf.

65. Motion to Recuse the Honorable Clay D. Land," Civil Action No: 09-106, Document 24, Oct. 2, 2009, p. 10, www.the-peoples-forum.com/cgi-bin/readart.cgi?ArtNum=14733.

66. Spencer Kornhaber, "Meet Orly Taitz, Queen Bee of People Obsessed With Barack Obama's Birth Certificate," *OC Weekly,* June 18, 2009.

67. Robert Farley, "Obama's birth certificate: Final chapter," *Politifact.com,* July 1, 2009, www.politifact.com/truth-o-meter/article/2009/jul/01/obamas-birth-certificate-final-chapter-time-we-mea/.

68. "Is this really smoking gun of Obama's Kenyan birth?" *WorldNet Daily*, Aug. 2, 2009, www.wnd.com/index.php?fa=PAGE.view&page Id=105764.

69. "Alleged Obama birth certificate is a hoax," *Politifact.com*, Aug. 21, 2009, www.politifact.com/truth-o-meter/statements/2009/aug/21/orly-taitz/alleged-obama-birth-certificate-kenya-hoax/; Jess Henig, "Born in the U.S.A.," Jess Henig, Factcheck.org, Aug. 21, 2008, http://factcheck.org/elections-2008/born_in_the_usa.html. *The St. Petersburg Times* is the former owner of CQ Press.

70. Joseph Farah, "Why I doubt Kenyan birth document," *WorldNet Daily,* Aug. 4, 2009, www.wnd.com/index.php?fa=PAGE.view&pageId=1 05902.

71. *Ibid.*

72. Quoted in Farley, *op. cit.*

73. *Ibid.*

74. Quoted in David Weigel, "Paglia: 'Birthers' Aren't Racist, and They Have a Point," *Washington Independent,* Sept. 17, 2009, http://washingtonindependent.com/59655/paglia-birthers-arent-racist-and-they-have-a-point.

75. Quoted in "Conservative media figures . . . ," *op. cit.;* Alex Koppleman, "Why the stories about Obama's birth certificate will never die," *Salon,* Oct. 13, 2009, /www.salon.com/news/feature/2008/12/05/birth_certificate/.

76. "Alex Jones — A Message to the Future," YouTube, Jan. 12, 2008, www.youtube.com/watch?v=I_6nz1Dhxn4.

77. *Ibid.*

BIBLIOGRAPHY

Selected Sources

Books

Barkun, Michael, *A Culture of Conspiracy: Apocalyptic Visions in Contemporary America,* University of California Press, 2003.
A leading conspiracy scholar at Syracuse University explores the links between conspiracism and "new age" beliefs.

Hofstadter, Richard, *The Paranoid Style in American Politics,* Vintage Books Edition, 2008.
The late Columbia University historian authored a key work in the study of American conspiracism.

Marrs, Jim, *Rule by Secrecy: The Hidden History That Connects the Trilateral Commission, the Freemasons, and the Great Pyramids,* Perennial-HarperCollins, 2001.

A former newspaper reporter lays out world history as one big conspiracy theory.

Olmsted, Kathryn S., *Real Enemies: Conspiracy Theories and American Democracy, World War I to 9/11*, Oxford University Press, 2009.
A University of California, Davis, historian explores how conspiracism grows out of real events and trends.

Pipes, Daniel, Conspiracy: *How the Paranoid Style Flourishes and Where It Comes From*, Free Press, 1997.
The director of a Middle East-related think tank analyzes the roots and consequences of U.S. and Western conspiracy theories.

Articles

Farley, Robert, "Obama's birth certificate: Final chapter. This time we mean it!" *Politifact.com*, July 1, 2009, www.politifact.com/truth-o-meter/article/2009/jul/01/obamas-birth-certificate-final-chapter-time-we-mea/.
A respected fact-checking organization says President Barack Obama's birthplace and nationality are definitively established.

Goldberg, Michelle, "Truther Consequences," *The New Republic*, Oct. 7, 2009, www.tnr.com/article/politics/truther-consequences.
An influential liberal profiles radio host Alex Jones, judging his influence to be growing.

Kornhaber, Spencer, "Anti-Obama 'Eligibility' Movement Members Are Breaking Ties With Laguna Niguel Attorney/Birther Orly Taitz," *OC Weekly*, Sept. 24, 2009.
Fights within the Obama-birthplace movement are becoming more intense, a Southern California weekly newspaper reports.

McManus, John F., "Speaker Pelosi Pushes 'New Order of the Centuries,'" John Birch Society, Jan. 8, 2007, www.jbs.org/jbs-news-feed/795-speaker-pelosi-pushes-qnew-order-of-the-centuriesq.
The president of the far-right John Birch Society links a Democratic Party leader and a globalist conspiracy.

Mosk, Matthew, "An Attack That Came Out of the Ether," *The Washington Post*, June 28, 2008, p. C1.
A *Washington Post* report chronicles an academic's exploration of the origins of a conspiracist notion of candidate Obama as a radical Muslim.

Shane, Scott, "C.I.A. Is Still Cagey About Oswald Mystery," *The New York Times*, Oct. 16, 2009, www.nytimes.com/2009/10/17/us/17inquire.html?hp=&pagewanted=all.
Even today, the intelligence agency is resisting disclosing some Kennedy assassination-related files.

Thomma, Steven, "Secret camps and guillotines? Groups make birthers look sane," McClatchy Newspapers, Aug. 28, 2009, www.mcclatchydc.com/336/story/74549.html.
A news organization with a track record of skepticism toward government takes an equally skeptical look at conspiracy theories.

Zaitchick, Alexander, "Meet the man who changed Glenn Beck's life," *Salon*, Sept. 16, 2009, www.salon.com/news/feature/2009/09/16/beck_skousen/print.html.
Zaitchick reports on the intellectual influence of the late W. Cleon Skousen on radio host Glenn Beck.

Reports and Studies

Berlet, Chip, "Toxic to Democracy: Conspiracy Theories, Demonization & Scapegoating," Political Research Associates, 2009, www.publiceye.org/conspire/toxic2democracy/Toxic-2D-all-rev-04.pdf.
A conspiracy expert concludes that the trend is on the rise and dangerous.

"Final Report on the Collapse of World Trade Center Building 7," National Institute of Standards and Technology, November 2008, http://wtc.nist.gov/NCSTAR1/PDF/NC-STAR%201A.pdf; and "Answers to Frequently Asked Questions — National Institute of Standards and Technology Federal Building and Fire Safety Investigation of the World Trade Center Disaster," National Institute of Standards and Technology, Aug. 30, 2006, http://wtc.nist.gov/pubs/fact sheets/faqs_8_2006.htm.
Two lengthy and technically detailed analyses of the Sept. 11 attacks attempt to answer questions raised by the "truther" movement.

For More Information

Alex Jones' Infowars.com. Offers access to conspiracy theorists' daily broadcasts, as well as interpretations of current events from the conspiracist perspective.

Conspiracy Science; http://conspiracyscience.com. Rebuts the leading conspiracy theories, in extensive detail.

Defend Our Freedoms Foundation, 29839 Santa Margarita Pkwy., Rancho Santa Margarita, CA 92688; (949) 683-5411; www.orlytaitzesq.com. The Web site of Orly Taitz, a leader among those claiming that President Obama wasn't born in the U.S.

911truth.org; (785) 597-5729; www.911truth.org. Assembles key "truther" documents to raise questions about the origin of the Sept. 11 attacks.

Political Research Associates, 1310 Broadway, Suite 201, Somerville, MA 02144; (617) 666-5300; www.publiceye.org. A liberal think tank that monitors conspiracism on the right but also reports critically on theories that attract left-wing followers.

Snopes.com; www.snopes.com. A nonpartisan Web site that investigates the veracity of rumors, "urban legends" and conspiracy theories.

11

Internet Accuracy

Is information on the Web reliable?

Marcia Clemmitt

Wikipedia, the phenomenally popular user-generated online information source, has come to symbolize the controversy over Internet accuracy. Supporters say wikis — along with blogs and other online postings — provide vast amounts of information and that factual errors are quickly corrected by readers. Critics say wikis are prone to manipulation, uncorrected errors and poorly written entries due to frequent, uncoordinated changes.

From *CQ Researcher,*
August 1, 2008

Is Barack Obama a Muslim? The answer, unequivocally, is no, he's a Christian who goes to church regularly. But according to some Internet sites — especially white-supremacist Web sites — the man who could be the next president of the United States not only practices Islam but is practically a terrorist.

Obama's campaign has fought back, launching a Web site — "fightthesmears.com" — to correct the misinformation about the candidate, including false claims that his campaign contributions largely have come from wealthy supporters in the Middle East.[1]

Obama isn't alone, of course, when it comes to inaccurate information on the Internet.

As millions of people and organizations around the world post information on the Internet, factual mistakes are alarmingly easy to find, and they don't just come from hate groups or "from shady, anonymous, Internet authors posing as reliable art historians," according to two historians at George Mason University in Fairfax, Va. Indeed, they say, misinformation often comes from highly reputable institutions.

In a study of Web sites highly ranked in Google searches, they found an incorrect date in a biography of the French Impressionist painter Claude Monet — the date he moved to Giverny, the small village west of Paris where he painted his famous images of water lilies. No less an authority than the Art Institute of Chicago posted an erroneous date (the correct date is 1883) while "the democratic (and some would say preposterously anarchical)" Web site Wikitravel got it right, according to the study.[2]

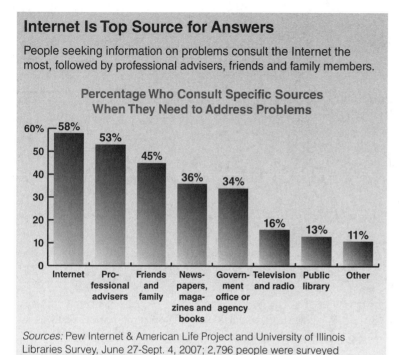

Internet Is Top Source for Answers

People seeking information on problems consult the Internet the most, followed by professional advisers, friends and family members.

Percentage Who Consult Specific Sources When They Need to Address Problems

Sources: Pew Internet & American Life Project and University of Illinois Libraries Survey, June 27-Sept. 4, 2007; 2,796 people were surveyed

Terrorist propaganda aside, "there are fewer signposts" online to signal reliability, such as newspaper brand names, says Larry Pryor, an associate professor of journalism at the University of Southern California's Annenberg School for Communications.

Wikis — user-generated online publications — like *Wikipedia* are edited by staff and other users only after they've been published online, unlike in traditional media, where editing comes before publication, notes Pryor. Furthermore, while some wiki entries are written by experts, others are contributed by people with no expertise in the subject matter, and it's difficult or impossible for unwary readers to tell the difference.

In a critique of *Wikipedia's* 2005 entry on "haute couture" — high fashion — *Vogue* magazine Editor Alexandra Shulman wrote that, "broadly speaking, it's inaccurate and unclear. . . . There are a few correct facts included, but every value judgment it makes is wrong."[5]

Nevertheless, not all so-called new media is inaccurate, says David Perlmutter, a professor at the University of Kansas' William Allen White School of Journalism. Take blogs, for example. "While some are merely sock puppets" spouting Republican or Democratic party talking points, "those are not very well-respected," while the most popular political blogs are the less biased ones, he says.[6]

In fact, online media frequently act as credibility watchdogs for traditional media, says Perlmutter. Many bloggers are experts, such as military officers and technology specialists, who are "big fact-checkers," using their specialized knowledge to spot false information in areas such as war reporting, he says.

For example, "it was . . . Russ Kick's *Memory Hole,* not *The New York Times,* that first broke pictures of military personnel brought home in [caskets] from Iraq," said Yochai Benkler, a professor at Yale Law School.[7]

Much online information also contains good clues with which to judge its credibility, says R. David Lankes,

In the past, a countable number of sources produced most of the world's information, and most readers and viewers took the names of top newspapers, magazines and television networks as a modest guarantee that they would be accurate.

But as information migrates onto the Internet and newspapers and network TV news outlets see their audiences declining, all that is changing.[3] Today the World Wide Web is a user-driven medium, where teenage videographers and political activists of all stripes can post their messages, often in formats as sophisticated-looking as the sites mounted by television networks and major newspapers. The tidal wave of citizengenerated content has made it much harder to ferret out the most credible sources, which has many people alarmed, including some policy makers.

For example, in May, Sen. Joseph I. Lieberman, I-Conn., asked Google to remove online YouTube videos that he says al Qaeda and other terrorist groups post to spread false and slanted anti-Western information. The company removed some videos but refused to block all videos from certain groups, as Lieberman requested.[4]

an associate professor at Syracuse University's School of Information Studies. For example, blogs usually contain biographies of their authors, and wikis have a history of the editing changes to posted articles.

Google News and Yahoo! News — sites that aggregate what are supposedly the days' top news stories — "are more scary" because they don't share the rules on which their rankings are based, says Lankes. But the online world is huge, and there's usually an alternate voice to consult on any issue, he says, "and that allays my fears a bit" about being misinformed.

The vast store of information available online has a major benefit: "We no longer have to rely on single authorities," says Lankes. The downside is that "we have to work harder to determine credibility."

But are Internet users prepared to be critical consumers of information? "The flaws in *Wikipedia* and other kinds of media are real" and "demonstrate how much we need to update our media literacy in a digital . . . era," said Dan Gillmor, director of the Center for Citizen Media, a project to support grassroots journalism jointly supported by Harvard and Arizona State universities.[8]

For example, when *Wikipedia*'s article on Pope Benedict XVI initially appeared — only a few hours after his election on April 19, 2005 — the page "suffered vandalism," with false statements and accusations popping up that very same day, said Gillmor. "Over time," the entry "will settle down to something all sides can agree on," Gillmor blogged later that day, but for the moment, "the vandals are having a good time mucking with the page, I'm sorry to report. What jerks they are."[9]

"Our internal b.s. meters . . . work, but they've fallen into a low and sad level of use in the Big Media world," Gillmor continued. "Many people tend to believe what they read. Others tend to disbelieve everything. Too few apply appropriate skepticism."

In fact, some online material can mislead readers into thinking it's from a more reliable source than it is.

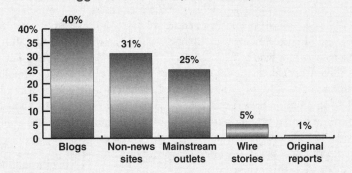

User-Driven News Sites Use Non-News Sources

Seven out of 10 stories posted on Internet sites that aggregate news items submitted by users come either from blogs or non-news sites, such as YouTube. Many of the stories users selected did not appear among the top stories in mainstream media coverage.

Sources of News Stories on Reddit, Digg and Del.icio.us, June 24-29, 2007*

* Figures do not total 100 due to rounding

Source: "The News You Choose," Pew Research Center, September 2007

For example, "a hospital Web site may not look any different from the herbal remedy store's Web site — or from an accomplished teenager's hobby page," said Frances Jacobson Harris, a professor of library administration at the University of Illinois at Urbana-Champaign. Even "relevancy ranking" — as in Google search results — can mislead, she said. For example, at one time a Google search for "Martin Luther King" pulled up a disguised anti-King hate site as its top result, partly because librarians had linked to the page as an example of untrustworthy information, said Harris.[10]

And despite young people's reputations as digital natives and Internet gurus, their "skills in effective navigation of today's information landscape are actually somewhat limited," Harris wrote. "They always find something when searching for information, just not always the best thing."[11]

For example, young researchers often "make credibility judgments that rely heavily on design and presentation features rather than content," he continued.[12]

Others argue that growing up online naturally makes one a savvier Internet user.

"Information overload" can overwhelm older generations, but the younger generation "doesn't know the phrase," says Penelope Trunk, a veteran blogger in Madison, Wis., who writes about careers in the Internet Age. Immersed in the online world practically from birth, "they're just smarter about information."

But "it's not how old you are but how long you've been online" that improves research skills, says Lankes. While some expect young people to be Internet experts, Lankes says, "I don't buy it. If we create this monolithic view of kids as technologically literate, we'll do a great disservice to kids who aren't."

Some fear that the double burden of teaching old-fashioned literacy, still vital online, plus the critical thinking required to sort through the vast amount of online information will increase the so-called digital divide, leaving low-income students — those who don't have computers or have limited computer literacy — further and further behind.[13]

"The industry argues that the digital divide is gone, but that's not true," says Erik Bucy, an associate professor of telecommunications at Indiana University. "We have to think of access to digital technology as a cognitive problem and a social problem," not just an issue of handing out computers, he says.

The Web was born in 1992, and "16 years in the evolution of man is not a long time," says Lankes. Nevertheless, "already we're seeing people learning to read it intelligently. Kids understand very well what they're seeing in *Wikipedia,*" he says, knowing they must judge credibility "article by article," rather than trusting the site as a whole, as one might do with the *Encyclopaedia Britannica,* he says.

The rules of collaborative, usergenerated media like wikis have been developing for less than a decade, so it's unrealistic to expect perfection, says Siva Vaidhyanathan, associate professor of media studies and law at the University of Virginia in Charlottesville. One promising approach is typified by Slash-dot — a Web site that posts technology news based on how many site users rate it as valuable, he says. Contributors get "reputation scores" based on votes from other site users, and it becomes clear over time that some "are more credible than others," he says.

Google's page-rank algorithm, which ranks pages based on how many other Web pages link to them, amounts to a public "vote on credibility," says Lankes. It

has turned out to be another kind of reliability test that is fairly accurate and "very powerful."

But some analysts call the idea that accurate information can arise from "collective intelligence" — the philosophy behind the Web's user-generated media and user-based ranking systems — a pipe dream.

"One need only look at the composition of the Internet to understand why the 'wisdom of crowds' will never apply," wrote Andrew Orlowski, a technology columnist for *The Register* in the United Kingdom. The Internet doesn't represent society because "only a self-selecting few" have any interest in information projects, which "amplifies groupthink," Orlowski charged. "Facts that don't fit beliefs are discarded."[14]

As readers, writers and technology experts grapple with the challenges of the new online world of information, here are some of the questions being asked:

Is information on the Internet reliable?

Clearly, Internet users have access to more information than at any time in history, but is high-quality information getting lost?

"I'm a great fan of the blogosphere," says the University of Southern California's Pryor. "You can find Web sites on any topic," and many bloggers are academics or technical experts, providing an unprecedented opportunity for the public to share the thinking of top minds, he says.

Many political blogs, like the *Huffington Post,* "allow the public to participate in news gathering," which benefits information-seekers, "since they come up with things that traditional journalists would never write about," Pryor says.

When it comes to breadth of coverage, "nothing comes close" to *Wikipedia,* "not even *Encyclopaedia Britannica,*" says Jim Jansen, an assistant professor in the College of Information Sciences and Technology at Pennsylvania State University.

Furthermore, worries that many people lie online are overblown, says Jeffrey T. Hancock, an associate professor of communications at Cornell University. "Reasons to lie on the Internet are the same ones we have in real life," such as enhancing our reputations or accomplishing some specific goal, he says. Few people actually say, "Hey, I'm online, why not just lie?" Even in online situations where lying is most likely — like postings on online dating sites — most who do lie only stretch the truth by about 15 percent, he says.

Some online media, such as wikis, have a transparent editing process that motivated readers can use to spot bias, says Jansen.[15] "With *Wikipedia*, the entire editing process is available to the consumer. You can see which articles are controversial" and why. And thanks to blogging traditions, even a strongly right- or a left-leaning blog usually links to the content that it's attacking, improving readers' chances of seeing the whole picture, says Perlmutter at the University of Kansas.

Moreover, fears that search-engine results will be skewed by who pays the most to get their sites listed have proven groundless, at least so far, says Jansen. The major search engines have resisted mixing pages they're paid to post with pages they turn up through unbiased searching, he says.

Nevertheless, there are many new digital forms of media content, and their credibility may be lower than the newspapers and magazines we're used to reading, says Pryor. For example, comment pages now exist on Web sites of all kinds, from traditional newspapers to blogs. "I think they're wonderful, but they are also particularly unreliable and dangerous" as an information source, Pryor says. "People cite all sorts of stuff in their comments that turn out to be absolutely wrong. But you can also find comments by people who are total experts and whose comments are like gold." Distinguishing between the two "is among the most treacherous issues" for readers, he says.

Some aspects of new media may make bias more likely. For example, most blogs have very small staffs that may reinforce each other's points of view and stifle other ideas, says Pryor. "As a reader, you may have a hard time figuring this out," he says.

In addition, wikis, such as *Wikipedia*, are vulnerable to malicious manipulation or errors that may be picked up and repeated by unwitting readers because they are checked by staff and other users only after being published online.

In one celebrated example, John Seigenthaler, Sr., former editorial director of *USA Today* and a former aide to Attorney General Robert F. Kennedy, was the victim of false information posted by an apparent *Wikipedia* prankster. For 132 days, Seigenthaler's entry included the false statement that "for a brief time," he "was

thought to have been directly involved in the Kennedy assassinations of both John, and his brother, Bobby. Nothing was ever proven."

After discovering the misinformation, Seigenthaler — whose son John is a journalist with NBC News — said, "It was mind-boggling when my son . . . phoned later to say he found the same scurrilous text on Reference.com and Answers.com. At my request, executives of the three Web sites now have removed the false content about me. But they don't know, and can't find out, who wrote the toxic sentences. . . . I am interested in letting many people know that *Wikipedia* is a flawed and irresponsible research tool."[16]

While Google "is generally accepted as being 'clean' in terms of separating paid advertisements from sponsored ones," a hidden factor that may bias results anyway is "search engine optimization," which enables corporate sites to get to the top of search results by paying fees that total in the billions of dollars annually, said British technology columnist Victor Keegan." For example, he said, typing in something like "quiet family hotel in Venice" will take the user to hotel groups or online travel sites rather than to a hotel.[17]

Others worry that governments worldwide increasingly filter citizens' online access, skewing the information they get, Ronald Deibert, editor of the book *Access Denied: The Practice and Policy of Global Internet Filtering*, told the BBC. "Countries are selectively blocking access to information around key events, such as demonstrations or elections," he said.[18]

The Internet's speed and multiple authors also give "the rumor mill enormous new potential to spread" misinformation, says Joseph Turow, a professor at the University of Pennsylvania's Annenberg School for Communication.

However, there's "a certain amount of irony" in questioning the reliability of online news, says John Newhagen, an associate professor of journalism at the University of Maryland in College Park. Even when people go online, "most are going to traditional news organization sites like CNN or *The New York Times,* and though the same information is on the Web site and in the paper, many people rate the information in the newspaper itself as more credible," he says.

Furthermore, "there have always been lots of schlocky, sleazy newspapers as well as great ones," says Jeff South, an associate professor of mass communications at Virginia Commonwealth University in Richmond.

And traditional news media are hardly unbiased, media critics say. In the non-Internet world, journalists "in survey after survey . . . report that they feel . . . pressures to avoid, slant or promote certain stories that might affect . . . powerful interests," such as suppressing negative stories about advertisers, government agencies and the media-company owners, said Fairness and Accuracy in Reporting, a left-leaning, New York City-based group.[19]

Is enough being done to teach people how to use the Web intelligently?

Many analysts say readers don't have the basic savvy to navigate online information. But others argue that experience is effectively educating Internet users, and that colleges, at least, are emphasizing critical analysis of information.

"We're increasingly creating a media-illiterate society," in which people trust what they've read on the Web and "don't know they're ill-informed," said Andrew Keen, English author of *The Cult of the Amateur,* which criticizes user-generated media.[20]

"An amazing number of people don't know that *Wikipedia* is user-generated," for example, says Richard H. Hall, a professor of information science at Missouri University of Science and Technology in Rolla.

"Despite the popularity of search engines, most users are not aware of how they work and know little about the implications of their algorithms," wrote researchers from Cornell University and the University of Charleston. "When Web sites rank highly in a search engine, they might not be authoritative, unbiased or trustworthy," and by repeatedly clicking only on the top-ranked sites users further cement those rankings, making it "more difficult for lesser-known sites to gain an audience," even if they are better.[21]

In the old-media world, "looking pretty" was a good sign that an information source was "produced by someone who has resources" and thus likely knew more, says Lankes of Syracuse. Online, however, "we're losing that shortcut. A 15-year-old kid can make a Web site that looks better than the ones put up by the federal government."

Many people indulge their own biases for or against online information, rather than conducting the kind of source-by-source consideration that's warranted, Hall

says. Some professors refuse to take any online sources seriously, "while some students won't accept anything that didn't come from the Web," he says.

"Why is it that teachers spend so much time talking about students' lack of Internet skepticism and . . . so little . . . examining their own?" wrote Elizabeth Losh, an instructor and writing consultant at the University of California, Irvine. For example, "My fellow instructors have fallen for self-righteous campaigns against 'Bonsai Kitten,'" a joke Web site that claims to raise misshapen miniature pets in bottles.[22]

"The empirical research I have done does not bear out that [young people, who've grown up with the Web] use multiple sources" to corroborate information unless a teacher explicitly requires it, says Steve Jones, a professor of communications at the University of Illinois at Chicago. "I'm happy when they look at both Google and *Wikipedia,"* he says. However, "you do need to separate the wheat from the chaff," so if "we are, in fact, using our critical faculty less, then it is a problem."

"A lot of people don't have the cognitive and social skills to exploit" what the Internet offers, says the University of Maryland's Newhagen. "And we're not going to solve access problems by carpet-bombing low-income people with computers," he says. A graduate student in one of his classes remarked that, as a substitute teacher in Washington, D.C., she'd "literally seen storerooms filled with computers because many teachers couldn't use them."

"The Web has lots of cognitive hurdles," requiring not only Internet literacy but also basic literacy, says Indiana University's Bucy. In fact, most of the population can't use the kinds of informational texts posted on the Internet, he adds.

Furthermore, "I'm not sure educational institutions have really got their minds around the problem, any more than society as a whole has," says South.

Currently, "there's little movement toward doing more with media literacy," says Bucy.

But at least some schools and colleges are beginning to teach online literacy.

"Despite the sometimes overwhelming challenges to teaching credibility assessment in today's school environment, many teachers and school librarians are finding ways to do so," said Harris of the University of Illinois.[23]

"I see plenty of efforts now — at least among the college ranks — to try to incorporate" critical-information searching into the curriculum, says Jones.

Furthermore, "we've only been doing this a short time, and we're going to get better at judging what we see out there," says the University of Virginia's Vaidhyanathan. Over the past decade "we've been steadily generating tactics to recognize quality" in information sites, such as user rankings, he says. "It's never going to work perfectly, but neither does *The New York Times*."

Many students are savvier information seekers than they get credit for, says Soo Young Rieh, an assistant professor at the University of Michigan's School of Information. Her research finds that most students have heard professors caution that sources aren't always credible, so they engage in "a lot of cross-checking" and "social" means of corroborating information, such as e-mailing a professor, parent or friend with relevant knowledge, Rieh says. Many "also rely on multiple sourcing," such as gauging information more credible if they've found it "in a library book and also in a blog."

"I'm actually very optimistic" about online users' concern for making sure that information is reliable, she says.

More frequent Internet users "are better at sniffing out what's dishonest" there, says Pryor. But high-school students, who've literally grown up on the Web, "absolutely are miles ahead" of even current undergraduate and graduate students when it comes to shrewd use of online sources, says Pryor. "They are more attuned to the Internet, can navigate it better and are more capable of sniffing out the b.s.," he says. "If something is [public relations] they smell it," he says. "Young people have a better nose for when they're being manipulated."

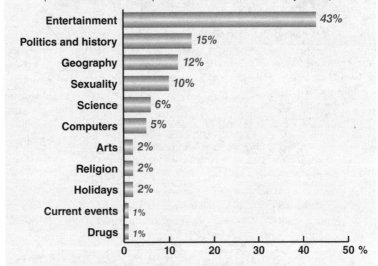

Entertainment Is the Most Popular Wiki Topic

Of the 230 most popular *Wikipedia* pages, 43 percent relate to entertainment — more than any other category. The politics and history category was a distant second, garnering only 15 percent of the total — or about a third of the pages devoted to entertainment.

Visits to Top 230 *Wikipedia* Pages, by Category
(Visited between September 2006 and January 2007)*

Category	Percent
Entertainment	43%
Politics and history	15%
Geography	12%
Sexuality	10%
Science	6%
Computers	5%
Arts	2%
Religion	2%
Holidays	2%
Current events	1%
Drugs	1%

* Percentages do not total 100 due to rounding

Source: Anselm Spoerri, "What is Popular on *Wikipedia* and Why?" *First Monday*, April 2, 2007

Can collaborative media like wikis be made reliable?

The philosophy behind collaborative media is that humans can arrive at better answers through "collective intelligence" than as individuals working alone. Some analysts call that notion a pipe dream, however.

"A core belief of the wiki world is that whatever problems exist in the wiki will be incrementally corrected as the process [of group editing] unfolds," wrote computer scientist and *Discover* magazine columnist Jaron Lanier. But "sometimes loosely structured collective activities yield continuous improvements, and sometimes they don't."[24]

The multiple authorship of wikis often squeezes out some points of view and produces text that is mostly disconnected, out-of-context facts, argues Lanier.

How to Evaluate Blogs and Online Information Sources

To begin with, ask basic questions.

With the huge variety of information sources available online, "critical thinking is more important than ever in sorting out what seems more reliable," says Doug Fisher, a former Associated Press news editor who teaches journalism at the University of South Carolina. Here are some tips to checking out the reliability of Web pages:

- **Look closely at the URL.** Many people mistakenly believe that an "org" suffix stands for something like "nonprofit organization," but in fact anyone can register an "org" domain, says Richard H. Hall, a professor of information science at Missouri University of Science and Technology in Rolla. By contrast, an "edu" suffix can only be held by an institution that has undergone some vetting by higher-education groups, he says. But even an "edu" page requires some caution, says Jeff South, associate professor of mass communications at Virginia Commonwealth University in Richmond, because the page could come from a professor, a freshman-class project or anyone working at the college, he says.

- **Locate the main Web site.** When you pull up a Web page, it's usually a good idea to check back to the main site to find out more about whoever posted the information, says South. To do that, simply lop off anything in the URL that follows the main domain suffix (such as .com or .edu). The main Web site should tell you clearly what person or group is responsible for its content. If a Web site doesn't do this, don't trust it, says Jeffrey T. Hancock, associate professor of communications at Cornell University, in Ithaca, N.Y. Posting one's identity is a good sign of trustworthiness in cyberspace, he says. "Can you Google this person or group and find out things about them?" If not, the Web site may not be trustworthy.

- **Can a real person be contacted?** "Check to see if you can contact a real person based on the Web site information," says Hall. "If there isn't a pretty detailed 'About' or 'About Me' page" or contact information, then there's reason to be suspicious.

- **Are there additional links?** Good online information "usually has references and links to additional information," both on other pages of its own site and on external Web pages, says Hall.

- **Are there misspellings and typos?** Grammatical errors on a Web page potentially indicate untrustworthy information, says South. "If they're breaking a lot of rules at the micro level, what does that suggest about the information they're presenting?"

- **Are there links to other sources?** For blogs, another test for reliability is whether writers cite or link to opinions of other writers that they disagree with, says Larry Pryor, an associate professor of journalism at the University of California's Annenberg School for Communications. "The more reliable blogs will reach out to other points of view" or at least point readers to pages where they can learn about them.

- **How long has the blogger been at it?** A blog will usually state how long the writer has been blogging, and longer is better, says Penelope Trunk, a veteran blogger in Madison, Wis., who writes about careers in the online age. "It takes time to resonate with the blogosphere and make changes" to improve your work, she says.

- **How many topics does the blog cover?** Blog sidebars usually list the main topic categories that the blog covers, says Trunk. "If there are too many and it's all over the place, then this is not an expert," she says.

- **What is the blog's format?** Formats can be clues to reliability too, says Trunk. Blogger Web sites generally have a default setting for organizing an individual blogger's page, and those who use the default may be less reliable "because they haven't put much time into" the project, says Trunk. Young readers in the blogosphere operate in a very different world of information than traditional media, Trunk argues. "Reliability" today means a writer who's developed a "personal brand" rather than one who operates under the "institutional brands" of the past, she says.

"I've participated in a number of elite, well-paid wikis . . . and have had a chance to observe the results," he wrote. "What I've seen is a loss of insight and subtlety, a disregard for the nuances of considered opinions, and an increased tendency to enshrine the official . . . beliefs of an organization."[25]

"It is one thing to say that *Wikipedia* is amazing and useful; it is quite another to say that we couldn't do better by adding a role" for credentialed, subject-matter experts and professional editors, said Larry Sanger, a co-founder of *Wikipedia* and editor-in-chief of Citizendium, a new, expert-guided, collaboratively created online encyclopedia.[26] From moment to moment, collaborative media can vary wildly, with no guarantee that material hasn't been recently vandalized, says *Wikipedia*'s own user-written article on "Why *Wikipedia* Is Not So Great." "Anyone can delete huge amounts of text from articles . . . or insert huge amounts of text into an article, destroying readability and all sense of proportion."[27]

Political topics on a wiki "can end up looking like CNN's 'Crossfire' rather than an encyclopedia article, with point-counterpoint in every sentence," says the user-written article on wiki faults. And even if peer review will improve the standard over time, "are there really enough good writers with enough time . . . to mitigate this weakness?"[28]

Furthermore, while *Wikipedia* has broad coverage, topics are idiosyncratically chosen, not picked on the basis of their importance to society at large. For example, many people with causes contribute "to 'get the word out,' because publishers laugh at their stuff," and putting up their own Web sites would cost money, says the *Wikipedia* faults entry. Meanwhile, "opposing establishment figures get stubs" — *Wikipedia*'s term for incomplete articles of only a few sentences — "whose content is a litany of all the evil things they've done to the obscure activists," says the article.[29]

"If *Wikipedia* follows the pattern of every other 'community forum' on the Net, small groups will become powerful to the exclusion of others," and the "inherent bias and hostility issues are likely to get worse," says the article.[30]

But *Wikipedia* is evolving into a system where many things are marked as "questionable" or "needs sourcing," allowing readers to judge an article's reliability, says Newhagen at the University of Maryland.

Admittedly, "some of the back and forth about editing gets uncivil, but that has happened in academia before," says Penn State's Jansen. But because *Wikipedia* posts such arguments publicly, "you can identify the articles that are controversial, and take them with a grain of salt." Meanwhile, many articles "have become stable," a good indicator of general accuracy, particularly for articles of high interest, which users would further edit and challenge if they disagreed, Jansen says.

Furthermore, *Wikipedia* requires contributors to post only information that has "already been published by reliable and reputable sources," which prevents too much outlandish misinformation, at least for frequently consulted articles, wrote John Willinsky, a professor of literacy and technology at the University of British Columbia.[31]

"*Wikipedia*'s long-lasting success is based not on anarchy but rather on a rigorous hierarchy," which should be the model for other collaborative and user-generated media, wrote Michael Maier, CEO of the German company Blogform Publishing. "Every article is strictly scrutinized before it is published and ultimately revised by the 'last editor,' who resides at the top of the hierarchy," he said."[32]

While the technology that allowed *Wikipedia* to be created also allows people to manipulate the content for their own agendas, by having a community vigilant against those sorts of edits, "they are, for the most part, kept in check," said Angela Beesley, chair of the Wikimedia Foundation's advisory board.[33]

The low barrier to entry for adding new content is vital to *Wikipedia*'s rapid growth and ability to cover many up-to-date topics and "works, . . . especially for non-controversial topics," said Virgil Griffith, a California Institute of Technology graduate student.

And although some recommend that anonymous edits be discontinued to ensure that information is unbiased, Griffith says *Wikipedia* should instead analyze controversial edits after the fact, tracking down and eliminating those that are false or self-serving. In fact, he invented a software program — WikiScanner — to trace anonymous *Wikipedia* edits to the originating organization, often a corporation or other group seeking to clean up its image.[34]

Moreover, some simple format clues can help alert readers to which wiki paragraphs are most likely to be accurate, according to Tom Cross, a founder of the social-networking site MemeStreams. For example, color-coded text could alert readers to "what assertions in an article have . . . survived the scrutiny of a large number of people, and what assertions are relatively fresh, and may not be as reliable."[35]

Wiki staff now understand that entries on major topics need to be held to a stricter standard of reliability, and "all the major entries are much more edited, vetted, and reliable today" than two or three years ago, says Marcus Messner, an assistant professor of communications at Virginia Commonwealth University.

Wikipedia is also open to a wider range of information than traditional encyclopedias, because it has no space limitations and has a different notion of what constitutes "neutrality," Messner says. For example, in a listing about a private company, *Wikipedia* will have "lots more about any scandals that have happened," than the *Encyclopaedia Britannica,* where "you don't see controversial content."

BACKGROUND

Information Deluge

Every communication media and technology has had powerful, wide-reaching effects on humanity, and, while its consequences are as yet largely unknown, the digital era will be no different.[36]

Throughout history, new media technologies have threatened — and even overturned — the powerful, says Irving Fang, a professor of communication history and broadcast journalism at the University of Minnesota. For example, the invention of the movable-type printing press in around 1450 changed Western history forever, not least by aiding the rise of Protestant reformers who challenged the Catholic Church.

"Without printing, Martin Luther could have ended up burned at the stake," like earlier would-be reformers, he says. Instead, printing "spread his words very fast," building support for his ideas first among German princes and laity, then quickly across Europe.

Media technologies throughout history have unexpectedly altered life for society and for individuals, he continues. For example, the telephone changed family relationships, allowing children to move far away, marry or find work while remaining in close touch. "If you retain a voice, you retain a lot," he says. The telephone also paved the way for other revolutionary developments, such as the skyscraper, which required communication devices for their construction and operation, Fang says.

Today, digital communication constitutes the biggest media revolution since the invention of printing and will bring with it changes of equal or even greater magnitude, says Jones of the University of Illinois. "Now that information is electronic, we're growing it exponentially," in both public and private domains, including the burgeoning digitization of everyday family life, says Jones. "Anybody born today is likely to have their whole life — photos, records, video — in digital form."

In 2002, for example, humans created a mound of new information equivalent in size to half a million libraries the size of the Library of Congress, about 92 percent of it digital and potentially available for Internet posting, according to researchers at the University of California, Berkeley.[37]

Computers were originally calculation devices. But humans are social beings with an insatiable desire to communicate, so media and communication uses were quickly devised after the first computers were linked into a network in the early 1970s.[38] The system was built to facilitate high-tech computing and government communications. But, to the surprise of many, high-tech users quickly adapted the network to a down-to-Earth pursuit — sending mail electronically for free. By 1973 e-mail made up 75 percent of network traffic.

By 1975, users, mostly scientists and academics, had developed another new application — mailing lists to broadcast individual messages to large numbers of subscribers. These discussion lists gave users their first taste of the new world to come, in which everyone with a computer could be a publisher. While some lists were work-related, many were not. The most popular of the early unofficial lists was SF-Lovers, a list for discussing science fiction.

With the 1992 introduction of the World Wide Web, Internet users for the first time could navigate among hyper-linked documents, images and multimedia. The explosion of information — plus the ability to place one's own creations online for others to see — drew ever-increasing numbers of the general public onto the Web.

"During the first few years . . . I was a taker; I looked for and found info I wanted," one pioneer computer user told researchers from the Pew Internet & American Life Project. But in the 1990s, "I developed my own Web

CHRONOLOGY

1990s *The public goes online.*

1990 Alan Emtage, a student at Montreal's McGill University, creates Archie, the first tool for searching Internet archives.

1992 World Wide Web expands, allowing Internet users to navigate among hyperlinked documents, images and multimedia.

1993 Massachusetts Institute of Technology student Matthew Gray creates the first automated search device for the hyperlinked Web, the World Wide Web Wanderer.

1996 American computer programmer Ward Cunningham creates wiki software, allowing users to create a Web site collaboratively.... eBay introduces user-generated ratings to ease fears about buying and selling online.

1997 Sergey Brin and Larry Page launch Google as a Stanford University research project. Its page rankings, based on how many other sites link to a page, quickly make it the most popular search tool.

1999 U.S. software engineer John Swapceinski is inspired by a professor he disliked to launch the user-generated Ratemyprofessors.com Web site.

2000s *Collaborative, user-produced media accelerate information production.*

2000 American Internet entrepreneur Jimmy Wales launches *Nupedia,* an online encyclopedia offering free online content written by volunteer experts.

2001 Wales launches *Wikipedia,* an encyclopedia to be written by the public and intended as a feeder source for *Nupedia.*

2003 With few articles completed, *Nupedia* folds.

2004 Finding that a Google search for "Jew" turned up the anti-Semitic Web site jewwatch.com as the No. 1 result, New York real estate agent Steven Weinstock launches an online petition asking Google to remove the site. Google refuses.... 11th Circuit Court of Appeals in

Georgia cites *Wikipedia* as a source in a ruling. A grassroots effort to link the word "Jew" on Web pages to *Wikipedia*'s entry for "Jew" pushes the *Wikipedia* article to the top spot a month later.

2005 Yahoo! indexes more than 20 billion items, including 1.6 billion images and over 50 million audio and video files.... Journalist John Seigenthaler Sr. complains about inaccuracies that remained for four months in his *Wikipedia* biography, including a false claim that he was involved in the assassination of President John F. Kennedy.... A non-peer-reviewed analysis in the British journal *Nature* concludes that *Wikipedia* and *Encyclopaedia Britannica* have comparable accuracy, but critics say the analysis was flawed.... *Los Angeles Times* opens a readers' comment section on its Web site op-ed page, then quickly closes it after it's flooded with obscene comments and pornographic spam.

2006 *Wikipedia* articles number more than 1 million.... *Wikipedia* bans comedian Stephen Colbert from editing articles after he makes joke edits and encourages his TV audience to do so.... Thai shopping blog — *Oh See What the Cat Drags In!* — posts photos of coup after military shuts down news outlets.

2007 Ryan Jordan, a member of *Wikipedia*'s Arbitration Committee — a group of experienced users who settle content disputes — is found to be a 24-year-old college dropout, not a theology professor with two Ph.Ds.... Number of active blogs stalls at around 15.5 million.... California Institute of Technology graduate student Virgil Griffith creates Wikiscanner, computer software that traces anonymous *Wikipedia* edits to the organizations where they originated, often corporations or government officials.

2008 Visits to online U.S. news sites increase by 22 percent over 2007.... Wikipedia ranks among top 10 most-visited Web sites worldwide.... English-language *Wikipedia* has more than 2.4 million articles, for a worldwide *Wikipedia* total of more than 9 million articles in 250 languages.... Citizen journalists using the new "microblogging" service Twitter report from the site of a May earthquake in China.... German publisher Bertelsman plans to print a book of German-language *Wikipedia* articles, the first time a wiki project will be published as a print product.

How to Improve Your Online Searches

Google has more to offer than you may think.

Yes, Google is a good place to start an online information quest and can provide much more information than many realize. But the number of other sources is almost endless. Here are some tips on improving your searches, starting with Google:

Getting the Most Out of Google

- A Google Alert lets you know whenever the search engine finds and indexes a new Web page on a topic you're interested in, such as blog entries or new videos of your favorite sports team or a research-paper topic. Click the pull-down menu under "more" at the top of the main Google search page, then click "even more" at the bottom of the menu. Then click on "Alerts" to pull up a Google Alert form and fill it out. You can choose alerts for the whole Web, or for news, blogs, videos or discussion groups only, and you can choose how often to receive alerts. Avoid the "as-it-happens" option for most topics, though, or you'll be overwhelmed with e-mails.
- Google allows you to limit searches so they provide information that's most relevant to your quest. For example, typing "intitle:" before your keywords will retrieve only pages with your search terms in the Web page's title.
- You can also narrow your search to a particular Web site or to a particular domain, such as higher-education or

government sites. To search only the Library of Congress site, for example, type "site:loc.gov" alongside your search terms, and you'll get back only Library of Congress pages relating to your query. To find your subject on higher-education sites only, type "site:edu" alongside your search terms.
- Typing "phonebook:" and a name in the search box asks the search engine to look up phone numbers. Typing "phonebook:" and a telephone number looks up the name associated with the number.
- Typing "define:" and a word returns definitions of the word.
- Typing "movie:" returns movie reviews. Typing "movie:" plus a movie title and the Zip code or a city name returns a list of local theatres and show times.[1]

Searching Beyond Google

- Some search sites are especially good for certain kinds of searches. For example, a search at www.USA.gov will return U.S. government-sponsored information. A search at www.scirus.com will turn up scientific material only, including journal articles and individual scientists' Web pages.
- To broaden your search horizons, http://bananaslug .com performs Google searches linking your search term

pages. First for work, then on my own. . . . I became a giver/publisher. What a thrill to contribute."[39]

The flood of people and information online has already changed the world, although much larger effects will surely come, says Fang. "E-mail has so obviously provided for worldwide community," he says, and the Web "has revolutionized commerce as well as propaganda."

"How many blogs are out there? Every political movement, no matter how small, now has one. It has been a godsend to [terrorist] organizations like al Qaeda," says Fang. "Just a few people can create cells all over the world. The Web has given voices to people who could otherwise be heard only as far as they could shout."

Cataloging Information

Having vast quantities of information at one's disposal always has its downside. In a vast sea of data, how do we locate the best answers to our questions? Of the tens of millions of information providers, how do we know which to trust?

"When I was a reporter, the problem was the scarcity of stuff," says South of Virginia Commonwealth University. "I remember going to the [newspaper] morgue and unfolding these yellow sheets of paper, trying to find scraps of information on a city council meeting," he says. "Now, we don't have a drought. It is a torrent," and sometimes that can be overwhelming.

to a randomly chosen word to pull up offbeat Web pages on your topic that never would have risen to the top of a simple Google search. "BananaSlug was designed to promote serendipitous surfing: finding the unexpected in the 8,058,044,651 Web pages indexed by Google," say the site's founders.[2]

- At http://clusty.com, the Clusty search engine returns results listed by popularity but also offers a sidebar that clusters all the search results into categories that may help you more easily find what you're looking for. Search results for the name of a pop singer, for example, may be grouped into categories including photos, lyrics, downloadable music and reviews, allowing the searcher to pull up all Web pages with song lyrics by that singer in a single click, for example.

- To find basic historical information, like what year the Civil War began or what Marie Curie was famous for, historians at George Mason University's Center for History and New Media are developing H-Bot, an artificial-intelligence program that sifts through information from many sites to arrive at the most likely right answer to such questions. Check out H-Bot at http://chnm .gmu.edu/tools/h-bot. Although it can't yet answer "how, where, or why" questions, it claims around 95 percent accuracy for birth or death years of famous people and brief biographies of famous people with relatively unique names and 60-to-80 percent accuracy on simple historical questions like "Who discovered oxygen?"[3]

- Interested in what's going on around the world? Global Voices (http://globalvoicesonline.org), a project of Harvard Law School's Berkman Center for Internet and Society, aggregates the work of bloggers and other citizen journalists around the globe to paint a daily picture of world events that goes beyond what mainstream American media publish.

- To search worldwide, pull up Search Engine Colossus (www.searchenginecolossus.com) to find an international directory of country-specific search sites and other online resources for countries and territories from Aaland to Zimbabwe, in English and many other languages.

- Oyez, at www.oyez.org, is a multimedia Supreme Court site where you can read the latest news and information on cases from 1793 to the present and also listen to recordings of recent oral arguments and take a virtual tour of the Supreme Court building.

- It's a wiki world today, with *Wikipedia* just one among thousands of collaborative, user-written sites on every imaginable topic, from Barbie dolls to economic development. User-written media can have the most up-to-date information but may also be only as accurate as the latest edit, which may or may not have been performed by an expert on the topic. For searchable lists, see WikiIndex, at http://wiki-index.org, and Wikimedia's list of the largest wikis at http://meta.wikimedia.org/ wiki/List_af_largest_wikis.

---

[1] "About BananaSlug," http://bananaslug.com.

[2] Rael Dornfest, Paul Bausch and Tara Calishain, *Google Hacks* (3rd ed., 2006), p. 9.

[3] "H-Bot," Center for History and New Media, http://chnm.gmu.edu/ tools/h-bot.

But "scholars have been complaining about too many books and journals since [16th Century English philosopher] Francis Bacon's day," said Christine Borgman, a professor of information studies at the University of California-Los Angeles. "The sifting problem . . . is not new. What is new is the declining availability of indicators to determine what's real, what's true, what's valuable and what will still be there the next time we look."[40]

Throughout history, every time there's been an increase in available information, people have had to invent tools to transmit, store, retrieve and navigate it, as well as gauge its accuracy, says Carolyn Marvin, a professor at the University of Pennsylvania's Annenberg School for Communication.

In ancient Greece and Egypt, for example, cities in developed large libraries, but in those vast collections "no one could find anything, save through extraordinary memory, for . . . there was no efficient system of book cataloging," wrote Steven Roger Fischer, director of the Institute of Polynesian Languages and Literature in Auckland, New Zealand. In the early 2nd century, B.C., the North African writer Callimachus of Cyrene established the first library catalog, at the Library of Alexandria in Egypt. It was divided into sections according to subject matter — such as legislation, medicine,

Internet Users Evaluate Sources on Many Levels

Credibility is no longer the only factor

As the world's information migrates online, Internet users are developing new expectations about information they get and what institutions like newspapers and libraries should provide.

Internet users can now access media of all kinds 24 hours a day, leaving many to tune out some of the old-media mainstays — such as major newspapers and network television — altogether, said Markus Prior, an assistant professor of politics and public affairs at Princeton University.

Traditional newspaper and TV news audiences are shrinking not because "shallow, loud or negative coverage of politics causes viewers to tune out in disgust," said Prior, but because for many people "shallow, loud entertainment . . . is available around the clock" online.[1]

The old notion that readers look for "credibility" when choosing an information source also is crumbling, says John Newhagen, an associate professor of journalism at the University of Maryland in College Park. In the days when television and newspapers were the primary media, he explains, "reaching deeply into primary sources was done for you by people called journalists, and the way to judge the information was something called credibility."

Online media, however, are an interactive experience in which scanning a Web page leads to clicking links and following them to other sites, says Newhagen. Accordingly, "interactivity" — the ease with which an online site allows one to gather the information that meets one's own needs — "may be taking the place of credibility" as Internet users' top criterion for judging media, he says.

"There are so many dimensions of news that can be measured besides credibility," says Erik Bucy, an associate professor of telecommunications at Indiana University. For instance, he asks, "How participatory is the medium? I think that's going to be as important going forward. How engaged am I?"

Having a Web site — or a paper publication — organized to provide clear, easy access to desired content is another important new standard, something that newspapers have not traditionally been good at in their paper editions, says Bucy. "That's another evaluation of news we need to look at. Does [the Web page] allow a quick scan of the news" and provide a clear path for readers to get more of whatever news they care about?

Accepting information as authoritative based on an institutional brand name simply doesn't fly today, says Doug Fisher, a former Associated Press news editor who teaches journalism at the University of South Carolina. "Some of your readers may be blogging and know more than you do," he says, even "if you're *The New York Times* or *The Washington Post.*"

New media's credibility is only as good as its latest report. And a willingness to listen to readers' views is another important new standard, he says, "because, frankly, there are a lot of people in the community who know a lot more than you do."

---

history and philosophy — and the books in each section were listed alphabetically, making the library for the first time "a systematized information center," according to Fischer.[41]

In England in the 11th through the 13th centuries, when written records of legal transactions first became common, retrieval methods taken for granted today — such as dating records and filing and indexing papers by date — had to be invented from scratch, says Marvin.

Over the years, librarians and others have kept improving the ways we catalog information so consumers can locate it. For example, the world's most commonly used library classification system, the Dewey Decimal System, was devised in the 1870s by Melvil Dewey, a 21-year-old student library assistant at

Increased communication between media producers and media consumers is a hallmark of the Internet world, which is far more "social" than past media, says R. David Lankes, an associate professor at Syracuse University's School of Information Studies.

For example, teenagers have told many libraries that they want reading recommendations in the form of blogs so they can find out about the person making the recommendations and evaluate them on the basis of their personalities, Lankes says.

The online world also is changing the scholarly enterprise, says Steve Jones, a professor of communication at the University of Illinois, Chicago. For example, soliciting reader comments on scholarly articles is now the norm and greatly expands the universe of people with whom researchers may end up communicating about their work, he says.

"In the long run, the peer-review process is going to change to community review," in which an entire scholarly group will decide whether to publish a paper, rather than just a handful of reviewers, says Jones. That change will have pluses and minuses for research, he says.

"If the research is iconoclastic, the community as a whole will be less likely to be open to it," potentially suppressing the most groundbreaking work, he says. In the past, some seminal research has seen the light of day in scholarly publications only after one influential scholar championed it in the face of general hostility, he says.

On the plus side, the Internet encourages much more collaborative research, as researchers post their data so that others can analyze and build on it. This process is already resulting in "a quite remarkable amplification" of scholarly efforts, says Jones.

Online storage of vast quantities of data — with the expectation that researchers worldwide can easily access it — is one of several new, complex jobs libraries are now being asked to undertake, says Christine L. Borgman, a professor of information studies at the University of California, Los Angeles. Online archivists face a "scientific data deluge" measuring in the terabytes — one terabyte equals 1,000 gigabytes — in fields ranging from astronomy's digital sky surveys to protein science, she explains.

"And managing data" for collaborative use by scholars around the world "is quite different from managing documents," she says. "Libraries are trying to convince researchers that 'I'll give it to the library' is not a data-management strategy" and that libraries need new financial support as science changes to a worldwide data-sharing enterprise.

With all the new expectations, some traditional — and vital — old-media functions are in danger of being lost, says Persephone Miel, a fellow at Harvard Law School's Berkman Center on Internet & Society. "Completeness of local news coverage," which people depend on without realizing it, could become a major casualty, says Miel. "It might be replaced by 10 personal blogs all obsessed with the same local issue," but that would leave many local-information needs unfilled, she says, such as news from zoning boards or local businesses' plans. "In-depth investigative reporting," which takes money, time and, perhaps, special training to accomplish could also be a casualty, along with international news reporting, says Miel.

But the overabundance of information in the online era along with the new expectations of Internet readers "makes it hard to convince people that important things may not be getting done," says Miel.

---

[1] Markus Prior, "The Real Media Divide," *The Washington Post,* July 16, 2007, p. A15.

Massachusetts' Amherst College. Today the system is in its 22nd edition.[42]

Internet information still awaits storage and retrieval methods equal to the vast volume of data and diversity of authors, Marvin says. And since digital documents are so easy to alter or remove from the Web, "each day's Internet is different," raising new problems of credibility and stability of information, she says. For example, if a writer points readers to a URL (Web address) as a reference today, there's no guarantee that the page will exist unchanged tomorrow.

But retrieval is the biggest problem, says Marvin. Endless information "doesn't do me any good," says Marvin. "The value of information to a society is not that it exists, but whether we can grab that information and use it."

Blog Readers Are Less Up-to-Date on News

The most-well-informed American audiences watch "The Daily Show" and "The Colbert Report" and read major newspapers online. The least knowledgeable audiences regularly view the network morning shows, Fox News Channel and local TV news.

Knowledge Levels by News Source

	High*	Moderate	Low
Nationwide	35%	31%	34%
Among the regular audience of ...			
The Daily Show/Colbert Report	54%	25%	21%
Major newspaper Web sites	54%	26%	20%
NewsHour with Jim Lehrer	53%	19%	28%
The O'Reilly Factor	51%	32%	17%
National Public Radio	51%	27%	22%
Rush Limbaugh's radio show	50%	29%	21%
News magazines	48%	27%	25%
TV news Web sites	44%	33%	23%
Daily newspaper	43%	31%	26%
CNN	41%	30%	29%
News from Google, Yahoo!, etc.	41%	35%	24%
Network evening news	38%	33%	29%
Online news discussion blogs	37%	26%	37%
Local TV news	35%	33%	32%
Fox News Channel	35%	30%	35%
Network morning shows	34%	36%	30%

* Answered at least 15 of 23 questions correctly.

Source: "What Americans Know: 1989-2007," Pew Research Center, April 2007

Search Engines Emerge

In the 1990s, technology innovators devised tools to help Internet users locate information in the ever-expanding online universe.[43] These "search engines" travel the Web looking at pages, following hyperlinks from page to page and assembling the pages found into an index that they store. When a search-engine user makes a query, the engine scans its indexed pages and returns a list of those that most closely match the query. Periodic scanning — "crawling" — of the Web keeps the index up to date.

The earliest search engines indexed the titles of Web pages only, but by the mid-1990s numerous engines and emerged that indexed full text, thus greatly increasing the amount of relevant material they could pull up to answer a query. These engines — including AltaVista and Yahoo! — vied with each other for popularity.

In 1997, Stanford University computer-science graduate students Sergey Brin and Larry Page launched a new engine, Google, as a research project. For the first time, Google "ranked" pages returned in answer to a query based on an algorithm that included information about how many other Web pages linked to the page in question. The method greatly increased the relevance of search results and quickly made Google the most popular search tool — and turned Brin and Page into billionaires.

But search engines are far from the perfect solution to finding good information online.

Perhaps surprisingly, much of the world's information is not yet online. Much more exists in databases that are inaccessible to the public, and some information — such as images and video — remain nearly impossible to adequately index and search.

"We had thousands of years of producing non-digital" material, and at this point academic articles back only to the 1970s have been converted into digital format, says Penn State's Jansen. "A mountain of tough grunt work" remains to be done to convert it all. Until then, "there will be a mixed way of getting information."

At present, automated information searches — unlike librarians — don't understand human language and may often fail to unearth the best available answers to a query. "Ideally, we would understand your question, we would understand all knowledge and match the two," but that vision is a long way from today's reality, said Udi Manber, a vice president of engineering at Google.[44]

For example, in his attempts to improve search, Manber said he's tested Google for queries including

Should online sites like YouTube ban postings by groups the government identifies as terrorists?

YES

Sen. Joseph I. Lieberman,
I-Conn Chairman, Senate Committee on Homeland Security and Governmental Affairs

From the Committee Web Site, May 19 And May 20, 2008, http://hsgac.senategov.

Islamist terrorist organizations rely extensively on the Internet to attract supporters and advance their cause. This Internet campaign is described in a bipartisan staff report by the Senate Committee on Homeland Security and Governmental Affairs.... The report explains how al-Qaeda manages an online media operation intended to enlist followers. Central to it is the branding of content with an icon to guarantee that the content was produced by al-Qaeda or allied organizations like al-Qaeda in Iraq. All of these groups have been designated Foreign Terrorist Organizations by the Department of State.

Searches on YouTube return dozens of videos branded with an icon or logo identifying the videos as the work of one of these Islamist terrorist organizations. A great majority document horrific attacks on American soldiers in Iraq and Afghanistan. Others provide weapons training, speeches by al-Qaeda leadership and general material intended to radicalize potential recruits.

In other words, Islamist terrorist organizations use YouTube to disseminate propaganda, enlist followers and provide weapons training — activities that are all essential to terrorist activity. The online content produced by al-Qaeda and other Islamist terrorist organizations can play a significant role in the process of radicalization, the end point of which is the planning and execution of a terrorist attack. YouTube also, unwittingly, permits Islamist terrorist groups to maintain an active, pervasive and amplified voice, despite military setbacks or successful operations by the law-enforcement and intelligence communities.

Protecting our citizens from terrorist attacks is a top priority for our government. The private sector can help us do that. By taking action to curtail the use of YouTube to disseminate the goals and methods of those who wish to kill innocent civilians, Google will make a singularly important contribution to this effort.

Google apparently has taken 80 videos off YouTube that violated the company's own guidelines against gratuitous violence. That is a start, but it is not enough. Videos produced by al-Qaeda and al-Qaeda affiliates showing attacks on American troops remain on YouTube's Web site and violate YouTube's own community guidelines. Those should be taken down immediately. Furthermore, Google continues to allow the posting of videos by organizations the State Department has designated as foreign terrorist organizations. No matter what their content, videos produced by terrorist organizations like al-Qaeda, that are committed to attacking America and killing Americans, should not be tolerated. Google must reconsider its policy.

NO

Leslie Harris and John Morris
President and CEO, General Counsel Center for Democracy & Technology

From The Huffington Post, May 28, 2008, www.huffingtonpost.com

Sen. Joe Lieberman took a step backward in America's "war on terrorism," by demanding that YouTube censor hundreds of videos allegedly posted by Islamic terrorist groups. And when the Google-owned site responded by promptly removing a large number of videos, which violated its guidelines against hate speech and violence, he insisted that action was "not enough."

What would be "enough" in the senator's estimation? The removal of all tainted videos, even those that were plainly constitutionally protected advocacy, albeit abhorrent, and a plan "to prevent the content from reappearing"?

Civil liberties continue to be a casualty in our efforts against terrorism. So far, broad Internet censorship has not taken root, but censorship is the path we would take if Google acceded to Lieberman's demand.

The system we have devised, in which online services establish rigorous terms of service and enforce them, is a wise one. Users help police the system, and sites that are notified of potentially offensive content generally take down content that violates their rules. In the spirit of self-policing, Lieberman's request to review specific videos is fair, but demanding ongoing review of all videos, and removal of those that don't meet with self-selected criteria, crosses the line....

For the last year, Congress has made the Internet a focus of anti-terrorism activities. The Violent Radicalization and Homegrown Terrorism Prevention Act, which has already passed the House, specifically finds that the Internet "aided in facilitating violent radicalization, ideologically based violence and the homegrown terrorism process in the United States by providing access to broad and constant streams of terrorist-related propaganda."

Congress can take away two diametrically opposed lessons from this finding. The first is that the Internet is an essential communications tool that America should learn to better use to counter terrorism and tout our values. The other is to fight terrorism by censoring the Internet and destroying our first freedom.

Ironically, while Lieberman's letter was being delivered to Google a Senate panel on human rights was hearing testimony on threats to Internet freedom from repressive regimes. Some, like China, have built a network of gatekeepers to block content that challenges the government's official messages. Congress cannot [advocate] Internet freedom with one voice and [call] for censorship with another.

"southeast Utah news-airplane crash 10/25/06; hair-styles for ears that stick out; inflammation and pain under my rib; what is answer to this math problem 6x/10x; how many calories in a pound." Of those, Google provided a really good answer only to the inflamed-rib question, he said.[45]

Furthermore, even when search engines do pull up the most relevant pages, the Internet Age "raises to a whole new level" the issue of whether the relevant information is also accurate and reliable, says Virginia Commonwealth's South. Online there's good information — even more of it than in the past — but also "a whole new set of things that are bad, including hoaxes" perpetrated by people "who simply want to mess with your mind," by posting legitimate-looking information that serves some poster's hidden agenda, and "stuff that's well-intentioned but not updated," a special pitfall for Internet users, who tend to assume that all online information is timely, he said.

"Google doesn't give you any sense of the reliability" of the Web sites it lists, says the University of Southern California's Pryor. "Instead, you've got to enter the blogosphere like it's a National Park and approach it like an adventure, going as far and as deep as you can" to develop your own sense of what can be trusted, he says.

In traditional media organizations, for instance, stories are vetted by editors before readers see them, but that's not true with most online information, where the entire burden of credibility checking is left to readers, he says.

Becoming a journalist in the traditional media "has always required jumping through a few hoops" to prove oneself, says Perlmutter of the University of Kansas. "But you can get on the Web and call yourself a journalist" without any scrutiny or credentials.

CURRENT SITUATION
Who Will Pay?

The age of online information is only dawning, so it's no surprise that we haven't yet hit upon the best ways to manage it. But the Internet is changing business and human expectations, as well, and some of those changes are shaking the old information infrastructure to its foundations without providing guidance on how to replace traditional institutions that strove to ensure information credibility, analysts say.

"For the next 20 years, we'll still be in the gestational, learning stage" of the digital era, says the University of Virginia's Vaidhyanathan. "People don't take enough of a historical view" and expect answers too fast, he says.

Part of the process will be figuring out how to pay people to provide organized, reliable information online, or deciding that we are willing to forgo such services because having a vast wealth of information available makes them less important to us.

In the past, taxpayers supported libraries and librarians to collect the materials they believed were most valuable and help readers find the ones they needed. Readers' and advertisers' dollars supported book, magazine and newspaper publishing, where editors and publishers chose and vetted writers and texts, publishing those they believed were best. Can the millions of people who voluntarily post content make up for the loss of such services?

Today, "the young generation will not pay for content on the Web," says Messner of Virginia Commonwealth. In part, that relates to another Internet-fueled expectation — that information will be updated nearly minute-by-minute — he says. "If you actually pay for the *Encyclopaedia Britannica,* your entries maybe [were] updated four or five years ago, while *Wikipedia* "is updated with things that happen today," Messner says, and it's free.

"Back in the olden days, people used to pay for newspapers. Now you can find everything for free," said a 19-year-old California man interviewed in an Associated Press survey on young adults' news habits.[46]

The ability of readers to search the Internet for information on their own, coupled with the availability of millions of Web pages appealing to every conceivable interest, also decrease advertisers' willingness to pay top dollar for space in newspapers, magazines or online information sites, say media scholars. That means the editorial judgment that formerly chose and edited news stories for the public often is no longer available.

"The evidence is mounting that the news industry must become more aggressive about developing a new economic model," said the Project for Excellence in Journalism. "Finding out about goods and services on the Web is an activity unto itself, like using the *Yellow Pages,* and less a byproduct of getting news, such as seeing a car ad during a newscast." As a result, advertisers may not need journalism as they once did, particularly online, depriving news organizations of their most important source of revenue.[47]

The wide variety of information outlets online and the ease of surfing from one to another mean that no one site alone can expect to draw many eyes or hold onto them, another reason advertisers will offer less money for ad placement, says Indiana University's Bucy. For example, "people don't watch MSNBC and then go online to MSNBC's Web site; they go elsewhere online," he says. For that reason, content producers, online and traditional, are seeing ad revenues dry up.

Citizen Journalists

Although much of today's online content is produced by volunteers, many analysts doubt they could fill the information gap that would occur if traditional news organizations go under. It's unlikely that unpaid citizen journalists and other content posters, working as volunteers, would have the same expertise, and professional dedication, to providing accurate, unbiased news coverage on a long-term basis, the analysts say. Much Internet content is in the form of blogs and other sites that don't seek out new information but comment on information turned up by traditional media like newspapers, says Virginia Commonwealth's South. Ironically, that leaves much of the reading audience, especially younger people, "unaware of the sweat that went into the original reporting," making it harder for media organizations to convince potential audiences that their work is worth paying for, he says.

New forms of media are developing, however, including ones staffed mainly by volunteers. Since 2004, so-called hyperlocal media — Web sites where citizens report on community issues, generally on a volunteer basis — "has really been building," says Jan Schaffer, executive director of Washington-based J-Lab: The Institute for Interactive Journalism. Her group has helped fund 40 hyperlocal projects, but received 845 proposals, Schaffer says.

Hyperlocal bloggers are filling some of the gap left by shrinking traditional-news coverage and also replacing old-media notions of credibility, which many believe have become bankrupt, says Schaffer.

For example, many hyperlocal reporters "have the aspiration to build community," something many feel that old media has worked against, she says. "They're not framing stories as conflicts, and don't do false 'yes-no' equivalencies on issues," Schaffer says. The yes-no paradigm is a traditional media storytelling strategy, intended to eliminate one-sidedness or bias, she says, but the new "citizen journalists" believe the strategy actually harmed media credibility and accuracy because it polarized issues and positions instead of finding the gray areas that often exist.

Some hyperlocal journalists are "getting so much credit in the community that they're being tapped to run for office in some places," Schaffer says.

But many analysts caution against hopes that the news reporting of the future will come from volunteer citizen reporters. "Most people will not become news producers," says Persephone Miel, a fellow at Harvard Law School's Berkman Center for Internet & Society. For one thing, "nobody has that much free time."

Evidence shows that only a handful of people who volunteer — perhaps 10 percent — either have the talent or motivation to produce journalistic-type work in collaborations that have been tried, according to New York University professor of journalism Jay Rosen.[48]

Another barrier to news volunteerism is the very real risk of being sued for libel, especially if reporters challenge powerful interests, as investigative journalists for mainstream media have traditionally done, says Miel. "What do you do when a small publication like *Chi-Town Daily News* [in Chicago] ends up with a libel lawsuit, and they don't have the same access to attorneys that *The Washington Post* has?"

Some outside groups, such as the Berkman Center's Citizen Media Law Project, have formed to help citizen media meet legal challenges, Miel says.

In the past, newspapers and other media companies have aggregated news, picking out and publishing what they deem the best material and the most important stories. This media function is also up for grabs online, with some user-based systems of news judgment potentially replacing institution-based ones.

For example, the nonprofit *NewsTrust* aggregates and presents the day's top news on its Web site, gleaned from traditional media Web sites as well as blogs and independent media. Billing itself as "Your Guide to Good Journalism," the site picks out what it deems the most credible stories based on ratings by both site users and a panel of experts.[49] Typically, they summarize the reports and then include a link to the original source, along with a 1-to-5-star ranking from their reviewers.

Nonprofit groups, including advocacy organizations, also may play a bigger role as actual reporters, as revenues for traditional news publishers shrink, even though advocacy groups' biases have long been thought to compromise the credibility of their writings.

Many charitable organizations would find it in their own interest to take on the cost of producing real news rather than the public-relations materials most produce today, said Martin Moore, director of the London-based Media Standards Trust, a new nonprofit group that's seeking ways to build credibility standards into new media. "Charities have an agenda . . . but they are also motivated by a sense of obligation to the public, have a keen interest in seeing injustice reported" and are "already on the ground" in trouble spots, he writes. "Plus, since they tend to wear their agenda on their sleeve . . . at least you know where their bias is coming from."[50]

Internet companies that depend on paid writers and other content producers to fill the Web with information have a stake in supporting credible journalism and should do so, said Neil Henry, a professor of journalism at the University of California, Berkeley. "It stands to reason that Google and corporations like it, who indirectly benefit so enormously from the expensive labor of journalists," should "somehow engage and support the traditional news industry" as "a public trust to society," he said. If not, "I can't help but fear a future — increasingly barren of skilled journalists — in which Google 'news' searches turn up not news but the latest snarky rants from basement bloggers, fake news reports from government officials and PR cleverly peddled as journalism by advertisers," said Henry.[51]

Others argue that traditional publishing values and organizations can flourish online, supported by advertising dollars, as long as revenue expectations are reasonable. The world of online information is "not the commercial desert it was feared to be a few years ago," says the University of Virginia's Vaidhyanathan. "People can make money" with online journalism, he says, although there are no windfalls any more, since advertisers are abandoning the dream of reaching everyone online and focusing instead on smaller, niche audiences on the Internet.

Online publishers must simply focus instead on content that draws in Internet users, he says. "Advertising is the only possible source of revenue," and "if content brings people to your site, advertisers will want to be there, too."

To create credible forms of media in the online world, "hybrid forms will be the strongest — openness with some controls, amateurs with some pros," said New York University's Rosen. "But that means we have to figure out how these hybrid forms work."[52]

OUTLOOK
Future of Search

The evolution of online searching will shape the future of information. But how that future plays out is anyone's guess.

Today, the world of search is totally dominated by Google, but that may not be true in the future and probably shouldn't be, says the University of Virginia's Vaidhyanathan.

"One of the central philosophical questions about digitizing" existing information is, "Should we focus on quantity or quality?" he says. Google has opted to digitize all the information it can find, rather than choosing the more "important" information first, a smart business move because "the more chaotic the world is, the more we need Google," Vaidhyanathan says. But the result is that "the Internet now feels like some weird combination of library, shopping mall and movie theater," he says.

Vaidhyanathan would like the world of online information to feel more like a library, where the most important works are archived according to a scheme set up by experts. "I'd like to see a publicly funded research system [for digitized, online information] based on collaboration of stakeholders that would be expertise-based and have values built in," such as human rights and privacy, he says.

Digitizing the world's information should be about "making a global library that privileges the needs of humanity over the next 50 years rather than the interests of a company in the next quarter," he says. "I love Google, too, but it's not enough; we shouldn't be relying on it totally."

The future could also bring a more sinister side of search-engine technology into play, says Turow of the University of Pennsylvania.

Search-engine and data-mining technology has "the ability to surround people with information based on what marketers and others think about them," without their being aware of it, he says. Virtually all U.S. media go digital with the analog-to-digital TV switch in February 2009.[53] After that, such clandestine targeting could happen "not just on the Web but on TV" and eventually in magazines and newspapers, which we will access digitally through portable electronic tablets, says Turow.

In fact, such targeting "is already happening in advertising, but it's troubling that people will be labeled and profiled, and, without our realizing it, we'll be sent news and information" as well, based on what someone else wants us to see, rather than what we choose, Turow says. "This is an issue that as a society we need to grapple with."

NOTES

1. For background, see Eli Saslow, "Hate Groups' Newest Target," *The Washington Post,* June 22, 2008, p. A6. For background, see "Fight the Smears," http://my.barackobama.com/page/con-tent/fightthesmearshome; Karen Tumulty, "Will Obama's Anti-Rumor Plan Work?" *Time,* June 12, 2008, www.time.com/time/printout/0,8816, 1813663,00.html.

2. Daniel J. Cohen and Roy Rosenzweig, "Web of Lies? Historical Knowledge on the Internet," *First Monday,* December 2005, www.first-monday.org/ISSUES/issue10_12/cohen.

3. For background, see Kenneth Jost, "Future of Newspapers," *CQ Researcher,* Jan. 20, 2006, pp. 49-72.

4. For background, see Dibya Sarkar, "Senator Urges Google To Remove Terrorist-Made YouTube Videos," The Associated Press, May 19, 2008.

5. Quoted in "Can You Trust *Wikipedia?*" *The Guardian* (United Kingdom), Oct. 24, 2005, www.guardian.co.uk/technology/2005/oct/24/comment.newmedia.

6. For background, see Kenneth Jost, "Blog Explosion," *CQ Researcher,* June 9, 2006, pp. 505-528.

7. Yochai Benkler, "Extracting Signal from Noisy Spin," *Edge: The Reality Club online journal,* www.edge.org/discourse/digital_maoism.html.

8. Jaron Lanier, "On 'Digital Maoism: The Hazards of the New Online Collectivism," *Edge: The Reality Club online journal,* May 30, 2006, www.edge.org/discourse/digital_maoism.html.

9. Dan Gillmor, "How the Community Can Work, Fast," *Dan Gillmor on Grassroots Journalism, Etc.* blog, April 19, 2005, http://dan-gillmor.typepad.com/dan_gillmor_on_grass-roots/2005/04/how_the_communi.html.

10. Frances Jacobson Harris, "Challenges to Teaching Credibility Assessment in Contemporary Schooling," in Miriam J. Metzger and Andrew J. Flanagin, eds., *Digital Media, Youth, and Credibility* (2008), p. 163.

11. *Ibid.,* p. 161.

12. *Ibid.*

13. For background, see Kathy Koch, "Digital Divide," *CQ Researcher,* Jan. 28, 2000, pp. 41-64.

14. Andrew Orlowski, "Junk Science — The Oil of the New Web," *The Register,* May 25, 2006, www.theregister.co.uk/2006/05/25/junk_science_and_the_wisdom_of_chimps.

15. For background, see Alan Greenblatt, "Media Bias," *CQ Researcher,* Oct. 15, 2004, pp. 853-876.

16. John Seigenthaler, "A False *Wikipedia* 'Biography,'" *USA Today,* Nov. 29, 2005, www.us-atoday.com/news/opinion/editorials/2005-11-29-wikipedia-edit_x.htm.

17. Victor Keegan, "I'm Searching for Google Alternatives," *The Guardian* (United Kingdom), June 12, 2008, www.guardian.co.uk.

18. Quoted in Clark Boyd, "How the Open Net Closed Its Doors," BBC News online, March 25, 2008, http://newsvote.bbc.co.uk. For background, see Marcia Clemmitt, "Controlling the Internet," *CQ Researcher,* May 12, 2006, pp. 409-432.

19. Julie Hollar, Janine Jackson and Hilary Goldstein, "Fear & Favor 2005," *Extra!* March/April 2006, www.fair.org.

20. "Web Trust Questioned," BBC News "News-night," June 5, 2007, www.bbc.co.uk/blogs/news-night/2007/06/the_cult_of_the_amateur_by_an-drew_keen_1.html.

21. Bing Pan, *et al.*, "In Google We Trust: Users' Decisions on Rank, Position, and Relevance, *Journal*

of Computer-Mediated Communication, April 2007, http://jcmc.indiana.edu/vol12/issue3/pan.html.

22. Liz Losh, "Do You Know that the Word 'Gullible' Isn't in the Internet?" VirtualPolitik blog, Jan. 23, 2006, http://virtualpolitik.blogspot.com.

23. Harris, *op. cit.*

24. Lanier, *op. cit.*

25. *Ibid.*

26. Larry Sanger, "Who Says We Know? On the New Politics of Knowledge," *Edge: The Third Culture,* www.edge.org/3rd_culture/sanger07.

27. "Why *Wikipedia* Is Not So Great," *Wikipedia,* http://en.wikipedia.org.

28. *Ibid.*

29. *Ibid.*

30. *Ibid.*

31. John Willinsky, "What Open Access Research Can Do For *Wikipedia*," *First Monday,* March 5, 2007, www.firstmonday.org/is-sues/issue12_3/willinsky/index.html.

32. Michael Maier, "Journalism Without Journalists: Vision or Caricature?" Joan Shorenstein Center on the Press, Politics, and Public Policy, discussion paper #D-40, November 2007, www.hks.harvard.edu/presspol/research_pub-lications/papers/discussion_papers/D40.pdf.

33. Quoted in *ibid.*

34. Virgil Griffith, "WikiScanner FAQ," http://vir-gil.gr/31.html.

35. Tom Cross, "Puppy Smoothies: Improving the Reliability of Open, Collaborative Wikis," *First Monday,* Sept. 4, 2006, www.firstmon-day.org/issues/issue11_9/cross.

36. For background, see Irving Fang, *A History of Mass Communication: Six Information Revolutions* (1997) and Clay Shirky, *Here Comes Everybody* (2008).

37. Peter Lyman, and Hal R. Varian, "How Much Information? 2003," School of Information and Management Sciences, University of California, Berkeley, October 2003, www2.sims.berke-ley.edu/research/projects/how-much-info-2003.

38. See Clemmitt, *op. cit.*

39. Amy Tracy Wells, "A Portrait of Early Internet Adopters: Why People First Went Online — and Why They Stayed," Pew Internet & American Life Project, Feb. 20, 2008, http://pewresearch.org.

40. Quoted in Scott Jaschik, "Scholarship in the Digital Age," *Inside Higher Ed,* Nov. 14, 2007, insidehighered.com.

41. Steven Roger Fischer, *A History of Reading* (2003), p. 58.

42. "How One Library Pioneer Profoundly Influenced Modern Librarianship," Online Computer Library Center, www.oclc.org/dewey/re-sources/biography.

43. For background, see "History of Search Engines: From 1945 to Google 2007," Search Engine History.com, www.searchenginehistory.com.

44. Quoted in Stephen Shankland, "Google's Search Challenge: Making Computers Think Like Humans," C/Net News.com, June 18, 2008, http://news.cnet.com.

45. *Ibid.*

46. "A New Model for News: Studying the Deep Structure of Young-Adult News Consumption," The Associated Press and Context-Based Research Group, June 2008, www.ap.org/newmodel.pdf.

47. "The State of the News Media 2008," Project for Excellence in Journalism, www.stateofthe-newsmedia.org.

48. Charlie Beckett, "Networked Journalism: For the People and With the People," *Press Gazette* (United Kingdom), Oct. 18. 2007, www.pressgazette.co.uk.

49. For background, see "About NewsTrust," NewsTrust.net, www.newstrust.net/about.

50. Martin Moore, "Why Charities Need to Become More Like News Organizations," Martin Moore Blog, May 28, 2008, http://mediastan-dardstrust.blogspot.com/2008/05/why-charities-need-to-become-more-like.html.

51. Neil Henry, "The Decline of News," *San Francisco Gate,* SFGate.com, May 29, 2007, www.sfgate.com.

52. Jay Rosen, "Open Systems, Closed Systems, and Trauma in the Press," "techPresident blog," *Personal Democracy Forum* Web site, June 23, 2008, www.techpresident.com.

53. For background, see Kenneth Jost, "Transition to Digital TV," *CQ Researcher,* June 20, 2008, pp. 529-552.

BIBLIOGRAPHY
Selected Sources
Books

Battelle, John, *The Search: How Google and Its Rivals Rewrote the Rules of Business and Transformed Our Culture,* Portfolio, 2005.
A technology journalist recounts the history of search engines and looks into the future of search technology.

Gillmor, Dan, *We the Media: Grassroots Journalism By the People, For the People,* O'Reilly Media, Inc., 2006.
The founder of the Center for Citizen Media argues the center of media power is shifting from media companies and professional journalists toward individual bloggers.

Shirky, Clay, *Here Comes Everybody: The Power of Organizing Without Organizations,* Penguin Press, 2008.
An adjunct professor of interactive telecommunications at New York University argues that collaborative media and other projects will create broad social change.

Stebbins, Leslie F., *Student Guide to Research in the Digital Age: How to Locate and Evaluate Information Sources,* Libraries Unlimited, 2005.
A Brandeis University reference librarian explains how to conduct online searches and evaluate research materials online.

Articles

"The New Media Effect on Political Participation: An Interview with Markus Prior," *Accuracy's Impact on Research: A Knowledge Networks Newsletter,* summer 2007, www.knowledgenetworks.com.
A Princeton University assistant professor of politics argues that the proliferation of new media means more people eschew news reading for easily accessible, 24-hour-a-day entertainment, and are thus less likely to vote or get involved in public affairs.

Cross, Tom, "Puppy Smoothies: Improving the Reliability of Open, Collaborative Wikis," *First Monday,* Sept. 4, 2006, www.firstmonday.org/issues/issue11_9/cross.
A computer security engineer argues that color coding paragraphs in collaborative media based on how long they've existed in their current form would help readers gauge credibility because bad information is unlikely to survive many edits.

Grubisch, Tom, "What Are the Lessons from Dan Gillmor's Bayosphere?" *Online Journalism Review,* Jan. 29, 2006, www.ojr.org/ojr/stories/060129 grubisich.
A San Francisco-area citizen-journalism project lasted less than a year because writers focused on technology rather than topics that interested more people.

Hessendahl, Arik, "Trends in Cybercensorship," *Business Week online,* March 26, 2008, www.business week.com.
Government censorship of the Internet is increasing around the world, becoming a standard policy option when officials fear dissent against government policies may spread.

Mihm, Stephen, "Everyone's a Historian Now," *The Boston Globe,* May 25, 2008, www.boston.com.
Historians hope the public can provide valuable details about archival photos being posted online by the Library of Congress and others.

Porter, Tim, "New Values for a New Age of Journalism," First Draft blog, April 10, 2005, http://timporter.com/first-draft/archives/000436.html.
A print reporter turned online-media analyst and entrepreneur says some traditional media values — like getting a "scoop" — must be replaced with values better suited to online reporting, such as explaining the context of stories.

Shankland, Stephen, "Google's Search Challenge: Making Computers Think Like Humans," C/Net News.com, June 18, 2008, http://news.cnet.com.
A Google executive says getting computers to understand what humans mean by the terms they type into a "search" box is his company's biggest challenge.

Reports and Studies

"What Americans Know: 1998-2007: Public knowledge of Current Affairs Little Changed by News and

Information Revolutions," Pew Research Center for the People & the Press, April 2007.
The explosion of online information and 24-hour news availability via computer and cable television haven't left Americans any better informed about public affairs than they were 20 years ago.

Maier, Michael, "Journalism Without Journalists: Vision or Caricature?" Discussion Paper #D-40, Joan Shorenstein Center on the Press, Politics and Public Policy, Harvard University, November 2007.

An online publisher examines the troubled history of collaborations between professional journalism and reader-contributed media and ways those collaborations can be improved.

Schaffer, Jan, "Citizen Media: Fad or the Future of News?" *J-Lab*, February 2007, www.kcnn.org/research/citizen_media_report.
The director of a nonprofit group that supports citizen journalism reports on the field's accomplishments.

For More Information

Berkman Center for Internet & Society, 23 Everett St., 2nd Floor, Cambridge, MA 02138; (617) 495-7547; http://cyber.law.harvard.edu. A Harvard Law School-based research group that studies the Internet and Internet-related law, including for online media.

Center for Citizen Media, www.citmedia.org. A university-backed group that provides support for and information about citizen-created journalism.

Credibility Commons, http://credibilitycommons.org. A foundation- and university-backed research group developing tools and standards for assessing credibility of online information.

Cyberjournalist.net, www.cyberjournalist.net. A group blog on online journalism and how technology is changing the media.

Digital Media and Learning, The MacArthur Foundation, 140 South Dearborn St., Suite 1200, Chicago, IL 60603; (312) 726-8000; http://digitallearning.macfound.org. Researches how digital technology is changing the way young people learn and participate in society.

First Monday, www.uic.edu/htbin/cgiwrap/bin/ojs/index.php/fm/index. A peer-reviewed online journal on Internet-related topics based at the University of Illinois, Chicago.

Global Voices, www.globalvoicesonline.org. Aggregates and publishes blogs from around the world; based at Harvard's Berkman Center.

J-Lab, The Institute for Interactive Journalism, 3201 New Mexico Ave., N.W., Suite 330, Washington, DC 20016; (202) 885-8100; www.j-lab.org. A foundation-backed group based at American University that works with news

organizations and citizens developing new media to increase citizen involvement in public affairs.

Media Standards Trust, Ground Floor, Discovery House 28-42 Banner St., London EC1Y 7QE, United Kingdom; www.mediastandardstrust.org. Researches ways to foster credibility and public trust in new media.

New Literacies Research Team, University of Connecticut, Neag School of Education, 019 Gentry, 249 Glenbrook Rd., Storrs, CT 06269; (860) 486-0202; www.newliteracies.uconn.edu. Studies the teaching and learning skills required by an Internet-based society.

NewsTrust.net, 775 East Blithedale, #320, Mill Valley, CA 94941; www.newstrust.net. A nonprofit group that aggregates the best daily news from traditional and new-media sources, based on ratings from site users and an expert panel.

Online Journalism Review, www.ojr.org. Contains the archives of a now-defunct online publication at the University of Southern California's Annenberg School for Communication that covered the switch from traditional to online journalism.

The Register, Situation Publishing Ltd., 33 Glasshouse St., London, W1B 5DG, United Kingdom; +44 (0)203 178 6500; www.theregister.co.uk. An online magazine that covers controversies and new developments in technology, including digital information.

Search Engine Land, http://searchengineland.com. An advertising-supported news site with news and commentary on search engines.

Wikimedia Foundation, http://wikimediafoundation.org. The nonprofit group that operates *Wikipedia* and supports worldwide development of wikis.